MULTIVARIATE ANALYSIS TECHNIQUES
in Social Science Research

D0620266

MULTIVARIATE ANALYSIS TECHNIQUES
in Social Science Research

FROM PROBLEM TO ANALYSIS

Jacques Tacq

Sage Publications

London • Thousand Oaks • New Delhi

English edition © Jacques Tacq 1997

First published in English 1997. Reprinted 1997, 1998

Originally published in Dutch as *Van Probleem naar Analyse* by Rotterdams
Instituut voor Sociologisch en Bestuurskundig Onderzoek, Rotterdam, 1991 and
© Academisch Boeken Centrum, ABC, De Lier 1991

 SAGE Publications Ltd
6 Bonhill Street
London EC2A 4PU

SAGE Publications Inc
2455 Teller Road
Thousand Oaks, California 91320

SAGE Publications India Pvt Ltd
32, M-Block Market
Great Kailash — I
New Delhi 110 048

British Library Cataloguing in Publication data

A catalogue record for this book is available from the British Library

ISBN 0 7619 5272 1

ISBN 0 7619 5273 X pbk

Library of Congress catalog card number 96-70412

Typeset by Paston Press Ltd, Loddon, Norfolk

Printed in Great Britain by
The Cromwell Press, Trowbridge, Wiltshire

Contents

Preface   xiii

Part I   From Theory to Methodology   **1**

1   TYPES OF RESEARCH PROBLEMS AND RESEARCH SITUATIONS   3

1.1   Preliminaries   3
    1.1.1   Units and Characteristics   3
    1.1.2   Units of Different Levels   4
    1.1.3   Characteristics of Different Measurement Levels   5
    1.1.4   The Dispersion of Units   6
    1.1.5   Many Characteristics   6
    1.1.6   Research Situations and Statement Systems   8
1.2   A Number of Research Examples and their Basic Format   8
    1.2.1   Humour as a Technique of Social Influence   8
    1.2.2   Childlessness   10
    1.2.3   Christian Beliefs and Anti-Semitism   12
    1.2.4   External Rewards and Intrinsic Motivation   15
    1.2.5   Poor and Rich Neighbourhoods   17
    1.2.6   Marital Adjustment   19
    1.2.7   Economic Inequality and Political Instability   23
    1.2.8   Styles in Furnishing the Living Room   26

2   A CLASSIFICATION OF CLASSICAL TECHNIQUES OF MULTIVARIATE ANALYSIS   31

2.1   Starting Points   32
    2.1.1   Our Notation System   32
    2.1.2   A First Acquaintance with Techniques   35
2.2   Subclassifications   35
    2.2.1   Dependent and Non-Dependent Techniques   35
    2.2.2   The Number of Dependent Variables   38
    2.2.3   The Measurement Level of Dependent Variables   39
    2.2.4   The Measurement Level of Independent Variables   40
    2.2.5   The Additive and Interactive Structure   40
    2.2.6   The Orthogonality of Independent Variables   41
    2.2.7   The Problem-Variable and the Problem-Relation   43
    2.2.8   One or More Hierarchical Steps   44
    2.2.9   Manifest and Latent Variables   46

2.2.10	The Number of Latent Variables	48
2.2.11	The Orthogonality of Latent Variables	50
2.2.12	The Measurement Level for Non-Dependent Techniques	51
2.2.13	Testing and Gauging	52
2.2.14	The Analysis of Variables and of Units	53
2.2.15	Linear and Non-linear Techniques of Analysis	54
2.2.16	The Analysis of Data and of Similarities	54
2.2.17	Other Classifications	55

3	THE ANALYSIS TECHNIQUE AS THE MIRROR OF THE RESEARCH PROBLEM	56
3.1	Research Examples	57
3.1.1	The Influence of Total Institutions on Self-Image	57
3.1.2	The Trade Union Militant	58
3.1.3	Occupational Sex Identification and the Assessment of the Male and Female Earnings Inequality	60
3.1.4	Student Evaluations of Teaching Merit	61
3.1.5	Interracial and Intraracial Rape	63
3.1.6	Organizational Mobility in a Nuclear Research Complex	64
3.1.7	Reform in Elementary Education: A Black Box	65
3.1.8	The Value and the Valuation of Jobs	67
3.1.9	A Classification of 16 Native-American Tribes	68
3.1.10	The Classical and Modern Role of Women in Matrimonial Advertisements	70
3.1.11	Absence Because of Illness	71
3.1.12	Are Non-Working People Socially Isolated?	72
3.1.13	Educational Level Achieved by Foreign Pupils	74
3.1.14	The Subjective Burden of Heart Attack Patients	75
3.2	The Dependency Theory: Manipulations of the Researcher	77
3.2.1	A Causal Analysis	78
3.2.2	Measurement Models	79
3.2.3	Causal Analysis without Hierarchical Steps	80
3.2.4	Degree of Development as a Trichotomy	80
3.2.5	Degree of Dependency as 'More' or 'Less'	81
3.2.6	A Model with Several Dependent Variables	81
3.2.7	A Dependency Set and a Development Set	82

Part II	**From Methodology to Analysis**	**85**
4	THE EXPERIMENTAL DESIGN: THE EFFECT OF HUMOUR ON FINANCIAL CONCESSION	90
4.1	The Standard Experiment	90
4.2	The OXO Notation	90
4.3	Implicit Multivariate Analysis	91
4.4	The Preliminary Investigation	91
4.5	Bivariate Association	92

4.6	The Data Matrix	92
4.7	The Causal Diagram	93
4.8	The *t* Test of Difference of Means	93
4.9	The Experimental Design in Research Practice	95
4.10	SPSS for Windows Output of Student's *t* Test	96
5	MULTIPLE REGRESSION ANALYSIS: THE CAUSES OF CHILDLESSNESS	99
5.1	The Research Problem and the Causal Diagram	99
5.2	The Data Matrix	99
5.3	Bivariate Regression Analysis: The Influence of Working on Childlessness	100
	5.3.1 The Model	100
	5.3.2 Geometric Approach	101
	5.3.3 Objectives of the Technique	104
	5.3.4 Calculation of the Regression Function	104
	5.3.5 The Strength of the Relationship and the Explained Variance	106
	5.3.6 Interpretations of the Correlation Coefficient	108
	5.3.7 Standardized Coefficients	110
	5.3.8 The Significance Test	113
5.4	Multiple Regression Analysis: The Influence of Working and Mean Age at Marriage on Childlessness	115
	5.4.1 The Model	115
	5.4.2 Geometric Approach	116
	5.4.3 Objectives of the Technique	118
	5.4.4 Preparatory Bivariate Analyses	118
	5.4.5 Calculation of the Regression Function	119
	5.4.6 The Strength of the Relationship and the Explained Variance	121
	5.4.7 Standardized Partial Regression Coefficients	122
	5.4.8 The Significance Test	124
	5.4.9 The Tests of Additivity and Linearity	126
	5.4.10 The Multicollinearity Problem	128
	5.4.11 The Analysis of Residuals	131
	5.4.12 Multiple Regression Analysis in Matrix Notation	132
	5.4.13 SPSS for Windows Output of Multiple Regression Analysis	135
6	PARTIAL CORRELATION AND PATH ANALYSIS: THE CAUSAL INFLUENCE OF CHRISTIAN BELIEFS ON ANTI-SEMITISM	140
6.1	The Research Problem and the Causal Diagram	140
6.2	The Data Matrix	142
6.3	Partial Correlation Analysis	142
	6.3.1 The Model	142
	6.3.2 Geometric Approach	145
	6.3.3 Objectives of the Technique	149
	6.3.4 Calculation of the Partial Correlation	149

	6.3.5	The Coefficient of Part Correlation	154
	6.3.6	The Significance Tests	157
6.4	The Simon–Blalock Procedure for Complex Causal Models		157
6.5	Path Analysis		159
6.6	SPSS for Windows Output of Partial Correlation and Path Analysis		179

| 7 | ANALYSIS OF VARIANCE AND COVARIANCE: THE EFFECT OF INTERACTION OF MONETARY REWARDS AND TASK INTEREST ON MOTIVATION | 183 |

7.1	The Research Problem and the Causal Diagram	183
7.2	The Data Matrix	184
7.3	The Model of Analysis of Variance	186
7.4	Geometric Approach	188
7.5	Objectives of the Technique	192
7.6	Calculations in One-Way ANOVA: Classical Approach	193
7.7	The ANOVA Summary Table	196
7.8	The t Test as Simplified F Test	196
7.9	Calculations in Two-Way ANOVA: Classical Approach	197
7.10	The Dummy Regression Approach	201
7.11	Testing the Global Model via the Regression Approach	204
7.12	Analysis of Covariance	206
7.13	The Factorial Experiment	209
7.14	The 2×2 Factorial Design	210
7.15	The 2×3 Factorial Design	212
7.16	Orthogonality, Homoscedasticity, Normality, Linearity	214
7.17	SPSS for Windows Output of ANOVA and ANCOVA	215

| 8 | TWO-GROUP DISCRIMINANT ANALYSIS: POOR AND RICH NEIGHBOURHOODS | 231 |

8.1	The Research Problem and the Causal Diagram	231
8.2	The Data Matrix	232
8.3	The Model of Discriminant Analysis	233
8.4	Geometric Approach	235
8.5	Objectives of the Technique	238
8.6	Preparatory Calculations: Matrices $\mathbf{T}$, $\mathbf{B}$, $\mathbf{W}$ and $\mathbf{C_w}$	239
8.7	Calculation of the Discriminant Function t	242
8.8	Classification and Prediction	246
8.9	Significance Testing: Preparatory Remarks	248
8.10	Significance Testing: Univariate Tests	249
8.11	Significance Testing: the Multivariate Test	250
8.12	Mahalanobis' Distance D^2	251
8.13	The Dummy Regression Approach	252
8.14	Equal Within-Groups Covariance Matrices: Box's M test	254
8.15	SPSS for Windows Output of Discriminant Analysis	255

9	FACTOR ANALYSIS: THE INVESTIGATION OF MARITAL ADJUSTMENT	266
9.1	Principal Components Analysis	266
	9.1.1 The Research Problem and the Diagram	266
	9.1.2 The Data Matrix	267
	9.1.3 The Model of Principal Components Analysis	268
	9.1.4 Geometric Approach	269
	9.1.5 Objectives of the Technique	270
	9.1.6 Examining the Eigenstructure of $\mathbf{X}$ or $\mathbf{R}$: Introductory Remarks on Singular Value Decomposition	271
	9.1.7 Eigenvalues and Eigenvectors of the Marital Adjustment Data	272
	9.1.8 Matrix $\mathbf{C}$ of Component Scores	274
	9.1.9 Matrix $\mathbf{A}$ of Component Loadings	276
	9.1.10 The measure of Redundancy of a Component	278
	9.1.11 Matrix $\mathbf{A}$ of Component Loadings and the Explained Variance	278
	9.1.12 How Many Components?	280
	9.1.13 Component Rotation	281
	9.1.14 Orthogonal Rotation	283
	9.1.15 Oblique Rotation	283
	9.1.16 SPSS for Windows Output of PCA	284
9.2	Principal Factor Analysis	290
	9.2.1 The Research Problem and the Diagram	290
	9.2.2 The Data Matrix	290
	9.2.3 The Model of Principal Factor Analysis	290
	9.2.4 The Reduced Correlation Matrix	292
	9.2.5 Eigenvalues and Eigenvectors of the Marital Adjustment Data	293
	9.2.6 The Factor Matrix $\mathbf{A}$ for all Factors: The Problem of Negative Eigenvalues	294
	9.2.7 Substantial Difference Between PFA and PCA	295
	9.2.8 Factor Matrix $\mathbf{A}$ for the First Factor and Further Iterations	295
	9.2.9 The Communalities	295
	9.2.10 Rotations and Factor Scores	296
	9.2.11 SPSS for Windows Output of PFA	297
9.3	Variations of Factor Analysis Methods	299
	9.3.1 The Diagonal Method	300
	9.3.2 The Centroid Method	303
	9.3.3 The Minimum Residuals Method (MINRES)	307
	9.3.4 Canonical Factor Analysis	308
	9.3.5 The Maximum Likelihood Method	310
	9.3.6 Alpha Factor Analysis	312
	9.3.7 Image Analysis	315
	9.3.8 The Multiple Group Method	317
9.4	Other Methods in the World of Factor Analysis	319
	9.4.1 R and Q Factor Analysis	320
	9.4.2 Non-linear and Non-metric Factor Analysis	321
	9.4.3 Higher-Order Factor Analysis	321

10	CANONICAL CORRELATION ANALYSIS: THE STUDY OF ECONOMIC INEQUALITY AND POLITICAL INSTABILITY	322
10.1	The Research Problem and the Causal Diagram	322
10.2	The Data Matrix	323
10.3	The Model of Canonical Correlation Analysis	324
10.4	Three Types of Correlations	325
10.5	Geometric Approach	326
10.6	Objectives of the Technique	328
10.7	Examination of the Eigenstructure of the $\mathbf{R}_{yy}^{-1}\,\mathbf{R}_{xy}^{-1}\,\mathbf{R}_{xx}^{-1}\mathbf{R}_{xy}$ Matrix	330
10.8	Examination of the Eigenstructure of Russett's Data	333
10.9	The **A** and **B** Matrices of Canonical Weights	335
10.10	The Canonical Variables x^* and y^*	336
10.11	A Causal Approach to Canonical Correlation Analysis	337
10.12	The Significance Tests	338
10.13	SPSS for Windows Output of Canonical Correlation Analysis	339
11	TECHNIQUES WITH MULTIPLE DEPENDENT VARIABLES	345
11.1	Multivariate Analysis of Variance; Where is the best place on earth to live?	345
11.1.1	The Research Problem and the Causal Diagram	345
11.1.2	The Data Matrix	346
11.1.3	Objectives of the Technique	346
11.1.4	Student's t, Fisher's F, Hotelling's T and Λ	347
11.1.5	Preparatory Calculations: the Matrices **W**, **B** and **T**	348
11.1.6	Wilks's Lambda Test	350
11.1.7	Alternatives for Wilks's lambda Test: Multivariate Analysis of Variance as the Reverse of Discriminant Analysis	352
11.1.8	Multivariate Analysis of Variance, an Entire World	353
11.1.9	Assumptions	354
11.1.10	SPSS for Windows Output of Multivariate Analysis of Variance	354
11.2	Multiple Discriminant Analysis: Enclaves of Cubans in Miami: The Triple Labour Market Model	356
11.2.1	The Research Problem and the Causal Diagram	356
11.2.2	The Data Matrix	358
11.2.3	Wilks's Lambda Test	358
11.2.4	Wilks's Lambda as the Ratio $|\mathbf{W}|/|\mathbf{T}|$	360
11.2.5	Wilks's Lambda Test from the Eigenstructure of $\mathbf{W}^{-1}\mathbf{B}$	360
11.2.6	Classification	362
11.2.7	Homoscedasticity	362
11.3	Multiple Discriminant Analysis as Canonical Correlation Analysis	363
11.3.1	SPSS for Windows Output of Multiple Discriminant Analysis	365
11.3.2	SPSS for Windows Output of Multiple Discriminant Analysis as Canonical Correlation Analysis	368

Appendix: Required Mathematical and Statistical Knowledge 371

Statistical Tables 401

Bibliography 405

Index 409

Preface

Many textbooks in statistics are indifferent to the content of research work. They focus upon the mathematical analyses, and artificial examples are glued to the techniques on an *ad hoc* basis. If this book entails something new, and we hope it does, then this lies in a reaction against such absence of content. Our contribution does not deal with chickens and coins, but with practical empirical research in the social sciences. We examined hundreds of examples of actual research and made an appropriate selection in order to illustrate how a social scientific research problem leads to the choice of a certain technique of multivariate analysis. This subject of the appropriate choice is dealt with in the first part (From Theory to Methodology), so that the reader gets an overview of the different types of research problems and of the many kinds of multivariate analyses. This part can be read separately and is suitable for lectures in non-university higher education and for the first years of a university education. It can also be of great help to researchers who want to find their way through the entirety of technical choices when faced with their research problem. We deal with examples from psychology, sociology, economics, political science, international comparative research and other disciplines.

The second part, Chapters 4 to 11, is more technical in nature. A number of multivariate analyses are calculated in detail. But, here, too, we make the link with the research problem in two ways. Firstly, the examples from the first part are the starting point for the treatment of statistical techniques. Using a research example, like the study on the discrimination between poor and rich neighbourhoods, we construct a mini data set which will lead to the same results as were found in the original inquiry. Thereafter, the whole analysis of this little data set is calculated by hand, so that the reader gains insight on the smallest details of the technical procedure. We also present the computer output in order to show that the computer has made the same calculations as we have by hand. Secondly, the link with the content of the social scientific research problem is also revealed in the interpretation of the results of analysis. Here, too, the statistical literature is very poor. Conversations with mathematically oriented statisticians have taught us how much difficulty they have in putting the results of their complex calculations into words. A statistician has no problems with providing an exact calculation of the Gini index for a certain country, but finds it difficult to interpret it in terms of income inequality. We will cope with this problem of mathematical one-sidedness, paying close attention to the verbal interpretation of the results and to the theoretical feedback on the social scientific research problem.

The techniques which are treated in detail are Student's *t* test in the experimental design, multiple regression analysis, partial correlation and path analysis, analysis of variance and covariance, two-group discriminant analysis, factor analysis, canonical correlation analysis, multiple discriminant analysis and multivariate analysis of variance and covariance. For each of these techniques, we follow the same presentation scheme: the introduction of the research problem, the visual representation by means of an arrow diagram, the geometrical representation in a Cartesian system of coordinates, the formal elaboration of the calculation procedure, the verbal interpretation of the results and the theoretical feedback, and, finally, the computer output.

The study of Part II presupposes an elementary knowledge of statistics. In the Appendix we give a brief description of the most important notions, as well as an introduction to matrix algebra. This should be sufficient for studying the technical parts of this book, since, in Chapters 4, 5 and 6, we give a review of some elementary techniques (Student's t test, regression analysis, analysis of variance) and, in dealing with the more advanced techniques, we follow a reader-friendly approach.

It is the custom to thank all those who have contributed existentially to the realization of this book. As this concerns so many people over so many years, we dare not attempt a summing up of names, because someone would most certainly be forgotten. The many colleagues who have given comments on certain parts of the text, the many student assistants who have done research work, the Social Faculty who paid for these student assistants, the many secretaries who have given support, all of them have played an important role. Thanks, therefore, to the Erasmus University of Rotterdam.

PART I

FROM THEORY TO METHODOLOGY

In this first part we focus upon the link between theory and methodology. Many examples of social science research are given and the question of which multivariate analysis is appropriate for each of the research problems is answered.

This subject of the appropriate choice is worked out in three chapters: one with research examples, one with statistical techniques and one where the link between the research problem and the technique is made.

In the first chapter, after treating a few introductory points, we discuss a number of problems from genuine empirical social research. These problems all have a typical formal structure, which we will call a basic format and which we will visualize in the form of an arrow diagram.

In the second chapter an overview of multivariate analyses is given and here, too, the basic formats are visualized by means of arrow diagrams. In doing so we make a great number of subclassifications. The existing literature is very limited in this respect, for in most textbooks only three classification criteria are used: the measurement level of the variables (interval, ordinal, nominal), the causal character of the associations (dependent, interdependent) and the nature of the phenomena investigated (variables, objects). In our approach 20 criteria for classification are treated, so that the research worker can find his way through the labyrinth of possibilities.

In the third chapter we make the connection between the research problems and the techniques of multivariate analysis. Many additional research examples are discussed, which serve as an exercise for the reader in using the classification criteria when making the appropriate choice for a statistical technique. Thereafter, all this is put into perspective, as the nice idea of making an appropriate choice proves to be hopelessly relative. Starting from the dependency theory in international comparative research, we show how the research worker, with the help of elementary manipulations, can find many different choices for one and the same social scientific research problem.

1

Types of Research Problems and Research Situations

Successful research is planned research. Many research projects end in futility because the researcher has plunged recklessly into the research activity — going to the library, making notes, gathering data, making computer analyses — with only a partially thought-out plan and an inconclusive design. What both research planning and architectural planning have in common is that a well-conceived conceptualization is required before work on the project can begin. For successful completion, a building requires plans which are clearly conceived and accurately drawn. A research project should be no less totally visualized and precisely detailed.

In this chapter attention is given to the conceptualization of social scientific research. We take the line that each simple statement about social reality reflects a formal structure, which gives direction to the research plan. For example, Robert Michels' statement 'Bureaucratization entails oligarchization' represents the structure $\Delta B \rightarrow \Delta O$, where B indicates the degree of bureaucracy, O the degree of oligarchy, Δ the change and $\rightarrow$ the causal relation, where the reference units of the statement (for example, institutions) remain implicit and where it is not indicated how B, O and Δ have to be measured.

It is our intention to map out a considerable number of social scientific statements and to point out the formal structure which they represent, just like $\Delta B \rightarrow \Delta O$. We believe that each statement ever brought forward by a social scientific researcher reflects such a formal structure, which we will call a format. We also believe that revealing this format can facilitate the planning of research and we hope that, in doing so, we will build a bridge between social theory and methodology.

1.1 Preliminaries

1.1.1 Units and Characteristics

Our first starting point is that each statement is composed of **units** and **characteristics**, that for each characteristic a number of (at least two) **distinctions** can be made and that these distinctions show a certain **dispersion**. Take, for example, the statement: 'In our country the proportion of better-paid occupations is higher for men than for women.' The units are all employed persons in our country. The characteristics are the gender and the occupational income. The distinctions for gender are: man and woman; for income: low and high. An example of the way in which the units are spread over the characteristics is shown in Figure 1.1.

Suppose this is a sample of 1600 employed persons with as many men as women (800 each). Then it appears firstly that a high occupational income occurs less

gender

		man	woman	
income	high	320	80	400
	low	480	720	1200
		800	800	1600

Figure 1.1   The dispersion of units over two characteristics

frequently (400 = 25% of 1600) than a low income (1200 = 75% of 1600). It also appears that the group of men shows a high proportion of high incomes (320 = 40% of 800) and the group of women contains less high incomes (80 = 10% of 800). Thus, given the marginal totals, the units are spread over the distinctions of the characteristics in a way in which the high frequencies are in the combinations man-high and woman-low.

It is our opinion that each statement can be elaborated in this way, with units, characteristics, distinctions and dispersion. For the sceptical reader, we give as a second example the statement: 'God is infinitely good.' As far as the units are concerned, we are confronted with a borderline case. There is only one unit: God. There is also only one characteristic: goodness. The distinctions of this characteristic go from infinitely bad to infinitely good. The dispersion is zero in this example because the units (only one here) are extremely situated at one side, the infinite goodness.

Summarized: each statement (research problem, hypothesis, research question) is syntactically composed of: units, characteristics, distinctions and dispersion.

1.1.2   Units of Different Levels

In the statement 'In our country the proportion of better-paid occupations is higher for men than for women', the units are persons. On the other hand, in Robert Michels' statement, 'Bureaucratization entails oligarchization', the reference units are of a higher level: organizations. It is very important for a research worker to have an exact notion of the reference units of his or her statements (hypotheses, research questions). (S)he should realize that many forms of indistinctness can be at stake here. Take, for example, the concept of 'bureaucracy'. This concept does not only refer to institutions, but also to persons in these institutions, to the written texts that are drawn up in such institutions and to the ordering and regulatory character of these texts, to the authority relations that are thereby implied, and so on. This ambiguity and multi-interpretability gives a researcher who is studying bureaucracy free play in making his/her choice. (S)he might, for instance, take the person as the observational unit, code for each person the status of official and count the number of officials for each institution. The unit of analysis would then be the institution, but the observational unit would be the individual. So, the concept of bureaucracy, measured as the number of officials, would be an aggregated characteristic of the institution. The same researcher could, however, also choose the texts that are being produced in an institution as a unit of observation or analysis. (S)he might also follow the strategy of questioning some persons, judges, on the regulating character of these texts and on the authority relations that are expressed in it. Each of these options places emphasis on one of the components of the concept of bureaucracy and these components are different when one chooses the institution instead of the person as the unit of reference.

It is of course evident that the theoretical concept is conclusive for making an adequate choice of the research units.

1.1.3   *Characteristics of Different Measurement Levels*

Referring back to our metaphor of the social scientist as architect, there is a relationship of tension between the concept of the planner and the factual realization of the building. A limited budget, the conflicting demands of the future owner and other obstacles will result in a situation where the execution of the plan is never optimal. The researcher is confronted with a comparable situation when (s)he tries to find adequate operationalizations for his/her concepts and, especially so when (s)he determines the measurement level of the indicators. Three measurement levels are usually distinguished. Characteristics are measured on a quantitative scale (age), on an ordinal scale (social status) or on a nominal scale (nationality). **Nominal** characteristics do not show any order in the distinctions (a Belgian is not higher in rank than a Dutchman or a Swiss), **ordinal** characteristics do show such an order (social status is high, median or low in rank). As well as an order, **quantitative** characteristics have the feature that the distances between the distinctions can be determined (George, six years of age, is four years older than Joanna, two years of age) as can the ratios (George is three times as old as Joanna). When this last condition is fulfilled, we speak of a ratio scale; if it is not, we have only an interval scale.

This last distinction is of minor importance for the social sciences. The Celsius and Fahrenheit scales are interval scales, because the ratios cannot be meaningfully determined (it is not twice as hot at 20 °C as at 10 °C). The absolute measurement of temperature in degrees Kelvin is a ratio scale because 0 °K is the absolute zero point (absence of Brownian movement; at 20 °K there is twice as much movement as at 10 °K). We will make no further distinction between the interval and ratio measurement level and will speak of the quantitative (or metric, or at least interval) measurement level.

The measurement level plays a very important role in the design and the execution of a research plan. The relationship of tension, which we mentioned above, is as follows. Certain characteristics can have a measurement level of their own, but the researcher can decide otherwise. A well-known example is given by the school results of pupils. The measurement level is in itself ordinal, because every teacher will admit that marks are relative in nature, that the distance from five to six on a maximum of ten is not the same as from seven to eight, and that the marking of exams is done according to a system of comparison in pairs. The analysis of school results thus implies a jump from the ordinal to the quantitative measurement level. The reverse occurs very often as well. The determination of age by means of the trichotomy young, median, old is a reduction of the quantitative to the ordinal measurement level.

The researcher can therefore do two things. Being a social architect, (s)he can use expensive and refined materials, whereas (s)he might have reached the same results with cheaper means. On the other hand, (s)he can prescribe materials that are too cheap and that affect the solidity of the building. Here, too, the theoretical concept should be conclusive.

1.1.4   The Dispersion of Units

Research doesn't make much sense when the distinctions of the characteristics are not spread over the units. The statement 'God is infinitely good' is not open for research because its validity could only be appreciated if bad gods existed with which a comparison could be made. A characteristic must have at least two distinctions (for example, sex: man, woman) and the units must be spread over these distinctions. In the planning of research, one should be very attentive in making sure that the characteristics show sufficient dispersion. An inquiry on the abortion debate makes sense when the opinions are divided, but not so when everybody holds the same opinion. The dispersion of school results, the distribution of incomes and the division of political opinions are sufficient in magnitude in most societies. But there are a great number of social phenomena for which the units are situated on one side of the characteristic. The 'occupational level of the father' of immigrant children in our country is predominantly 'low'. The 'social origin' of female students at universities is predominantly 'high'. In such cases, where the units are insufficiently spread over the distinctions of a characteristic, the researcher might have to drop the characteristic from the research. (S)he might of course think of other solutions, such as the extension of the number of units. When adding males to the university file of female students, the social origin will have a higher dispersion. However, in doing so, it is possible that the research problem itself will be changed. The latter must evidently remain the ultimate guideline.

1.1.5   Many Characteristics

The format of a statement becomes more complicated when it contains more than two characteristics. Take our example of the relationship between gender and occupational income and suppose that this relationship does hold for salaried employees, but not for those in small businesses or for the self-employed. Then the statement becomes more complex, for, in addition to gender (man, woman) and occupational income (low, high), a new characteristic comes into play: the nature of the occupation (salaried, self-employed). For salaried employees there is a higher proportion of men with high incomes than women with high incomes, but for the self-employed this relationship is absent (or reversed). The research hypothesis now shows a higher degree of complexity. Figure 1.1 now becomes Figure 1.2.

For salaried employees the proportions of high incomes for men and women are $260/680 = 0.38$ and $20/680 = 0.03$ respectively. For the self-employed these proportions are: $60/120 = 0.50$ and $60/120 = 0.50$. This situation is an example of what we will call an effect of interaction: the relation between two characteristics X and Y behaves differently for the distinctions of a third characteristic Z.

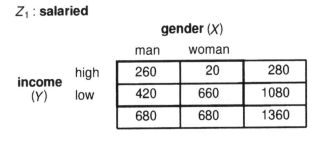

Z_1 : **salaried**

gender (X)

		man	woman	
income (Y)	high	260	20	280
	low	420	660	1080
		680	680	1360

Z_2 : **self-employed**

gender (X)

		man	woman	
income (Y)	high	60	60	120
	low	60	60	120
		120	120	240

Figure 1.2   *The dispersion of units over three characteristics*

This is only one of the many formats that can be encountered in a statement with three characteristics. Another possibility is given in the following example. There is a higher proportion of suicides in the group of entrepreneurs who go bankrupt than in the group of entrepreneurs with flourishing businesses. The units are entrepreneurs. The two characteristics are bankruptcy X (yes, no) and suicide Y (yes, no). A causal relation $X \rightarrow Y$ is postulated. But this relation disappears if we introduce age Z (young, old). It no longer holds, neither for the younger nor older entrepreneurs, that bankruptcy causes suicide. But, on the other hand, there is a strong relationship between Z and X (older entrepreneurs go bankrupt more frequently than younger ones) and between Z and Y (older entrepreneurs commit suicide more frequently than younger ones).

The format is now different from the one given in Figure 1.2. There is no effect of interaction in this case, for the relationship between bankruptcy and suicide is no different for young and old entrepreneurs. On the contrary, the relationship disappears in both age groups. And, as there is a strong relationship between age and each of the two characteristics, age now plays the role of partialling out: the originally postulated causal connection $X \rightarrow Y$ disappears and the relations $Z \rightarrow X$ and $Z \rightarrow Y$ take its place. In the literature, such a formal structure is known as 'spuriousness' (spurious causal relation).

One can conceive of many other formats. The situation becomes still more complicated when the number of characteristics is more than three. Before developing any systematics on the most important types of formal structure contained in statements, we must first dispel the idea that this chapter will be limited to some sort of ennobled proposition logic. Research is naturally not restricted to little statements. The architect not only concentrates on bricks and walls, but (s)he has to raise a whole building. Therefore, it is important that (s)he doesn't lose sight of the basic configuration.

1.1.6   Research Situations and Statement Systems

In view of the fact that research is not restricted to the testing of merely one or a few hypotheses, one can hardly speak of 'the' format. A whole battery of characteristics and statements are incorporated in a research plan. Certain small groups of statements will require separate attention and will display a specific format. Therefore, many formal structures will be met with in one and the same scientific study/research. But, just as the architect wants to give a certain character to the building, the research worker, too, will have a basic format in mind.

An inquiry of the spread of incomes in our society is an analysis of dispersion. An historical study of the influence of feudalism on capitalism is causal research. An investigation of the opinions in a population on the subject of euthanasia is a descriptive analysis of the common factors. A study of the subordination of women as compared to men in our society is an analysis of discrimination. These are a few examples from which it is apparent that an investigation always begins with a global research problem, to which a basic format is linked. In our typology, we will be predominantly guided by this global structure of the research problem. It is of course evident that such a basic structure involves a whole battery of subhypotheses, so that a complex system of statements emerges, just like the basic concept of a building is subdivided into dining rooms, bedrooms, kitchens, living rooms and garden sheds. This analysis of subsystems is part of the more refined methodology of research. But one should never lose sight of the fundamentals. Let us imagine that a researcher–contractor sits at the table with a methodologist–architect: they first draw up a global research plan, and the more detailed elaborations follow at a later stage.

1.2   A Number of Research Examples and their Basic Format

1.2.1   Humour as a Technique of Social Influence

It is said of Henry Kissinger that he used humour as a tool of diplomacy. According to Valeriani (1979) Kissinger's banter inspired banter in others and usually led to a more relaxed atmosphere in the private, formal discussions or negotiations with world leaders. More generally, students of social behaviour have suggested for years that humour may facilitate social influence.

O'Quin and Aronoff (1981) tried to test this hypothesis scientifically. They set up an experiment where the task was to reach agreement on the price of a painting. They preprogrammed the presence and absence of humour in the bargaining situation and they measured the degrees of financial concessions being made. An equal number of men and women participated in the experiment. A number of persons (here, too, equal frequencies of men and women) were trained as experimenter, confederate or observer. Four members comprised a team: the experimenter, a confederate, and two observers. Prior to the manipulation, many conditions were planned: humour or no-humour, man or woman as confederate and a small, medium or large financial demand for the painting. The subjects were randomly assigned to the conditions (randomization). A faked draw always assigned the subject to the position of 'Buyer' and the confederate to the position of 'Seller'. Each participant received 'private instructions'. The confederate's sheet contained a programmed script that detailed each bid, beginning at 70 000 dollars, plus a short verbalization on each bid. The subject's private instructions assigned a starting bid of 25 000 dollars and made it clear that, after the first, bids might be of any size or number. During the bargaining, the experimenter was seated behind a small wooden partition. The observers, stationed in observation rooms behind the mirrors, recorded each instance of the subject's laughing/smiling behaviour on a four-step rating scale. They also recorded each of the subject's verbalizations. The free bargaining portion of the session was over when the participants had bargained to within 10 000 dollars of each other. At this point, the experimenter broke in on them to say time was nearly up and that agreement must be reached shortly. Immediately after time was called, the confederate introduced the independent manipulation. In the no-humour condition, the confederate said: 'Well, my final offer is ... dollars.' In the humour condition, he or she smiled and said: 'Well, my final offer is ... dollars, and I'll throw in my pet frog.' The size of the demand was varied, thus asking the subject for a small, medium or large concession. Bargaining then continued; the confederate made 2000 dollar concessions on each postmanipulation bid until final agreement was reached. Immediately after the session, participants received a postexperimental questionnaire with 30 Likert items asking for self-reports of nervousness, liking for the partner, liking for the task, perceived humorousness of the situation and perceived restrictions on bargaining freedom.

In analysing the results of this experiment, the researchers built in an enormous number of controls. Examples of control variables were the sex of the experimenter and the confederate, the interobserver reliability for the coding of laughter, the questionnaire variables, the degree of commitment of the subjects and other factors that could cause disturbance. None of these control variables showed a significant effect on the making of concessions.

The most important result of this research was that, controlling for all these factors, the subjects in the humour condition made a larger proportional concession than no-humour subjects. This effect of humour remained stable in each of the three demand conditions and in each of the sex groups. As far as gender is concerned, females both smiled and laughed more than males and males took longer to reach agreement, but both sexes made the same financial concessions in the end.

The results establish that humour may indeed be used to influence others. We should of course not conclude that the formula for success is to mix one's request with a mild joke to create compliance, for it is clear that the context in which an influence attempt is made should be considered. But in this research it is scientifically supported that humour contributes to compliance.

We have started with this research example because the basic format of the research problem contains **only two characteristics**, the humour and the financial concession. A causal relation between these two characteristics is postulated: the use of humour causes higher financial concessions.

However, there are in fact **other characteristics** that play a role in this research, like the sex, the demand price, the 30 items of the questionnaire and others. These characteristics are explicitly made use of in the analysis, but they are only **implicitly**

Figure 1.3   The bivariate causal structure

contained in the basic research problem, notably as control factors. The controls reach even much further than the factors that were just mentioned, because the random assignment of the persons to the different experimental conditions (randomization) sees to it that other unknown factors cannot show more than random differences. So, in fact, in addition to the controlling factors that are explicitly designed in the experiment (by matching), there are unknown, latent control factors as well (by randomization). But the basic structure of the research problem contains only one causal factor and only one effect factor, as is shown in Figure 1.3.

The research in discussion is an example of a well-controlled standard experiment and, strictly speaking, is out of place in this book, for the basic research problem deals with merely two characteristics. In all the examples to follow, the basic format will contain three or more characteristics. The corresponding difficulties that will arise in the analyses will be greater. We must therefore realize that the design of this first research example is a sort of ideal, from which all following designs will deviate.

1.2.2   Childlessness

The changing pattern of fertility in the United States during the past decade and some of the reasons for this change have been widely discussed in the demographic literature. An impetus to recent considerations has been the approach of zero population growth — the average two-child family as compared to the average three-child family of a decade or so ago. The change in childlessness, which is a component of the larger trend in fertility, has been relatively ignored in the analysis of these fertility trends. Although in recent years it has been noted that fewer women live through their childbearing years without giving birth, the trends in childlessness for the 1970–1974 period are differentiated by age group. For women of 30 years of age and over, a trend toward declining childlessness is apparent, and it has been the concentration on women who have completed childbearing that has led some researchers to suggest that voluntary childlessness is nearly non-existent. But common sense would indicate that the incidence of childlessness in western society might be expected to increase, because of the changing status and role of women and because of the improvement of birth control techniques.

We refer to two researchers, G.F. de Jong and R.R. Sell. According to them it seems as if we are dealing with a paradox: in spite of the trends that would be in favour of childlessness, exactly the reverse seems to have happened. They argue that it concerns only an apparent paradox, for the demographic inquiries, which are concentrated on married women of 30 years and older over a long time-period, in fact choose the wrong frame of validity. It is apparent that part of the paradox lies in the differential trends in marital childlessness for different age cohorts. For women aged 30 and over, in the period 1940–1974, the percentage of women who were ever married remaining childless declines almost constantly, but for the younger age cohorts a different pattern emerges: up to 1960 this percentage declines, but since 1960 it has started to increase. This result was reason enough for a number of researchers in the United States to study the Census data and Public Use Samples of 1960 as compared to those of 1970 and to analyse the changes (increase and decline) in the percentage of childless women as functions of the changes in a number of explanatory factors. One such study was undertaken in 1975 by the two researchers mentioned above, G.F. de Jong and R.R. Sell. They considered white women who were ever married, aged 18 to 40, at two time points, 1960 and 1970. The unit of analysis was the quarter-year age from ages 18.00 to 40.75, so that 92 age categories were distinguished. For the operationalization of the characteristics a difference between 1960 and 1970 was made for each age category. This means that a characteristic measures the change over a decade. For example, the characteristic 'change in the percentage of childless women' has 92 scores, one for each age category, and each score is the difference between the percentage of childless women in 1970 and the percentage of childless women in 1960.

Referring to the foregoing section, where the distinction between units, characteristics, distinctions and dispersion was made, we are dealing with a special case here, because the units in this research are situated on the macro-level. They are not individuals, but 92 groups of persons. The persons of a group all have the same age within a quarter-year. The characteristics of the macro-units are measured as a change between 1960 and 1970, in the form of a difference of means or proportions. These differences are the distinctions of a characteristic. The measurement level is therefore quantitative.

We select a few causal factors for the explanation of childlessness:

X_1 = decade change in percentage of labour-force participation,
X_2 = decade change in mean number of years of school completed,
X_3 = decade change in percentage of disrupted marriages,
X_4 = decade change in mean age at first marriage.

The characteristic of childlessness itself is:

Y = decade change in percentage of childless women.

The basic format of this research is the **convergent causal structure**, as is represented by Figure 1.4. We call this structure convergent because there are many causes and only one effect, so that the arrows converge in one point. This outline is the reverse of the divergent structure with one cause and many effects. The characteristic to explain is Y, the change in childlessness. Explanatory factors are the characteristics X_1 to X_4. The arrows indicate the cause–effect relations. The causal factors are conceived of as mutually independent in principle, which means that the addition of a new factor offers an extra explanation for childlessness. For, suppose that X_2 and X_4 were strongly connected, because women who marry at young age have a low level of education, then the addition of X_4 to X_2 would hardly offer an extra explanation for childlessness, as there would be an overlap between the causal factors. In technical language, we will say that there must be **no multicollinearity**.

It must also not be the case that the causal factors execute their effect 'in combination'. It is expected that they each have explanatory power 'on their own',

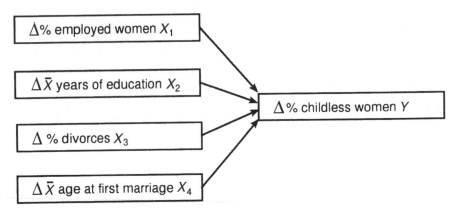

Figure 1.4   The convergent causal structure

so that the sum of all the factors offers a global explanation. This means that the conceptual model is **additive**.

This basic format of the convergent causal structure is paramount in the social sciences. Not only increasing childlessness, but countless social changes, such as increasing criminality, income inequality, environmental pollution, suicide, youth unemployment and other factors, give rise to the need for a causal explanation of the convergent, multicausal type. The new social situation is experienced as a disequilibrium and a number of causal factors are conceived of in order to give an explanation for the distorted situation.

1.2.3   Christian Beliefs and Anti-Semitism

Christian ethics stresses the brotherhood of all men, yet research reveals strong prejudice among Christians, even more among church members than non-members. One aspect of the linkage between religiosity and prejudice is the part played by Christian beliefs in producing anti-Semitism today.

Past research has come to several conclusions, of which two explanatory factors are predominant: theology and teaching. Elements clearly exist in Christian theology which feed anti-Semitism, especially the portrayal of the Jews' rejection of Jesus in the New Testament. Historical accounts of anti-Semitism throughout Western history demonstrate convincingly how the New Testament tradition encouraged this. Elements of anti-Semitism are also clearly present in Christian teaching today. Analysts of the content of Sunday school materials and other church publications, both Protestant and Catholic, have found some very negative portrayals of Jews.

The presence of negative references to Jews in the New Testament or in present-day Christian publications, however, does not prove that Christian beliefs are an important source of secular anti-Semitism in our society today. Many Christians have limited acquaintance with, or commitment to, the New Testament teachings. And even if it can be demonstrated that certain beliefs about Jews held by Christians today correlate with secular anti-Semitism, it is possible that the relationship is **not causal but spurious**. It is always possible that other factors — economic, social or social–psychological — are the sources of both the Christian faith and anti-Semitism.

Many researchers have investigated this spuriousness. They have stressed a great number of factors which might overshadow the causal relation between religion and anti-Semitism. Educational level, occupation of head of household, income, size of community of origin, region of origin, age, political tendency and sex are predominantly used as control variables in the social sciences. But the final link remained in spite of these controls. More important were a number of social–psychological measures, such as authoritarianism, dogmatism and anomia. Many research studies have shown that most of the relationship between the religious variables and anti-Semitism was rendered spurious by these personality characteristics.

The basic format of these investigations is that of spurious causality, as is shown in Figure 1.5.

The question mark in Figure 1.5 indicates that the originally postulated relationship is apparently causal. True, there is a relationship between Christian belief and anti-Semitism, but this should not be conceived as a direct cause–effect relationship. As far as causality is concerned, the socio-psychological characteristics (dogmatism and others) produce anti-Semitism (replacement causality): dogmatic personalities have a dislike for Jews, non-dogmatic personalities do not have this dislike or have it much less. The same characteristics also produce Christian belief: dogmatic personalities are more inclined to Christian belief than non-dogmatic personalities. In this way the relationship between religion and anti-Semitism is literally overshadowed by the socio-psychological characteristics. True, the relationship exists, but in causal terms it has to be conceived of from these characteristics (it is explained away by these characteristics).

The subject of anti-Semitism is of course far more complex than has been outlined so far. We selected part of an American study done by Hoge and Carroll (1975) in order to illustrate the structure of spurious causality. In the same study another format is examined, that of **indirect causality**. The idea is that, although religious orthodoxy is not a direct cause of anti-Semitism, the causal effect runs indirectly through intermediate factors. Libertarianism is such a factor. Adherents of Christian belief are less libertarian and a non-libertarian attitude produces anti-Semitism. Figure 1.6 represents this structure of indirect causality.

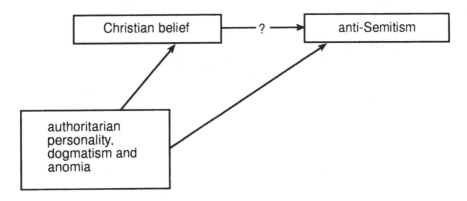

Figure 1.5 Spurious causality

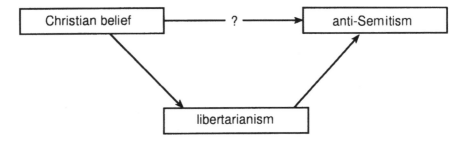

Figure 1.6   Indirect causality

In Hoge and Carroll's research the formats of Figures 1.5 and 1.6 are combined, which results in a rather complex model.

For example, age and educational level appeared to have an important role in explaining away the relationship, but this spurious causality evolved indirectly through libertarianism. Therefore a combination of the two formats had to be considered, as follows: on the one hand educated people are more libertarian and therefore less anti-Semitic and on the other hand educated people are less inclined to the Christian doctrine. Figure 1.7 gives a visual representation of this complex argument.

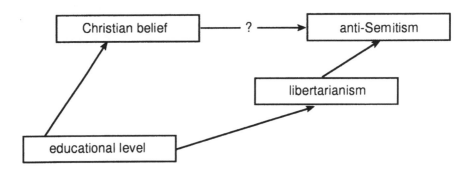

Figure 1.7   Spurious and indirect causality in combination

These two basic formats are very important for the social sciences. The search for factors that can explain away the originally postulated relationship (spurious causality) or that can help to explain it (indirect causality) is a critical activity that enhances the scientific quality of causal research.

The reader who wants to practise distinguishing the two formats, can do this for the following triads of characteristics, where the first is always the causal factor, the second the effect factor and the third the antecedent or intermediate control factor:

– social level, number of children, effectiveness of birth control;
– marital state, absenteeism, number of children;
– bankruptcy, suicide, age;
– motivation, achievement, presence in lectures at college education;
– marital state, absenteeism, age;

- educational level, duration of holidays abroad, income;
- number of children, divorce, duration of marriage;
- consumption of butter, heart attack, north or south of Belgium;
- frequent occurrence of storks, birth-level, rurality.

1.2.4 External Rewards and Intrinsic Motivation

Is there an effect of external rewards, for example monetary rewards, on intrinsic motivation? This issue has been the focal point of a great deal of controversy among psychologists. The traditional belief is that external and internal rewards act on intrinsic motivation in an additive fashion. This means that the award of an amount of money for the performance of a task brings about an extra increase in intrinsic motivation, even if the person was already very motivated because of the internal rewards of the activity (such as intellectual satisfaction, self-realization and the like). Recent findings seem to be breaking down this traditional belief. In fact, evidence seems to indicate that contingent external rewards cause a decrease in intrinsic motivation.

Intrinsic motivation is usually defined as the motivation to perform a task or activity when no apparent reward is received, except that which is directly involved with the task itself. Extrinsic motivation, on the other hand, is defined as the motivation to perform a task or activity strictly for the external rewards that are received.

Intrinsic motivation can be observed in many different ways. A behavioural measure can be used, i.e., the amount of free time spent on a task. But attitudinal measures of intrinsic motivation are also possible, i.e., ratings of interest and liking for a task.

Behavioural measures as well as attitudinal measures showed similar results: subjects who received a contingent monetary reward for performing a task demonstrated significantly less intrinsic motivation to do the task than subjects who received no reward. Additional research has demonstrated this effect with nursery school children, elementary school children, high school students and college students.

Cognitive evaluation theory states that intrinsically motivated behaviour is behaviour that allows a person to feel competent and self-determining. When an external reward is introduced, the perceived locus of causality shifts from within the person to the external reward. Once this change occurs, the individual no longer feels self-determining; therefore, intrinsic motivation is decreased. If this shift in one's locus of causality occurs and then the reward is removed, the major justification for performing the task is also removed.

The present research expands the previous research by considering previously neglected variables: the type of task and the task structure. As far as the type of task is concerned, a distinction should be made between interesting and boring tasks. Although monetary rewards tend to decrease intrinsic motivation on interesting tasks, rewards may actually increase intrinsic motivation on boring tasks. Additionally, when the reward is perceived as an integral part of the task itself (e.g., a game such as poker), the reward may lead to an increase in one's motivation.

These results, too, can be interpreted in terms of a direct reinforcement–effect model. When the negative effects of a change in one's locus of causality are minimal (as in tasks of low initial interest) or prevented (as in tasks in which the reward is integral), the major effect of rewards is to associate pleasant effect (aroused by the reward) with the task, thereby increasing the attractiveness of the task. However, when this shift is substantial (as in interesting tasks), the effect will be the reverse.

Another task characteristic is the task structure. Task structure refers to the manner in which a task supervisor organizes and defines worker activities and the way he/she plans the role that workers are to assume. In the high-task-structure condition, subjects were not given much freedom. They were given written instructions providing explicit rules detailing the procedures to be used. In the low-task-structure condition, on the contrary, the subjects could complete the task in whatever fashion they felt was most efficient.

Research by T.L. Daniel and J.K. Esser (1980) demonstrated that external rewards bring about a significant decrease in intrinsic motivation in the low-task-structure condition. In the high-task-structure condition, on the other hand, this effect of a monetary reward on intrinsic motivation remained absent. A reasonable speculation is that the external constraints inherent in high task structure provide an external locus of control (an effect that parallels that of rewards according to the cognitive evaluation theory). It is further speculated that the provision of an external reward for work on a task of high structure cannot further undermine intrinsic motivation because the locus of control is already external (as in boring tasks). The reverse holds for tasks of low structure.

The research dealt with concentrates on the relationship between external rewards (X_1) and intrinsic motivation (Y). The other characteristics, the task interest (X_2) and the task structure (X_3), play a very special role in the argument. They are not just control factors, but bring about a modification in the relationship between X_1 and Y.

The basic format of such an argument is the **interactive structure**, as is shown in Figure 1.8.

The format of the interactive structure is more complex than all foregoing formats. It is not only stated that X_1 has a causal effect on Y and that X_2 (or X_3) has an extra causal effect on Y, in an additive fashion, but combinations of X_1 and X_2 are also considered and the effect of these combinations on Y is under discussion.

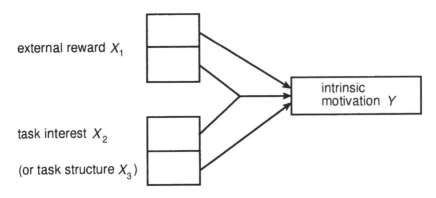

external reward X_1

intrinsic motivation Y

task interest X_2

(or task structure X_3)

Figure 1.8   The interactive structure

The combination 'external reward, interesting task' has a negative effect on intrinsic motivation. The combination 'external reward, boring task' has a positive effect on intrinsic motivation. The absence of an external reward, when combined with an interesting task, leads to a high motivation and, when combined with a boring task, to a low motivation. Thus, what characterizes the interactive structure is that the effect of a factor X_1 on Y is not only executed by itself, but in combination with another factor X_2.

For the social sciences this argumentation, which parallels the format of the interactive structure, is very important but underestimated. Researchers often forget that the relationships between social phenomena should not be studied in themselves, but have to be investigated in combination with the background factors and conditions.

Another example of interaction is the combined effect of gender and discipline on success and failure in the first year of college. Male students have a higher probability of success than female students (effect of gender). Students of the hard sciences have a higher probability of success than students of the social sciences (effect of discipline). In addition to these separate effects, combinations of sex and discipline have to be considered. He in the hard sciences and she in the social sciences have a higher probability of success than she in the positive sciences and he in the social sciences (effect of interaction).

1.2.5   Poor and Rich Neighbourhoods

Everyone is able to picture the rich villa districts and the poor slums in our large cities. When we walk through these districts we are predominantly struck by outward appearances: the town-planning and technical qualities and defects; the low or high density of building; the area amenities; the playgrounds for children; the amount of public green areas. What we do not see, but what undoubtedly plays an important role, are the differences in income level and educational level of the inhabitants, their position in the labour market, their age and nationality. We are also in the dark about the provisions for education, social service and healthcare. Of course we expect that all of this will be rather satisfactory in the rich neighbourhoods and disappointing in the poor ones. In other words, we are dealing with discrimination.

The observation that certain groups of the population are favoured above other groups brings us, especially when the social inequalities are dramatic, to the ethical principle of social (in)justice. In our view, government policy should give priority to the groups of society with the fewest chances. A positive discrimination is straightforward: the greatest efforts for the least welfare. With regard to the neighbourhoods, this means that policy measures should be taken in favour of social work in situations with the fewest chances.

If we want to stimulate such government policies, it is very important that we make maps, upon which the poor neighbourhoods are clearly distinguished from the other neighbourhoods. In other words, the discrimination needs to be literally mapped out. This requires intensive scientific work, in which the criteria for the definitions of poverty and wealth have to be elaborated. The geographical unit — the neighbourhood or district — has to be determined and, for all neighbourhoods, comparable statistical data have to be gathered.

Such a scientific investigation was conducted by the researcher F. Provoost (1979) for the neighbourhoods of the Dutch-speaking part of Belgium and the district of Brussels capital. In order to map out the discrimination between the poor and rich neighbourhoods, indicators were used with regard to the financial situation of the inhabitants (income level), the educational situation (educational level, continuation of studies), the labour situation (position in the working process), the housing situation (state of the houses, technical features of town-planning and living, density of building, mean occupations of dwellings and rooms, number of telephone subscribers, spatial and social engagement), the participation (degree of participation of the inhabitants in the decision-making) and the presence and functioning of services (with regard to education, area amenities, recreation, playgrounds for children, amount of public green, social services and health-care). Some additional specific indicators were included with regard to town-renovation, problems of a psycho-social nature and presence of particular subpopulations. The idea was that neighbourhoods with specific problems, such as demolition and a high concentration of foreign labourers, might show a high probability of poverty and distress.

This research deals with the discrimination of population groups.[1] Therefore, the basic format will be called **the discrimination structure**. It is represented in Figure 1.9.

The argumentation of the discrimination structure consists of three parts: the prior classification in groups, the analysis by means of discriminating characteristics and the classification of new cases. Let us go back to our walk through the residential quarters. We will spontaneously make a prior classification of two groups: poor and rich. This is, in a certain sense, the **first step**. In a scientific study, this first step will of course not be left to our feelings, but we will make an appeal to judges (persons who have a special knowledge of the problem investigated) in making the prior classification.

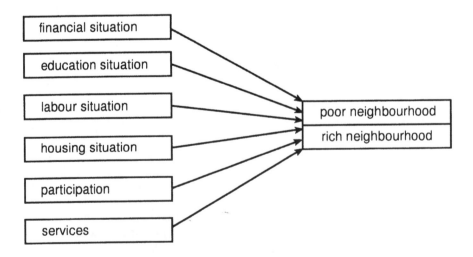

Figure 1.9   The discrimination structure

[1] The research was conducted in another way than we have outlined here. But it is merely our intention to illustrate the basic format of discrimination research.

The **second step** is the analysis by means of the many discriminating characteristics: the financial situation, the housing situation and others. The analysis of all these statistical data for each neighbourhood will enable us to verify our prior classification. That means that we will be able to check if the discriminating characters do indeed discriminate between the two groups of districts. It will prove, for example, that one characteristic (e.g., the labour situation) has a higher capacity of discriminating between the poor and rich neighbourhoods than the other (e.g., the educational level). Our argument also implies that an accumulation of characteristics will bring about more discrimination than each characteristic separately, because the poorest neighbourhoods will have low scores on all the characteristics, and vice versa. As the characteristics will not have equal discriminating powers, we would like to assign a weight to each of them, which is an expression of their discriminating capacity. Reckoning with these weights, we could then make a weighted sum of the characteristics. This weighted sum would be the most promising instrument of discrimination between the neighbourhoods.

This brings us to the **third step** of the argument, the classification of new cases. Making use of our instrument, we can determine whether any new neighbourhood not included in our analysis is poor or rich in nature. To do so, we merely have to gather the scores on the income level, the educational level and all the other discriminating characteristics and apply the weights to make the weighted sum. The making of maps is part of this third step.

Recapitulating, in a research problem with discrimination structure and in the scientific research of the characteristics that discriminate between population groups in society, we follow an argument in which three steps are involved. Firstly, we make, as reliably as possible, a prior classification of groups. Secondly, we gather statistical data for a great number of characteristics, we statistically analyse their discriminating capacities and we make a weighted sum. Thirdly, if the analysis of the second step is successful (significant discriminating capacity of the characteristics and of their weighted sum), then we have a good instrument for classifying new cases in one of the groups.

1.2.6 Marital Adjustment

Marital adjustment has been defined as the presence of such characteristics in a marriage as a tendency to avoid or resolve conflicts, a feeling of satisfaction with the marriage and with each other, the sharing of common interests and activities, and the fulfilling of the marital expectations of the husband and the wife. Operationally, it is generally defined as that which is measured by a marital-adjustment test. The latter consists of a number of questions in which husbands and wives are asked how they perceive or assess their marriages. These questions relate to leisure time spent together, choice of friends, finances, religious matters, sexual relations, character, goals in life and other subjects. Now, what do we think about when we keep all these subjects in mind? We may wonder whether all these questions could be reduced to one single question, such as, 'How is life going with both of you?' In other words, we would like to know if the tens of specific indicators of marital adjustment all measure nearly the same. For, if that is the case, it will not matter which question a couple is asked. If adjusted, they will give positive answers to all questions, and vice versa. But it might, of course, be possible that the subjects are split into mutually exclusive subgroups, in such a way that the measures of the indicators are approximately the same within a subgroup, but are different between subgroups. This would mean that the concept of marital adjustment, as it is conceived by the respondents, splits into a certain number of different dimensions.

Such an investigation was conducted by Locke and Williamson (1958). The cases of the sample consisted of 349 spouses, 171 husbands and 178 wives. For greater homogeneity, people of 50 years of age and older were eliminated. The sample came from three social areas of Los Angeles: a lower class area, a lower-middle class area and an upper-middle class area, with an equal number of persons in each area. The marital-adjustment test was composed of 20 items:

X_1: Check the place on the scale from 1 to 5 which best describes the degree of happiness of your present marriage.

X_2: Check any of the following things which you think cause serious difficulties in your marriage: attempt to control your spending money, insincerity, excessive criticism, narrow-mindedness, untruthfulness, paying attention to another person, being easily influenced by others, religious differences, different amusement interests, lack of mutual friends, ill-health, constant bickering, lack of mutual affection, selfishness, adultery, other things.

X_3: How often do you and your mate 'get on each other's nerves'?

X_4: Do you ever wish you had not married?

X_5: If you had your life to live over, do you think you would marry the same person, a different person or not marry at all?

X_6: When disagreements arise, do they result in agreement by mutual give and take, husband giving in, wife giving in or neither giving in?

X_7: Extent of agreement on handling family finances.

X_8: Agreement on matters of recreation.

X_9: Agreement on religious matters.

X_{10}: Agreement on the amount of time spent together.

X_{11}: Agreement on choice of friends.

X_{12}: Agreement on sexual relations.

X_{13}: Agreement on ways of dealing with in-laws.

X_{14}: Agreement on conventional behaviour.

X_{15}: Agreement on aims, goals, and things believed important in life.

X_{16}: Do you confide in your mate: always, almost always, rarely, almost never?

X_{17}: In leisure time, do husband and wife both prefer: to stay at home, to go out, or does one prefer to go out and the other to stay at home?

X_{18}: Do you and your mate engage in outside activities together?

X_{19}: Do you kiss your mate every day, occasionally or almost never?

X_{20}: What things does your mate do that you do not like?

The analysis of the responses showed that the 20 items do not measure the same thing but split into subgroups. These clusters of items are, however, not entirely disjunctive. There is some overlap, for some items belong in fact to two or more clusters. The difficult task of the researcher consists of discovering which dimensions of the concept of marital adjustment are represented by the subgroups of indicators. As the items of one cluster all measure the same thing, the thought is that there must be a latent characteristic, a dimension of marital adjustment, which serves as a representative shelf for the items. The assignment of a label to a cluster is, however, not at all an easy task. The researchers discovered a first dimension A, based on the items X_5, X_6, X_{14}, X_{17}, X_{18} and X_{19} and they assigned it the label 'companionship'. A second dimension B, consisting of X_4, X_5, X_7, X_8, X_9, X_{10}, X_{11}, X_{12}, X_{13}, X_{14} and X_{15}, was labelled 'agreement', because nearly all agreement questions are contained in this subgroup. A third dimension C was predominantly composed of the affective or emotional items X_1, X_2, X_3, X_5, X_{12}, X_{18} and X_{19} and was labelled 'affectionate intimacy'. There was also a cluster D, composed of X_{10}, X_{14}, X_{16} and X_{18}, with which the researchers did not know what to do at first. This factor was apparently the only one that elicited different responses from wives and husbands. The husbands were more likely to respond favourably on these items; wives presumably were accommodative. Therefore the label 'masculine interpretation' (or feminine accommodation) was chosen. A last cluster E had six items: X_1, X_3, X_4, X_5, X_{16} and X_{19}. It was called 'Halo Effect', because it seemed to be composed of items toward which people have a euphoric tendency. In other words, some persons react to these questions with great enthusiasm and perceive all marital relationships as perfect.

Now, what is the **basic format** of this research? Strictly speaking, there is **none**! For, the investigators were not searching for a number of causal factors of marital adjustment, as in the convergent causal structure, or for an explanation of discrimination between the adjusted and the non-adjusted, as in the discrimination structure. They did not have a clearly structured prior conception of the research problem. The only thing they did was to conceive of 20 items that were in some respect related to marital adjustment, and left the rest for statistical analysis to decide whether these items were divisible into subgroups with strong within-relationships. In other words, they merely had the intention to search for a hidden structure in the data.

The basic format is, therefore, the **latent structure**. The concept of marital adjustment was apparently divisible into a number of dimensions, which we will call 'latent characteristics'. We use the adjective 'latent' because the dimensions only emerge *after* the statistical analysis (latent structure analysis). In Figure 1.10 we give a visual representation of the format of the latent structure. The 'latent characteristics' (A to E) are encircled, the 'manifest characteristics' (the actually measured indicators X_1 to X_{20}) are enframed.

If it were the case that all 20 items measured something different, then they could in principle be reduced to 20 latent characteristics. But it is of course the hope of every researcher that the analysis results in a small number of characteristics, such as companionship, agreement and affectional intimacy, for, we do not learn from the reduction of 20 indicators to 20 latent characteristics. It would mean, so to speak, that we had reduced multiplicity to multiplicity. We can only learn from an analysis when a great number of indicators is reduced to a small number of latent characteristics, so that multiplicity ends up in unity. For this reason, 'latent structure' could also be called the structure of **dimension-reduction**.

In our opinion, the investigation of the latent structure is too widespread in the social sciences. For, if we recall the metaphor of researcher as architect, it would mean that a building is erected without the architect having a clear concept. However, not everybody is in agreement with our opinion. According to some scientists and methodologists, the analysis of the latent structure is much better than any other

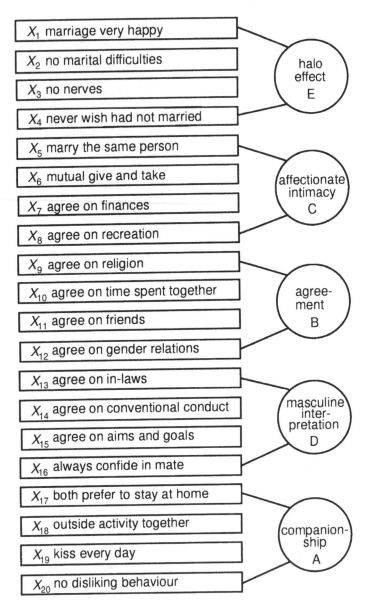

Figure 1.10   The latent structure

analysis, for the very reason that social reality itself (the respondents), and not the researcher, introduces structure in the research theme. The reader is free to share one or the other opinion. In the context of this discussion, it is worth mentioning that a form of research exists in which the latent characteristics are determined *a priori* by the researcher, and in which the analysis takes the form of a test of this prior structure.

We would like to make a final remark. The basic format of this research consisted of splitting up many characteristics (20 in number) into subgroups, where each subgroup represented a dimension of a general concept (marital adjustment). Now, another possibility exists, namely, splitting the many units–individuals (349 spouses here) into subgroups in such a way that the units of a specific subgroup (e.g., the marital-adjusted persons) have more or less equal scores on the 20 characteristics (e.g., all agree, kisses every day, mutual give and take, and so on). The basic format would then be a latent structure analysis of the units instead of the characteristics.

1.2.7 Economic Inequality and Political Instability

At least since the ancient Greeks many thinkers have regarded a great diversity of wealth as incompatible with stable government.

In this context, Russett (1969) quotes Euripides:

> In a nation there be orders three:
> The useless rich, that ever crave for more;
> The have-nots, straitened even for sustenance,
> A dangerous folk, of envy overfull,
> Which shoot out baleful stings at such as have,
> Beguiled by tongues of evil men, their 'champions':
> But of the three the midmost saveth states;
> They keep the order which the state ordains.

Alexis de Tocqueville, writing many centuries later, declared: 'Remove the secondary causes that have produced the great convulsions of the world and you will almost always find the principle of inequality at the bottom. Either the poor have attempted to plunder the rich, or the rich to enslave the poor. If, then, a state of society can ever be founded in which every man shall have something to keep and little to take from others, much will have been done for the peace of the world.'

Both Plato and Karl Marx so despaired of the pernicious effects of wealth that they saw no way to abolish the evil except by abolishing private property itself. Tocqueville, on the other hand, thought that he found in America a society which had been able to reach another solution: 'Between these two extremes [very few rich men and few poor ones] of democratic communities stands an innumerable multitude of men almost alike, who, without being exactly either rich or poor, possess sufficient property to desire the maintenance of order, yet not enough to excite envy. Such men are the natural enemies of violent commotions; their lack of agitation keeps all beneath them and above them still and secures the balance of the fabric of society.'

Yet, according to Russett (1969), the answer is not so clear-cut when we check the matter empirically with present-day politics. Is economic inequality incompatible with stable government, or merely with democratic or good government? If we mean stable government, do we mean regimes in which the rulers themselves remain in power for long periods despite the chronic outbreak of violence (Colombia and South Vietnam), or simply the avoidance of significant violence even though governments may topple annually (France throughout most of the Third and Fourth Republics)? Or must 'stable' government be both peaceful and reasonably long-term? Finally, what do we mean by the government? A particular individual (Spain), a particular party (Uruguay), the essential maintenance of a particular coalition (France under the system of 'replastering'), or the continued dominance of a particular social stratum (Jordan)?

Another part of the difficulty stems from the absence of the necessary data or from the non-comparability of the available data.

Russett claims to be the first who has gathered a great amount of data by which the relationship between economic inequality and political instability can be tested. For the measure of inequality he uses the following indicators:

X_1: The percentage of landholders who collectively occupy one-half of all the agricultural land, starting with the farmers with the smallest plots of land and working toward the largest.

X_2: The Gini index of concentration: this is a number which expresses in which measure the economic distribution of a land deviates from the ideal distribution of perfect equality.

X_3: Farm households that rent all their land as a percentage of the total number of farms.

X_4: GNP per capita in 1955, in dollars.

X_5: Percentage of the labour force employed in agriculture.

It is even more difficult to find a satisfactory operational definition of stability than a measure of inequality. In an effort to account for different aspects of stability, quite different indices were used:

Y_1: Instability of personnel: measured as the number of years during the period 1945–1961 in which a country was independent, divided by the number of individuals who held the post of chief executive during the same period.

Y_2: Internal group violence: measured as the number of people killed per 1 000 000 people, during the period 1950–1962, as a result of civil wars, revolutions and riots.

Y_3: Internal War, measured as the total number of violent incidents, from plots to protracted guerilla warfare.

Y_4: Stability of democracy: stable democracies are defined as states that have been characterized by the uninterrupted continuation of political democracy since World War I, and the absence over the past 30 years of a totalitarian movement, either Fascist or Communist, which at any point received as much as 20% of the vote. Unstable democracies are countries which, although unable to meet the first criteria, nevertheless have a history of more or less free elections for most of the post-World War I period. Dictatorships are those countries in which, perhaps despite some democratic interludes, free elections have been generally absent.

As well as Russett, Gifi (1980) also made an analysis of the associations between the economic and political characteristics of the 47 countries. The results are mainly as follows. The economic characteristics that are by far the most important variables, because they are strongly associated with nearly all the political characteristics, are first the Gini index (X_2) and then the percentage of the population employed in agriculture (X_5). The most important political variables in the equations for predicting economic inequality are the stability of a democratic regime (Y_4) and of leadership (Y_1). The latter, Y_4 and Y_1, are, however, not strongly correlated. This is not so strange, according to Gifi, because dictatorships are characterized by either varying political leaders (military coups), or by having the same political leader for years (Yugoslavia) and democracies have a varying leadership.

A special place is occupied by the percentage of tenant-farmers (X_3). Although this characteristic is strongly associated with the distribution of agricultural land, it appears, none the less, to contribute little to the explanation of political stability. According to Gifi, this is understandable with regard to the stability of democracy (Y_4), for there are dictatorships where a great amount of land is rented from rich landowners (South American peasants) and there are dictatorships without any tenants at all (Yugoslavia, Poland).

Apart from X_3, the other economic characteristics play an important role in the explanation of stability of democracy (Y_4). Russett's general conclusion is, therefore, that Tocqueville's basic observation appears to be correct: no state can maintain a democratic form of government for a long time if the major sources of economic gain are divided very unequally among its citizens.

We will now deal with the **basic format** of the general research problem of this investigation. Two sets of characteristics, an economic set and a political set, are being related to each other. The first set is composed of five indicators of the concept of 'economic inequality'. This concept itself can be conceived of as a latent characteristic. The second set contains four indicators of the latent concept of 'political instability'. The researchers were above all interested in the associations between the sets, not in the associations within a set. For, it was their intention to examine whether the economic characteristics (the X set) are related to the political characteristics (the Y set). They presumably wanted to take even one step further in postulating a causal influence of the X set on the Y set (and not in the reverse order). We do not want to go that far here. Therefore, in order to indicate that the causal question remains open, we draw a double-sided curved arrow in Figure 1.11.

The formal structure of a research problem, in which two sets of indicators, each represented by a latent characteristic, are related to each other, will be called the

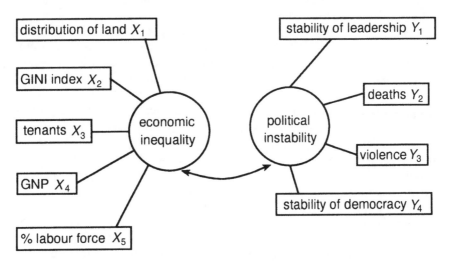

Figure 1.11 The canonical structure

canonical structure. The term 'canonical' stems from pure mathematics, but one can also think of a canon as a piece of vocal music for two voices in which the voices join in one after the other, singing and continually repeating the same theme.

Please note that the conceptual structure of the canon runs across the sets. It has to do with the relationship between indicators of economic inequality (such as GINI and % labour force in agriculture) and indicators of political instability (such as personnel instability and government form) and not the relationship between indicators within a set (such as GINI and GNP). Note also that Figure 1.11 merely shows the simplest version of the basic structure, for, in cases where the concepts of economic inequality and political instability are multidimensional, there will be more than one latent characteristic for each set. It is furthermore possible that the canon is a piece of music for more than two voices; in that case the research problem will be composed of more than two sets of characteristics.

1.2.8   Styles in Furnishing the Living Room

For years and years sociologists have been dealing with the phenomena of style and fashion, predominantly in relation to social status and prestige. A well-known example is the hypothesis of the 'trickling effect' (not to be confused with Reagan-omics), according to which the higher social levels set the tone in questions of fashion, which is adopted (as it trickles down) by the lower social levels, whereafter the higher levels once again introduce a new fashion, which is once again adopted, etc.

Instead of explaining short cycles of fashion, one might also be interested in the prestige function of fashionable behaviour. Demonstrative consumption as a dissipation of goods has, in line with the famous Veblen thesis of conspicuous consumption, the function that the riches of the spender are made visible to all.

The close relationship between fashion and social level has also been examined by Simmel. In his view fashions are class-related. They evoke the affiliation with the equalized and the unity of a circle and, therefore, they exclude the lower situated groups, for the latter are characterized as not belonging to the circle. In this way, social recognition and social differentiation go hand in hand.

Unlike the classical sociologists Veblen, Simmel and others, recent contributions place more emphasis on the fashion industry, which is given a more important and even a decisive role in the formation of norms and good taste. The thesis does not state, however, that the cultural industries dictate fashion to the consumers, but that a complex process of collective selection replaces the simple class differentiation. In line with this argument, many authors observe a class-exceeding trend towards homogeneity. Schelsky even speaks of a levelling middle class society, where material and immaterial goods of social civilization are made use of in a uniform fashion. Enzensberger mentions the cultural hegemony of a petite bourgeoisie, which has superseded the grand bourgeoisie and which has simultaneously infected the life-forms and aspirations of the proletariat.

Pappi and Pappi (1978) investigated the above-mentioned theses. In their contribution they focus upon the furnishings of the living room. The term 'fashion' or 'taste' is too broad for this research subject of decoration styles, but according to them it can be conceived of as a fashion in a more narrow sense of the word. The main purpose of their research is the falsification of the thesis of homogeneization. They defend the hypothesis that the levelling of styles in different social levels has not occurred and that the status-symbolism has not come to an end, but has rather been refined. With regard to the decoration of the living room, they even speak of a status-specific dichotomy of the market. This status-dependence of the living styles can only be investigated by the researchers after they have first traced the existing styles. They first have to make observations in the living rooms of a large number of families in order to make an objective description, which could be replicated by other researchers, of the styles that are found in families. Such an empirical classification is not fixed in a prior fashion, but is inductively inferred from unprejudiced observations of style characteristics in the living rooms of a sample of households. The discussion in the next sections will concentrate on this empirical identification of the styles of decoration.

Pappi and Pappi collected their data in Jülich, a small village in the Rhineland, Germany. They made use of two data collection methods: questioning and observing. A list of 29 attitudinal statements was presented to a representative random sample of 582 households, in such a way that the respondents could indicate their agreement or disagreement. During the interview, the interviewer had the opportunity to observe the furnishings of the living room. In order to guarantee a maximum of reliability, the interviewers had been trained for these observations. With the help of illustrative material, they had been practising to observe the style, the room, the order, the state of the furniture and other things. A total of 70 observations had to be made. A little more than one-third were mere inventories, for which it was sufficient to indicate the presence or absence of the objects. Other observations had a bearing on style-elements, like the pattern and the colour of the floor-covering, the curtains and other things.

Contrary to what is customary in the social sciences, the unit of analysis in this research is not the person or the group of persons, but the living room (582 in number). The characteristics are the elements that are being observed or questioned. A total of 49 characteristics were subjected to an analysis. For some of these characteristics, like a piano, it sufficed to check its presence or absence. For other characteristics, like the size of the living room, a score was assigned. The following 49 characteristics were appointed: size of the living room, size of the windows, furniture kept in repair, parquet floor, pvc floor, carpet, Persian carpet, carpet with geometrical motif, small Persian carpet, walls with big motif, walls with flower-motif, walls without a motif, leather sofa, sofa of imitation leather, television on a piece of furniture, television of synthetic material, number of books, glass curtains with fringe, glass curtains of lace, curtains with fringe, glossy curtains, curtains with a flower pattern, curtains without a pattern, over-furnished, very tidy, luxurious, painting with mountain landscape, no paintings, engraving, abstract paintings, paintings with heavy frames, modern lamps, candlestick, wall with inlaid cupboards, wall of fibre-board, show-window, sideboard, dresser, rocking chair, armchair, house-bar, piano, tinware, imitation flowers, flower arrangement, Gobelin tapestry, cushions, beautiful ceiling, family pictures.

The similarities between the style characteristics formed the starting point of the analysis. For example, the Persian carpet and the parquet floor go together in most of the living rooms, but this is not the case for the Persian carpet and the pvc floor. Examples of characteristics that will show strong similarities are the walls without a motif, the many books, the abstract paintings and the television of synthetic material. This group of characteristics represents a more general dimension, which we will indicate as the 'modern style'. In an analogical sense, the paintings with mountain landscape and heavy frames, the beautiful ceiling, the cushions and the imitation flowers will represent a 'traditional Old German style'. In making an analysis of all the bivariate associations between the 49 characteristics, the researchers investigated whether groups of associated characteristics could be found which represented different and separate styles. The **format** of this research problem is comparable with the one in our example in 1.2.6 of marital adjustment, with this distinction that the starting point is now given by the $\binom{49}{2} = 1176$ two by two associations.

Kruskal and Wish (1978) put this in a very expressive fashion as follows.

> Suppose you are given a map showing the locations of several cities in the United States, and are asked to construct a table of distances between these cities. The task will be a simple matter. Now consider the reverse problem, where you are given the table of distances between the cities, and are asked to produce the map.

In essence, the researchers are faced with this reverse problem.

In their research, the distances are the 1176 similarities between the 49 style characteristics. If they succeeded in making a map of style characteristics, then all these characteristics could be placed in a two-dimensional solution, in which the north–south axis and the east–west axis are the two dimensions and have to be interpreted as two general life-styles. It is of course possible that more than two dimensions have to be provided for. In this research example, a three-dimensional solution appeared to show the best fit with the data. In Figure 1.12, this three-dimensional solution is drawn in the form of a diagram. The structure is comparable with that of Figure 1.10, for, as in the investigation of marital adjustment, the researchers want to discover the latent dimensions of living-style. However, as in this example the starting point is not formed by the 49 characteristics, but by the 1176 similarities,[2] we will speak of '**the latent structure of similarities**'. The similarities are indicated by double-sided curved arrows. It is of course impossible to draw all 49 style characteristics, let alone all 1176 arrows.

The 'quality dimension' is in fact economic in nature. It stands for the power to pay for the attributes. The big living room, the parquet and the Persian carpet are expensive. In the higher social levels of the population, they appear together in the house. The other extreme is formed by the households without paintings and with sofas of imitation leather and glaring curtains as affordable substitutes. The mountain landscape, the heavy frames and the cushions are strongly and positively related, but each of these characteristics seldom occurs in relation to walls without a motif, abstract paintings and many books. The latter three are strongly interrelated and represent the 'modern style', in contradistinction to the former three, which represent the 'traditional style'. The third dimension initially caused some problems for the researchers. Looking at the piano, they firstly conceived of the 'use' as a dimension.

---

[2] The example of marital adjustment was a preparation for factor analysis, whereas the example of living-styles prepared for multidimensional scaling. However, we will show that the association matrix can be used as a input of factor analysis as well. Therefore, the distinction made here is relative in a technical sense.

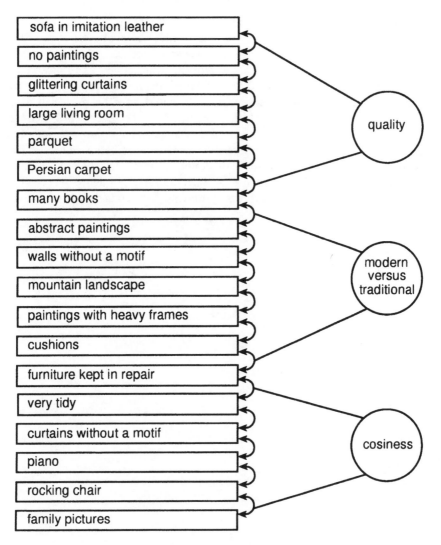

sofa in imitation leather

no paintings

glittering curtains

large living room

parquet

Persian carpet

many books

abstract paintings

walls without a motif

mountain landscape

paintings with heavy frames

cushions

furniture kept in repair

very tidy

curtains without a motif

piano

rocking chair

family pictures

quality

modern versus traditional

cosiness

Figure 1.12   The latent structure of similarities

However, in contrast with the excessive upkeep of the furniture, the extremely clean-looking living room and the absence of motifs, they decided to choose 'kind-heartedness or cosiness' as the third style-dimension.

As in the example of marital adjustment, it can be inferred from the foregoing that the strategy of searching for dimensions proceeds in total absence of a prior basic structure. Characteristics of living-style are gathered and the more general style-dimensions are inductively inferred. In the sections above, we have given our negative verdict upon this strategy, because we are strongly opposed to the piling up at random of observations without theory. We would, however, do the researchers an injustice if we did not mention that, in addition to the inductive analysis, they also followed another strategy. The interviewers were also given a prior classification with seven living-styles: simple light, heavy representative, Old German, modern, Scandinavian, mixed with separate antique pieces and the residual category other mixed style. Making use of illustrative materials, the interviewers were trained to recognize these styles and for each living room they had to indicate which style was applicable. In the aforementioned inductive analysis, a three-dimensional solution was found with the dimensions quality, modernity and cosiness. It would have been ideal if a seven-dimensional solution were found which coincided with the seven *a priori* conceived living-styles. But in confronting the empirically acquired solution with the *a priori* dimensional structure, which was inferred from magazines like *Schöner Wohnen*, a strong correspondence still emerged. This double strategy, in which a deductive as well as an inductive analysis is made and in which the correspondence between them is tested, leads us to conclude that this investigation has to be considered as a research of the better sort.

2

A Classification of Classical Techniques of Multivariate Analysis

In the first chapter we discussed a number of examples of empirical research. In doing so, we intended to show that every research problem has an underlying basic format, in other words a structure or syntax. We thereby carefully avoided any use of technical language. We did not speak of multiple regression analysis, but of the convergent causal structure; not of partial correlation analysis and spurious correlation, but of spurious and indirect causality; not of analysis of variance and covariance, but of the interactive structure; not of discriminant analysis, but of the discrimination structure; not of factor or cluster analysis, but of the latent structure; not of canonical correlation analysis, but of the canonical structure; not of multi-dimensional scaling techniques, but of the latent structure of similarities.

We thus tried to avoid so-called variable language. It was our purpose to write a reader-friendly introduction to multivariate analysis with examples of several social–scientific disciplines as a starting point. One of my scientific friends has typified such a purpose as attempting to square the circle. The reader is free to judge whether this attempt has been successful.

In this chapter, we make a classification of classical techniques of multivariate analysis which correspond with the research examples. We take the line that a research problem with a certain basic format (e.g. the convergent causal structure) leads to the choice of a technique of multivariate analysis which corresponds to that format (in this example the multiple regression analysis). Therefore, the first and most important criterion for the classification of techniques is the underlying format. In order to make a justified classification, many other criteria will have to be considered as well. An obvious criterion is the measurement level of the variables: quantitative, ordinal or nominal (see 1.1.3). Another criterion of frequent occurrence is the presence or absence of dependency, in other words the causal asymmetry, whereby the distinction between independent and dependent variables is made. The measurement level and the dependency are the two most widely used criteria for the classification of techniques. This is very understandable, for, in using different measurement levels or in choosing for dependency versus non-dependency, the analyses are calculated in a different manner. So, these two criteria are inspired by arithmetic considerations. The same holds for many other criteria, such as the number of dependent variables, the linearity, and others.

These technical and arithmetic criteria are of course decisive in making the appropriate choice of a technique of analysis. Therefore, we will have to include them in our classification. Nevertheless, we hold the opinion that the basic format is the most important criterion, because it ensures the correspondence with the conceptual structure of a social–scientific research problem.

In preparing our classification, we will first make a number of agreements with regard to a notation system, which will be continually used in the following chapters. After that, we will make a classification for each criterion separately. This will, in the end, lead to a classification system in which many criteria are dealt with simultaneously.

We still want to note the limitations of this book. Only the 'classical' techniques of analysis are dealt with, regression analysis, analysis of variance, discriminant analysis and the like. The recently developed advanced techniques, like loglinear modelling, homogeneity analysis and LISREL (LInear Structural Relations System) are not included, for two reasons. Firstly, the problem of space. The treatment of these techniques would lead to a separate second volume. Secondly, the problem of overlap. The recently developed techniques have their roots in the classics, which we discuss here. For example, loglinear modelling, which is suited for variables measured at a low level, can be conceived of, *qua format*, from the analysis of variance with interactive structure. In other words, the development of these most advanced procedures of analysis has always been modelled on the classical techniques. We hope, therefore, to lay the foundations which should enable the interested reader to study the moderns, thereby recognizing the historical roots.

2.1 Starting Points

2.1.1 Our Notation System

For the presentation of the basic format of a technique (or of a research problem), we will agree on the following:

stands for a latent variable, which is a non-measured characteristic, for example 'companionship' in the research on marital adjustment (see 1.2.6) or 'economic inequality' in the research of the canonical structure (see 1.2.7) or 'quality' in the research on the furnishing of the living room (see 1.2.8).

stands for a manifest variable, which is a directly measured characteristic, like the example of anti-Semitism among Americans (see 1.2.3) or happiness with marriage among spouses (see 1.2.6). We take the line that a square or a rectangle indicates a variable of quantitative measurement level (interval or ratio-scale). For lower measurement levels we subdivide the rectangle in a manner which is explained below.

stands for a dummy variable with two categories, gender, for example, with categories man, woman (control factor in 1.2.1) or poorness with categories rich and poor (see 1.2.5). A dummy variable with two categories is a variable which is coded as 0 and 1, for example 0 for man and 1 for woman, or the reverse: 0 for woman and 1 for man. It does not matter which category is assigned the 0- or the 1-score, for it is merely the intention to 'calculate' with the numerical values 0 and 1. In doing so, a dichotomous variable (gender: man, woman) is artificially lifted to a higher measurement level. The nominal measurement level is conceived of as quantitative and means and variances are calculated, as with the interval scaled characteristic 'age'. Such calculations are evidently 'fake', for it cannot be said of a man that he is a 0 and of a woman that she is a 1, or vice versa. The same holds for poor and rich neighbourhoods. We will however show that this dummy coding has great advantages in a technical respect. As no consequences of substance are involved, we might as well call a dummy variable a 'stupid' variable.

 stands for a variable with three categories (a trichotomy), which is represented by means of two dichotomous dummy variables. An example of a trichotomy arises when not two but three kinds of neighbourhood are distinguished: poor, neutral and rich. This variable is then represented by means of two dummies D_1 and D_2, as follows:

	D_1	D_2
poor	1	0
neutral	0	1
rich	0	0

A poor neighbourhood is assigned the code 1 for dummy variable D_1 and the code 0 for D_2. A neutral neighbourhood is coded 0 and 1 for D_1 and D_2 respectively. A rich neighbourhood is assigned the code 0 for both dummies. Please note that two dummy variables are sufficient in order to distinguish between the three categories. It also does not matter which categories are assigned which codes, for the variable is allowed to be non-ordinal, so that the categories may be interchanged. In general, a polytomous variable with k categories can be represented by $k - 1$ dummies.

As an illustration, we give the codes of the (non-ordinal) variable nationality with five categories.

	D_1	D_2	D_3	D_4
Belgian	1	0	0	0
British	0	1	0	0
Italian	0	0	1	0
Dutch	0	0	0	1
Swiss	0	0	0	0

It is clear that one category, the Swiss, is assigned the code 0 for all dummies and that the other categories are assigned the code 1 for one dummy and the code 0 for all others. In this way, the five categories can be distinguished by means of the codes they are assigned to for the four dummies. This dummy coding will be used frequently in calculating multivariate analyses. It will give us the opportunity to gain more insight into the techniques by mutual comparison.

——— stands for a statistical relationship between two variables that is not causal in nature. An example is the relationship between an indicator (the GINI index) and the latent variable (economic inequality) which it represents (see 1.2.7).

⌣ stands, just like ———, for a statistical relationship that is not conceived of in terms of cause and effect. By the double-sided curved arrow, it is stressed that the asymmetry of the relationship is not considered. Not asymmetry, but symmetry. Not dependency, but interdependency. An example is the canonical correlation between economic inequality and political instability (see 1.2.7). It is important not to confuse the double-sided curved arrow with feedback. The latter is indicated by the symbol $\rightleftarrows$ and means double dependency, once from X to Y and once from Y to X.

⟶ stands for a dependent relationship in terms of cause and effect. It is the convention to write $X \rightarrow Y$, where X is called the independent variable (or: predictor, causal factor, explaining factor, *explanans*) and Y the dependent variable (or: criterion, effect factor, factor to be explained, *explanandum*). The pre-eminent example of a dependent relationship is the influence of humour on financial concession (see 1.2.1), for, according to some students, the controlled standard experiment is the only research design suited to give empirical support to causal relationships. Not everybody agrees with this rigorous opinion. Those who find the classical techniques of multivariate analysis suitable for causal research will find a good example of dependent relationship in the influence of $\Delta\%$ working women on $\Delta\%$ childless women (see 1.2.2).

⟩⟶ stands for effect of interaction, which means the combined effect of two independent variables on the dependent variable. An example is the interaction of external rewards and task interest in their effect on intrinsic motivation (see 1.2.4).

The argument that is implied by an effect of interaction is more complex than that of a relation of dependency. An effect of interaction is not merely the effect of external rewards in itself, or of task interest, but it expresses the effect of combinations of external rewards and task interest. This can also be represented in another fashion, as is made clear in the following figure.

$X_1 \rightarrow X_2$
$\quad\uparrow$
X_3
is an arrow on an arrow and stands, just like $\genfrac{}{}{0pt}{}{X_1}{X_3} \rightarrowtail X_2$, for an effect of interaction. The interpretation is now that the factor X_3 exercises influence on the dependent relationship between X_1 and X_2. The latter, that is, the influence of external rewards on intrinsic motivation, behaves differently for different categories of the factor X_3. For

interesting tasks this influence of X_1 on X_2 is negative, and, on the other hand, for uninteresting tasks this influence is positive.

So, the structure of the effect of interaction is not as in the causal chain $X_3 \rightarrow X_1 \rightarrow X_2$, nor is it similar to convergent causality. It is more complex than each of these. Using brackets, it can be represented as follows: $X_3 \rightarrow (X_1 \rightarrow X_2)$. The arrow on an arrow expresses that the dependent relationship $X_1 \rightarrow X_2$ is influenced by X_3.

In this approach the independent variables X_1 and X_3 can be interchanged, thus producing the structure $X_1 \rightarrow (X_3 \rightarrow X_2)$. This means that the effect of task interest on intrinsic motivation is positive when external rewards remain absent, and negative when external rewards are assigned. This interchangeability of the independent variables renders the symbol of the forked arrow $\rightarrowtail$ acceptable.

2.1.2   A First Acquaintance with Techniques

Making use of our notation system, we can now indicate the format of the most important techniques of multivariate analysis.

2.2   Subclassifications

2.2.1   Dependent and Non-Dependent Techniques

The discussion on the experiment as the only suited design for the investigation of causal relationships is left aside here. We take the line that multivariate analyses, too, are open to causal research.

Multiple and partial analysis of correlation and regression, analysis of variance and covariance and discriminant analysis are typical examples of dependent techniques. Path analysis and LISREL are more advanced dependent methods of analysis, which are a further elaboration of multiple regression and come down to it in their most simple form.

Canonical correlation analysis can be conceived of as dependent, when the two latent variables—economic inequality and political instability—of the canonical structure (see 1.2.7) are causally connected. As this is not necessarily the case and as the arithmetic of the technique is not built upon asymmetry, we will regard canonical correlation analysis as non-dependent.[1]

Factor analysis, cluster analysis and multidimensional scaling are by definition non-dependent. These techniques are mostly called interdependent, but this term can only be confusing. Non-dependent would be a better term, because the associations between the variables are not conceived of in cause–effect terms. The examples of marital adjustment (1.2.6) and of the furnishing of the living room (1.2.8) serve as models. The analyses are symmetrical. From the bivariate associations between a battery of variables a latent structure is inferred, without there being question of dependency.

---

[1] It should be noted, however, that an asymmetrical version of canonical correlation analysis has been developed, based on multiple regression in one direction. This version is of course dependent.

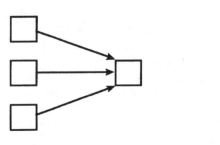

multiple regression analysis
(convergent causal structure)

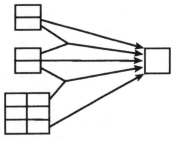

analysis of variance (ANOVA)
(the interactive structure)

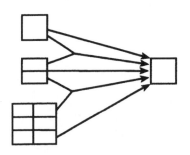

analysis of covariance (ANCOVA)
(interactive structure)

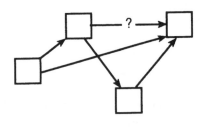

partial correlation analysis
(spurious or indirect causality)

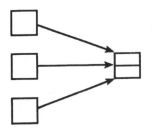

discriminant analysis
(discriminant structure)

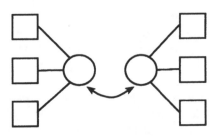

canonical correlation analysis
(the canonical structure)

Figure 2.1   The formal structure of techniques of multivariate analysis

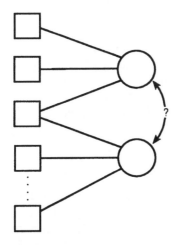

factor and cluster analysis
(latent structure)

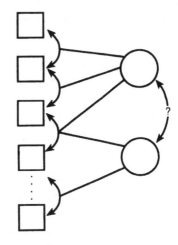

multidimensional scaling
(latent structure of similarities)

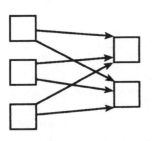

multivariate multiple regression
(convergent causal structure two
or several times)

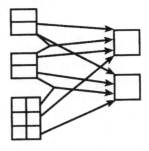

multivariate analysis of variance
(interactive structure two or
several times)

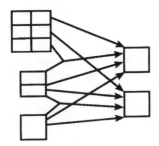

multivariate analysis of covariance
(interactive structure two or
several times)

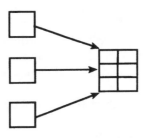

multiple discriminant analysis
(discrimination structure with more than
two population groups)

Figure 2.1   continued

A first subclassification is therefore as follows:

dependent techniques	non-dependent techniques
multiple regression	factor analysis
partial correlation	cluster analysis
analysis of variance	multidimensional scaling
analysis of covariance	canonical correlation analysis
discriminant analysis	

2.2.2   The Number of Dependent Variables

It sometimes happens that the dependent variable of a dependent research problem is measured in many ways. An example is the school results of pupils, measured by many different tests. It is also possible that a research problem refers to several dependent variables simultaneously. This would be the case, for example, if not only the influence of Christian beliefs on anti-Semitism had been investigated (see 1.2.3), but also on anti-Communism.

Therefore, for a number of dependent techniques, some complex versions have been developed which deal with several dependent variables. Referring to Chapter 1, we give three examples.

Firstly, the convergent causal structure in the research on childlessness (see 1.2.2) is analysed by means of multiple regression. If, next to $\Delta\%$ childless women, we added $\Delta\overline{X}$ number of children as an extra dependent variable (which would, of course, mean that the research problem is enlarged from childlessness to birth-control), then we would have to perform a multivariate multiple regression analysis, where 'multi-variate' stands for the presence of several dependent variables.

Secondly, the interactive structure in the research on intrinsic motivation (see 1.2.4) is analysed by means of analysis of variance. Now, if intrinsic motivation is measured in two ways, as the amount of free time spent on a task (behavioural measure) and as ratings of interest and liking for a task (attitudinal measure), then we would have to perform a multivariate analysis of variance. Here, too, the adjective 'multivariate' refers to the presence of several dependent variables.

Thirdly, the discrimination structure in the research on poor neighbourhoods (see 1.2.5) is analysed by means of two-group discriminant analysis. If not two, but three, kinds of neighbourhood are distinguished, the trichotomous variable can be represented by two dummies (see 2.1.1). The latter then function as two dependent variables. In that case we perform a multiple discriminant analysis, where 'multiple' indicates that there is more than one dependent variable (more than two groups).

Another subclassification of dependent techniques is therefore as follows:

one dependent	several dependent variables
multiple regression	multivariate multiple regression
analysis of variance	multivariate analysis of variance
analysis of covariance	multivariate analysis of covariance
discriminant analysis	multiple discriminant analysis
(two groups)	

2.2.3 The Measurement Level of Dependent Variables

Another criterion for the subclassification of dependent techniques is the measurement level of the (one or several) dependent variables. In view of the fact that in almost all dependent techniques means and variances of the dependent variable are calculated, its measurement level is quantitative in principle. In fact, there is only one exception: discriminant analysis. Our example of poor and rich neighbourhoods (see 1.2.5) makes it clear that the dependent variable is dichotomous. In enlarging the research problem to several kinds of neighbourhood it becomes polytomous.

We can, therefore, state that discriminant analysis (of two or several groups) is the pre-eminent example of a dependent technique with dependent variable(s) of low measurement level, as distinct from other dependent techniques like multiple regression and analysis of variance and covariance, where the dependent variable 'has to be' quantitative (at least an interval scale).

There are, however, other alternatives for the analysis of models with a dependent variable measured at a low level, like the logit model, the probit model and others. These alternatives are reducible to attempts to lift a non-quantitative dependent variable to the quantitative measurement level by means of a mathematical transformation, so that a classical technique like multiple regression can be performed.

In restricting ourselves to the classical basic techniques, we come to the following subclassification of dependent techniques of analysis (for one as well as several dependent variables):

quantitative **nominal dependent variable**
multiple regression discriminant analysis
partial correlation
analysis of variance
analysis of covariance

It should be pointed out that the measurement level of the dependent variable is not always quantitative or nominal, but can also be ordinal. An example is social prestige with low, median or high rank. These ordinal characteristics are mostly dealt with as if they were nominal. The dummy coding is then straightforward. This, however, involves a lowering of the measurement level, so that the information of order, which is contained in the dependent variable, is simply not used.

The number of techniques in which the ordinal character of the variables is respected is very small. True enough, there exist some ordinal versions of the analysis of variance, like Kruskal and Carmone's (1968) monotonic analysis of variance, and Kruskal and Wallis' (1952) analysis of variance for ranks. An ordinal equivalent for multiple regression and path analysis has also been developed by Somers (1968) and others. But, these contributions are either very complicated in arithmetic, or their ins and outs are not yet elaborated from an inferential point of view (i.e., for generalization from the sample to the population). It is therefore understandable that almost everybody takes the easy way of dummy coding.

The ordinal measurement level remains the blind spot of multivariate analysis. Alas!

2.2.4 The Measurement Level of Independent Variables

In using this criterion, the analysis of variance is the exception. Almost all dependent techniques are designed for independent variables of quantitative measurement level. Not so for (univariate or multivariate) analysis of variance. The calculation of the variance refers to the dependent variable, which 'has to be' quantitative in principle. This variance is calculated within and between categories of the independent variables. The latter represent groups, which is why they are measured at a lower level.

In our research example on intrinsic motivation (see 1.2.4) the external rewards and the task interest are the two independent variables: an external reward is or is not assigned and a task is interesting, neutral or uninteresting. Of these two independent variables, the external reward is dichotomous. The task interest has three categories, or even better: ranks, for it concerns an ordinal variable. It is typical for analysis of variance that both independent variables are measured at a level which is lower than interval.

A nuance is introduced here by the analysis of covariance. The prefix 'co' indicates that not all the independent variables are measured at a lower level, but that at least one of them is quantitative, so that 'co'variances can be calculated. In other words, in analysis of covariance there is a mix of measurement levels on the side of the independent variables. In analysis of variance, on the contrary, the situation is clear: all independent variables are dichotomous or polytomous (or eventually ordinal). In all other dependent techniques the situation is clear as well: all independent variables are quantitative.

All this leads to the following subclassification of dependent techniques (for one as well as for more dependent variables):

Measurement level of the independent variables:

nominal	quantitative	mixed
analysis of variance	multiple regression	analysis of
	partial correlation	covariance
	discriminant analysis	

2.2.5 The Additive and Interactive Structure

In the foregoing pages we have repeatedly stressed the importance of the interactive structure. Analysis of variance and covariance (univariate and multivariate) are the suitable techniques for the investigation of effects of interaction. Referring to the research example on intrinsic motivation (see 1.2.4), we indicated that the argument which corresponds to an effect of interaction is rather complex. It becomes still more complicated when the model contains more than two independent variables. In these cases, we speak of higher-order interactions. With one dependent variable Y and three independent variables X_1, X_2 and X_3 it means that the effect of X_1 on Y is different for the categories of X_2 and that these differences are again different for the categories of X_3. It will be apparent from this argument that the interpretation of, say, an interaction of seventh order would be nothing less than a summum of intellectual gymnastics.

In ANOVA, MANOVA, ANCOVA and MANCOVA these effects of interaction are calculated and tested for significance.

All other techniques, dependent as well as non-dependent, are additive 'in principle', which means that the effects of interaction are not calculated and not reckoned with.[2] Our distinction between additive and interactive structures leads to the following subclassification:

additive structure	interactive structure
multiple regression	analysis of variance
partial correlation	analysis of covariance
discriminant analysis	multivariate analysis of variance
factor and cluster analysis	multivariate analysis of covariance
multidimensional scaling	

2.2.6 The Orthogonality of Independent Variables

Rather than a classification, we want to give a warning in this section, namely, the preservation of the requirement of orthogonality.

That two variables are orthogonal means, literally, that they are perpendicular. This means that they have nothing in common, so their relationship is zero.

This orthogonality of independent variables is of special importance for dependent techniques. The use of multiple regression is disreputable in this respect. The basic format of this technique is the convergent causal structure. We gave the research example of childlessness (see 1.2.2). We stated there that the independent variables must not overlap in principle. However, we suspected that the factors education (X_2) and age at marriage (X_4) might be strongly associated.

Such an association between independent variables in a multiple regression model is called 'multicollinearity'. A perfect association = 1 would mean that one or both variables is sufficient for the explanation of childlessness, so that one of them can be removed from the analysis (perfect multicollinearity). On the other hand, a perfect absence of association would mean that both factors offer their explanation 'separately', without any overlap (no multicollinearity). Figure 2.2 on the following page gives a visualization of the argument.

When reading hundreds of examples of multiple regression analysis, it appeared that the presence of multicollinearity was the rule rather than the exception. We therefore called the research using this technique 'disreputable'.

We have found just one example in which the independent variables could be considered as orthogonal on substantial grounds and in which the empirical correlation between these variables was indeed approximately zero. It is an investigation by Elmar Lange, who observed that the number of sociologists at Bielefeld University had increased by almost 200% in the period 1961–1970, while this proportional increase was only 40% for all disciplines put together (Lange, 1978). In his analysis, with choice of study as the dependent variable, the two exogenous (= independent)

---

[2] In the following chapters we will weaken this argument. For example, a multiple regression in which the independent variables have a lower measurement level and are coded as dummies and in which product terms are introduced, will appear to be identical with the analysis of variance. We therefore write: 'in principle'.

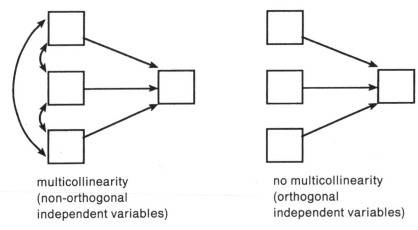

multicollinearity   no multicollinearity
(non-orthogonal   (orthogonal
independent variables)   independent variables)

Figure 2.2   Multiple regression with and without multicollinearity

variables were gender and social origin (measured as the occupational level of the
father). The empirical correlation between gender and social origin appeared to be
0.03. At most universities in the world, the reverse is the case: if female students get to
university, they come predominantly from high social levels. The researcher was,
however, aware of the fact that Bielefeld University was an exception: female and
male students stem from higher social levels in equal proportions.

It is evident that a researcher will not always be able to avoid multicollinearity, as
Elmar Lange did. (S)he will therefore have to resort to procedures of orthogonalization, in which the non-orthogonal independent variables are made orthogonal
artificially, such that multiple regression can be performed in a justified way. We will
discuss this matter in dealing with principal components analysis.

The requirement of orthogonality of the independent variables holds in principle
for all dependent techniques with convergent causal structure. So for discriminant
analysis, just as for multiple regression, the independent variables must not show any
strong associations. In regression literature one uses the expression 'absence of
multicollinearity', although the meaning is identical to 'orthogonality of the independent variables'. On the other hand, in analysis of variance the term orthogonality is
used. This divergent use of language has to do with historical roots. In techniques
with quantitative independent variables there is a tradition of thinking in terms of
linear dependencies. Two independent variables that are linearly dependent are called
collinear. For several variables the term multicollinearity is, then, straightforward.

Analysis of variance stems from a totally different tradition of thinking in terms of
experimental designs. In the research example on the influence of humour on financial
concessions (see 1.2.1), we discussed the standard experiment and saw that it focusses
principally on two variables, one independent and the other dependent. Its structure
is bivariate. The limited nature of this design was the concern of Sir Ronald Fisher in
the 1930s. It was his idea to include several independent variables (called factors) in
one design simultaneously, and to consider not only the dependent relationships but
the effects of interaction as well. This factorial design, which was called factorial
experiment at that time, developed into the analysis of variance. Such a design had to

remain a copy of the controlled experiment as much as possible. One of the requirements was orthogonality. Referring to the research on intrinsic motivation (see 1.2.4) this means that all combinations of categories of independent variables ($2 \times 3 = 6$ combinations here) have to be represented by equal numbers of persons. On this condition of equal cell frequencies, the independent variables are uncorrelated. It follows logically that this orthogonality has the same meaning as the absence of multicollinearity, though referring now to lower measurement levels.

A final remark can be made. From our annual experience with students we learn that they do not always succeed in making a sharp distinction between the effect of interaction and multicollinearity. The reason might be that in both terms something like an interacting process between independent variables is involved. We repeat that the argument of an effect of interaction is much more complex: for one dependent variable Y and two independent variables X and Z it means that the causal effect of X on Y is different for different categories of Z, so that combinations of X and Z have to be considered in explaining Y. Multicollinearity or non-orthogonality, on the other hand, means simply that X and Z are associated. No more, no less.

2.2.7   The Problem-Variable and the Problem-Relation

For most dependent techniques, the explanandum is a problem-variable. Increasing childlessness is such an example (see 1.2.2). The characteristic '$\Delta\%$ childless women' is conceived of as a dependent variable and, by means of multiple regression, it is investigated to what extent it can be explained by several causal factors in a multicausal model. Intrinsic motivation is another example of a problem-variable (see 1.2.4), which has to be explained by external rewards, task interest and their interaction. Still another example of a problem-variable is the poorness of neighbourhoods (see 1.2.5). It is coded as a dummy variable, which is dichotomous with the categories poor and rich. A number of discriminating characteristics of neighbourhoods are advanced for explanation.

In the example of the influence of Christian beliefs on anti-Semitism (see 1.2.3) the situation is different. The starting point of the research problem is now a problem-relation and not a problem-variable. Either it is questionable whether there is a causal relationship between Christian beliefs and anti-Semitism and antecedent variables are therefore considered which render the causal relationship spurious (spurious causality), or the validity of the causal effect is convincing and so intermediate variables are included which are helpful in explaining the causal connection (indirect causality). The technique used in the investigation of spurious and/or indirect causality is partial correlation analysis. A more advanced version of it, which will be discussed in Part II, is the Simon–Blalock procedure. Path analysis and LISREL are suitable as well. The starting point of these techniques is a problem-relation, not merely a problem-variable.

This leads to the following classification of dependent techniques:

problem-variable	**problem-relation as starting point**
multiple regression	partial correlation analysis
analysis of variance	(Simon–Blalock procedure)
analysis of covariance	
discriminant analysis	

2.2.8   *One or More Hierarchical Steps*

Up to this point, we have considered only one hierarchical step in multiple regression analysis. With childlessness as the dependent variable (see 1.2.2), a number of causal factors were brought up, but there was no further search for causes that lay deeper. Each of the series of independent variables, education, age at marriage, and others, was conceived of as executing a 'direct' influence on childlessness. Such an investigation of direct causal influences is termed an analysis with one hierarchical step.

When several hierarchical steps are involved, we not only search for causes, but also for causes of these causes. In the next step we can again search for the causes of the latter. It is of course impossible to continue this search indefinitely. The model is limited. The variables that are situated most to the left of the causal chain, and for which the causes are no longer investigated, are called exogenous variables.

In the research example on childlessness we might introduce several hierarchical steps by looking at the causal mechanisms between the independent variables. In groups with high Δ mean age at marriage, there will be less $\Delta\%$ divorces than in groups of women where the change in mean age at marriage is low. X_4 is therefore a direct cause of X_3. We can also expect that X_2 is a direct cause of X_4, because groups of women with higher mean education show a higher mean age at marriage, as they postpone their marriage. Looking at these two causal relationships, the convergent causal structure of multiple regression analysis would be converted into Figure 2.3 involving several hierarchical steps.

The change in educational attainment and the change in the number of working women are the two exogenous variables. A non-causal association is postulated between them (double-sided curved arrow). The model contains three hierarchical

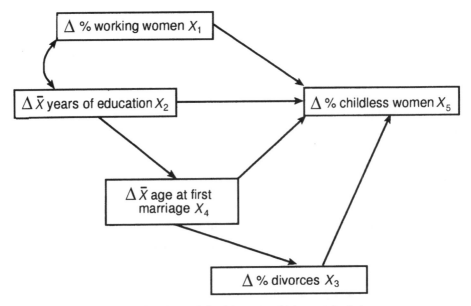

Figure 2.3   A model with several hierarchical steps

steps, from education to age at marriage, from age at marriage to divorce and from divorce to childlessness.

For the analysis of such a model with several hierarchical steps, the global model is subdivided into submodels. Each submodel has the format of the convergent causal structure, with one dependent variable and one or more direct causes. For each submodel a mathematical equation is constructed, with the dependent variable (for example X_5) as a function of the direct causes (X_1, X_2, X_3 and X_4). In this way a system emerges of as many equations as there are submodels:

$$X_5 = f(X_1, X_2, X_3, X_4)$$
$$X_3 = f(X_4)$$
$$X_4 = f(X_2)$$

Such a system of equations is called a 'structural equation model' or a 'simultaneous equation model'. Of the techniques of multivariate analysis suitable for such a system, the path analysis is the prototype. A more advanced procedure of analysis is called 'linear structural relations system', in short LISREL. For lower measurement levels some analogues of the simultaneous equation approach have been developed. Examples are pathals and the path analytic version of the loglinear model.

Another technique, in which several hierarchical steps are analysed in principle, is partial correlation analysis and its more advanced version, the Simon–Blalock procedure. In the format of indirect causality (see 1.2.3) two hierarchical steps are involved: from Christian beliefs to libertarianism ($X_1 \to X_3$) and from libertarianism to anti-Semitism ($X_3 \to Y$). However, this presence of several hierarchical steps is only implicit. Indeed, as we have stated in 2.2.7, the starting point of this technique is not the problem-variable 'anti-Semitism', but the problem-relation 'religion -? $\to$ anti-Semitism'. The investigation of causes of causes is not at stake here.

On the other hand, it is possible to analyse the scheme of indirect causality by means of path analysis, with a system of structural equations. In that case, anti-Semitism would be the problem-variable of a first step, with Christian beliefs and libertarianism as causal factors. In a second hierarchical step the causal influence of Christian beliefs on libertarianism would be investigated. The expectation of this analysis would then be that the causal effect of Christian beliefs on anti-Semitism is weakened. So, as in partial correlation analysis, the same result would be reached from this approach, as the causal relationship would be rendered spurious here as well. In any case the procedure of analysis is different. On the one hand, it corresponds less to the research problem, because the problem-variable and not the problem-relation is the starting point. On the other hand, it corresponds better, as the two hierarchical steps are more explicitly involved in the arithmetic of the technique. Another advantage is the fact that asymmetrical coefficients are used in the calculations (path coefficients), unlike partial correlation analysis, which makes use of symmetrical measures (correlation coefficients). In Part II we will discuss even more differences. Here, we can confine ourselves to advising the researcher to try out both procedures of analysis.

In making a classification, the techniques with interactive structure have to be left out of the argument, because all analyses with several hierarchical steps presuppose additivity (= absence of effects of interaction). The subclassification is therefore restricted to the distinction between multiple regression and the systems of analysis with more than one hierarchical step:

one hierarchical step	**several hierarchical steps**
multiple regression	simultaneous equation models
	• path analysis
	• LISREL
	partial correlation analysis
	Simon–Blalock procedure

2.2.9   *Manifest and Latent Variables*

We remind the reader that a manifest variable is enframed and a latent variable encircled. A manifest variable is a characteristic which is directly observed and measured. The most obvious example of a manifest variable is the question in a questionnaire.

A latent variable, conversely, is not directly measured, but is conceived of as a hypothetical term which is added to or inferred from the analysis. We therefore speak of a hypothetical variable, hypothetical concept or hypothetical construct. Other synonyms are: theoretical variable, theoretical term, theoretical concept, theoretical construct, factor and unmeasured variable. The adjective 'theoretical' indicates that the latent variable is part of a theory, while the manifest variable is only an instrument of measurement on the operational level. For example, the relation between economic inequality and political instability (see 1.2.7) is situated on the level of political theory. But the GINI index is an observation term, serving as an indicator of the concept of economic inequality. The synonyms 'factor' and 'unmeasured variable' are more limited. Factor refers to the technique of factor analysis. Unmeasured variable indicates that the latent variable is not directly observed. We prefer the term 'latent variable' because it refers to the hidden structure in the research material. We give a few examples with reference to Chapter 1.

The idea that a great amount of research material can contain a hidden structure was introduced in the research example on marital adjustment (see 1.2.6). The technique used in this research is factor analysis. In this technique latent variables are called 'factors'. A factor is a linear combination, which means a weighted sum of indicators. The weights indicate to what extent each indicator is related to the factor under consideration. In Figure 1.10 we might draw connecting lines for the highest weights. Making use of these lines we could try to give an interpretation of each factor, in other words we could try to find a name which serves as a summarizing concept for the indicators.

How the factors are calculated will be illustrated in detail in Part II. Such a great number of calculation methods have been developed that we can speak of a whole world of factor analyses. Generally, factors are determined in such a way that they have — in accordance with some criterion — the highest possible explanatory power. This could mean, for example, that they extract the highest possible proportion out of the variance of the answers on interview questions. There is mostly an order of magnitude: the factor companionship (A) has the highest explanatory power, the next in magnitude are agreement (B) and affectional intimacy (C). The proportion of the variance that is extracted by all three factors in a three-factor solution then gives an idea of the explanatory power of the factor model as a whole.

Another example of a latent variable is each of the canonical variables in canonical correlation analysis. Economic inequality and political instability form such a pair of canonical variates (see 1.2.7). The X set of five economic indicators and the Y set of four political indicators are the measured variables.

A canonical variate, like a factor, is a linear combination of indicators. So, economic inequality is a linear combination of the five X variables and political instability is a linear combination of the four Y variables. The weights of both linear combinations are calculated in such a way that the (canonical) correlation between them is maximal. So, the introduction of latent variables is a means of solving the technical problem of maximizing the correlation between the X set and the Y set. The assignment of a name to each of the canonical variates is strictly a subordinate matter in this procedure. In the example, the names are admittedly postulated in a prior fashion. They are convenient as summarizing terms. But, contrary to factor analysis, it is not the purpose in canonical correlation analysis to search for a summarizing concept for one battery of indicators, e.g., the X set. The mechanism of the technique is different. The focus is not on the associations within a set, but on the associations between sets. The problems of interpretation and name-giving will play a role from the moment that a second pair of canonical variates can be distinguished from the first pair.

There are many other cases where latent variables come into play, but where it is impossible or unintended to consider them as theoretical concepts. A typical example is given by the unknown control factors in the example of humour as a technique of social influence (see 1.2.1). These characteristics are factors in an experiment, which are unknown by definition and the effect of which will hopefully be eliminated by randomization. Such residual factors can in fact be distinguished in every technique, which we have not done in Chapter 1 for reasons of parsimony.

There are still other reasons to justify the proposition that a technique of multivariate analysis without latent variables is non-existent. Take, for example, multiple regression analysis in its application to the research on childlessness (see 1.2.2, Figure 1.4). It would seem as if there are no latent variables in this convergent causal structure. However, in Part II we will look at multiple regression from the technical side and it will be shown there that the technique can be seen as a special case of canonical correlation analysis, in which latent variables do play a role in the form of linear combinations of manifest variables. The causal factors X_1, X_2, X_3 and X_4 can be conceived of as a first set of indicators. The second set is a singleton here, containing only one indicator, which is the dependent variable Y. The latent variable is in fact redundant for this second singleton set, because it coincides and is even identical with that one indicator. But for the first X set, we are searching for a linear combination of X_1 up to X_4, in such a way that the correlation with Y is maximal. In other words, the formal structure of multiple regression can also be represented as in Figure 2.4.

In Figure 2.4 we have drawn a causal arrow from latent variable X^* to Y^*. But, focussing on the technique of canonical correlation analysis for which it was suggested that the arithmetic is not asymmetrical, we would have to eliminate this

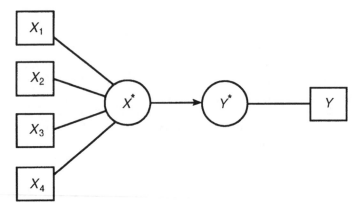

Figure 2.4 Multiple regression with latent variables

high-handed arrow *a fortiori*. It is only in the face of additional information that we get indications on the problem of causality.

In the foregoing paragraphs we made some remarks on the relativity of the distinction between manifest and latent variables: residuals, too, appear to be latent variables and there is in fact no multivariate analysis without them. It thus seems impossible to make a classification of techniques with and without latent variables. It is, however, the tradition to look at factor analysis, canonical correlation analysis and multidimensional scaling as typical examples of techniques with latent variables. The latent variables are called, respectively, factors, canonical variates and dimensions. They can be introduced *a priori* as theoretical concepts or they can be inferred from the analysis and interpreted in an *ad hoc* fashion.

The classification (see the encircled variables in 2.1.2) is as follows:

techniques without and	**with latent variables**
multiple regression	factor analysis
analysis of variance	canonical correlation analysis
analysis of covariance	multidimensional scaling
discriminant analysis	
partial correlation analysis	

2.2.10   *The Number of Latent Variables*

In canonical correlation analysis there is more than one latent variable, by definition, because 'pairs' of canonical variates are investigated. The first pair in the example from 1.2.7 was economic inequality and political instability. When the explained variance (squared canonical correlation) of the first pair is not very high, it can be worthwhile looking for other pairs. Each next pair is uncorrelated with the previous one and a pair is calculated in such a way that the (canonical) correlation is maximal.

It is possible not only to investigate several pairs of latent variables, but to compare more than two sets of variables as well, e.g., a Z set in addition to an X set and a Y set. In that case, several trios of latent variables are dealt with in a generalized canonical correlation analysis.

There are no pairs in factor analysis or in scaling techniques. Here, the starting point is 'one set' of variables and a latent structure is searched for. Estimates are made in order to reduce the variable set to a small number of latent variables. These are called 'factors' in factor analysis and 'dimensions' in scaling techniques. The number and the names of these latent variables can be defined *a priori* or can be inferred from the analysis in an inductive–explorative fashion. It is thereby possible that merely one factor or dimension is at stake. In these cases, we are dealing with a one-factor solution or a unidimensional scale. It might therefore have been possible in the example on marital adjustment that all indicators had high loadings on one factor 'companionship' and that this factor extracted a high proportion out of the variance of the variables. In that case, a one-factor solution might have been preferable, which would have meant that all indicators measured nearly the same and were interchangeable. The same holds for the dimension 'quality' in the investigation of the styles in furnishing the living room.

The technique of factor analysis is not restricted to the unidimensional case. A one-factor solution is chosen only in those cases where one single factor is postulated *a priori* or where one single factor is inferred from the data *a posteriori*. In scaling analyses, on the other hand, some of the techniques are explicitly designed to be unidimensional, such as the Guttman scaling technique and its probabilistic version, the Mokken scaling technique. It is therefore convention to speak of 'uni' and of 'multidimensional scaling' (MDS). In the latter MDS techniques several dimensions can be inferred simultaneously from the analysis.

A varying number of latent variables is not only possible for the non-dependent techniques, but also for the advanced versions of dependent techniques of analysis. Jöreskog's LISREL model contains several latent variables, each represented by multiple indicators. If one and only one latent variable is present, LISREL coincides with the simpler factor analysis with a one-factor solution. If several latent variables are present, they can be interconnected in a causal model. Now, if each of these latent variables in a recursive causal model is represented by one and only one indicator, so that only 'manifest' variables come into play, then LISREL coincides with the much simpler path analysis. In making a classification, we could thus distinguish versions without, with one and with several latent variables.

There is still another way to augment the number of latent variables, i.e., performing a 'higher-order factor analysis'. In cases where the number of factors in a first factor analysis is rather high and where it is suspected that these factors measure the same in part, a second factor analysis might be chosen with the factors as indicators. The technique which follows this strategy is called 'second-order factor analysis'.

Summarizing, we have the following possibilities:

no latent variable	**one latent variable**
multiple regression analysis	unidimensional scaling
partial correlation analysis	(Guttman, Mokken and others)
path analysis	factor analysis, one-factor-model
ANOVA and ANCOVA	
discriminant analysis	

several latent variables	**groups of latent variables**
factor analysis	canonical correlation analysis
multidimensional scaling	(pairs)
LISREL	generalized canonical
higher-order factor analysis	correlation analysis (trios)

2.2.11 *The Orthogonality of Latent Variables*

The dimensions which are inferred from a latent structure analysis need not necessarily be orthogonal or perpendicular, but it is of course nice when this is the case. For example, in principal components factor analysis (PCA), orthogonality is built-in by definition. Take the research example on marital adjustment from 1.2.6 and suppose that we perform such a PCA, then the factors 'companionship', 'agreement' and 'affectional intimacy' would be mutually uncorrelated, i.e., orthogonal. This would mean that the three factors represent three 'separate' dimensions, without there being any overlap. The latter is naturally seldom the case. The dimensions that are inferred from a technique of dimension reduction are usually not uncorrelated: not geometrically so because they are not perpendicular, not statistically so because they do share common variance, and not in terms of contents because they share the same meaning in part (think of companionship and agreement).

In confirmatory factor analysis, which is a special case of LISREL developed by Jöreskog, the correlations between the factors are an explicit part of the analysis. They are collected in a matrix of factor correlations. It is therefore possible in confirmatory factor analysis to decide *a priori* whether the factors will or will not be correlated.

In classical exploratory factor analyses (PCA, PFA and others), the question of factor correlations arises in rotating. Rotating is the turning of the factor axes until they fit better with the data and provide for a clearer interpretation. Such a rotation can be performed orthogonally, so that the factors remain perpendicular. It is, however, also possible to rotate in an 'oblique' fashion, in such a way that the factor axes form an angle unequal to 90° (oblique = slanting, askew, cunning, ambiguous). True enough, the factors fit better with the data after oblique rotation, but on the other hand the interpretations become more ambiguous because of the overlap due to factor correlations.

For multidimensional scaling a comparable explanation holds as for factor analysis. Here too, the dimensions can be orthogonal or non-orthogonal and the situation of orthogonality leads to a less ambiguous interpretation.

The case of canonical correlation analysis is clearly different when compared to factor analysis and MDS. In searching for a first pair of latent variables (canonical variates), the aim is not orthogonality but rather the opposite, for the (canonical) correlation between this pair is maximized. It is not until the next pair of canonical variates, which are themselves maximally correlated, that this pair needs to be uncorrelated with the first pair.

From the foregoing we infer the following classification:

techniques of analysis with latent variables:

uncorrelated variables	correlated variables
principal components analysis and other factor analyses (with orthogonal rotation)	confirmatory factor analysis (LISREL) exploratory factor analyses (with oblique rotation)
multidimensional scaling (only in principle)	
canonical correlation analysis (across pairs)	canonical correlation analysis (each pair)

2.2.12 *The Measurement Level for Non-Dependent Techniques*

In dealing with dependent techniques we indicated that variables might be measured at a level lower than interval and that these can often be represented by means of dummy coding. For example, when the dependent variable has a lower measurement level, we will make use of discriminant analysis. When this is the case for all the independent variables, we make use of analysis of variance, and when some but not all independent variables are nominal or ordinal, we use analysis of covariance.

The possibility of including variables of lower measurement level, some or all of them, also holds for the non-dependent techniques such as factor analysis and canonical correlation analysis.

The number of procedures for ordinal and nominal variables has become so elaborate these days that, if we were to discuss them all, this book would have to be augmented with a second volume.

In this context we would like to praise the pioneering work of Leo Goodman on the one hand and of the Gifi Group on the other hand.

In an extensive series of articles, Leo Goodman of the University of Chicago has developed a lower measurement analogue for almost all classical multivariate analyses, dependent as well as non-dependent. These analogues are known as the loglinear model. This is an extremely clever model, because the stringent conditions of classical techniques, like normality, homo-scedasticity and others, are no longer stipulated and because a profound statistical basis is made at the same time, even in inferential terms. The working procedure of loglinear analysis consists of testing different models successively and of estimating the parameters of the selected model. These parameters are effects of zero, first, second up to n-th order, when there are n variables. Therefore, higher-order interactions can be explored with this technique.

The Gifi Group of the Department of Data Theory at Leiden University, under the leadership of Jan de Leeuw, has built on the work of Benzecri, Guttman, Kruskal and many others. Their pioneering efforts concern the non-metric and non-linear multivariate analysis. Using the names Homals (= Anacor), Princals, Canals, Morals, Criminals, Pathals and others, this group of data analysts has developed an analogue for almost all classical techniques, including user-friendly software. The names of the corresponding classical techniques are implicitly contained in the new names: principal components analysis (Princals), canonical correlation analysis (Canals), multiple correlation and regression analysis (Morals), discriminant analysis (Criminals).

The working method of the Gifi Group is different from Goodman's. Their emphasis is less on structural representation, more on simplification and reduction; less on inferential statistics, more on descriptive statistics; less on the deductive, more on the inductive approach; less on stringent testing, more on searching with an open-minded spirit; and less founded on the basis of philosophy of science, more on geometrical representation. Theory is left to the theoretician or the investigator. The members of the Gifi Group define themselves as data analysts. They analyse data that are handed to them by the investigator. According to them, the structure of these data does not have to be linear, normal or orthogonal. They visualize in circles, horseshoes and all possible structures. The work is always performed by computer and after the analysis the data are mostly plotted in a two-dimensional space. The geometrical plot decides whether a certain structure in the data can be recognized and how this is to be interpreted.

In addition to the recent work of Leo Goodman and the Gifi Group, cluster analysis should be mentioned as the prototype of non-dependent techniques for variables of lower measurement level. As in the case of factor analysis, a whole world of techniques of cluster analysis is involved. It is, however, worth mentioning that most of these techniques perform an analysis on the units of the data matrix, so that clusters of individuals are obtained. But a cluster analysis of variables also exists, which takes the association matrix as a starting point, so that clusters of variables are obtained. It is the latter cluster analysis that we are focussing on in this section.

Without attempting to be complete, we arrive at the following classification of non-dependent techniques with variables of metric and non-metric (ordinal or nominal) measurement level:

non-dependent techniques of analysis:

metric	**non-metric**
factor analysis	cluster analysis,
canonical correlation	Homals, Princals, Canals
multidimensional scaling	loglinear analysis
(in principle)	

2.2.13   *Testing and Gauging*

Throughout the previous sections we alluded to the distinction between *a priori* and *a posteriori*, between a deductive and an inductive approach, between confirmation and exploration. For example, in the research example on marital adjustment from 1.2.6 we stated that the latent structure was inferred by means of factor analysis from the 20 variables on an *ad hoc* basis, without the researchers having any clear vision. We poked fun at this situation, for it is, according to us, scientifically more sound to start from theory and to subject this theory to a test. There is a characteristic joke in this respect, where many researchers performing a factor analysis are not able to come up with a name for a given factor, like 'companionship', and so simply decide to add up the many variables with high factor loadings, resulting in the factor 'kisses every day/together out/together at home/legitimate behaviour/give and take/marry the same person'. At a later stage this condemnation of factor analysis was toned down, because a prior theory is explicitly required in Jöreskog's confirmatory factor analysis.

Another example, where testing and gauging are concerned, is the furnishing of the living room from 1.2.8. We praised the researchers, because in addition to the inferring of dimensions from the data inductively, they had postulated these dimensions priorally in order to investigate, testing deductively whether they could be given empirical support.

A further example was the investigation of the canonical correlation between economic inequality and political instability of countries. There, too, we stated that the names of the canonical variates were determined *a priori*, but we cautiously added that it would be difficult to find names for the next pair of canonical variates.

We also discussed the issue of testing and gauging when dealing with non-metric non-dependent techniques (see 2.2.12). We praised the loglinear model of Leo Goodman for its statistical testing merits and we pointed to the unique approach of the Gifi Group, whose emphasis is placed less on inferential and more on descriptive statistics. This is, unfortunately, the weak point of Homals, Princals and other 'als'-techniques.

The remarks made in this section do not lead to a classification, for, in principle, we can use any technique in either an exploratory or deductive fashion. It will thereby have become clear that the latter, if possible, has our preference.

2.2.14 The Analysis of Variables and of Units

So far we have taken it for granted that a multivariate analysis is an analysis of several variables. For example, in the investigation of marital adjustment 20 questions were put to a sample of 349 people. Each of these 20 questions was a variable. For each variable a distribution of the individuals was made with a mean and a variance. For the variables two by two correlations were calculated. These correlations were collected in a matrix and from this correlation matrix a factor analysis was performed. A subgroup of strongly associated variables represents a factor. This type of working-method is called R factor analysis.

Now, instead of variables, we can also analyse units. We could indeed investigate for each two people to what extent they resemble each other, making use of their scores on the 20 posed questions. Persons having approximately equal scores on the different variables could then be placed in the same group. Groups of persons would then be formed instead of groups of variables. This type of working method is called Q factor analysis.

Most techniques of cluster analysis are of this Q-type. For, 'clusters' usually indicate groups of units. Clusters are homogeneous inwardly, because the inter-person-correlations within a cluster are strong, and heterogeneous outwardly, because the inter-person-correlations over clusters are weak.

The recently developed techniques of the Gifi Group, of which Homals is the prototype, make possible an analysis of units as well as variables and their categories. They are therefore R-type as well as Q-type.

A classification is as follows:

analysis of variables	of units	of both
all techniques up to now	Q factor analysis	Homals, etc.
R factor analysis	most cluster analyses	

2.2.15   Linear and Non-linear Techniques of Analysis

Regression, factor analysis, canonical correlation analysis and other classical techniques are metrical and linear. We know from 2.2.12 that a non-metric variant has been developed for each metric technique. The pioneering work of Leo Goodman and the Gifi Group was praised in this respect. There is really no need to make a distinction between the adjectives 'non-metric' and 'non-linear', for these non-metric techniques are also non-linear. This is implied in the expression 'loglinear model', because the model only becomes linear after taking the logarithm. The title of Gifi's book *Non-linear Multivariate Analysis* also speaks for itself.

Linearity is an old sore in statistics. In applications of classical regression analysis it became clear all too often that the plots of the data seldom follow the pattern of a nice straight line or a flat plane. To understand what is meant here, we only have to think of the exponential functions applied by the Club of Rome in the analysis of increasing environmental pollution. And, in addition to regression, the same holds of course for discriminant analysis, factor analysis and other classical techniques. A linearity test is, therefore, always an obligation.

A linear function is naturally handy, as it is easy to calculate and to interpret. One can therefore consider — in cases of non-linearity — performing certain transformations on the data in such a way as to obtain linearity. Taking the logarithm is an example of such a transformation. It is, however, also possible to fit a non-linear function, which will be a quadratic function, a function of the third degree or, in general, a polynomial of the n-th degree, depending on the number of curves that are detected in the scatterplot: one, two or $n - 1$ respectively. It has become possible for nearly all existing techniques to fit such a nonlinear function.

Our conclusion is that, especially in recent decades, a non-linear analogue has been developed for almost all multivariate analyses, so that for each technique we can make a subclassification in the linear and the non-linear versions.

2.2.16   The Analysis of Data and of Similarities

The starting point for most techniques of analysis is the data matrix. This matrix contains properties in the head column, units in the front column and scores in the body. Multidimensional scaling (MDS) techniques form an exception here, because the similarities between properties and not the properties themselves are the input of analysis. For this reason the computer program 'ALSCAL', which is part of SPSS, is preceded by the program 'PROXIMITIES'. The latter calculates similarities, dissimilarities and distances, and this output can be used in the form of input matrices in the ALSCAL procedure.

As far as contents are concerned, multidimensional scaling is especially applied to preference data. In marketing research, for example, a number of products are presented to a sampling of people, and the individuals have to give their preference for each combination of two products. Input of the analysis is then the matrix of two by two similarities between the products.

Such similarities were also the starting point in the investigation of the furnishing of the living room. Therefore, the analysis chosen in this research was multidimensional scaling (MDS). All two by two associations were calculated for 49 characteristics of the living rooms. Remember, for example, the association of the Persian carpet and the parquet floor. These associations formed the input of the MDS analysis.

We must, however, qualify our observations. For, the distinction between the input of multidimensional scaling and of other latent structure analyses is in fact relative. The matrix of bivariate associations can be used as a starting point in factor analysis as well as cluster analysis. Think of the correlations between the indicators of marital adjustment, e.g., between staying at home and having outside activities together, or between happiness in marriage and getting on each other's nerves.

There is still a difference in research strategy. When the characteristics are presented to the respondents by two's and preferences are asked, the data already have the form of similarities in the observation phase. In this case, MDS is generally chosen. When, on the other hand, scores of separate characteristics are observed, we then in fact perform two analyses. A first analysis results in the matrix of similarities and the latter is used as the input of a second latent structure analysis. In this case, either factor analysis or cluster analysis is generally chosen.

These choices are predominantly related to research traditions.

From the qualifications made above, we come to a subclassification of analyses of data (all techniques except MDS) and analyses of data similarities (MDS).

2.2.17 *Other Classifications*

Many other subclassifications can be made. We limit ourselves to a short list of possibilities.

Models of analysis can be static, when all data are observed at one moment in time, or dynamic, when the time variable is explicitly taken into the analysis. Examples of the latter are time series analyses, panel studies, longitudinal approaches and dynamic causal models.

The dependent techniques can be subdivided further into recursive models, when all causal arrows go in the same direction, and non-recursive models, when direct and/or indirect feedbacks occur. The LISREL procedure is one of the possibilities for the investigation of non-recursive models. In this textbook we restrict ourselves to partial correlation analysis and path analysis, which can only be applied to recursive models.

Other distinctions are: the use of parametric versus non-parametric statistics, the investigation of the sample or of the population, the presence or absence of transformations and the presence or absence of stringent assumptions.

3

The Analysis Technique as the Mirror of the Research Problem

In this chapter a link is made between the research problems and the techniques of analysis. We will discuss the appropriate choice of a technique of multivariate analysis for a number of social scientific research problems. Almost all examples are taken from empirical investigations that were actually conducted. For each investigation we first give an outline of the researcher's motives in choosing the subject and we indicate how the research problem was structured. Next, we make use of the classification schemes of Chapter 2 and of the causal diagram of a research problem in order to discuss the appropriate technique of analysis. In doing so the reader can practise recognizing the structure of a research problem (basic format), making an appropriate research design and anticipating an appropriate technique of analysis.

In the second part of this chapter we leave the rather scholastic idea behind that there is only one appropriate technique of multivariate analysis for a research problem. We take as a starting point the dependency theory, which is a causal theory in international political science, and show how the researcher executes several manipulations in practice, so that the choice of an appropriate technique becomes relative. In its pure form, the dependency theory leads to the application of a path analysis (or LISREL). Disregarding the causal mechanisms between the independent variables we obtain multiple regression analysis. By shrinking the dependent variable into a dichotomy or polytomy we end up in two-group or multiple discriminant analysis. On the other hand, when performing all kinds of shrinkages on the side of the independent variables, we obtain the design of ANOVA or ANCOVA, with or without the effects of interaction. When several dependent variables are entered into the model simultaneously, the design changes into MANOVA or MANCOVA. These dependent variables can also be conceived of as a set, so that an analysis of the association between the set of dependent and the set of independent variables can be made. This is a canonical correlation analysis. For lower measurement levels it is a canals analysis.

It follows that our title 'The Analysis Technique as the Mirror of the Research Problem' becomes relative. In research practice there is never a nice one to one correspondence between the theoretical ideas and the technical choices, for all sorts of pragmatic decisions bring the researcher from one technique to another. We should therefore take care that the original ideas which are contained in the research problem are not denied.

3.1 Research Examples

3.1.1 The Influence of Total Institutions on Self-Image

In his volume *Asylums*, the sociologist Erving Goffman introduces the concept of the 'total institution'. Examples of total institutions are monasteries, barracks, prisons and mental hospitals. They are defined as places of residence and work cut off from the rest of society, where a large number of uniform individuals lead an enclosed, formally administered life for an appreciable period of time. In Goffman's view, the consequences of institutionalization are devastating. The confinement is characterized by an inevitable process of resocialization. The individual passes through a series of humiliation ceremonies, isolation techniques and uniformization demands, the purpose of which is to strip him of his past statuses and roles and provide him with a new identity appropriate to his institutional status and in which the measure of obedience is linked with rewards and punishments. It is important to recognize that Goffman's view on total institutions is essentially an extension of the labelling theory, in which the social re-construction of the individual's identity (by significant others) implies an alteration of the ego-identity (by himself).

John F. Myles (1978), an investigator at Carleton University, wants to address Goffman's theory empirically. He regards institutions for the aged as total institutions organized according to the medical model. He formulates the thesis that the institutionalized, regardless of their objective health status, will gradually come to define themselves as ill, and that a quite different picture will emerge for the non-institutionalized. To test this institutionalization thesis empirically he draws a random sample, stratified by residential status (institutionalized, non-institutionalized), of 3851 persons aged 65 and over from the Province of Manitoba. All respondents are asked, on a scale from 1 to 10, to what extent they perceive and evaluate the state of their health (subjective health). Objective health is measured by a series of tests, which, together with other observations, result in a battery of health indicators. These indicators are analysed by means of a classical R-type factor analysis and for the resulting one-factor solution the factor scores are calculated. Controlling for sex, marital status, income and education appeared to be unnecessary, so that these background characteristics could be excluded from the analysis.

Design 3.1.1

Controlling for the objective health status, the research problem is that there will be a significant difference between the subjective health perceptions of institutionalized and non-institutionalized aged persons (higher level of sick role identification for the institutionalized):

- The research problem is dependent. The dependent variable (Y) is the subjective health. The independent variables are the residential status (X_1: institutionalized or not) and the objective health (X_2). Therefore, the non-dependent designs can be eliminated.
- The number of dependent variables is restricted to one. So, the designs with several dependent variables are no longer considered.
- The dependent variable has been measured at the interval level. For that reason, discriminant analysis can be eliminated.

- Two groups are formed, one of aged persons in a total institution à la Goffman and one of non-institutionalized persons. The effect of institutionalization on patterns of sick role identification is investigated, controlling for many other variables. We are therefore dealing with a quasi-experimental design.
- There is a mix of measurement levels among the independent variables: X_1 is dichotomous and X_2 has been measured at the interval level. In the quasi-experiment the variable X_2 plays the role of an important control variable in the form of a covariate. The structure of the research problem might eventually be interactive, for example if the effect of the total institution on the ego-identity is different for different levels of objective health.

Conclusion: a quasi-experimental ANCOVA design.

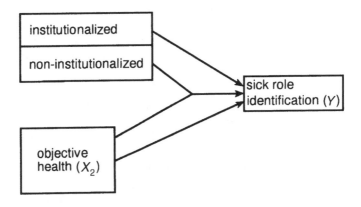

3.1.2   The Trade Union Militant

The workers of the 'Cerro de Pasco Corporation' (CPC) concern in Peru, together with the Bolivian mine workers, are known as the most militant in Latin America. D. Kruijt and M. Vellinga want to investigate this militantism empirically. They wonder how an adequate measurement of the trade union militant can be achieved. The distinction between the member of the union who has paid his contribution, and the non-member, who has not contributed, is not necessarily the same as the distinction between the militant and the docile worker. It is indeed possible that the category of paying members of the union contains active workers as well as less active workers, and the group of non-members can consist of non-active as well as militant workers.

In order to investigate whether the payment of union dues is a valid indicator of militantism, the researchers gather supplementary data for 13 000 workers of the CPC. This extra information is taken from the individual registration cards and contains seniority, hierarchical level in the industry, educational level, debts to the CPC and the number of penalties for undisciplined behaviour. The theoretical hypothesis is that the workers with higher seniority are less militant, firstly because the repressive and anti-unionist character of the CPC has gradually resulted in an expulsion of the radical workers, caused by procedures of dismissal and lock-out, and secondly because the workers with a long service record show a higher probability of absorption into the complex system of co-optation and incorporation of the CPC family. It is further hypothesized that militantism is higher for workers with higher educational level, lower hierarchical level in the industry, less debts and more penalties.

Design 3.1.2
We gave an outline of only a part of a large-scale investigation. The research problem here is whether the prior classification of member and non-member of the union coincided with the distinction between the militant and the docile worker, where militantism is measured by means of the indicators seniority, hierarchical level in the industry, educational level, debts to the CPC and penalties for undisciplined behaviour:

- The research problem is dependent. The dependent variable (Y) is the membership of the union (member or non-member). The independent variables are the indicators of militantism.
- The number of dependent variables is restricted to one.
- The dependent variable is measured at the nominal measurement level. It is a dichotomous variable, which represents the two groups of members and non-members of the union.
- The independent variables seniority, level in the hierarchy, educational level and numbers of debts and penalties (X_1 to X_5) have all been measured at the interval level.
- No effects of interaction are mentioned in the research problem. The researchers merely intend to investigate whether the indicators of militantism as a whole (weighted sum of X variables) give rise to a classification of two groups of workers, which coincide approximately with the *a priori* designed groups of members and non-members of the union.

Conclusion: a two-group discriminant analysis.

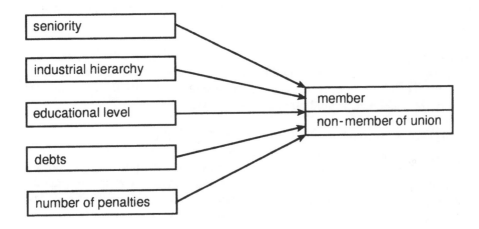

3.1.3   Occupational Gender Identification and the Assessment of the
Male and Female Earnings Inequality

Steven McLaughlin (1978) criticizes recent research on sex differences in the process of the attainment of earnings, because the individual is taken as the unit of analysis and two separate regression analyses are performed, one for men and one for women, of earnings as determined by education, prestige and other variables. According to him this approach may lead to misspecification and 'ecological fallacy'. One potential threat to a discrimination interpretation of these individual-level findings may be found in differences that exist in the nature of the occupations typically held by males and females. They may be paid at different rates, but a portion of the gap may be due to occupational characteristics. So, if there are income-relevant differences in the occupational tasks, then the lower earnings of the occupations dominated by females may be due to these occupational characteristics, regardless of gender. Investigations have provided evidence that occupations dominated by females tend to include incumbents with a higher mean education than the labour force at large, but also that earnings were lower for both men and women who worked in these occupations. Given this equal income discrimination for both men and women in occupations of equal prestige, the lower earnings have to be attributed to other occupational characteristics.

For these and other reasons, McLaughlin concludes that the occupation and not the individual should be chosen as the unit of analysis. From the American *Dictionary of Occupational Titles* and from the US Bureau of the Census he draws data for 4000 occupations on mean income (*Y*), gender identification of the occupation (male, female, mixed), occupational prestige and a great number of occupational characteristics. The aptitudes recorded for each occupation were the following: complexity, necessary training, intelligence demands, social skills, verbal and numerical skill, spatial comprehension ability, form perception, motor coordination, finger dexterity, manual skill, eye–hand–foot coordination, colour discrimination and also a number of working conditions, like the need to climb, the exposure to hot and cold, loud noises and fumes, and the requirement to work inside, outside or both.

The main object of the research was to make a refined analysis in which the differences in earnings between the three gender groups (m, f, mixed) are controlled and modified by occupational prestige and the other occupational characteristics.

Design 3.1.3
Research problem: Are there significant differences in the attaining of earnings between the occupations of the three gender groups (m, f, mixed), when controlling for occupational prestige and other occupational characteristics?
    Preparation:
    The first step is to reduce the great number of occupational characteristics to a few dimensions. A principal factor analysis with varimax rotation may be of great help here (orthogonal rotation in order to obtain mutually independent dimensions with a clear interpretation). A three-dimensional solution may, for example, lead to the following three factors: cognitive, manipulative and social skills. Factor scores are calculated and the three factors are entered into the design.

Design:

- The research problem is dependent. The dependent variable (Y) is the earnings attainment of the occupation. The independent variables are gender identification (X_1), prestige (X_2) and occupational characteristics (factors, indicated as X_3).
- There is only one dependent variable.
- The dependent variable has been measured at the interval level.
- There are three gender groups: male, female and mixed. The independent variable X_1 is trichotomous. The other independent variables X_2 and X_3 function as covariates. So, there is a mix of measurement levels among the independent variables.
- An effect of interaction is possible, when the effect of gender identification on earnings attainment is different for occupations of varying prestige and/or for occupations with different characteristics.

Conclusion: an ANCOVA design.

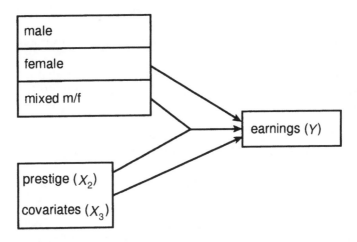

3.1.4 Student Evaluations of Teaching Merit

Lecturers at university fulfil three main tasks: teaching, research and management. Instruction often suffers as a result of the pressure to give priority to research (publish or perish!) and of the enlargement of the management tasks. Therefore, evaluation systems were developed, especially in the 1970s, at many universities in the world, allowing students to judge the quality of their lecturers.

Richard Shingles (1977) of Virginia State University tried to construct an instrument for these student evaluations. Questionnaires were obtained from a random sample of ± 1000 students, with questions on the lecturer's knowledge in his field, communication of the course objectives, use of examples and illustrations in explaining ideas, emphasizing understanding rather than memorizing, interpretation of abstract ideas and theories, enthusiasm of the lecturer, clarification of questioned material without embarrassing the student, interest in the individual student, availability outside of class, use of reading material and assignments, intellectual growth and development, the extent to which the course facilitates the understanding and evaluation of the arguments on the topics in the field, the effect on eagerness to learn and the recommendatory value of the course.

The researcher hoped to extract a number of dimensions from the material which best coincided with the following four dimensions commonly reported in the literature on student evaluations: the lecturer's competence, the structure and organization of the course, the effort the lecturer displays and the benefit to the student of having taken the course. He realized that these dimensions would not be mutually independent, firstly because the lecturer's competence, his enthusiasm and the benefits to the student are not very different in reality, and secondly because the students do not separate these dimensions in their answers.

Design 3.1.4
The research problem consists of reducing a large number of data on student evaluations to a small number of non-independent dimensions:

- The research problem is non-dependent. No distinction is made between dependent and independent variables.
- The measurement level of the variables: let us assume that all variables have been measured at the interval level.
- A prior theory is strictly absent, but there is the expectation that the dimensions that result from the material will be mutually correlated (non-orthogonal latent variables).

Conclusion: (a) without explicit *a priori* theory:
                        explorative factor analysis with oblique rotation
             (b) with explicit *a priori* theory:
                        confirmatory factor analysis (rotation unnecessary).

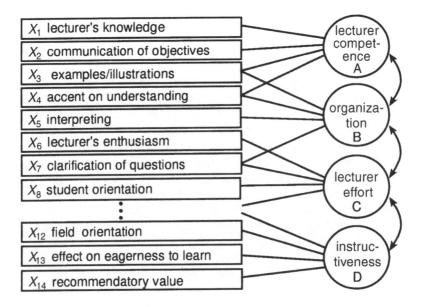

3.1.5 Interracial and Intraracial Rape

Gary LaFree (1983) refers to empirical studies which have shown a substantial increase in the rates of black offender–white victim rapes (BW). In these studies researchers have been particularly concerned with sanctions: black men accused of sexually assaulting white women receive more serious sanctions than other sexual assault suspects.

According to LaFree, paranoia concerning the protection of white women from sexual assault by black men is a legacy of American slavery that has frequently served as a focus for racist exaggerations about black men. This may explain why most empirical research on interracial rape is limited to questions of whether and to what extent agents of the law discriminate against black men. For, all studies have shown substantially higher rates of black offender–white victim (BW) than white offender–black victim rapes (WB) as well as increasing rates of BW rapes every year. But no research has examined whether interracial rapes are in fact different from intraracial rapes (WW and BB).

This is what LaFree wants to do. His data consist of 453 reports of rape and attempted rape derived from the National Crime Panel survey of crime victims, undertaken by the U.S. Bureau of the Census. He distinguishes three racial groups: BW, WW and BB. For each report he also collects measures of victims' characteristics (age, education, marital status), of the interpersonal context of the crime (whether or not offender and victim were strangers, whether the offender had a right to be at the scene of the offence as a guest or workman, whether the incident did or did not occur in the victim's home, during the night or day, with or without accessories) and of the amount of violence (physical injury, use of weapons, victim resistance, required medical attention). Where necessary, dummy coding with 0 and 1 was applied to these data, so that they could all be conceived of as measured on the interval level.

The main object of this investigation was to examine whether the scores of the report data show significant differences for the three racial groups of rapes: BW, WW and BB.

Design 3.1.5

The research problem is whether the report data of the victim, the interpersonal context and the amount of violence show significant differences for the three groups of rapes: one interracial group BW and two intraracial groups WW and BB:

- The research problem is dependent. The dependent variable (Y) is formed by the three groups BW, WW and BB. The independent variables are the data of the reports of rape.
- The number of dependent variables is restricted to one. (Remark: when the three groups are represented by two dummies, the model may be seen as having two dependent variables.)
- The dependent variable has been measured at the nominal level. It is a trichotomy, which represents the three groups BW, WW and BB.
- The independent variables are all conceived of as measured at the interval measurement level, using codes 0 and 1. Most of them are in fact dichotomous variables.

- There is no question of effects of interaction in the research problem. The researcher merely wants to examine whether the data of the reports (weighted sum of X variables) bring about significant differences between the three *a priori* postulated groups.

Conclusion: A multiple discriminant analysis.

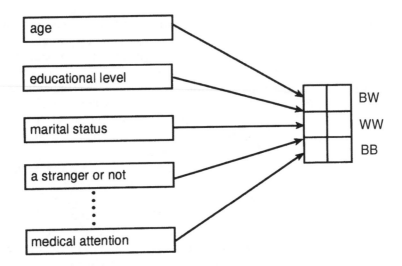

3.1.6 *Organizational Mobility in a Nuclear Research Complex*

The researcher Klingemann (1979) examined organizational mobility in a nuclear research complex at Jülich, Western Germany. For a random sample of 295 natural scientists he examined to what extent they were inclined to change their occupational position (e.g., go on to teach at a university or move to industry) or to change places within the same occupation. It was his purpose to find an explanatory model for the inclination towards mobility. The hypothesis that scientists and other working men are subject to the same mobility conditions had to be tested and the researcher expected it to be falsified. Family characteristics, general labour satisfaction, satisfaction with the community and seniority had to be weighed against more science-orientated factors like the career concept, intrinsic labour satisfaction, priority for fundamental research in the natural sciences and the perception that the organizational ends are attained. According to the prior expectations of the researcher the organization–internal factors (research motivation, priority for fundamental research, individual achievement and intrinsic labour satisfaction) would exhibit a stronger effect on the mobility of the natural scientists than the organization–external factors (duration of residence, satisfaction with the community, seniority and family pressure), this in contradistinction to other labourers.

Moreover, there would be causal relationships among these factors, for instance the effect of individual achievement on research motivation, of research motivation on the priority for fundamental research, of the duration of residence on the satisfaction of the community and (negatively) of the duration of residence on the research motivation and of the duration of residence on the priority for fundamental research.

All variables were measured at the interval measurement level.

The object of the research was to test the global causal model, in which the causal mechanisms are outlined that give an explanation for the inclination towards organizational mobility.

Design 3.1.6

The research problem is that organizational mobility can be explained by means of a complex entirety of causal contributions, i.e., individual achievement via motivation and priority for fundamental research, duration of residence via satisfaction with the community, as well as duration of residence (negatively) via motivation and priority for fundamental research:

- The research problem is dependent. The dependent variable (Y) is the inclination towards organizational mobility.
- Among the independent variables, too, dependency is postulated. So, causes of causes are investigated and therefore there are several hierarchical steps.
- All variables have been measured at the interval level.
- There is no question of effects of interaction. The causal model is additive.

Conclusion: a path analysis (perhaps LISREL).

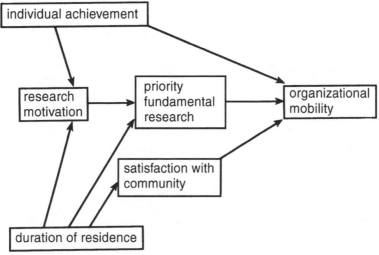

Diagram shows only part of the investigation

3.1.7 Reform in Elementary Education: A Black Box

Three Belgian researchers, R. Vandenberghe, H. Denoo and F. De Roo (1978) come to the conclusion that reform in education, like the development of curriculum, is not always realized as the 'innovators' had imagined. This phenomenon of non-implementation is caused by the politics of the school that accepts the reform as well as by a series of obstacles involving the teachers responsible for the realization of the reform. According to the researchers the process of reform is not rational and linear in character, but, rather, a socio-political transaction from the intended reform to the final realization. The process of transition itself is a black box, so that the following scheme emerges: intended reform → black box → actual implementation. The black box contains all positive and negative factors that operate at school and that either stimulate or hinder actual reform. These factors are predominantly characteristics of the teachers, because in the end it is they who must realize the reform and put it into practice. Examples of positive factors are the cooperation of the schools inspectorate, colleagues at school, the headmaster, the parents and the psycho–medical–social centre, as well as the presence of publications, stimulating textbooks, didactic material and the possibility of additional schooling. Some of the inhibitory factors are the disproportionate number of pupils in a class, lack of space, lack of cooperation by the teachers, lack of information on the reform, lack of support by the schools inspectorate, insufficiency and inaccessibility of publications, textbooks and didactic material, lack of additional schooling, shortage of financial means, the compelling character of the curriculum and a sceptical attitude towards educational reform.

The researchers want to get more insight into the black box and they hope to attain this objective by questioning a random sample of 1100 teachers on all these factors (31 positive and 45 negative) and have them indicate on a scale to what degree they are influenced by each of the factors.

Design 3.1.7
The research problem consists of reducing a great number of factors, stimulating or inhibiting educational reform, to a small number of independent dimensions in order to achieve more insight into the black box process from the intended reform to the actual realization:

- The research problem is non-dependent (also called interdependent). No distinction is made between dependent and independent variables.

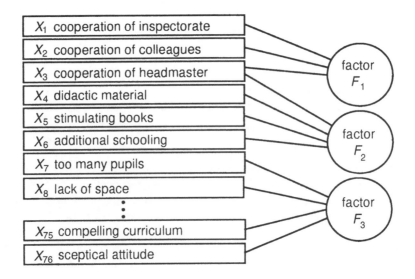

- All variables are measured at the interval measurement level, in the form of scales presented to the teachers.
- There is obviously a total absence of theory, which is clearly expressed by the term 'black box'.

Conclusion: an exploratory factor analysis with orthogonal rotation (orthogonal in order to obtain 'independent' dimensions).

3.1.8 The Value and the Valuation of Jobs

In his research on job satisfaction, Arne L. Kalleberg (1977) of Indiana University discusses several approaches in occupational sociology. One group of researchers has sought to explain the variation in job satisfaction solely in terms of the personalities of individual workers, and another group in terms of the nature of the jobs people perform. None of these approaches is adequate; for instance, the second approach does not consider individual differences in the satisfaction experienced by people with the same job characteristics.

Therefore, Kalleberg wants to introduce a new approach, in which a distinction is made between the subjective 'valuation' and the objective 'value' of the jobs. The 'valuation' question was presented to a sample of 1496 persons from the 'Quality and Employment Survey' of 1972–1973 in the United States. These persons were asked to give scores of their perceptions regarding their occupational situation for a great number of job characteristics, and means were calculated for each job. The 'value' of the jobs was determined by an independent team of scientists. These were given the same job characteristics and for each job they had to compose scores for the characteristics.

In his research Arne Kalleberg wants to investigate whether the scores of the labourers (valuation) correspond to the scores of the independent team (value). The presented job characteristics pertain to the following: intrinsic features (whether the task is interesting, allows the worker to develop their abilities, whether the worker can see the results of the work); convenience (convenient travel to and from work, good hours, freedom from conflicting demands, pleasant physical surroundings, no excessive amounts of work, enough time to do the work, opportunity to forget about personal problems); financial aspects (the pay, fringe benefits and job security); career perspective (whether the chances for promotion are good, whether promotions are handled fairly and whether the employer is concerned about giving everyone a chance to get ahead); relationships with co-workers (whether the job allows for opportunities to make friends, whether co-workers are friendly and helpful and whether one's co-workers take a personal interest in oneself); and resource adequacy (whether the help, equipment and information required for job performance are adequate).

Design 3.1.8

The research problem consists of investigating the association between two identical sets of job characteristics, whereby one set is scored by the workers and the second set by an independent team. The units of analysis are jobs:

- The research problem is non-dependent. The association between the value and the valuation of jobs is investigated, not the causal effect of one on the other. There is no question of dependent and independent variables.
- There are two sets of variables and the association between the sets is studied rather than the association within each of the sets.
- The research problem has bearing on pairs of latent variables, one representing the first set and one representing the second set. A first pair of latent variables is named *a priori* 'value' and 'valuation' by the researcher. Names for other possible pairs cannot be given until the results of analysis are considered.
- The variables have been measured at the interval level, on the condition that the scores are measured on an interval scale.

Conclusion: (a) with variables of interval measurement level:
      a canonical correlation analysis,
  (b) with variables of lower measurement level:
      a canals analysis (see Gifi, 1980 for details of this technique).

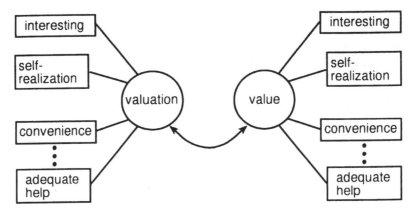

3.1.9   A Classification of 16 Native American Tribes

Karl Schuessler and Harold Driver (1956) collected statistical data for 16 geographically contiguous tribes in northwest California. The names of the tribes are: Tolowa, Yurok 1 and 2, Karok 1 and 2, Hupa 1 and 2, Chilula, Wiyot, Van Duzen, Chimariko, Sinkyone 1 and 2, Mattole, Coast Yuki and Kato.

There was little or no prior theory. The researchers merely wanted to carry out a study of Native American culture in California. 2500 items were applied to each of the 16 tribes. The items ranged over important phases of social life such as subsistence, housing, transportation, weapons, courting, marriage, ceremonies, crime, and others.

They may be illustrated by a few items on kinship avoidances between mother-in-law and son-in-law: do not speak at all, speak little, plural address, speak through third person, turn away from one another on trail, must not eat together, must not laugh together.

As it was only possible to establish the presence or absence of a trait and not to measure its magnitude, a tribe was not represented by a set of values, as a conventional variable, but merely by the number of traits present, and the number absent. For example, when a mother-in-law and son-in-law in a tribe speak to each other but may not eat or laugh together, then this tribe is assigned the score 2, while another tribe, in which all seven kinship avoidances occur, is assigned the score 7. This is analogous for other areas of social life, like subsistence, housing and others.

Consequently, the correlations calculated by the researchers did not express the degree of similarity between paired measurements, but the correlation between any two tribes and each such correlation expressed the number of traits jointly present. In other words, the intercorrelations were between the tribes rather than between the traits. In calculating these similarities between Native American tribes and in analysing the matrix of similarities, the researchers hoped to obtain a justified classification. Thus, their purpose was the making of a natural classification.

Design 3.1.9
The research problem consists of studying the similarities between any two of 16 Native American tribes, using the scores on a large number of characteristics, which should result in a natural classification of such societies:

- The research problem is non-dependent. No distinction is made between dependent and independent variables.
- There is no prior theory. The investigators do not have the intention of 'testing', but rather of 'gauging'.
- The analysis is not performed on the variables, but on units (tribes). This is justified, since there are many items and few units. If an analysis were made of the (2500)(2499)/2 inter-item-correlations, the calculation would only be based on 16 units which would lead to very unreliable results. The purpose is to make a classification of tribes (subdivision in clusters) and not to reduce the 2500 items to a number of dimensions (reduction to factors).

Conclusion: a Q-type factor analysis (or possibly a cluster analysis of units or a homals analysis); analysis of the front column of the classical data matrix.

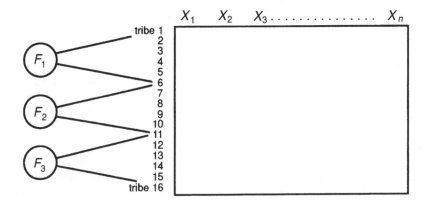

3.1.10   The Classical and Modern Role of Women in Matrimonial
Advertisements

In the magazine *Brigitte* journalist Suzanne Bontemps set up an inquiry into the role of the spouse as represented in matrimonial advertisements. (The example is fictitious and borrowed from lectures at college.) The journalist made a distinction between two role patterns: (1) the classical role: in need of protection, accent on subordination, affection, cherishing, romance; (2) the modern role: objective attitude, no need for protection, accent on the idea of equality, cooperation on a rational basis.

The journalist's hypothesis was that men predominantly accept the classical role. In other words, she hypothesized a causal effect of the nature of the role pattern on the measure of acceptance by men. In order to test this causal hypothesis she first subdivided all advertisements by women into classical and modern. A few examples follow. Advertisement 1 (classical): Wanted: strong shoulders to support weak woman, age 32, 1.56 m, attractive, girlish, feminine, slender but no model's figure, likes painting, theatre, walking, people and nice things. What soft and thoughtful man with personality is looking for a non-liberated woman to share weal and woe? Advertisement 2 (classical): Female creature, age 26, 1.65 m, with class, charm and spirit, seeks male protector with wedding plans. Advertisement 3 (modern): Woman teacher, with vocation, age 25, 1.68 m, is looking for tolerant, wise wedding partner, who accepts my professional practice. Advertisement 4 (modern): Individualist, age 36, 1.60 m, slender, physician, versatile, interest in nature and technology, theatre and politics, seeks responsive husband.

A selection of advertisements from each of these two groups was made by means of a combination of matching and random sampling. As much care as possible was taken to distribute the two groups equally over several control variables, such as height, age, occupation and length of advertisement. The number of respondent men was counted for each advertisement and it was investigated whether the mean number of responses was significantly higher for ads in which women took the classical role.

Design 3.1.10
The hypothesis is that the mean number of men reacting to the classical female role is significantly higher than for advertisements of the modern female role:

● The research problem is dependent. The dependent variable (Y) is the measure of acceptance by men, operationalized as the number of men who react to a matrimonial advertisement. The independent variable is the nature of the role pattern (classical or modern). The units of analysis are advertisements.
● The number of dependent variables is restricted to one. So, the designs with several dependent variables no longer have to be considered.
● The dependent variable is measured at the interval level. Therefore, discriminant analysis can be eliminated.
● Two groups have been formed, one of advertisements portraying the classical female role and one of the advertisements representing the modern female role. There is thus question of a quasi-experimental design (quasi, because no real randomization has taken place, because no prior research on the male attitude is

possible and because the stimulus is not introduced by the researcher him/herself).
The independent variable representing the two groups is dichotomous.

- In this simplified example, the line has been taken that the two groups show an
equal distribution on control variables like height, age, occupation and length of
advertisement. If these variables had been explicitly admitted into the analysis in
the form of covariates, the performance of an ANCOVA design would have been
appropriate. But here we are limited to a bivariate causal analysis.

Conclusion: a quasi-experimental design;
Student's *t*-test on difference of means.

3.1.11   *Absence Because of Illness*

H. Philipsen conducted an investigation into the causes of differences in mean
absenteeism of 83 medium-sized industries in the Netherlands (1969). He performed
an analysis in which the dependent variable Y was the frequency of illness (the mean
number of illnesses recorded per person per year) and some of the independent
variables were the following: X_1 = the technological commitment of the production
process (the measure of mechanization/ automatization); X_2 = the shift system (the
percentage of shift-workers); X_3 = the educational level of the work (the measure of
training or schooling required for the work); X_4 = the delegation to the non-executive
staff (the measure of delegation of responsibilities to subordinates); X_5 = the
autonomy of conduct of business (a score of autonomy with the family business at
one end of the continuum which is a closed limited liability company and operates
independently and at the other end the local establishment of large concerns);
X_6 = the conditions of benefit and continuance of payment (the financial opportunity
to report ill, with at one end the industries where full continuance of payment is the
rule and at the other end industries where the worker carries a substantial and
unconditional risk); X_7 = the link with the industrial insurance board (a score with, at
one end, the industries where the employee's illness is checked by the insurance board
and, at the other end, the industries organizing their own checks); X_8 = term of
service (the percentage of workers with a term of service shorter than one year); and
X_9 = the urbanization (the measure of urbanization of the community where the
industry is established as a measure of the global mentality of the population: in cities
there is a broader view on illness).

Variable X_1 is an indicator of stable working relations, X_2 of working objections,
X_3, X_4 and X_5 of the opportunities of self-realization and social ties, X_6 and X_7 of the
economic and insurance–technical opportunity of absenteeism, X_8 and X_9 of the
(negative) chances of social control of absenteeism.

Philipsen's intention was to find a multicausal model for the explanation of
frequency of illness (Y) in medium-sized industries in the Netherlands.

Design 3.1.11

The research problem consists of finding an explanation for the differences in mean numbers of illnesses recorded in medium-sized industries, using nine causal factors which are observed at the industry level:

- The research problem is dependent. The dependent variable (Y) is the frequency of illness, measured as the mean number of illnesses recorded per person per year. The independent variables are the nine causal factors (X_1 to X_9).
- The number of dependent variables is restricted to one. Therefore, the designs with several dependent variables can be eliminated.
- The dependent variable has been measured at the interval level. Therefore, discriminant analysis can be eliminated.
- The starting point is formed by a problem-variable (absenteeism because of illness Y) and not by a problem-relation.
- All independent variables have been measured at the interval level (or can be conceived of as quantitative because they are dichotomous with codes 0 and 1).
- In the research problem there is no question of effects of interaction. The conceptual model is clearly additive. (Remark: This does not free the researcher from the obligation of testing the possible effects of interaction in the empirical data. The same holds, moreover, for several other tests of linearity, homoscedasticity and random pattern of the residuals.)

Conclusion: a multiple regression analysis (perhaps a path analysis if mutual relations of dependency between the causal factors are considered).

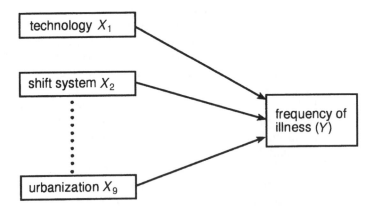

3.1.12   Are Non-Working People Socially Isolated?

Researchers D. Houtman and A.J. Steijn (1990) of Erasmus University Rotterdam have criticized recent scientific studies of minimum wage-earners and the unemployed, and especially the hypothesis that the condition of these population groups leads to a decrease in their social participation. Some investigators even speak of modern poverty. The relative deprivation and particularly the low income, in their view, lead to a decrease in social contact and of socio-cultural participation: leisure activities and social occasions are restricted and memberships in clubs and associations are terminated. According to others the lack of social participation is not caused by the difficult financial situation but rather by the need for the reduction of psychological tension: their contact with other unemployed people in particular is deliberately cut down. Still others follow a more structural approach in their explanation: the unemployed do not retreat purposely from social relations, but are forced to do so because they have less objective opportunities for maintaining social contacts.

Houtman and Steijn tried to unmask this thesis of social isolation. For, the connection between unemployment and social isolation might disappear when controlling for a number of background variables, which are related to Bourdieu's concept of cultural capital (educational level, cultural and social participation of parents) and to the composition of the household (number of children, single parent status) as well as to age. Take, for example, the cultural capital. On the one hand, it is expected that persons with low cultural capital have a higher chance of unemployment and/or social minimum benefit, and on the other hand that lower cultural capital leads to a decreased social participation. Accordingly, the social isolation of the unemployed and the minimum wage-earners should be conceived of as the continuation of a life-style, which stems from the period before dependence took place.

In supplementary research this argument will be extended for duration of unemployment (instead of the employed/unemployed) and its presumed effect on social participation.

Design 3.1.12
The research problem is whether the relationship between unemployment (and duration of unemployment) and social participation should be conceived of as a direct causal effect, or as a result of the cultural capital received from home:

- The research problem is dependent. The dependent variable (Y) is social participation.

The causal effect of the independent variables unemployment and duration of unemployment on Y is examined, controlling for cultural capital:

- The problem relation $X \rightarrow Y$ is the focus question (spurious causality), rather than the problem variable Y.
- The dependent variable Y, one in number, has been measured at the interval level.
- The independent variable unemployment can be conceived of as a dichotomy (the employed/unemployed). The researchers make a further distinction of the unemployed into RWW and ABW (Dutch social security laws), so that a trichotomy emerges. But this is not very important. What is important here is that not only the unemployed, but also the employed are taken into the design, so that a comparison is possible.
- The independent variable 'duration of unemployment' of the supplementary research has been measured at the interval level.
- The control variable 'cultural capital' is a factor which has been inferred from a factor analysis on the background characteristics and for which the factor scores were calculated. Therefore, it is a variable of interval measurement level.

Conclusions: (a) for the research with the three groups of unemployment: an
ANCOVA design;

(b) for the supplementary research with duration of unemployment: a
partial correlation analysis. The causal diagram of the latter is
drawn here.

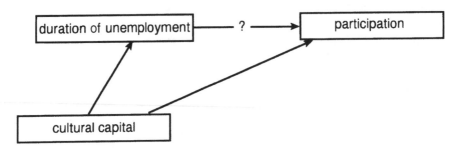

3.1.13   Educational Level Achieved by Foreign Pupils

Under the title 'What have they achieved?', M.J. De Jong (1982) of Erasmus
University Rotterdam analysed the educational achievements of 15-year-old foreign
pupils in Rotterdam. A scale of 'achieved educational level' (Y) was constructed using
combinations of years of apprenticeship and school type attended by the pupils. The
'nationality' of the pupils was represented by three groups: Surinamese, South
Europeans (Italy, Portugal, Spain and others) and the Third World group (especially
Turkey and Morocco). It was expected that the mean educational level would be the
highest for Surinamese, because of the absence of language barriers, and the lowest
for the Third World groups, because of the greater cultural distance compared to
Dutch society. Two groups of 'duration of residence' were also made: 1 = present
before 1973, 2 = arrived 1973 or later. The argument here was that achievements at
school need some time and improve along with the duration of residence. Furthermore, two groups of 'socio-economic status' were the result of dichotomizing an
index, which was constructed on the basis of the occupational and educational level of
father and mother, the number of books at home and the amount of living space at
home. It was evidently expected that pupils from families with relatively high socio-
economic status would perform better at school. In addition to the factors just
mentioned — effects of nationality, duration of residence and socio-economic status
on the achieved educational level — some modifying higher-order relationships were
expected. An example is the combined effect of nationality and duration of residence
on the achieved educational level. For instance, the better achievements of Surinamese pupils, who surpass the South Europeans and the Third World group, hold for
the short term, but not for pupils with a long duration of residence. In the long run the
Surinamese are overtaken by the South Europeans, so that both groups draw level. It
was expected that the Third World group would require a still longer term than the
duration of residence used in the research to realize this equilibrium.

Design 3.1.13

The research problem is that the mean educational level achieved by foreign pupils of
15 years of age is significantly different for the three nationality groups, the two

duration-of-residence groups and the two groups of socio-economic status. More-over, combinations of these groups offer an additional explanation:

- The research problem is dependent. The dependent variable (Y) is the educational level achieved. The independent variables are nationality, duration of residence and socio-economic status.
- The number of dependent variables is restricted to one. Therefore the designs with several dependent variables can be eliminated.
- The dependent variable has been measured at an interval level.
- The independent variables are nominally scaled measurements. Nationality is a trichotomy. Duration of residence and socio-economic status are dichotomous. They represent groups. We have a three-way design, because there are three independent variables. We have a three-way $3 \times 2 \times 2$ design, because the independent variables consist of one trichotomy and two dichotomies.
- Effects of interaction are provided for in the research problem.

Conclusion: a three-way $3 \times 2 \times 2$ analysis of variance.

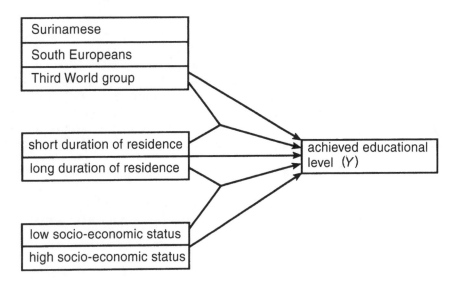

3.1.14   *The Subjective Burden of Heart Attack Patients*

Researchers Johannes Siegrist and Klaus Dittman were dissatisfied with research in medical sociology into the etiology of heart attacks. Investigations dealing with such rough variables as social level, social isolation and social mobility have contributed distressingly little to our knowledge of the genesis of illness. Essential variables such as 'subjective assimilation', 'routine in dealing with situations of crisis', 'social support' and 'vulnerability' are absent in most studies, and the treatment of the interaction between chronic difficulties and conflicts in the private and occupational context, on the one hand, and subacute changes, on the other hand, is insufficient in conceptual as well as operational terms.

The researchers designed a study in which these measures of the subjective burden were taken into account. They constructed two groups of 190 men, who were German-speaking, who had an occupation and were between 30 and 55 years of age. One of these groups was a random sample of heart attack patients (who had survived an attack), the other group consisted of persons without circulatory difficulties. Data were collected for both groups on the subjective valuation of several events in the person's life, for example: other diseases, accidents, robbery, death of an acquaintance, loss of job, substantive changes at work, moving, financial losses, termination of private relations, acute conflicts in the family or the circle of close friends. A distinction was made between the items related to the person himself and those related to family members and friends, in order to distinguish and control for the ego versus alter localization. The points in time of the events were also precisely recorded.

Although the data of the burden (number of fatal events, character of fatal events, distribution in time and subjective burden) did in fact precede the outbreak of the disease, they were nevertheless conceived of as retrospectively acquired dependent variables. The researchers investigated whether there were significant differences between the mean burden of the two groups, controlling for the ego versus alter-localization.

Design 3.1.14
The research problem is that, in controlling for the ego versus alter localization, there will be a significant difference between the group of heart attack patients and the group of persons without circulatory difficulties with regard to the number of fatal events, the character of fatal events, the distribution in time and the subjective burden (the heart attack patients endure, on average, more fatal events, stronger events, higher proportional burden shortly before the attack and a higher subjective burden):

- The research problem is dependent. A distinction is made between dependent and independent variables.
- There are several dependent variables of interval measurement level: number and character of fatal events, distribution in time and subjective burden (retrospectively acquired!).

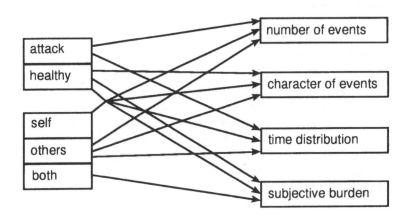

- The dichotomous independent variable is formed by the two groups: heart attack patients and healthy persons. The design is quasi-experimental. Remark: it is a problem that the researchers had to restrict themselves to patients who had survived the attack; this can lead to biases in the results.
- The control variable is formed by the distinction between persons for whom events are related to the person himself and those for whom events are related to family members and friends. Persons who are confronted with both kinds of event form a third group. The control variable is therefore a trichotomy. Effects of interaction are possible.

Conclusion: a (quasi-experimental) MANOVA-design.

3.2 The Dependency Theory: Manipulations of the Researcher

Starting from the dependency theory, which is a causal theory in international political science, we will now show how the researcher executes several manipulations in practice. We leave the idea behind that one and only one technique of multivariate analysis fits a research problem. The appropriate choice of a technique becomes relative.

We first give an outline of the main ideas of the dependency theory.

Many scientists have been concerned with the question of which factors influence the economic development of countries. In the 1960s and 1970s attention was focussed on a non-economic approach: the dependency theory of Andre Gunder Frank. This theory states that the causes of underdevelopment of Third World countries are not to be found in the characteristics of these countries, but in the structure of the economic world system, i.e., in the international division of labour.

The dependency approach encompasses many different conceptions, such as holism versus particularism, the emphasis on external versus internal factors, socio-political versus economic analysis, sectoral/regional oppositions versus oppositions of class, underdevelopment versus development, voluntarism versus determinism (see Hettne, 1982). However, if we restrict ourselves primarily to the economic aspects, we can still distinguish a certain common root.

A distinction is made between the centre or metropolis on the one hand and the periphery or satellite countries on the other hand. There are relations of dependency, rather than interdependency, between the countries of both subsystems. 'Dependency' is presented as: 'a situation in which the economy of a certain group of countries is conditioned by the development and expansion of another economy, to which their own economy is subjected... which shapes a certain structure of the world economy such that it favors some countries to the detriment of others and limits the development possibilities of the subordinate economies' (Bodenheimer, 1973).

This dependency leads to the underdevelopment of the peripheral countries, because the centre is able to take the surplus from the periphery and transfer it to itself. Therefore development and underdevelopment are two sides of the same coin; the one doesn't exist without the other.

The practical advice that was given by several dependency theoreticians to the Third World countries with regard to economic policy consisted accordingly of withdrawal from the world system by cutting off economic relationships with the centre countries, so that the relations of dependency could be broken.

The most general hypothesis that can be inferred from the dependency theory is that an increase in dependency causes an increase in underdevelopment, in other words that there is a negative causal effect of the degree of dependency on the level of development, where the units are Third World countries.

Christopher Chase-Dunn (1975) makes a distinction between three mechanisms by which this causal relationship is made more explicit. (1) Exploitation of the peripheral countries by the countries of the centre takes place by means of decapitalization and unequal exchange. Profits and returns on capital and credits disappear into the countries of the centre. This exploitation leads to the withdrawal from the peripheral countries of the very resources that are necessary for development. (2) A structural disruption of the economy of the peripheral countries emerges, because integration and therefore development are hindered by forced specialization in raw materials, differentiation and the outwardly oriented infrastructure (export). (3) A political situation exists whereby an autonomous mobilization in favour of national develop-ment is prevented, i.e., there are more common interests between the elites of the centre and the periphery than between the elites and other population groups within the peripheral countries.

Chase-Dunn compares the dependency approach with the neoclassical economic theories and the (more sociological) modernization theory, which both see a positive relationship between dependency and development, invoked by the following mechanisms. (1) Import of foreign capital leads to increased production in industries where the capital arrives, and subsequently to growth and increased production in other sectors, because the initially increased production results in a higher demand. (2) With the aid of foreign credits it becomes possible to finance the infrastructure necessary for development. (3) There is a transfer from the countries of the centre to the peripheral countries of technology, modern work habits, modern rational forms of organization and modern conceptions that are necessary for the development of the economy.

3.2.1 A Causal Analysis

Many hypotheses can be formulated in an attempt to test the dependency theory using empirical data of countries. In his doctoral research dissertation, Hout (1984) tried to summarize the theory into nine basic hypotheses. We make a selection:

1. As the dependency of the satellite countries on the metropole increases, the satellites become more and more underdeveloped.
2. As the dependency of the satellite countries on the metropole increases, the instability of the political system of the satellites increases.
3. The instability of the political system has a negative effect on development.
4. As the satellites become more orientated towards export, the development of their national economies will be more unbalanced.

These four hypotheses can be linked together into a causal model, which can be tested by means of path analysis (or LISREL):

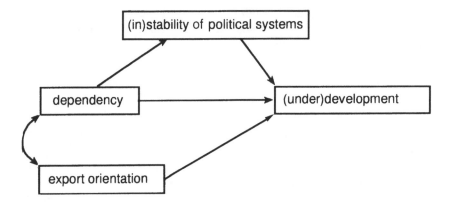

3.2.2 Measurement Models

The central concepts used in the dependency theory, the 'measure of dependency' and the 'degree of development', are very complex. For instance, many authors distinguish several dimensions of the concept of dependency: dependency on foreign capital and trade (Kaufman, Chernotsky, Geller); dependency on loans and on investments (Chase-Dunn); dependency on economic power and on markets (McGowan, Smith); financial–technological and cultural dependency (Duvall *et al.*).

Using factor analysis it is possible to investigate to what degree the theoretical dimensions distinguished by the authors are supported empirically. Many indicators have to be supplied for that purpose. W. Hout collected the following data:

 1. export as a percentage of the GNP;
 2. export specialization with regard to goods;
 3. import as a percentage of the GNP;
 4. external debts of the government;
 5. total foreign direct investments;
 6. foreign direct investments in industry;
 7. foreign direct investments in mining and oil;
 8. foreign direct investments in agriculture;
 9. total capital invested by multinationals;
10. patents in foreign hands.

A principal factor analysis with orthogonal rotation resulted in a two-factor solution of which the first dimension was the dependency on finances, investments and technology (high loadings for indicators 4 to 10) and the second dimension was the dependency on trade (indicators 1 to 3).

Likewise, several indicators can be supplied for the concept 'degree of development'. Although the concept of development is usually operationalized by simply using data on the GNP or the GNP per capita, some doubts have arisen during the last decades because this concept is multifaceted. Other indicators that have been mentioned are: consumption of energy per capita, level of literacy, level of gross internal investments, stock of capital goods, number of people aged 15 years or older who attend school, number of people aged 15 years or older participating in a

vocational training, calorie consumption per capita, life expectancy and medical care
measured as the number of hospital beds per 1000 inhabitants. Principal components
analysis of these indicators results in a single-component solution, so that the concept
of 'development' can be viewed as unidimensional.

3.2.3   Causal Analysis without Hierarchical Steps

Supposing that the central concepts of the causal theory are measured carefully and
that each dimension is represented by one separate variable, a causal analysis can be
performed in the form of a path analysis. When several indicators are foreseen in the
model, the concepts 'dependency' and 'development' can be conceived of as latent
variables, thus making the global causal model much more complex and requiring the
application of a more advanced technique such as LISREL.

   On the other hand, a researcher can also decide that an analysis of the causal
mechanisms is much too complicated and (s)he can limit (her)himself to the analysis
of the factors that influence the 'degree of development': dependency (or the two
dimensions of dependency), political instability, and export orientation. This would
result in a multiple regression analysis in which the causal relationships between the
independent variables are not investigated:

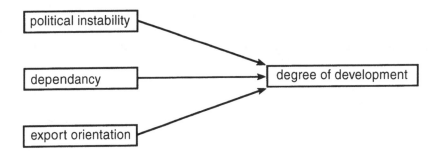

3.2.4   Degree of Development as a Trichotomy

Instead of measuring the dependent variable 'degree of development' on the interval
level, the researcher can also apply the following strategy. It is untrue that Third
World countries form a homogeneous group. This is apparent from the phenomenon
of NICs (newly industrializing/industrialized countries) and near-NICs; NICs are
countries that are accountable for an increasing part of the world production in the
industrial sector. Examples are Brazil, Mexico, Korea, and Taiwan. The category of
near-NICs is illustrated by Chile, Indonesia, Morocco, Peru, Tunisia, and Uruguay.

   If the dependency theory were correct, then these NICs and near-NICs would have
detached themselves from the world system, i.e., they would have become less
dependent. In order to test the value of the approach, one would have to investigate
whether there are significant differences between the means of the variables (dependency and others) of the three groups of countries: NICs, near-NICs and the least
developed nations. This is a multiple discriminant analysis:

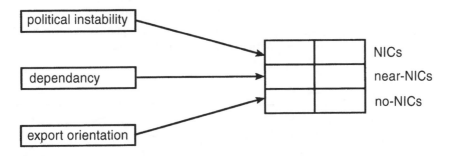

3.2.5 Degree of Dependency as 'More' or 'Less'

Instead of the dependent variable, the researcher can also shrink the independent variables into a dichotomy or trichotomy. This shrinkage is not always self-evident for data at the interval measurement level. Unless there are plausible theoretical reasons, it is always better to include as many distinctions of a variable as possible in the analysis, either to avoid biases by shrinkage or to prevent information loss. If, however, the researcher maintains that the concept of 'dependency' is not a question of exact figures, but should be conceived of as 'more dependent' or 'less dependent', then a shrinkage to a dichotomy can be considered. Something similar can be done with the political variable, for instance, in the form of a trichotomy stable, not very stable and unstable. When the dependent variable 'development' is at the interval measurement level, this leads to a two-way 2×3 ANOVA design. With 'export orientation' as a covariate, which remains at the interval measurement level, it would be an ANCOVA design. Effects of interaction could indicate that the effect of dependency on development is different for varying degrees of political stability.

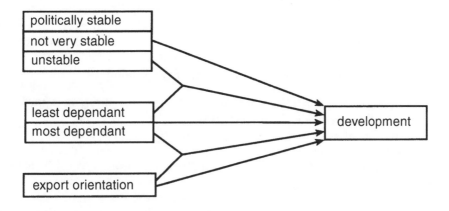

3.2.6 A Model with Several Dependent Variables

A researcher could conceivably be confronted with more than one dependent variable if, for example, the degree of dependency of the satellite countries on the central countries not only influences the degree of development, but also causes a disequilibrium in the development (a 'monoculture' which is orientated towards a rather small number of products) and furthermore leads to a higher economic inequality within the satellite countries. In order to test all this in a single model with two groups of dependency and three groups of political stability as the independent variables, a two-way MANOVA design emerges. With export orientation as the covariate it becomes a MANCOVA design.

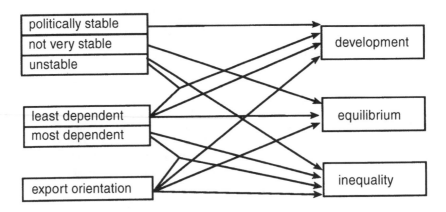

3.2.7   *A Dependency Set and a Development Set*

The dependent variables of the MAN(C)OVA design can be conceived of as a set. And if the independent variables, with their original interval measurement level, are also taken as a set, then a canonical correlation analysis can be performed. (For lower measurement levels this would be a canals analysis.) Such a canonical correlation analysis can be useful for testing the global hypothesis, i.e., the association between dependency and development, in which both central concepts are measured by multiple indicators and might eventually split up into several dimensions.

An example of such a conceptual pattern can be found in Alschuler (1976). He uses the concepts satellization and stagnation, which coincide with dependency and (under)development, respectively.

Alschuler takes four indicators of the concept of satellization:

1. concentration of commercial goods (ccg: export of the three most important categories of goods divided by total export);
2. concentration of business partner (cbp: export to the most important business partner divided by total export);
3. penetration of capital (pcp: income paid to foreign countries divided by national income);
4. vertical trade [vtr: $(a+b-c-d)/(a+b+c+d)$, where a = input value of raw materials, b = export value of processed materials, c = export value of raw materials, d = input value of processed materials].

Three indicators are used for the concept of stagnation:

1. income growth (i: ΔBNP per capita);
2. growth of urbanization (u: Δpopulation growth in locations with more than 2000 inhabitants);

3. growth of education (e: Δpercentage of the population in elementary and other education).

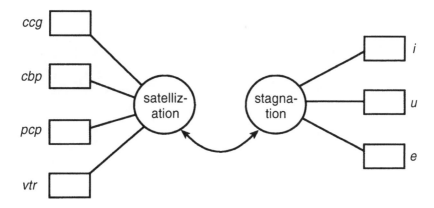

   In this canonical analysis it is self-evident to assume a causal influence of 'satellization' on 'stagnation', but, strictly speaking, the technique is not designed asymmetrically, as a canonical correlation coefficient is a symmetrical measure which does not indicate a causal direction.

PART II

FROM METHODOLOGY TO ANALYSIS

In the first three chapters we gave a non-technical overview of existing techniques of multivariate analysis. In Chapter 1 eight types of research problems were distinguished and their basic format was presented by means of a causal diagram with an arrow structure. In Chapter 2 a personal notation system was used to make several classifications of classical techniques of multivariate analysis that coincide with the formats.

Next we discussed the necessary linkage between the research problems of Chapter 1 and the techniques of Chapter 2 that the researcher must make when faced with the choice of an appropriate technique for their research problem. This resulted in Chapter 3, in which this question of the appropriate choice was dealt with using additional examples of social scientific investigations.

The Research Examples

In the following chapters these subjects are worked out from the statistical–technical side. To this end, we will use the research examples from Chapter 1. The procedure for these examples is as follows. We start with the research on humour as a technique of social influence. This is the example involving the simplest research problem because the basic format contains only two characteristics: humour and financial concession.

Next follows the investigation into the causes of increasing childlessness. The format is now a little less simple, because not one but several causal factors are considered. The following investigation deals with the relationship between Christian belief and anti-Semitism. This research problem, too, is less simple than that of the humour example, because other factors are explicitly added to the bivariate scheme, either as antecedent variables that factor out the causal connection (spurious causality) or as intermediary variables that help to explain the causal connection (indirect causality). In the following research on intrinsic motivation a new extension is made, for, not only many factors but the combined interactions of these factors are considered as well in the explanation of intrinsic motivation. The research example on poor and rich neighbourhoods is *qua* structure not fundamentally different from the research on childlessness, for here, too, a number of causal factors are considered which together offer an explanation of poverty versus wealth. What is new here is that the dependent variable is conceived of as a classification into a number of groups. This means that the dependent variable has a lower measurement level.

In the last three examples we let go of the idea of causality. We now deal with the search for a latent structure of relationships between variables within one set, as in the research on marital adjustment and on living styles, or between several sets, as in the research on the relationship between economic inequality and political instability.

The Techniques of Analysis

For each of these research examples there is an appropriate technique of analysis. The technique that fits with the humour example is the classical experimental design with a simple *t* test or another test of association between two variables, depending on the measurement level. The extension to several independent variables in the research on childlessness brings us to multiple regression analysis. If the extension consists of adding a number of control variables, as in the research on anti-Semitism, the appropriate technique becomes partial correlation analysis. In the research on intrinsic motivation, the effects of interaction are considered and therefore analysis of variance and covariance is applied. These can be conceived of as multiple regression analyses with product terms. The investigation into the discrimination between poor and rich neighbourhoods is performed by means of discriminant analysis. This technique can be conceived of as a multiple regression analysis with dichotomous dependent variables.

   The latent structure of marital adjustment is investigated by means of factor analysis. As factor analysis implies not only one but a great many techniques, one could speak of an entire world of factor analysis methods. This will be elaborated in the following chapters.

   In cases where the search for a latent structure is started with similarity data, as in the investigation of living styles, the appropriate technique is multidimensional scaling. Here, too, we can speak of an entire world. In the investigation into the latent structure of relationships between two or more sets of factors, e.g., a set of factors of economic inequality and a set of characteristics of political instability, we perform a canonical correlation analysis.

   Summarized, this results in the following scheme:

Research example	Basic format	Technique of analysis
humour and financial concession	$X \longrightarrow Y$ bivariate causal structure	test of association between two variables
causes of childlessness	X_1 $X_2 \longrightarrow Y$ X_3 convergent causal structure	multiple regression analysis

Research example	Basic format	Technique of analysis

Christian beliefs and
anti-Semitism

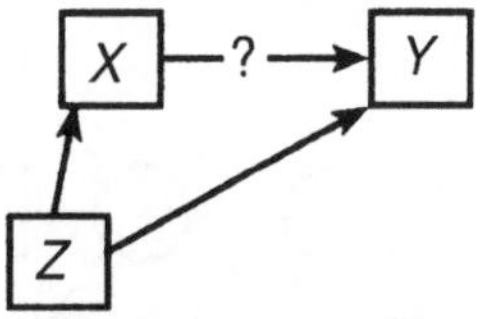

spurious causality

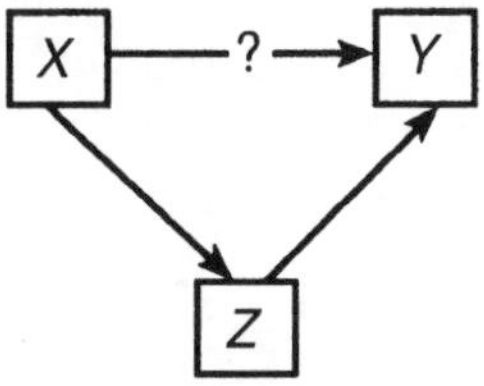

indirect causality

partial correlation
analysis

external rewards and
intrinsic motivation

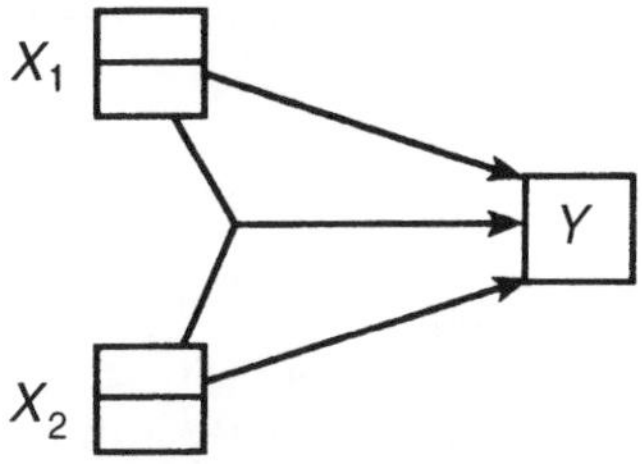

interactive structure

analysis of variance
and covariance

poor and rich
neighbourhoods

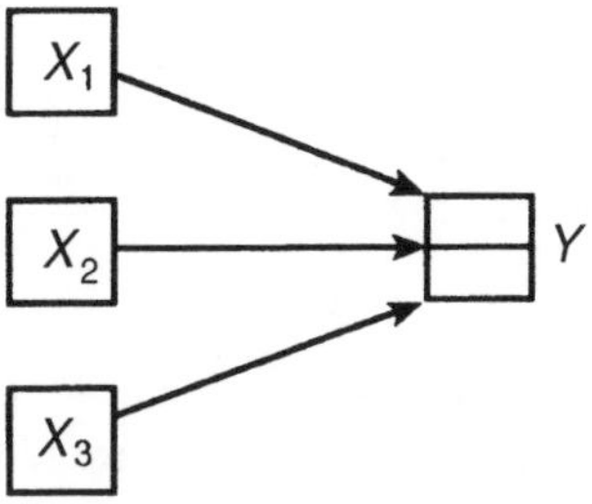

discrimination structure

two group discriminant
analysis

marital adjustment

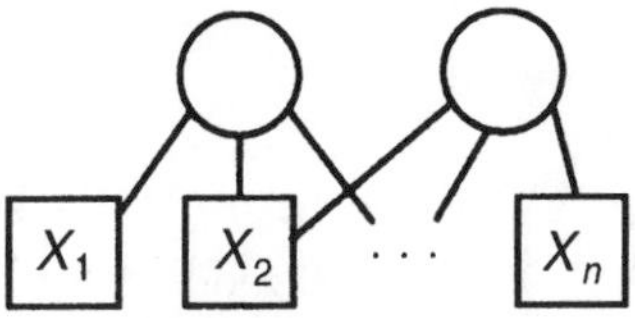

latent structure

factor analysis

Research example	Basic format	Technique of analysis
economic inequality and political instability	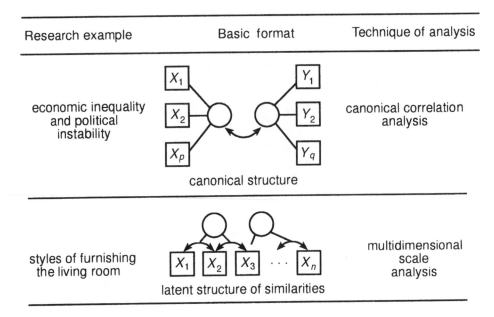 canonical structure	canonical correlation analysis
styles of furnishing the living room	latent structure of similarities	multidimensional scale analysis

Mini Data Sets

In the following chapters the techniques of multivariate analysis are calculated by hand. Mini data sets are used, for instance of eight units and three variables, in order to enable the reader to check every step of the algorithm.

Our working procedure is as follows. We give a short recapitulation of the research problem and, assuming that the variables are well operationalized and that the appropriate technique is chosen, we write down the (fictitious) data matrix and we perform the whole analysis by hand. Special and careful attention is paid to the interpretation of the results obtained. Now and then it will be necessary to include a short situation for the technique being discussed, but long introductions and elaborations will be avoided.

After the demonstration of the arithmetic, the computer output will be added in order to show that the computer has come to exactly the same results as we have obtained by hand. In this way we hope to discourage widespread uncritical use of the computer.

Required Mathematical Knowledge

The mathematical and statistical knowledge necessary for the successful reading of this second part is very limited. Secondary school algebra and elementary introductions in descriptive and inferential statistics of the first years of any university or school of higher education should be amply sufficient. In the Appendix we give a brief recapitulation of the most important concepts.

For the elementary algebra, involution, logarithms, functions and the like, we confine ourselves to an enumeration. An initiation can be found in Van Raaij (1968).

For the elementary descriptive and inferential statistics we give a short recapitulation in telegraphese. A detailed treatment can be found in Hays (1972), but it should be mentioned that Hays' notation system is very different from the more contemporary notations of Blalock (1960) and Green (1976, 1978), to which we are partial.

Matrix Algebra

As far as matrix algebra is concerned, we assume that the reader has no prior knowledge. Therefore, the simplest techniques — multiple regression, analysis of variance and certain elements of two-group discriminant analysis — are presented in the usual algebraic fashion. For the more complex analysis procedures — multivariate analysis of variance, multiple discriminant analysis, canonical correlation analysis and others — it would, in principle, be possible to maintain this algebraic presentation. The number of pages in this book, however, would increase drastically. Matrix notation is simply a compact representation of algebraic notation. We therefore give a treatment in the Appendix of the relevant matrix operations, i.e., operations that will enable us to determine the eigenstructure of a matrix. For a detailed treatment we warmly recommend Green (1976).

With this we have also answered the question that I have been asked again and again by students every year, the question of the necessity of matrix algebra. The answer is touchingly simple. Matrix algebra is not a necessity. It offers no surplus value compared to the familiar algebraic approach. It is only more compact, handier. It fills less pages. Clearly put: a matrix consisting of 500 rows and 50 columns, which fills many pages, is written down by means of a single bold-faced letter X (or a little curl under the X, which indicates that it should be read as bold). No more, no less.

We hereby hope to have dispelled the myth that matrix algebra is capable of doing more than our own common sense, as well as the myth that the computer is in a position to do more than we are able to do by hand.

4

The Experimental Design: The Effect of Humour on Financial Concession

4.1 The Standard Experiment

In the investigation into the effect of humour on concessions in negotiations the researchers made use of an experimental design. In the standard experiment there were, strictly speaking, only two variables involved in the analysis: the use of humour (X) and the financial concession (Y). The causal factor X is, in this case, dichotomous with the following categories: the humour condition and the no-humour condition. The effect factor Y is at the quantitative measurement level, measured as the proportion of the number of dollars that was conceded after the use of humour from the number of dollars that could maximally be conceded. The scores of this proportional concession vary from 0 to 1.

The idea in an experimental design is that if X is a cause of Y and if all other possible causes of Y are kept constant, then a change in X produced by manipulation (the joke about the pet frog) should be accompanied by a significant change in Y (the proportional concession). This change in Y must not occur before the manipulation of X, but after. Therefore, there are two groups: an experimental group in which X is manipulated and a control group in which no manipulation takes place. In order to ensure that the two groups do not differ on Y before the assignment of stimulus X, they have to be equal for all other possible causes of Y. This equalization is realized by randomization and/or matching. It can also be controlled by a preliminary investigation on Y. After manipulation of X, the change in Y should occur in the experimental group and not in the control group.

4.2 The OXO Notation

In imitation of Cook and Campbell (1979) the OXO notation was used for the standard experiment. R stands for randomization, i.e., the determination on a purely random basis of which persons are assigned to the experimental group and which to the control group. M stands for matching, i.e., the *a priori* equalization of the two groups for the factors that have to be controlled. O stands for the observation of Y, O_i for the *i*-th observation.

The resultant scheme has the following form, in which the upper line represents the experimental group, the bottom line the control group, and in which one should imagine a researcher time-axis from the left to the right:

R/M	O_1	X	O_2
R/M	$O_{1'}$		$O_{2'}$

4.3 Implicit Multivariate Analysis

This scheme makes it clear why the standard experiment involved only a bivariate analysis and why an explicit multivariate analysis was not used. The factors, for which the two groups must not be significantly different before the assignment of stimulus X, are only implicitly at stake. This is expressed in the randomization and matching.

In randomizing, one does not even know for which factors the equalization is realized. Chance determines the assignment to groups and in this way it is ensured that only random differences exist between the two groups for all possible factors.

In matching, a certain amount of implicitness is sacrificed. For the equalization of the factor age the experimental design is planned in such a way that the inclusion of an 18-year-old person in the experimental group necessitates the inclusion of an 18-year-old person in the control group, etc. (precise matching). As this precise matching is all but impossible, it is common practice to follow a cruder approach in taking care that the age distributions of the two groups are not significantly different. It is also possible to combine matching and randomization. But, whatever the approach, the important point here is that the factors for which a matching procedure is performed are not explicitly involved in a multivariate analysis. True, age distributions are equalized at the beginning of the experiment, but the causal effect of age (higher concessions for the older persons as compared to the younger ones) is not focussed upon. This leaves only the effect of humour on concession.

4.4 The Preliminary Investigation

The two groups should be priorally equal, not only for several disturbing factors such as age, sex, educational level and others, but also for the dependent variable itself.

In randomizing, significant differences between the two groups — including the dependent variable financial concession — are compensated for. A preliminary investigation would therefore be, strictly speaking, redundant, because the difference $O_1 - O_{1'}$ in the OXO scheme does not exceed random differences. So, the investigation can be restricted to a test of the significant difference between O_2 and $O_{2'}$. If, however, there already was a prior difference between the readiness to concessions in both groups (O_1 and $O_{1'}$), then a preliminary investigation would be necessary in order to compare the initial difference $O_1 - O_{1'}$ with the post-stimulus difference $O_2 - O_{2'}$. This comparison with the preliminary investigation is also necessary when the magnitude of the humour-effect is being measured. Such a procedure will be applied in the analysis of covariance. But there will then, in fact, already be three variables involved in the analysis: the prestimulus concession O_1, the poststimulus concession O_2 and the stimulus X.

In this chapter, we will treat only the simplest experimental design without a preliminary investigation.

4.5 Bivariate Association

The techniques used in the simplest experimental design are related to two variables. For the test of association a great number of procedures are available, dependent on the measurement level of each of the variables. If both variables are measured at least at the interval level, then bivariate correlation and regression analysis are appropriate. This is reviewed shortly in the next chapter in the form of an introduction to multiple regression analysis. If both variables are measured at a lower level, ordinal or nominal, then a large number of association measures are available with corresponding significant tests.

In the humour example, the dependent variable Y is quantitative and the independent variable X is dichotomous. This is the most common situation in experimental designs. The procedure used in this case is the t test of difference of means. This test will be reviewed briefly below, thereby providing an opportunity for the preparation of analysis of variance and two-group discriminant analysis.

4.6 The Data Matrix

The humour variable X has two categories: the humour condition and the no-humour condition. These coincide with the experimental group and the control group and are given the codes 1 and 0, respectively. The proportional concession Y is a quantitative variable with scores between 0.00 and 1.00.

The (fictitious) data matrix for an experimental group with five persons and a control group with six persons is given in Table 4.1.

The numbers are kept small to give the reader the opportunity to verify all calculations by hand. The groups have been made unequal in size, as this is the most general case.

Table 4.1   Data matrix

X	Y
1	0.60
1	0.70
1	0.60
1	0.50
1	0.60
0	0.50
0	0.40
0	0.40
0	0.30
0	0.40
0	0.50

mean $\bar{Y} = 0.50$

variation $\sum(Y - \bar{Y})^2 = 0.14$

variance $s_y^2 = \dfrac{1}{n-1}\sum(Y - \bar{Y})^2 = 0.014$

4.7 The Causal Diagram

The causal diagram which coincides with the research problem is the bivariate causal structure shown in Figure 4.1. The causal factor X is dichotomous. The effect factor Y is quantitative.

Figure 4.1 Causal diagram

The appropriate technique in the situation where the dependent variable is quantitative and the independent variables are measured at a lower level is the analysis of variance. In cases with only one independent variable, it is called a one-way analysis of variance. If this single independent variable has only two categories, then we can perform the t test. It follows that the t test is the simplest form of analysis of variance, i.e., the one-way analysis of variance with dichotomous independent variable.

4.8 The t Test of Difference of Means

We want to investigate whether the mean financial concession in the experimental group $(X = 1)$ is significantly higher than the mean concession in the control group $(X = 0)$. In order to show better what is meant here, we rearrange the data matrix. We place the two groups next to each other, we order the persons according to the measure of concession they made and we indicate the numbers of persons for each score of concession. In doing so, we obtain two frequency distributions as shown in Table 4.2.

Table 4.2 Frequency distributions

Financial concession (variable Y)	Control group ($X = 0$) no-humour condition		Exp. group ($X = 1$) humour condition	
0.30	1		–	
0.40	3		–	
0.50	2		1	
0.60	–		3	
0.70	–		1	
$\bar{Y} = 0.42$	$\bar{Y} = 0.60$			
$\sum(Y - \bar{Y})^2 = 0.03$	$\sum(Y - \bar{Y})^2 = 0.02$			
$s_y^2 = 0.006$	$s_y^2 = 0.005$			

There is a difference between the means: $0.60 - 0.42 = 0.18$.
The two groups are unequal: $n_0 = 6$ and $n_1 = 5$.

The dispersions are unequal: variances 0.006 and 0.005. In order to perform a t test legitimately, the distributions should be approximately normal (in the case of small groups) and the variances must not be significantly different. For both conditions there exist several test procedures, the test of normality and the test of homoscedasticity (= homogeneity of variances), respectively. Assuming that both conditions are fulfilled, the calculations are as follows.

A mean (pooled average) of the two dispersions is calculated:

$$s_w^2 = \frac{\text{variation group } 0 + \text{variation group } 1}{(n_0 - 1) + (n_1 - 1)}$$

$$= \frac{0.03 + 0.02}{(6 - 1) + (5 - 1)} = 0.006$$

In order to obtain the sampling distribution, we consider all theoretically possible pairs of a select and independent samples (with sizes n_0 and n_1) that could have been drawn from a theoretical population (i.e., a population under H_0, for which the difference in means of both samples would be purely random). For each of the countless number of pairs of samples, we consider the difference of mean concessions. In this way we obtain a sampling distribution of differences of means. The variance of such a sampling distribution appears to be equal to the sum of the variances of the two sampling distributions of means separately (one for samples with size n_0 and one for samples with size n_1), thus:

$$\sigma_{diff}^2 = \sigma^2/n_0 + \sigma^2/n_1$$

The term σ^2, i.e., the variance of the theoretical population out of which both samples would have been drawn according to H_0, is not known and it is therefore estimated. The estimator used is the pooled average s_w^2 which was calculated above. In order to use tables, we apply standardization: from each difference of means, the mean of the sampling distribution of differences of means (which is equal to 0 under H_0) is subtracted and the result is divided by the standard error σ_{diff} (which is equal to the square root of the estimated variance of the sampling distribution). Instead of classical z scores, we obtain t scores, because the sampling distribution of differences of means does not have the shape of a normal distribution but of a t distribution, see Figure 4.2. The reasons for this are that the variance of the population has to be estimated and that the groups are rather small, which results in a deviation from the normal distribution. If we now calculate the t score for our pair of samples, we can then situate it in the sampling distribution and come to a conclusion.

$$t = \frac{|\bar{Y}_{(1)} - \bar{Y}_{(0)}| - 0}{\left(\frac{s_w^2}{n_0} + \frac{s_w^2}{n_1}\right)^{1/2}} = \frac{|0.60 - 0.42| - 0}{\left(\frac{0.006}{6} + \frac{0.006}{5}\right)^{1/2}} = 3.84$$

For a priorally postulated type I error of $\alpha = 0.05$ and for $(n_0 - 1) + (n_1 - 1) = (6 - 1) + (5 - 1) = 9$ degrees of freedom, and using a one-tailed test, we find in the t table a critical value of $t^* = 1.833$. The absolute value of t that we have calculated (which is 3.84 and differs from 4.13 in the computer output, due to rounding errors) is higher and is therefore situated in the rejection region. Thus, with an *a priori* 95% likelihood of not being mistaken, there is a significant difference between the mean

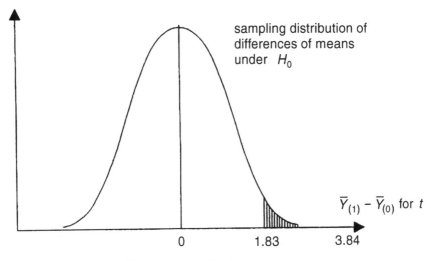

sampling distribution of differences of means under H_0

$\overline{Y}_{(1)} - \overline{Y}_{(0)}$ for t

0   1.83   3.84

Figure 4.2   *t* distribution curve

financial concessions of the humour condition and the no-humour condition (even with these small groups).

4.9   The Experimental Design in Research Practice

Actual experimental analysis is much more complex than our treatment in this chapter. In the original research on the humour effect, O'Quin and Aronoff (1981) did in fact explicitly control for several disturbing factors. We will discuss how this was done in our introduction to partial correlation analysis. They also searched for the presence of the effects of interaction. This will be dealt with in our chapter on analysis of variance and covariance. The researchers also included several dependent variables, like negotiation time, laughter and the use of words by subjects in the experiment. Such an analysis with several dependent variables will be discussed in our chapter on multivariate analysis of variance and covariance. These and other techniques were in fact applied in the experimental design. Therefore, the suggestion that only two variables are subjected to analysis in the experimental form should not be taken too literally. The idea is that only two characteristics are focussed upon in the experimental 'logic' and that all other control factors serve as a background. From the moment that these background variables are explicitly involved in the analysis, we find ourselves in multivariate analysis.

Experimental research does not always follow the nice OXO scheme of the standard experiment. Many variants are in use and are extensively discussed in Cook and Campbell (1979). In order to avoid the test effect, it is possible to leave out the preliminary investigation. To avoid compensating competition between the groups, the control group can be left out or the control group can be given a stimulus in a way that precludes compensating competition. It is also possible to add certain steps to the standard experiment. For example, the addition of groups without preliminary investigation offers the possibility of measuring the magnitude of the test effect. Furthermore, time series analyses as well as schemes with repeated intervention have been designed, with or without a control group.

Thus, we should not speak of 'the' experiment, but rather of an entire world of quasi-experiments. Cook and Campbell's book, entitled *Quasi-Experimentation*, is hereby warmly recommended.

4.10   SPSS for Windows Output of Student's *t* Test

For the mini-example of the effect of humour on financial concession we now present the SPSS for Windows output. The reader can easily verify whether our results calculated by hand coincide with the output.

Opening an SPSS session
We open an SPSS session by double-clicking the mouse on the SPSS icon. The Data Editor opens automatically in the form of a spreadsheet.

Now, there are two possibilities.

Choosing an existing data file
If the data file already exists, you can choose it as follows. Click on File. Click on Open. Click on Data. Click on the ↓ arrow next to Stations and click on the directory path where the existing data file is to be found. Click on the ↓ arrow next to File type and click on *.sys, *.sav or whatever the type of your data file is. Your data file should now appear in the list, e.g. *humour.sys*. Click on it. Click on OK. You can now run the statistical procedure.

Creating a new data file
If the data file does not exist, the data have to be entered first. Just type them in the spreadsheet, beginning with the first data cell (below the variable name) in the first column. Each time you press Enter the value is entered in the cell and you automatically move down to the next row. When the first column is completed, use the → and ↑ key to move the cursor to the first data cell of the next empty column.

The variables have to be given names. The default names for the variables are var00001, var00002, etc. To change a variable name, double-click on that name and a Define Variable dialog box appears. If you simply type the new variable name (X for the humour variable and Y for the financial concession variable), the old one will be overridden.

Click on Type and a Define Variable Type dialog box appears. By default SPSS assumes that all variables are numeric, which is indicated by a radio button next to the choice Numeric. This will suit you.

The default format of the variables is F8.2, i.e., the width is 8 and the number of decimal places is 2. Width is the maximum number of characters, including one position for the decimal indicator. Decimal places is the number of decimal positions for display purposes. To change the width, click on the numeral 8, use the ← backspace key to eliminate it and type the new numeral. To change the decimal places, click on the numeral 2, use the ← backspace key to eliminate it and type the new numeral. In this example, the format of X is F1.0 and the format of Y is either F3.1, if you used numbers like 0.6, or F4.2, if you used 0.60. Click on Continue.

To assign a variable label, click on Labels. Type the variable label (humour for X and financial concession for Y) and click on Continue. Click on OK: name, type and label are now assigned and you return to the spreadsheet.

Repeat the choice of variable name, variable type and variable label for other variables.

You can now save the data file. Click on File. Click on Save as. Type the file name with extension *.sav*, for example *humour.sav*. Click on the ↓ arrow next to Stations and click on your choice of directory path where you want to save the data file. Click on OK. You can now run the statistical procedure.

Running the statistical procedure
To perform a Student's *t* test, click on Statistics. Click on Compare Means. Click on Independent-Samples T Test. A subdialog box for the Independent-Samples T Test appears. On the left of this box you find a Source Variable list. Click on the grouping variable (X) and click on the ▶ push button of the Grouping Variable. Do the same for the test variable, i.e., click on the test variable (Y) and click on the ▶ push button of the Test Variable. Both variables are now selected. The grouping variable is, however, not yet defined, which is shown by two question marks between brackets. Click on the grouping variable to make it highlighted and click on Define Groups. Type the value 1 of the humour group 1. Click on the value of the non-humour group 2 and type the value 0. Click on Continue.

Click on Options and make your choices, if you want to, and click on Continue to go back to the Independent-Samples T Test dialog box. Click on OK. SPSS now runs the statistical procedure and an output window appears with the results of Student's *t* test. Clicking on the arrows at the margins of the output window will help you to go up, down, left and right all through the text.

Running the statistical procedure by means of SPSS commands
For those who are used to running a statistical procedure by means of SPSS commands, the foregoing actions can be replaced as follows. Click on File. Click on New. Click on SPSS Syntax. This opens a syntax window. In this window you can type the SPSS statements, just as in SPSS/PC +. These statements will be given below for Student's t test. If you then put the cursor on the first command line and click on the ▶ push button on the icon bar at the top of the syntax window (for the SPSS for Windows 6.1 version) or click on the run push button (for the SPSS for Windows 5.0 version), you obtain the same output as above.

Saving the output
You should not forget to save the output. Click on File. Click on Save as. Type the file name with extension *.lst*, for example *humour.lst*. Click on the ↓ arrow next to Stations and make your choice of directory path where you want to save the list file, which contains the output. Click on OK.

If you now want to end this SPSS session, click on File and click on Exit. You will be asked if you want to save the contents of the open windows. Click on No, because you already have saved everything there is to save.

The 'statements' to type in the syntax window are:

```
1   LIST.
2   T-TEST GROUPS = X (0,1)/
3   VARIABLES  = Y.
```

In statement 1 the data matrix is requested with 'list'.

Statements 2 and 3 request the t test. Statement 2 indicates that the humour variable X represents the groups. The numbers 0 and 1 between brackets indicate the minimum and maximum value of the groups, respectively. These could have been 1 and 2 as well, on the condition that these numbers were used in the data matrix.

In the computer output we can see that an F test is performed. This is a test of homoscedasticity (= homogeneity of variances). As we know, the variances must not be significantly different. Notice, therefore, that the empirical significance level must not be smaller but greater than 0.05 (if $\alpha = 0.05$). As it appears to be 0.929, there is no problem of heteroscedasticity in our example.

The output is as follows:

```
X   Y

1   .6
1   .7
1   .6
1   .5
1   .6
0   .5
0   .4
0   .4
0   .3
0   .4
0   .5
```

```
Number of cases read =     11    Number of cases listed =      11
Independent samples of  X          HUMOUR


Group 1:  X  EQ 0          Group 2:  X  EQ 1

t-test for:  Y             FINANCIAL CONCESSION

                    Number                 Standard    Standard
                    of Cases    Mean     Deviation       Error

        Group 1       6        .4167       .075          .031
        Group 2       5        .6000       .071          .032
```

			Pooled Variance Estimate			Separate Variance Estimate		
F	2-Tail		t	Degrees of	2-Tail	t	Degrees of	2-Tail
Value	Prob.		Value	Freedom	Prob.	Value	Freedom	Prob.
1.13	.929		−4.13	9	.003	−4.16	8.83	.003

5

Multiple Regression Analysis: The Causes of Childlessness

5.1 The Research Problem and the Causal Diagram

In the investigation into the causes of childlessness several causal factors are included which together should offer an explanation for the phenomenon that the percentage of childless women (Y) increased during the period 1960–1970. For reasons of simplicity we restrict ourselves to two causal factors: the decade change in percentage of labour-force participation (X_1) and the decade change in mean age at first marriage (X_2). Consequently, there are three variables involved in the analysis, one dependent variable Y and two independent variables X_1 and X_2. All three variables have been measured at the interval level. The technique applied in such a case is multiple regression analysis. The basic format is the convergent causal structure, as is represented in the diagram below.

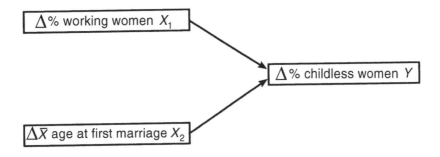

5.2 The Data Matrix

The units of analysis are groups of white women of the same age who were ever married. In our (fictitious) mini data set (Table 5.1) we consider $n = 10$ units of analysis.

Variable X_1 is the difference between the percentage of working women in 1970 and the percentage of working women in 1960.

Variable X_2 is the difference between the mean age at first marriage in 1970 and the mean age at first marriage in 1960.

The dependent variable Y is the difference between the percentage of childless women in 1970 and the percentage of childless women in 1960.

Table 5.1   Data Matrix

	X_1	X_2	Y
	1	1	2
	2	6	3
	3	3	2
	4	2	2
	5	2	4
	6	5	10
	6	9	12
	7	4	8
	9	1	3
	9	7	14
mean	$\bar{X}_1$ = 5.2	$\bar{X}_2$ = 4	$\bar{Y}$ = 6
variation	$\sum(X_1 - \bar{X}_1)^2 = 67.6$	$\sum(X_2 - \bar{X}_2)^2 = 66$	$\sum(Y - \bar{Y})^2 = 190$
variance	s_1^2 = 7.51	s_2^2 = 7.33	s_y^2 = 21.11
standard deviations	s_1 = 2.74	s_2 = 2.71	s_y = 4.59

5.3   Bivariate Regression Analysis: the Influence of Working on Childlessness

In order to prepare multiple regression we first give a short recapitulation of the simple correlation and regression analysis for two variables. We choose X_1 and Y and we study the influence of the increase in the proportion of working women on the increase in the proportion of childless women.

The causal diagram is now simply $X_1 \rightarrow Y$ and the data matrix contains only the two columns of X_1 and Y.

5.3.1   The Model

We formulated the research problem as the investigation of the influence of working on childlessness. The idea seems to be that a small increase in the percentage of working women will invoke a small increase in the percentage of childless women and that a high increase in the one will bring about a high increase in the other, according to a stable pattern. This idea has to be formalized. If the pattern is approximately a straight (ascending) line, then it is represented by means of a linear model.

This model is as follows for the population:

$$Y_i = \beta_0 + \beta_{y1} X_{i1} + \varepsilon_i$$

In this formula Y is the dependent variable; X_1 the independent variable; i the considered unit of analysis; β_0 the intercept, i.e., the value of Y when X_1 is equal to zero, in other words the increase in childlessness when there is no increase in labour-force participation; β_{y1} the regression coefficient, i.e., the change in Y per unit increase in X_1, in other words the degree of change of the childlessness variable for every unit increase in labour-force participation; ε the error term, i.e., a term which is added because the prediction of Y based on the linear model is seldom perfect; in other words the model is probabilistic and not deterministic.

In this model the independent variable X_1 is treated as fixed, which means that the scores of X_1 are assumed known. For each of these fixed values of X_1 the expected value of Y is situated on the straight line. The symbol for this expected value of Y is $E(Y)$ or $\hat{Y}$. The expression for $E(Y)$ is 'expectation of Y' and with $\hat{Y}$ it is indicated that Y is estimated. We read $\hat{Y}$ as 'Y estimated' or 'Y hat'. It follows from the foregoing that:

$$E(Y_i) = \hat{Y}_i = \beta_0 + \beta_{y1}X_{i1}$$

The difference between Y_i and $\hat{Y}_i$ is the error term:

$$\varepsilon_i = Y_i - \hat{Y}_i$$

The observed values Y_i are consequently the sum of a fixed part $\beta_0 + \beta_{y1}X_{i1}$ and a random part ε_i. The errors ε_i should follow a random pattern. This means that they are scattered around the straight line in a random fashion with an expected value of $E(\varepsilon_i) = 0$ and a constant variance σ_ε^2.

Thus far the model for the population has been discussed. Greek letters β_0, β_{y1} and ε have been used.

But when estimations are made, the analysis is based on a sample of units. The model is then formulated in Latin letters as follows:

$$Y_i = b_0 + b_{y1}X_{i1} + e_i$$
$$E(Y_i) = \hat{Y}_i = b_0 + b_{y1}X_{i1}$$
$$e_i = Y_i - \hat{Y}_i$$

5.3.2 Geometric Approach

The linear model can be represented in a Cartesian coordinate system with a horizontal X_1 axis and a vertical Y axis. From the data matrix we obtain the ten (X_1, Y) pairs of numbers: (1,2), (2,3), (3,2) ... (9,14). When we draw these pairs in the coordinate system we obtain a cloud of dots, called a scatter diagram.

An inspection of this scatter diagram should always be our first mandatory task. For, if the points do not follow a linear pattern, then another non-linear model has to be chosen as the starting point. Another issue is that the dispersions of the Y values for each of the X_1 values have to be approximately equal (assumption of homoscedasticity). We also have to check whether there are no units of analysis that deviate from the linear pattern. Such units are called 'outliers'. Dependent on the subject of research they can be analysed separately or removed from the data file. In addition to non-linearity, heteroscedasticity and the presence of outliers, many other problems can be encountered in a scatter diagram. The forming of clusters can be an indication of distinctive groups in the data file. Parallel lines sometimes reveal a hidden variable, non-parallel lines an effect of interaction. A systematic study of the linear pattern will be made in the analysis of residuals, which will be discussed in the following sections. Let us initially be content with a naked-eye view. We do this for the ten (X_1, Y) pairs. We see in Figure 5.1 that the scatter diagram of the ten points only approximately follows the required linear pattern.

The pair (9,3) seems to be an outlier: high decade increase of working women, low decade increase of childlessness. Without this outlier the pattern is approximately linear, but there seem to be two groups, below to the left and above to the right. This

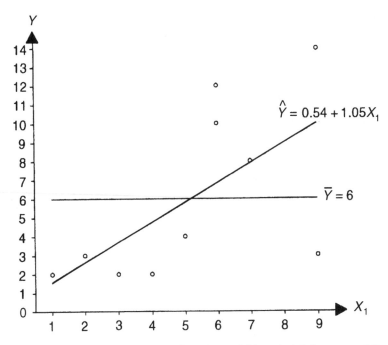

Figure 5.1   Scatter diagram of working (X_1) and childlessness (Y)

is due to the discontinuity of the Y values: the increase in childlessness jumps from 4% to values of 8% to 14%. Values between 4% and 8% do not appear.

If this group formation is due to another (dichotomous) variable, for example because the lower part of the scatter diagram is related to one of its categories, then this variable should have been included in the analysis. It might then have become apparent that the pair (9,3) is much less of an outlier than appeared at first sight. For, the analysis could then have been split into two separate subanalyses, one for the group below and one for the group above (see Figure 5.2). For the group below there would then be almost no relationship between X_1 and Y, for, whatever the increase in working from 1% to 9%, the increase in childlessness remains moderate from 2% to 4%. For the group above there would be a strong relationship, because an increase in the proportion of working women from 6% to 9% brings about an increase in the proportion of childless women from 10% via a small decrease to 8% going up to 14%. Geometrically, the subanalyses would result in Figure 5.2.

These subanalyses only have the status of supposition and they are of course only meaningful if the necessary information on the assumed groups — information that would make an interpretation possible — is present. For, the human eye can be greatly mistaken and might see groups that are in fact non-existent. After all, the variables themselves might be the cause of the strange pattern. In our example, the apparent group formation can be due to the discontinuity of the Y variable and not necessarily to the effect of another hidden factor.

Therefore, each bivariate analysis should be preceded by an anlysis of each variable separately.

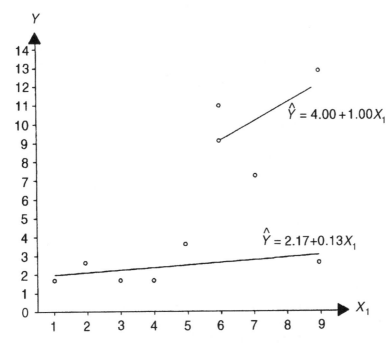

Figure 5.2   Scatter diagram of working (X_1) and childlessness (Y): two sub-analyses

Going back to the global scatter diagram and supposing that it shows a linear pattern, we try to find a straight line that gives the best fit with the scatter diagram. In the coordinate system we drew that line $\hat{Y} = 0.54 + 1.05\ X_1$. The calculation follows below. Some of the points (1,2), (2,3) and (7,8) are very close to the straight line. Other points are very far from the line. Take, for example, the pair (9,3): for $X_1 = 9$ the real value of Y is equal to 3 and the value of Y that is estimated on the basis of the regression line is $\hat{Y} = 0.54 + (1.05)(9) = 9.99$. The deviation of the point from the regression line is the error $e_i = Y_i - \hat{Y}_i = 3 - 9.99 = -6.99$. This error is negative, because point (9,3) lies under the regression line. Point (9,14), on the other hand, lies above the regression line and the error $e_i = Y_i - \hat{Y}_i = 14 - 9.99 = 4.01$ is positive.

The errors compensate each other in such a way that the algebraic sum of the ten errors, both positive and negative, is equal to zero: $\sum e_i = 0$.

However, the fact that $\sum e_i = 0$ is not sufficient as a means for finding the linear regression function that best fits the scatter diagram. For, there are other straight lines for which it also holds that $\sum e_i = 0$ but for which the fit with the points is much worse. An extreme example of such a line is the function $\hat{Y} = 6$, indicated in Figure 5.1, which runs through $\bar{Y}$ and is parallel with the X_1 axis. For this function the relationship between X_1 and Y would be nil, because nowhere does an increase in X_1 bring about an increase or decrease in Y.

We are thus in need of another criterion to find the best line. This will be the least squares criterion. It will be discussed in the calculation of the regression function.

5.3.3   Objectives of the Technique

Bivariate regression analysis as a calculation technique is used for three objectives. Looking at the example of childlessness and restricting ourselves to one independent variable X_1 these objectives are the following:

1. We look for a function $Y_1 = b_0 + b_{y1}X_{i1}$ which represents the linear relationship between X_1 and Y better than any other function. This comes down to the calculation of the regression coefficient b_{y1} and the intercept b_0.
2. We investigate the magnitude of the relationship between X_1 and Y and we also want to know, with prediction in view, which part of the variance of Y is explained by the variance of X_1. This comes down to the calculation of the correlation coefficient r_{y1} and its square r_{y1}^2 respectively.
3. We investigate whether the relationship between X_1 and Y that is found in the sample can be generalized to the population. This comes down to the application of a significance test of the relationship.

5.3.4   Calculation of the Regression Function

We stated above that the algebraic sum of the errors with respect to the best fitting regression line is equal to zero, but that this also holds for many other straight lines. In order to find the best line we need another criterion. Many other criteria can be conceived of.

The one most widely applied is the ordinary least squares criterion (OLS), according to which the sum of the squared errors $\sum e^2$ has to be minimal.

We know that squares are always positive and that therefore the sum $\sum e^2$ will also be positive, in contradistinction to the sum $\sum e_i$ of errors, which is zero because the positive and negative errors cancel each other out. It might of course have also been possible to minimize the sum $\sum |e_i|$ of absolute values, but the squares have interesting features that cannot be equalled by the absolute values.

We now apply the OLS criterion to the function $Y = b_0 + b_{y1}X_1 + e$ and we thus calculate b_0 and b_{y1}. (The indices i are removed for the sake of simplicity).

$$e = Y - \hat{Y}$$
$$e = Y - (b_0 + b_{y1}X_1) = Y - b_0 - b_{y1}X_1$$
$$e^2 = Y^2 + b_0^2 + b_{y1}^2 X_1^2 - 2b_0 Y - 2b_{y1}X_1 Y + 2b_0 b_{y1} X_1$$
$$\sum e^2 = \sum Y^2 + \sum b_0^2 + \sum b_{y1}^2 X_1^2 - 2\sum b_0 Y - 2\sum b_{y1}X_1 Y + 2\sum b_0 b_{y1} X_1$$

This sum of squared errors has to be minimized. This is done by setting the partial derivatives equal to zero and solving the equations. In other words, we first consider b_0 as being a constant term, we take the derivative with respect to b_{y1}, make it equal to zero and solve:

$$\delta_{b_{y1}}\left(\sum e^2\right) = 2b_{y1}\sum X_1^2 - 2\sum X_1 Y + 2b_0 \sum X_1 = 0$$

from which follows:

$$b_0 = \left(\sum X_1 Y - b_{y1}\sum X_1^2\right)\Big/ \sum X_1 \qquad (1)$$

After that we consider b_{y1} as being a constant term, we take the derivative with respect to b_0, set it equal to zero and we solve:

$$\delta_{b_0}\left(\sum e^2\right) = 2nb_0 - 2\sum Y + 2b_{y1}\sum X_1 = 0$$

from which follows:

$$b_0 = \left(\sum Y - b_{y1}\sum X_1\right)/n \tag{2}$$

Equalization of (1) and (2) results in one equation with one unknown b_{y1}:

$$\left(\sum X_1 Y - b_{y1}\sum X_1^2\right)/\sum X_1 = \left(\sum Y - b_{y1}\sum X_1\right)/n$$

$$n\sum X_1 Y - nb_{y1}\sum X_1^2 = \sum Y\sum X_1 - b_{y1}\sum X_1\sum X_1$$

$$n\sum X_1 Y - \sum Y\sum X_1 = nb_{y1}\sum X_1^2 - b_{y1}\left(\sum X_1\right)^2$$

$$b_{y1} = \frac{n\sum X_1 Y - \sum Y\sum X_1}{n\sum X_1^2 - \left(\sum X_1\right)^2}$$

$$\boxed{b_{y1} = \frac{\sum X_1 Y - n\bar{Y}\bar{X}_1}{\sum X_1^2 - n\bar{X}_1^2}}$$

This is the so-called computational formula, which is generally used for the calculation of the regression coefficient. It can easily be shown that it is equal to the well-known formula, in which the covariance of X_1 and Y is divided by the variance of X_1:

$$\boxed{b_{y1} = \frac{\sum(X_1 - \bar{X}_1)(Y - \bar{Y})}{\sum(X_1 - \bar{X}_1)^2}}$$

From (2) we can now derive b_0:

$$b_0 = \left(\sum Y - b_{y1}\sum X_1\right)/n$$

$$\boxed{b_0 = \bar{Y} - b_{y1}\bar{X}_1}$$

For the application of these formulae in the research of childlessness, we bring the calculations of $\bar{X}_1$, $\bar{Y}$, $\sum X_1^2$ and $\sum X_1 Y$ together in Table 5.1.

After the calculation of b_{y1} and b_0 we can determine the expected value $\hat{Y}_i = b_0 + b_{y1}X_{i1}$ for each unit of analysis as well as the residuals $e_i = Y_i - \hat{Y}_i$. The squares e_i^2 of the residuals are added for later calculation.

The regression function is $\hat{Y} = 0.54 + 1.05X_1$.

The intercept $b_0 = 0.54$ is the value of Y when X_1 is zero: if there is no decade change in the proportion of working women, then the proportion of childless women increases with 0.54%.

The regression coefficient $b_{y1} = 1.05$ is the change of Y for every unit increase of X_1: if the decade change in the proportion of working women increases with one unit, then the decade change in the proportion of childless women is expected to increase

Table 5.2   Calculation of the regression function

X_1	Y	X_1^2	$X_1 Y$	$\hat{Y}$	e	e^2
1	2	1	2	1.59	0.41	0.17
2	3	4	6	2.64	0.36	0.13
3	2	9	6	3.69	−1.69	2.85
4	2	16	8	4.74	−2.74	7.51
5	4	25	20	5.79	−1.79	3.20
6	10	36	60	6.84	3.16	9.98
6	12	36	72	6.84	5.16	26.62
7	8	49	56	7.89	0.11	0.01
9	3	81	27	9.99	−6.99	48.88
9	14	81	126	9.99	4.01	16.07
sum	52	60	338	383		0	115.43
mean	5.2	6.0				0	
standard deviation	2.74	4.59				3.58	

$$b_{y1} = \frac{383 - 10(6.0)(5.2)}{338 - 10(5.2)^2} = 1.05$$

$$b_0 = 6.0 - 1.05(5.2) = 0.54$$

with 1.05 units. For example, we read in the table that an increase of X_1 from 3 to 4 is accompanied by an increase of Y from 3.69 to 4.74; and an increase of X_1 from 6 to 7 by an increase of $\hat{Y}$ from 6.84 to 7.89.

We see that the sum $\sum e_i$ of the residuals is equal to zero. Their standard deviation s_e is 3.58, which indicates to what degree the points of the scatter diagram are dispersed around the regression line. As it is smaller than $s_y = 4.59$, there is a linear relationship between X_1 and Y.

The sum $\sum e^2$ of the squared errors is 115.43 and is smaller than any other such sum for other linear functions, which follows from the OLS criterion.

5.3.5   The Strength of the Relationship and the Explained Variance

We now discuss the second objective of bivariate regression analysis: the calculation of the magnitude of the relationship and the proportion of variance explained, by means of the correlation coefficient r_{y1} and its square, respectively. We start with the latter, because the interpretation of the square, as will become apparent, is more comprehensible. The squared correlation coefficient, which is also called the determination coefficient, varies from 0 to 1 and can be interpreted in two ways: as a prediction measure and as a measure of explained variance.

The first predictive interpretation runs as follows.

We try to predict the increase in childlessness Y on the basis of the increase in labour-force participation X_1 for one randomly drawn unit of analysis. If we have no information on X_1 for that unit of analysis, then the mean $\bar{Y}$ is the best prediction. The probability of error of this prediction can be represented by the variation of Y values around their mean: $\sum (Y - \bar{Y})^2$.

If we do have information on X_1, then we can rely on the regression line in making the prediction. We then predict the value $\hat{Y}_i$ on the regression line which coincides with the value X_{i1} of the unit of analysis i. The probability of error of this prediction is represented by the variation of Y values around the $\hat{Y}$ values of the regression line: $\sum(Y - \hat{Y})^2$. If this probability of error is smaller than the original probability of error, then the regression function offers an improvement in the prediction.

The difference $\sum(Y - \bar{Y})^2 - \sum(Y - \hat{Y})^2$ is the reduction of the probability of error. When we divide this reduction by the original probability of error, we obtain the proportional reduction of the probability of error. This is r_{y1}^2.

$$r_{y1}^2 = \frac{\sum(Y - \bar{Y})^2 - \sum(Y - \hat{Y})^2}{\sum(Y - \bar{Y})^2}$$

In the research on childlessness we found that $\sum(Y - \hat{Y})^2 = \sum e^2 = 115.43$. The variation of Y values around their mean is $\sum(Y - \bar{Y})^2 = 190$. It follows that $r_{y1}^2 = (190 - 115.43)/190 = 0.39$.

This means that in the prediction of the decade change of childlessness, there is a proportional reduction of 39% in the probability of error when we rely on the labour variable as opposed to not relying on it. In the literature this interpretation is indicated as the PRE-interpretation: proportional reduction in error.

The second interpretation, in terms of explained variance, is obtained by splitting the total variation of Y values into two parts: the part that is due to the regression line itself (explained variation, sum of squares due to regression SSR) and the remaining part of the variation around the regression line (unexplained variation, sum of squares due to error SSE). This splitting corresponds with SST = SSB + SSW, which is elaborated in the appendix.

$$
\begin{array}{llll}
\text{SST} & = \text{SSR} & + \text{SSE} \\
\sum(Y - \bar{Y})^2 & = \sum(\hat{Y} - \bar{Y})^2 & + \sum(Y - \hat{Y})^2 \\
\text{Total} & = \text{explained} & + \text{unexplained variation} \\
190 & = 74.57 & + 115.43
\end{array}
$$

When we divide the explained variation by the total variation of Y values, we obtain the proportion of the variation of childlessness changes that is explained by the labour variable.

This is r_{y1}^2.

$$r_{y1}^2 = \frac{\sum(\hat{Y} - \bar{Y})^2}{\sum(Y - \bar{Y})^2} = \frac{74.57}{190} = 0.39$$

Most textbooks speak of explained variance rather than explained variation. However, if we take the formula of r_{y1}^2 and divide the numerator as well as the denominator by the number of degrees of freedom $n - 1$, then we obtain variances instead of variations. It follows that r_{y1}^2 can also be interpreted as the proportion of the variance of Y that is explained by X_1.

From the foregoing it is apparent that the square of the correlation coefficient can be interpreted very well, either as a prediction measure (PRE-interpretation) or as a proportion of explained variance (or variation). The fact that these nice interpretations can be made is due to the additive splitting of the total variation $\sum(Y - \bar{Y})^2$ into an explaining part $\sum(\hat{Y} - \bar{Y})^2$ and a residual part $\sum(Y - \hat{Y})^2$, where the double product $2\sum(\hat{Y} - \bar{Y})(Y - \hat{Y})$ is dropped (on the one hand, because the value of

$\hat{Y} - \bar{Y}$ is constant for each value of X_1 and can be brought before the summation sign and, on the other hand, because $\sum(Y - \hat{Y}) = 0$).

Such an 'additive' splitting, into a sum of an explained and an unexplained part and without a double product, is possible for the total variation or variance, but not for the standard deviation. This is why the square of r_{y1} can be interpreted so well, while the correlation coefficient r_{y1} itself cannot. The latter varies between -1 and $+1$. A value $r_{y1} = 0$ means absence of relationship between Y and X_1. The value $r_{y1} = 1$ indicates a perfect positive relationship, $r_{y1} = -1$ a perfect negative relationship. In the example we obtained $r_{y1} = 0.63$, which indicates a moderate positive relationship between the childlessness change and the change in labour-force participation (the higher the one, the higher the other or the lower the one, the lower the other).

5.3.6 Interpretations of the Correlation Coefficient

We mentioned above that the product moment correlation coefficient r_{y1} is less interpretable than its square. There are, however, many ways to look at r_{y1}. Here we restrict ourselves to three views: r_{y1} as the covariance corrected for the variances, r_{y1} as the covariance of standardized variables and r_{y1} as the geometric mean of the regression coefficients.

Firstly, it can be easily derived from the foregoing formulae that r_{y1} is equal to the covariation divided by the square root of the product of variations. The derivation is as follows.

$$r_{y1}^2 = \frac{\sum(\hat{Y} - \bar{Y})^2}{\sum(Y - \bar{Y})^2}$$

$$= \frac{\sum(b_0 + b_{y1}X_1 - \bar{Y})^2}{\sum(Y - \bar{Y})^2}$$

$$= \frac{\sum(\bar{Y} - b_{y1}\bar{X}_1 + b_{y1}X_1 - \bar{Y})^2}{\sum(Y - \bar{Y})^2}$$

$$= \frac{b_{y1}^2 \sum(X_1 - \bar{X}_1)^2}{\sum(Y - \bar{Y})^2}$$

$$= \frac{\left[\sum(X_1 - \bar{X}_1)(Y - \bar{Y})\right]^2 \sum(X_1 - \bar{X}_1)^2}{\left[\sum(X_1 - \bar{X}_1)^2\right]^2 \sum(Y - \bar{Y})^2}$$

$$= \frac{\left[\sum(X_1 - \bar{X}_1)(Y - \bar{Y})\right]^2}{\sum(X_1 - \bar{X}_1)^2 \sum(Y - \bar{Y})^2}$$

$$\boxed{r_{y1} = \frac{\sum(X_1 - \bar{X}_1)(Y - \bar{Y})}{\left[\sum(X_1 - \bar{X}_1)^2 \sum(Y - \bar{Y})^2\right]^{1/2}} = \frac{\text{covariation } X_1, Y}{[(\text{variation } X_1)(\text{variation } Y)]^{1/2}}}$$

The numerator in this formula is the covariation of X_1 and Y, which expresses in what way (positively or negatively) and to what extent X_1 and Y vary together. If we draw the centre of gravity $(\bar{X}_1, \bar{Y})$ in the $X_1 - Y$ coordinate system, then a positive relationship means that the points of the scatterplot are predominantly situated above and to the right and below and to the left of this point, because positive deviations

$X_1 - \bar{X}_1$ go together with positive deviations $Y - \bar{Y}$ and negative deviations with negative deviations, so that the products $(X_1 - \bar{X})(Y - \bar{Y})$ have to be positive. For a negative relationship, positive deviations in one variable go together with negative deviations in the other one.

The denominator in the formula is a correction for the degree of dispersion of each of the variables around their mean. That the latter comes down to standardization will become clear in the second view.

The correlation coefficient is also the covariance of the standardized variables (z scores z_1 and z_y). This follows from rewriting the foregoing formula as follows.

$$r_{y1} = \frac{\sum(X_1 - \bar{X}_1)(Y - \bar{Y})}{[\sum(X_1 - \bar{X}_1)^2 \sum(Y - \bar{Y})^2]^{1/2}}$$

$$= \frac{[1/(n-1)]\sum(X_1 - \bar{X}_1)(Y - \bar{Y})}{\{[1/(n-1)]\sum(X_1 - \bar{X}_1)^2[1/(n-1)]\sum(Y - \bar{Y})^2\}^{1/2}}$$

$$= \frac{1}{n-1} \frac{\sum(X_1 - \bar{X}_1)(Y - \bar{Y})}{s_1 s_y}$$

$$= \frac{1}{n-1}\sum \frac{X_1 - \bar{X}_1}{s_1} \frac{Y - \bar{Y}}{s_y}$$

$$\boxed{r_{y1} = \frac{1}{n-1}\sum z_1 z_y}$$

So, the correlation coefficient is the covariance of the z scores. This formula will play an important role in most formal derivations of multivariate analyses.

According to the third view, the correlation coefficient r_{y1} is the geometric mean (the square root of the product) of the two regression coefficients b_{y1} and b_{1y}.

Regression coefficient b_{y1} is an asymmetric association measure with Y as the dependent and X_1 as the independent variable. The regression function $Y = 0.54 + 1.05X_1 + e$ was calculated above. If, on the other hand, X_1 is regarded as the dependent and Y as the independent variable, then we obtain another regression function $X_1 = b_0 + b_{1y}Y + e$ with another regression coefficient b_{1y}. It is easily calculated that this function is $X_1 = 2.96 + 0.37Y + e$.

Now, the product of b_{y1} and b_{1y} appears to be equal to the determination coefficient (the square of the correlation coefficient): $(1.05)(0.37) = 0.39$. The correlation coefficient r_{y1} is the square root of this product. We infer the formal derivation from the formulae for b_{y1}, b_{1y} and r_{y1} as follows.

$$b_{y1} = \frac{\sum(X_1 - \bar{X}_1)(Y - \bar{Y})}{\sum(X_1 - \bar{X}_1)^2} \quad \frac{\text{covariation}}{\text{variation } X_1}$$

$$b_{1y} = \frac{\sum(X_1 - \bar{X}_1)(Y - \bar{Y})}{\sum(Y - \bar{Y})^2} \quad \frac{\text{covariation}}{\text{variation } Y}$$

$$r_{y1} = \frac{\sum(X_1 - \bar{X}_1)(Y - \bar{Y})}{[\sum(X_1 - \bar{X}_1)^2 \sum(Y - \bar{Y})^2]^{1/2}} = \frac{\text{covariation}}{[(\text{variation } X)(\text{variation } Y)]^{1/2}}$$

so that:

$$r_{y1} = (b_{y1}b_{1y})^{1/2}$$

   Geometrically, this means that there are two regression functions with regression coefficients b_{y1} and b_{1y}, which usually differ from one another. They are only equal when the variances of X_1 and Y are equal. The two functions intersect in the centre of gravity: $(\bar{X}_1, \bar{Y}) = (5.2, 6)$, as in Figure 5.3.

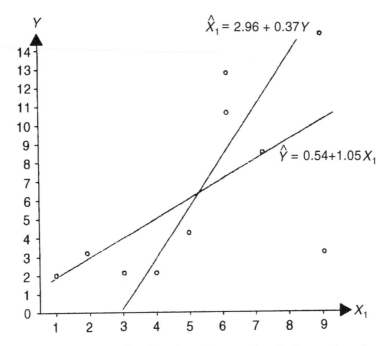

Figure 5.3   Two regression functions, intersecting in the centre of gravity

   As r_{y1} is the geometric mean of the two asymmetric coefficients b_{y1} and b_{1y}, it is consequently a symmetric association measure. It is therefore possible to reverse the order of the indices and write r_{1y}. In terms of causal diagrams, this symmetrical character is indicated as a double-sided curved arrow. The following three diagrams with corresponding coefficients can be drawn.

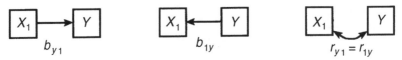

5.3.7   Standardized Coefficients

In discussing the correlation coefficient as the covariance of standardized variables, X_1 and Y were written as z scores. We will now look at what happens to the regression coefficients when the variables are standardized. In that case we speak of 'standardized regression coefficients' or 'betas' and we indicate them by an asterisk as b^*_{y1} and b^*_{1y}, in order to distinguish them from ordinary regression coefficients.

Standardization is performed in two steps: subtraction of the mean and division by the standard deviation.

In the first step we subtract the mean $\bar{Y} = 6$ from each value of variable Y and we subtract the mean $\bar{X} = 5.2$ from each value of X_1.

Geometrically, we obtain Figure 5.4.

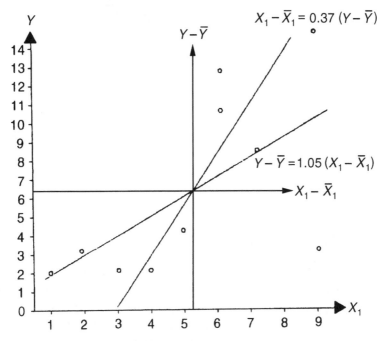

Figure 5.4   Regression analysis with $X_1 - \bar{X}_1$ and $Y - \bar{Y}$ as the axes

We see that the configuration of points as well as the two regression lines remain in their place. Only the two axes have shifted by a translation from Y to $Y - \bar{Y}$ and from X_1 to $X_1 - \bar{X}_1$.

The two regression functions now run through the origin. In other words, the intercepts drop and the regression coefficients remain the same. The two resulting functions are $(Y - \bar{Y}) = 1.05 (X_1 - \bar{X}_1)$ and $(X_1 - \bar{X}_1) = 0.37 (Y - \bar{Y})$.

In the second step, the configuration of points does change, because each value of $Y - \bar{Y}$ is divided by $s_y = 4.59$ and each value of $X_1 - \bar{X}_1$ is divided by $s_1 = 2.74$ and, as s_y is much greater than s_1, the points are squeezed together much more along the Y axis than along the X_1 axis. The variances are made equal.

In Figure 5.5 the new configuration of points is drawn with z_1 and z_y as the axes. This figure corresponds to the data matrix for standardized variables, which is given in Table 5.3.

The values of z_1 and z_y were plotted in the figure. Their mean is 0 and their standard deviation is 1. If we apply the classical correlation and regression procedure to these z_1 scores and z_y scores according to the formulae that were used in this chapter, then

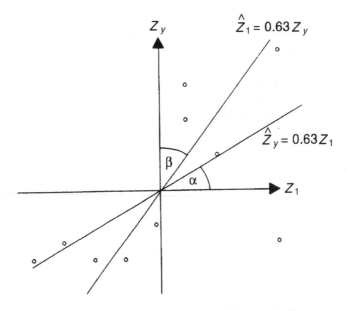

Figure 5.5   Regression with standardized variables as axes

we obtain the following results. The correlation between z_1 and z_y appears to be 0.63. This is the same as the correlation between X_1 and Y. Regression of z_y on z_1 also results in a slope of 0.63; the standardized regression coefficient b^*_{y1} is thus equal to the correlation coefficient r_{y1} (in the bivariate case). Regression of z_1 on z_y also results in 0.63; so we also have $b^*_{1y} = r_{y1}$. This is understandable. We remember from above that the correlation coefficient r_{y1} is equal to the geometric mean of the regression coefficients b_{y1} and b_{1y} and that the latter usually differ, except when the variances of X_1 and Y are equal. This equality of variances holds by definition for the standardized variables z_1 and z_y, for their standard deviations are 1. Therefore $b^*_{y1} = b^*_{1y} = r_{y1} = 0.63$.

Table 5.3   Data matrix

X_1	Y	$z_1 = \dfrac{X_1 - \bar{X}_1}{s_1}$	$z_y = \dfrac{Y - \bar{Y}}{s_y}$
1	2	-1.53	-0.87
2	3	-1.17	-0.65
3	2	-0.80	-0.87
4	2	-0.44	-0.87
5	4	-0.07	-0.44
6	10	0.29	0.87
6	12	0.29	1.31
7	8	0.66	0.44
9	3	1.39	-0.65
9	14	1.39	1.74
mean 5.2	6	0	0
standard deviation 2.74	4.59	1	1

The latter can also be seen when we look at the angles in the figure with the $z_1 - z_y$ co-ordinate system. The regression coefficient, which expresses the change in the dependent variable per unit increase of the independent variable, is the tangent of the angle formed by the regression line and the axis of the independent variable. As we can see in the figure, the angle α between $\hat{z}_y = 0.63\, z_1$ and the z_1-axis is equal to the angle β between $\hat{z}_1 = 0.63\, z_y$ and the z_y axis. Consequently, the slopes are equal.

5.3.8 The Significance Test

We now discuss the third objective of bivariate regression analysis: the generalizability of sample association between X_1 and Y.

The coefficient $b_{y1} = 1.05$ is a sample statistic which offers an estimation of the population statistic $\beta_{y1}.r_{y1} = 0.63$ and $r_{y1}^2 = 0.39$ are also estimates of ρ_{y1} and ρ_{y1}^2.

In general, two significance tests can be performed: a test for the correlation coefficient (or determination coefficient) with the null hypothesis H_0: $\rho_{y1} = 0$ and a test for the regression coefficient with the null hypothesis H_0: $\beta_{y1} = 0$.

In the bivariate case these tests coincide. We make the distinction here because it will play an important role in multivariate analysis. We will not discuss the traditional significance tests for ρ_{y1} and β_{y1}, as they can be found in any statistics textbook. In imitation of Green (1978, p. 46), we will use the model comparison procedure, which leads to identical results and is generalizable for the multivariate case. In this model comparison approach, two models are compared, the restricted model and the full model. According to the restricted model the term $\beta_{y1}X_1$ is unnecessary for the prediction of Y. This corresponds to the null hypothesis H_0: $Y = \beta_0 + \varepsilon$. In the full model, on the other hand, the term $\beta_{y1}X_1$ *is* included. This results in the alternative hypothesis H_a: $Y = \beta_0 + \beta_{y1}X_1 + \varepsilon$.

The two models, the restricted and the full model, can also be compared geometrically (see Figure 5.6).

In the restricted model β_0 is equal to $\bar{Y}$. The dispersion around the mean line, which gives an idea of the prediction error, is represented by the variation $\text{SSE}_r = \sum(Y - \bar{Y})^2 = 190$, which was calculated above. In the full model we do not predict $\bar{Y}$ but, rather, Y. The prediction error is now $\text{SSE}_f = \sum(Y - \hat{Y})^2 = 115.43$. The two variations are compared with each other. If the difference $\sum(Y - \bar{Y})^2 - \sum(Y - \hat{Y})^2$ is substantial, then the full model is better than the restricted model. We will divide this difference by the prediction error SSE_f, after having divided the numerator and the denominator by the appropriate numbers of degrees of freedom, which are respectively $d_r - d_f$ and d_f.

The number of degrees of freedom for the restricted model is $d_r = n - 1 = 9$, because we loose one degree of freedom at the mean $\beta_0 = \bar{Y}$, for which it holds that $\sum(Y - \bar{Y}) = 0$. For the full model the number of degrees of freedom is $d_f = n - 2 = 8$, because both β_0 and β_{y1} have to be estimated. This results in the following F value:

$$F = \frac{(\text{SSE}_r - \text{SSE}_f)/(d_r - d_f)}{\text{SSE}_f/d_f}$$
$$= \frac{(190 - 115.43)/(9 - 8)}{115.43/8} = 5.17$$

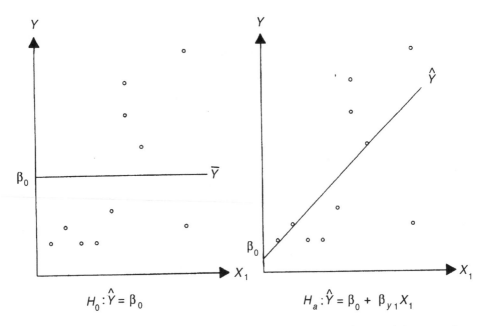

Figure 5.6   Geometry of significance testing according to the model comparison procedure

For a priorly postulated significance level of 0.05 and for one and eight degrees of freedom for numerator and denominator respectively, we find a critical F value (under H_0) of 5.32 in the F table. The F value $F = 5.17$ found in our sample is smaller than the F value in the table, so that we cannot reject the null hypothesis.

Why the F test contains $SSE_r - SSE_f$ in the numerator and SSE_f in the denominator will become clear after we have discussed analysis of variance. The denominator SSE_f/df_f is the error variance s_e^2 and is an estimation of σ_e^2. This is the dispersion of the individual values that remains after the full model has been applied. The numerator of F is related to the surplus value of the regression model ($\hat{Y}$) compared to the absence of this model ($\bar{Y}$). If this surplus value equals the dispersion of the individual values as such ($F = 1$), or if it differs from it only randomly ($F < 5.32$), then the model cannot be accepted.

The numerator and denominator of F can also be obtained in another way, by making use of coefficients of determination. The error variance in the denominator is also equal to the variance that remains when the proportion of variance r_{y1}^2 explained by the model is subtracted from 1, so that $s_e^2 = (1 - r_{y1}^2)/df_f$. The surplus value of the model in the numerator, if divided by the appropriate number of degrees of freedom, can be expressed as the difference between the proportion of explained variance for the full model ($r_f^2 = r_{y1}^2$) and for the restricted model ($r_r^2 = 0$). This results (with $r_f^2 = 0.393$ instead of 0.39 in order to set bounds to rounding errors) in the identical outcome as above:

$$F = \frac{(r_f^2 - r_r^2)/(d_r - d_f)}{(1 - r_f^2)/d_f}$$

$$= \frac{(0.393 - 0)/(9 - 8)}{(1 - 0.393)/8} = 5.17$$

This formula according to the model comparison method is of great generalizing value. It will be applied in multiple regression analysis, analysis of variance and other linear models of multivariate analysis.

5.4   Multiple Regression Analysis: The Influence of Working and Mean Age at Marriage on Childlessness

After the recapitulation of bivariate regression analysis we now turn to multiple regression. 'Multiple' means that there is more than one independent variable, measured of course at the quantitative level. At the beginning of this chapter we gave the research problem, the causal diagram and the data matrix for the association between the dependent variable Y (decade change in childlessness) and the two independent variables X_1 (change in labour-force participation) and X_2 (change in mean age at marriage). The treatment of multiple regression analysis, which now follows, proceeds almost analogously to that of bivariate regression analysis.

5.4.1   The Model

The linear model is now more complex, because there are three variables. The pattern represented by the model is no longer a straight line in an $X_1 - Y$ coordinate system, but a plane in the three-dimensional $X_1 - X_2 - Y$ space. For the population, this model is as follows: $Y_i = \beta_0 + \beta_{y1.2}X_{i1} + \beta_{y2.1}X_{i2} + \varepsilon_i$. The symbols Y, X_1, i, β_0 and ε have the same meaning as in the bivariate case. The regression coefficient β_{y1} has, however, undergone a change. It is now a partial regression coefficient and is written as $\beta_{y1.2}$; that means the change of $E(Y)$ for every unit increase of X_1 when controlling for X_2, in other words the degree of change of the childlessness variable for every unit increase of the labour variable when the age at marriage variable remains constant. In a similar way $\beta_{y2.1}$ is interpreted as the change of $E(Y)$ for every unit increase of X_2 when controlling for X_1, in other words the degree of change of the childlessness variable for every unit increase of the age at marriage variable when the labour variable remains constant. The formulations can become cumbersome here, because they deal with changes while the three variables themselves are already operationalized as a decade change (from 1960 to 1970). An exercise in accurate usage of language is called for in this example. We maintain the opinion that even complicated calculations can be conveyed by language in such a way that they remain mathematically exact, while still communicable to a large population. *Ce qui se conçoit bien, s'énonce clairement.*

The expected values of Y are written as $E(Y)$ or $\hat{Y}$:

$$E(Y) = \hat{Y} = \beta_0 + \beta_{y1.2}X_1 + \beta_{y2.1}X_2$$

The difference between Y and $\hat{Y}$ is the error term: $\varepsilon = Y - \hat{Y}$.

This error term has an expected value of $E(\varepsilon) = 0$ and a constant variance of σ_ε^2. It is considered to be uncorrelated with each of the independent variables X_1 and X_2. This means that this residual term ε is the orthogonal complement of X_1 and X_2 with respect to Y.

In the sample that follows, Latin letters are used instead of Greek letters:

$$Y = b_0 + b_{y1.2}X_1 + b_{y2.1}X_2 + e$$
$$E(Y) = \hat{Y} = b_o + b_{y1.2}X_1 + b_{y2.1}X_2$$
$$e = Y - \hat{Y}$$

5.4.2 Geometric Approach

The linear model is now situated in a three-dimensional space. The image to keep in mind is not a flat plane with two axes, in which a straight line is estimated, but rather a space with three axes, in which a plane is estimated.

In Figure 5.7 we have drawn the three axes X_1, X_2 and Y, as well as the flat plane $\hat{Y} = -2.68 + 0.78X_1 + 1.16X_2$. For each unit of analysis, the couple of numbers (X_1, X_2) is indicated as a cross in the bottom plane, the real Y value as a bold point and the estimated $\hat{Y}$ value as a dash. The latter $\hat{Y}$ values lie in the flat plane and are calculated by filling in the values of X_1 and X_2 in the linear function. For example, for the tenth and last unit of analysis we obtain $\hat{Y} = -2.68 + 0.78(9) + 1.16(7) = 12.43$. The real Y value ($Y = 14$) is greater and lies therefore above the plane (highest point in the figure). On the other hand, for the ninth (second to last) unit of analysis we obtain $\hat{Y} = -2.68 + 0.78(9) + 1.16(1) = 5.47$ and $Y = 3$. Here Y is smaller than $\hat{Y}$ and so it lies under the flat plane (the point situated most to the left in the figure). Just as in the bivariate case, the errors $e_i = Y_i - \hat{Y}_i$ are now alternatively positive and negative, so that their sum is equal to zero: $\sum e_i = 0$. In order to find the best plane that fits better than any other plane to the points, the least squares criterion will be applied.

As one can see, the inspection of the scatter diagram with the naked eye is now much more difficult than in a two-dimensional space. The cloud of points is now situated in the space under and above the flat plane. With four of more variables, it even becomes impossible to draw such a figure. The linear function that is estimated in these cases is called a 'hyperplane' and escapes our visual imagination. The principle, however, remains the same.

If one imagines a plane that is parallel to the $X_1 - X_2$ bottom plane and runs through $\bar{Y} = 6$, perpendicular to the Y axis, then this would represent the situation in which there is no relationship between X_1 and X_2 on the one hand and Y on the other hand. The points of the scatter diagram lie partly under and partly above this plane. The dispersion of the points with respect to this plane is simply the dispersion of the Y values around their mean, without X_1 and X_2 coming into play, and is represented by the total variation $\sum(Y - \bar{Y})^2$.

The estimated plane $\hat{Y}$ is, however, not parallel to the bottom plane, but shows an upwards slope with respect to both the X_1 and the X_2 axis. The dispersion of the points around this estimated plane is the residual variation $\sum(Y - \hat{Y})^2$, i.e., the dispersion that remains after having estimated the best fitting plane through the points.

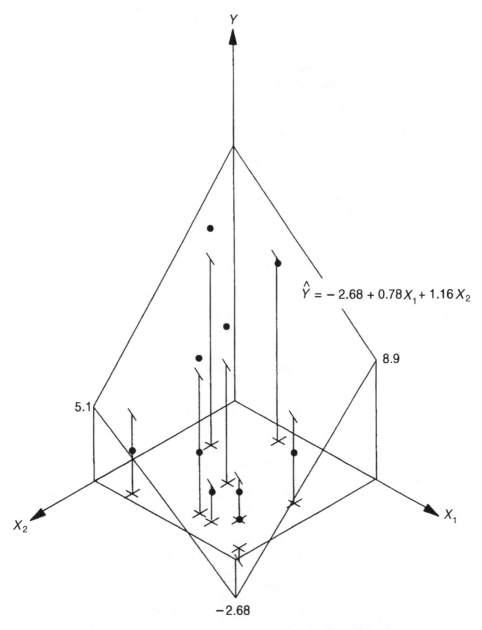

Figure 5.7   The multiple regression plane in the X_1–X_2–Y space

The difference between the total and the residual variation indicates to what measure the estimated $\hat{Y}$ plane is better than the $\bar{Y}$ plane and is represented by the explained variation $\sum(\hat{Y} - \bar{Y})^2$. We know that the splitting of the total variation into an explained part and a residual part is additive: $\sum(Y - \bar{Y})^2 = \sum(\hat{Y} - \bar{Y})^2 + \sum(Y - \hat{Y})^2$ or SST = SSR + SSE (T for total, R for regression, E for error).

It should be mentioned, moreover, that in the multivariate case as well, in which an inspection with the naked eye becomes impossible, the fulfilment of the assumptions of linearity, homoscedasticity and absence of outliers is required as well as other assumptions like additivity and absence of multicollinearity. For the tests of these requirements, arithmetic procedures exist which will be discussed in the next sections.

A visual aid is given by the inspection of the scatterplot of the residuals against $\hat{Y}$ or against an independent variable X_j. More about this below.

The geometric approach that has been given here takes the variables (Y, X_1, X_2) as axes and the units of analysis as points within this variable space. In this case we speak of the 'response surface model'. The reverse case, in which the ten units of analysis form the axes and in which the three variables are taken as points in this ten-dimensional space, is called a 'vector model'. We will restrict ourselves here to the treatment of the 'response surface model'.

5.4.3   Objectives of the Technique

Multiple regression analysis as a calculation technique is used for four objectives. Three of them have been dealt with in bivariate regression analysis and a fourth objective is now added because there are several independent variables.

Looking at the example of childlessness and with X_1 and X_2 as the independent variables, these objectives are the following:

1. We search for a function $Y = b_0 + b_{y1.2}X_1 + b_{y2.1}X_2 + e$ which represents the linear association between X_1, X_2 and Y better than any other function. This comes down to the calculation of the two regression coefficients $b_{y1.2}$ and $b_{y2.1}$ and the intercept b_0.
2. We examine the strength of the relationship between the linear combination of X_1 and X_2 on the one hand and Y on the other hand, and we also want to know, in view of prediction, which share of the variance of Y is explained by the variances of X_1 and X_2 together. This comes down to the calculation of the multiple correlation coefficient $R_{y.12}$ and its square, respectively.
3. We investigate whether the associations found in the sample are generalizable to the population. This comes down to the application of significance tests.
4. We examine which independent variable is most important in the explanation of Y, i.e., we want to make a comparison of the effects of X_1 on Y and X_2 on Y. This is done by the calculation of the beta weights (which we indicate by an asterisk: b^*).

5.4.4   Preparatory Bivariate Analyses

In order to prepare the calculation of the multiple regression function, we first carry out a number of additional bivariate analyses, of Y on X_2, of X_1 on X_2 and of X_2 on X_1.

These analyses are performed in the same way as the analysis of Y on X_1, which was treated extensively in the foregoing sections. The results are the following:

$Y = 0.54 + 1.05X_1 + e$, with $b_0 = 0.54$, $b_{y1} = 1.05$ and $r_{y1} = 0.63$
$Y = 0.61 + 1.35X_2 + e$, with $b_0 = 0.61$, $b_{y2} = 1.35$ and $r_{y2} = 0.79$
$X_1 = 4.23 + 0.24X_2 + e$, with $b_0 = 4.23$, $b_{12} = 0.24$ and $r_{12} = 0.24$
$X_2 = 2.77 + 0.24X_1 + e$, with $b_0 = 2.77$, $b_{21} = 0.24$ and $r_{21} = 0.24$

It may be noted in passing that one shouldn't be surprised by the equality of b_{12} and b_{21} (both are equal to 0.24), for the dispersions of X_1 and X_2 are $s_1 = 2.74$ and $s_2 = 2.71$ respectively and we know from the foregoing that, in the case of equal dispersions, $b_{12} = b_{21}$ holds. The correlation coefficient r_{12} is also equal to 0.24, as it is the geometric mean of the two regression coefficients. And, moreover, we can already expect that the standardized regression coefficients b_{12}^* and b_{21}^* will be both equal to 0.24, because they are equal to r_{12} in the bivariate case.

5.4.5 Calculation of the Regression Function

The first objective of multiple regression analysis is the calculation of $b_{y1.2}$, $b_{y2.1}$ and b_0. The coefficients $b_{y1.2}$ and $b_{y2.1}$ are 'partial' regression coefficients, which means that the asymmetrical relationship between two variables is controlled for a third variable. This control is necessary for the following reason. Take, for example, b_{y1}. This coefficient expresses to what extent the decade change in childlessness (Y) varies for every unit increase of the labour variable (X_1). But the variation of the age at marriage variable (X_2) plays tricks on us here. For X_2 is associated with both X_1 and Y. Take, on the other hand, b_{y2}. Here X_1 plays a disturbing role. For X_1 is related to both X_2 and Y. It becomes apparent that the coefficient b_{y1} does not express to what extent Y is influenced by X_1, for in order to make a judgement of this influence in its pure form we would have to remove the contaminating influence of X_2. The same holds for b_{y2} and the contamination by X_1. The procedure for the calculation of 'partial' regression coefficients will therefore first consist of removing the contamination in order to find the asymmetrical relationship in its pure form.

In order to calculate $b_{y1.2}$ we will first remove the influence of X_2 on Y and of X_2 on X_1. After that we will be able to make a judgement of the influence of X_1 on Y which is free of contamination. The coefficient $b_{y2.1}$ will be calculated in the same way. After that, the calculation of b_0 will be straightforward.

It is, however, possible to show that the removal of the influence on Y is unnecessary. If only the influence of X_2 on X_1 is removed (and not the influence of X_2 on Y) in the calculation of $b_{y1.2}$, then the result appears to be the same. The same holds for $b_{y2.1}$. The procedure is therefore as follows.

In a first step we conduct a bivariate regression analysis of X_1 on X_2. The estimated $\hat{X}_1$ values are calculated and the difference $X_1 - \hat{X}_1$ offers the residual scores. The dispersion of these residual scores indicates to what extent X_1 still varies when the common variance with X_2 is removed. After that a bivariate regression analysis of Y on $X_1 - \hat{X}_1$ is conducted. This results in the coefficient $b_{y1.2}$.

The calculations are brought together in Table 5.4. From the preparatory bivariate analyses we know that: $\hat{X}_1 = 4.23 + 0.24\, X_2$.

Bivariate regression analysis of Y on $X_1 - \hat{X}_1$ results in: $\hat{Y} = 6 + 0.78\,(X_1 - \bar{X}_1)$. It follows that $b_{y1.2} = 0.78$.

In a second step we analogously calculate the partial regression coefficient $b_{y2.1}$, which represents the effect of X_2 on Y when controlling for X_1. We know that $\hat{X}_2 = 2.77 + 0.24\, X_1$. See Table 5.5.

Bivariate regression analysis of Y on $X_2 - \hat{X}_2$ results in: $\hat{Y} = 6 + 1.16\,(X_2 - \hat{X}_2)$. It follows that $b_{y2.1} = 1.16$.

Table 5.4

X_1	X_2	$\hat{X}_1$	$X_1 - \hat{X}_1$	Y
1	1	4.47	−3.47	2
2	6	5.68	−3.68	3
3	3	4.96	−1.96	2
4	2	4.72	−0.72	2
5	2	4.72	0.28	4
6	5	5.44	0.56	10
6	9	6.41	−0.41	12
7	4	5.20	1.80	8
9	1	4.47	4.53	3
9	7	5.93	3.07	14

Table 5.5

X_1	X_2	$\hat{X}_2$	$X_2 - \hat{X}_2$	Y
1	1	3.01	−2.01	2
2	6	3.24	2.76	3
3	3	3.48	−0.48	2
4	2	3.72	−1.72	2
5	2	3.95	−1.95	4
6	5	4.19	0.81	10
6	9	4.19	4.81	12
7	4	4.43	−0.43	8
9	1	4.90	−3.90	3
9	7	4.90	2.10	14

For the calculation of the intercept b_0 an analoguous formula holds as in the bivariate case:

$$b_0 = \bar{Y} - b_{y1.2}\bar{X}_1 - b_{y2.1}\bar{X}_2 = 6 - (0.78)(5.2) - (1.16)(4) = -2.68$$

We can now write down the multiple regression function which represents the best flat plane estimated by means of OLS, best because it fits better than any other plane with the ten points of the scatter diagram:

$$\hat{Y} = -2.68 + 0.78X_1 + 1.16X_2 \quad \text{or} \quad Y = -2.68 + 0.78X_1 + 1.16X_2 + e$$

The interpretations for the investigation of childlessness are as follows. When the decade changes in labour-force participation and in mean age at marriage of women are equal to 0, then there is a decrease in the decade change in percentage of childless women of − 2.68. When the decade change in mean age at marriage remains constant, then a unit increase of the labour variable entails an increase of 0.78 in the childlessness change. And when the decade change in percentage of working women remains constant, then there is an increase of 1.16 in the childlessness change for every unit increase of the decade change in mean age at marriage.

It cannot be automatically inferred from these results that the effect of the age at marriage factor (1.16) is greater than the effect of the labour factor (0.78). For, the coefficients $b_{y1.2}$ and $b_{y2.1}$ are not suitable for mutual comparison of the effects. Such a comparison of the importance of the causal factors is only permitted when the dispersions of the variables X_1 and X_2 are equal, which is accidentally the case in our example. This weighing of the effects will be calculated by means of the beta weights when we discuss the fourth objective.

Recapitulating, we have now dealt with the first objective of multiple regression analysis in calculating the partial regression coefficients and the intercept. A partial regression coefficient is obtained by conducting a bivariate analysis, in which Y is the dependent variable and the independent variable is the residual $X_i - \hat{X}_i$, in which the linear association of X_i with other independent variables is removed. This decontamination is only unnecessary when the independent variables are uncorrelated, because in that case the partial regression coefficient is equal to the bivariate regression coefficient b_{yi}.

5.4.6   The Strength of the Relationship and the Explained Variance

We now come to the second objective of multiple regression analysis, the calculation of the linear association between Y on the one hand and X_1 and X_2 on the other, by means of the multiple correlation coefficient $R_{y.12}$. The square of $R_{y.12}$ is called the multiple determination coefficient and represents the proportion of explained variance in a way analogous to the bivariate analysis. We start with the calculation of $R_{y.12}$.

The multiple correlation coefficient $R_{y.12}$ is a measure of the linear association between Y and the combination of X_1 and X_2. Therefore, we first calculate the scores of the linear combination $\hat{Y} = b_0 + b_{y1.2}X_1 + b_{y2.1}X_2$. After that we calculate the zero-order correlation r_y between Y and $\hat{Y}$. This is $R_{y.12}$. In the table below, the scores of $\hat{Y}$ are obtained by filling in the X_1 and X_2 values in the function: $\hat{Y} = -2.68 + 0.78 X_1 + 1.16 X_2$.

In order to prepare other calculations to follow, we also add the residuals $Y - \hat{Y}$ and their square (Table 5.6).

Simple calculation of the correlation coefficient (zero-order correlation) between Y and $\hat{Y}$ gives us a coefficient $r_{y\hat{y}} = 0.91$. It follows that $R_{y.12} = 0.91$. So, there is a positive linear association between the decade change in childlessness and the combination of decade changes in labour-force participation and mean age at

Table 5.6

X_1	X_2	$\hat{Y}$	Y	$Y - \hat{Y}$	$(Y - \hat{Y})^2$
1	1	−0.74	2	2.74	7.50
2	6	5.84	3	−2.84	8.06
3	3	3.13	2	−1.13	1.28
4	2	2.75	2	−0.75	0.56
5	2	3.52	4	0.48	0.24
6	5	7.78	10	2.22	4.97
6	9	12.42	12	−0.42	0.18
7	4	7.40	8	0.60	0.36
9	1	5.47	3	−2.47	6.08
9	7	12.43	14	1.57	2.47
sum				0	31.70

marriage. This relationship is very strong, for, just like the zero-order correlation coefficient, the coefficient $R_{y.12}$ has a maximum of 1 (its minimum, however, is 0).

Geometrically, this coefficient indicates to what extent the ten points in three-dimensional space fit the estimated flat plane.

In the vector model, which is not treated here, $R_{y.12}$ is the cosine of the angle formed by Y and $\hat{Y}$ in ten-dimensional space.

We know that the square of $R_{y.12}^2$ can be interpreted as the proportion of explained variance. This multiple determination coefficient can be calculated in many ways. A first way, of course, is by calculating $R_{y.12}$ as above and taking its square. The result is $R^2 = 0.83$. Consequently, 83% of the variance of the decade change in childlessness is explained by the variance of the decade changes in working and mean age at marriage in combination.

This interpretation becomes clearer when we consider the additive splitting of the variation of Y in an explained and an unexplained part, in an identical fashion as in the bivariate analysis:

$$\begin{aligned}
\sum(Y - \bar{Y})^2 &= \sum(\hat{Y} - \bar{Y})^2 &+ \sum(Y - \hat{Y})^2 \\
\text{SST} &= \text{SSR} &+ \text{SSE} \\
\text{Total} &= \text{explained} &+ \text{unexplained variation}
\end{aligned}$$

We already calculated the total variation of Y-values: $\sum(Y - \bar{Y})^2 = 190$. The explained variation $\sum(Y - \bar{Y})^2$ can easily be inferred in three ways from the table with $\hat{Y}$ scores. Either we subtract $\bar{Y}$ from the $\hat{Y}$ scores and we make the sum of the squares of these differences, or we simply calculate the variation of the $\hat{Y}$ scores $\sum(\hat{Y} - \bar{\hat{Y}})^2$, for the mean $\bar{\hat{Y}}$ of the $\hat{Y}$ scores is always equal to $\bar{Y}$. A third possibility is to take the unexplained variation $\sum(Y - \hat{Y})^2 = 31.70$ and subtract it from the total variation $\sum(Y - \bar{Y})^2 = 190$. The result is $\sum(\hat{Y} - \bar{Y})^2 = 158.30$.

The multiple determination coefficient is equal to the explained variation divided by the total variation:

$$R_{y.12}^2 = \frac{\sum(\hat{Y} - \bar{Y})^2}{\sum(Y - \bar{Y})^2} = \frac{158.30}{190} = 0.83$$

If the numerator as well as the denominator is divided by $10 - 1$, then we naturally obtain a ratio of variances instead of variations, which comes down to the same.

There are still many other ways to calculate R^2. The PRE interpretation, which we treated above, applies here as well. Other possibilities for obtaining the multiple determination coefficient are:

via correlation coefficients and betas: $R_{y.12}^2 = r_{y1}b_{y1.2}^* + r_{y2}b_{y2.1}^*$

via correlations and partial correlations: $R_{y.12}^2 = r_{y1}^2 + r_{y2.1}^2(1 - r_{y1}^2)$

These interpretations presuppose the treatment of betas and partial correlation coefficients. A still more extensive elaboration of these topics will be given in path analysis (see Chapter 6).

5.4.7   Standardized Partial Regression Coefficients

We will now first treat the fourth objective of multiple regression analysis and then go into the problem of statistical generalization from the sample to the population.

We stated above that, strictly speaking, the partial regression coefficients $b_{y1.2}$ and $b_{y2.1}$ are not mutually comparable and that this is only the case when the dispersions of X_1 and X_2 are equal, which — exceptionally — happens to be the case in our example. So, for a mutual comparison of the effect of X_1 on Y and of X_2 on Y, the scores should have equal dispersions. Now, we know that standardization is a procedure in which the standard deviation is made equal to 1. Consequently, if we first standardize the variables and then perform a multiple regression analysis, the resulting regression coefficients will be mutually comparable so that an appreciation of the importance of the effects will become possible. These regression coefficients are called 'standardized partial regression coefficients' or 'betas' and they are indicated by an asterisk as b^*.

The rather elaborate procedure for the calculation of the betas is thus as follows. Firstly, the scores of X_1 are transformed into z scores $z_1 = (X_1 - \bar{X}_1)/s_1$, the scores of X_2 into $z_2 = (X_2 - \bar{X}_2)/s_2$ and the scores of Y into $z_y = (Y - \bar{Y})/s_y$. After that the calculation of the multiple regression function, which has already been demonstrated in this chapter (see 5.4.5), is performed again on these z scores. This results in an equation without intercept (because z scores involve deviations of mean and deviations of mean involve a translation to the origin) and with betas as the regression coefficients: $z_y = b^*_{y1.2}z_1 + b^*_{y2.1}z_2 + e$.

The application of this procedure is a good exercise for the reader. The results are $b^*_{y1.2} = 0.46$ and $b^*_{y2.1} = 0.68$.

But, with the definition of the mathematician as an 'intelligent lazy-bones' in mind, we want to pursue a shorter method. For, it can easily be shown that a beta coefficient is equal to the corresponding b coefficient multiplied by the ratio s_x/s_y, i.e., the standard deviation of the independent variable X divided by the standard deviation of the dependent variable Y. We now demonstrate this for the bivariate case (with variables X and Y) and the derivation is identical for the multivariate case.

We know that

$$b_{yx} = \frac{\text{covariation } X, Y}{\text{variation } X}$$

$$b_{yx} = \frac{\sum(X - \bar{X})(Y - \bar{Y})}{\sum(X - \bar{X})^2}$$

For standardized variables, the mean is equal to 0. In an analogous fashion, we can therefore write:

$$b^*_{yx} = \frac{\text{covariation } z_x, z_y}{\text{variation } z_x} = \frac{\sum(z_x - 0)(z_y - 0)}{\sum(z_x - 0)^2}$$

$$= \frac{\sum z_x z_y}{\sum z_x^2} = \frac{\sum\left(\dfrac{X - \bar{X}}{s_x}\right)\left(\dfrac{Y - \bar{Y}}{s_y}\right)}{\sum\left(\dfrac{X - \bar{X}}{s_x}\right)^2}$$

$$= \frac{(1/s_x s_y)\sum(X - \bar{X})(Y - \bar{Y})}{(1/s_x^2)\sum(X - \bar{X})^2} = \frac{s_x}{s_y}b_{yx}$$

It is therefore easy to infer the betas from the b's:

$$b^*_{y1.2} = b_{y1.2}\frac{s_1}{s_y} = 0.78\frac{2.74}{4.59} = 0.46$$

$$b^*_{y2.1} = b_{y2.1}\frac{s_2}{s_y} = 1.16\frac{2.71}{4.59} = 0.68$$

These beta weights are most suitable for determining the relative importance of the predictors X_1 and X_2. It appears that the decade change in mean age at marriage has the greatest effect on the decade change in childlessness. Nevertheless, the labour variable still has an important effect of almost half a unit increase in the childlessness variable for every unit increase in the labour variable, both being standardized.

Contrary to the b's, the betas must not be greater than 1, in principle, because of the standardization procedure. If a beta greater than 1 *is* obtained, which sometimes happens, then please sound the alarm. An excessively strong association between the causal factors X_1 and X_2 (multicollinearity) is frequently a reason for this artefactual result.

5.4.8 The Significance Test

We now come to the third objective of multiple regression analysis: the generalizability of the relationships found in the sample to the population. Several significance tests can be performed. We will deal here with two kinds of test:

1. a test of the global model, in which both independent variables are included;
2. a test of each independent variable separately.

Both significance tests can be performed using the model comparison procedure. One should always start with the test of the global model, for if this doesn't show a significant result, then the regression function is unfit for use. The analysis should then be terminated. Only in the second instance, when R^2 is significant, does it become legitimate to investigate whether this is also the case for each of the predictors separately.

For the global test the null hypothesis can be written as:

$$H_0 : R^2_{y.12} = 0 \quad \text{or as} \quad H_0 : \beta_{y1.2} = \beta_{y2.1} = 0$$

The restricted model $Y = \beta_0 + \varepsilon$ is compared with the full model:

$$Y = \beta_0 + \beta_{y1.2}X_1 + \beta_{y2.1}X_2 + \varepsilon$$

The number of degrees of freedom for the restricted model is $d_r = 10 - 1 = 9$, because one degree of freedom is lost to the mean, and the number for the full model is $d_f = 10 - 3 = 7$, because two additional parameters $\beta_{y1.2}$ and $\beta_{y2.1}$ have to be estimated.

We have already calculated that $\text{SSE}_r = \sum(Y - \bar{Y})^2 = 190$ and $\text{SSE}_f = \sum(Y - \hat{Y})^2 = 31.70$. The F test for the full model leads to the following result:

$$F = \frac{(SSE_r - SSE_f)/(d_r - d_f)}{SSE_f/d_f}$$

$$= \frac{(190 - 31.70)/(9 - 7)}{31.70/7} = 17.5$$

For a priorally postulated type I error of $\alpha = 0.05$ and for two degrees of freedom for the numerator and seven for the denominator, we find a critical F^* value (under H_0) of 4.74 in the F table. The calculated value $F = 17.5$ is much higher than the F^* value of the table, so that we can reject the null hypothesis. Therefore, with a priorally postulated probability of 95%, there is a significant relationship between the labour and age at marriage variable, together, and the childlessness variable. So, the full model is generalizable to the population. In the computer output of most standard programs we can read this as 'SIGNIFICANCE $F = 0.0019$'. This value represents the empirical significance level, i.e., the probability of exceeding. Geometrically, it is the area under the curve of the sampling distribution of F values (under H_0) which is situated to the right of the F value found in the sample. If this area is smaller than 0.05, then we have a significant result, because the probability of finding the sample F value or an even more extreme value under H_0 is so small that we can reject H_0.

The test which was performed above can also be written in terms of determination coefficients. For the restricted model we have $R_r^2 = 0$ and for the full model $R_f^2 = 0.833$. The following formula leads to the same result as above:

$$F = \frac{(R_f^2 - R_r^2)/(d_r - d_f)}{(1 - R_f^2)/d_f}$$

$$= \frac{(0.833 - 0)/(9 - 7)}{(1 - 0.833)/7} = 17.5$$

It should be mentioned that in the case of a great number of independent variables, we will sometimes have to use an adjusted formula for R^2 (adjusted R square). For, if new independent variables are added to the multiple regression equation, then R^2 can become artificially high because of a mechanism of capitalizing on chance. A correction for this artificial mechanism is contained in the formula below.

$$\text{adjusted } R^2 = 1 - (1 - R^2)\frac{n - 1}{n - p - 1}$$

This formula results in R^2 when the number of independent variables p is equal to 0. As p increases, the downward 'correction for shrinkage' becomes greater. In our example the correction is not very substantial, because there are only two independent variables:

$$\text{adjusted } R^2 = 1 - (1 - 0.83)\frac{10 - 1}{10 - 2 - 1} = 0.79$$

As the global model is significant, we can turn to the second step, the testing of each predictor separately. For, simply because X_1 and X_2 together have a significant effect on Y, this is not necessarily the case for each of them separately. In the output of most computer programs these separate tests are performed in a traditional fashion by means of a classical t test. 'SIGNIFICANCE T' shows a value of 0.0226 for variable

X_1 and 0.0035 for X_2. With a prior type I error of $\alpha = 0.05$ both effects are thus significant.

Such a t test can also be performed for the constant term β_0. The empirical significant level is 0.1551. The null hypothesis $\beta_0 = 0$ cannot be rejected. Our interpretation of $b_0 = -2.68$, according to which the decade change in childlessness Y decreases with 2.68% when X_1 and X_2 are equal to 0, must therefore be taken with a grain of salt, for the intercept cannot be generalized to the population.

In testing the separate effects, we can also use the same model comparison procedure as above, instead of the classical t test. The results are identical. When testing the separate effect of X_1, the null hypothesis is $H_0: \beta_{y1.2} = 0$. The full model is now $Y = \beta_0 + \beta_{y1.2}X_1 + \beta_{y2.1}X_2 + \varepsilon$ and the restricted model is $Y = \beta_0 + \beta_{y2.1}X_2 + \varepsilon$, in which the effect of X_1 is removed null-hypothesis-wise. The determination coefficients for the full model are $R_f^2 = 0.833$, and for the restricted model $R_r^2 = r_{y2}^2 = 0.632$.

The numbers of degree of freedom are $d_f = 10 - 3 = 7$ and $d_r = 10 - 2 = 8$.

The F value in our sample is the following:

$$F = \frac{(R_f^2 - R_r^2)/(d_r - d_f)}{(1 - R_f^2)/d_f}$$

$$= \frac{(0.833 - 0.632)/(8 - 7)}{(1 - 0.833)/7} = 8.43$$

The critical F^* value in the table for one and seven degrees of freedom and for a prior type I error α of 0.05 is equal to 5.59. The F value of 8.43 found in the sample is greater. The effect of the labour variable in the explanation of childlessness is therefore significant. Please note that the calculated F value of 8.43 is equal to the square of the t value of 2.91 from the classical t test. With one degree of freedom for the numerator, we can perform the F test as well as the t test. The tests are identical because of the fixed relationship $F = t^2$.

The test of the effect of X_2 is performed in the same way.

$$F = \frac{(0.833 - 0.393)/(8 - 7)}{(1 - 0.833)/7} = 18.46$$

We see that the effect of the decade change in mean age at marriage is also significant, for the calculated F value is much greater than the value 5.59 of the table for one and seven degrees of freedom.

5.4.9   The Tests of Additivity and Linearity

In the model $Y = \beta_0 + \beta_{y1.2}X_1 + \beta_{y2.1}X_2 + \varepsilon$ the assumption is made that the effects of X_1 and X_2 in the explanation of Y can be added up. A weighted sum (linear combination) of both variables is made. In that case the model is called additive.

If, however, it could be hypothesized that the effects of working and age at marriage reinforce each other in their explanation of childlessness, so that there is an effect of interaction, then their product $X_1 \cdot X_2$ would offer an explanation for Y. In such a case the additive model would no longer be adequate. We would then want a multiplicative model, because not the weighted sums but the products offer an explanation.

With more than two independent variables in the model, several product terms can be included for every two, three or more variables. A simple test of additivity consists of the construction of a regression equation in which all possible product terms are added to the additive model, and by comparing this equation to the simple additive model without product terms, according to the model comparison approach.

In our example only one product X_1X_2 can be made, so that the following two models are compared:

full model: $\quad\quad Y = b_0 + b_1X_1 + b_2X_2 + b_3X_1X_2 + e$
restricted model: $\quad Y = b_0 + b_1X_1 + b_2X_2 + e$

The multiple determination coefficient for the restricted model has been calculated above and is equal to 0.833. (Note that this was R^2 for the full model in the other significance tests.) For the calculation of the multiple determination coefficient of the full model, we have to perform the regression analysis with X_1, X_2 and X_1X_2 as the independent variables. The result is $R^2 = 0.947$.

The numbers of degrees of freedom are $d_r = 7$ and $d_f = 6$.

The test leads to the following result:

$$F = \frac{(R_f^2 - R_r^2)/(d_r - d_f)}{(1 - R_f^2)/d_f}$$

$$= \frac{(0.947 - 0.833)/(7 - 6)}{(1 - 0.947)/6} = 12.91$$

For $\alpha = 0.05$ and for one and six degrees of freedom, we find a critical F^* value of 5.99 in the F table. The calculated F value of the sample (12.91) is greater and we decide that the whole of the interaction effects (only one here) offers a significant contribution to the explanation of childlessness. The additive model was therefore inadequate.

For further literature on the testing of additivity we refer to Opp and Schmidt (1976, pp. 218–225) and Nie *et al.* (1975, p. 373). It should be mentioned that the testing of the effects of interaction in regression analysis is usually neglected, not only in research practice but also in the theoretical textbooks by methodologists.

In addition to a test of additivity, one must also perform a test of linearity, for, the assumption that a linear model adequately represents the structure of relationships in the childlessness data is not necessarily fulfilled. A simple way to check the requirement of linearity is the inspection of residual plots. More about this in the following sections.

There also exist explicit linearity tests. The model comparison approach, with which we have become familiar, can be applied as follows. Take as an example the relationship between X_i and Y and suppose that we want to investigate whether a quadratic function $Y = b_0 + b_1X + b_2X^2$ represents this relationship better than a straight line $Y = b_0 + b_1X$. Then the parabolic function (polynomial of the second degree) represents the full model and the linear function (polynomial of the first degree) the restricted model, and the F test is performed exactly as it was in the cases above.

It is also possible to test the adequacy of polynomials of the second, third, fourth, ..., up to the k-th degree, successively. For example, the function

$Y = b_0 + b_1 X + b_2 X^2 + b_3 X^3 + b_4 X^4 + e$ is a polynomial of the fourth degree, because the highest power of X appearing in the function is equal to 4. Such a function makes three curves, one less than its degree. So, a polynomial of the third degree has two curves and the polynomial of the second degree, which we dealt with above and which is a parabolic function, has one curve upwards ($\cap$) or downwards ($\cap$) with one maximum or one minimum. It is customary to start with a test of a polynomial of the second degree, then the third, then the fourth, and so on until further testing becomes redundant.

There are still many other ways to deal with the problem of non-linearity. Examples are taking the logarithms of certain variables, taking the inverses, or another adjusted transformation. For further literature we refer to Opp and Schmidt (1976, pp. 189 *et seq.*), Nie *et al.* (1975, p. 372) and Green (1978, pp. 201 *et seq.*).

One should be aware of the fact that the testing of additivity as well as linearity creates the problem whereby the added terms, the product term $X_1 X_2$ or the term of the second degree X^2, for example, can be strongly associated with the independent variables that were already in the equation (X_1 for example).

This creates the thorny problem of multicollinearity, which means that the independent variables in a multiple regression equation are too strongly interrelated, so that the estimations of the regression coefficients become unreliable. We will now deal with this problem separately.

5.4.10 The Multicollinearity Problem

The problem of the independent variables X_1 ($\Delta\%$ working women) and X_2 (Δ mean age at marriage) being strongly associated, and therefore making them partly interchangeable, is called the multicollinearity problem. The concept of 'multicollinearity' is geometrical in nature. It means that many things are all situated on one straight line. Referring to the vector model, in which the ten units of analysis span a ten-dimensional space and in which the three variables are seen as points in this space (endpoints of vectors from the origin), we can represent this as follows. The most general case, in which X_1 and X_2 are moderately correlated and where the correlation is not perfect and not zero, is the case in which the vectors x_1 and x_2 do not coincide and are not perpendicular, but form an angle between $0°$ and $90°$, so that they jointly form a base. The cosine of the angle α between these two vectors is the correlation coefficient r_{12}. The orthogonal projection of the endpoint of vector y at the base is the endpoint of the vector of expected values $\hat{y}$. When the scores are expressed as deviations of mean, so that the intercept drops, this projection is also equal to the weighted sum $b_{y1.2}\, x_1 + b_{y2.1}\, x_2$. This general case is shown in Figure 5.8.

Now, if X_1 and X_2 were perfectly correlated, so that $r_{12} = 1$ and the angle α was equal to zero, then the vectors x_1 and x_2 would coincide. The endpoints of these two vectors would either fall together or lie on one straight line. This explains the term multicollinearity: several endpoints lie on one straight line and are therefore colinear. In that case there would no longer be a base. The two independent variables would be identical and therefore interchangeable.

It can be shown that multicollinearity in multiple regression analysis creates serious problems, not in the descriptive, but rather in the inferential sense of generalization from sample to population. For, as the correlations between independent variables

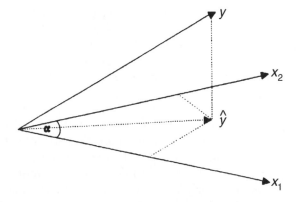

Figure 5.8   Multiple regression analysis in the vector model

become stronger, the estimations of the partial regression coefficients become less precise. In order to demonstrate this, let us first introduce the concept of tolerance. We take one of the independent variables, the labour variable X_1 for example, and we calculate the multiple determination coefficient with X_1 as the dependent variable and all the other independent variables (only one here: age at marriage) as independent variables. In our mini example this is $R^2_{1.2}$, i.e., the proportion of the variance of X_1 that is explained by all other independent variables (only X_2 here). The remainder $1 - R^2_{1.2}$ is the proportion of the variance of X_1 that is not explained by the other independent variables. This is the tolerance. It is a measure of the absence of multicollinearity. In our example it is: $1 - R^2_{1.2} = 1 - r^2_{12} = 1 - (0.24)^2 = 0.94$.

This tolerance plays a crucial role in the calculation of the confidence interval of the partial regression coefficients. With a priorly postulated probability of $1 - \alpha = 0.95$, the population coefficient $\beta_{y1.2}$ is situated between the values 0.15 and 1.41 (df = $n - p - 1$):

$$b_{y1.2} \pm t_{\alpha/2}\hat{\sigma}_{b1}$$

$$b_{y1.2} \pm t_{\alpha/2}\frac{s_y}{s_1}\left[\frac{1 - R^2_{y.12}}{(1 - R^2_{1.2})(n - p - 1)}\right]^{1/2}$$

$$0.78 \pm 2.365\frac{4.59}{2.74}\left[\frac{1 - 0.833}{(1 - 0.24^2)(10 - 2 - 1)}\right]^{1/2}$$

$$0.78 \pm 2.365(0.27), \text{ thus } 0.15 \text{ and } 1.41$$

We see that the tolerance $1 - R^2_{1.2}$ is part of the denominator and thus jointly determines the estimated precision (standard error $\hat{\sigma}_{b1} = 0.27$). As multicollinearity increases, tolerance will decrease and therefore the standard error will become greater, so that the precision becomes smaller.

In the same fashion we obtain a 95% confidence interval for the effect of age at marriage $\beta_{y2.1}$, which is situated between 0.52 and 1.80 with a precision of 0.27.

High multicollinearity thus creates a thorny problem where the estimates of the partial regression coefficients of the population become very unprecise. This is especially a problem when we want to make a mutual comparison of the effects of the independent variables, for the large confidence intervals of the different partial regression coefficients bring about overlap and ambiguity.

If such a weighing of the relative importance of the causal factors is not one's purpose, then multicollinearity is no problem. But we personally know of no research example where this purpose is indeed absent.

Now, what do we have to do in research practice when the data show high multicollinearity with correlations between the independent variables of, say, 0.60 or higher? Many procedures exist. The first and most drastic one is the removal of one or several of the independent variables, i.e., those that are too strongly associated with others. The second procedure consists of assigning the common variance to one of the independent variables and removing it from the others. In our example, this would mean that the labour variable X_1 remains what it is and that we would remove the part that the age at marriage variable X_2 shares with X_1, which means that the residual variable $X_2 - \hat{X}_2$ remains, resulting in the performance of a multiple regression analysis of Y in function of X_1 and $X_2 - \hat{X}_2$. The third procedure is the splitting of the common variance between the different independent variables. The way this distribution must occur is not always clear. The fourth procedure is the separate treatment of the shared variance. If we indicate the latter by G, then in our example we would make an analysis of Y as a function of $X_1 - \hat{X}_1$, $X_2 - \hat{X}_2$ and G, where X_1 and X_2 are both decontaminated.

Many other procedures, like Bayes' regression and others, have been developed. We would like to mention a final and often used strategy, the use of factor analysis. When there are a great number of independent variables of the appropriate measurement level (interval), then it is customary, in cases of high multicollinearity, to perform a factor analysis on these independent variables (mostly a principal components analysis).

This technique will be dealt with in one of the following chapters. It consists of bringing together the shared variances of the original variables into newly created variables, called factors (or components). These factors can be mutually correlated again, but it is possible to choose a factor analysis procedure in which the factors are orthogonal. These factors are smaller in number than the original variables. Each factor acts as a representative of a group of variables that are strongly interconnected. Now, if we perform a multiple regression analysis with Y as the dependent variable and with the factors as the independent variables, then the multicollinearity problem is solved, for the factors are mutually uncorrelated. One could compare the factors with political parties with a seat in Parliament. The original variables then represent the opinions of the population.

The problem is, however, that a factor analysis must inductively distil the coherent and mutually uncorrelated (or are they?) party opinions from the opinions of the population and that, in doing so, it cannot make use of a well-organized nation, which is based on party-systems. It is therefore often a problem to find a suitable name for an inferred factor, for one is only aware of the variables that have 'high loadings' on such a factor. From this group of strongly interrelated variables one has to infer the meaning of such a factor. So, in the end, the problem of multicollinearity has been avoided, but the meaning of the newly created independent variables (factors) is open to interpretation. Every medal has its reverse.

5.4.11   *The Analysis of Residuals*

A helpful tool in the investigation of whether the assumptions of linearity, homoscedasticity, absence of outliers, etc., are fulfilled, is the analysis of residuals. In most computer programs plots can be requested of the residuals e_i against one of the independent variables X_j or against the weighted sum $\hat{Y}$ of the independent variables (not against Y!). Most used is the plot of the residuals e_i against the predicted values $\hat{Y}$, in which e_i as well as $\hat{Y}$ are standardized. The idea is that the residuals must not show a systematic pattern with regard to the hyperplane $\hat{Y}$. It holds by definition that e_i and $\hat{Y}$ are each other's orthogonal complement. In other words, the residual component is orthogonal to the linear combination of independent variables. The correlation between both components is exactly equal to 0. A correlation of zero can, however, be established in many ways. It would be ideal if the residuals compensated each other with regard to the hyperplane in an equitable fashion, so that the plot showed a sort of random pattern without abnormalities. But all sorts of unlikely situations can occur, of which Figure 5.9 below shows a few examples.

In each of the figures, the correlation between e and $\hat{Y}$ is equal to 0, but the pattern nevertheless contains certain abnormalities. In Figure 5.9(a) the scatterplot shows a non-linear pattern. A non-linear regression function with a quadratic term might be more appropriate in fitting the data.

From Figure 5.9(b) it appears that the assumption of constant residual variance is not met (violation of the requirement of homoscedasticity). The dispersion of the residual variable increases with the linear combination of independent variables $\hat{Y}$, so that the pattern shows divergence. There is only absence of heteroscedasticity when the hypothetical band around the residual plots consists of two parallel horizontal lines. A transformation of the dependent variable Y into $Y^{1/2}$ is one of the possible strategies for avoiding this problem. Another strategy is called weighted least squares (WLS). See Chatterjee and Price (1977, p. 49) for a treatment of this topic.

In Figure 5.9(c) we see that the values are clustered. A polytomous variable with as many categories as there are clusters, which lies behind the data and is not taken into the analysis, might be the cause of this awkward pattern. We might obtain more insight from a separate analysis of each of the different clusters.

Figure 5.9(d) shows a nice random pattern, as it should be, but at the top and to the right there is an 'outlier' for which the residual value is more than two standard

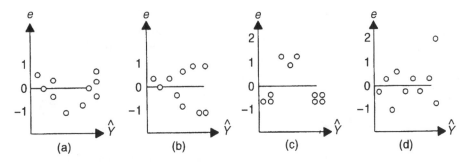

Figure 5.9   Residual plots in regression analysis

deviations away from the mean 0. Just as in the case of the formation of clusters, a separate analysis of these deviating units is the correct method. We wish to dispel the misunderstanding here that quantitatively orientated methodologists have the habit of throwing away the 'outliers', because they do not fit the model. On the contrary, just as the qualitatively oriented methodologist rightly recommends, we should perceive the deviating units as exceptional discoveries, as interesting specimens that have to be submitted for a separate analysis and from which we learn to what extent our models have to be adjusted and elaborated.

In addition to the plotting of the residual term against the independent variables X_j and their linear combination $E(Y)$, there are still many other ways to investigate the model-adequacy of the residuals. A standard procedure is the so-called 'casewise plot'. This is a plot of the residuals, for each case and in standardized form. The cases, for which the residual is removed more than two standard deviations from 0, can be selected from this plot at a first glance. Most computer programs also offer the possibility of retrieving such 'outliers' separately. In that case, only the truly deviating cases are given, with their identification numbers and their standardized residual scores. This produces more convenient and restricted output, for, in cases of large samples a 'casewise plot' would take up an enormous number of pages.

One can also investigate whether the residuals are dispersed in the form of a random pattern around their mean 0. This is done by means of a histogram of standardized residuals. Ideally, this histogram should take the form of a normal distribution. In cases of serious deviation from such a Gauss curve pattern, we should sound the alarm. Most computer programs make a plot of the empirical histogram as well as the ideally expected curve in one figure.

Another way to investigate whether the observed distribution of residuals coincides with the distribution that is expected under the assumption of normality is the so-called 'normal probability plot'. This is a plot of two cumulative distributions against each other. The horizontal axis shows cumulative probabilities of occurrence of standardized residuals in the expected ideal case of normality. The vertical axis shows the same cumulative probabilities in the observed situation. If these two cumulative distributions are identical, then a 45° line emerges. The way in which the points are scattered with respect to this expected straight line gives an indication of the possible violation of the normality assumption.

5.4.12   *Multiple Regression Analysis in Matrix Notation*

In the foregoing sections we have made use of the ordinary least squares criterion for the estimation of the multiple regression function. We used so-called OLS estimates. The units were situated in three-dimensional space and through the plots a plane was estimated. This estimation was a BLUE, i.e., a Best Linear Unbiased Estimate, Best because of all linear unbiased estimates it has the smallest variance, Linear because a linear function is estimated and Unbiased because the expected value $E(b)$ of each sample parameter is equal to the corresponding population parameter β. According to the Gauss–Markoff theorem, the vector **b** of ordinary least squares estimators is a BLUE.

The plane for which the sum $\sum(Y - \hat{Y})^2$ of squared residuals is minimal (OLS) fits the points better than any other plane. For the calculation of this regression plane the partial derivatives are set equal to zero and the resulting system of equations is solved. This leads to a solution for b_0, $b_{y1.2}$ and $b_{y2.1}$, which together form the vector **b**.

All this can be represented much more briefly when using matrix notation. We let **y** denote the (10×1) vector of dependent variable scores Y. The scores of the independent variables are collected in a matrix **X**, which contains two columns with scores of X_1 and X_2 as well as a first column with 1 scores for finding the intercept. We see that matrix **X** is in fact an augmented (10×3) matrix. The (3×1) vector **b** contains the three parameters b_0, $b_{y1.2}$ and $b_{y1.2}$. This is β for the population. The (10×1) vector **e** collects the residual scores. This is ε for the population.

So, the general linear model can be written as $\mathbf{y} = \mathbf{X}\boldsymbol{\beta} + \boldsymbol{\varepsilon}$ for the population and $\mathbf{y} = \mathbf{Xb} + \mathbf{e}$ for the sample. Let us continue with the sample notation. For the mini data set of the childlessness research we have:

$$
\begin{array}{ccccc}
\mathbf{y} & = & \mathbf{X} & \mathbf{b} & + & \mathbf{e} \\
\begin{bmatrix} 2 \\ 3 \\ 2 \\ 2 \\ 4 \\ 10 \\ 12 \\ 8 \\ 3 \\ 14 \end{bmatrix}
& =
& \begin{bmatrix} 1 & 1 & 1 \\ 1 & 2 & 6 \\ 1 & 3 & 3 \\ 1 & 4 & 2 \\ 1 & 5 & 2 \\ 1 & 6 & 5 \\ 1 & 6 & 9 \\ 1 & 7 & 4 \\ 1 & 9 & 1 \\ 1 & 9 & 7 \end{bmatrix}
& \begin{bmatrix} b_0 \\ b_{y1.2} \\ b_{y2.1} \end{bmatrix}
& +
& \begin{bmatrix} e1 \\ e2 \\ e3 \\ e4 \\ e5 \\ e6 \\ e7 \\ e8 \\ e9 \\ e10 \end{bmatrix} \\
(10 \times 1) & & (10 \times 3) & (3 \times 1) & & (10 \times 1)
\end{array}
$$

The estimated values $\hat{Y}$ together form the (10×1) vector $\hat{\mathbf{y}}$. From the model, we can derive that $\hat{\mathbf{y}} = \mathbf{Xb}$ and $\mathbf{e} = \mathbf{y} - \hat{\mathbf{y}}$.

For the calculation of the vector **b**, the ordinary least squares criterion is applied: the sum $\sum e^2$ of squared residuals must be as small as possible. This sum is written in matrix algebra as the scalar product $\mathbf{e'e}$. The vector which minimizes this scalar product $\mathbf{e'e}$ is obtained by calculating the partial derivatives of $\mathbf{e'e} = (\mathbf{y} - \mathbf{Xb})'(\mathbf{y} - \mathbf{Xb})$, setting these equal to zero and solving for the resulting system of equations. The result is: $\mathbf{b} = (\mathbf{X'X})^{-1}\mathbf{X'y}$.

We first calculate the product of the transposed matrix $\mathbf{X'}$ and **X**, as well as the product of $\mathbf{X'}$ and **y**:

$$
\mathbf{X'X} = \begin{bmatrix} 1 & 1 & 1 & 1 & 1 & 1 & 1 & 1 & 1 & 1 \\ 1 & 2 & 3 & 4 & 5 & 6 & 6 & 7 & 9 & 9 \\ 1 & 6 & 3 & 2 & 2 & 5 & 9 & 4 & 1 & 7 \end{bmatrix}
\begin{bmatrix} 1 & 1 & 1 \\ 1 & 2 & 6 \\ 1 & 3 & 3 \\ 1 & 4 & 2 \\ 1 & 5 & 2 \\ 1 & 6 & 5 \\ 1 & 6 & 9 \\ 1 & 7 & 4 \\ 1 & 9 & 1 \\ 1 & 9 & 7 \end{bmatrix}
= \begin{bmatrix} 10 & 52 & 40 \\ 52 & 338 & 224 \\ 40 & 224 & 226 \end{bmatrix}
$$

$$X'y = \begin{bmatrix} 1 & 1 & 1 & 1 & 1 & 1 & 1 & 1 & 1 & 1 \\ 1 & 2 & 3 & 4 & 5 & 6 & 6 & 7 & 9 & 9 \\ 1 & 6 & 3 & 2 & 2 & 5 & 9 & 4 & 1 & 7 \end{bmatrix} \begin{bmatrix} 2 \\ 3 \\ 2 \\ 2 \\ 4 \\ 10 \\ 12 \\ 8 \\ 3 \\ 14 \end{bmatrix} = \begin{bmatrix} 60 \\ 383 \\ 329 \end{bmatrix}$$

We calculate the inverse of matrix **X'X**:

$$(X'X)^{-1} = \cfrac{\begin{bmatrix} \begin{vmatrix} 338 & 224 \\ 224 & 226 \end{vmatrix} & -\begin{vmatrix} 52 & 224 \\ 40 & 226 \end{vmatrix} & \begin{vmatrix} 52 & 338 \\ 40 & 224 \end{vmatrix} \\[6pt] -\begin{vmatrix} 52 & 40 \\ 224 & 226 \end{vmatrix} & \begin{vmatrix} 10 & 40 \\ 40 & 226 \end{vmatrix} & -\begin{vmatrix} 10 & 52 \\ 40 & 224 \end{vmatrix} \\[6pt] \begin{vmatrix} 52 & 40 \\ 338 & 224 \end{vmatrix} & -\begin{vmatrix} 10 & 40 \\ 52 & 224 \end{vmatrix} & \begin{vmatrix} 10 & 52 \\ 52 & 338 \end{vmatrix} \end{bmatrix}}{10\begin{vmatrix} 338 & 224 \\ 224 & 226 \end{vmatrix} - 52\begin{vmatrix} 52 & 224 \\ 40 & 226 \end{vmatrix} + 40\begin{vmatrix} 52 & 338 \\ 40 & 224 \end{vmatrix}}$$

$$= \cfrac{\begin{bmatrix} 26212 & -2792 & -1872 \\ -2792 & 660 & -160 \\ -1872 & -160 & 676 \end{bmatrix}}{42056}$$

$$= \begin{bmatrix} 0.623 & -0.066 & -0.045 \\ -0.066 & 0.016 & -0.004 \\ -0.045 & -0.004 & 0.016 \end{bmatrix}$$

The product of $(X'X)^{-1}$ and $(X'y)$ is vector **b**:

$$b = (X'X)^{-1}X'y = \begin{bmatrix} 0.623 & -0.066 & -0.045 \\ -0.066 & 0.016 & -0.004 \\ -0.045 & -0.004 & 0.016 \end{bmatrix} \begin{bmatrix} 60 \\ 383 \\ 329 \end{bmatrix}$$

$$= \begin{bmatrix} -2.68 \\ 0.78 \\ 1.16 \end{bmatrix}$$

So, in using matrix algebra, we have obtained the multiple regression function $\hat{Y} = -2.68 + 0.78X_1 + 1.16X_2$ in a much shorter way.

5.4.13   SPSS for Windows Output of Multiple Regression Analysis

For the mini example of childlessness research we now present the SPSS for Windows output (some of which will be suppressed for reasons of space). The reader can easily verify whether our results calculated by hand coincide with the output.

Choosing or creating a data file
How to open an SPSS session and how to choose a data file or, if a data file does not yet exist, how to enter data, to choose name, type and label of variables and to save the data file with extension *.sav*, is shown in Chapter 4.

Running the statistical procedure
Click on Statistics. Click on Regression. Click on Linear. A subdialog box for Linear Regression appears. Click on variable Y in the Source Variable list on the left and click on the ▶ push button of the Dependent Variable. Click on the variables X_1 and X_2 in the Source Variable list (either separately or together by means of the click and drag technique) and click on the ▶ push button of the Independent Variables. The default method is Enter. This will suit you.

Click on Statistics. A subdialog box Linear Regression: Statistics appears. You will see that Estimates and Model Fit are already selected. You can click on Confidence Intervals, Covariance Matrix, Descriptives, Block Summary, Durbin Watson and Collinearity Diagnostics, depending on your choices. Click on Continue.

Click on Plots. Click on *ZPRED and click on the ▶ push button of Y. Click on *ZRESID and click on the ▶ push button of X. A plot of the standardized predicted values as a function of the standardized residuals is now requested. Click on Next and do the same for the standardized predicted values and the studentized residuals (*SDRESID), if you want to. Click on Histogram to obtain a histogram of the standardized residuals. Click on Normal Probability Plot. Click on Casewise Plot and then on the radio button next to All Cases. Click on Continue. Click on OK.

SPSS now runs the statistical procedure and an output window appears with the results of multiple regression analysis. Do not forget to save it: click on File, click on Save as, type *chldln.lst* and click on OK.

Alternatively, you can run this statistical procedure by opening a syntax window and typing SPSS commands. Click on File, click on New, click on SPSS Syntax, type the statements, put the cursor anywhere in the first command line and click on ▶ (or on Run for the 5.0 version).

The 'statements' are:

```
1 REGRESSION /DESCRIPTIVES ALL
2     /VARIABLES Y, X1, X2
3     /STATISTICS ALL
4     /DEPENDENT Y
5     /METHOD ENTER X1 X2
6     /SCATTERPLOT      (*ZPRED *ZRESID)
7                       (*ZPRED *SDRESID)
8     /RESIDUALS DEFAULTS
9     /CASEWISE ALL.
```

Statement 1 requests all 'descriptives': means, standard deviations, variances, number of units, correlation matrix, covariance matrix, matrix of sums of squares and cross products (= matrix of variations and covariations) and one-tailed significance levels for the correlation coefficients.

Statements 2, 4 and 5 indicate that three variables are in play, where Y is the dependent variable and where the independent variables X_1 and X_2 are entered together in a single step (enter). Other methods besides 'enter', are 'forward', in which variables are entered one at a time, 'backward', in which all variables are entered and then removed one at a time, and 'stepwise', in which variables are examined at each step for entry or removal. The stepwise method is the most intelligent. The entry or removal of variables is based on priorally specified criteria with regard to the F test of model significance. In the decision as to whether a variable should be entered, the default values of F and the empirical significance level of F (probability of F-to-enter) are, respectively, 3.84 and 0.05, and in a decision for removal, these values are 2.71 and 0.10.

Statement 3 requests all 'statistics': the multiple correlation coefficient, its square, adjusted R square, its standard error, the analysis of variance table with F value and empirical significance level p, the change in R^2, F and p between steps, the partial regression coefficients, their standard error, their standardized version 'beta', their confidence interval, t value and two-tailed significance level of t, the zero-order correlations, partial correlations (see following chapter), tolerance and other statistics.

Statements 6, 7, 8 and 9 focus on the analysis of residuals. 'Casewise = all' requests a plot of the standardized residuals of all ten cases. We see in the display that limits are set at a deviation of three standard deviations from the mean 0. The actual deviations are much smaller. Note that values of $\hat{Y}$ and of $e = Y - \hat{Y}$ coincide perfectly with the values we calculated by hand. They are represented in the output as *PRED and *RESID. The standardized residuals are indicated as *ZRESID. These are printed as a result of the 'Residuals' subcommand. (Remark: instead of standardized residuals, Studentized residuals can also be calculated and sometimes give more precise results.)

The 'Residuals' statement also displays, firstly, a histogram of standardized residuals for confrontation with the normal distribution, secondly, a normal probability plot, which is also used for testing the normality assumption, and a number of descriptive measures. The program ends with the requested 'scatterplots'. The model assumptions are not violated. The (intentionally limited) output follows below.

```
* * * *   M U L T I P L E   R E G R E S S I O N   * * * *

Listwise Deletion of Missing Data
Mean  Std Dev  Label

Y          6.000    4.595  change in % childlessness
X1         5.200    2.741  change in labour participation
X2         4.000    2.708  change in mean age at marriage
```

```
N of Cases =    10
Correlation:
                Y           X1          X2
Y            1.000        .626        .795
X1            .626       1.000        .240
X2            .795        .240       1.000


Equation Number 1    Dependent Variable..   Y   change in % childlessness
Block Number  1.  Method:  Enter      X1       X2
Equation Number 1    Dependent Variable..   Y   change in % childlessness

Variable(s) Entered on Step Number
    1..   X2         change in mean age at marriage
    2..   X1         change in labour participation
Multiple R           .91292
R Square             .83342
Adjusted R Square    .78583
Standard Error       2.12636
Analysis of Variance
                     DF      Sum of Squares      Mean Square
Regression           2           158.35020         79.17510
Residual             7            31.64980          4.52140


F =      17.51119        Signif F =  .0019
------------------ Variables in the Equation ------------------

Variable             B          SE B        Beta        T   Sig T

X2            1.160453      .269585     .683947     4.305   .0035
X1             .775632      .266376     .462650     2.912   .0226
(Constant)   -2.675100     1.678698                -1.594   .1551

Casewise Plot of Standardized Residual
*: Selected    M: Missing

             -3.0      0.0      3.0
Case #    0:.......:........:0      Y       *PRED       *RESID
    1    .          .   *     .     2     -.7390       2.7390
    2    .      *    .         .     3     5.8389      -2.8389
    3    .        * .         .     2     3.1332      -1.1332
    4    .         *.         .     2     2.7483       -.7483
    5    .          .*        .     4     3.5240        .4760
    6    .          .   *     .    10     7.7810       2.2190
    7    .         *.         .    12    12.4228       -.4228
    8    .          .*        .     8     7.3961        .6039
    9    .      *    .         .     3     5.4660      -2.4660
   10    .          . *       .    14    12.4288       1.5712
Case #    0:.......:........:0      Y       *PRED       *RESID
             -3.0      0.0      3.0

Residuals Statistics:
                     Min         Max      Mean    Std Dev    N

*PRED              -.7390     12.4288    6.0000     4.1946   10
*RESID            -2.8389      2.7390     .0000     1.8753   10
*ZPRED            -1.6066      1.5326     .0000     1.0000   10
*ZRESID           -1.3351      1.2881     .0000      .8819   10
Total Cases =       10
```

```
Durbin-Watson Test =    2.28958

Outliers - Standardized Residual
Case #        *ZRESID

      2        -1.33509
      1         1.28812
      9        -1.15975
      6         1.04359
     10          .73893
      3         -.53291
      4         -.35193
      8          .28399
      5          .22387
      7         -.19882
```

Normal Probability (P-P) Plot
Standardized Residual

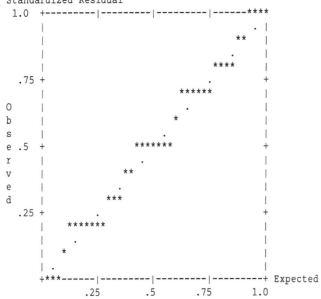

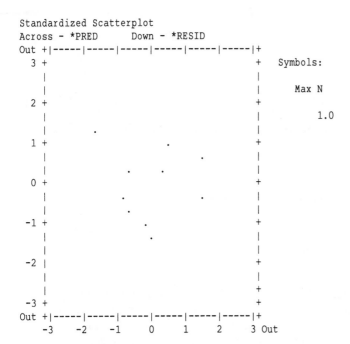

```
Standardized Scatterplot
Across - *PRED      Down - *RESID
Out +|-----|-----|-----|-----|-----|-----|+
  3 +                              +      Symbols:
    |                              |
    |                              |        Max N
  2 +                              +
    |                              |          1.0
    |        .                     |
  1 +                 .            +
    |                              |
    |             .     .          |
  0 +                              +
    |          .            .      |
    |           .                  |
 -1 +              .               +
    |                .             |
    |                              |
 -2 |                              +
    |                              |
    |                              +
 -3 +                              +
Out +|-----|-----|-----|-----|-----|-----|+
      -3    -2    -1    0     1     2     3 Out
```

Partial Correlation and Path Analysis: The Causal Influence of Christian Beliefs on Anti-Semitism

6.1 The Research Problem and the Causal Diagram

In most social scientific research problems, a problem-variable is postulated and a series of causal factors is sought which together offer an explanation for the problematic phenomenon. The basic format of such a research problem is the convergent causal structure with one effect variable and several causal factors. Now, instead of a problem-variable it is also possible to take a problem-relation as the starting point. An example of a problem-relation is the causal influence of Christian beliefs on anti-Semitism. The question under discussion is whether the correlation between Christian beliefs and secular anti-Semitism in present-day society can be seen as a direct causal effect. For it might be possible that other antecedent factors produce Christian beliefs as well as anti-Semitism. In that case, the relationship between religious orthodoxy (X_1) and anti-Semitism (Y) is explained away by these factors. It is only apparently causal. An example of such an antecedent variable is dogmatism (X_2). There is a positive causal effect of X_2 on X_1 (the more dogmatic, the more orthodox) and of X_2 on Y (the more dogmatic, the greater the dislike of Jews). This mechanism of spurious causality is represented by Figure 6.1. The plus signs indicate a positive relationship (the more, the more and the less, the less). The question mark indicates that the originally postulated relationship between X_1 and Y might be spuriously causal.

So, three variables are involved in the analysis. Let us assume that all three have been measured at the interval level. The technique which is applied in that case is partial correlation analysis. The antecedent factor dogmatism (X_2) is the control variable. The general idea is that the original relationship between religion (X_1) and anti-Semitism (Y) will almost disappear when controlling for X_2. This means that

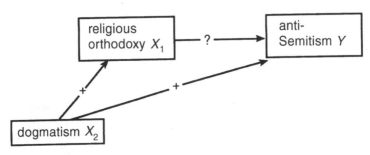

Figure 6.1   Mechanism of spurious causality

persons showing differences in religious orthodoxy will also differ in their degree of anti-Semitism, but that this covariation is almost entirely due to differences in dogmatism. For subgroups of persons with equal scores on dogmatism, this relationship between religion and anti-Semitism should disappear. This is the mechanism of partial correlation analysis in its ideal form. The initial correlation between X_1 and Y is said to be 'spurious' and it is therefore common to speak of 'spurious correlation'.

Taking the problem-relation between religious orthodoxy and anti-Semitism as the starting point and supposing that it is not directly causal: it is also possible that this relationship will not appear to be spurious, but that a form of indirect causality is at work, via intermediate factors. An example of an intermediate variable is the libertarian attitude (X_3). There is a negative causal effect of X_1 on X_3 (the more orthodox, the less libertarian) and of $\dot{X}_3$ on Y (the less libertarian, the stronger the dislike for Jews). The causal diagram in Figure 6.2 represents this mechanism of indirect causality.

The minus signs in Figure 6.2 indicate a negative relationship (the more, the less and the less, the more). The question mark points out that the originally postulated association between X_1 and Y might not be direct but indirectly causal in nature. Partial correlation analysis is applied here as well. As in the case of spurious causality, the common variance of X_1 and Y for indirect causality is almost completely due to the variance that they share with the control variable (here X_3). For subgroups of persons with identical scores on the libertarian attitude, the relationship between religion and anti-Semitism will almost disappear. Thus, the calculating mechanism is the same for both indirect causality and spurious causality. The order of the causal arrows, however, is different. The control variable X_3 now lies between X_1 and Y. In other words, the scheme is now causal-friendly, for religious orthodoxy does have a causal effect on anti-Semitism, albeit not directly, but indirectly via the libertarian attitude as the intermediate factor.

In the investigation into the causal influence of Christian beliefs on anti-Semitism, both schemes of spurious and indirect causality were in fact applied in combination. Social–psychological characteristics, like dogmatism, acted as antecedent variables and other factors, like the libertarian attitude, played the role of intermediate variables. Moreover, several background variables, like age, educational level and others, were included in the causal model. These are sometimes called exogenous variables. They are mostly situated to the left of the causal diagram, because they are considered deeper-lying causal factors, which themselves are not causally influenced

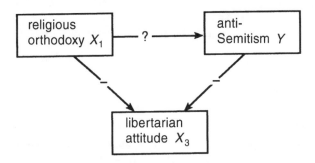

Figure 6.2 Mechanism of indirect causality

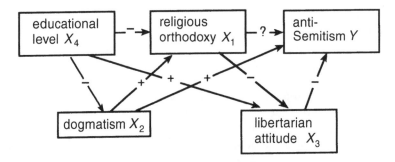

Figure 6.3   System of causal chains

by other factors. For example, the educational level (X_4) has a positive causal effect on the libertarian attitude and a negative causal effect on dogmatism and religious orthodoxy. Its causal effect on anti-Semitism is not direct, but indirect and negative via dogmatism (the higher the education, the less dogmatic and therefore the less anti-Semitic) and via libertarianism (the higher the education, the more libertarian and therefore the less anti-Semitic).

The causal diagram, in which not only anti-Semitism, religion and dogmatism, but also the educational level is included, now becomes a complex system of causal chains, as is represented in Figure 6.3.

Such a complex causal model is investigated by means of path analysis, with which we will deal in the following sections. We start with the simple mechanism of partial correlation analysis.

6.2   The Data Matrix

The units of analysis are persons. In our (fictitious) mini data set we consider $n = 10$ units. All variables have been measured at the quantitative level with scores from 0 to 9.

Variable Y is the degree of anti-Semitism.
X_1 is the degree of religious orthodoxy.
X_2 is the degree of dogmatism.
X_3 is the libertarian character of the attitude toward life.
X_4 is the educational level.

The data matrix is as shown in Table 6.1. This yields the correlation matrix shown in Table 6.2.

6.3   Partial Correlation Analysis

6.3.1   The Model

Let us first refer to the investigation of the partial correlation between religion (X_1) and anti-Semitism (Y), controlling for dogmatism (X_2).

There are many ways to look at this partial correlation. We obtain the best

Table 6.1   Data matrix

	Y	X_1	X_2	X_3	X_4
	3	2	1	8	9
	3	1	2	8	6
	2	5	3	6	4
	6	2	3	5	7
	4	3	4	7	6
	5	6	5	4	4
	6	5	6	4	5
	4	8	7	6	5
	9	7	8	2	1
	8	3	9	5	6
mean	5.0	4.2	4.8	5.5	5.3
standard deviation	2.261	2.348	2.658	1.900	2.111

Table 6.2   Correlation matrix

	Y	X_1	X_2	X_3	X_4
Y	1.000	0.251	0.777	−0.802	−0.442
X_1	0.251	1.000	0.612	−0.623	−0.731
X_2	0.777	0.612	1.000	−0.704	−0.582
X_3	−0.802	−0.623	−0.704	1.000	0.762
X_4	−0.442	−0.731	−0.582	0.762	1.000

understanding from the viewpoint according to which the influence of X_2 is removed from X_1 as well as from Y, so that the partial correlation becomes the simple zero-order correlation between the residual terms $X_1 - \hat{X}_1$ and $Y - \hat{Y}$. This mechanism involves three steps.

In the first step a bivariate regression analysis is performed from X_1 on X_2. The estimated $\hat{X}_1$ values are calculated and the difference of $X_1 - \hat{X}_1$ yields the residual scores. The dispersion of these residual scores indicates to what measure X_1 still varies when the common variance with X_2 is removed. In terms of the model, this first step can be represented by the figure below, in which the dashes through the arrow indicate that the influence of X_2 is removed.

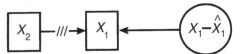

In the second step, a bivariate regression analysis of Y on X_2 is performed. The estimated $\hat{Y}$ values are calculated and the difference of $Y - \hat{Y}$ yields the residual scores that are freed from X_2.

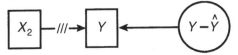

In the third step $X_1 - \hat{X}_1$ and $Y - \hat{Y}$ are correlated. This zero-order correlation between the residuals is the partial correlation coefficient $r_{y1.2}$. If we indicate this coefficient as a double-sided arrow and if we bring all three steps together in one model, then we obtain the picture represented in Figure 6.4.

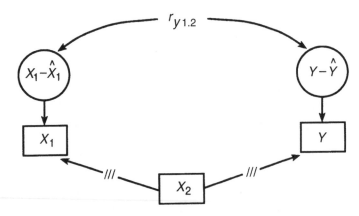

Figure 6.4   The model of partial correlation analysis

Therefore, the partial correlation coefficient $r_{y1.2}$ is the zero-order product-moment correlation coefficient between Y and X_1, after the common variance with X_2 is removed from both variables.

Instead of X_2 (dogmatism), it is also possible that X_3 (libertarianism) or X_4 (educational level) is the control variable. In these cases, the partial correlation coefficients are $r_{y1.3}$ and $r_{y1.4}$, respectively. These partial correlations are first-order coefficients, because one controls for only one variable. The model can be extended for higher-order partial correlations with several control variables. In the third-order coefficient $r_{y1.234}$, the partial correlation between Y and X_1 is calculated, controlling for X_2, X_3 and X_4. In that case, the first step is not a bivariate, but a multiple regression analysis of X_1 on X_2, X_3 and X_4, resulting in the residual term $X_1 - \hat{X}_1$. The second step is a multiple regression analysis of Y on X_2, X_3 and X_4, yielding the residual term $Y - \hat{Y}$. The zero-order correlation between $X_1 - \hat{X}_1$ and $Y - \hat{Y}$ is, then, the coefficient $r_{y1.234}$. The visual representation is given in Figure 6.5.

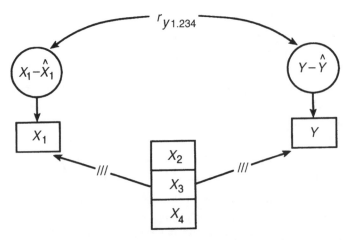

Figure 6.5   The model of higher-order partial correlation analysis

For the population, Greek instead of Latin letters are used. The sample coefficients $r_{y1.2}$, $r_{y1.3}$, $r_{y1.4}$ and $r_{y1.234}$, which are indicated above, are then written as ρ instead of r.

6.3.2 Geometric Approach

The foregoing model of the partial correlation as the zero-order correlation between the residuals can be represented in three-dimensional space for the first-order partial correlation (with one control variable). In Figure 6.6, the three axes are drawn for religion (X_1), anti-Semitism (Y) and the control variable dogmatism (X_2). Together, they form a $10 \times 10 \times 10$ cube. On the lateral face at the front and to the left, the bivariate association between X_2 and X_1 is represented. The encircled points are the (X_2, X_1) couples of numbers. The straight line through these points is the regression function $\hat{X}_1 = 1.60 + 0.54X_2$, which is estimated from OLS and which has X_1 as the dependent and X_2 as the independent variable. The distances of the couples of numbers to this $\hat{X}_1$ line are indicated as line segments and represent the scores $X_1 - \hat{X}_1$. In the figure, these residuals are lifted to the upper surface of the cube, making use of parallel translations.

Analogously, the bivariate association between X_2 and Y is represented on the lateral face at the front and to the right. The encircled points are the (X_2, Y) couples. The estimated regression function with Y as the dependent and X_2 as the independent variable is $\hat{Y} = 1.83 + 0.66X_2$. Here, too, the residuals $Y - \hat{Y}$ are transposed to the upper surface by means of translation. Encircled points are drawn in the upper surface at the place where the residuals of the (X_2, X_1) plane and the residuals of the (X_2, Y) plane meet. The residual axes $X_1 - \hat{X}_1$ and $Y - \hat{Y}$ are also indicated in the upper surface by means of transposition of the regression functions.

If we perform a bivariate regression analysis between the residual scores $X_1 - \hat{X}_1$ and $Y - \hat{Y}$, then we obtain two regression functions: $Y - \hat{Y} = -0.346(X_1 - \hat{X}_1) + e$ and $X_1 - \hat{X}_1 = -0.587(Y - \hat{Y}) + e$. These two regression lines are shown in the upper surface as dashed lines. The regression coefficients -0.346 and -0.587 are both negative. The geometric mean $[(-0.346)(-0.587)]^{1/2} = -0.450$ is, as we know, the correlation coefficient between $X_1 - \hat{X}_1$ and $Y - \hat{Y}$. This is the partial correlation coefficient $r_{y1.2}$.

We can also obtain the latter by applying the formula for the zero-order correlation coefficient for the $X_1 - \hat{X}_1$ scores and the $Y - \hat{Y}$ scores.

On the upper surface, we have also drawn the bivariate analysis between X_1 and Y, without controlling for X_2. The (X_1, Y) couples are indicated as crosses and for the two regression functions $\hat{Y} = 3.98 + 0.24X_1$ and $\hat{X}_1 = 2.90 + 0.26Y$ full lines have been used. Both regression coefficients b_{y1} and b_{1y} are positive, as is the correlation coefficient $r_{y1} = 0.25$, which is the geometric mean of 0.24 and 0.26.

We clearly see here how drastic the mechanism of partial correlation analysis can be. While the original association between religion and anti-Semitism was positive ($r_{y1} = 0.25$), it appears not only to become stronger when controlling for dogmatism, but, moreover, it changes sign ($r_{y1.2} = -0.45$). In terms of contents, this would mean that the relationship between religion and anti-Semitism originally appeared to be moderate and positive (the more religious, the more anti-Semitic), but this relationship turns out to be strong and negative for persons with the same score on dogmatism (the more religious, the less anti-Semitic). The reason for this drastic

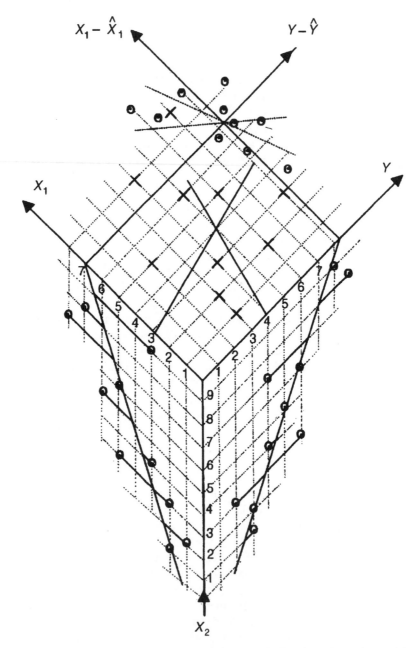

Figure 6.6   Partial correlation as zero-order correlation between the residual
scores

difference between the correlation and the partial correlation is that there is a strong association between the control variable X_2 and each of the variables X_1 and Y. We saw this in the figure on the two lateral faces of the cube, which represent the association between X_2 and X_1 and between X_2 and Y, respectively. The correlation coefficients $r_{21} = 0.61$ and $r_{2y} = 0.78$ are both very strong. Therefore, the correlation $r_{1y} = 0.25$ presents a misleading idea of the association between religion and anti-Semitism, for the variance that is shared by both variables is predominantly produced by the variance that they share with dogmatism.

This example shows that the mechanism of 'spurious correlation' should not be naively understood as the disappearance of a relationship when controlling for an antecedent factor. It appears that a weak relationship can also become stronger after the control and even that the sign of the relationship can change. The reader can imagine a table with 25 possibilities, in which both the original relationship and the partial relationship are rated as strongly negative, weakly negative, zero, weakly positive or strongly positive. Our example of religion and anti-Semitism shows one of these possibilities: the original relationship is weakly positive and the partial relationship is strongly negative.

Another way to represent the mechanism of partial correlation analysis geometrically follows the line of thought that one can form many subgroups of individuals with equal scores on dogmatism. In order to be able to draw this in a figure, we would have to work with many numbers (not $n = 10$ as in the mini example, but, e.g., $n = 2000$). For we would have to perform a bivariate analysis between X_1 and Y for each value of X_2 separately. Geometrically, this would mean that the (X_1, Y, X_2) cube would be cut into horizontal slices, one for each score on dogmatism, and that a $X_1 - Y$ scattergram with corresponding regression function would be plotted for each slice. Such a relationship between X_1 and Y for a fixed score of X_2 is called a 'conditional relationship', because the relationship between X_1 and Y is investigated under the 'condition' that $X_2 = k$. In Figure 6.7, it is shown how, for a fictitious data set of $n = 30$ individuals, a negative association between X_1 and Y can be split into ten positive conditional relationships. The 30 individuals are drawn in the upper surface. The total relationship is negative, which is indicated by the dashed regression line, for which increasing values of X_1 coincide with decreasing values of Y. Each of the ten planes below, one for $X_2 = 1$, one for $X_2 = 2$, one for $X_2 = 3$, etc., contains three individuals and the regression lines are indicated by dashed lines. It appears that these conditional $X_1 - Y$ relationships are all positive.

The geometric interpretation of the partial correlation can also be made in the vector model, in which the individuals form the axes and in which the three variables are located as points (endpoints of vectors) within this space of individuals. In this vector model the partial correlation coefficient $r_{1y.2}$ is equal to the cosine of the angle Θ between the projections of the vectors $\vec{x}_1$ and $\vec{y}$ on the surface that is perpendicular to the vector $\vec{x}_2$. Figure 6.8 is borrowed from J. Van de Geer (1971, p. 107). A further elaboration for higher-order coefficients can be found in M.G. Kendall and A. Stuart (1969, p. 328).

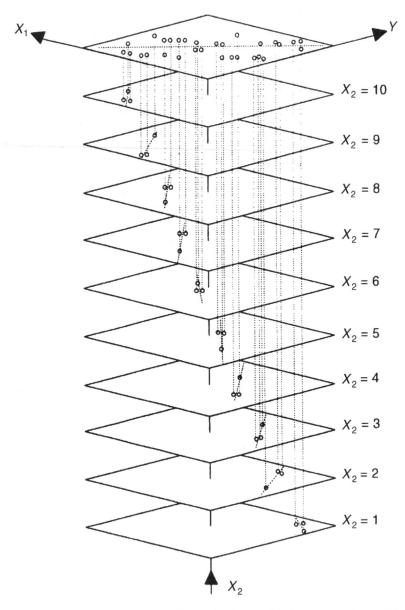

Figure 6.7   The unravelling of a total relationship into several conditional relationships

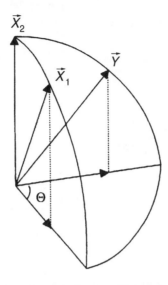

Figure 6.8 The partial correlation coefficient in the vector model

6.3.3 *Objectives of the Technique*

Partial correlation analysis as a calculation technique has three objectives. With the example of the causal influence of Christian beliefs (X_1) on anti-Semitism (Y) as background and restricting ourselves to one control variable (dogmatism X_2 or libertarianism X_3), the purposes of partial correlation analysis can be summarized as follows:

1. We investigate whether the relationship between X_1 and Y is spurious. This comes down to the comparison of the original correlation coefficient r_{1y} and the partial correlation coefficient $r_{1y.2}$, in which the control variable X_2 is an antecedent test variable, i.e., a variable that is causally prior to X_1 and Y.
2. We want to know whether the association between X_1 and Y is indirectly causal. In this case we compare the original correlation coefficient r_{1y} with the partial correlation coefficient $r_{1y.3}$. The control variable X_3 is now an intermediate test variable, lying between X_1 and Y with respect to causal order.
3. We analyse whether the partial correlation coefficient found in the sample can be generalized for the population. This means that we perform a significance test.

6.3.4 *Calculation of the Partial Correlation*

We will first calculate the first-order coefficient $r_{1y.2}$ and in doing so will follow the procedure of the foregoing sections according to the model of partial correlation analysis. In a first step, a bivariate regression analysis of X_1 as a function of X_2 is performed, the estimated values of X_1 are calculated and the difference of $X_1 - \hat{X}_1$ gives us the residual scores. In a second step, a bivariate regression analysis of Y as a function of X_2 is performed, the estimated $\hat{Y}$ values are calculated and the difference of $Y - \hat{Y}$ provides the residual scores, which are decontaminated from X_2. In a third step, the zero-order correlation coefficient between $X_1 - \hat{X}_1$ and $Y - \hat{Y}$ is calculated.

Table 6.3   Calculating the partial correlation

Step 1: $\hat{X}_1 = 1.60 + 0.54X_2$				Step 2: $\hat{Y} = 1.83 + 0.66X_2$			
X_1	X_2	$\hat{X}_1$	$X_1 - \hat{X}_1$	Y	X_2	$\hat{Y}$	$Y - \hat{Y}$
2	1	2.15	−0.15	3	1	2.49	0.51
1	2	2.69	−1.69	3	2	3.15	−0.15
5	3	3.23	1.77	2	3	3.81	−1.81
2	3	3.23	−1.23	6	3	3.81	2.19
3	4	3.77	−0.77	4	4	4.47	−0.47
6	5	4.31	1.69	5	5	5.13	−0.13
5	6	4.85	0.15	6	6	5.79	0.21
8	7	5.39	2.61	4	7	6.45	−2.45
7	8	5.93	1.07	9	8	7.11	1.89
3	9	6.47	−3.47	8	9	7.77	0.23

Step 3: $\qquad r_{(X_1-\hat{X}_1)(Y-\hat{Y})} = r_{y1.2} = -0.45$

This is the partial correlation coefficient $r_{y1.2}$. All these operations are brought together in Table 6.3.

We have already discussed in the geometric approach the fact that the effect of partial correlation analysis is very drastic here: the relationship between religion and anti-Semitism, which was originally weak and positive ($r_{1y} = 0.25$), becomes strong and negative when controlling for dogmatism ($r_{1y.2} = -0.45$).

The investigation of indirect causality, in which an intermediate test variable (X_3) rather than an antecedent test variable (X_2) is used, is performed in the same way. The results of the three steps are as follows:

Step 1: $\hat{X}_1 = 11.96 - 0.77X_3$
Step 2: $\hat{Y} = 10.25 - 0.95X_3$
Step 3: $r_{1y.3} = -0.53$

Here, too, we see that the association between Christian belief and anti-Semitism, which was initially weak and positive ($r_{1y} = 0.25$), changes into a strong and negative relationship after having controlled for libertarianism ($r_{1y.3} = -0.53$). The reason for this drastic turn has to be found in the strong and negative correlations between X_3 and each of the original variables X_1 and Y ($r_{13} = -0.62, r_{y3} = -0.80$): the more religious, the less libertarian and the less libertarian, the more anti-Semitic.

A Computational Formula for the Partial Correlation Coefficient
It can easily be shown that the partial correlation coefficient ($r_{y1.2}$) is equal to a fraction, of which the numerator is the difference between the original correlation (r_{y1}) and the product of the marginal relationships ($r_{y2}r_{12}$) and of which the denominator is the geometric mean (the $\sqrt{}$ of the product) of the proportions of variance of the original variables Y and X_1 that cannot be explained by the control variable X_2 (i.e., of the residual variances: $1 - r_{y2}^2$ and $1 - r_{12}^2$) :

$$r_{y1.2} = \frac{r_{y1} - r_{y2}r_{12}}{[(1 - r_{y2}^2)(1 - r_{12}^2)]^{1/2}}$$

The **derivation**, in which some prior knowledge of correlation and regression analysis is presupposed, runs as follows.

We start with the formula for the zero-order correlation coefficient:

$$r_{y1} = \frac{\frac{1}{n}\sum(X_1 - \bar{X}_1)(Y - \bar{Y})}{\frac{1}{n}[\sum(X_1 - \bar{X}_1)^2 \sum(Y - \bar{Y})^2]^{1/2}}$$

In this formula, the numerator is the covariance s_{1y} and the denominator is the product $s_1 s_y$ of the standard deviations (or the geometric mean of the variances), so that:

$$r_{1y} = \frac{s_{1y}}{s_1 s_y} = \frac{s_{1y}}{(s_1^2 s_y^2)^{1/2}}$$

The formula for the partial correlation coefficient can be constructed in the same manner:

$$r_{1y.2} = \frac{s_{1y.2}}{s_{1.2} s_{y.2}} = \frac{s_{1y.2}}{(s_{1.2}^2 s_{y.2}^2)^{1/2}}$$

We first develop the numerator $s_{1y.2}$. We know that the general formula for a covariance between X_1 and Y is:

$$s_{1y} = \frac{1}{n}\sum(X_1 - \bar{X}_1)(Y - \bar{Y}) = \frac{1}{n}\sum x_1 y$$

For reasons of simplicity we write $X_1 - \bar{X}_1$ as x_1 and $Y - \bar{Y}$ as y; in other words we use lower case letters for deviations of the mean. Another advantage of using these 'deviation of mean' scores is that the intercepts of the regression equations drop.

Now, we do not need s_{1y}, but rather $s_{1y.2}$. This covariance is the mean of the products of residual scores, after having removed the effect of X_2 on each of the variables X_1 and Y:

$$s_{1y.2} = \frac{1}{n}\sum(x_1 - \hat{x}_1)(y - \hat{y})$$
$$= \frac{1}{n}\sum(x_1 - b_{12}x_2)(y - b_{y2}x_2) \qquad \text{[no intercepts!]}$$
$$= \frac{1}{n}\sum\left(x_1 - r_{12}\frac{s_1}{s_2}x_2\right)\left(y - r_{y2}\frac{s_y}{s_2}x_2\right)$$
$$= \frac{1}{n}\left[\sum x_1 y - r_{12}\frac{s_1}{s_2}\sum x_2 y - r_{y2}\frac{s_y}{s_2}\sum x_1 x_2 + r_{12}r_{y2}\frac{s_1 s_y}{s_2^2}\sum x_2^2\right]$$
$$= s_{1y} - r_{12}\frac{s_1}{s_2}s_{2y} - r_{y2}\frac{s_y}{s_2}s_{12} + r_{12}r_{y2}s_1 s_y r_{22}$$

In the denominator we first develop $s_{1.2}^2$. The general formula for a variance in our abbreviated notation is $s_1^2 = 1/n \sum x_1^2$. Similar to this formula, the variance $s_{1.2}^2$ is the summation of the squared residual scores of X_1, after having removed the effect of X_2:

$$s_{1.2}^2 = \frac{1}{n}\sum(x_1 - \hat{x}_1)^2$$

$$= \frac{1}{n}\sum(x_1 - b_{12}x_2)^2$$

$$= \frac{1}{n}\sum\left(x_1 - r_{12}\frac{s_1}{s_2}x_2\right)^2$$

$$= \frac{\sum x_1^2}{n} + r_{12}^2\frac{s_1^2}{s_2^2}\frac{\sum x_2^2}{n} - 2r_{12}\frac{s_1}{s_2}\frac{\sum x_1 x_2}{n}$$

$$= s_1^2 + r_{12}^2\frac{s_1^2}{s_2^2}s_2^2 - 2r_{12}\frac{s_1}{s_2}r_{12}s_1 s_2$$

$$= s_1^2 + r_{12}^2 s_1^2 - 2r_{12}^2 s_1^2$$

$$= s_1^2 - r_{12}^2 s_1^2$$

$$= s_1^2(1 - r_{12}^2)$$

Similarly, we have:

$$s_{y.2}^2 = s_y^2(1 - r_{y2}^2)$$

Hence, the denominator is:

$$(s_{1.2}^2 s_{y.2}^2)^{1/2} = [s_1^2(1 - r_{12}^2)s_y^2(1 - r_{y2}^2)]^{1/2}$$

$$= s_1 s_y[(1 - r_{12}^2)(1 - r_{y2}^2)]^{1/2}$$

Division of numerator by denominator gives us the promised formula:

$$r_{y1.2} = \frac{s_{1y} - r_{12}\frac{s_1}{s_2}s_{2y} - r_{y2}\frac{s_y}{s_2}s_{12} + r_{12}r_{y2}s_1 s_y r_{22}}{s_1 s_y[(1 - r_{12}^2)(1 - r_{y2}^2)]^{1/2}}$$

$$= \frac{r_{1y} - r_{12}r_{2y} - r_{y2}r_{12} + r_{12}r_{y2}}{[(1 - r_{12}^2)(1 - r_{y2}^2)]^{1/2}}$$

$$= \frac{r_{1y} - r_{12}r_{y2}}{[(1 - r_{12}^2)(1 - r_{y2}^2)]^{1/2}}$$

In our example, this leads to the desired result:

$$r_{1y.2} = \frac{0.251 - (0.612)(0.777)}{[(1 - 0.612^2)(1 - 0.777^2)]^{1/2}} = -0.451$$

We can obtain this formula in many other ways. One other method is the use of the formula of the normal distribution. For one variable, we would speak of the 'univariate normal distribution'. For example, for X_1 this distribution has the following formula (in which the expression $\exp[-y]$ stands for e^{-y}) :

$$f(X_1) = \frac{1}{\sigma_1\sqrt{2\pi}}\exp\left[-\frac{1}{2}\frac{(X_1 - \mu_1)^2}{\sigma_1^2}\right]$$

This distribution is a function of two parameters: μ_1 and σ_1, i.e., the mean and the standard deviation of X_1. The formula can be extended for two or more variables. For two variables, we speak of 'bivariate normal distribution' and, for several variables, of 'multivariate normal distribution'. The number of parameters is much larger now: many means $\mu_1, \mu_2, \ldots$, many standard deviations $\sigma_1, \sigma_2, \ldots$ and, in addition, the associations — covariances or correlations — between each pair of variables (only one such association in the bivariate case).

The formula of the partial correlation coefficient $r_{1y.2}$ is then found by applying the product rule $p(A, B) = p(A|B)p(B)$ of probability calculus, in which $A = \{X_1, Y\}$ and $B = X_2$. Thus, the factor $p(A|B)$ is the bivariate normal probability distribution of X_1 and Y for a fixed X_2, i.e., $f(\{X_1, Y\}|X_2)$, and this can be written as $p(A, B)$ divided by $p(B)$, i.e., as the quotient of the trivariate normal probability distribution $f(X_1, Y, X_2)$ and the univariate normal probability distribution $f(X_2)$. Manipulation of the naturally rather complex formulae appears to result in a bivariate normal distribution of $X_1|X_2$ and $Y|X_2$, of which the correlation parameter is $r_{1y.2}$ and is equal to the formula that we have derived above for the partial correlation coefficient. The derivation can be found in matrix notation in Kendall and Stuart (1969, pp. 317–318) and, in more elaborate algebraic notation, in Brownlee (1965, pp. 429–430).

Kendall and Stuart (1969, pp. 328–329) also succeeded in deriving the formula geometrically in the vector model, a derivation that is warmly recommended to the reader who enjoys intellectual pieces of art.

Still another way to find the formula for $r_{1y.2}$ is the one used in path analysis, which will be dealt with in the next sections. Path coefficients are standardized partial regression coefficients and these can be expressed as functions of zero-order correlation coefficients as follows:

$$b^*_{y1.2} = (r_{y1} - r_{12}r_{y2})/(1 - r^2_{12})$$

With X_1 as the dependent and Y as the independent variable, this is:

$$b^*_{1y.2} = (r_{y1} - r_{12}r_{y2})/(1 - r^2_{y2})$$

Just as the zero-order correlation coefficient r_{1y} is the geometric mean of the two regression coefficients b_{y1} and b_{1y}, in the same way the first-order partial correlation coefficient $r_{1y.2}$ is the geometric mean of the two partial regression coefficients $b_{y1.2}$ and $b_{1y.2}$ or of their standardized versions $b^*_{y1.2}$ and $b^*_{1y.2}$. Indeed, we see that:

$$(b^*_{y1.2}b^*_{1y.2})^{1/2} = \left[\frac{(r_{y1} - r_{12}r_{y2})}{(1 - r^2_{12})}\frac{(r_{y1} - r_{12}r_{y2})}{(1 - r^2_{y2})}\right]^{1/2}$$

$$= \frac{(r_{y1} - r_{12}r_{y2})}{[(1 - r^2_{12})(1 - r^2_{y2})]^{1/2}} = r_{1y.2}$$

This formula can easily be extended for higher-order coefficients. For example, if we, in addition to X_2, introduce X_4 as a control variable in the investigation of the relationship between X_1 and Y, then we simply write down the formula of $r_{1y.2}$ and we add the control for X_4 to each zero-order correlation in the formula, or, reversing the order: we write the formula for $r_{1y.4}$ and we add the control for X_2 everywhere:

$$r_{1y.24} = \frac{r_{1y.4} - r_{12.4}r_{y2.4}}{[(1 - r^2_{12.4})(1 - r^2_{y2.4})]^{1/2}}$$

$$= \frac{r_{1y.2} - r_{14.2}r_{y4.2}}{[(1 - r^2_{14.2})(1 - r^2_{y4.2})]^{1/2}}$$

We see that the second-order partial correlation coefficient is a function of first-order coefficients. Each higher-order coefficient can be written in this way, i.e., in terms of coefficients of which the order is one lower.

In our example, we have $r_{1y.4} = -0.118$, $r_{12.4} = 0.337$ and $r_{y2.4} = 0.712$, so that:

$$r_{1y.24} = [-0.118 - (0.337)(0.712)]/[(1 - 0.337^2)(1 - 0.712^2)]^{1/2} = -0.541$$

6.3.5   The Coefficient of Part Correlation

The part correlation coefficient $r_{y(1.2)}$, which is also called the semipartial correlation coefficient by Hays, differs from the partial correlation coefficient $r_{y1.2}$ in the following respect: the influence of the control variable X_2 is removed from X_1, but not from Y.

Referring to the model of partial correlation analysis, the three steps are now reduced to two. In the first step, the residual scores $X_1 - \hat{X}_1$ from a bivariate regression analysis of X_1 on X_2 are calculated. In the second and last step we calculate the zero-order correlation coefficient between these residual scores $X_1 - \hat{X}_1$ and the original Y scores. This, then, is the part correlation coefficient $r_{y(1.2)}$. For higher-order coefficients, like $r_{y(1.24)}$, it holds in the same way that the influence of the control variables X_2 and X_4 (plural!) is removed from X_1, but not from Y. In our research example of anti-Semitism this means that a correlation coefficient is calculated between the original scores on anti-Semitism, on the one hand, and the scores on religion, cleared of dogmatism and educational level, on the other hand.

When dealing with considerations of content, part correlation finds little application. One reason why part correlation could be preferred to partial correlation in practical empirical research is that the variance of Y would almost disappear when removing the influence of the control variable X_2 from it, so that there would be little left to explain. In such a case, the control variable would of course be a very special one, because it would share its variance almost entirely with one of the considered variables. For instance, dogmatism would then be interchangeable with anti-Semitism and the part correlation between the religion score, purified of dogmatism, and anti-Semitism would then come down to the part correlation between the religion score, purified of dogmatism, and dogmatism itself.

An example of a more appropriate use of the part correlation coefficient can be found in the research of Colson (1977, p. 216) into the influence of the age structure on natality in a sample of countries. The age structure was operationalized as the mean age (A) and natality as the gross birth coefficient (B). But as the latter is not independent of the age structure, and vice versa, as the mean age A contains a fertility component, a problem of contamination arose. This problem can be solved in two ways if we include fertility as a variable, which is measured as the raw reproduction figures (R) and of which we know that it is independent of the age structure. A first procedure is the calculation of the correlation coefficient between A and R, i.e., the association between the age structure and age-free fertility. A second procedure, which was chosen by the author because he wanted to explain natality, is the calculation of the part correlation coefficient $r_{B(A.R)}$ between natality (measured as B) and the fertility-free age structure (residual scores of A after removing the influence of R).

This is an example of the appropriate use of part correlation analysis, provided that one is aware that one does not always know which concepts remain after the decontamination procedure. It is therefore advisable, if possible, to preserve a conceptual distance between the original concepts (age structure and natality).

Computational Formulae for Partial and Part Correlation

In the foregoing we attempted to demonstrate the relevance of the part correlation in terms of contents. However, its power is predominantly formal in nature. Many formulae can be developed for the part correlation coefficient, and for each of these formulae an equivalent for the partial correlation coefficient can be derived. We will now make some derivations for the coefficient $r_{y(1.24)}$ of the anti-Semitism research example.

The part correlation is, in its squared form, the increase in the proportion of the explained variance of Y that emerges when adding X_1 to the $\{X_2, X_4\}$ set:

$$r^2_{y(1.24)} = R^2_{y.124} - R^2_{y.24}$$
$$= 0.720 - 0.604 = 0.116$$

We get a bit more insight into this formula when we rewrite it as follows:

$$R^2_{y.124} = R^2_{y.24} + r^2_{y(1.24)}$$

The multiple determination coefficient $R^2_{y.124}$ is the proportion of the variance of Y that is explained by X_1, X_2 and X_4 together. This is 0.720. This proportion can be split additively into two parts. The first part $R^2_{y.24}$ is the proportion of the variance of Y that is explained by X_2 and X_4 together. This is 0.604. The second part is the proportion that is additionally due to X_1, after the latter is freed from the influence of X_2 and X_4. This is the squared part correlation coefficient $r^2_{y(1.24)} = 0.116$.

If X_1 is uncorrelated with X_2 and X_4, then this increase in R^2 is simply equal to r^2_{y1}. On the other hand, if X_1 is strongly associated with X_2 and X_4, then the squared part correlation will be very different from the original squared correlation r^2_{y1}. This is indeed the case in our example ($r^2_{y1} = 0.063$ against $r^2_{y(1.24)} = 0.116$).

Now, if the other variables X_2 and X_4 together explain a substantial proportion of the variance of Y, then there is not much left for X_1 to explain. In such a case, the part correlation $r^2_{y(1.24)}$ is unfairly small and will be hardly comparable with the situation in which the control variables do not explain a great amount. It is therefore wiser to divide the 'absolute' increase in R^2 by the proportion of the variance of Y that is not explained by X_2 and X_4. In doing so, we obtain the squared partial correlation coefficient, which is thus equal to the 'relative' increase in the proportion of the explained variance of Y that emerges when adding X_1 to the $\{X_2, X_4\}$ set:

$$r^2_{y1.24} = \frac{R^2_{y.124} - R^2_{y.24}}{1 - R^2_{y.24}}$$

$$= \frac{0.720 - 0.604}{1 - 0.604} = 0.293$$

Consequently, the squared partial correlation is obtained by dividing the squared part correlation by the part that is not explained by the control variables:

$$r^2_{y1.24} = \frac{r^2_{y(1.24)}}{1 - R^2_{y.24}} \quad \text{whence} \quad r_{y1.24} = \frac{r_{y(1.24)}}{(1 - R^2_{y.24})^{1/2}}$$

In our example:

$$0.293 = \frac{0.116}{1 - 0.604} \quad \text{and} \quad -0.541 = \frac{-0.341}{(1 - 0.604)^{1/2}}$$

Let us now discuss yet another way to compare the partial and part correlation. This time, we start with the partial correlation coefficient $r_{y1.24}$. Our starting point is the general knowledge from bivariate analysis that $r_{y1} = b_{y1}(s_1/s_y)$. This formula can be extended for the partial correlation coefficient $r_{y1.24}$, which is consequently equal to the partial regression coefficient $b_{y1.24}$ multiplied by the ratio of two standard deviations. The latter are, however, not the standard deviations s_1 and s_y as in the bivariate case, but the standard deviations of the residual scores after regression of X_1 and Y on the control variables X_2 and X_4. These are, respectively, $s_1(1 - R^2_{1.24})^{1/2}$ and $s_y(1 - R^2_{y.24})^{1/2}$. Hence, the formula becomes:

$$r_{y1.24} = b_{y1.24} \frac{s_1(1 - R^2_{1.24})^{1/2}}{s_y(1 - R^2_{y.24})^{1/2}}$$

$$= -0.511 \frac{2.348(1 - 0.587)^{1/2}}{2.261(1 - 0.604)^{1/2}} = -0.541$$

In this formula

$b_{y1.24}(s_1/s_y)$ is equal to $b^*_{y1.24}$, whence:

$$r_{y1.24} = b^*_{y1.24} \frac{(1 - R^2_{1.24})^{1/2}}{(1 - R^2_{y.24})^{1/2}}$$

$$= -0.531 \frac{(1 - 0.587)^{1/2}}{(1 - 0.604)^{1/2}} = -0.541$$

As we will see in the next sections, the standardized partial regression coefficient $b^*_{y1.24}$ is equal to the path coefficient p_{y1} in an analysis with Y as the dependent and X_1, X_2 and X_4 as the independent variables.

The part correlation coefficient, for which the control on X_2 and X_4 is performed for X_1, but not for Y, can be derived simply from the foregoing formulae by removing the factor $(1 - R^2_{y.24})^{1/2}$:

$$r_{y(1.24)} = b_{y1.24} \frac{s_1}{s_y} (1 - R^2_{1.24})^{1/2} = b^*_{y1.24}(1 - R^2_{1.24})^{1/2}$$

$$= -0.511 \frac{2.348}{2.261} (1 - 0.587)^{1/2} = -0.531(1 - 0.587)^{1/2}$$

$$= -0.341$$

6.3.6 The Significance Tests

We saw in multiple regression analysis how the test of a significant contribution of one predictor can be performed by means of the model comparison approach. The significance tests of $r_{y1.24}$, $r_{y(1.24)}$ and $b_{y1.24}$ are identical.

6.4 The Simon–Blalock Procedure for Complex Causal Models

In his famous article 'Spurious Correlation, a Causal Interpretation', Herbert Simon (1954) demonstrated that the same statistical evidence is required for the scheme $X \leftarrow Z \rightarrow Y$ of spurious causality as for the scheme $X \rightarrow Z \rightarrow Y$ of indirect causality. Both causal mechanisms obtain empirical support when the partial correlation coefficient $r_{xy.z}$ is equal to zero.

In our example, the relationship between religion (X_1) and anti-Semitism (Y) is explained away by dogmatism (X_2) if the correlation r_{y1} changes into a negligibly small partial correlation $r_{y1.2}$, as a result of the control for X_2. And, similarly, the relationship between X_1 and Y is intermediated by the libertarian attitude (X_3) if $r_{y1.3}$ tends to zero. The fact that X_2 is causally prior to both variables and that X_3 is situated in between, is determined on non-statistical grounds. The statistical test only decides whether the direct causal effect of X_1 on Y can be removed, i.e., whether the arrow $X_1 \rightarrow Y$ should be removed in both schemes.

Following in Simon's footsteps, this idea that the omission of an arrow in a causal model can be tested by setting a partial correlation equal to zero, has been further developed by Hubert Blalock for complex causal models. His most widely cited contribution in this field is the chapter entitled 'Evaluating Causal Models' of his book *Causal Inferences in Nonexperimental Research* (Blalock, 1961).

The rationale proposed by Blalock for the evaluation of causal models only holds when all arrows run in the same direction, i.e., when dealing with recursive models without direct or indirect feedback. We will make it a rule to visualize this recursivity in all figures in imagining an axis of causal order from the left to the right. Causes will always be drawn to the left of their effects, causes of causes still more to the left, etc. The factors that are situated most to the left are called exogenous variables, because they are no longer influenced by causal factors within the model. In our example, the educational level is such an exogenous variable. The causal diagram is shown in Figure 6.9.

This model can be represented by a system of regression equations. A first equation contains Y as the dependent variable and X_1, X_2 and X_3 as direct causal factors. The second equation shows X_3 as a function of X_1 and X_4. In the third equation, X_1 is a function of X_2 and X_4. And the last equation represents the direct causal effect of X_4

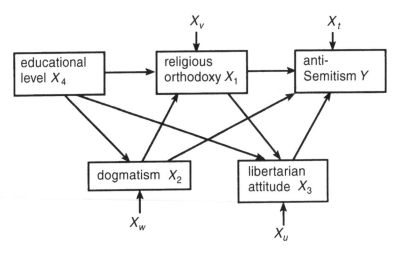

Figure 6.9   Causal diagram

on X_2. So, there is one equation for each dependent variable where arrows arrive, and the independent variables of an equation are the 'direct' causal factors from which the arrows take their departure.

Moreover, a residual variable is added in each regression equation. For example, X_t indicates which portion of Y remains to be explained after X_1, X_2 and X_3 together have executed their causal influence. We assume that a residual variable (X_t) is not associated with the other causal factors in the regression equation (X_1, X_2, X_3).

The system of regression equations that coincides with our causal model can now be written down. As the variables are written as deviations of their mean (lower case letters!), the intercepts can be left out.

$$\begin{bmatrix} y = b_{y1.23}x_1 + b_{y2.13}x_2 + b_{y3.12}x_3 + b_{yt.123}x_t \\ x_3 = b_{31.4}x_1 + b_{34.1}x_4 + b_{3u.14}x_u \\ x_1 = b_{12.4}x_2 + b_{14.2}x_4 + b_{1v.24}x_v \\ x_2 = b_{24}x_4 + b_{2w.4}x_w \end{bmatrix}$$

Blalock argues that the omission of an arrow in the causal model coincides with equating the corresponding partial regression coefficient to zero. For instance, in the first equation, in which Y is the dependent variable, the direct causal effect of X_4 on Y is missing. It must therefore be assumed that $b_{y4.123} = 0$. For the second equation, X_1, X_2 and X_4 are the potential direct causes of X_3, because they are situated more to the left of the causal order axis. However, only X_1 and X_4 are included in the equation. Consequently, the assumption is that $b_{32.14} = 0$.

Note that one should never control for dependent variables. We also do not need to control for factors that are not related to the variables under consideration, because it would be unnecessary to control for factors that do not have the power to bring about the mechanism of spurious or indirect causality.

In the last two regression equations there are no omitted factors, so that no partial regression coefficients can be set at zero.

Now, the formulae of a partial regression coefficient and the corresponding partial correlation coefficient have the same numerator. For example, the formulae for $b_{y2.14}$ and $r_{y2.14}$ both have $r_{y2.4} - (r_{y1.4})(r_{21.4})$ as their numerator.[1] A fraction is equal to 0 if the numerator is 0. So, the assumption that $b_{y2.14} = 0$ comes to the same thing as $r_{y2.14} = 0$. It follows that the omission of an arrow in the causal model can also be represented by equating a partial correlation to zero.

In the recursive model of our research example, two arrows are omitted: $X_4 \rightarrow Y$ and $X_2 \rightarrow X_3$. Consequently, the assumptions are that $r_{y4.123}$ and $r_{32.14}$ are both equal to 0. These assumptions are predictions which can be used to test the validity of the causal model. By way of illustration, we take $r_{32.14} = 0$. The numerator of $r_{32.14}$ is $r_{32.4} - (r_{31.4})(r_{21.4})$. In the computer output we can read that $r_{32.4} = -0.494$, $r_{31.4} = -0.149$ and $r_{21.4} = 0.337$. So, the numerator of $r_{32.14}$, which should be equal to zero according to the postulated model, is in fact equal to $-0.494 - (-0.149)(0.337) = -0.444$. The difference between what was expected according to the model and what was in fact observed is so substantial here that the validity of the model should be rejected. The arrow $X_2 \rightarrow X_3$ cannot be omitted with impunity.

In summary, the Simon–Blalock procedure offers the opportunity to test the validity of a complex causal model. For each arrow that is omitted, we examine whether the corresponding (higher-order) partial correlation coefficient is equal to zero. In doing so, we only have to control for factors that are related to both variables under consideration. One should not control for dependent variables.

The procedure is only appropriate for recursive causal models. A number of assumptions have to be made, for instance the absence of correlations between residual variables and 'direct' causal factors. This and other assumptions will be dealt with extensively in the section on path analysis.

6.5 Path Analysis

The procedure developed by Simon and introduced into sociology by Blalock, according to which partial correlations are set equal to zero, has a prehistory as well as a posthistory. In taking the viewpoint that regression coefficients are asymmetrical in nature and are therefore better suited for the representation of causal effects than are correlation coefficients, Blalock and his followers took the step from the Simon-procedure to path analysis.

In fact, this path analysis, in which the path coefficients are equal to the standardized partial regression coefficients, had already been developed a long time ago by Sewell Wright (1918, 1921, 1934) for problems in genetics. In the 1950s, this path analysis was introduced into econometrics by Herman Wold (1954, 1956, 1960) under another name: 'Structural Equation Models' or 'Simultaneous Equation Models'.

---

[1] For the non-standardized partial regression coefficient, s_y is in the numerator as well, but that does not alter the argument.

Whereas Simon and Goldberger remained within econometrics with their contributions, it was Blalock who opened up the causal model approach to other scientific disciplines.

Following in his footsteps, Raymond Boudon (1965, 1967) developed his dependency analysis, which can also be applied to variables of non-metric measurement levels.

Lazarsfeld (1955, 1961, 1968) and Coleman (1964) have also contributed indirectly to these developments, although they are not associated with causal analysis.

Nowadays, the further development of path analysis has been overrun by the introduction of Jöreskog's (1973) 'linear structural relations system' (LISREL), in which a solution is proposed for each of the rigid assumptions of path analysis; Feedback, inclusion of latent variables, associations among residuals and other possibilities which were unimaginable in the past decades are provided in LISREL.

Before dealing with path analysis, let us first discuss a number of classifications made in methodological literature. Some of these classifications have already been dealt with in multiple regression analysis. Here, we are concerned with the problem of causality. In preparation for path analysis, we ask ourselves whether the proposed classifications are related to causality. In our opinion, this is not the case for classification on the basis of the **measurement level of variables** (quantitative, ordinal, nominal or mixed). There are, however, some authors who wish to restrict causal statements to quantitative regularities, and other authors are inclined to restrict themselves to dichotomous variables, because they are reasoning from a bivalent logic. Both viewpoints are unrealistic, certainly when keeping methodology for social–scientific research in mind. Causal models for each of the measurement levels are indeed provided for. The distinction is purely statistical and technical in nature and has nothing to do with the causality problem as such.

This is also the case for the classification of causal models according to their **identification status** (over, under or perfect identification). Identification refers to the possibility of finding a solution for the system of mathematical equations that coincides with the postulated causal model and is therefore simply a working-condition. For instance, overidentification (more equations than unknowns) is a condition for forming extra test equations in addition to the global evaluation of the model, through which, according to some authors, causal order may be tested.

Another classification gives the different **estimation procedures** which can be used in solving the system of mathematical equations representing the causal model. As a general rule, we apply the ordinary least squares estimation (OLS), which was discussed in multiple regression analysis. But, in applying OLS to non-recursive models, serious problems of bias arise, so that other estimation procedures have to be chosen, such as indirect least squares and the instrumental variable method. An additional problem emerges when such a non-recursive model is overidentified, because the same system of equations will then lead to several solutions. In such cases even more estimation procedures are required, such as two-stage least squares estimation or maximum likelihood estimation.

Another number of classifications in methodological literature are directly related to causality. The pre-eminent example is the distinction between **recursive** models, in which all causal influences run in the same direction, and **non-recursive** models, in which this is not the case.

Another classification, closely related to the problem of recursive vs. non-recursive systems, distinguishes between **static** models, in which all variables, causal factors as well as effect factors, are observed at the same moment in time, and **dynamic** models, in which the observations are performed at different moments in time. Philosophically speaking, we know that the causal category is of the dynamic type, but that the dynamics are not necessarily or not exclusively represented by the time dimension (*post hoc ergo propter hoc* sophism). The restriction to temporal order, however, is built-in in the methodological literature for operational reasons. Panel research and time series analysis serve as model designs. The fact that social–scientific researchers seldom use dynamic models and have the habit of designing one-moment surveys, may give rise to criticism. But that does not alter the fact that static models can still represent causal dynamics in many cases.

A more recent classification distinguishes between causal models with **observed** variables and models with **non-observed** variables, which are also called latent variables, hypothetical constructs or theoretical concepts. The latter group of models form a combination of causal structure analysis (CSA) and latent structure analysis (LSA). The idea is that causal arguments are situated on the theoretical level and that observations are merely practical indications or manifestations of these underlying theoretical relationships between concepts. In this viewpoint, which is built-in in Jöreskog's LISREL, the distinction between cause and indicator plays an important role.

In the last few decades, more and more attention has been paid to the distinction between **linear** and **non-linear** causal models. The performance of a linearity test, which we discussed in multiple regression analysis, should become a standard procedure.

Closely linked to linearity is the **problem of additivity**. Here, a distinction is made between additive and non-additive models. The latter category refers to systems in which interaction terms are included. We already know from multiple regression analysis that these interaction effects take the form of product terms. We will give an additional explanation of these non-additive mechanisms in the treatment of analysis of variance and covariance.

Another topic of great controversy is the question of whether the variables included in a causal model should be **standardized**. Standardization means that the variables are transformed in such a way that their mean becomes 0 and their standard deviation becomes 1, so that they become mutually comparable. The classification, then, distinguishes between causal models with standardized variables and models with unstandardized variables. According to some authors, the parameters or coefficients of models with unstandardized variables should be called structural or fundamental. This distinction is, in our opinion, an exaggeration. Standardization is simply a question of the verification and stamping of weights and measures in order to reach comparability. If we aim at the mutual comparison of the influences of different causal factors in one and the same causal model, then it is better to standardize, because the raw scores of these factors have different units of measurement. If, on the other hand, it is the objective to compare one or more parameters of a causal model in different populations, then it is better to use unstandardized coefficients. One technical reason is that unstandardized coefficients are invariant for different popula-tions, even when the variances of exogenous and residual variables of these populations differ, whereas this is not the case for standardized coefficients (see Opp and Schmidt, 1976, p. 127).

A last subject, which is receiving more and more attention, is the problem of **multicollinearity**. Collinearity or, in the case of several variables, multicollinearity, means that there are substantial correlations among the causal factors of a multi-causal model. We know from multiple regression analysis that multicollinearity is a real problem, because the estimations of the sample parameters become very inefficient, as they entail large standard errors. And, consequently, we are left in uncertainty as to the value and the sign of the corresponding parameters in the population. These problems are not only technical in nature, but are also related to content. For, the requirement that multicollinearity should remain low really means that the causal factors in a multicausal model have to execute their causal influence independently. It is evident that this gives rise to the question of whether such causal models without multicollinearity are in fact realistic for social science data. Pleas have been made both for and against this idea.

Thus far, we have discussed a number of classifications which have been made in the methodology of social science research and upon which strategies of causal research are grounded. With these classifications in mind, we can say that the 'prototype' of the causal models is **quantitative** (in order to apply correlation and regression analysis), **identified** (in order to find a solution for the model), **recursive** (in order to use the ordinary least squares estimation), **static** (because one-moment surveys are common practice, so that no extra problems of autocorrelation arise), **directly observed** (so that no distinction should be made between cause and indicator or between latent and manifest variables), **linear** (so that the interpretations remain simple and linear correlation and regression analysis can be applied), **additive** (so that no interaction terms have to be included), **standardized** (for comparability in one and the same population) and **without multicollinearity** (in order to avoid inefficient estimations). This 'prototype' is **path analysis**.

Our representation of this technique is adopted from the work of Karl-Dieter Opp and Peter Schmidt (1976). They have given an outline of the working method in 13 steps.

Step 1: *A priori formulation of the hypotheses, the causal diagram and the structural equations*

We have already made these formulations in the treatment of the Simon-Blalock procedure. The hypotheses are:

1. Religious orthodoxy has a direct and positive causal effect on anti-Semitism.
2. The effect of religion on anti-Semitism is cancelled, to a large extent, by the direct and positive causal effect of dogmatism on each of the variables (spurious causality).
3. The effect of religion on anti-Semitism is, to a large extent, indirect because of the direct and negative causal effect of religious orthodoxy on libertarianism on the one hand and the direct and negative causal effect of the libertarian attitude on anti-Semitism on the other hand.

4. The causal effects of the educational level on anti-Semitism all run indirectly via religion, dogmatism and libertarianism. These indirect causal effects are all negative. For, the direct causal effects of the educational level on religion and dogmatism are both negative and the direct causal effect of the educational level on the libertarian attitude is positive. As a result, the indirect effects of the educational level on anti-Semitism are, respectively, as follows:

$$
\begin{aligned}
&\text{education} \xrightarrow{-} \text{religion} \xrightarrow{+} \text{anti-Semitism} \\
&\text{education} \xrightarrow{-} \text{dogmatism} \xrightarrow{+} \text{anti-Semitism} \\
&\text{education} \xrightarrow{+} \text{libertarianism} \xrightarrow{-} \text{anti-Semitism}
\end{aligned}
$$

Application of the sign rule $(-.+ = -$ and $+.- = -)$ results in a negative causal effect in all cases. The postulated causal diagram (with signs included) is shown in Figure 6.10.

We can now write the structural equations that coincide with this diagram (omitting the control factors in the partial regression coefficients for reasons of simplicity):

$$
\begin{bmatrix}
y = b_{y1}x_1 + b_{y2}x_2 + b_{y3}x_3 + b_{yt}x_t \\
x_3 = b_{31}x_1 + b_{34}x_4 + b_{3u}x_u \\
x_1 = b_{12}x_2 + b_{14}x_4 + b_{1v}x_v \\
x_2 = b_{24}x_4 + b_{2w}x_w
\end{bmatrix}
$$

Variable X_4 is called exogenous, because it is no longer influenced by other causal factors in the model. Y, X_1, X_2 and X_3 are endogenous or dependent variables, because they are influenced by at least one causal factor. X_t, X_u, X_v and X_w are residual variables. The status of variables X_1, X_2 and X_3 is double. They are independent as well as dependent, i.e., cause as well as effect. If their effect character

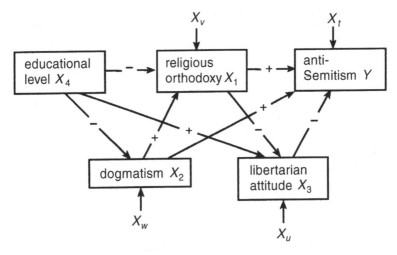

Figure 6.10   Causal diagram with signs included

is stressed, they are called predetermined variables. On the other hand, when their causal character is emphasized, they are 'predetermining variables', because they are not residual and they have a causal effect on an endogenous variable. This effect can be direct or indirect. For example, with respect to the endogenous variable Y, the variables X_1, X_2 and X_3 are directly predetermining, whereas X_4 is indirectly predetermining. Another element of the causal diagram is the double-sided curved arrow, which stands for the correlation between two variables, leaving it an open question whether a causal interpretation is involved. Such a double-sided curved arrow is absent in our causal diagram, but referring to the results of the Simon–Blalock analysis, according to which the relationship $X_2 - X_3$ should not be omitted, we may imagine such a correlation between dogmatism and libertarianism.

We can read in the diagram that the *a priori* formulation of the hypotheses is sometimes restricted to the indication of the signs of the causal influences. For instance, it is expected that religion and dogmatism have a positive causal effect on anti-Semitism. The effect of libertarianism, on the other hand, is expected to be negative. This mostly involves an interpretation of the form 'The more ..., the more ...' and 'the more ..., the less ...' respectively. Strictly speaking, the regression coefficients (b) or the **path coefficients** (p), which will be inferred in step 3, ought to be postulated *a priori*. Now, we can imagine that this might be possible for certain coefficients in econometrics, for example the consumption rate, which measures the effect of income on consumption from an underlying linear regression viewpoint and which shows some degree of stability for certain periods in western countries. But for sociology we cannot imagine such an example. Instead of postulating the exact prior values, one might simply be satisfied with the indication of the **intervals** within which the coefficients are expected to lie. Another possibility, which is applied more and more in social sciences, is the *a priori* **arrangement** of coefficients according to their magnitude. This strategy contains the idea that certain causal factors execute a greater influence than others. The last possibility is the restriction to the indication of **signs**, as was done in our example. For any hypothetical–deductive argument, this is a minimum requirement that really must be fulfilled. If not, we are no longer testing hypotheses, but are rather following a *post factum* procedure, which leads to the *a posteriori* conclusion that X_3 has the greatest influence, that X_2 has a positive effect, etc.

It should be mentioned here that the term *a priori* (or *a posteriori*) is not used in the Kantian but in the Bayesian sense, which means that the hypotheses are formulated before (or after) taking cognizance of the empirical results in a practical research context. De Finetti (1964) proposed using the terms initial and final, which may be more adequate. However, the terms *a priori* and *a posteriori* are of such frequent use that a deviating use would be unwarranted.

Step 2: Verify whether the conditions for application of path analysis are fulfilled

All variables are measured at the **quantitative** (interval or ratio) level. The postulated model is **recursive**, i.e., there is no direct or indirect feedback. The determination of the **identification status** of a model is not always simple, for, even in the case of perfect identification in a theoretical respect, it may appear afterwards that a model shows empirical underidentification. A model is considered to be identified when there are as many correlations between observed variables $[\binom{5}{2} = 10]$ as there are parameters in the model. The number of parameters is equal to the number of paths, including the correlations between exogenous variables, but exclusive of the paths from residual to endogenous variables. In our example, the model is overidentified, because the number of informative data (10) is greater than the number of parameters to be estimated (8). The model contains only **directly observed** variables. The relationships between these variables are considered to be **linear** and **additive**. We know that there are tests, making use of the data, to check afterwards whether these assumptions of linearity and additivity are falsified. These tests can be found in Opp and Schmidt (1976, pp. 194 and 221). It is also assumed that there is **absence of high multi-collinearity**. This is especially a problem in models with several exogenous variables, but, even in our model, in which only one exogenous variable is present, each equation should be checked separately to determine whether the intercorrelations among the independent variables are not too high.

If all these conditions are fulfilled, then path analysis can be applied. It may be mentioned, too, that the causal model is **static**. Temporal dynamics is not a strict requirement for the application of the technique, because static models may represent a process of causal dynamics. Sometimes dynamic models create extra interpretation problems because of built-in autocausation. An additional requirement is that **residual** and **directly predetermining** variables are **uncorrelated**. This will be discussed separately in step 6.

Step 3: Standardization of the variables

In standardizing each variable, i.e., subtracting the mean and dividing by the standard deviation, z scores are obtained $[z = (X - \mu)/\sigma]$. In doing so, the regression coefficients (b) become path coefficients (p), which can also be obtained by multiplying the regression coefficients by the standard deviation of the independent variable and dividing it by the standard deviation of the dependent variable. We get more insight into this mechanism in the following derivation:

$$\begin{bmatrix} Y = b_{y1}X_1 + b_{y2}X_2 + b_{y3}X_3 + b_{yt}X_t + \text{a constant} \\ X_3 = b_{31}X_1 + b_{34}X_4 + b_{3u}X_u + \text{a constant} \\ X_1 = b_{12}X_2 + B_{14}X_4 + b_{1v}X_v + \text{a constant} \\ X_2 = b_{24}X_4 + b_{2w}X_w + \text{a constant} \end{bmatrix}$$

We will now do three things for each equation of this system. Firstly, we express each variable as a deviation of its mean, so that the constant terms disappear. Secondly, the dependent variable to the left of the equal sign is divided by its standard deviation. In order to restore the equality, we must then also divide all terms to the right of the equal sign by this standard deviation of the dependent variable.

Thirdly, we divide each independent variable $X_i - \bar{X}_i$ by its standard deviation s_i and we immediately multiply by s_i in order to render the term unchanged. In this way, the foregoing system is rewritten as follows.

$$\frac{Y - \bar{Y}}{s_y} = b_{y1}\frac{s_1}{s_y}\frac{X_1 - \bar{X}_1}{s_1} + b_{y2}\frac{s_2}{s_y}\frac{X_2 - \bar{X}_2}{s_2} + b_{y3}\frac{s_3}{s_y}\frac{X_3 - \bar{X}_3}{s_3} + b_{yt}\frac{s_t}{s_y}\frac{X_t - \bar{X}_t}{s_t}$$

$$\frac{X_3 - \bar{X}_3}{s_3} = b_{31}\frac{s_1}{s_3}\frac{X_1 - \bar{X}_1}{s_1} + b_{34}\frac{s_4}{s_3}\frac{X_4 - \bar{X}_4}{s_4} + b_{3u}\frac{s_u}{s_3}\frac{X_u - \bar{X}_u}{s_u}$$

$$\frac{X_1 - \bar{X}_1}{s_1} = b_{12}\frac{s_2}{s_1}\frac{X_2 - \bar{X}_2}{s_2} + b_{14}\frac{s_4}{s_1}\frac{X_4 - \bar{X}_4}{s_4} + b_{1v}\frac{s_v}{s_1}\frac{X_v - \bar{X}_v}{s_v}$$

$$\frac{X_2 - \bar{X}_2}{s_2} = b_{24}\frac{s_4}{s_2}\frac{X_4 - \bar{X}_4}{s_4} + b_{2w}\frac{s_w}{s_2}\frac{X_w - \bar{X}_w}{s_w}$$

The expressions $(X_i - \bar{X}_i)/s_i$ are z scores of the form z_i and the expressions $b_{yi}(s_i/s_y)$ are path coefficients of the form p_{yi}. So, the system can also be written in the following form.

$$\begin{bmatrix} z_y = p_{y1}z_1 + p_{y2}z_2 + p_{y3}z_3 + p_{yt}z_t \\ z_3 = p_{31}z_1 + p_{34}z_4 + p_{3u}z_u \\ z_1 = p_{12}z_2 + p_{14}z_4 + p_{1v}z_v \\ z_2 = p_{24}z_4 + p_{2w}z_w \end{bmatrix}$$

Step 4: Multiplication of the equations by each of the directly predetermining variables

The result of this operation is a system for each of the four equations.

$$\begin{bmatrix} z_yz_1 = p_{y1}z_1z_1 + p_{y2}z_2z_1 + p_{y3}z_3z_1 + p_{yt}z_tz_1 \\ z_yz_2 = p_{y1}z_1z_2 + p_{y2}z_2z_2 + p_{y3}z_3z_2 + p_{yt}z_tz_2 \\ z_yz_2 = p_{y1}z_1z_3 + p_{y2}z_2z_3 + p_{y3}z_3z_3 + p_{yt}z_tz_3 \end{bmatrix} \quad \text{first system}$$

$$\begin{bmatrix} z_3z_1 = p_{31}z_1z_1 + p_{34}z_4z_1 + p_{3u}z_uz_1 \\ z_3z_4 = p_{31}z_1z_4 + p_{34}z_4z_4 + p_{3u}z_uz_4 \end{bmatrix} \quad \text{second system}$$

$$\begin{bmatrix} z_1z_2 = p_{12}z_2z_2 + p_{14}z_4z_2 + p_{1v}z_vz_2 \\ z_1z_4 = p_{12}z_2z_4 + p_{14}z_4z_4 + p_{1v}z_vz_4 \end{bmatrix} \quad \text{third system}$$

$$[z_2z_4 = p_{24}z_4z_4 + p_{2w}z_wz_4] \quad \text{fourth system (only one equation)}$$

Step 5: Calculation of the means (summation and division by n) and formation of the r equations (r as a function of p)

In each of the equations of each of these systems we make the sum of values across all n individuals and we then divide by n, so that we obtain a number of expressions in which each term $(\sum z_iz_j)/n$ is equal to a correlation coefficient r_{ij}. This operation is demonstrated here for the first system only:

$$\begin{bmatrix} \frac{\sum z_yz_1}{n} = p_{y1}\frac{\sum z_1z_1}{n} + p_{y2}\frac{\sum z_2z_1}{n} + p_{y3}\frac{\sum z_3z_1}{n} + p_{yt}\frac{\sum z_tz_1}{n} \\ \frac{\sum z_yz_2}{n} = p_{y1}\frac{\sum z_1z_2}{n} + p_{y2}\frac{\sum z_2z_2}{n} + p_{y3}\frac{\sum z_3z_2}{n} + p_{yt}\frac{\sum z_tz_2}{n} \\ \frac{\sum z_yz_3}{n} = p_{y1}\frac{\sum z_1z_3}{n} + p_{y2}\frac{\sum z_2z_3}{n} + p_{y3}\frac{\sum z_3z_3}{n} + p_{yt}\frac{\sum z_tz_3}{n} \end{bmatrix} \quad \text{first system}$$

$$\begin{bmatrix} r_{y1} = p_{y1} & + p_{y2}r_{21} + p_{y3}r_{31} + p_{yt}r_{t1} \\ r_{y2} = p_{y1}r_{12} + p_{y2} & + p_{y3}r_{32} + p_{yt}r_{t2} \\ r_{y3} = p_{y1}r_{13} + p_{y2}r_{23} + p_{y3} & + p_{yt}r_{t3} \end{bmatrix} \quad \text{first system}$$

This is a system of r equations (r being a function of p), which is derived from the first structural equation. Such a system of r equations can be formed for each of the four structural equations. Consequently, there are as many systems of r equations as there are endogenous variables. These systems can also be derived from the **fundamental theorem** of path analysis, i.e., $r_{ij} = \sum_q p_{iq}r_{qj}$, in which the indices i and j indicate the two variables and where index q refers to each variable from which direct paths run to X_i. The equations could be further elaborated, if r_{qj} were developed analogously.

For recursive models this fundamental theorem simply comes down to the following **tracing rule**: the correlation between X_i and X_j is the sum of products of path coefficients for all possible tracings from X_j to X_i. The set of tracings includes all the possible routes from X_j to X_i given that: (a) the same variable is not entered twice and (b) a variable has not simultaneously entered and left through an arrowhead, i.e., given that the scheme $\rightarrow X_q \leftarrow$ is absent.

This decomposition of a correlation into products of path coefficients will be discussed again in step 10. We will pay special attention to the fact that we do not merely obtain products of path coefficients in our example here, but rather products of path coefficients and correlation coefficients. (The latter correlation coefficients will be decomposed further.)

For reasons of completeness, we also write down the second, third and fourth systems of r equations.

$$\begin{bmatrix} r_{31} = p_{31} & + p_{34}r_{41} + p_{3u}r_{u1} \\ r_{34} = p_{31}r_{14} + p_{34} & + p_{3u}r_{u4} \end{bmatrix} \quad \text{second system}$$

$$\begin{bmatrix} r_{12} = p_{12} & + p_{14}r_{42} + p_{1v}r_{v2} \\ r_{14} = p_{12}r_{24} + p_{14} & + p_{1v}r_{v4} \end{bmatrix} \quad \text{third system}$$

$$[r_{24} = p_{24} \quad + p_{2w}r_{w4}] \quad \text{fourth system}$$

Step 6: Assumption of zero correlation between residual and directly predetermining variables

Let us take the first system as the example. There are three equations with four parameters to estimate, so that the system is underidentified. In making the assumption that $r_{t1} = r_{t2} = r_{t3} = 0$, the system becomes perfectly identified:

$$\begin{bmatrix} r_{y1} = p_{y1} & + p_{y2}r_{21} + p_{y3}r_{31} \\ r_{y2} = p_{y1}r_{12} + p_{y2} & + p_{y3}r_{32} \\ r_{y3} = p_{y1}r_{13} + p_{y2}r_{23} + p_{y3} \end{bmatrix} \quad \text{first system}$$

For the other systems, all terms to the right-hand side can be omitted analogously.

However, if this requirement of zero correlation between residual and direct causal factors is in fact not fulfilled, then the estimations of the path coefficients are biased.

For instance, if $r_{t1} \neq 0$, then the path coefficient p_{y1} of the first equation would not be equal to $r_{y1} - p_{y2}r_{21} - p_{y3}r_{31}$ but rather to $r_{y1} - p_{y2}r_{21} - p_{y3}r_{31} - p_{yt}r_{t1}$. And it goes without saying that the bias is very serious if r_{t1} is substantial.

We should mention here that the determination of the identification status of the first two systems of r equations does not involve the same argument as for the last two systems. We will come to this point in steps 7 and 11.

Step 7: Calculation of the path coefficients by solving the systems of r equations

Let us start with the fourth system. This is an amazingly simple one. There is only one r equation and, after having assumed that $r_{w4} = 0$, this is reduced to $r_{24} = p_{24}$. It follows that path coefficient p_{24} is equal to correlation coefficient r_{24}, i.e., to -0.582.

The third system contains two r equations in which we substitute the known correlation coefficients:

$$\left[\begin{array}{l} 0.612 = p_{12} + p_{14}(-0.582) \\ -0.731 = p_{12}(-0.582) + p_{14} \end{array} \right.$$

Solution of this system yields: $p_{14} = -0.567$ and $p_{12} = 0.282$.

There are, however, some problems for the first two systems. For, in step 4 we have multiplied by each of the directly predetermining variables, i.e., those appearing in the right-hand term of the structural equation. But, we can also multiply by the indirectly predetermining variables, which are situated still more to the left in the causal diagram and which do not appear in the structural equation. For the third system, there were no such variables. But for the second system, in which X_3 is multiplied by X_1 and X_4, X_2 is such an extra variable.

Now, suppose that we multiply by X_2 as well. We would then obtain (having made the assumption of step 6) an overidentified system of three r equations with two unknowns. The extra r equation is $r_{32} = p_{31}r_{12} + p_{34}r_{42}$.

For the first system, in which Y is multiplied by X_1, X_2 and X_3, X_4 is an extra variable. The additional r equation is $r_{y4} = p_{y1}r_{14} + p_{y2}r_{24} + p_{y3}r_{34}$.

For the present, these extra r equations will not be used, but we would like to point out the fact that they will be used in step 11 in order to perform some tests of the model. For the purpose of estimation of the path coefficients, we will merely follow the same procedure as in the third system. Moreover, it will be shown that this is indeed the most correct procedure.

After substitution of the known correlation coefficients, the second system is as follows:

$$\left[\begin{array}{l} -0.623 = p_{31} + p_{34}(-0.731) \\ 0.762 = p_{31}(-0.731) + p_{34} \end{array} \right.$$

Solution of this system yields: $p_{31} = -0.141$ and $p_{34} = 0.658$. Substitution of the correlation coefficients in the first system results in:

$$\begin{bmatrix} 0.251 = p_{y1} + p_{y2}(0.612) + p_{y3}(-0.623) \\ 0.777 = p_{y1}(0.612) + p_{y2} + p_{y3}(-0.704) \\ -0.802 = p_{y1}(-0.623) + p_{y2}(-0.704) + p_{y3} \end{bmatrix}$$

The solution of this system is: $p_{y1} = -0.582$, $p_{y2} = 0.621$, $p_{y3} = -0.727$.

It is worth mentioning that path coefficients can be given an interesting interpretation, one that was proposed by Wright (1934, p. 164) for squared coefficients. According to him, a squared path coefficient is equal to the proportion of variance of the dependent variable, for which the independent variable is directly responsible, provided that a correction is built in the following fashion. Let us take p_{y1}. Its square, according to Wright, is:

$$p_{y1}^2 = \frac{s_{y.23t}^2}{s_y^2} \cdot \frac{s_1^2}{s_{1.23t}^2}$$

In this formula, $s_{y.23t}^2/s_y^2$ expresses the proportion of the variance of Y which remains after X_2, X_3 and X_t have been kept constant, which is due to X_1. However, if X_2 and X_3 are kept constant, it may be that the variance of X_1 will thereby be reduced as a consequence of the correlations of X_1 with X_2 and X_3. The additional part $s_1^2/s_{1.23t}^2$ is a correction for this reduction. If r_{12} and r_{13} are zero, then this part is equal to 1. If r_{12} and r_{13} are not equal to zero, then $s_1^2/s_{1.23t}^2$ is a correction factor, which restores the reduction of the variance of X_1 that had resulted from keeping X_2 and X_3 constant. Consequently, the squared path coefficient p_{y1}^2 expresses the proportion of the variance of Y, which would be due to X_1 if all other sources of the variance of Y were kept constant and if X_1 kept its variance entirely.

Step 8: Check whether the *a priori* expectations are falsified by the results of step 7

We now have to verify whether the signs of the path coefficients coincide with the signs postulated *a priori* in step 1. As we can read from Figure 6.11, no signs except one are falsified. We only appeared to be wrong about the influence of religion on anti-Semitism. This influence is in fact negative after controlling for dogmatism and the libertarian attitude.

If we had postulated an arrangement or intervals or exact values, then we would have had to verify these as well. How large the deviations would then have to be hasn't been described anywhere in an adequate fashion. After all, this problem is two-faced. As well as a hypothetical–deductive side (comparison of the *a priori* formulated hypotheses and the empirical results), it also has an inferential side (generalization from sample to population). For, if the data set of $n = 10$ units of analysis constitutes a simple random sample of a larger population, then the path coefficients obtained are not necessarily a confident reproduction of the corresponding coefficients in the population. Let us suppose that the 95% confidence interval of $p_{31} = -0.14$ is situated between the limits -0.34 and $+0.06$, then zero or even a positive coefficient would be possible for the population; in other words the result -0.14 would not be significant and might possibly have an unreliable sign. In the methodological

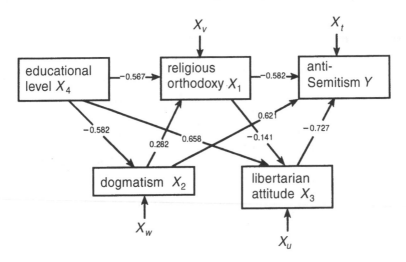

Figure 6.11   Causal diagram with values included

literature, this inferential side of the matter is dealt with under the heading 'significance of a path coefficient'. As statistical significance is a minimum condition of generalizability of the sample results to the population, it forms an essential part of this falsification-step.

Step 9: Calculation of the explained variance and the residual path coefficient

Our original system contained a structural equation for each endogenous (= dependent) variable. In multiplying these structural equations in an analogous way as in steps 4 and 5, this time by the dependent and the residual variable, we make a calculation of the residual path coefficient and the multiple correlation coefficient.

The first structural equation was:

$$z_y = p_{y1}z_1 + p_{y2}z_2 + p_{y3}z_3 + p_{yt}z_t$$

This equation is multiplied by z_y and z_t, which yields the following two equations:

$$
\begin{bmatrix}
r_{yy} = 1 = p_{y1}r_{1y} + p_{y2}r_{2y} + p_{y3}r_{3y} + p_{yt}r_{ty} \\
r_{yt} = p_{y1}r_{1t} + p_{y2}r_{2t} + p_{y3}r_{3t} + p_{yt}r_{tt} \\
\quad = p_{yt} \quad \text{(for } r_{1t} = r_{2t} = r_{3t} = 0 \text{ according to step 6)}
\end{bmatrix}
$$

According to the second of these two equations, r_{yt} and p_{yt} can be equated. In doing so, the residual path coefficient p_{yt} can be derived from the first equation:

$$1 = p_{y1}r_{1y} + p_{y2}r_{2y} + p_{y3}r_{3y} + p_{yt}^2$$
$$p_{yt} = [1 - (p_{y1}r_{1y} + p_{y2}r_{2y} + p_{y3}r_{3y})]^{1/2}$$
$$\quad = \{1 - [(-0.582)(0.251) + (0.621)(0.777) + (-0.727)(-0.802)]\}^{1/2}$$
$$\quad = 0.284$$

And, as $p_{y1}r_{1y} + p_{y2}r_{2y} + p_{y3}r_{3y} = R^2_{y.123}$, it also holds that:

$$p_{yt} = (1 - R^2_{y.123})^{1/2}, \text{ in which } R^2_{y.123} = 0.919$$

Starting from the other three structural equations, we obtain the residual path coefficients in the same fashion:

$$p_{3u} = (1 - R^2_{3.14})^{1/2}, \text{ where } R^2_{3.14} = p_{31}r_{13} + p_{34}r_{43}$$

$$p_{1v} = (1 - R^2_{1.24})^{1/2}, \text{ where } R^2_{1.24} = p_{12}r_{21} + p_{14}r_{41}$$

$$p_{2w} = (1 - r^2_{24})^{1/2}, \text{ where } r_{24} = p_{24} \text{ (bivariate analysis!)}$$

As the square of the multiple correlation coefficient, for instance $R^2_{y.123}$, is interpreted as the proportion of the variance of the dependent variable Y that is explained by X_1, X_2 and X_3 together, so p^2_{yt} expresses the proportion of the variance that remains unexplained. Two sources of unexplained variance are usually distinguished: (1) random factors; (2) causal factors, which were not included in the causal model and are considered as if they merely bring about random dispersion. A requirement is of course that the explained variance (for the sample as well as for the population) is sufficiently high.

Duncan (1975, pp. 63 ff.), however, warns us of the restricted usefulness of the multiple correlation coefficient in a causal model as compared to a predictive model. For, we know that R^2 can be split into predictive contributions of each of the predictors in such a way that the proportions of explained variance are added successively, controlling each time for all foregoing variables and in which each new partial coefficient is operating on the part of the variance that until then had remained unexplained:

$$R^2_{y.123} = r^2_{y1} + r^2_{y2.1}(1 - r^2_{y1}) + r^2_{y3.12}(1 - R^2_{y.12})$$

Such a partition of $R^2_{y.123}$ enables verification of the prediction capacities of each of the variables X_1, X_2 and X_3 in predicting Y, but, according to Duncan, this is far from a partition in causal components. For, the causal effects of X_1 and X_2 operate indirectly for the most part. Therefore, the causal structure is not contained by R^2. Moreover, R^2 is not only a function of path coefficients, but also of the variances and covariances of the included variables, so that different values of R^2 would be obtained for the same causal model with identical path coefficients in different populations, for which the variances of the exogenous variables are different. Besides, the value of R^2 depends on the number of independent variables included in a multiple regression model. For instance, in an article by Gordon (1968) it is shown how misleading R^2 can be in this respect. He considers a model with five independent variables, which all have the same correlation (0.60) with the dependent variable and which are mutually correlated in such a way that, for two subgroups of three and two independent variables, respectively, the within-intercorrelations are 0.80 and the between-intercorrelations are 0.20. If we add one variable to such a model, which shows the same strong correlation (0.60) with the dependent variable and a weak correlation (0.20) with each of the independent variables, then R^2 increases from 0.644 to 0.821. It also appears that the highest regression coefficients are obtained for the smallest subgroup of independent variables. So, if an independent variable happened to be at hand and was not included in a consideration of causality, then it could nevertheless give an impression of great importance and could increase R^2 substantially.

In our opinion, the foregoing arguments of Duncan and Gordon have to be amended in some respects. In adding independent variables to a model, much higher demands of significance will be made on R^2. Therefore, the arguments of Duncan and Gordon are not acceptable as far as inferential statistics is concerned.

Nor can we conclude from the relativity of R^2 that we can be satisfied with a small value of R^2. In the foregoing, we played devil's advocate in citing Duncan's arguments against R^2 (Duncan, 1975), for the same author (Blau and Duncan, 1967) tried to explain occupational stratification, and the proportion of explained variance in his causal model was only 0.43. Woelfel and Haller (1971) wrote a daring article in this respect. After a critical attack on a series of research studies by American sociologists, they reported that the world record for R^2 among sociologists appeared to be approximately 0.60.

The use of R^2 also has a psychological side. In passing criticism on a causal model, one is inclined to use $R^2 = 0.43$ and not $R = 0.66$, because the latter is the square root of a number between 0 and 1 and is therefore always higher. On the other hand, in presenting one's own research work, the temptation to launch out about $R = 0.66$ instead of $R^2 = 0.43$ is difficult to resist. The same holds for the proportion of unexplained variance $1 - R^2 = 0.57$ as compared to its square root $(1 - R^2)^{1/2} = 0.75$. The latter, the residual path coefficient, is more demanding as a criterion of falsification of the model than its square, the proportion of unexplained variance. It appears to us that the squares R^2 and $1 - R^2$ are most appropriate, because they have a clear (albeit predictive) interpretation. This follows from the fact that the partition in an explained and an unexplained part is only possible for the squares (see any textbook on statistics).

Step 10: The decomposition of causal influences in direct, indirect and spurious parts

The r equations, which were derived from the fundamental theorem of path analysis in steps 4 and 5 and which were further simplified in step 6, can be elaborated still further. This is done by substitution of as many correlation coefficients to the right of the equal sign as possible, so that in the end what is left consists almost exclusively of path coefficients. For example, for the r_{y1} equation, this operation yields the following result:

$$r_{y1} = p_{y1} + p_{y2}r_{21} + p_{y3}r_{31}$$

with:

$$r_{21} = p_{12} + p_{14}r_{42}$$
$$r_{31} = p_{31} + p_{34}r_{41}$$

so that:

$$r_{y1} = p_{y1} + p_{y2}(p_{12} + p_{14}r_{42}) + p_{y3}(p_{31} + p_{34}r_{41})$$
$$r_{y1} = p_{y1} + p_{y2}p_{12} + p_{y2}p_{14}r_{42} + p_{y3}p_{31} + p_{y3}p_{34}r_{41}$$

with:

$$r_{42} = p_{24} \quad \text{and} \quad r_{41} = p_{14} + p_{12}r_{24} = p_{14} + p_{12}p_{24}$$

whence, in the end:

$$r_{y1} = p_{y1} + p_{y2}p_{12} + p_{y2}p_{14}p_{24} + p_{y3}p_{31} + p_{y3}p_{34}p_{14} + p_{y3}p_{34}p_{12}p_{24}$$

Here

p_{y1} $= -0.582$ is the direct causal effect of X_1 on Y,
$p_{y3}p_{31} = (-0.727)(-0.141)$ the indirect causal effect via X_3,
$p_{y2}p_{12} = (0.621)(0.282)$ the spurious effect because of X_2,
$p_{y2}p_{14}p_{24}$, $p_{y3}p_{34}p_{14}$ and $p_{y3}p_{34}p_{12}p_{24}$, the more complex combinations of indirect and spurious causal effects.

We can do the same for all other r equations. Thus, a total correlation (here r_{y1}) can be decomposed into different sorts of effects: direct, indirect, spurious and complex. These can be simply read in the diagram by means of the tracing rule. In our example, the correlation coefficient r_{y1} could be entirely written as a function of p's. Sometimes, however, when the diagram contains not only straight arrows, but double-sided curved arrows as well, it will not be possible to eliminate all correlation coefficients. Suppose, for example, that a curved arrow was placed between X_2 and X_3 in our diagram, indicating a relationship but not necessarily a causal connection, then $p_{y2}p_{y3}r_{23}$ would be an 'indirectly correlated effect'.

The direct and indirect effects take on a 'causal' status. Their sum is called the total causal effect. The spurious and indirectly correlated effects are not causal in nature.

It should be mentioned that the combined presence of direct, indirect, spurious and indirectly correlated effects in a complex causal model can cause serious interpretation problems. This is especially the case for the transitive parts of the model. A transitive structure has the form: $A \rightarrow B$ and $B \rightarrow C$, and also $A \rightarrow C$. An example in our model is: $X_2 \rightarrow X_1$ and $X_1 \rightarrow Y$, and also $X_2 \rightarrow Y$; in plain language: dogmatism causes religious orthodoxy, religious orthodoxy causes anti-Semitism, and also: dogmatism causes anti-Semitism. This transitive mechanism is somewhat ambiguous. On the one hand, the relationship between religion and anti-Semitism is partly a direct causal effect and partly a spurious causal relationship because of dogmatism. On the other hand, the same mechanism can be read in such a way that the relationship between dogmatism and anti-Semitism is partly direct and partly an indirect causal effect via religious orthodoxy. In this last interpretation, it is the relationship between dogmatism and anti-Semitism which is focussed upon. As this was in no way the purpose of this research example, because the relationship between religion and anti-Semitism was the starting point in the form of what we have called a problem-relation in section 2.2.7, the first interpretation has naturally been chosen by the researchers. But in fact both interpretations are legitimate and, consequently, a transitive mechanism always remains impure with respect to interpretation. Strictly speaking, only the mechanisms $X_1 \leftarrow X_2 \rightarrow Y$ and $X_2 \rightarrow X_1 \rightarrow Y$ are really pure. In the first mechanism the arrow $X_1 \rightarrow Y$ is absent (spurious causality) and in the second mechanism the arrow $X_2 \rightarrow Y$ is absent (indirect causality). This omission of arrows is the reason why a causal model is overidentified. As stated, the restrictions that result from this overidentification will be considered as test equations. This is discussed in the following step.

Step 11: The test of causal order

The causal model consists of four substructures, one with Y, one with X_3, one with X_1 and one with X_2 as the dependent variable. The latter two substructures are perfectly identified. The resulting r equations offer a unique solution for p_{12} and p_{14} (third substructure) and for p_{24} (fourth substructure). The first two substructures, on the contrary, are overidentified (see also step 7). For, the first structural equation with Y as the dependent variable can be multiplied by X_1, X_2 and X_3 as well as by X_4. As a result, we obtain four r equations (for r_{y1}, r_{y2}, r_{y3} and r_{y4}) with three unknowns (p_{y1}, p_{y2} and p_{y3}). And the second structural equation with X_3 as the dependent variable can be multiplied by X_1 and X_4 as well as by X_2. This yields three r equations (for r_{31}, r_{34} and r_{32}) with two unknowns (p_{31} and p_{34}). The resulting surplus of information can be understood in two ways, as an estimation problem or as a test-possibility. Firstly, it may be considered annoying that no unique solution can be found for p_{31} and p_{34} in the second substructure (see step 7). In such a case one will be worried about the estimation of the path coefficients. Several estimation procedures have been proposed. A simple or weighted average of the different solutions has generally been rejected. Boudon (1967, p. 103) proposed to consider all r equations simultaneously and to calculate the estimators of p_{31} and p_{34} by means of the ordinary least squares procedure in such a way that the deviation between the observed r values and the r values calculated from the r equations would be minimal. It was, however, Goldberger (1970) who showed that the ordinary least squares estimators obtained from simple regression analysis are equally unbiased as Boudon's estimators and are even more precise, i.e., have a smaller standard error. This proposition by Goldberger is what we have in fact been doing in step 7, for solving the system with the r_{31} and r_{34} equations gives the same result as calculating the standardized partial regression coefficients of the regression equation of X_3 as a function of X_1 and X_4. In the same fashion, the b^*'s can be calculated in the first substructure of Y as a function of X_1, X_2 and X_3. These are, then, the best estimators of the path coefficients p_{y1}, p_{y2} and p_{y3}.

We now come to the second viewpoint, the use of the surplus information for testing purposes. For example, from the second system with r_{31} and r_{34} equations we obtained the ordinary least squares solution $p_{31} = -0.141$ and $p_{34} = 0.658$. If we substitute these values in the extra r_{32} equation, then we can verify whether the value of r_{32} does not deviate too much from the corresponding observed correlation coefficient:

model expectation	**observed**	**difference**
$r_{32} = p_{31}r_{12} + p_{34}r_{42}$	$r_{32} = -0.704$	0.235
$\quad = (-0.141)(0.612) + (0.658)(-0.582)$		
$\quad = -0.469$		

The first substructure can be tested in an analogous way. From the system with the r_{y1}, r_{y2} and r_{y3} equations we obtained the ordinary least squares solution $p_{y1} = -0.582$, $p_{y2} = 0.621$ and $p_{y3} = -0.727$. We substitute these values in the r_{y4} equation and we verify whether the value of r_{y4} expected from the model does not deviate too much from the corresponding observed value:

model expectation   **observed**   **difference**

$r_{y4} = p_{y1}r_{14} + p_{y2}r_{24} + p_{y3}r_{34}$ $r_{y4} = -0.442$ -0.048

$= (-0.582)(-0.731) + (0.621)(-0.582)$

$+ (-0.727)(0.762) = -0.490$

If the r values calculated from the model show large deviations from the observed r values, then the model is falsified. For the r_{y4} equation, falsification is not obvious (the difference is only -0.048), but for the r_{32} equation the difference is more substantial (0.235). The same result has already been obtained in applying the Simon–Blalock procedure.

As we have seen, the additional r equations offer the opportunity to test the validity of the model. For this reason they are called test equations. But the name is misleading. For, the operation is not really a statistical test. There is only a rule of thumb (Weede calls it a solution of embarrassment), according to which the difference must not be higher than 0.10. It is therefore understandable that the use of test equations has been criticized from the standpoint of inferential statistics and has been replaced by significance tests of the path coefficients *and* by a goodness of fit test of the global model (Jöreskog, 1973). Opp and Schmidt (1976, p. 155) raise objections to this argument, for significance tests, too, have only limited value, because the result always depends on the sample size and, we add, on the postulated probability of type I error α (a small path coefficient is still significant for a sufficiently large sample size n, and sufficiently low prior probability $1 - \alpha$, and a high path coefficient is no longer significant for small n and high $1 - \alpha$). Therefore, Opp and Schmidt still plead in favour of the use of test equations.

They even go a step further. According to them, the test equations offer the opportunity to give a decisive answer with respect to the **causal order** of the variables.

For example, for the models $\begin{array}{c} C \\ \swarrow \searrow \\ A \leftarrow B \end{array}$ and $\begin{array}{c} C \\ \swarrow \searrow \\ A \rightarrow B \end{array}$ the r_{AB} equations would be:

$r_{AB} = p_{AC}r_{BC} + p_{AB}$ and $r_{AB} = p_{BC}r_{AC} + p_{BA}$, respectively. If the causal effect of B on A or of A on B were absent, i.e., for the model $A \leftarrow C \rightarrow B$, these r equations would be reduced to $r_{AB} = p_{AC}r_{BC}$ and $r_{AB} = p_{BC}r_{AC}$, respectively. In this way, it would be possible to test for the presence or absence of a causal effect as well as for the causal order. The possibilities of testing are, however, very limited. For example, the model

$A \rightarrow C \rightarrow B$ may discriminate against the model $\begin{array}{c} C \\ \nearrow \searrow \\ A \rightarrow B \end{array}$, but not against the model

$\begin{array}{c} C \\ \nearrow \searrow \\ A \leftarrow B \end{array}$, because the latter is not recursive, so that the estimation procedures and the assumption of step 6 (zero correlation between residual and directly predetermining variables) are no longer valid.

Nevertheless, some attempts have been made (Ammerman, and others, 1975) to form test equations for non-recursive models as well, but there, too, the possibilities of testing the causal order appear to be very limited.

Moreover, there are still recursive models for which a test equation cannot be formulated, even if they are overidentified. For instance, the model $\begin{smallmatrix} C \\ \searrow B \\ A \nearrow \end{smallmatrix}$ does not

contain the indirectly predetermining variables that are necessary to form the test equations through multiplication. If we add to all this that the same data matrix can give empirical support to different models with unequal causal orders, then we come to the unsatisfactory conclusion that the heading of step 11, namely, 'the test of causal order', is rather premature. This may be the reason why methodological literature resorts to the more careful expression 'the test of restrictions resulting from over-identification'.

Step 12: The comparison of several causal models

Strictly speaking, one may not formulate and test more than one model for each data set. From the viewpoint of inferential statistics, a mechanism of capitalization on chance comes into operation as soon as different causal models are tried out for the same data. For, if a prior probability of 0.99 is postulated, then the probability of falsification of an invalid model for two independent tests becomes $(0.99)^2 = 0.98$; for three tests $(0.99)^3 = 0.97$; for four tests $(0.99)^4 = 0.96$, etc. This probability becomes lower, so that, conversely, the probability of non-falsification of an invalid model becomes higher. It follows that one will always score a success as soon as one tries out a sufficient number of models. The moral might be that only one test is allowed for each data matrix. Another possibility is to test more and more conservatively as more models are tried out: for instance, to postulate in each of three tests a probability of 0.99 for calculation purposes and to use a prior probability of 0.97 in the interpretation of the results. A widely recommended method is the 'split-half procedure'. The sample is randomly split into two halves. The one half serves to try out several models and the acquired knowledge is used to formulate a model, which is tested in the second half. This second half thus obtains in fact the status of new research.

But, it is not always possible to use the split-half procedure in practice. Firstly, for three variables, taking the signs into account, no less than 96 linear recursive models can be formulated. For models with more variables and in which non-linear and non-recursive relationships are allowed, this number becomes so large that a very sophisticated computer program would be needed to select fitting models. Opp and Schmidt (1976, p. 160): 'As far as we know, such a computer program doesn't yet exist.' Secondly, in trying out several models, a split-half procedure will not suffice. For, in performing multiple tests in one half of the sample, the tolerated probability of type I error becomes so high that the selected model could be brought about merely by chance. The probability of finding this model reconfirmed in the second half then becomes very low. We might imagine that the sample is still further split, so that a split-10 or maybe even a split-50 procedure would be applied. However, the required sample size would then have to be 10 or 50 times as high as the planned one. So, the proposition avoids capitalization on chance, but it requires capital.

It appears that nothing is left to the researcher but to make their own selection of the most plausible models. There are no precise rules for the way in which this has to be done. Methodologists refer for this to the theory formulated in step 1. We quote Otis Duncan (1975, p.151): 'Your models can be no better than your ideas.' 'There is no formula for "doing science". If such a formula were paradoxically to be discovered, we could program it for a computer and have done with the tedious business of thinking for ourselves' (p. 149). 'A formal analysis can only reveal formal conditions that a good model must satisfy (or satisfy approximately). Whether it is really any good must be determined on substantive grounds, with the guidance of the best theory available' (p. 99).

Duncan and other methodologists appear to be very conscious of the well-known distinction made in the philosophy of science between the 'context of discovery' and the 'context of justification'. Causal analysis doesn't give us rules for the 'discovery' of causal hypotheses, but it helps to 'justify' postulated causal hypotheses. Sewall Wright (1921) had already considered his path analysis in this manner, viz., as a method of analysis which combines the knowledge which we possess with respect to causal relations, with the knowledge of the magnitude of the relations which is provided by the correlation coefficients.

Many considerations can of course play a role in the comparison of different causal models: the removal or addition of causal arrows, the removal or addition of variables, the rearrangement of the variables by changing the causal order, and other operations. Theory, results of previous research, one's own preliminary research and common sense can help us make the appropriate choices. For the determination of the causal order, the criterion of temporal succession is mostly used in practice, even if one is aware of the *post hoc ergo propter hoc* sophism. However, other criteria exist which are proposed in philosophical treatises on causality. Examples are: production, action, intervention, fixation, dispersion, nature of the variables (cause vs. indicator, event vs. characteristic, macro vs. micro variable, fundamental variable or not). For a discussion of these criteria, see Tacq (1984).

Step 13: Modification of the model

After the mutual comparison of different models, it can be decided in a definitive step to remove a causal arrow from the original model (if the corresponding path coefficient is extremely low and non-significant), to add a causal arrow (if it can be suspected on the basis of the test equations that it was unjustly omitted), to eliminate a variable (if all direct and indirect effects of this variable are extremely small) and/or to add a new variable (if the explained variance R^2 is too small). For the latter, a new research is in fact required, because no data are available for the variables that must be added.

In our example we suggest that a double-sided curved arrow between dogmatism (X_2) and libertarianism (X_3) should be added.

6.6   SPSS for Windows Output of Partial Correlation and Path Analysis

We now present the SPSS for Windows output for the mini example of the anti-Semitism inquiry. The reader can easily verify whether our results calculated by hand coincide with this output.

Choosing or creating a data file

How to open an SPSS session and how to choose a data file or, if a data file does not yet exist, how to enter data, to choose name, type and label of variables and to save the data file with extension *.sav*, is shown in Chapter 4.

Running the statistical procedure

Click on Statistics. Click on Regression. Click on Linear. A subdialog box for Linear Regression appears. Click on variable Y in the Source Variable list on the left and click on the ▶ push button of the Dependent Variable. Click on the variables X_1, X_2 and X_3 in the Source Variable list (either separately or together by means of the click and drag technique) and click on the ▶ push button of the Independent Variables. The default method is Enter. This will suit you.

You can click on Statistics and make further choices, if you want to. You can also click on Plots and choose for plots of standardized residuals. We will not do so here. Just click on Continue to come back in the subdialog box for Linear Regression. Click on OK. SPSS then runs a multiple regression analysis of Y as a function of X_1, X_2 and X_3.

Repeat the same procedure:

- for X_3 as a function of X_1 and X_4,
- for X_1 as a function of X_2 and X_4 and
- for X_2 as a function of X_4.

You have now performed the path analysis. The partial correlations can be calculated as follows. Click on Statistics. Click on Correlate. Click on Partial. This opens the Partial Correlations dialog box. Click on the two variables of the Source Variable list that are to be correlated and click on the ▶ push button of Variables. Click on the one or more variables that are to be controlled for and click on the ▶ push button of Controlling For. Click on OK. SPSS now calculates the partial correlations you requested for.

As for the part correlations, you will have to open a syntax window and type the appropriate SPSS commands. You click on File, click on New, click on SPSS Syntax, type the statements, put the cursor anywhere in the first command line and click on ▶ (or on Run in the SPSS for Windows 5.0 version).

We give the statements below, also for the path analysis.

```
1    REGRESSION /VARIABLES Y X1 X2
2       /STATISTICS ZPP /DEPENDENT Y /METHOD ENTER X1 X2.
3    REGRESSION /VARIABLES Y X1 X3
4       /STATISTICS ZPP /DEPENDENT Y /METHOD ENTER X1 X3.
5    REGRESSION /VARIABLES Y X1 X2 X4
6       /STATISTICS ZPP /DEPENDENT Y /METHOD ENTER X1 X2 X4.
7    REGRESSION /VARIABLES Y X1 X2 X3
8       /DEPENDENT Y /METHOD ENTER X1 X2 X3.
9    REGRESSION /VARIABLES X1 X3 X4
10      /DEPENDENT X3 /METHOD ENTER X1 X4.
11   REGRESSION /VARIABLES X1 X2 X4
12      /DEPENDENT X1 /METHOD ENTER X2 X4.
13   REGRESSION /VARIABLES X2 X4
14      /DEPENDENT X2 /METHOD ENTER X4.
```

In statements 1 to 6, the zero-order, partial and part correlations are given by means of 'statistics = zpp'. The first-order coefficient $r_{y1.2}$ is requested in statements 1 and 2, the first-order coefficient $r_{y1.3}$ in statements 3 and 4. In the regression analysis of statements 5 and 6, the second-order coefficient $r_{y1.24}$ is requested as well as the part correlation $r_{y(1.24)}$.

The next four regression analyses in statements 7 to 14 form the basis of the path analysis. The output is as follows.

```
Listwise Deletion of Missing Data
Equation Number 1    Dependent Variable..   Y   degree of anti-Semitism
Block Number  1.  Method: Enter     X1      X2


Variable(s) Entered on Step Number
   1..    X2          degree of dogmatism
   2..    X1          degree of religious orthodoxy


----- Variables in the Equation -----

Variable     Correl Part Cor  Partial

X2            .776501  .787654  .813752
X1            .251224 -.283829 -.450439

********************************************************************************
Listwise Deletion of Missing Data
Equation Number 1    Dependent Variable..   Y   degree of anti-Semitism
Block Number  1.  Method: Enter     X1      X3


Variable(s) Entered on Step Number
   1..    X3          libertarian attitude
   2..    X1          degree of religious orthodoxy


----- Variables in the Equation -----

Variable     Correl Part Cor  Partial

X3           -.801754 -.824711 -.852037
X1            .251224 -.316943 -.530312

********************************************************************************

Listwise Deletion of Missing Data
Equation Number 1    Dependent Variable..   Y   degree of anti-Semitism
Block Number  1.  Method: Enter     X1      X2      X4


Variable(s) Entered on Step Number
   1..    X4          educational level
   2..    X2          degree of dogmatism
   3..    X1          degree of religious orthodoxy
```

```
----- Variables in the Equation -----

Variable      Correl Part Cor  Partial

X4          -.442387 -.188801 -.335602
X2           .776501  .715732  .803679
X1           .251224 -.340681 -.540759
```

****


```
Listwise Deletion of Missing Data
Equation Number 1    Dependent Variable..   Y   degree of anti-Semitism
Block Number  1.  Method:  Enter      X1        X2        X3
```


```
Variable(s) Entered on Step Number
   1..   X3          libertarian attitude
   2..   X1          degree of religious orthodoxy
   3..   X2          degree of dogmatism
```


```
Multiple R            .95862
R Square              .91896
Adjusted R Square     .87844
Standard Error        .78823
```


```
Analysis of Variance
                    DF       Sum of Squares      Mean Square
Regression           3            42.27218         14.09073
Residual             6             3.72782           .62130

F =      22.67929       Signif F =  .0011
```


```
Equation Number 1    Dependent Variable..   Y   degree of anti-Semitism


------------------ Variables in the Equation ------------------

Variable             B        SE B        Beta        T   Sig T

X3          -.864541    .207067    -.726689    -4.175  .0058
X1          -.560336    .150622    -.581849    -3.720  .0099
X2           .528463    .146522     .621390     3.607  .0113
(Constant)  9.571763   1.817108                 5.268  .0019
```

****

```
Listwise Deletion of Missing Data
Equation Number 1    Dependent Variable..   X3   libertarian attitude
Block Number  1.  Method:  Enter      X1        X4
```

```
Variable(s) Entered on Step Number
    1..   X4        educational level
    2..   X1        degree of religious orthodoxy


Multiple R              .76785
R Square                .58959
Adjusted R Square       .47233
Standard Error         1.38039


Analysis of Variance
                    DF      Sum of Squares      Mean Square
Regression          2           19.16163          9.58081
Residual            7           13.33837          1.90548


F =      5.02803        Signif F =  .0443



Equation Number 1    Dependent Variable..   X3    libertarian attitude



------------------ Variables in the Equation ------------------

Variable              B        SE B        Beta        T   Sig T

X4               .592745     .319441     .658413     1.856  .1059
X1              -.114446     .287225    -.141384     -.398  .7022
(Constant)      2.839128    2.738262                 1.037  .3343

*****************************************************************************

Listwise Deletion of Missing Data
Equation Number 1    Dependent Variable..   X1   degree of religious orthodoxy
Block Number  1.  Method:  Enter      X2      X4


Variable(s) Entered on Step Number
    1..   X4        educational level
    2..   X2        degree of dogmatism


Multiple R              .76628
R Square                .58718
Adjusted R Square       .46924
Standard Error         1.71029

Analysis of Variance
                    DF      Sum of Squares      Mean Square
Regression          2           29.12432         14.56216
Residual            7           20.47568          2.92510


F =      4.97835        Signif F =  .0452



Equation Number 1    Dependent Variable..   X1   degree of religious orthodoxy
```

```
----------------- Variables in the Equation ------------------

Variable                B        SE B       Beta        T    Sig T

X4              -.629893    .332177   -.566367    -1.896   .0998
X2               .249703    .263763    .282756      .947   .3753
(Constant)      6.339858   2.755024                2.301   .0549
```

```
********************************************************************************
```

Listwise Deletion of Missing Data
Equation Number 1   Dependent Variable..   X2   degree of dogmatism
Block Number 1. Method: Enter   X4

Variable(s) Entered on Step Number
   1..   X4   educational level


```
Multiple R          .58217
R Square            .33892
Adjusted R Square   .25628
Standard Error     2.29251
```

Analysis of Variance
```
                    DF      Sum of Squares     Mean Square
Regression           1           21.55511        21.55511
Residual             8           42.04489         5.25561

F =       4.10135       Signif F =  .0774
```


Equation Number 1   Dependent Variable..   X2   degree of dogmatism


```
----------------- Variables in the Equation ------------------

Variable                B        SE B       Beta        T    Sig T

X4              -.733167    .362026   -.582166    -2.025   .0774
(Constant)      8.685786   2.051124                4.235   .0029
```

Analysis of Variance and Covariance: The Effect of Interaction of Monetary Rewards and Task Interest on Motivation

7.1   The Research Problem and the Causal Diagram

In the investigation into the intrinsic motivation of people in the performance of a task, the causal effect of external rewards was examined. The effect of task interest was also investigated: interesting, moderately interesting and boring tasks were distinguished. It was expected that both causal factors would have a positive effect on intrinsic motivation: higher motivation if an amount of money is awarded than in the absence of it (effect of external rewards) and increasing motivation the more captivating the task is (effect of task interest).

In addition to these separate effects, a combined effect of both factors was also expected, which is known as an effect of interaction. The latter is much more complex. It means that the effect of one variable has to be shaded by the other variable. For, the positive effect of external rewards on intrinsic motivation would hold for boring tasks, but for moderately interesting tasks the effect would be absent, and for captivating tasks the effect would even be negative. Or conversely, and resulting in the same thing, the effect of task interest is different for the two categories (absence or presence) of monetary awards. In the case of a significant effect of interaction, combinations of the two causal factors have to be considered in their effect on intrinsic motivation. For instance, the combination 'monetary award, boring task' will show another mean motivation than the combination 'monetary award, captivating task'. There are six such combinations and there is an effect of interaction if the motivational levels of these six combinations are significantly different.

Three variables are involved in our example: one dependent variable, Y (intrinsic motivation); and two independent variables, X_1 (external rewards) and X_2 (task interest). The dependent variable Y is measured at the quantitative level. On the other hand, the independent variables are both measured at a lower level. Monetary reward X_1 is dichotomous (categories: absence, presence of reward) and task interest X_2 is ordinal (ranks: high, moderate, low).

The format of the argument is the interactive structure, as is represented in Figure 7.1 below, in which X_1 is drawn as a dichotomy and X_2 as a trichotomy:

The arrow $X_1 \rightarrow Y$ represents the direct causal effect of external rewards on intrinsic motivation. The arrow $X_2 \rightarrow Y$ represents the direct causal effect of task interest on intrinsic motivation.

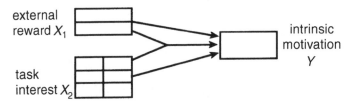

Figure 7.1   Causal diagram of the interactive structure

The forked arrow $\genfrac{}{}{0pt}{}{X_1}{X_2} \!\!\rightarrowtail Y$ represents the effect of interaction, i.e., the effect of combinations of external rewards and task interest on intrinsic motivation.

In order to explain the different possibilities of the application of analysis of variance and covariance, we will now look at the **diagram** in more detail and make a number of distinctions.

Firstly, there are two independent variables. Therefore, the applied technique is the **two-way** analysis of variance. In the case of only one independent variable we perform a one-way ANOVA and, for n independent variables an n-way ANOVA.

Secondly, in one-way designs the independent variable can be dichotomous, as is external rewards X_1. In that case the classical t test is performed. However, the independent variable may also be a trichotomy or polytomy, as is task interest X_2. In that case the **F** test is performed.

Thirdly, the diagram contains a forked arrow, which indicates an effect of interaction. In the absence of interaction, the separate effects of external rewards and task interest would operate in an additive fashion. A weighted sum could then be made to determine their joint effect on intrinsic motivation (as is done in multiple regression analysis). The model would therefore be called additive. In our example, on the contrary, we have a **non-additive model**.

Fourthly, both independent variables are measured at a low level, nominal or ordinal. In such a case, analysis of variance (ANOVA) is used. However, if one or some independent variables have been measured at the quantitative level, then these are called 'covariate' and the appropriate technique is **analysis of covariance** (ANCOVA). This would be the case in our example if the external rewards variable were expressed in amounts of money.

To sum up, the possible research designs in the form of causal diagrams and the corresponding techniques of analysis are presented in Figure 7.2.

In connection with the investigation into intrinsic motivation, we will now deal with two-way analysis of variance including an effect of interaction. Here, the models we encounter will automatically be simpler.

7.2   The Data Matrix

In our (fictitious) mini data set we consider $n = 24$ persons as units of analysis. The dependent variable Y is intrinsic motivation and is measured as an interval scale with scores from 0 to 9. External rewards X_1 has two categories: the absence (score $= 1$) or

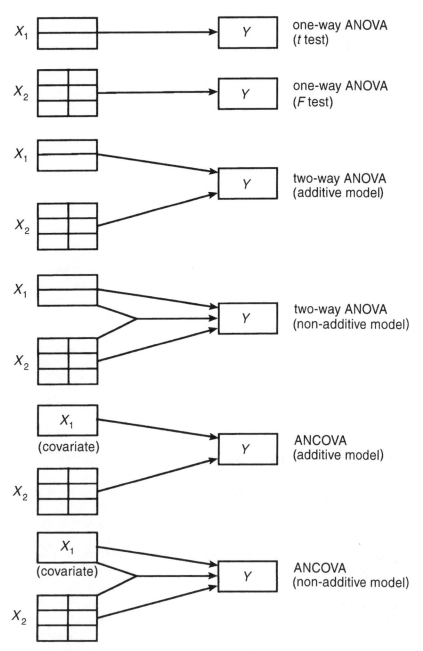

Figure 7.2   Causal diagrams for ANOVA and ANCOVA

Table 7.1   Data matrix

Y	X_1	X_2
6	1	1
4	1	1
3	1	1
3	1	1
4	1	2
3	1	2
3	1	2
2	1	2
3	1	3
2	1	3
2	1	3
1	1	3
9	2	1
9	2	1
8	2	1
6	2	1
7	2	2
5	2	2
4	2	2
4	2	2
4	2	3
2	2	3
1	2	3
1	2	3

presence (score $= 2$) of an amount of money. Task interest has three ranks: high (score $= 1$), moderate (score $= 2$) and low (score $= 3$).

The data matrix is as shown in Table 7.1.

7.3   The Model of Analysis of Variance

Correlation and regression analysis and the related path analysis are mostly treated as a part of descriptive statistics. The fact that the correlation coeffients, the regression coefficients and the global causal model have to be tested for significance is often neglected and, if not, is at most added as a supplementary warning.

This all has to do with tradition. The habit of treating regression analysis mainly as a predictive model and, later on in path analysis, as a causal model, is a growing one. Attention has predominantly been paid to the mutual comparison of the predictive capacities of the predictors or of the causal effects of the causal factors. Questions of generalization from sample to population disappeared — erroneously — from sight.

The reverse holds for analysis of variance, for it was originally presented by Sir Ronald Fisher as a part of inferential statistics. And so the question of generalization from sample to population is literally built-in in the ANOVA model. The technique centres on the *F* test (*F* for Fisher), which is an extension of the *t* test used in experimental designs. We thus see that analysis of variance should be situated within the experimental tradition. No wonder that psychologists — the most versed in the designing of experiments — frequently used this technique.

With the classical Student's t test in mind, Fisher asked himself two things. Firstly, instead of two groups, an experimental group and a control group, three or several groups can sometimes be formed, which are exposed to varying experimental conditions. The comparison of every pair of mean scores of these groups by means of t tests creates the thorny problem of repeated testing, which is called 'multiple comparisons' in statistical literature and which entails capitalization on chance. Moreover, these t tests are not independent. How can a solution be found for this problem?

Secondly, instead of exposing the experimental subjects to the varying conditions of one factor, it is also possible to do this for two or more factors simultaneously in one and the same experimental design (two-factor and multiple-factor experiment). In considering this possibility, Fisher realized that an effect of interaction can appear in addition to the effects of each of the factors. A solution had to be found for that extension as well.

It is from these two considerations that the F test emerged.

To explain the **general model** of analysis of variance, we first quote Kendall and Stuart (1969, p. 3), who point out rightly that the term 'analysis of variation' would in fact be more appropriate. For, it is the total variation which is partitioned into the within-groups variation and the between-groups variation (TOTAL = WITHIN + BETWEEN). For instance, let us take the three groups of task interest. Each group consists of eight individuals. The extent to which eight individuals within a group differ from each other is expressed by the sum of squared deviations of their motivation scores from the group mean. This is a **within-groups variation** and there are three of them, one for each group. The mean of these three within-groups variations gives an idea of the differences between the individuals, without this having any bearing on the group, for the latter has been kept constant.

Conversely, we can also examine the differences between the groups, without this having any bearing on the individuals. To do so, we take the group means and we calculate the sum of squared deviations of these mean motivation scores from the grand mean. If this variation is multiplied by the group size (for reasons explained later), we obtain the **between-groups variation**.

It appears that the sum of this between-groups variation and the within-groups variation is equal to the **total variation**. The latter is the sum of squared deviations of all 24 individual scores from the grand mean and thus gives an idea of the differences that have to do with individuality as well as with group identity.

In analysis of variance, the differences between groups are compared with the differences between individuals. The between-groups variation indicates that part of the differences that is exclusively due to the groups. In dividing it by the number of degrees of freedom (here $d_B = 3 - 1$, because there are three groups and the grand mean is fixed), we obtain the **between-groups variance**.

The within-groups variation indicates that part of the differences that is exclusively due to the individuals. In dividing it by the number of degrees of freedom (here $d_W = 3(8 - 1) = 21$, because for each of the three groups there are eight individuals, for which the group mean is fixed), we obtain the **within-groups variance**.

The quotient of the between-groups variance and the within-groups variance is the **F score**, which will be used in the F test. The numerator of this F score contains group differences, the denominator contains the differences between individuals. If $F = 1$, so that the groups differ as much as the individuals already differ from each other, then the groups of task interest have no effect on intrinsic motivation. Such an effect only exists if the numerator is greater than the denominator, i.e., if $F > 1$, because in that case the variance of groups rises above the variance of individuals. How much greater than 1 the F score has to be will become clear in the discussion of the F test. Our intention here is merely to present the line of the general model. This consists of three parts: decomposition of the total variation of Y scores into a between- and within-variation, division by the numbers of degrees of freedom to obtain variances and calculation of the ratio of the between- and within-variance in order to confront the group differences with the differences among individuals.

This model is a variant of the **general linear model**, which was dealt with in regression analysis. In matrix notation, it was written as $y = X\beta + \varepsilon$ for the population and as $y = Xb + e$ for the sample. The component X, which contained the independent variables in regression analysis, refers to the groups. Dummy variables will be used here. The elements of the vector b indicate the group effects. The variation $(Xb)'(Xb)$, which was called the explained variation in regression analysis[1] and which was indicated as SSR (Sum of Squares due to Regression), is formally identical to the between-groups variation SSB (Sum of Squares Between Groups).

The component e is the residual term, just as in regression analysis. The variation $e'e$ is the unexplained variation SSE (Sum of Squares due to Error) and is formally identical to the within-groups variation SSW (Sum of Squares Within Groups).

The vector y contains the scores of the dependent variable. The variation $y'y$ is the total variation SST (Sum of Squares for the Total sample). The decomposition SST = SSR + SSE thus changes here to: SST = SSB + SSW.

If, in addition to the three groups of task interest, represented by variable X_2, the two groups of external rewards (X_1) are included as well, then the foregoing decomposition of the total variation is **more complex**. Several F tests will then have to be performed in addition to the F test for the effect of X_2: an F test for the effect of X_1 and possibly an F test for the effect of interaction. In this last case, the concept of 'interaction variation' SSI (Sum of Squares due to Interaction) will have to be introduced. The decomposition then becomes: $SST = SSB_{(x1)} + SSB_{(x2)} + SSI + SSW$.

In each of the three F tests it is customary to use SSW in the denominator of F. The numerators contain the three other components, respectively.

7.4   Geometric Approach

We will first consider the model according to which the total variation of Y scores is partitioned into a between- and within-variation. After that, we will consider analysis

---

[1] We assume that the variables are expressed as deviations of their mean.

of variance as a variant of the general linear model and discuss the analogy with regression analysis. We will give a geometrical visualization of both approaches.

We start with the most simple case: one-way ANOVA for two groups. The effect of external rewards on intrinsic motivation is investigated. There are two groups: the no-money group and the money group. According to the null hypothesis, these two groups are random samples from the same population, so that there would only be random differences between their motivation means. This situation is visualized in Figure 7.3.

The distributions of each of the two groups are shown to the left. Each has a within-dispersion. The pooled average of these two within-dispersions offers a first estimation of the dispersion of the population put forward in the null hypothesis. To the right, the group means are brought together in one distribution. The dispersion of these group means is much smaller than the within-dispersions, for an artificial reason. For, the situation obtained here is comparable to a sampling distribution of means, in which the means are more tightly packed than the original individual scores (variance n times smaller for samples of size n). In multiplying the dispersion of means by the group size ($n = 12$) we obtain a fair second estimation of the dispersion in the population. If this second estimation is significantly higher than the first one, then the group means lie too far apart to be attributed to chance. The monetary award then has a significant effect.

In the same fashion, the effect of task interest on intrinsic motivation can be presented as a decomposition (see Figure 7.4). There are now three groups, each containing eight persons: one with interesting tasks, one with moderate tasks and one with boring tasks

If the effects of external rewards and task interest on intrinsic motivation are examined in combination, then we obtain a more complex two-way ANOVA design with $2 \times 3 = 6$ groups of four persons each (see Figure 7.5).

We can represent this by means of a 2×3 contingency table, in which a within-distribution is drawn in each of the six cells. The foregoing two one-way designs are now situated at the margins of the table. The total distribution stands below to the right. The means are indicated by *.

This representation of analysis of variance with means and within-distributions in each of the cells will be the starting point for the calculations in the classical approach.

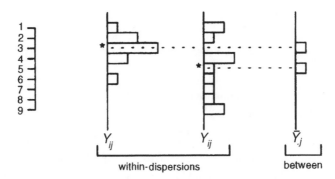

Figure 7.3 Within- and between-distributions for one-way ANOVA (I)

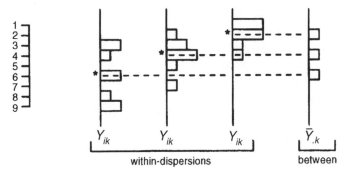

Figure 7.4   Within and between-distributions for one-way ANOVA (II)

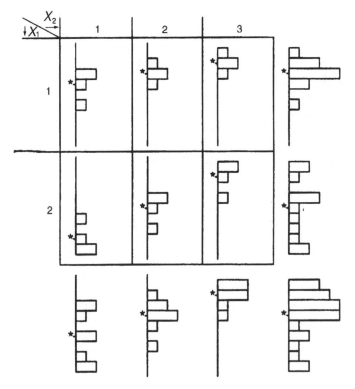

Figure 7.5   Within-distributions for two-way ANOVA

We now turn to the **regression approach**. From this viewpoint the technique is seen as a variant of the general linear model. For that purpose, dummies will be used. The external rewards variable X_1 is represented as the dummy variable D_1 with scores 0 (no money) and 1 (money). The task interest X_2 is replaced by two dummies D_2 and D_3 with scores 1 and 0 for interesting tasks, 0 and 1 for moderately interesting tasks and 0 and 0 for boring tasks, respectively. For a non-additive model (with the effect of interaction), extra product terms $D_4 = D_1D_2$ and $D_5 = D_1D_3$ have to be added. We thus obtain a six-dimensional space, for the regression model has one dependent variable (Y) and five independent variables (D_1 to D_5). As this can no longer be drawn, we restrict ourselves here to a geometric representation, firstly of the effect $X_1 \rightarrow Y$ in (Y, D_1) space and, after that, of the effect $X_2 \rightarrow Y$ in the three-dimensional (Y, D_2, D_3) space.

Let us start with the most simple case: the effect of external rewards (X_1) on intrinsic motivation (Y). Variable X_1, replaced by D_1, has only two scores: 0 (no monetary award) and 1 (monetary award). The regression model is represented in Figure 7.6.

The regression-interpretation is straightforward here, especially because the independent variable D_1 only has two scores (0 and 1). The intercept is equal to 3. This means that the predicted value of Y for $D_1 = 0$ is equal to 3: if no amount of money is rewarded we predict a motivation score of 3. This is the mean of Y for the no-money group. The regression coefficient b_{y1} is equal to 2. This is the increase of motivation for every unit increase of D_1. As the increase from $D_1 = 0$ to $D_1 = 1$ is in fact a unit increase, we are dealing here with the move from the no-money group to the money group. In other words, coefficient b_{y1} expresses that the reward of an amount of money increases the motivation by 2 on the average. So, the mean of Y for the money group is 2 higher than for the no-money group: $3 + 2 = 5$.

For the visualization of the effect of task interest (X_2) on intrinsic motivation (Y), we need a three-dimensional (Y, D_2, D_3) space, as is represented in Figure 7.7.

The regression function $Y = 2 + 4D_2 + 2D_3 + e$ will be worked out in the sections below. The intercept is equal to 2. This means that the predicted value of Y for $D_2 = 0$ and $D_3 = 0$ is equal to 2: the mean motivation of the group with boring tasks is 2. The regression coefficient $b_{y2.3}$ is equal to 4. This means that in moving to the group with interesting tasks ($D_2 = 1$ and $D_3 = 0$), the motivation increases by 4 on the average. Indeed, the mean motivation of this group is 4 higher than that of the (0,0) group: $2 + 4 = 6$. The regression coefficient $b_{y3.2}$ is equal to 2. This is the increase of Y for every unit increase of D_3 ($D_3 = 1$) when keeping D_2 constant ($D_2 = 0$). In other

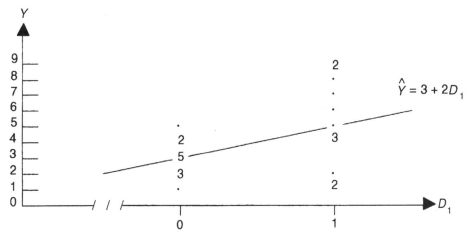

Figure 7.6   One-way ANOVA as regression with one dummy variable

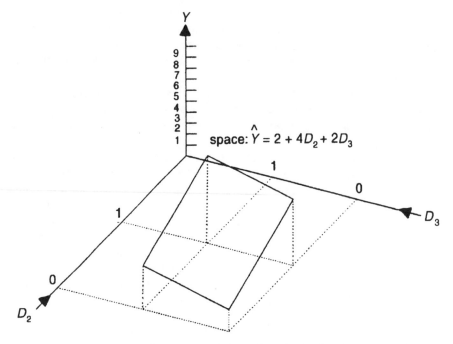

Figure 7.7 The geometric representation of analysis of variance as a dummy regression model

words, in moving to the group with moderately interesting tasks ($D_2 = 0$ and $D_3 = 1$) the motivation increases by 2 on the average as compared to the (0,0) reference group: $2 + 2 = 4$.

7.5 Objectives of the Technique

In analysis of variance the accent is placed more on testing than on description. Keeping the motivation example in mind and restricting ourselves to the two independent variables X_1 and X_2, the technique has the following objectives:

1(a). Is there a significant difference between the mean motivation scores of the money group and the no-money group, without regard to task interest? This comes down to the performance of a simple t test in a one-way design.

1(b). Is there a significant difference between the mean motivation scores of the money group and the no-money group, when controlling for task interest? Here, we will have to perform a two-way design.

2(a). Is there a significant difference between the mean motivation scores of the three groups of task interest, regardless of external rewards? This comes down to the performance of an F test of significant difference between the means of three groups in a one-way design.

2(b). Is there a significant difference between the mean motivation scores of the three groups of task interest when controlling for external rewards? Here, the same question must be applied to a two-way design.

3.   Is there a significant effect of interaction? In other words, are the differences between the mean motivation scores of the three groups of task interest for the money group significantly different from the same differences for the no-money group? This comes down to an F test of interaction in a two-way design.

4.   Has the correct model been chosen, one that fits best with reality? Do all three of the aforementioned effects, the effect of X_1, the effect of X_2 and the effect of interaction, have to be included in the model? From the viewpoint of the dummy regression approach this comes down to the search for a linear function with Y as the dependent variable and with the dummy-coded predictors X_1 and X_2 together with their product terms (D_1 to D_5) as the independent variables. An F test of this global model shows whether an adequate model has been chosen, or whether this model has to be revised.

7.6   Calculations in One-Way ANOVA: Classical Approach

We first deal with objectives 1(a) and 2(a) of the one-way design. As a simple t test can be performed to answer question 1(a), we will first illustrate the calculation by means of 2(a). We will investigate whether there are significant differences between the mean motivation scores of the three groups of task interest. For the sake of clarity, we rewrite the data matrix, so that the groups appear in three separate columns (Table 7.2).

The null hypothesis states that the groups are three random samples of one and the same population, so that their means would be situated in the same sampling distribution and would therefore merely show random differences:

$$H_0 : \mu_1 = \mu_2 = \mu_3 = \mu.$$

To test this null hypothesis, two sources of variation of the motivation scores are compared: the between-variation between the mean scores of the groups and the within-variation between the scores of individuals within each of the groups. This

Table 7.2

Group 1	Group 2	Group 3
6	4	3
4	3	2
3	3	2
3	2	1
9	7	4
9	5	2
8	4	1
6	4	1
$\bar{Y}_{.1} = 6$	$\bar{Y}_{.2} = 4$	$\bar{Y}_{.3} = 2$

comparison can be made because both variations are the result of an additive partition of the total variation of motivation scores:

$$\text{SST} = \text{SSB} + \text{SSW} \text{ (derivation in Appendix)}.$$

The procedure consists of making two separate estimations of the variance of the population stated in the null hypothesis. The first estimation, $\hat{\sigma}_w^2$, is based on the within-variation. The second estimation, $\hat{\sigma}_b^2$, is based on the between-variation. Each of these estimations contains three steps: (a) variation = sum of squares, (b) degrees of freedom, (c) estimation of population variance. Next, the ratio of these two estimations is calculated. This is the F ratio, which will be situated in the theoretical F distribution to arrive at a conclusion with regard to the null hypothesis.

1. First estimation of the population variance, via the within:

(a)   Within-variation SSW
The variation of individual scores as compared to their group mean is calculated for each group separately:

$$\sum_i (Y_{ij} - \bar{Y}_{.1})^2 = (6-6)^2 + (4-6)^2 + \ldots = 44$$

$$\sum_i (Y_{ij} - \bar{Y}_{.2})^2 = (4-4)^2 + (3-4)^2 + \ldots = 16$$

$$\sum_i (Y_{ij} - \bar{Y}_{.3})^2 = (3-2)^2 + (2-2)^2 + \ldots = 8$$

We find the sum of the three within-variations and thus obtain SSW:

$$\sum_j \sum_i (Y_{ij} - \bar{Y}_{.j})^2 = (44 + 16 + 8 + = 68$$

(b)   Degrees of freedom d_W
If the mean (or the sum) is fixed in a series of n_j scores, then $n_j - 1$ scores have freedom of variation. Only the last score is determined, for it is equal to the sum total minus the sum of the other scores. In our example, there are three groups of eight individuals. In each group the local mean is fixed, so that $8 - 1$ scores have freedom of variation. Therefore, the number of degrees of freedom is: $3(8 - 1) = 21$.

(c)   Population variance, estimated via the within
In dividing the within-variation SSW by the number of degrees of freedom d_W we obtain MSW (mean sum of squares within). This is a first estimation of the population variance ($\hat{} = $ estimation): $\hat{\sigma}_w^2 = \text{SSW}/d_W = 68/21 = 3.24$.

2. Second estimation of the population variance, via the between

(a)   Between-variation SSB
The three group means are 6, 4 and 2. The grand mean, i.e., the sum of the 24 scores divided by 24, can also be calculated as the mean of the three group means, provided that group sizes are equal: $(6 + 4 + 2)/3 = 4$.

We calculate the variation of the three group means as compared to the grand mean:

$$\sum_{j}(\bar{Y}_j - \bar{Y}_{..})^2 = (6 - 4)^2 + (4 - 4)^2 + (2 - 4)^2 = 8$$

This variation is, however, artificially small. For, just as in a sampling distribution, the means are by definition more tightly packed than the original individual scores. In multiplying the calculated variation by the group size (here $n_j = 8$) we obtain a fair estimation of the population variance via the between:

$$\text{SSB} = \sum_{j} n_j(\bar{Y}_j - \bar{Y}_{..})^2 = 8 \times 8 = 64$$

We are happy to verify that

$$\text{SST} = \text{SSB} + \text{SSW} : 132 = 64 + 68$$

(b) Degrees of freedom d_B

Three group means are involved in the calculation. We lose one degree of freedom, because the grand mean is fixed. Therefore, $d_B = 3 - 1 = 2$.

(c) Population variance, estimated via the between

In dividing the between-variation SSB by the number of degrees of freedom d_B we obtain MSB (mean sum of squares between). This is a second estimation of the population variance: $\hat{\sigma}_b^2 = \text{SSB}/d_B = 64/2 = 32$.

3. The performance of the F test

Division of the two estimations of the population variance yields the F ratio, which has the between-estimation in the numerator and the within-estimation in the denominator: $F = 32/3.24 = 9.88$.

We can now arrive at a conclusion with regard to the null hypothesis. On the assumption that the null hypothesis is true, the sampling distribution of F ratios appears to follow a theoretical F distribution, for which tables can be found in any statistics textbook. For an *a priori* postulated probability (e.g., $1 - \alpha = 0.95$) and for a number of degrees of freedom in numerator and denominator (which, here, are 2 and 21, respectively) these tables contain the critical values F^*. For the sake of clarity: if the F ratio in our sample is greater than F^* in the table, then the null hypothesis is rejected. In our example, for $\alpha = 0.05$ and for $d_B = 2$ and $d_W = 21$, we find a critical value $F^* = 3.47$ in the table. The F ratio in our sample, $F = 9.88$, is much higher. Consequently, we can conclude that a significant relationship exists between task interest and intrinsic motivation. The mean motivation scores of the three groups of task interest are significantly different.

In the computer output we do not find a critical F^* value, but rather the expression: SIGNIF OF $F = 0.001$. This is the empirical significance level, which represents a probability of exceeding, i.e., the probability of finding an F ratio of 9.88 or an even more extreme value under H_0. If this probability is very low (less than $\alpha = 0.05$), then we can reject the null hypothesis.

It may be noted in passing that this F test only confirms the existence of significant differences among the three means. It does not follow necessarily that every subset of two means shows a significant difference. The latter is investigated by means of separate 'tests of contrasts' (also termed multiple comparison tests), in which the testing is more conservative (with smaller α).

7.7 The ANOVA Summary Table

The results of the foregoing F test can be represented concisely in an ANOVA summary table, which is also used in every computer output (Table 7.3).

Table 7.3 ANOVA table

	SS	df	MS	F
between	64	2	32	
within	68	21	3.24	9.88
total	132	23		

7.8 The *t* Test as Simplified *F* Test

For the analysis of the relationship between external rewards and intrinsic motivation, a simple t test can be performed (objective 1(a)).

We might, however, follow the foregoing procedure of the F test as well. We will do this briefly. Firstly, we rearrange the data matrix so that the two groups appear in separate columns (Table 7.4).

Table 7.4

Group 1	Group 2
6	9
4	9
3	8
3	6
4	7
3	5
3	4
2	4
3	4
2	2
2	1
1	1
$\bar{Y}_{.1} = 3$	$\bar{Y}_{.2} = 5$

1. First estimation of the population variance, via the within

(a) Within-variation SSW: $SSW = (6-3)^2 + (4-3)^2 + \ldots + (9-5)^2 + (9-5)^2 + \ldots = 108$,

(b) Degrees of freedom: $d_W = 2(12-1) = 22$,

(c) Population variance, estimated via the within: $SSW/d_W = 108/22 = 4.91$.

2. Second estimation of the population variance, via the between:

(a) *Between-variation SSB:* $\text{SSB} = 12[(3-4)^2 + (5-4)^2] = 24$,
(b) *Degrees of freedom:* $d_B = 2 - 1 = 1$,
(c) *Population variance, estimated via the between:* $\text{SSB}/d_B = 24/1 = 24$.

3. The performance of the *F* test

We find $F = 24/4.91 = 4.89$. In the F table, for $\alpha = 0.05$ and for $d_B = 1$ and $d_W = 22$, we read a critical value $F^* = 4.30$. The F ratio calculated in the sample is slightly higher. Thus, the mean motivation scores of the money group and the no-money group are significantly different.

If we perform a *t* **test** in this example for $(12-1) + (12-1) = 22$ degrees of freedom, we find the following t score (formula chapter 4): $t = (5-3)/[(4.91/12 + 4.91/12)^{1/2}] = 2.21$. In the t table, for $\alpha = 0.05$ and for $df = 22$, we find a critical value $t^* = 2.074$ (two-tailed test).

We see that $t = \sqrt{F}$ and $t^* = \sqrt{F^*}$. So, the square of a variable, which is distributed as t with $n - 2$ degrees of freedom, also appears to be distributed as F with 1 and $n - 2$ degrees of freedom. Consequently, the t test of the difference between two groups is identical to the F test. We can also verify in the tables that the F^* values for $d_B = 1$ are the squares of the corresponding t^* values.

Note that this correspondence between the t test and the F test only holds for the case of two groups, i.e., for $d_B = 1$. As soon as there are more than two groups, it would become possible to perform several t tests for the multiple comparison of pairs of means. However, such a procedure would not be allowed, for two reasons. Firstly, we capitalize on chance when we perform repeated tests. Secondly, the multiple tests of contrasts are not independent.

7.9 Calculations in Two-Way ANOVA: Classical Approach

In order to answer questions 1(b), 2(b), 3 and 4, a more complex decomposition of the total variation (SST) of the motivation scores is required. For, in the two-way design we deal with three possible effects: the effect of external rewards (X_1), the effect of task interest (X_2) and the effect of interaction. The decomposition is now as follows:

$$\text{SST} = \text{SSB}_{(x1)} + \text{SSB}_{(x2)} + \text{SSI} + \text{SSW}$$

This time, we rewrite the data matrix in the form of a 2×3 cross table with four motivation scores in each of the six cells (Table 7.5).

There are 24 individual scores Y_{ijk}. There are $r = 2$ groups of external rewards (r for rows). Group j is any of these. There are $c = 3$ groups of task interest (c for columns). Group k is any of these. There are $n = 4$ individual scores for each combination of external rewards and task interest. Individual i is any of these. There are four kinds of means:

$\bar{Y}_{j.}$ for each reward group, regardless of task interest,
$\bar{Y}_{.k}$ for each group of task interest, regardless of rewards,
$\bar{Y}_{jk}$ for each combination of external rewards and task interest,
$\bar{Y}_{...}$ for the grand mean.

Table 7.5

external rewards	task interest group 1		group 2		group 3		
group 1	6 4 3 3	$\bar{Y}_{.11} = 4$	4 3 3 2	$\bar{Y}_{.12} = 3$	3 2 2 1	$\bar{Y}_{.13} = 2$	$\bar{Y}_{.1.} = 3$
group 2	9 9 8 6	$\bar{Y}_{.21} = 8$	7 5 4 4	$\bar{Y}_{.22} = 5$	4 2 1 1	$\bar{Y}_{.23} = 2$	$\bar{Y}_{.2.} = 5$
	$\bar{Y}_{..1} = 6$		$\bar{Y}_{..2} = 4$		$\bar{Y}_{..3} = 2$		$\bar{Y}_{...} = 4$

The reader can see that we make use of the dot notation. A dot means that a summation is made over the units in question (individuals i, rows j or columns k).

We can now deal with **objectives 1(b), 2(b) and 3**:

1(b). Are there, on the average, significant differences between the $r = 2$ row means across columns? In other words, is there a significant relationship between external rewards and intrinsic motivation, controlling for task interest?

2(b). Are there, on the average, significant differences between the $c = 3$ column means across rows? In other words, is there a significant relationship between task interest and intrinsic motivation, controlling for external rewards?

3. Is there a significant effect of interaction?

For each of these three tests we will follow the same procedure as applied in the one-way analysis: the population variance is estimated in two ways, via the within and via the between, and the ratio of these two estimations provides the F ratio, which is used to test whether there are significant differences between the means.

The estimation of the population variance via the within-variation is, however, different from the one-way design. For now there are six cells of four individuals each in a 2×3 cross-table. As this estimation of the population variance via the within is identical for each of the three tests, we will first calculate it separately:

(a)   Within-variation SSW

In each of the six groups we calculate the variation of the individual scores as compared to their local mean. We make the sum of these six within-variations, thus obtaining SSW:

$$\begin{aligned}
\text{SSW} = & (6-4)^2 + (4-4)^2 + (3-4)^2 + (3-4)^2 \\
& + (4-3)^2 + (3-3)^2 + (3-3)^2 + (2-3)^2 \\
& + (3-2)^2 + (2-2)^2 + (2-2)^2 + (1-2)^2 \\
& + (9-8)^2 + (9-8)^2 + (8-8)^2 + (6-8)^2 \\
& + (7-5)^2 + (5-5)^2 + (4-5)^2 + (4-5)^2 \\
& + (4-2)^2 + (2-2)^2 + (1-2)^2 + (1-2)^2 = 28
\end{aligned}$$

(b)   Degrees of freedom d_W

There are $2 \times 3 = 6$ groups of four individuals each involved in the calculation. In each group, the number of degrees of freedom is equal to $4 - 1 = 3$, because of the fixation of the local group mean. Consequently, the total number of degrees of freedom is: $d_W = rc(n - 1) = 2.3(4 - 1) = 18$.

(c)   Population variance, estimated via the within

$$SSW/d_W = MSW = 28/18 = 1.556$$

1(b)   Are there significant differences between the row means?

1. First estimation of the population variance, via the within:

This was just calculated a moment ago: $MSW = 1.556$.

2. Second estimation of the population variance, via the between:

This calculation is identical with the one-way design and was performed in the section entitled 'The t Test as Simplified F Test'. The result is: $MSB = SSB/d_B = 24/1 = 24$.

3. The performance of the F test

This test is not the same as in the one-way design, because the calculation of the denominator MSW of F now involves six and not merely two groups. We find $F = 24/1.556 = 15.42$. In the F table, for $\alpha = 0.05$ and for one and 18 degrees of freedom, we read a critical value $F^* = 4.41$. As $F = 15.42$ is much higher, we can conclude that the mean motivation scores of the money group and the no-money group are significantly different, also after the control for task interest.

2(b)   Are there significant differences between the column means?

1. First estimation of the population variance, via the within

This was calculated above: $MSW = 1.556$.

2. Second estimation of the population variance, via the between

This calculation is identical to the one-way design and was performed in the section entitled 'Calculations in One-Way ANOVA: Classical Approach': $MSB = SSB/d_B = 64/2 = 32$.

3. The performance of the F test

We point out again that this test is not the same as in the one-way design, because six cells, and not merely the three groups of task interest, are now involved in the denominator of F. We find $F = MSB/MSW = 32/1.556 = 20.57$. In the F table, for $\alpha = 0.05$ and for two and 18 degrees of freedom, we read a critical value $F^* = 3.55$. As $F = 20.57$ is much higher, we conclude that the mean motivations of the three groups of task interest are significantly different, also after the control for external rewards.

3. Is there a significant effect of interaction?

1. First estimation of the population variance, via the within

This was calculated above: $\text{MSW} = 1.556$.

2. Second estimation of the population variance, via the interaction

(a)   Interaction-variation SSI
As the effect of interaction can be seen as differences between the differences of means, the interaction-variation can be calculated in a corresponding manner. Looking at the 2×3 cross table, we see for each of the three columns a difference between the money group and the no-money group: $\bar{Y}_{.21} - \bar{Y}_{.11}$, $\bar{Y}_{.22} - \bar{Y}_{.12}$ and $\bar{Y}_{.23} - \bar{Y}_{.13}$. These differences of means are: $8 - 4 = 4$, $5 - 3 = 2$ and $2 - 2 = 0$, respectively. The difference between the two reward groups at the margin of the table is $\bar{Y}_{.2.} - \bar{Y}_{.1.} = 5 - 3 = 2$. The interaction-variation could then be calculated by comparing the three differences between the row means per column with this marginal difference between the row means. A more general method of calculating, which comes down to the same, is as follows. Instead of differentiating the money group and the no-money group per column (e.g., $8 - 4 = 4$), we differentiate the money group and the marginal column mean ($8 - 6 = 2$). This gives us the same information, for, if two groups do not differ, then they are not different from the column mean. At the margin of the table, we do something similar. Instead of differentiating the two-row means ($5 - 3 = 2$), we differentiate a row mean and the grand mean ($5 - 4 = 1$). All this results in the following formula: $(\bar{Y}_{jk} - \bar{Y}_{.k}) - (\bar{Y}_{j.} - \bar{Y}_{...})$. Such a difference between a difference per column and a difference at the margin of the table can be calculated six times. The summation of these six differences of differences is made. Here too, we have to multiply by the group size ($n_jk = 4$) in order to obtain the interaction-variation:

$$\text{SSI} = \sum\sum n_{jk}[(\bar{Y}_{jk} - \bar{Y}_{.k}) - (\bar{Y}_{j.} - \bar{Y}_{...})]^2$$
$$= 4\{[(4 - 6) - (3 - 4)]^2 + [(3 - 4) - (3 - 4)]^2$$
$$+ [(2 - 2) - (3 - 4)]^2 + [(8 - 6) - (5 - 4)]^2$$
$$+ [(5 - 4) - (5 - 4)]^2 + [(2 - 2) - (5 - 4)]^2\} = 4 \times 4 = 16$$

(b)   Degrees of freedom d_I
A number of $r \times c = 2 \times 3 = 6$ cell means are involved in the calculation. In each column we lose one degree of freedom at the column mean. In each row we lose one degree of freedom at the row mean. Therefore, the number of degrees of freedom is:

$$d_I = (r - 1)(c - 1) = (2 - 1)(3 - 1) = 2$$

(c)   Population variance, estimated via the interaction
This is obtained by dividing the interaction-variation SSI by the number of degrees of freedom d_I: $\text{MSI} = \text{SSI}/d_I = 16/2 = 8$.

3. The performance of the F test

We find $F = \text{MSI}/\text{MSW} = 8/1.556 = 5.14$. In the F table, the critical value for $\alpha = 0.05$ and for two and 18 degrees of freedom, is $F^* = 3.55$. As the sample value $F = 5.14$ is higher, we conclude that there is a significant effect of interaction of external rewards and task interest on intrinsic motivation. In terms of the subject matter, this means the following. Looking at the cross table, we see that there is an effect of task interest: the mean motivations decrease as the tasks become more boring, at the margin of the table $(6, 4, 2)$ as well as within the table $(4, 3, 2$ and $8, 5, 2)$. However, this decline is less drastic in the no-money group $(4, 3, 2)$ than in the money group $(8, 5, 2)$. This mechanism, according to which the relationship between task interest and motivation is less strong in reward group 1 than in reward group 2, is called effect of interaction and appears to be significant.

Here we conclude the classical approach. The attentive reader will have noted that $\text{SSB}(x_1) + \text{SSB}(x_2) + \text{SSI} + \text{SSW} = 24 + 64 + 16 + 28 = 132$. This is SST.

7.10 The Dummy Regression Approach

In the foregoing we repeatedly alluded to the formal equivalence of the regression model and the analysis of variance model, on the understanding that dummy coding had been used in the latter. For the sake of preliminary illustration, let us at first restrict ourselves to the effect of external rewards (X_1) on intrinsic motivation (Y) and begin by rewriting the $X_1 - Y$ data matrix. Variable X_1 is replaced by D_1 and is assigned the scores 0 and 1 instead of the scores 1 and 2 (for the no-money group and the money group, respectively) as shown in Table 7.6.

If we present this matrix with dummy coding for D_1 to the computer and request a regression analysis, then we obtain exactly the same results as we do when we present the original data matrix with 1–2 coding for X_1 and request a classical analysis of variance. We will now demonstrate this by way of introduction, thus illustrating that regression analysis and analysis of variance are two variants of the general linear model.

For the classical analysis of variance approach we refer to the foregoing section entitled 'The t Test as Simplified F Test'. The mean motivation of the money group was 5 and the mean motivation of the no-money group was 3. The difference between these two means $(5 - 3 = 2)$ appeared to be significant. We found an F ratio of 4.89, which was greater than the critical value $F^* = 4.30$ of the F table (for $\alpha = 0.05$ and $d_B = 1$ and $d_W = 22$).

Keeping these results in mind, we now perform the regression analysis, using the matrix with dummy coding. For briefness' sake we choose the matrix approach. We first calculate the regression function and, after that, perform the F test, using the model comparison procedure.

(a) Calculation of the regression function
The regression coefficients b_0 and b_{y1} together form a vector $\mathbf{b}$, which is derived from: $\mathbf{b} = (\mathbf{X}'\mathbf{X})^{-1}\mathbf{X}'\mathbf{y}$. In this formula, $\mathbf{y}$ is the (24×1) column vector of Y scores and $\mathbf{X}$ is the augmented (24×2) matrix, which not only contains the D_1 scores, but also a first

Table 7.6

Y	D_1
6	0
4	0
3	0
3	0
4	0
3	0
3	0
2	0
3	0
2	0
2	0
1	0
9	1
9	1
8	1
6	1
7	1
5	1
4	1
4	1
4	1
2	1
1	1
1	1

column with 1 scores (augmented matrix). We first calculate the product of the transposed matrix $\mathbf{X}'$ and $\mathbf{X}$, as well as the product of $\mathbf{X}'$ and $\mathbf{y}$:

$$\mathbf{X}'\mathbf{X} = \begin{bmatrix} 1 & 1 & 1 & \cdots & 1 \\ 0 & 0 & 0 & \cdots & 1 \end{bmatrix} \begin{bmatrix} 1 & 0 \\ 1 & 0 \\ 1 & 0 \\ \vdots & \vdots \\ 1 & 1 \end{bmatrix} = \begin{bmatrix} 24 & 12 \\ 12 & 12 \end{bmatrix}$$

$$\mathbf{X}'\mathbf{y} = \begin{bmatrix} 1 & 1 & 1 & \cdots & 1 \\ 0 & 0 & 0 & \cdots & 1 \end{bmatrix} \begin{bmatrix} 6 \\ 4 \\ 3 \\ \vdots \\ 1 \end{bmatrix} = \begin{bmatrix} 96 \\ 60 \end{bmatrix}$$

The inverse of matrix $\mathbf{X}'\mathbf{X}$ is found by means of standard methods:

$$(\mathbf{X}'\mathbf{X})^{-1} = \frac{\begin{bmatrix} 12 & -12 \\ -12 & 24 \end{bmatrix}'}{144} = \begin{bmatrix} 1/12 & -1/12 \\ -1/12 & 1/6 \end{bmatrix}$$

The product of $(\mathbf{X'X})^{-1}$ and $(\mathbf{X'y})$ is vector $\mathbf{b}$:

$$\mathbf{b} = (\mathbf{X'X})^{-1}(\mathbf{X'y}) = \begin{bmatrix} 1/12 & -1/12 \\ -1/12 & 1/6 \end{bmatrix} \begin{bmatrix} 96 \\ 60 \end{bmatrix} = \begin{bmatrix} 3 \\ 2 \end{bmatrix}$$

The regression function $\hat{Y} = b_0 + b_{y1}D_1$ thus becomes: $\hat{Y} = 3 + 2D_1$. In this equation the intercept 3 is the mean of the no-money group (with 0 scores). The regression coefficient 2 is the increase of the mean motivation for a unit increase of D_1. As the change from score 0 to score 1 of D_1 is in fact a unit increase, this means that the mean motivation of the money group (with 1 scores) lies 2 higher than for the no-money group: $3 + 2 = 5$. All this has already been explained in the section entitled 'Geometric Approach'.

(b) The F test according to the model comparison procedure

In the regression approach, the significance of a model is tested by making a distinction between the full model and the restricted model and by performing an F test. In this simple example, the full model contains only one independent variable D_1. The explained variance (see computer output) appears to be 0.182. In the restricted model, D_1 is absent. It follows naturally that the explained variance is equal to 0 in this model, for there is nothing to explain.

Thus, the full model is: $Y = b_0 + b_{y1}D_1 + e$ with $R_f^2 = 0.182$.
The restricted model is: $Y = b_0 + e$ with $R_r^2 = 0$.
The degrees of freedom are $d_f = 22$ and $d_r = 23$, respectively.
The F test of the model with D_1 gives us the following result:

$$F = \frac{(R_f^2 - R_r^2)/(d_r - d_f)}{(1 - R_f^2)/d_f} = \frac{(0.182 - 0)/(23 - 22)}{(1 - 0.182)/22} = 4.89$$

This is exactly the same result as we found in the section entitled 'The t Test as Simplified F Test'. The correspondence between the classical approach and the dummy regression approach is complete.

The regression function for the **effect of task interest on intrinsic motivation** can be calculated in an analogous fashion. The full model is now $Y = b_0 + b_{y2}D_2 + b_{y3}D_3 + e$ and the restricted model is $Y = b_0 + e$. The data matrix with variables Y and X_2 is first rewritten as a data matrix (Table 7.7), in which X_2 (with scores 1, 2, 3) is replaced by D_2 and D_3 (with scores 1 and 0, 0 and 1, 0 and 0 respectively).

The calculation of the multiple regression function can be performed in three ways: via the separate calculation of the partial regression coefficients, via the correlation approach of path analysis or via the matrix approach. We obtain: $Y = 2 + 4D_2 + 2D_3 + e$. This equation has already been discussed. The intercept 2 is the mean motivation of the 0–0 group with boring tasks. This mean is 4 higher $(b_{y2.3} = 4)$ for the 1–0 group with interesting tasks and 2 higher $(b_{y3.2} = 2)$ for the 0–1 group with moderately interesting tasks.

The explained variance of this model with D_2 and D_3 appears to be 0.485 (please calculate yourself or see computer output). The explained variance without D_2 and D_3 is naturally equal to 0. The numbers of degrees of freedom are $d_f = 21$ and $d_r = 23$,

Table 7.7

Y	D_2	D_3
6	1	0
4	1	0
3	1	0
3	1	0
9	1	0
9	1	0
8	1	0
6	1	0
4	0	1
3	0	1
3	0	1
2	0	1
7	0	1
5	0	1
4	0	1
4	0	1
3	0	0
2	0	0
2	0	0
1	0	0
4	0	0
2	0	0
1	0	0
1	0	0

respectively. The F test according to the model comparison procedure results in an F score of:

$$F = [(0.485 - 0)/(23 - 21)]/[(1 - 0.485)/21] = 9.88$$

This result is identical to the one found in the section entitled 'Calculations in One-Way ANOVA: Classical Approach'.

7.11   Testing the Global Model via the Regression Approach

Once again making use of the formal equivalence of the model of analysis of variance and the regression model, we can now answer objective 4 (including objective 3): the F test of the global model, in which the dummies D_1, D_2 and D_3 as well as the product terms $D_4 = D_1 D_2$ and $D_5 = D_1 D_3$, are included. The data matrix is shown in Table 7.8.

According to the model comparison procedure of regression analysis, the full model (with D_1 to D_5) is compared with the restricted model (without independent variables):

Full model: $Y = b_0 + b_{y1}D_1 + b_{y2}D_2 + b_{y3}D_3 + b_{y4}D_4 + b_{y5}D_5 + e$

Restricted model: $Y = b_0 + e$

Table 7.8

Y	D_1	D_2	D_3	D_4	D_5
6	0	1	0	0	0
4	0	1	0	0	0
3	0	1	0	0	0
3	0	1	0	0	0
4	0	0	1	0	0
3	0	0	1	0	0
3	0	0	1	0	0
2	0	0	1	0	0
3	0	0	0	0	0
2	0	0	0	0	0
2	0	0	0	0	0
1	0	0	0	0	0
9	1	1	0	1	0
9	1	1	0	1	0
8	1	1	0	1	0
6	1	1	0	1	0
7	1	0	1	0	1
5	1	0	1	0	1
4	1	0	1	0	1
4	1	0	1	0	1
4	1	0	0	0	0
2	1	0	0	0	0
1	1	0	0	0	0
1	1	0	0	0	0

To find the degrees of freedom we subtract the number of parameters of a model from the total number of observations (24). In the restricted model there is only one parameter (b_0), whereas in the full model there are six parameters. Consequently, $d_r = 23$ and $d_f = 18$. The explained variance (R^2) of the restricted model is equal to 0 and for the full model it is 0.788 (please calculate yourself or see computer output).

Thus, the F score is: $F = [(0.788 - 0)/(23 - 18)]/[(1 - 0.788)/18] = 13.37$. In the F table, for $\alpha = 0.05$ and five and 18 degrees of freedom, we read a critical value $F^* = 2.77$. As our F value is much higher, the global model appears to be significant.

Making use of the same model comparison procedure, we can also test whether there is a **significant effect of interaction**. When dummy coding has been applied, this effect of interaction is represented by the two product terms $D_4 = D_1D_2$ and $D_5 = D_1D_3$. These two product terms are included in the full model, but not in the restricted model. The difference between the two models then consists of the two product terms D_4 and D_5:

Full model: $Y = b_0 + b_{y1}D_1 + b_{y2}D_2 + b_{y3}D_3 + b_{y4}D_4 + b_{y5}D_5 + e$

Restricted model: $Y = b_0 + b_{y1}D_1 + b_{y2}D_2 + b_{y3}D_3 + e$

The explained variances are 0.788 and 0.667, respectively (please calculate yourself or see computer output). The degrees of freedom are $d_f = 18$ and $d_r = 20$. The calculation of the F ratio is straightforward: $F = [(0.788 - 0.667)/(20 - 18)]/[(1 - 0.788)/18] = 5.14$.

Please note that this result is identical to the one found in the section entitled 'Calculations in Two-Way ANOVA: Classical Approach', when we answered the question: Is there a significant effect of interaction? The effect of interaction indeed appears to be significant, for $F = 5.14$ is greater than $F^* = 3.55$, for $\alpha = 0.05$ and two and 18 degrees of freedom.

This test of significant interaction can also be performed for more complex models by means of the same model comparison approach. A warning is, however, appropriate here. It is not recommendable to subject all possible effects of interaction (and other effects) to a test one at a time. For, in doing so we commit the sin of 'repeated testing', through which the probability of success is artificially enhanced. Therefore, it is better to start with one test, in which the full model contains all product terms (by twos, by threes, by fours etc.) and in which not one product term is included in the restricted model. This way one tests whether there is any interaction at all. If this is not the case, then we can continue with the additive model without product terms. On the other hand, if significant interactions exist, then we have no choice but to perform multiple tests. These tests will then have to be more conservative (with a smaller probability of type I error α). But, then, too, we can group these tests a little in order to avoid capitalization on chance. For example, we can test first whether the three-, four- and higher-order interactions, taken together, show a significant result. If not, then we have already eliminated all these product terms by means of one single test and can concentrate further on the two-order interactions.

In formulating a **substantial conclusion** we have to face the fact that our initial expectations of the effect of interaction are refuted by the empirical data. There is indeed a significant interaction, but it is substantially different in character than was formulated *a priori*. For, it was postulated that the positive effect of an amount of money would hold for boring tasks, but that it would be absent for moderately interesting tasks and even be negative for captivating tasks. However, the results of our analyses show that rewards and task interest reinforce each other in a positive fashion: highest mean motivation for interesting tasks *and* a monetary reward!

7.12 Analysis of Covariance

If one or several independent variables in an ANOVA-design are measured at the interval level, then these are called 'covariate' and the applied technique is analysis of covariance ($=$ ANCOVA). Suppose that intrinsic motivation (Y) as well as the three groups of task interest (X_2) are left unaltered in our example, but that variable X_1, which was a dichotomy (no money or money), is changed into an interval variable with gradual awards of amounts of money (varying from 1000 to 9000 BF (Belgian francs)). Then we obtain an ANCOVA design.

As X_1 and Y are measured as interval scales, we can calculate a mean and a variation for each of these variables within the three groups of task interest (SSW) as well as between these groups (SSB). Not only the variations (sum of squares), but also the covariation of X_1 and Y can be calculated, within and between. A complex number of covariance theorems can be set up in this manner with corresponding F tests. This is the way in which analysis of covariance was presented in earlier days. This working method stems from an experimental tradition. For, keeping the OXO-model of the standard experiment in mind, covariate X_1 has to be seen as the score of the dependent variable in the preliminary investigation: the means of the groups should not differ significantly *before* the introduction of the experimental stimulus. This applies to the dependent variable (pre-test score of Y) and various other variables. And, in so far as such differences exist, controls should be performed. The dependent variable Y is the post-test score in this model: there is a significant difference between the mean Y scores of the groups *after* the introduction of the stimulus.

This classical approach will not be followed here, for it is too cumbersome. As an alternative, the regression approach offers us the opportunity to present analysis of covariance as a new variant of the general linear model. And in this way we can be very brief. Firstly, code the independent variables of lower measurement level in the form of dummies (one dummy less than the number of categories). Secondly, leave the dependent variable and the covariates with the interval measurement level unaltered (or express them as deviations of their means). Thirdly, present this data matrix, with or without product terms, to the computer and perform a regression analysis. The results of this analysis, with corresponding F tests, will be the same as in the classical analysis of covariance.

For example, the test of the global non-additive model consists of comparing the following models according to the model comparison procedure: (a) the full model with covariate X_1 (the awarded amount of money), with the dummies D_2 and D_3 (which represent the three groups of task interest) and with the product terms $X_1 D_2$ and $X_1 D_3$; (b) the restricted model without these independent variables. The only difference with ANOVA is that X_1 is no longer treated as a dummy variable, but as a variable of interval measurement level (with amounts of money as scores).

One remark is, however, in place here. The **dummy coding** does not always have to proceed according to the proposed 0–1 pattern. The possibilities are innumerable. The coding has to be set up in such a way that no linear dependencies occur among the independent variables (including the dummies). This can be inspected in the correlation matrix, which will contain zeros for all correlations between independent variables. Such a construction of dummy variables in a way in which linear dependencies among dummies and predictors are absent is known as the construction of an orthogonal design matrix $\mathbf{X}$. It means that the product $\mathbf{X'X}$ is diagonal, i.e., that the off-diagonal elements are all zero. Until now we have used 1–0, 0–1 and 0–0 for the coding of D_2 and D_3. This indeed does not produce linear dependencies among the dummies:

$$\begin{bmatrix} 1 & 0 & 0 \\ 0 & 1 & 0 \end{bmatrix} \begin{bmatrix} 1 & 0 \\ 0 & 1 \\ 0 & 0 \end{bmatrix} = \begin{bmatrix} 1 & 0 \\ 0 & 1 \end{bmatrix}$$

We will now show another way of coding of D_2 and D_3, namely 1 1, 0 −2 and −1 1, for which $\mathbf{X'X}$ is diagonal as well:

$$\begin{bmatrix} 1 & 0 & -1 \\ 1 & -2 & 1 \end{bmatrix} \begin{bmatrix} 1 & 1 \\ 0 & -2 \\ -1 & 1 \end{bmatrix} = \begin{bmatrix} 2 & 0 \\ 0 & 6 \end{bmatrix}$$

We will follow this method of coding below.

Table 7.9

Y	X_1	D_2	D_3
6	8	1	1
4	5	1	1
3	2	1	1
3	3	1	1
9	9	1	1
9	7	1	1
8	6	1	1
6	4	1	1
4	8	0	-2
3	7	0	-2
3	6	0	-2
2	4	0	-2
7	5	0	-2
5	9	0	-2
4	3	0	-2
4	2	0	-2
3	4	-1	1
2	9	-1	1
2	8	-1	1
1	2	-1	1
4	6	-1	1
2	7	-1	1
1	5	-1	1
1	3	-1	1

The data matrix, in which X_1 is operationalized as x times 1000 BF, is as shown in Table 7.9.

Multiple regression analysis of the global model with product terms yields the following regression equation: $\hat{Y} = 4 + 0.35(X_1 - \bar{X}_1) + 2D_2 + 0D_3 + 0.35D_2(X_1 - \bar{X}_1) + 0.14D_3(X_1 - \bar{X}_1)$ with $R^2 = 0.71$ and a significant result ($F = 8.98$, df: 5,18).

A test of interaction is performed by comparing this global model with the restricted model without product terms: $\hat{Y} = 4 + 0.35(X_1 - \bar{X}_1) + 2D_2 + 0D_3$ with $R^2 = 0.60$ and a significant result ($F = 10.05$, df: 3,20).

Using the model comparison approach, this test of interaction yields a result which is just shy of being significant: $F = [(0.71 - 0.60)/(20 - 18)]/[(1 - 0.71)/18] = 3.41$ (df: 2,18; $\alpha = .05$).

Geometrically, an effect of interaction means that the magnitude of the relationship between X_1 and Y is different for the three groups. For our fictitious data the figure is as shown in Figure 7.8.

There is an effect of interaction if the slopes of the three within-groups regression lines are different, i.e., if the three regression lines are not parallel. We see in the figure that the effect of monetary rewards on motivation is much stronger for the first group with interesting tasks ($b_{y1} = 0.83$) than for the other two groups ($b_{y1} = 0.07$ and 0.14). It appeared, however, from the F test performed a moment ago, that this effect of interaction is not significant.

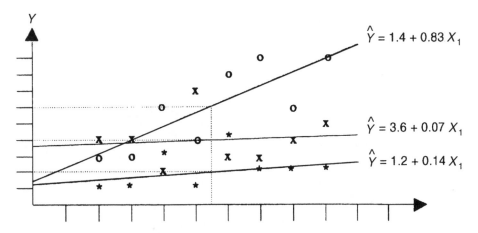

Figure 7.8   Effect of external rewards on motivation for three groups of task interest

We can also derive the other relationships from the figure. For example, the mean amount of money (X_1) is equal to 5.5 for each of the three groups, which can be indicated by projection on the X_1 axis. So, there is no relationship between covariate X_1 and the groups.

The mean motivations (Y) are 6, 4 and 2, respectively; looking at the projections on the Y axis, we can see that the three group means are indeed situated one above the other. Thus, there is a relationship between Y and the groups of task interest.

The existence of a positive relationship between covariate X_1 and the dependent variable Y can be seen when we look at the slopes of the three regression lines: for each of the three groups, motivation increases as the amount of money increases. It may be noted in passing that the regression coefficient of X_1 is a partial coefficient, which is an average of the local coefficients: the number 0.35 indeed lies midway between 0.83, 0.07 and 0.14.

It follows from our analyses that the model with the three groups and the covariate and without the product terms is most adequate. The model also appears to be safeguarded against relationships among the independent variables, a nice feature which we called 'orthogonality' in analysis of variance and 'absence of multicollinearity' in regression analysis. By way of conclusion in Figure 7.9 we now draw the causal diagram of the best fitting model.

7.13   The Factorial Experiment

The analysis of variance model belongs especially to 'inferential' statistics. An F ratio of two variances, the between-groups and the within-groups variance, is tested for significance. Up to now there has been no mention of a measure of the strength of an effect or of a mutual comparison of the effects, contrary to regression analysis, in which the correlation and regression coefficients — and especially the betas — played this role.

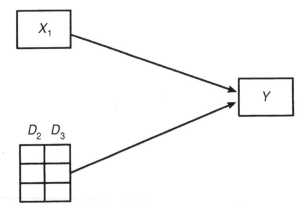

Figure 7.9　Causal diagram

In an attempt to develop this 'descriptive' side of analysis of variance, the **'factorial experiment'** has been designed. The expression 'factorial design' is sometimes used as well. The term 'experiment' refers to the experimental tradition. The so-called 'factors' are the stimuli, which are introduced in the experiment. They are the independent variables. The term 'design' refers to the construction of a design matrix **X**, of which we have given some examples in the foregoing sections. The latter will now receive the most attention, for it will become clear from the design matrix which effects we intend to calculate.

7.14　The 2 × 2 Factorial Design

In our example of analysis of variance the external rewards variable (X_1) was a dichotomy and the task interest (X_2) was a trichotomy. So, we were dealing with a two-way 2 × 3 design. For didactical reasons we will, however, start with a two-way 2 × 2 design, in which each of the two factors are dichotomous. We do so by omitting the group of moderately interesting tasks. We speak of a two-way design because there are two independent variables. We call it a 2 × 2 design or, in general a 2^k design, because all independent variables have two categories.

The strength of an effect will be represented by a difference of means, for example the mean motivation of the money group minus the mean motivation of the no-money group. Such a difference of means is a linear combination with coefficients $+1$ and -1: $\bar{Y}_1 - \bar{Y}_2 = (+1)\bar{Y}_1 + (-1)\bar{Y}_2$. The design matrix will therefore exist of 1s and -1s. The story is, however, somewhat more complicated, because we will have to calculate partially. We will demonstrate this in the data matrix, which is given in the form of a cross-table (Table 7.10).

Without calculating partially, the effect of external rewards would simply be the difference of the means of group 2 (5) and group 1 (3). We would then pretend there were no groups of task interest and would only perform a bivariate analysis of the effect of money on motivation, regardless of task interest.

To calculate partially means that the difference in means of group 2 and group 1 is calculated twice, once for the group with interesting tasks $(8 - 4 = 4)$ and once for the

Table 7.10

	task interest		
external rewards	group 1	group 3	
group 1	6 4 3 3 $\bar{Y}_{11} = 4$	3 2 2 1 $\bar{Y}_{13} = 2$	$\bar{Y}_{1.} = 3$
group 2	9 9 8 6 $\bar{Y}_{21} = 8$	4 2 1 1 $\bar{Y}_{23} = 2$	$\bar{Y}_{2.} = 5$
	$\bar{Y}_{.1} = 6$	$\bar{Y}_{.3} = 2$	$\bar{Y}_{..} = 4$

group with uninteresting tasks $(2 - 2 = 0)$, and that we calculate the mean of these two differences $[(4 + 0)/2 = 2]$. In doing so, we have controlled for task interest. In an analogous fashion the effect of task interest can be calculated, either regardless of or controlling for external rewards.

Let us indicate external rewards as 'factor A' and its effect d_A. And let task interest be indicated as 'factor B' and its effect d_B. Then the partial calculation of the effects is as follows:

$$d_A = \tfrac{1}{2}[(\bar{Y}_{21} - \bar{Y}_{11}) + (\bar{Y}_{23} - \bar{Y}_{13})] = \tfrac{1}{2}[(8 - 4) + (2 - 2)] = 2$$
$$d_B = \tfrac{1}{2}[(\bar{Y}_{13} - \bar{Y}_{11}) + (\bar{Y}_{23} - \bar{Y}_{21})] = \tfrac{1}{2}[(2 - 4) + (2 - 8)] = -4$$
$$d_{AB} = \tfrac{1}{2}[(\bar{Y}_{23} - \bar{Y}_{21}) - (\bar{Y}_{13} - \bar{Y}_{11})] = \tfrac{1}{2}[(2 - 8) - (2 - 4)] = -2$$

or equally:

$$\tfrac{1}{2}[(\bar{Y}_{23} - \bar{Y}_{13}) - (\bar{Y}_{21} - \bar{Y}_{11})] = \tfrac{1}{2}[(2 - 2) - (8 - 4)] = -2$$

The last effect d_{AB} is the effect of interaction and is calculated as a difference of differences of means. The division by 2 (multiplication by $\tfrac{1}{2}$) serves the purpose of maintaining comparability with the main effects d_A and d_B.

The foregoing can be greatly simplified by the construction of a **design matrix** with 1s and -1s as shown in Table 7.11.

Four cells are indicated in the column at the front. For the main effect, d_A, we write 1 where a_2 is (the money group) and -1 where a_1 is (the no-money group). For the main effect, d_B, we write 1 where we see b_3 (uninteresting tasks) and -1 where we see

Table 7.11

	d_A	d_B	d_{AB}
cell $a_1 b_1$ ($\bar{Y}_{11} = 4$)	-1	-1	1
$a_1 b_3$ ($\bar{Y}_{13} = 2$)	-1	1	-1
$a_2 b_1$ ($\bar{Y}_{21} = 8$)	1	-1	-1
$a_2 b_3$ ($\bar{Y}_{23} = 2$)	1	1	1
	4	-8	-4

b_1 (interesting tasks). For the effect of interaction, $d_A B$, we simply take the product of the first two columns.

After that we add up the products of the cell means with the 1s and -1s, per column. For example, for the effect $d_A B$ we obtain: $(1)(4) + (-1)(2) + (-1)(8) + (1)(2) = -4$. Dividing the three sums of products $(4, -8, -4)$ by 2 yields the three effects of A, B and the product AB, which were calculated above $(2, -4, -2)$.

Note that the design matrix $\mathbf{X}$ with 1s and -1s is orthogonal, because $\mathbf{X'X}$ is diagonal. Therefore, we might apply the regression approach with this dummy coding as well.

It should also be pointed out that the sign of an effect is relative. For example, for the effect of task interest, the mean motivation of the group with interesting tasks was subtracted from the mean motivation of the group with uninteresting tasks. The result was negative: $\frac{1}{2}(-8) = -4$. This result would, however, have been positive if we had subtracted the group with uninteresting tasks from the group with interesting tasks, for the latter group has the highest mean motivation. The same holds for the effect of external rewards.

The construction of a design matrix is handy for a quick calculation of the effects. So is the set up of a **tree diagram**, as shown in Figure 7.10. The effects can be read at a

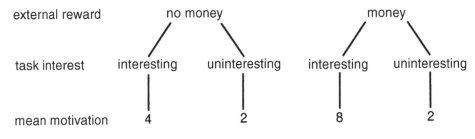

Figure 7.10   Tree diagram

glance in the bottom row of mean motivations. For instance, the effect of money is the mean of the two differences between the money group and the no-money group: 8–4 and 2–2. The effect of task interest is the mean of the two differences between the uninteresting and the interesting task group: 2–4 and 2–8. The effect of interaction is the difference between two differences of means.

7.15   The 2 × 3 Factorial Design

We now return to the original example of two-way analysis of variance, in which factor A is dichotomous (external rewards: no-money or money) and factor B a trichotomy (task interest: interesting, moderately interesting or uninteresting). Such a 2×3 design is less easy to manage, for the trichotomy of factor B causes multi-interpretability. What exactly does the effect of B mean? Do we want to compare the interesting task group with the other two groups? Do we want to compare the three groups by twos? Or do we want to take the uninteresting task group as the reference group and examine whether the motivations of the other two groups are different

Table 7.12

external rewards (A)	task interest (B) group 1		group 2		group 3		
group 1	6 4 3 3	$\bar{Y}_{.11} = 4$	4 3 3 2	$\bar{Y}_{.12} = 3$	3 2 2 1	$\bar{Y}_{.13} = 2$	$\bar{Y}_{.1.} = 3$
group 2	9 9 8 6	$\bar{Y}_{.21} = 8$	7 5 4 4	$\bar{Y}_{.22} = 5$	4 2 1 1	$\bar{Y}_{.23} = 2$	$\bar{Y}_{.2.} = 5$
	$\bar{Y}_{..1} = 6$		$\bar{Y}_{..2} = 4$		$\bar{Y}_{..3} = 2$		$\bar{Y}_{...} = 4$

from this group? We will follow this last strategy below and construct an appropriate design matrix.

The data matrix, in the form of a cross-table, is as shown in Table 7.12. For the main effect, d_A, we now have to calculate three differences of means, one for each group of task interest. We then calculate their mean. For factor B we cannot speak of 'the' main effect d_B, because there are three groups. We take group 3 with uninteresting tasks as the reference group. We first compare group 1 with group 3, putting group 2 at zero. Next we compare group 2 with group 3, putting group 1 at zero. In this way, the effect of B is represented by two differences of means with the third group: one for group 1 and one for group 2.

As the contribution of factor B is represented by two effects, the effect of interaction will also consist of two parts.

$$d_A = \tfrac{1}{3}[(\bar{Y}_{.21} - \bar{Y}_{.11}) + (\bar{Y}_{.22} - \bar{Y}_{.12}) + (\bar{Y}_{.23} - \bar{Y}_{.13})]$$
$$= \tfrac{1}{3}[(8 - 4) + (5 - 3) + (2 - 2)] = 2$$
$$d_{B_1} = \tfrac{1}{2}[(\bar{Y}_{.11} - \bar{Y}_{.13}) + (\bar{Y}_{.21} - \bar{Y}_{.23})] = \tfrac{1}{2}[(4 - 2) + (8 - 2)] = 4$$
$$d_{B_2} = \tfrac{1}{2}[(\bar{Y}_{.12} - \bar{Y}_{.13}) + (\bar{Y}_{.22} - \bar{Y}_{.23})] = \tfrac{1}{2}[(3 - 2) + (5 - 2)] = 2$$
$$d_{AB_1} = \tfrac{1}{2}[(\bar{Y}_{.21} - \bar{Y}_{.23}) - (\bar{Y}_{.11} - \bar{Y}_{.13})] = \tfrac{1}{2}[(8 - 2) - (4 - 2)] = 2$$
$$d_{AB_2} = \tfrac{1}{2}[(\bar{Y}_{.22} - \bar{Y}_{.23}) - (\bar{Y}_{.12} - \bar{Y}_{.13})] = \tfrac{1}{2}[(5 - 2) - (3 - 2)] = 1$$

This cumbersome working method can be systematized and abbreviated by constructing a **design matrix**. The latter now not only contains 1s and −1s, but 0s as well, for in calculating the differences of means for factor B a third group is left out of consideration (put at zero). The coefficients for the effect of interaction are simply the products AB_1 and AB_2.

The sums of products of cell means and coefficients give us the magnitudes of the different effects. These then still have to be divided by the number of differences of means involved in the calculation, in order to obtain mean effect sizes.

All this has been collected in the design matrix shown in Table 7.13.

Most computer programs offer the possibility to choose other design matrices, depending on which differences of means one wants to examine. This possibility is generally indicated under the subprogram 'contrast', because the design matrix

Table 7.13

	d_A	d_{B_1}	d_{B_2}	d_{AB_1}	d_{AB_2}
cell a_1b_1 ($\bar{Y}_{.11} = 4$)	-1	1	0	-1	0
a_1b_2 ($\bar{Y}_{.12} = 3$)	-1	0	1	0	-1
a_1b_3 ($\bar{Y}_{.13} = 2$)	-1	-1	-1	1	1
a_2b_1 ($\bar{Y}_{.21} = 8$)	1	1	0	1	0
a_2b_2 ($\bar{Y}_{.22} = 5$)	1	0	1	0	1
a_2b_3 ($\bar{Y}_{.23} = 2$)	1	-1	-1	-1	-1
	6	8	4	4	2

indicates which specific contrasts between cell means will be calculated. The corresponding significance tests (tests of contrasts) are also provided and these tests are more conservative if several contrasts are examined.

The 'default' option generally expresses each effect as a difference between the local mean and the grand mean, so that contrasts do not have the form $\mu_2 - \mu_1$, but rather $\mu_i - \mu$. This working method, which we have not followed here, can be found in most classical statistics textbooks.

7.16   Orthogonality, Homoscedasticity, Normality, Linearity

As in multiple regression analysis, it is very important to submit the assumptions of the model to a test. In the foregoing sections we have often performed a test of **additivity** (absence of effect of interaction), as well as various tests of the separate effects, with the intention of obtaining the most adequate model.

Linearity and **normality** are two other important assumptions that have to be submitted to a test, without which application of the technique may lead to the wrong conclusions. An analysis of the residuals can be extremely helpful here and most modern computer programs are much better equipped to perform these analyses than they used to be. A residual plot is sometimes sufficient, for a random pattern of the residuals indicates that the distribution is approximately normal and a non-linear pattern of the residuals indicates that the linear model is inadequate for the empirical data.

Orthogonality has been treated at length in the foregoing sections. In multiple regression analysis it was called 'absence of multicollinearity', whereas in analysis of variance the term 'orthogonality' was used. For the design matrix **X** this required that the product **X'X** be diagonal, i.e., that the off-diagonal elements are all zero. This simply means that the independent variables are mutually uncorrelated. In analysis of variance, in which the independent variables constitute nominal scales, because they represent groups, this requirement is fulfilled if all cells contain an equal number of units. In research practice, however, this is seldom the case. Which strategy should then be followed if the cells show unequal frequencies? A first possibility is the construction of a non-orthogonal design. We will, however, often depend on the consultation of a specialist here, for few textbooks treat this topic explicitly and computer programs leave the elaboration to the user under the heading 'user-defined contrast', adding the remark that 'orthogonal contrasts are the most useful'. Another possibility is to draw random samples from the cells with highest frequencies, using sample sizes equal to the mean of the sizes of the other cells. This strategy naturally entails loss of information, but the units that have not been selected can be kept in reserve for the performance of controls.

The assumption of **homoscedasticity**, which is also called 'homogeneity of variances', means that the dispersions of the dependent variable Y within cells must not differ significantly. If differences occur, we use the term 'heteroscedasticity'. This violation, too, can be controlled at a glance in the analysis of residuals. An example is the investigation of the smoking behaviour of men and women, in which women use tobacco between two and four times a day (three on the average) and men between six and 16 (11 on the average), so that the range is $4 - 2 = 2$ for women and $16 - 6 = 10$ for men. The standard deviations, which are mostly about one-quarter of the ranges (because 4 standard deviations span almost the whole, i.e., 95.5% of the statistical population of a normal distribution), are then approximately 0.5 and 2.5. A test of significant difference between the group variances is included in each computer program. This test of homogeneity of variances must not lead to a significant result. In the expression 'significance $= \ldots$', indicated in the computer output, we should read at $\ldots$ a number which is greater — preferably much greater — than 0.05. If this is not the case, then we should either conclude that the technique was not appropriate for application, or that some transformation of the dependent variable has to be performed in order to avoid this problem.

In our example with fictitious data we have cautiously seen to it that the dispersions of each of the six cells are not too different: ranges $6 - 3 = 3$, $4 - 2 = 2$, $3 - 1 = 2$, $9 - 6 = 3$, $7 - 4 = 3$, $4 - 1 = 3$.

To avoid misunderstandings we still want to point out that differences in dispersion are not necessarily evil. Sometimes they themselves are the subject of investigation. An example is the sleeping behaviour of students. In an inquiry among students at Leuven University, Belgium, three months before exams, one month before exams and during exams, the mean numbers of sleeping hours and the ranges appeared to be, respectively: (a) 8 and $14 - 2 = 12$, (b) 7.5 and $10 - 5 = 5$ and (c) 7 and $8 - 6 = 2$. The decreasing range (12, 5, 2) here indicates that the sleeping behaviour becomes more homogeneous as the exams come nearer.

7.17 SPSS for Windows Output of ANOVA and ANCOVA

The SPSS computer output for this mini example of motivation research consists of three parts: (a) a classical analysis of variance, (b) an analysis of variance in the form of a dummy regression analysis with 0s and 1s and (c) an analysis of covariance as dummy regression analysis, now using another orthogonal design matrix.

Choosing or creating a data file
How to open an SPSS session and how to choose a data file or, if a data file does not yet exist, how to enter data, to choose name, type and label of variables and to save the data file with extension *.sav*, is shown in Chapter 4.

Running the classical ANOVAs

Click on Statistics. Click on ANOVA Models. Click on Simple Factorial. This opens the Simple Factorial ANOVA dialog box. Click on variable Y in the Source Variable list and click on the ▶ push button of Dependent. Click on X_1 in the Source Variable list and click on the ▶ push button of Factors. Click on Define Range. This opens the Define Range dialog box. Enter the minimum value 1. Click on the value of Maximum and enter the maximum value 2. Click on Continue.

You may click on Options to see the possibilities, but these will not be used at this stage. Click on Continue to go back to the Simple Factorial ANOVA dialog box. Click on OK.

SPSS now runs a one-way analysis of variance with intrinsic motivation (Y) as the dependent variable and external rewards (X_1) as the independent variable.

You can now run other classical ANOVAs in the same way:

- of intrinsic motivation (Y) by task interest (X_2 with ranges 1 and 3);
- of intrinsic motivation (Y) by X_1 and X_2; and
- of intrinsic motivation (Y) by X_1 and X_2, suppressing interactions.

For the suppression of interactions, you click on Options and you click on the radio button next to None. Click on Continue. After that, click on OK to run the procedure.

Running the ANOVAs by means of dummy regression

To run the dummy regressions, you will first have to compute the product of external rewards (represented by dummy D_1) and task interest (represented by dummies D_2 and D_3). To do so, click on Transform and click on Compute. This opens the Compute Variable dialog box. Click on D_1 and on ▶. Click on *. Click on D_2 and on ▶. Click on Target Variable and give it the name D_4. You have now calculated D_4 as the product of D_1 and D_2. Do the same for D_5 as the product of D_1 and D_3.

Now you can run the regression analyses in the familiar way, as shown in the preceding chapters, Chapters 5 and 6. You will run:

- Y as a function of D_1;
- Y as a function of D_2 and D_3;
- Y as a function of D_1, D_2 and D_3; and
- Y as a function of D_1, D_2, D_3, D_4 and D_5.

Running analysis of covariance

ANCOVA, too, will be performed here by means of dummy regression analysis, so that nothing new is coming up. You can easily infer the actions from the commands in the syntax window below. Please note that another orthogonal design matrix is used for a change.

The statements for the classical ANOVA are as follows:

```
1  LIST.
2  ANOVA /VARIABLES Y BY X1 (1,2).
3  ANOVA /VARIABLES Y BY X2 (1,3).
4  ANOVA /VARIABLES Y BY X1 (1,2) X2 (1,3).
5  ANOVA /VARIABLES Y BY X1 (1,2) X2 (1,3)
6          /MAXORDERS NONE.
```

In statement 1 the data matrix is requested by 'list'. This matrix contains scores 1 and 2 for variable x_1 and scores 1, 2 and 3 for variable x_2.

Statements 2 and 3 request the one-way ANOVAs.

In statement 4 a two-way ANOVA is calculated for the non-additive model with the effect of x_1, the effect of x_2 and the effect of interaction.

In statements 5 and 6 'maxorders none' (which used to be 'options 3') means that the effect of interaction has to be omitted, so that the additive model is requested.

The statements of the dummy regression analysis are as follows:

```
1  LIST.
2  COMPUTE D4 = D1 * D2.
3  COMPUTE D5 = D1 * D3.
4  REGRESSION /VARIABLES Y D1 /DEPENDENT Y /METHOD ENTER D1.
5  REGRESSION /VARIABLES Y D2 D3 /DEPENDENT Y /METHOD ENTER D2 D3.
6  REGRESSION /VARIABLES Y D1 D2 D3 /DEPENDENT Y /METHOD ENTER D1 D2 D3.
7  REGRESSION /VARIABLES Y D1 D2 D3 D4 D5 /DEPENDENT Y
8                /METHOD ENTER D1 D2 D3 D4 D5.
```

The data matrix, requested in statement 1 by means of 'list' now contains 0s and 1s. External rewards is represented by dummy d_1 and task interest by dummies d_2 and d_3.

In statements 2 and 3 the two product terms are calculated.

The regression analysis of statement 4 calculates the effect of external rewards (d_1) on intrinsic motivation.

The regression analysis of statement 5 calculates the effect of task interest (d_2 and d_3 together) on motivation.

Next, the effects of d_1 on the one hand and d_2 and d_3 on the other hand are analysed together in a more complex model, first without product terms (statement 6: additive model) and then with the product terms d_4 and d_5 (statements 7 and 8: non-additive model).

For the analysis of covariance as dummy regression analysis, the statements are:

```
1   LIST.
2   COMPUTE NEWY = Y - 4.
3   COMPUTE NEWX1 = X1 - 5.5.
4   COMPUTE NEWD4 = NEWX1 * D2.
5   COMPUTE NEWD5 = NEWX1 * D3.
6     REGRESSION /VARIABLES NEWY NEWX1 /DESCRIPTIVES ALL
7          /STATISTICS ALL /DEPENDENT NEWY /METHOD ENTER NEWX1.
8     REGRESSION /VARIABLES NEWY D2 D3 /DESCRIPTIVES ALL
9          /STATISTICS ALL /DEPENDENT NEWY /METHOD ENTER D2 D3.
10    REGRESSION /VARIABLES NEWY NEWX1 D2 D3 /DESCRIPTIVES ALL
11         /STATISTICS ALL /DEPENDENT NEWY /METHOD ENTER NEWX1 D2 D3.
12    REGRESSION /VARIABLES Y NEWX1 D2 D3 NEWD4 NEWD5
13         /DESCRIPTIVES ALL /STATISTICS ALL /DEPENDENT Y
14         /METHOD ENTER NEWX1 D2 D3 NEWD4 NEWD5.
```

The expression 'list' in statement 1 requests the data matrix. The dependent variable y and the covariate x_1 are measured as interval scales with scores from 0 to 9. We might have coded the dummies d_2 and d_3 with 0s and 1s, but for a change we used a design matrix with other codes: 1, 0, -1 for d_2 and 1, -2, 1 for d_3. This coding implies that the mean of d_2 as well as that of d_3 is equal to 0, which can be checked in the computer output, as the statement 'descriptives' requests the means of all the variables. Moreover, the sum of products of the scores of d_2 and d_3 is equal to 0, which means that the cross product matrix $\mathbf{X}'\mathbf{X}$ of the design matrix $\mathbf{X} = [\mathbf{d}_2\mathbf{d}_3]$ is diagonal, so that orthogonality is ensured. This orthogonality can also be verified in the correlation matrix, in which d_2 and d_3 appear to be uncorrelated. The statement 'descriptives' provides a print of this correlation matrix in the computer output. Another way to verify the orthogonality of independent variables is given in the 'statistics' statement, which provides the tolerance for each independent variable of the regression model. This tolerance is a measure of the absence of multicollinearity (read: orthogonality of independent variables). If this tolerance is equal to 1, then the association between the considered variable and all other independent variables is equal to 0, which is perfect. If, on the other hand, it is 0, then there is perfect multicollinearity, which is dramatic.

In statements 2 and 3, y and x_1 are expressed as deviations of their mean (newx_1 and new$y$). For, the mean of y is 4 and the mean of x_1 is 5.5. Note that d_2 and d_3 do not have to be expressed as deviations of mean, because the system of coding is set up in such a way that their mean is equal to 0.

In statements 4 and 5 the product terms newd_4 and newd_5 are calculated. They represent the products of the covariate newx_1 and each of the dummies d_2 and d_3. In statements 6 and 7 the effect of the covariate newx_1 is analysed, regardless of other variables.

The effect of task interest appears from statements 8 and 9, in which dummies d_2 and d_3 are the independent variables.

The additive analysis of covariance model is examined in statements 10 and 11, which includes the covariate newx_1 as well as the dummies d_2 and d_3, but not the product terms.

In statements 12 to 14, not only the covariate newx_1 and the dummies d_2 and d_3, but the product terms newd_4 and newd_5 are also included. Thus, this is the most complex global model. For variety's sake, we have not included the dependent variable 'motivation' as deviation of mean (new$y$), but in the form of original (raw) y scores. We can see in the computer output that the intercept of the regression function is consequently not 0, but the mean motivation (4). With our knowledge of multiple regression analysis we could anticipate this outcome.

The output of the three analyses is as follows.

```
Y  X1 X2
6   1  1
4   1  1
3   1  1
3   1  1
4   1  2
3   1  2
3   1  2
2   1  2
3   1  3
2   1  3
2   1  3
1   1  3
9   2  1
9   2  1
8   2  1
```

```
6  2  1
7  2  2
5  2  2
4  2  2
4  2  2
4  2  3
2  2  3
1  2  3
1  2  3
```

Number of cases read =   24   Number of cases listed =   24

	Y	intrinsic motivation				
BY	X1	external rewards				
Source of Variation		Sum of Squares	DF	Mean Square	F	Signif of F
Main Effects		24.000	1	24.000	4.889	.038
X1		24.000	1	24.000	4.889	.038
Explained		24.000	1	24.000	4.889	.038
Residual		108.000	22	4.909		
Total		132.000	23	5.739		

24 Cases were processed.
0 Cases (.0 PCT) were missing.

	Y	intrinsic motivation				
BY	X2	task interest				
Source of Variation		Sum of Squares	DF	Mean Square	F	Signif of F
Main Effects		64.000	2	32.000	9.882	.001
X2		64.000	2	32.000	9.882	.001
Explained		64.000	2	32.000	9.882	.001
Residual		68.000	21	3.238		
Total		132.000	23	5.739		

24 Cases were processed.
0 Cases (.0 PCT) were missing.

	Y	intrinsic motivation				
BY	X1	external rewards				
	X2	task interest				
Source of Variation		Sum of Squares	DF	Mean Square	F	Signif of F
Main Effects		88.000	3	29.333	18.857	.000
X1		24.000	1	24.000	15.429	.001
X2		64.000	2	32.000	20.571	.000
2-way Interactions		16.000	2	8.000	5.143	.017
X1 X2		16.000	2	8.000	5.143	.017
Explained		104.000	5	20.800	13.371	.000
Residual		28.000	18	1.556		
Total		132.000	23	5.739		

24 Cases were processed.
0 Cases (.0 PCT) were missing.

```
            Y          intrinsic motivation
      BY    X1         external rewards
            X2         task interest
```

Source of Variation	Sum of Squares	DF	Mean Square	F	Signif of F
Main Effects	88.000	3	29.333	13.333	.000
X1	24.000	1	24.000	10.909	.004
X2	64.000	2	32.000	14.545	.000
Explained	88.000	3	29.333	13.333	.000
Residual	44.000	20	2.200		
Total	132.000	23	5.739		

****

```
Y D1 D2 D3

6  0  1  0
4  0  1  0
3  0  1  0
3  0  1  0
4  0  0  1
3  0  0  1
3  0  0  1
2  0  0  1
3  0  0  0
2  0  0  0
2  0  0  0
1  0  0  0
9  1  1  0
9  1  1  0
8  1  1  0
6  1  1  0
7  1  0  1
5  1  0  1
4  1  0  1
4  1  0  1
4  1  0  0
2  1  0  0
1  1  0  0
1  1  0  0
```

```
Number of cases read =     24    Number of cases listed =     24
```

```
Listwise Deletion of Missing Data
Equation Number 1    Dependent Variable..   Y    intrinsic motivation
Block Number  1.  Method: Enter      D1
```

```
Variable(s) Entered on Step Number
    1..    D1         external rewards

Multiple R            .42640
R Square              .18182
Adjusted R Square     .14463
Standard Error       2.21565

Analysis of Variance
                     DF      Sum of Squares      Mean Square
Regression            1            24.00000         24.00000
Residual             22           108.00000          4.90909

F =      4.88889        Signif F =  .0377
```

```
Equation Number 1    Dependent Variable..   Y   intrinsic motivation

------------------ Variables in the Equation ------------------

Variable              B        SE B        Beta        T   Sig T

D1             2.000000     .904534     .426401     2.211   .0377
(Constant)     3.000000     .639602                 4.690   .0001
```

```
****************************************************************************

Listwise Deletion of Missing Data
Equation Number 1    Dependent Variable..   Y   intrinsic motivation
Block Number  1.  Method:  Enter      D2       D3
```

```
Variable(s) Entered on Step Number
    1..    D3         interest-dummy 2
    2..    D2         interest-dummy 1

Multiple R            .69631
R Square              .48485
Adjusted R Square     .43579
Standard Error       1.79947

Analysis of Variance
                     DF      Sum of Squares      Mean Square
Regression            2            64.00000         32.00000
Residual             21            68.00000          3.23810

F =      9.88235        Signif F =  .0009

Equation Number 1    Dependent Variable..   Y   intrinsic motivation
```

```
------------------ Variables in the Equation ------------------

Variable              B          SE B        Beta        T   Sig T

D3             2.000000     .899735     .402015    2.223  .0373
D2             4.000000     .899735     .804030    4.446  .0002
(Constant)     2.000000     .636209                3.144  .0049
```

```
***************************************************************************
```

```
Listwise Deletion of Missing Data
Equation Number 1   Dependent Variable..   Y   intrinsic motivation
Block Number  1. Method:  Enter       D1        D2        D3
```

```
Variable(s) Entered on Step Number
   1..   D3          interest-dummy 2
   2..   D1          external rewards
   3..   D2          interest-dummy 1
```

```
Multiple R            .81650
R Square              .66667
Adjusted R Square     .61667
Standard Error       1.48324
```

```
Analysis of Variance
                    DF      Sum of Squares      Mean Square
Regression           3            88.00000         29.33333
Residual            20            44.00000          2.20000
```

```
F =     13.33333      Signif F =  .0001
```

```
Equation Number 1   Dependent Variable..   Y   intrinsic motivation
```

```
------------------ Variables in the Equation ------------------

Variable              B          SE B        Beta        T   Sig T

D3             2.000000     .741620     .402015    2.697  .0139
D1             2.000000     .605530     .426401    3.303  .0036
D2             4.000000     .741620     .804030    5.394  .0000
(Constant)     1.000000     .605530                1.651  .1143
```

```
***************************************************************************
```

```
Listwise Deletion of Missing Data
Equation Number 1   Dependent Variable..   Y   intrinsic motivation
Block Number  1. Method:  Enter
   D1        D2        D3        D4        D5
```

```
Variable(s) Entered on Step Number
     1..    D5
     2..    D4
     3..    D3        interest-dummy 2
     4..    D2        interest-dummy 1
     5..    D1        external rewards


Equation Number 1    Dependent Variable..   Y   intrinsic motivation


Multiple R           .88763
R Square             .78788
Adjusted R Square    .72896
Standard Error      1.24722

Analysis of Variance
                   DF      Sum of Squares     Mean Square
Regression          5           104.00000       20.80000
Residual           18            28.00000        1.55556


F =      13.37143      Signif F =  .0000


Equation Number 1    Dependent Variable..   Y   intrinsic motivation

------------------ Variables in the Equation ------------------

Variable             B         SE B       Beta        T  Sig T

D5            2.000000    1.247219    .317821     1.604  .1262
D4            4.000000    1.247219    .635642     3.207  .0049
D3            1.000000     .881917    .201008     1.134  .2717
D2            2.000000     .881917    .402015     2.268  .0359
D1         -5.89523E-15     .881917 -1.257E-15     .000 1.0000
(Constant)    2.000000     .623610                3.207  .0049


**************************************************************************************
Y X1 D2 D3

6  8  1  1
4  5  1  1
3  2  1  1
3  3  1  1
4  8  0 -2
3  7  0 -2
3  6  0 -2
2  4  0 -2
3  4 -1  1
2  9 -1  1
2  8 -1  1
1  2 -1  1
9  9  1  1
9  7  1  1
8  6  1  1
6  4  1  1
```

```
7  5  0 -2
5  9  0 -2
4  3  0 -2
4  2  0 -2
4  6 -1  1
2  7 -1  1
1  5 -1  1
1  3 -1  1
```

Number of cases read =   24   Number of cases listed =   24

Listwise Deletion of Missing Data

              Mean   Std Dev   Variance   Label

NEWY   .000   2.396   5.739
NEWX1   .000   2.341   5.478

N of Cases =   24

Correlation, Covariance, 1-tailed Sig, Cross-Product:

                   NEWY   NEWX1

NEWY   1.000   .341
                 5.739   1.913
                    .   .051
               132.000   44.000

NEWX1   .341   1.000
                 1.913   5.478
                  .051   .
                44.000   126.000

Equation Number 1   Dependent Variable..   NEWY
Block Number 1. Method: Enter   NEWX1
Equation Number 1   Dependent Variable..   NEWY

Variable(s) Entered on Step Number
   1..   NEWX1

Multiple R   .34118
R Square   .11640   R Square Change   .11640
Adjusted R Square   .07624   F Change   2.89820
Standard Error   2.30252   Signif F Change   .1028

Analysis of Variance
                         DF   Sum of Squares   Mean Square
Regression   1   15.36508   15.36508
Residual   22   116.63492   5.30159

F =   2.89820   Signif F = .1028

Equation Number 1   Dependent Variable..   NEWY

--------------------- Variables in the Equation ----------------------

Variable	B	SE B	95% Confdnce Intrvl B		Beta
NEWX1	.349206	.205125	-.076196	.774609	.341178
(Constant)	.000000	.469999	-.974719	.974719	

-------------------- Variables in the Equation ---------------------

Variable	SE Beta	Correl	Part Cor	Partial	Tolerance	VIF
NEWX1	.200408	.341178	.341178	.341178	1.000000	1.000

Equation Number 1   Dependent Variable..   NEWY

----------- in ------------

Variable	T	Sig T
NEWX1	1.702	.1028
(Constant)	.000	1.0000

****

Listwise Deletion of Missing Data

	Mean	Std Dev	Variance	Label
NEWY	.000	2.396	5.739	
D2	.000	.834	.696	interest-dummy 1
D3	.000	1.445	2.087	interest-dummy 2

N of Cases =   24

Correlation, Covariance, 1-tailed Sig, Cross-Product:

	NEWY	D2	D3
NEWY	1.000	.696	.000
	5.739	1.391	.000
	.	.000	.500
	132.000	32.000	.000
D2	.696	1.000	.000
	1.391	.696	.000
	.000	.	.500
	32.000	16.000	.000

```
D3                    .000        .000       1.000
                      .000        .000       2.087
                      .500        .500          .
                      .000        .000      48.000
```

```
Equation Number 1    Dependent Variable..   NEWY
Block Number   1.  Method:  Enter      D2        D3
Equation Number 1    Dependent Variable..   NEWY
```

```
Variable(s) Entered on Step Number
   1..   D3         interest-dummy 2
   2..   D2         interest-dummy 1
```

```
Multiple R            .69631
R Square              .48485       R Square Change    .48485
Adjusted R Square     .43579       F Change          9.88235
Standard Error       1.79947       Signif F Change    .0009
```

```
Analysis of Variance
                      DF      Sum of Squares      Mean Square
Regression             2          64.00000         32.00000
Residual              21          68.00000          3.23810
```

```
F =      9.88235       Signif F =  .0009
```

```
Equation Number 1    Dependent Variable..   NEWY
```

```
---------------------- Variables in the Equation ----------------------
```

```
Variable              B        SE B     95% Confdnce Intrvl B       Beta

D3                .000000    .259731    -.540141     .540141     .000000
D2               2.000000    .449868    1.064449    2.935551     .696311
(Constant)        .000000    .367315    -.763874     .763874
```

```
-------------------- Variables in the Equation ----------------------
```

```
Variable     SE Beta   Correl Part Cor  Partial  Tolerance      VIF

D3           .156624  .000000  .000000  .000000  1.000000      1.000
D2           .156624  .696311  .696311  .696311  1.000000      1.000
```

```
Equation Number 1    Dependent Variable..   NEWY
```

```
----------- in ------------
```

```
Variable        T  Sig T

D3            .000 1.0000
D2           4.446  .0002
(Constant)    .000 1.0000
```

****

Listwise Deletion of Missing Data

```
          Mean  Std Dev  Variance  Label

NEWY      .000   2.396    5.739
NEWX1     .000   2.341    5.478
D2        .000    .834     .696    interest-dummy 1
D3        .000   1.445    2.087    interest-dummy 2

N of Cases =    24
```

Correlation, Covariance, 1-tailed Sig, Cross-Product:

```
              NEWY      NEWX1       D2         D3

NEWY         1.000      .341       .696       .000
             5.739     1.913      1.391       .000
               .        .051       .000       .500
           132.000    44.000     32.000       .000

NEWX1         .341     1.000       .000       .000
             1.913     5.478       .000       .000
              .051       .         .500       .500
            44.000   126.000       .000       .000

D2            .696      .000      1.000       .000
             1.391      .000       .696       .000
              .000      .500        .         .500
            32.000      .000     16.000       .000

D3            .000      .000       .000      1.000
              .000      .000       .000      2.087
              .500      .500       .500        .
              .000      .000       .000     48.000
```

```
Equation Number 1    Dependent Variable..  NEWY
Block Number  1.  Method:  Enter      NEWX1    D2        D3
Equation Number 1    Dependent Variable..  NEWY
```

Variable(s) Entered on Step Number
```
   1..    D3          interest-dummy 2
   2..    D2          interest-dummy 1
   3..    NEWX1
```

Equation Number 1   Dependent Variable.. NEWY

```
Multiple R            .77540
R Square              .60125      R Square Change    .60125
Adjusted R Square     .54144      F Change          10.05227
Standard Error       1.62227      Signif F Change     .0003
```

```
Analysis of Variance
                    DF       Sum of Squares      Mean Square
Regression           3           79.36508         26.45503
Residual            20           52.63492          2.63175


F =      10.05227       Signif F =  .0003



Equation Number 1    Dependent Variable..   NEWY

--------------------- Variables in the Equation ----------------------

Variable              B       SE B     95% Confdnce Intrvl B      Beta

D3               .000000    .234154     -.488436     .488436    .000000
D2              2.000000    .405566    1.154003    2.845997     .696311
NEWX1            .349206    .144523     .047737     .650676     .341178
(Constant)       .000000    .331144    -.690753     .690753



-------------------- Variables in the Equation ----------------------

Variable      SE Beta   Correl Part Cor  Partial  Tolerance       VIF

D3            .141200  .000000  .000000  .000000  1.000000      1.000
D2            .141200  .696311  .696311  .740757  1.000000      1.000
NEWX1         .141200  .341178  .341178  .475349  1.000000      1.000



Equation Number 1    Dependent Variable..   NEWY


----------- in ------------

Variable         T   Sig T

D3             .000 1.0000
D2            4.931  .0001
NEWX1         2.416  .0254
(Constant)     .000 1.0000

*************************************************************************************


Listwise Deletion of Missing Data

            Mean  Std Dev  Variance  Label

Y          4.000   2.396    5.739   intrinsic motivation
NEWX1       .000   2.341    5.478
D2          .000    .834     .696   interest-dummy 1
D3          .000   1.445    2.087   interest-dummy 2
NEWD4       .000   1.911    3.652
NEWD5       .000   3.310   10.957

N of Cases =    24
```

```
Correlation, Covariance, 1-tailed Sig, Cross-Product:
```

	Y	NEWX1	D2	D3	NEWD4	NEWD5
Y	1.000	.341	.696	.000	.275	.192
	5.739	1.913	1.391	.000	1.261	1.522
	.	.051	.000	.500	.096	.185
	132.000	44.000	32.000	.000	29.000	35.000
NEWX1	.341	1.000	.000	.000	.000	.000
	1.913	5.478	.000	.000	.000	.000
	.051	.	.500	.500	.500	.500
	44.000	126.000	.000	.000	.000	.000
D2	.696	.000	1.000	.000	.000	.000
	1.391	.000	.696	.000	.000	.000
	.000	.500	.	.500	.500	.500
	32.000	.000	16.000	.000	.000	.000
D3	.000	.000	.000	1.000	.000	.000
	.000	.000	.000	2.087	.000	.000
	.500	.500	.500	.	.500	.500
	.000	.000	.000	48.000	.000	.000
NEWD4	.275	.000	.000	.000	1.000	.000
	1.261	.000	.000	.000	3.652	.000
	.096	.500	.500	.500	.	.500
	29.000	.000	.000	.000	84.000	.000
NEWD5	.192	.000	.000	.000	.000	1.000
	1.522	.000	.000	.000	.000	10.957
	.185	.500	.500	.500	.500	.
	35.000	.000	.000	.000	.000	252.000

```
Equation Number 1    Dependent Variable..  Y   intrinsic motivation

Block Number  1.  Method:  Enter
   NEWX1    D2       D3       NEWD4    NEWD5

Equation Number 1    Dependent Variable..  Y   intrinsic motivation

Variable(s) Entered on Step Number
   1..    NEWD5
   2..    NEWD4
   3..    D3       interest-dummy 2
   4..    D2       interest-dummy 1
   5..    NEWX1

Equation Number 1    Dependent Variable..  Y   intrinsic motivation

Multiple R            .84494
R Square              .71392      R Square Change    .71392
Adjusted R Square     .63446      F Change          8.98411
Standard Error       1.44841      Signif F Change     .0002
```

```
Analysis of Variance
                     DF      Sum of Squares      Mean Square
Regression           5            94.23810          18.84762
Residual            18            37.76190           2.09788


F =      8.98411       Signif F =  .0002
```

Equation Number 1   Dependent Variable..   Y   intrinsic motivation

---------------------- Variables in the Equation ----------------------

Variable	B	SE B	95% Confdnce Intrvl B		Beta
NEWD5	.138889	.091241	-.052802	.330579	.191903
NEWD4	.345238	.158034	.013221	.677256	.275405
D3	.000000	.209060	-.439218	.439218	.000000
D2	2.000000	.362102	1.239252	2.760748	.696311
NEWX1	.349206	.129034	.078115	.620298	.341178
(Constant)	4.000000	.295655	3.378852	4.621148	

Equation Number 1   Dependent Variable..   Y   intrinsic motivation

--------------------- Variables in the Equation ----------------------

Variable	SE Beta	Correl	Part Cor	Partial	Tolerance	VIF
NEWD5	.126068	.191903	.191903	.337711	1.000000	1.000
NEWD4	.126068	.275405	.275405	.457787	1.000000	1.000
D3	.126068	.000000	.000000	.000000	1.000000	1.000
D2	.126068	.696311	.696311	.793044	1.000000	1.000
NEWX1	.126068	.341178	.341178	.537786	1.000000	1.000

Equation Number 1   Dependent Variable..   Y   intrinsic motivation

----------- in ------------

Variable	T	Sig T
NEWD5	1.522	.1453
NEWD4	2.185	.0424
D3	.000	1.0000
D2	5.523	.0000
NEWX1	2.706	.0145
(Constant)	13.529	.0000

8

Two-Group Discriminant Analysis: Poor and Rich Neighbourhoods

8.1   The Research Problem and the Causal Diagram

In an investigation into the discrimination between poor and rich neighbourhoods, six discriminating variables were distinguished (the financial situation, the educational situation, the labour situation, the housing situation, the participation level and the presence of services) and these six variables, taken together, were examined for their capability to discriminate significantly between the two kinds of neighbourhood.

For the sake of simplicity we restrict ourselves to two discriminating variables: the financial situation (X_1) and the level of services (X_2). In section 1.2.5 it was stated that scientific research on the characteristics that bring about discrimination between population groups in society involves an argument which consists of three steps. Firstly, and as reliably as possible, we make an *a priori* **classification** of groups. As this classification is the subject of explanation, it represents the (dictotomous) dependent variable Y with the categories poor and rich. Secondly, statistical data are gathered for a great number of characteristics (only two here), their discriminating capacity is determined by means of statistical **analysis** and a weighted sum is calculated. These characteristics are the independent variables X_1 and X_2, their weights are k_1 and k_2, respectively, and the weighted sum is $k_1X_1 + k_2X_2$. Thirdly, if the analysis of the second step appears to be successful (significant discriminating capacities of the weighted sum and of each of the characteristics separately), then we have a good instrument for classifying additional units into one of the groups. This last step, **classification**, offers the opportunity for a well-founded determination of whether the neighbourhoods not included in the analysis are poor or rich.

It follows from the foregoing that the structure of discriminant analysis is the same as that of multiple regression analysis, except for one point: the dependent variable Y is now dichotomous instead of quantitative. The causal diagram, which coincides with the research problem, is shown below.

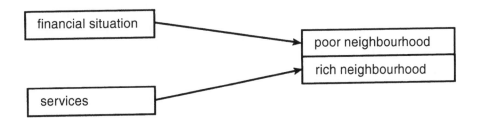

The discriminating variables, the financial situation (X_1) and the level of services (X_2), are measured at the interval or ratio level. As in multiple regression analysis, they can be considered as causal factors in a multicausal model. The dependent variable Y represents the two groups. It can be seen as the dichotomous variable 'poorness' with the categories poor and rich. For this reason we no longer speak of the prediction of Y scores, but rather of the classification into one of the two groups. As in multiple regression analysis, the model is also additive. This means that there are no effects of interaction in principle, i.e., a weighted sum of X_1 and X_2 is sought and the product term $X_1 X_2$ is not considered.

8.2　The Data Matrix

The units of analysis are districts or neighbourhoods. In our (fictitious) mini data set we consider a number of $n = 15$ neighbourhoods.

The independent variables X_1 and X_2, which are also called discriminating variables, are measured as an interval scale with scores from 0 to 9. The financial situation (X_1) is operationalized as the average income of the inhabitants. And the level of services (X_2) is a quantitative index, derived from measures of the services with respect to education, spatial accommodations, recreation, playgrounds for children, public green, social services and health-care. The dependent variable 'poorness' (Y) is measured at the qualitative level with categories poor and rich. Anticipating the dummy approach, we will already use the codes 0 and 1, respectively. The data matrix is given in Table 8.1.

Table 8.1　Data matrix

Y	X_1	X_2
0	1	1
0	1	4
0	2	1
0	4	5
0	5	5
0	5	9
1	4	2
1	4	4
1	5	6
1	6	3
1	6	6
1	7	6
1	8	7
1	9	7
1	9	8

8.3   The Model of Discriminant Analysis

In two-group discriminant analysis we want to examine whether a set of variables (X_1 and X_2) is capable of distinguishing (= discriminating in the neutral sense) between the two groups. Therefore, we search for a linear combination of the discriminating variables (X_1 and X_2) in such a way that the two groups (poor and rich neighbour-hoods) are maximally distinguished. Such a linear combination is called a discriminant function and generally has the following form:

$$T - \bar{T} = k_1(X_1 - \bar{X}_1) + k_2(X_2 - \bar{X}_2) + \ldots + k_p(X_p - \bar{X}_p)$$

or

$$t = k_1 x_1 + k_2 x_2 + \ldots + k_p x_p$$

In this formula t and x_i are expressed as deviations of mean (lower case letters). The coefficients k_i are called discriminant weights. The variables x_1 to x_p are the discriminating variables. Their number is p. In our example, we have $p = 2$, so that the discriminant function is simplified to: $t = k_1 x_1 + k_2 x_2$.

This can be written much more simply in matrix notation as $\mathbf{t} = \mathbf{Xk}$, in which $\mathbf{t}$ is a 15×1 column vector of discriminant scores, $\mathbf{X}$ is a 15×2 matrix of scores of the discriminating variables and $\mathbf{k}$ is a 2×1 column vector of discriminant weights:

$$\begin{bmatrix} t_1 \\ t_2 \\ \vdots \\ t_{15} \end{bmatrix} = \begin{bmatrix} 1 - 5.067 & 1 - 4.933 \\ 1 - 5.067 & 4 - 4.933 \\ \vdots & \vdots \\ 9 - 5.067 & 8 - 4.933 \end{bmatrix} \begin{bmatrix} k_1 \\ k_2 \end{bmatrix}$$

In the case of two groups, there is only one discriminant function. If, on the other hand, several groups were to be compared, then the number of discriminant functions would maximally be equal to min $(g - 1, p)$. For example, if $g = 4$ groups are analysed by means of $p = 5$ discriminating variables, then we have $g - 1 = 3$ and $p = 5$, so that the maximum number of discriminant functions is equal to 3.

After the discriminant function or functions is/are calculated, the two main objectives of discriminant analysis come up for discussion: analysis and classification.

In the phase of analysis, one tests whether and to what extent the x variables are capable of discriminating between the groups. In the phase of classification one first examines whether the discriminant function imparts a good classification of the 15 considered units in the different groups. After that, new units can be classified in the groups. For example, if the average income and the service level of a neighbourhood which does not belong to our 15 analysed units is known, then one can determine to which group it belongs: poor or rich. The latter is in fact a form of prediction, for which all sorts of classification rules can be set up. In doing so, it is customary to make use of probability calculus, and especially of Bayesian statistics.

For purposes of explanation, the model of discriminant analysis can be looked at from many different angles. We will first follow the classical approach according to Fisher. In a later stage we will present the dummy regression approach.

Let us keep the following data matrix in mind as a visual reference point:

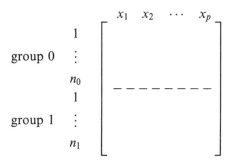

There are two groups, group 0 with n_0 units and group 1 with n_1 units. The discriminant function t is a linear combination of the p discriminating variables $(x_1, x_2, \ldots, x_p)$ and must be calculated in such a way that it brings about a maximal distinction between the two groups. Consequently, we need a criterion according to which the highest possible discrimination between the groups is imparted. To determine this criterion, we refer to the terminology of classical analysis of variance and especially, to one-way ANOVA.

Remember that analysis of variance includes an F test of the differences between the means of a number of groups and that F is calculated as the ratio of two dispersions: the dispersion of the group means (SSB) and the dispersion of the units within groups (SSW-pooled), each divided by the appropriate degrees of freedom. So, the criterion for a good discrimination between the group means was determined as the highest possible ratio of the between- and within-variance.

The same criterion will be used in discriminant analysis, except that in one-way ANOVA the dependent variable constitutes an interval or ratio scale and the independent variable, which represents several groups, is measured at a weaker level. In discriminant analysis it is the other way round: the dependent variable represents the groups and the independent variables $x_1 \ldots x_p$ are measured as an interval scale. However, consider the following two artifices. Firstly, replace the series of $x_1 \ldots x_p$ by a linear combination t, so that only one variable of interval measurement level remains. (Remark: the case of several discriminant functions is left out of the consideration for the moment.) Secondly, perform the analysis in the other direction, i.e., take the dependent variable as independent. In this way discriminant analysis is converted into a one-way ANOVA problem, at least for the formal statistical-technical side.

This is the way in which Sir Ronald Fisher originally approached the technique (in 1936). In the next sections the calculations will be performed in accordance with this ANOVA-like approach. The ratio of the between- and within-variance will be maximized. It should, however, by pointed out that many other approaches exist nowadays, such as the multiple regression approach with nominal dependent variable, the approach by means of Mahalanobis' extended version of Euclidian distance, and many others. These approaches will be discussed in later sections, but we will start with Fisher's procedure, after the paragraphs on geometry and the objectives of the technique.

8.4 Geometric Approach

We first make a scatterplot of the data in Figure 8.1. We consider a coordinate system with X_1 and X_2 as axes. The scores of group 0 are indicated as a circle (○), the scores of group 1 as an asterisk (*).

Looking at this scatterplot, it becomes clear at a glance that the second group of rich neighbourhoods has higher scores than the first group for X_1 as well as X_2, for the asterisks (*) are situated uppermost and furthest to the right. In other words, this group predominantly contains neighbourhoods with a high level of incomes and services, in contrast to the first group of poor neighbourhoods (○) which primarily contains neighbourhoods with a low score on both variables.

We also want to mention that the association between the financial situation and the level of services is positive in both groups with about an equal magnitude, for if we were to estimate a regression line through the points of each group, then both lines would go up (the higher the income level, the higher the level of services) and be approximately parallel (about the same strength of association between the levels of income and services within the two groups).

If we look at the dispersions of variables X_1 and X_2 in each of the groups, then we see that the income level varies from 1 to 5 in the first group (range = 4) and from 4 to 9 in the second group (range = 5) and that the level of services varies from 1 to 9 in the first group (range = 8) and from 2 to 8 in the second group (range = 6). Thus it appears that the difference between the dispersions is not too large for the financial situation (ranges 4 and 5, respectively) and is somewhat larger but still limited for the level of services (ranges 8 and 6, respectively). This is extremely important, for the approximate equality of the dispersions of X_1 and X_2 and of the associations between X_1 and X_2 within-groups are required for the application of discriminant analysis. (Compare the requirement of homoscedasticity in analysis of variance.) Expressed in more technical language: the variance–covariance matrices of group 0 and group 1 must not be significantly different. We will see in the next sections that this is the case in our example.

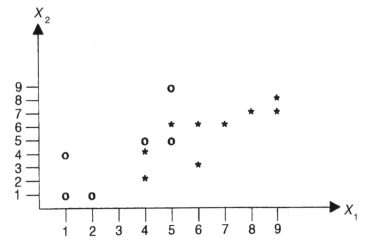

Figure 8.1   Scatterplot of six poor and nine rich neighbourhoods

We can give yet another clarification in visualizing the argument. We assume samples of observations whose scatterplots have the form of 95% concentration ellipses, i.e. ellipses which enclose 95% of the observations. In Figure 8.2 we have drawn such ellipses. This kind of representation is borrowed from Cooley and Lohnes (1971, p. 245).

In each of the three parts of Figure 8.2(a), (b) and (c), our data are plotted in x_1–x_2 space. The scores of x_1 and x_2 are now expressed as deviations of mean. For each group a concentration ellipse has been drawn. In the middle of each ellipse we have indicated the letter c, which represents the centroid, i.e., the place where the means come together. The total centroid for the entire group of 15 neighbourhoods lies in the origin, for the scores are deviations of the grand mean. (Remark: one might also draw a big concentration ellipse for this total group.) The ellipses go up to the right, because x_1 and x_2 are positively associated within each group, and the main axes of the ellipses are approximately parallel, because this association is about equally strong in both groups.

We will now search for a linear combination $t = k_1x_1 + k_2x_2$ i.e., an axis through the origin in x_1–x_2 space, in such a way that t brings about the best discrimination between the two groups. The latter can be verified by projecting the neighbourhoods of each group onto the t axis (orthogonal projections) and by inspecting the between- and within-variances. Our criterion is that the ratio of the between- and within-variance should be the highest possible. To gain more insight into this mechanism we have tried out a candidate t axis in each part of Figure 8.2. The axes are drawn in dashed lines and are drawn again below the figure after parallel translation in order to represent the projections separately in the form of a normal distribution for each of the two groups.

In Figure 8.2(a) we have considered x_1 as a possible candidate for a good t axis. Looking at the projections, we see that the two group centroids are far removed from each other. A rough estimation with a ruler is 1.4 cm. A good discrimination is therefore established. However, the dispersions of the neighbourhood projections within each group are rather large and, consequently, there is a substantial overlap between the two groups. A rough estimation of the within-dispersions is 2.8 cm. The ratio between/within would then be equal to $1.4/2.8 = 0.5$.

In Figure 8.2(b) the connection between the two centroids is considered as a possible t axis. This centroid connection axis appears to be an extremely bad choice. For, although the two group centroids are even further removed from each other than in the foregoing figure (estimation: 1.6 cm), the within-dispersions are dramatically higher (estimation: 4.0 cm) and so is, consequently, the overlap between the two distributions of projections. The between/within ratio here would be equal to $1.6/4.0 = 0.4$.

The best t axis is represented in Figure 8.2(c). It is the linear combination $t = 0.897x_1 - 0.442x_2$, the calculation of which will be demonstrated below. We see in the figure that the two group centroids are now rather close to one another (estimation 1.0 cm). So, if we were to mistakenly restrict the analysis to the inspection of the between-dispersion, we would expect a smaller discrimination between the groups. But, taking the within-dispersions into account as well, we see that these are drastically smaller than in the foregoing two figures (estimation: 1.5 cm). The ratio between the between- and within-dispersion is therefore much larger: $1.0/1.5 = 0.67$. This ratio is greater than 0.4 (Figure 8.2(b) and 0.5 (Figure 8.2(a)).

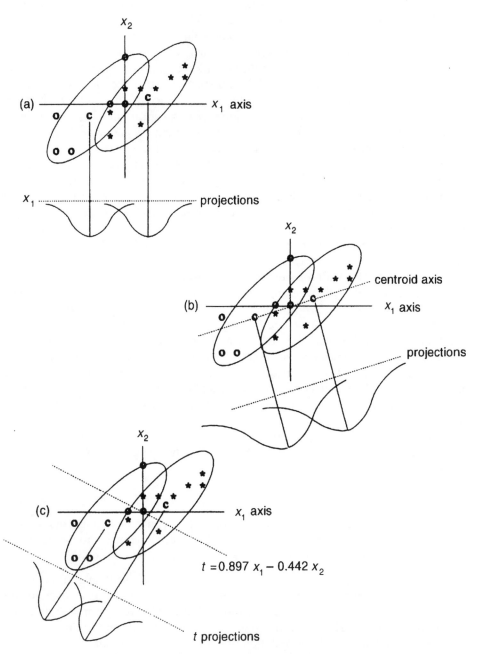

Figure 8.2   Geometry of two-group discriminant analysis

Some general statements can be derived from the foregoing. Firstly, the best axis is not necessarily the one for which the centroid projections are furthest removed from each other. In other words, the **centroid axis**, which connects the two group centroids, is not necessarily the best axis. The latter is only the case when the two concentration ellipses both have the form of a circle, i.e., when two requirements are fulfilled for each of them: (1) equal variances for the variables x_1 and x_2; (2) covariance between the variables x_1 and x_2 equal to 0. We will see below that the variance of x_1, the variance of x_2 and the covariance of x_1 and x_2 are collected in a matrix for each group, the so-called within-groups covariance matrix. If a concentration ellipse has the form of a circle, then the off-diagonal elements of such a matrix are all zero (absence of covariance) and the elements on the main diagonal are equal scalars (equal variances). In that case we speak of a scalar matrix. If the ellipses are not circular, but cigar-shaped and if these oblong cigars are not going up or down obliquely (as in our example), but stand upright or lie flat, then the within-groups covariance matrices are diagonal, but not scalar. Diagonal, because the relationship between x_1 and x_2 is equal to 0. Not scalar, because the dispersions of x_1 and x_2 are not equal (highest variance for the variable in the direction of the lengthwise axis of the cigar). In this case, too, the discriminant function is not the connection of the centroids, but an axis for which the variable with the smaller variance receives more weight.

A second general statement refers to **the sign of k_1 and k_2** in the discriminant function $t = k_1 x_1 + k_2 x_2$. We saw in Figure 8.9(b) that the centroid axis was not a good choice. This axis is oblique and goes up to the right, so that the weights k_1 and k_2 are both positive. For example, the linear function $t = 7x_1 + 3x_2$ approximately represents this line connecting the two centroids. On the other hand, in Figure 8.2(c) the oblique t axis goes down. Here, the linear composite is represented by the function $t = 0.897x_1 - 0.442x_2$ in which k_1 is positive and k_2 negative. The reason is that the relationship between variables x_1 and x_2 is positive: the best axis runs in the direction opposite to the x_1–x_2 correlation.

In summary: k_1 and k_2 have opposite signs if the within-groups correlations are positive, and equal signs if the within-groups correlations are negative.

8.5 Objectives of the Technique

The purposes of discriminant analysis are threefold. Keeping the example of poor and rich neighbourhoods (two groups) in mind and restricting ourselves to two discriminating variables (x_1 and x_2), these purposes can be summarized as follows:

1. We search for a linear function $t = k_1 x_1 + k_2 x_2$, called a discriminant function, in such a way that the scores of the neighbourhoods on this function t (discriminant scores) exhibit the property of maximizing the ratio of between-groups and within-groups variability. This comes down to the calculation of the discriminant weights k_1 and k_2 and, next, to the calculation of the 15 discriminant scores.
2. We examine whether the discrimination established by the function can be generalized to the population. Is there a significant difference between the two group centroids, i.e., between the means of the two groups for variables X_1 and X_2 taken together? This comes down to the performance of Hotelling's T^2 test, which is an extension of the simple Student's t test.

3. Making use of the discriminant function *t*, we also want to determine for each neighbourhood, and eventually for new neighbourhoods, to which of the two groups they belong. Given our knowledge of a neighbourhood's score of income and level of services, can we predict whether it is poor or rich? This comes down to determining a cutoff point and verifying whether the discriminant scores are situated to the left or to the right of this point. If a discriminant score is equal to the cutoff point, then the corresponding neighbourhood can be randomly assigned to one of the two groups.

This process of classification of units in groups is mostly considered in the broader context of statistical decision theory and of Bayesian statistics. For these procedures, we refer to more advanced textbooks.

8.6 Preparatory Calculations: Matrices T, B, W and C_w

To find the discriminant function *t*, we first have to do some preparatory calculations. We calculate the means, dispersions and associations for the discriminating variables X_1 and X_2, for the total group of 15 neighbourhoods and for each of the groups separately (see Table 8.2). The outcomes are then collected in vectors and in the matrices **T**, **B** and **W** and an important property, $T = B + W$, is demonstrated.

Table 8.2 Means, dispersions and associations of variables X_1 and X_2

Total sample

Y	X_1	X_2
0	1	1
0	1	4
0	2	1
0	4	5
0	5	5
0	5	9
1	4	2
1	4	4
1	5	6
1	6	3
1	6	6
1	7	6
1	8	7
1	9	7
1	9	8

sum	$\sum X_i =$	76	74
mean	$\bar{X}_i =$	5.067	4.933
variation	$\sum(X_i - \bar{X}_i)^2 =$	90.933	82.933
variance	$s_i^2 =$	6.495	5.924
covariation	$\sum(X_1 - \bar{X}_1)(X_2 - \bar{X}_2) = 63.067$		
covariance	$s_{12} = 4.505$		

(continues)

Table 8.2   *continued*

Group 0

Y	X_1	X_2
0	1	1
0	1	4
0	2	1
0	4	5
0	5	5
0	5	9

sum	$\sum X_i =$	18	25
mean	$\bar{X}_i =$	3	4.167
variation	$\sum (X_i - \bar{X}_i)^2 =$	18	44.833
variance	$s_i^2 =$	3.6	8.967
covariation	$\sum (X_1 - \bar{X}_1)(X_2 - \bar{X}_2) = 22$		
covariance	$s_{12} = 4.4$		

Group 1

Y	X_1	X_2
1	4	2
1	4	4
1	5	6
1	6	3
1	6	6
1	7	6
1	8	7
1	9	7
1	9	8

sum	$\sum X_1 =$	58	49
mean	$\bar{X}_i =$	6.444	5.444
variation	$\sum (X_i - \bar{X}_i)^2 =$	30.222	32.222
variance	$s_i^2 =$	3.778	4.028
covariation	$\sum (X_1 - \bar{X}_1)(X_2 - \bar{X}_2) = 25.222$		
covariance	$s_{12} = 3.153$		

Let us first look at the means. There are several variables (two here) and, consequently, several means. These are collected in a vector and such a vector of means is called a centroid, which is indicated as $\bar{x}'$. The lower case boldface letter denotes a vector, the prime indicates that this column vector is transposed to a row vector and the bar indicates means. There are three centroids, one for group 0, one for group 1 and one for the total group:

Group 0: $\bar{x}_0'$ $= (3 \qquad 4.167)$
Group 1: $\bar{x}_1'$ $= (6.444 \quad 5.444)$
Total sample: $\bar{x}'$ $= (5.067 \quad 4.933)$

Note that the differences between the two group centroids can also be collected in a difference vector **d** (**d** for difference), in which the differences of the means of the two groups are brought together.

$$d = \bar{x}_0 - \bar{x}_1 = \begin{bmatrix} 3 \\ 4.167 \end{bmatrix} - \begin{bmatrix} 6.444 \\ 5.444 \end{bmatrix} = \begin{bmatrix} -3.444 \\ -1.277 \end{bmatrix}$$

Next we look at the variations and covariations. These are collected in a matrix of variations and covariations, also called a 'sum of squares and cross products matrix' (SSCP matrix), because the variations are the sums of squares and the covariations are the sums of cross products. We begin with the total sample. The variation of X_1 is 90.933, the variation of X_2 is 82.933 and the covariation of X_1 and X_2 is 63.067. These outcomes are collected in matrix $\mathbf{T}$ ($\mathbf{T}$ for total):

$$\mathbf{T} = \begin{bmatrix} \text{variation } X_1 & \text{covariation} \\ \text{covariation} & \text{variation } X_2 \end{bmatrix} = \begin{bmatrix} 90.933 & 63.067 \\ 63.067 & 82.933 \end{bmatrix}$$

To compose the within-groups SSCP matrix $\mathbf{W}$ ($\mathbf{W}$ for within), the variations and covariations of group 0 and group 1 are added together. The within-variation of X_1 is thus equal to $18 + 30.222 = 48.222$, the within-variation of X_2 is $44.833 + 32.222 = 77.056$ and the within-covariation is $22 + 25.222 = 47.222$:

$$\mathbf{W} = \begin{bmatrix} 18 & 22 \\ 22 & 44.833 \end{bmatrix} + \begin{bmatrix} 30.222 & 25.222 \\ 25.222 & 32.222 \end{bmatrix} = \begin{bmatrix} 48.222 & 47.222 \\ 47.222 & 77.056 \end{bmatrix}$$

To change variations and covariations into variances and covariances we have to divide by the appropriate number of degrees of freedom. For the within-groups calculations we lose one degree of freedom at the mean of group 0 and one at the mean of group 1, so that the appropriate number is $n_0 - 1 = 6 - 1 = 5$ for group 0 and $n_1 - 1 = 9 - 1 = 8$ for group 1. For the calculations in which both groups are involved it is: $\sum(n_j - 1) = (6 - 1) + (9 - 1) = 13$. If we divide matrix $\mathbf{W}$ by 13, we obtain matrix $\mathbf{C}_w$, i.e., the 'pooled within-groups covariance matrix'. The expression 'pooled within' means that the variances and covariances of $\mathbf{C}_w$ are a sort of average (pooled average) of the ones from group 0 and group 1 (more exactly: a weighted mean with weights 5 and 8). The within-groups covariance matrices $\mathbf{C}_0$, $\mathbf{C}_1$ and the 'pooled within' $\mathbf{C}_w$ are given below.

$$\mathbf{C}_0 = \begin{bmatrix} 18/5 & 22/5 \\ 22/5 & 44.833/5 \end{bmatrix} = \begin{bmatrix} 3.6 & 4.4 \\ 4.4 & 8.967 \end{bmatrix}$$

$$\mathbf{C}_1 = \begin{bmatrix} 30.222/8 & 25.222/8 \\ 25.222/8 & 32.222/8 \end{bmatrix} = \begin{bmatrix} 3.778 & 3.153 \\ 3.153 & 4.028 \end{bmatrix}$$

$$\mathbf{C}_w = \begin{bmatrix} 48.222/13 & 47.222/13 \\ 47.222/13 & 77.056/13 \end{bmatrix} = \begin{bmatrix} 3.709 & 3.632 \\ 3.632 & 5.927 \end{bmatrix}$$

We will now compose matrix $\mathbf{B}$, i.e., the 'between-groups SSCP matrix' ($\mathbf{B}$ for between). Note that the data matrix is now a matrix of only two units, group 0 and group 1. And the variables are not X_1 and X_2, but their means. The scores in the body of the data matrix are the means within groups (Table 8.3).

In these calculations a procedure of weighing is applied, because the frequencies in group 0 and group 1 are unequal ($n_0 = 6$ and $n_1 = 9$). For example, the grand mean of the income variable was calculated as: $[3(6) + 6.444(9)]/15 = 5.067$. A similar calculation is performed for the services variable.

The between-variation of the group means of variable X_1 refers to no more than two cases, for there are only two groups. For the sake of comparability with matrices $\mathbf{T}$ and $\mathbf{W}$, the between-variation is calculated in such a way that it would refer to 15

Table 8.3   Between-data matrix

	Y	$\bar{X}_1$	$\bar{X}_2$
	0	3	4.167
	1	6.444	5.444
grand mean		5.067	4.933
between-variation		42.711	5.878
covariation	15.844		

cases by applying the weights 6 and 9: $[6(3 - 5.067)^2] + [9(6.444 - 5.067)^2] = 42.711$. A similar calculation is performed for variable X_2.

The calculation of the covariation is analogous: $[6(3 - 5.067)(4.167 - 4.933)] + [9(6.444 - 5.057)(5.444 - 4.933)] = 15.844$. The matrix of between-variations and -covariations brings all these calculations together:

$$\mathbf{B} = \begin{bmatrix} 42.711 & 15.844 \\ 15.844 & 5.878 \end{bmatrix}$$

We see that $\mathbf{T} = \mathbf{W} + \mathbf{B}$. Hence, we could also have calculated $\mathbf{B}$ as the difference of $\mathbf{T} - \mathbf{W}$.

We can now move on from preparatory calculations to determine the discriminant function.

8.7   Calculation of the Discriminant Function t

We already know that the function t is a linear combination of x_1 and x_2. We use lower case letters for t and x_i, because they are expressed as deviations of mean. If, on the other hand, original X_i scores were used, then the function t would also contain a constant term (intercept). The latter will not be the case here and so, in accordance with the geometric approach, the discriminant axis will run through the origin. The unknown discriminant weights are k_1 and k_2. Hence, the discriminant function has the following form:

$$t = k_1 x_1 + k_2 x_2$$

This function t will be calculated in such a way that it shows the highest possible discrimination between the two groups, i.e., that the ratio of the between- and within-dispersion is maximal. For that purpose, the variation of t is split into a between- and within-part, as follows.

We know that a variation (sum of squares) is equal to the summation of squared deviations of mean. As t is already expressed as a deviation of mean, the variation of t is simply the summation of t squares:

$$t = k_1 x_1 + k_2 x_2$$
$$\sum t^2 = \sum [k_1 x_1 + k_2 x_2]^2$$
$$= \sum [k_1^2 x_1^2 + k_2^2 x_2^2 + 2k_1 x_1 k_2 x_2]$$
$$= k_1^2 \sum x_1^2 + k_2^2 \sum x_2^2 + 2k_1 k_2 \sum x_1 x_2$$

where

$$\sum x_1^2 = 90.933$$

$$\sum x_2^2 = 82.933$$

$$\sum x_1 x_2 = 63.067$$

which is calculated above and brought together in matrix $\mathbf{T}$. We substitute these values in the equation: $\sum t^2 = 90.933k_1^2 + 82.933k_2^2 + 63.067(2k_1k_2)$. Remember that $\mathbf{T} = \mathbf{B} + \mathbf{W}$ and hence, each value of $\mathbf{T}$ can be partitioned into a between- and a within-part:

$$\sum t^2 = (42.711 + 48.222)k_1^2 + (5.878 + 77.056)k_2^2 + (15.844 + 47.222)(2k_1k_2)$$

$$= [42.711k_1^2 + 5.878k_2^2 + 31.688k_1k_2] + [48.222k_1^2 + 77.056k_2^2 + 94.444k_1k_2]$$

$$= \text{between-part} \qquad\qquad + \text{within-part}$$

In the geometric approach we projected the two concentration ellipses onto a t axis and we made a rough estimation of the dispersion between and within groups with a ruler. These are the dispersions which are calculated here as the between- and within-parts of $\sum t^2$.

The foregoing calculations can be represented in contracted form by means of matrix notation. The discriminant function then simply becomes $\mathbf{t} = \mathbf{X}\mathbf{k}$ (in which a capital letter $\mathbf{X}$ is now used, because it indicates a matrix instead of a vector and for which we assume the use of deviations of mean). The variation of t is now written as $\mathbf{t}'\mathbf{t}$. The foregoing derivations now look as follows:

$$\mathbf{t}'\mathbf{t} = (\mathbf{X}\mathbf{k})'(\mathbf{X}\mathbf{k})$$

$$= \mathbf{k}'\mathbf{X}'\mathbf{X}\mathbf{k}$$

$$= \mathbf{k}'\mathbf{T}\mathbf{k}$$

$$= \mathbf{k}'(\mathbf{B} + \mathbf{W})\mathbf{k}$$

$$= \mathbf{k}'\mathbf{B}\mathbf{k} + \mathbf{k}'\mathbf{W}\mathbf{k}$$

$$= \text{between} + \text{within}$$

The weights k_1 and k_2 have to be calculated so that the ratio between/within is as high as possible. Hence, we have to find the maximum of the following ratio:

$$\lambda = \frac{\mathbf{k}'\mathbf{B}\mathbf{k}}{\mathbf{k}'\mathbf{W}\mathbf{k}} = \frac{42.711k_1^2 + 5.878k_2^2 + 31.688k_1k_2}{48.222k_1^2 + 77.056k_2^2 + 94.444k_1k_2}$$

To solve this problem of maximizing, the partial derivatives of the ratio λ are calculated (find the derivative with respect to k_1 and k_2, respectively). These are set equal to zero, so that two equations with two unknowns, k_1 and k_2, are obtained. This system of two equations can be written in matrix algebra format as: $(\mathbf{W}^{-1}\mathbf{B} - \lambda\mathbf{I})\mathbf{k} = \mathbf{0}$.

The trivial solution $\mathbf{k} = \mathbf{0}$ (discriminant weights k_1 and k_2 both equal to zero) is naturally not considered.

The system has the form $\mathbf{A}\mathbf{k} = \mathbf{0}$, where $\mathbf{A} = \mathbf{W}^{-1}\mathbf{B} - \lambda\mathbf{I}$. For the non-trivial case ($k_1 \neq 0$ and/or $k_2 \neq 0$) it can be shown that the determinant of $\mathbf{A}$ has to be equal to 0 (see Appendix). Hence:

$$|W^1 B - \lambda I| = 0$$

This equation is called a characteristic equation and it will offer us the opportunity to calculate the highest possible λ. We set the determinant of $W^{-1}B - \lambda I$ equal to zero and from the solutions for λ we take the maximum. Next, we substitute the value of λ in the original equations of the system and from this we determine the values of k_1 and k_2. These operations are now performed one by one.

There are three matrices involved in the characteristic equation: W, B and I. W and B were calculated above. I is the identity matrix, having all its components equal to 0 except the diagonal components, which are equal to 1. These three matrices are written once more below:

$$W = \begin{bmatrix} 48.222 & 47.222 \\ 47.222 & 77.056 \end{bmatrix}$$

$$B = \begin{bmatrix} 42.711 & 15.844 \\ 15.844 & 5.878 \end{bmatrix}$$

$$I = \begin{bmatrix} 1 & 0 \\ 0 & 1 \end{bmatrix}$$

We first calculate the inverse of W:

$$W^{-1} = \frac{\text{adj } W}{|W|} = \frac{\begin{bmatrix} 77.056 & -47.222 \\ -47.222 & 48.222 \end{bmatrix}'}{(48.222)(77.056) - (47.222)^2} = \begin{bmatrix} 0.052 & -0.032 \\ -0.032 & 0.032 \end{bmatrix}$$

Next we form the characteristic equation:

$$|W^{-1}B - \lambda I| = 0$$

$$\left| \begin{bmatrix} 0.052 & -0.032 \\ -0.032 & 0.032 \end{bmatrix} \begin{bmatrix} 42.711 & 15.844 \\ 15.844 & 5.878 \end{bmatrix} - \lambda \begin{bmatrix} 1 & 0 \\ 0 & 1 \end{bmatrix} \right| = 0$$

$$\left| \begin{bmatrix} 1.711 - \lambda & 0.635 \\ -0.843 & -0.313 - \lambda \end{bmatrix} \right| = 0$$

$$(1.711 - \lambda)(-0.313 - \lambda) - (-0.843)(0.635) = 0$$

$$\lambda^2 - 1.399\lambda = 0$$

$$\lambda_{max} = 1.399$$

This value of λ is called the 'eigenvalue'. To determine k_1 and k_2, we substitute this value into the original equations of the system:

$$(W^{-1}B - \lambda I)k = 0$$

$$\left[\begin{bmatrix} 1.711 & 0.635 \\ -0.843 & -0.313 \end{bmatrix} - 1.399 \begin{bmatrix} 1 & 0 \\ 0 & 1 \end{bmatrix} \right] \begin{bmatrix} k_1 \\ k_2 \end{bmatrix} = \begin{bmatrix} 0 \\ 0 \end{bmatrix}$$

$$\begin{bmatrix} 0.313 & 0.635 \\ -0.843 & -1.711 \end{bmatrix} \begin{bmatrix} k_1 \\ k_2 \end{bmatrix} = \begin{bmatrix} 0 \\ 0 \end{bmatrix}$$

$$0.313k_1 + 0.635\,k_2 = 0$$

$$-0.843k_1 - 1.711\,k_2 = 0$$

These two equations are not linearly independent, because the ratios $0.313/0.635$ and $-0.843/(-1.711)$ are equal. Therefore, there are an infinite number of solutions and so it is impossible to determine k_1 and k_2 exactly. It is only possible to indicate their ratio. For instance, looking at the first equation, $k_1 = 0.635$ and $k_2 = -0.313$ would be a solution. Vector $\mathbf{k}$ would then be:

$$\mathbf{k} = \begin{bmatrix} k_1 \\ k_2 \end{bmatrix} = \begin{bmatrix} 0.635 \\ -0.313 \end{bmatrix}$$

However, other authors will find other solutions, such as $k_1 = 1.711$ and $k_2 = -0.843$ if they rely on the second equation. For all these solutions, the ratio k_1/k_2 will be the same. In other words, k_1 and k_2 are unique but for a transformation of scales.

We will therefore have to make an agreement, so that everybody obtains the same values for the discriminant weights. Such an agreement consists of normalizing vector $\mathbf{k}$. Normalizing means that the vector is divided by its length $\|\mathbf{k}\|$ to obtain a vector with unit length. In Figure 8.3 it can be easily verified that the length of $\mathbf{k}$ is equal to $[k_1^2 + k_2^2]^{1/2}$:

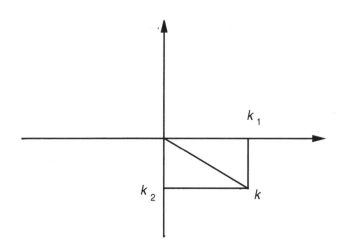

Figure 8.3   Vector k

Hence, vector $\mathbf{k} = \begin{bmatrix} 0.635 \\ -0.313 \end{bmatrix}$ has to be divided by: $[(0.635)^2 + (-0.313)^2]^{1/2} = 0.708$.

$$\mathbf{k} \text{ (normalized)} = \frac{\mathbf{k}}{\|\mathbf{k}\|} = \frac{1}{0.708} \begin{bmatrix} 0.635 \\ -0.313 \end{bmatrix} = \begin{bmatrix} 0.897 \\ -0.442 \end{bmatrix}$$

We have now found, finally, the discriminant function:

$$t = 0.897x_1 - 0.442x_2$$

Vector $\mathbf{k}$ is called an eigenvector. The weights k_1 and k_2, collected in this vector, determine the direction of the discriminant axis. In the normalized version, in which the length of **k** is equal to 1, they are equal to the cosine of the angle formed by t and each of the axes. For that reason they are also called direction cosines.

We notice that k_1 is positive and k_2 negative. We know from the geometric approach that this is so because the correlation between income and services is positive within each of the groups, as the direction of the discriminant axis is opposite to the direction of the correlation.

Function t does not contain a constant term, because the variables are expressed as deviations of mean. We might have performed the whole operation on the raw scores as well, thus working in the original space of Figure 8.1 instead of the space around the origin of Figure 8.2. In that case, the function would have contained a constant term and the weights k_1 and k_2 would have been the same as above. Notice that certain parts of the computer output, which is given below, contain such a constant term.

Instead of raw scores (X_i) or deviations of mean (x_i), one can also start from standardized scores (z_i). Apart from the fact that the discriminant function then has no constant term, this also creates the advantage whereby the weights of vector **k** are mutually comparable, so that it becomes possible to determine which discriminating variable has the highest capacity of discriminating between the poor and rich neighbourhoods. (We can make a comparison here with the beta weights of regression analysis and/or the path coefficients of path analysis.)

8.8   Classification and Prediction

Now that we have found the discriminant function, we can calculate the expected t value (= discriminant score) of each of the 15 individual neighbourhoods. For example, for the first neighbourhood the score of X_1 is equal to 1 and the score of X_2 is also equal to 1. So, the expected t value is 0.897 $(1 - 5.067) - 0.442(1 - 4.933) = -1.910$. We perform these calculations for each of the 15 neighbourhoods (see Table 8.4).

Table 8.4   Discriminant scores of the 15 neighbourhoods

X_1	$x_1 = X_1 - \bar{X}_1$	X_2	$x_2 = X_2 - \bar{X}_2$	t	predicted group
1	-4.067	1	-3.933	-1.910	0
1	-4.067	4	-0.933	-3.236	0
2	-3.067	1	-3.933	-1.013	0
4	-1.067	5	0.067	-0.987	0
5	-0.067	5	0.067	-0.090	1
5	-0.067	9	4.067	-1.858	0
4	-1.067	2	-2.933	0.339	1
4	-1.067	4	-0.933	-0.545	0
5	-0.067	6	1.067	-0.532	0
6	0.933	3	-1.933	1.691	1
6	0.933	6	1.067	0.365	1
7	1.933	6	1.067	1.262	1
8	2.933	7	2.067	1.718	1
9	3.933	7	2.967	2.615	1
9	3.933	8	3.067	2.173	1

The same operation can also be performed for the group centroids. We then obtain the projections onto the t axis of the points indicated as c in Figure 8.2. For group 0 the centroid is (3   4.167) and for group 1 it is (6.444   5.444). Hence:

$$\bar{t}_0 = 0.897(3 - 5.067) - 0.442(4.167 - 4.933) = -1.516$$
$$\bar{t}_1 = 0.897(6.444 - 5.067) - 0.442(5.444 - 4.933) = 1.009$$

The point in the middle of these two projections of the group centroids can be chosen as the 'cutoff point': $t_c = [(-1.516) + 1.009]/2 = -0.254$. If the two groups had been of equal size, then this cutoff point would have lain in the origin, i.e., $t_c = 0$. Here, it lies to the left of the origin, because group 0 contains less neighbourhoods ($n_0 = 6$) than group 1 ($n_1 = 9$).

Looking at the discriminant scores of the 15 neighbourhoods, we can classify each neighbourhood in one of the two groups. Those scoring to the right of $t_c(t_i > t_c)$ are assigned to group 1 and those to the left of t_c ($t_i < t_c$) are classified in group 0. In Table 8.2 we have indicated the predicted group membership. Comparing this with the original Y scores, we see that 12 of the 15 neighbourhoods, i.e. 80%, are correctly classified. The discriminant function is not capable of a perfect classification, because there is some overlap between the two groups, which we already saw in a first inspection of the scatterplot (see Figure 8.2(c)). For example, the ninth neighbourhood, with scores $X_1 = 5$ and $X_2 = 6$, and which belonged *a priori* to group 1, is assigned to group 0 by the function t. We can see in the scatterplot that this neighbourhood indeed belongs to group 0, rather than group 1. In the projections onto the t axis this neighbourhood lies in the zone of overlap between the two groups and, therefore, its t score ($t_9 = -0.532$) lies very close to the cutoff point ($t_c = -0.254$).

Making use of the discriminant scores, we can also verify the between- and within-dispersions on the t axis. The variation (sum of squares) of the first six t scores of group 0 is 5.79. The variation of the last nine t scores of group 1 is 10.62. (Please calculate by hand or by means of a pocket calculator.) The sum of these two within-groups variations, which is the within-dispersion on the t axis, is 16.41 and it is indeed equal to the denominator of the eigenvalue λ, which we have maximized:

$$\mathbf{k}'\mathbf{Wk} = 48.222k_1^2 + 77.056k_2^2 + 94.444k_1k_2$$
$$= 48.222(0.897)^2 + 77.056(-0.442)^2 + 94.444(0.897)(-0.442)$$
$$= 16.41$$

For the calculation of the between-variation of the two group centroid projections on t, we use the weighing procedure with weights 6 and 9. Hence, this between-variation is equal to: $6(-1.516 - 0)^2 + 9(1.009 - 0)^2 = 22.95$, which equates the numerator of the eigenvalue λ:

$$\mathbf{k}'\mathbf{Bk} = 42.711k_1^2 + 5.878k_2^2 + 31.688k_1k_2$$
$$= 42.711(0.897)^2 + 5.878(-0.442)^2 + 31.688(0.897)(-0.442) = 22.95$$

We also verify that the ratio $\lambda = (\mathbf{k}'\mathbf{Bk})/(\mathbf{k}'\mathbf{Wk}) = 22.95/16.41 = 1.40$ is equal to the eigenvalue, which was calculated from the characteristic equation.

8.9 Significance Testing: Preparatory Remarks

We want to examine whether there is a significant difference between the two group centroids, i.e., between the means of the two groups for the income variable and the level of services variable, taken together. This is a test of the global model. In addition, we want to perform separate significance tests of the difference of income means and of means of levels of services. The latter two tests are called 'univariate tests', because the x variables are considered one at a time.

Before performing these tests, we will first present a brief summary of some tests dealt with in foregoing chapters and, making use of this knowledge, anticipate the tests of subsequent chapters and bring everything together in a system.

In Chapter 4, **Student's *t* test** was performed. There were only **two groups**, the humour group and the no-humour group, and there was only **one variable** of interval measurement level: financial concession.

In Chapter 7 the **F test of one-way ANOVA** was discussed. There were **several groups**, with interesting, moderately interesting and boring tasks, and there was **one** (dependent) **variable** of interval measurement level: intrinsic motivation. In the simple case of two groups, the money group and the no-money group, the F test appeared to be identical to Student's t test. Remember that $F = t^2$. The computer output of the corresponding dummy regression analysis still printed the results of the t test, with $d_f = n_0 - 1 + n_1 - 1 = n - 2$ degrees of freedom, but we know that the F test, according to the model comparison approach with 1 and $n - 2$ degrees of freedom, is the same.

We learn from the foregoing that the F test, which is more complex than the t test and which is meant for more than two groups, can also be applied in the simple case of two groups. The reverse, that the t test could be used in more complex cases, does not hold.

This is a principle which will hold for each of the following extensions. In **two-group discriminant analysis** the number of variables, rather than the number of groups, is more complex. There are **two groups**, the poor and the rich group, and there are **several variables** of interval measurement level: average income, level of services and possibly many others. The test, which will now be performed, is **Hotelling's T^2 test**. Just like the F test of analysis of variance, this test is an extension of the simple Student's t test. Here, too, it will hold that the more complex test applies to the simpler case, for, in the simple case of one discriminating variable, Hotelling's T^2 is identical to the square of Student's t. The reverse does not hold: Student's t test cannot be applied in the case of two groups and several discriminating x variables.

In the chapters to follow, not only the number of variables, but also the number of groups will be extended. For instance, in **multiple discriminant analysis**, the adjective 'multiple' indicates the presence of **several groups**, given that there are **several variables** of interval measurement level. In this most complex case, **Wilks's lambda (Λ) test** is applied. This test will not only be used in multiple discriminant analysis, but also in canonical correlation analysis and multivariate analysis of variance. Here, too, the indicated principle holds: t, F and T^2 are special cases of Wilks's lambda and not the other way round.

By way of summary, we make a scheme of the four tests (Figure 8.4), according to the two principles of complexity: the number of groups and the number of variables.

variables

	one	several
two	Student's t	Hotelling's T^2
several	Fisher's F	Wilks's lambda

groups

Figure 8.4 Sorts of tests in multivariate analysis

8.10 Significance Testing: Univariate Tests

In a univariate test, one pretends that there is only one variable. Other variables are simply left out of consideration. (Note that this is not the same as testing the effect of one out of many variables in a multivariate model.)

It is in fact always wise to perform the test of the global model before looking at the contributions of the separate variables. But for didactical purposes we will start here with the simpler 'univariate tests'.

Let us take the income variable X_1. We want to examine whether there is a significant difference between the mean income levels of the poor and the rich group of neighbourhoods. This is a simple problem with two groups and one variable, so that Student's t test can be applied. The mean income of group 0 is 3. The variation is 18 and the variance is 3.6. The mean income of group 1 is 6.444. The variation is 30.222 and the variance is 3.777. The pooled average of within-variances is:

$$s_w^2 = \frac{18 + 30.222}{(6 - 1) + (9 - 1)} = 3.709$$

The test of the difference between the mean income levels is performed by calculating the t score:

$$t = \frac{(3 - 6.444) - 0}{[(3.709/6) + (3.709/9)]^{1/2}} = -3.393$$

For $(6 - 1) + (9 - 1) = 13$ degrees of freedom and $\alpha = 0.05$ we find a value of $t^* = 1.771$ in the t table. The absolute value of the t score found in our sample is much greater than t^*. Hence, we conclude, with a prior probability of 95%, that the mean income levels of the poor and the rich group are significantly different.

Now, notice that the SPSS computer output of discriminant analysis does not print a t test, but rather: 'Wilks' lambda (U-statistic) and univariate F-ratio'. Let us first discuss the F test. We already know that the univariate F test is identical to the t test and that $F = t^2$, which is indeed verified: $F = (-3.393)^2 = 11.51$. The empirical probability of obtaining this value or higher values under H_0, for 1 and 13 degrees of freedom, is given in 'significance $= 0.0048$'. This probability is so small that we can reject the null hypotheses and speak of a significant result.

Instead of squaring t, we can also find the F score another way. We know from analysis of variance that F is the ratio of two variances: the between- and the within-variance. These variances can be read in matrices **B** and **W**. We find the variation of X_1 in the upper left part of these matrices: the between-variation is 42.711 and the within-variation is 48.222. The appropriate degrees of freedom are $g - 1 = 2 - 1 = 1$ for the between-dispersion and $n - g = 15 - 2 = 13$ for the within-dispersion. Hence, $F = [(42.711/1)/(48.222/13)] = 11.51$.

Similar comparisons can be made for Wilks' lambda. The computer output contains a value of Wilks's lambda $= 0.530\,30$ with respect to the income variable. When discussing the more advanced techniques in the chapters to follow, it will be shown that Wilks's lambda is equal to the ratio of two determinants: the determinant of **W** and the determinant of **T**. As there is only one variable in our simple case, we only consider the upper left element of matrices **W** and **T**, which contains the income data: the within-variation and the total variation are 48.222 and 90.933, respectively. Hence, the value of Wilks's lambda is $48.222/90.933 = 0.530\,30$. We will see in later chapters which theoretical probability distribution has to be used for this statistic and how it has to be tested.

For the level of services variable X_2, Student's t test or the corresponding F test and Wilks's lambda test can be performed in a similar manner. The reader can verify that $t = -0.996$, $F = 0.9916$ and Wilks's lambda $= 0.929\,13$. The result is not significant. Hence, there is no significant difference between the mean levels of services of the poor and the rich group of neighbourhoods.

8.11 Significance Testing: the Multivariate Test

We will now look at variables X_1 and X_2 together. We will examine whether there is a significant difference between the centroid of group 0 and the centroid of group 1. This time, we are confronted with several problems: not only the problem that the dispersions of a variable in the two groups can be different (so that the pooled within-variance, i.e., the square of s_w, has to be used), but also the problem that the variables can be mutually correlated within groups and, moreover, the problem that the dispersions of the variables within groups can be unequal. In other words: the within-groups covariance matrices $\mathbf{C}_0$, $\mathbf{C}_1$ and $\mathbf{C}_w$ (pooled within) are not necessarily diagonal (think of cigars standing upright or lying flat) and not necessarily scalar (think of circles).

It was the commendable accomplishment of Hotelling to design a multivariate extension of Student's t test in which all these problems are taken into consideration. The inverse of matrix $\mathbf{C}_w$ plays a crucial role in his contribution. Analogous to the formula of t (squared), he constructed a statistic, called Hotelling's T^2, in which not only X_1, but also X_2 and other possible discriminating variables, are included, in which a difference of group means now becomes a difference of group centroids, because there are several variables, and in which $1/s_w^2$ is replaced by the inverse of $\mathbf{C}_w$, containing not only the dispersions but also the mutual associations between the discriminating variables. For any X, the formula of t^2 was given in Chapter 4:

$$t^2 = \frac{(\bar{X}_0 - \bar{X}_1)^2}{\dfrac{s_w^2}{n_0} + \dfrac{s_w^2}{n_1}} = \frac{n_0 n_1}{n_0 + n_1}(\bar{X}_0 - \bar{X}_1)\frac{1}{s_w^2}(\bar{X}_0 - \bar{X}_1)$$

The analogous formula for Hotelling's T^2 is:

$$T^2 = \frac{n_0 n_1}{n_0 + n_1} \mathbf{d}' \mathbf{C}_w^{-1} \mathbf{d}$$

We first calculate the inverse of $\mathbf{C}_w$:

$$\mathbf{C}_w = \begin{bmatrix} 3.709 & 3.632 \\ 3.632 & 5.927 \end{bmatrix} \quad |\mathbf{C}_w| = (3.709)(5.927) - (3.632)^2 = 8.792$$

$$\mathbf{C}_w^{-1} = \text{adj } \mathbf{C}_w / |\mathbf{C}_w| = \frac{1}{8.792} \begin{bmatrix} 5.927 & -3.632 \\ -3.632 & 3.709 \end{bmatrix}'$$

$$= \begin{bmatrix} 0.674 & -0.413 \\ -0.413 & 0.422 \end{bmatrix}$$

Vector $\mathbf{d}$, the difference vector between group centroids, was calculated before:

$$\mathbf{d} = \bar{\mathbf{x}}_0 - \bar{\mathbf{x}}_1 = \begin{bmatrix} 3 \\ 4.167 \end{bmatrix} - \begin{bmatrix} 6.444 \\ 5.444 \end{bmatrix} = \begin{bmatrix} -3.444 \\ -1.277 \end{bmatrix}$$

We can now derive $\mathbf{d}' \mathbf{C}_w^{-1} \mathbf{d}$. This will be Mahalanobis' distance D^2.

$$D^2 = \mathbf{d}' \mathbf{C}_w^{-1} \mathbf{d} = (-3.444 \quad -1.277) \begin{bmatrix} 0.674 & -0.413 \\ -0.413 & 0.422 \end{bmatrix} \begin{bmatrix} -3.444 \\ -1.277 \end{bmatrix}$$

$$= 5.051$$

Hotelling's T^2 can be derived from the foregoing:

$$T^2 = \frac{n_0 n_1}{n_0 + n_1} \mathbf{d}' \mathbf{C}_w^{-1} \mathbf{d} = \frac{(6)(9)}{6 + 9} (5.051) = 18.182$$

Hotelling proved that the value $[(n - p - 1)/p(n - 2)]T^2$ is distributed as F with p and $n - p - 1$ degrees of freedom. In our example we have $p = 2$, because there are two discriminating variables, and $n = 15$, because there are 15 neighbourhoods, from which we obtain the following F value: $F = [(n - p - 1)/p(n - 2)]T^2 = [(15 - 2 - 1)/2(15 - 2)](18.182) = 8.392$. For two and 12 degrees of freedom and for $\alpha = 0.05$, we find a critical F value of 3.89 in the F table. It follows that there is a significant difference between the centroids of the two groups, i.e., between the mean income levels and the mean levels of services, taken together and taking their dispersions and mutual associations into consideration. Hence, the global model is significant.

8.12 Mahalanobis' Distance D^2

Hotelling's T^2 formula includes Mahalanobis D^2:

$$D^2 = \mathbf{d}' \mathbf{C}_w^{-1} \mathbf{d}$$

$$T^2 = \frac{n_0 n_1}{n_0 + n_1} \mathbf{d}' \mathbf{C}_w^{-1} \mathbf{d} = \frac{n_0 n_1}{n_0 + n_1} D^2$$

Therefore, the foregoing F test could have been performed by means of D^2 as well:

$$F = \frac{n-p-1}{p(n-2)} \cdot \frac{n_0 n_1}{n_0 + n_1} D^2$$

Most interesting is the geometric interpretation of Mahalanobis' distance D^2. For, it is an extension of Euclidian distance $\mathbf{d'd}$. To explain this we look back at the scatterplot of Figure 8.1, in which we now draw concentration ellipses and indicate the centroids as c.

In discussing the discriminant function t, it appeared that the best t axis is not necessarily the connection of the two centroids. This is only the case when the two concentration ellipses are in fact circles, i.e., when the within-groups covariance matrices are not only diagonal (absence of $X_1 - X_2$ association), but also scalar (equal X_1 and X_2-dispersions). Such a situation is drawn in Figure 8.5(a). The between-distance between the circles can be simply calculated as the Euclidian distance between the two centroids, (3 4.167) and (6.444 5.444). It can easily be read from the figure that the square of the Euclidian distance is equal to the sum of squares of mean differences for variables X_1 and X_2:

$$\text{(Euclidian distance)}^2 = (3 - 6.444)^2 + (4.167 - 5.444)^2 = 13.50$$

In vector notation:

$$\mathbf{d'd} = (-3.444 \quad -1.277) \begin{bmatrix} -3.444 \\ -1.277 \end{bmatrix} = 13.50$$

However, the Euclidian distance between the group centroids is not a good measure of the group distance, for neither the unequal dispersions of X_1 and X_2 (oblong cigars instead of circles) nor the relationship between X_1 and X_2 (oblique cigars) are taken into account. Such a situation is drawn in Figure 8.5(b). Because of the unequal dispersions and the association, it is no longer possible to represent the group distance by the Euclidian distance between centroids. This is what Mahalanobis' distance is about. The inclusion of the inverse of $\mathbf{C}_w$ in the calculation of the distance entails a correction for the within-groups variances and covariances. The following result was obtained above:

$$D^2 = \mathbf{d'C_w^{-1}d} = 5.051$$

We see that the calculation according to Mahalanobis results in a substantial reduction of the squared distance between the groups as compared with the (squared) Euclidian distance, which is 13.50.

8.13 The Dummy Regression Approach

Just like analysis of variance, discriminant analysis can be converted into multiple regression analysis if we make use of dummy coding. At the beginning of this chapter we anticipated this 0–1 coding in the data matrix of 15 neighbourhoods. The independent variables X_1 and X_2 are measured at the interval level and the two groups are represented by the dependent variable Y. If the scores 0 and 1 are given to the poor and rich group, respectively, then the application of multiple regression

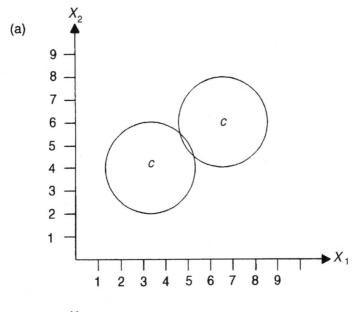

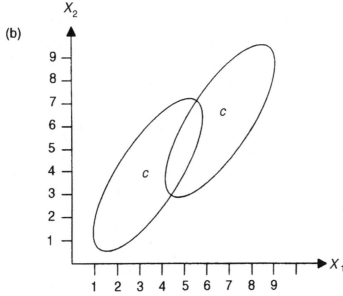

Figure 8.5 Geometry of Mahalanobis' distance D^2

analysis is straightforward. True, the obtained output then refers to a regression problem and not to a discrimination problem, but the outcomes are the same. We will discuss the multiple regression function and the F test of the global model, successively.

The computer output gives us the following multiple regression function:

$$\hat{Y} = 0.539 + 0.207X_1 - 0.102X_2$$

The constant term is left out of consideration, for, if we had made our calculations with deviations of mean, then it would have been equal to 0 and the regression coefficients would have been the same. The two regression coefficients are brought together in a vector **b** and this vector is normalized:

$$\mathbf{b} = \begin{bmatrix} b_{y1} \\ b_{y2} \end{bmatrix} = \begin{bmatrix} 0.207 \\ -0.102 \end{bmatrix}$$

Vector **b** is divided by its length:

$$||\mathbf{b}|| = [(0.207)^2 + (-0.102)^2]^{1/2} = 0.231$$

$$\mathbf{b} \text{ (normalized)} = \frac{\mathbf{b}}{||\mathbf{b}||} = \frac{1}{0.231} \begin{bmatrix} 0.207 \\ -0.102 \end{bmatrix} = \begin{bmatrix} 0.897 \\ -0.422 \end{bmatrix}$$

We see that **b** is equal to **k**. Hence, the multiple regression function is equal to the discriminant function t.

It also holds that the F test of a multiple regression analysis with dummy dependent variable is exactly the same as the F test associated with Hotelling's T^2. In the regression output we indeed find an F value of 8.392 with two and 12 degrees of freedom and an empirical significance level of 0.0053. It follows that the multivariate test of the global model can also be obtained via the dummy regression approach.

The same holds for the tests of the separate contributions of X_1 and X_2. Notice, however, that the t tests of multiple regression analysis are not the same as the univariate tests of discriminant analysis, for the latter are really univariate. To make the comparison, one has to look at the separate bivariate regressions, of Y and X_1 one the one hand and of Y and X_2 on the other hand.

There are also several analogues with the multiple determination coefficient $R^2 = 0.583$. We know from multiple regression analysis that R^2 is equal to the ratio of two variations: the explained variation SSR and the total variation SST (where $SST = SSR + SSE$). We know from the dummy regression approach of analysis of variance that the analogue of R^2 in the case of groups is equal to the ratio of the between-variation SSB and the total variation SST (where SST = SSB + SSW). The latter holds in discriminant analysis as well. In the calculation of the eigenvalue λ, the numerator was equal to $SSB = \mathbf{k'Bk} = 22.95$ and the denominator was $SSW = \mathbf{k'Wk} = 16.41$. Consequently, $SST = SSB + SSW = 22.95 + 16.41 = 39.36$. The ratio $SSB/SST = 22.95/39.36 = 0.583$ is indeed equal to R^2. This can also be written as $R^2 = \lambda/(1 + \lambda) = 1.399/2.399 = 0.583$, from which we can see that there is a fixed relationship between the eigenvalue and the multiple determination coefficient. This also holds for Hotelling's T^2 and Mahalanobis' D^2, for the eigenvalue λ is obtained by dividing Hotelling's T^2 by $n_0 + n_1 - 2$: $\lambda = 18.182/13 = 1.399$. The other analogues follow automatically.

8.14 Equal Within-Groups Covariance Matrices: Box's M Test

The application of discriminant analysis is in fact not allowed if the within-groups covariance matrices are significantly different. Bartlett and Box have each developed a 'test for equality of covariance matrices'. Box's test is most general in nature and is printed in the computer output. A look at the empirical significance level is sufficient. Notice that, for $\alpha = 0.05$, it must not be smaller but greater than 0.05, for the difference between the matrices should *not* be significant.

In Norušis's, *SPSS Statistical Algorithms* (an addendum with formulae) (1978) it is indicated where Box's M is used, which is distributed as F, and where Bartlett's B is used, which is distributed as chi-square. In our example we can use Bartlett's test. Besides, the formulae of B and M are identical here:

$$M = (n - g) \ln |\mathbf{C}_w| - \sum_{j=1}^{g} (n_j - 1) \ln |\mathbf{C}_j|$$

This statistic M is distributed as chi-square with $d_f = 1/2(g - 1)(p)(p + 1)$ degrees of freedom. Applied to our example:

$$\mathbf{C}_0 = \begin{bmatrix} 3.6 & 4.4 \\ 4.4 & 8.967 \end{bmatrix} \qquad |\mathbf{C}_0| = 12.92 \qquad n_0 = 6$$

$$\mathbf{C}_1 = \begin{bmatrix} 3.778 & 3.153 \\ 3.153 & 4.028 \end{bmatrix} \qquad |\mathbf{C}_1| = 5.276 \qquad n_1 = 9$$

$$\mathbf{C}_w = \begin{bmatrix} 3.709 & 3.632 \\ 3.632 & 5.927 \end{bmatrix} \qquad |\mathbf{C}_w| = 8.792 \qquad n = 15$$

$$M = (15 - 2) \ln 8.792 - [(6 - 1) \ln 12.92 + (9 - 1) \ln 5.276]$$
$$= (13)(2.174) - (5)(2.559) - (8)(1.663) = 2.161$$

This Box's M value can be verified in the computer output. For $\alpha = 0.05$ and $d_f = 1/2(2 - 1)(2)(2 + 1) = 3$ the critical value of chi-square is 7.81.

As M is much smaller, there is no significant difference between $\mathbf{C}_0$ and $\mathbf{C}_1$, so that the performance of discriminant analysis is allowed.

In cases in which the covariance matrices do differ significantly, a quadratic discriminant function might be more appropriate.

8.15 SPSS for Windows Output of Discriminant Analysis

The output of our mini example of poor and rich neighbourhoods consists of two parts: (a) a discriminant analysis and (b) a regression analysis with dummy dependent variable.

Choosing or creating a data file
How to open an SPSS session and how to choose a data file or, if a data file does not yet exist, how to enter data, to choose name, type and label of variables and to save the data file with extension .*sav*, is shown in Chapter 4.

Running the discriminant analysis
Click on Statistics. Click on Classify. Click on Discriminant. Click on variable Y in the Source Variable list on the left and click on the ▶ push button of the Grouping Variable. Click on Define Range. Type the minimum value 0. Click on the value of Maximum and type 1. Click on Continue. You now return to the Discriminant Analysis dialog box. Click on the variables X_1 and X_2 in the Source Variable list (either separately or together by means of the click and drag technique) and click on the ▶ push button of the Independents.

Click on Statistics. A Discriminant Analysis Statistics dialog box appears. Click on everything. Click on Continue.

You don't have to click on Method, because we are not going to select a stepwise analysis. Click on Classify. A Discriminant Analysis Classification dialog box appears. You will see under Prior Probabilities that All Groups Equal is chosen. Click on Compute from Group Sizes and a radio button will show that you have chosen this option. Click on Continue.

If you now click on OK in the main Discriminant Analysis dialog box, SPSS will run the statistical procedure and an output window will appear with the results of discriminant analysis.

Running discriminant analysis in the form of a regression analysis with dummy dependent variable
You can do this in the familiar way. Click on Statistics. Click on Regression. Click on Linear. Choose Y as the dependent variable. Choose X_1 and X_2 as the independent variables. Click on OK.

Do not forget to save the output: click on File, click on Save as, type *poor.lst* and click on OK.

Running the statistical procedures with SPSS commands
As you already know, you can run the foregoing statistical procedures by opening a syntax window and typing SPSS commands. Click on File, click on New, click on SPSS Syntax, type the statements, put the cursor anywhere in the first command line and click on ▶ (or on Run for the 5.0 version).

The statements for discriminant analysis are as follows:

```
1 LIST
2 DISCRIMINANT/GROUPS Y (0.1)
3    /VARIABLES XI X2
4    /ANALYSIS X1 X2
5    /METHOD DIRECT
6    /STATISTICS ALL.
```

In statement 1 we request the data matrix with 'list'. Statement 2 indicates that the variable Y of the data matrix represents groups. The numbers 0 and 1 between brackets indicate the minimum and maximum value of the groups, respectively. These could have been 1 and 2 as well, on the condition that these numbers were used in the data matrix. For more than two, say five, groups, the statement could have indicated Y (1,5). In other words, only the lowest and the highest scores are written.

In statement 3 the discriminating variables are indicated. Statements 4 and 5 are in fact superfluous in our simple example for 'analysis' requests analyses of subsets of variables, which is not the purpose here, and 'method = direct' includes all mentioned variables in the analysis, which is 'default'. In statement 6 we request all 'statistics', for in addition to the eigenvalue and the significance tests we also want to look at the centroids, the standard deviations, the covariance matrices, the univariate tests, Box's M test and the unstandardized discriminant weights.

For the multiple regression analysis with a dummy dependent variable we need not offer the computer a new data matrix, for we have already coded Y with scores 0 and 1. The statements are as follows:

```
7    REGRESSION /VARIABLES Y X1 X2
8       /DESCRIPTIVES DEFAULT
9       /DEPENDENT Y
10      /METHOD ENTER X1 X2.
11   REGRESSION /VARIABLES Y X1 X2
12      /DEPENDENT Y
13      /METHOD ENTER X1.
14   REGRESSION /VARIABLES Y X1 X2
15      /DEPENDENT Y
16      /METHOD ENTER X2.
```

In statements 7 to 10, the analysis of the global model is requested. The comparison with discriminant analysis has been discussed extensively. The F test is exactly the same. For a comparison of the regression coefficients and the discriminant weights one should not forget to first collect them in a vector and to normalize this vector.

Statements 11 to 16 are added for a comparison with the univariate tests of discriminant analysis.

The output is as follows:

```
LIST.
Y X1 X2
0  1  1
0  1  4
0  2  1
0  4  5
0  5  5
0  5  9
1  4  2
1  4  4
1  5  6
1  6  3
1  6  6
1  7  6
1  8  7
1  9  7
1  9  8
Number of cases read =    15   Number of cases listed =    15


This Discriminant Analysis required 1272 (1.2K) BYTES of workspace.

On groups defined by Y poor/rich

             15 (unweighted) cases were processed.
              0 of these were excluded from the analysis.
             15 (unweighted) cases will be used in the analysis.
```

```
Number of Cases by Group
                Number of Cases
    Y         Unweighted     Weighted Label
          0        6            6.0
          1        9            9.0
      Total       15           15.0
```

```
Group Means
    Y              X1              X2
          0      3.00000        4.16667
          1      6.44444        5.44444
      Total      5.06667        4.93333
```

```
Group Standard Deviations
    Y              X1              X2
          0      1.89737        2.99444
          1      1.94365        2.00693
      Total      2.54858        2.43389
```

```
Pooled Within-Groups Covariance Matrix with        13 degrees of freedom
              X1              X2
    X1      3.709402
    X2      3.632479        5.927350
```

```
Pooled Within-Groups Correlation Matrix

              X1              X2
    X1      1.00000
    X2       .77478         1.00000
```

Correlations which cannot be computed are printed as'.'

```
Wilks' Lambda (U-statistic) and univariate F-ratio
with   1 and        13 degrees of freedom

    Variable   Wilks' Lambda          F        Significance
    --------   -------------    -------------   ------------

    X1             .53030          11.51           .0048
    X2             .92913           .9916          .3375
```

```
Covariance Matrix for Group        0,

              X1              X2
    X1      3.600000
    X2      4.400000        8.966667
```

```
Covariance Matrix for Group        1,

              X1              X2
    X1      3.777778
    X2      3.152778        4.027778
```

```
Total Covariance Matrix with        14 degrees of freedom

              X1              X2
    X1      6.495238
    X2      4.504762        5.923810
```

On groups defined by Y   poor/rich

Analysis number   1
Direct method: All variables passing the tolerance test are entered.
     Minimum Tolerance Level .... .00100

Canonical Discriminant Functions

     Maximum number of functions.............   1
     Minimum cumulative percent of variance... 100.00
     Maximum significance of Wilks' Lambda   1.0000

Prior probability for each group is .50000

Classification Function Coefficients
(Fisher's Linear Discriminant Functions)

Y   =   0   1

X1   .3010369   2.095269
X2   .5184705   -.3655217
(constant) -2.224849   -6.449538

                    Canonocal Discriminant Functions

              Pct of   Cum Canonical After Wilks'

 Fcn Eigenvalue Variance Pct   Corr   Fcn Lambda Chisquare DF Sig
                                         :   0 .4169   10.499   2 .0053
  1*   1.3986 100.00 100.00   .7636 :

  * marks the   1 canonical discriminant functions remaining in the analysis.

Standardized Canonical Discriminant Coefficients

            FUNC 1
X1   1.53766
X2   -.95765

Structure Matrix:

Pooled-within-groups correlations between discriminating variables
                         and canonical discriminant functions
(Variables ordered by size of correlation within function)

            FUNC 1
X1   .79579
X2   .23354

Unstandardized Canonical Discriminant Function Coefficients

            FUNC 1
X1   .7983764
X2   -.3933485
(constant) -2.104588

Canonical Discriminant Functions evaluated at Group Means (Group Centroids)

```
Group      FUNC   1
  0        -1.34841
  1         .89894
```

Test of equality of group covariance matrices using Box's M

The ranks and natural logarithms of determinants printed as those
of the group covariance matrices.

```
Group Label              Rank   Log Determinant
      0                    2        2.558776
      1                    2        1.663176
Pooled Within-Groups
Covariance Matrix          2        2.173845
```

```
Box's M       Approximate F  Degrees of freedom  Significance
2.1607          .59074          3,       4817.6     .6211
```

Case Number	Mis Val	Sel	Actual Group		Highest probability Group P(D/G) P(D/G)			2nd Highest Group P(G/D)		Discrim Scores
1			0		0	.7255	.9649	1	.0351	-1.6996
2			0		0	.1257	.9974	1	.0026	-2.8796
3			0		0	.6547	.8206	1	.1794	-.9012
4			0		0	.6379	.8127	1	.1873	-.8778
5			0	**	1	.3279	.5809	0	.4191	-.0794
6			0		0	.7608	.9612	1	.0388	-1.6528
7			1		1	.5507	.7657	0	.2343	.3022
8			1	**	0	.3876	.6419	1	.3581	-.4845
9			1	**	0	.3812	.6359	1	.3641	-.4728
10			1		1	.5441	.9799	0	.0201	1.5056
11			1		1	.5664	.7750	0	.2250	.3256
12			1		1	.8220	.9540	0	.0460	1.1240
13			1		1	.5287	.9809	0	.0191	1.5290
14			1		1	.1532	.9968	0	.0032	2.3274
15			1		1	.3006	.9922	0	.0078	1.9340

Symbols used in Plots

```
Symbol  Group  Label
------  -----  --------------------
  1       0
  2       1
```

```
Histogram for Group        0
          Canonical Discriminant Function 1
   4 +                                        +
     |                                        |
     |                                        |
     |                                        |
   3 +                                        +
     |                                        |
     |                                        |
     |                                        |
   2 +              1 1                       +
     |              1 1                       |
     |              1 1                       |
     |              1 1                       |
   1 +           1  1 1 1                     +
     |           1  1 1 1                     |
     |           1  1 1 1                     |
     |           1  1 1 1                     |
     X----|----|----|----|----|----|----|----X
      Out -6.0 -4.0 -2.0   .0  2.0  4.0  6.0    Out
 Class   1111111111111111111122222222222222222222
Centroids                  1


            Histogram for Group        1
          Canonical Discriminant Function 1
   4 +                                        +
     |                                        |
     |                                        |
     |                                        |
   3 +                                        +
     |                                        |
     |                                        |
     |                                        |
   2 +              2 2  2                    +
     |              2 2  2                    |
     |              2 2  2                    |
     |              2 2  2                    |
   1 +              2 2 2222                  +
     |              2 2 2222                  |
     |              2 2 2222                  |
     |              2 2 2222                  |
     X----|----|----|----|----|----|----|----X
      Out -6.0 -4.0 -2.0   .0  2.0  4.0  6.0    Out
 Class   1111111111111111111122222222222222222222
Centroids                      2
```

```
                     All-groups stacked Histogram

                  Canonical Discriminant Function 1
         4 +                                                 +
           |                                                 |
           |                                                 |
           |                                                 |
         3 +                                                 +
           |                                                 |
           |                                                 |
           |                                                 |
         2 +               1 12 2  2                         +
           |               1 12 2  2                         |
           |               1 12 2  2                         |
           |               1 12 2  2                         |
         1 +          1  1 1212 2222                          +
           |          1  1 1212 2222                         |
           |          1  1 1212 2222                         |
           |          1  1 1212 2222                         |
           X----|----|----|----|----|----|----|----X
           Out -6.0 -4.0 -2.0   .0  2.0  4.0  6.0   Out
     Class    111111111111111111112222222222222222222222
   Centroids                      1     2
```

Classification Results -

| | No. of | Predicted Group Membership | |
Actual Group	Cases	0	1
Group 0	6	5	1
		83.3%	16.7%
Group 1	9	2	7
		22.2%	77.8%

Percent of "grouped" cases correctly classified: 80.00%

Classification Processing Summary
        15 Cases were processed.
         0 Cases were excluded for missing or out-of-range group codes.
         0 Cases had at least one missing discriminating variable.
        15 Cases were used for printed output.

****

Now follows the output of the regression analysis with dummy dependent variable.

Listwise Deletion of Missing Data

```
        Mean  Std Dev  Label
Y        .600    .507  poor/rich
X1      5.067   2.549  financial situation
X2      4.933   2.434  Level of services

N of Cases =    15
```

```
Correlation:

                 Y          X1          X2

Y             1.000        .685        .266
X1             .685       1.000        .726
X2             .266        .726       1.000


Equation Number 1    Dependent Variable..   Y   poor/rich
Block Number  1. Method:  Enter      X1       X2
Equation Number 1    Dependent Variable..   Y   poor/rich

Variable(s) Entered on Step Number
   1..     X2        level of services
   2..     X1        financial situation

Multiple R          .76361
R Square            .58309
Adjusted R Square   .51361
Standard Error      .35365

Analysis of Variance
                    DF       Sum of Squares      Mean Square
Regression           2           2.09914          1.04957
Residual            12           1.50086           .12507

F =      8.39174        Signif F =  .0053

Equation Number 1    Dependent Variable..   Y  poor/ rich


------------------ Variables in the Equation ------------------

Variable              B        SE B         Beta        T   Sig T

X2              -.102058    .056490    -.489845    -1.807  .0959
X1               .207146    .053948    1.041084     3.840  .0024
(constant)       .053947    .223775                  .241  .8136


****************************************************************************


Listwise Deletion of Missing Data

Equation Number 1    Dependent Variable..   Y poor/ rich

Block Number  1. Method:  Enter      X1


Equation Number 1    Dependent Variable..   Y poor/ rich


Variable(s) Entered on Step Number
   1..    X1        financial situation
```

```
Multiple R            .68534
R Square              .46970
Adjusted R Square     .42890
Standard Error        .38321
```

Analysis of Variance

	DF	Sum of Squares	Mean Square
Regression	1	1.69091	1.69091
Residual	13	1.90909	.14685

F = 11.51429 Signif F = .0048

Equation Number 1 Dependent Variable.. Y poor/rich

------------------- Variables in Equation -------------------

Variable	B	SE B	Beta	T	Sig T
X1	.136364	.040186	.685344	3.393	.0048
(Constant)	-.090909	.226380		-.402	.6945

****

Listwise Deletion of Missing Data
Equation Number 1   Dependent Variable..   Y   poor/rich
Block Number 1.   Method: Enter   X2

Equation Number 1   Dependent Variable..   Y   poor/rich

Variable(s) Entered on Step Number
   1..   X2   level of services

```
Multiple R            .26622
R Square              .07087
Adjusted R Square    -.00060
Standard Error        .50724
```

Analysis of Variance

	DF	Sum of Squares	Mean Square
Regression	1	.25514	.25514
Residual	13	3.34486	.25730

F =   .99164   Signif F = .3375

Equation Number 1   Dependent Variable..   Y poor/ rich

```
------------------ Variables in the Equation ------------------

Variable              B        SE B       Beta        T   Sig T

X2                .055466    .055700    .266221     .996   .3376
(Constant)        .326367    .304401               1.072   .3031
```

Factor Analysis: The Investigation of Marital Adjustment

This chapter is divided into three parts. Using the research example of marital adjustment as our basis (section 1.2.6), we first discuss **principal components analysis** (PCA). Next we deal with **principal factor analysis** (PFA). These two forms of factor analysis, PCA and PFA, have different underlying models, but the method for the calculation of the factor solution is the same. Besides, a great number of calculation-methods have been developed, so that we can in fact speak of an entire world of factor analyses. Therefore, in the third part, an overview is given under the heading **'Variations of Factor Analysis Methods'**.

In dealing with PCA and PFA, we will follow the same scheme as in previous chapters, with the research problem and the causal diagram, the mini data matrix, the model, the geometric approach, research objectives, calculations by hand, assumptions and the computer output, respectively. However, various subjects will now be described more succinctly and now and then an appeal will be made to the prior knowledge of certain mathematical methods, such as matrix algebra and, especially, the SVD operation (singular value decomposition).

9.1 Principal Components Analysis

9.1.1 The Research Problem and the Diagram

In the investigation of marital adjustment, a random sample of 349 spouses was given 20 questions to answer. A research problem was in fact absent in this study. The only thing the researchers did was to conceive of 20 items related to marital adjustment. They left it to statistical analysis to decide whether a hidden structure could be recognized in the material.

This basic format, or perhaps we should say this absence of a basic format, was entitled **latent structure**. Factor analysis can indeed be considered a technique of latent structure analysis. This can be extremely helpful if we want to examine whether a concept like marital adjustment can be split into a number of latent characteristics (dimensions). The 20 indicators (= manifest variables = items = observations = questions in the questionnaire) are then grouped, as it were, in different subgroups. The indicators of such a subgroup have high within-correlations and, therefore, are considered to represent the same dimension, which finds expression in their high 'loadings' on the related latent variable.

There are many conceivable situations between two extremes. According to one extreme, all 20 indicators measure nearly the same and hence their mutual correlations are very high, so that they are almost interchangeable. Whichever question is asked, 'agreement on finances' or 'kisses every day', nearly the same answer is given by the spouses–respondents. In such a case the research materials would have a one-dimensional structure, for all 20 indicators would have high loadings on one latent variable (factor). The other extreme is a situation in which all 20 indicators measure something different. These 20 indicators would then be subdivided into 20 singletons, i.e., 20 sets containing only one element. From this 20-dimensional factor solution we would learn nothing, for the latent structure of the materials would be as complex as the original manifest structure. Reality usually lies in between these two extremes: in the practice of research a great number of observed indicators can be reduced to a smaller number of dimensions. For example, the 20 questions on marital adjustment are reduced to three dimensions, 'companionship', 'agreement' and 'affectional intimacy'.

For didactical reasons we will restrict ourselves to three of the 20 questions and a two-factor solution will emerge. These three questions are:

X_6: give and take; this variable will be X_1 below;
X_7: agreement on finances; this variable will be X_2 below;
X_{17}: both prefer stay at home; this variable will be X_3 below.

We start with the treatment of principal components analysis (PCA), in which the three variables can essentially be reduced to a solution with the same number, i.e., three dimensions. Next, in principal factor analysis (PFA), dimension reduction, i.e., the reduction of the variables to a smaller number of dimensions, will receive more attention.

The diagram is no longer a 'causal' diagram, because principal components analysis (and factor analysis in general) is a non-dependent technique. Some authors propose to draw a causal arrow from the latent variables to the indicators. They defend the thesis that a factor (companionship) exercises a causal influence on the manifest behaviour (give and take). We do not agree with this thesis. We understand a factor as a mother-concept which gives a summary of a subgroup of indicators that measure largely the same. In other words, we consider a factor analysis diagram as a measuring model and not as a causal model.

In principal components analysis we do not speak of 'factors', but rather of 'components'. For the three variables, X_1, X_2 and X_3, three components, C_1, C_2 and C_3, are provided. It will appear in later stages that we do not need all three components, but in its full form the PCA model has as many components as variables. The diagram is shown in Figure 9.1.

9.1.2   The Data Matrix

In our (fictitious) mini data set we consider $n = 12$ persons, to which three statements are presented: X_1, X_2 and X_3. We assume that these three variables are measured at the interval level. The scores from 1 to 9 indicate to what extent the respondent gives a 'maritally-adjusted' answer. We make an exception for X_3, which has been inverted for reasons that will become clear in later sections.

X_1 is the extent to which disagreements are resolved by mutual give and take. X_2 is the measure of agreement on finances. X_3 is the extent to which husband and wife

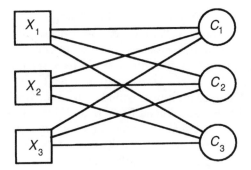

Figure 9.1   Principal components analysis (PCA) diagram

Table 9.1   Data matrix

X_1	X_2	X_3
8	9	1
5	5	5
4	4	5
8	7	2
7	1	4
4	5	7
5	5	5
2	6	8
6	5	3
3	2	6
2	8	9
6	3	5

both prefer '*not*' to stay at home during leisure time. The data matrix is shown in Table 9.1.

9.1.3   The Model of Principal Components Analysis

In PCA an attempt is first made to find a linear combination of the three variables X_1, X_2 and X_3, in such a way that a maximum of variance is extracted from these three variables. Such a linear combination is indicated as C_1 (C for component). The three variables are presented in standardized form, as a z score:

$$C_1 = u_{11}z_1 + u_{12}z_2 + u_{13}z_3$$

In the exceptional situation in which C_1 would extract 100% of the variance of the three variables, this first component would be sufficient, because it would exhaustively represent all the information of the data matrix. This is of course seldom the case. Take, for example, the situation in which the first component shares only 60% of the variance with the three variables. We then look for a second component, perpendicular to the first, in such a way that a maximum is extracted from the remaining 40%. Next, we look for a third component, perpendicular to the foregoing two, so that the remaining variance is used up. The three components together extract 100% of the variance of the three variables.

Thus, in PCA we look for as many linear combinations as there are variables, under two restricting conditions:

1. The components have to be perpendicular (orthogonality).
2. The first component has to extract as much variance as possible from the original variables, the second component as much as possible from the remaining variance, etc., until all variance is used up (**principal axis method**).

In our example there are three components:

$$C_1 = u_{11}z_1 + u_{12}z_2 + u_{13}z_3$$
$$C_2 = u_{21}z_1 + u_{22}z_2 + u_{23}z_3$$
$$C_3 = u_{31}z_1 + u_{32}z_2 + u_{33}z_3$$

In matrix notation, this model is:

$$\boxed{\mathbf{C = XU}}$$

In this model, $\mathbf{X}$ is the (12×3) matrix of scores of variables X_1, X_2 and X_3, i.e., the original data matrix, albeit in standardized scores. $\mathbf{U}$ is the (3×3) matrix of factorscore coefficients u_{ij}. If the latter were known, then the scores of the 12 persons on each of the three components could be calculated. These component scores are collected in the (12×3) matrix $\mathbf{C}$.

The PCA model can also be considered the other way round. Each original variable can be conceived of as a linear combination of the three components:

$$z_1 = a_{11}C_1 + a_{12}C_2 + a_{13}C_3$$
$$z_2 = a_{21}C_1 + a_{22}C_2 + a_{23}C_3$$
$$z_3 = a_{31}C_1 + a_{32}C_2 + a_{33}C_3$$

In matrix notation, this model is:

$$\boxed{\mathbf{X = CA'}}$$

The coefficients of matrix $\mathbf{A}$ are called component loadings. They are the beta weights of a multiple regression of a (standardized!) variable as a function of the three components. We will see, in PCA, that these beta weights are equal to the correlations between variables and components. This is why matrix $\mathbf{A}$ is mostly used for the interpretation of the PCA solution. For, inspection of this matrix will show that certain variables have high correlations with (have high loadings on) a component, whereas other variables do not. In this way it becomes possible to determine which variables are best represented by the component in question.

9.1.4 *Geometric Approach*

The PCA model becomes extremely clear if it is approached from the geometric point of view. For, to perform a principal components analysis is in fact simply the rotation of a cube. The three variables X_1, X_2 and X_3 can be represented by a three-dimensional space, which takes the form of a cube with the three variables as sides. If the variables are standardized, then the origin lies in the centroid, i.e., the point inside the cube where the means come together. The 12 points lie around this origin, one for each person.

In PCA we try to draw a straight line through the origin in such a way that the projections of the 12 points onto the line have the highest possible dispersion (maximal variance). This first straight line is the linear combination C_1. If the 12 points were already lying on a straight line (perfect multicollinearity), then this first component would exhaustively represent all the information of the data matrix. This is of course seldom or never the case. In general, the points are scattered around C_1, e.g., in the form of a cigar.

Therefore, we look for a second straight line, C_2, through the origin and perpendicular to the first, in such a way that the projections of the 12 points on this second line have maximal variance. Next we look for a third straight line, C_3, through the origin and perpendicular to C_1 and C_2, for which the projections similarly have maximal dispersion.

The three components C_1, C_2 and C_3 are the sides of a new cube. The old cube, with X_1, X_2 and X_3 as axes, is rotated round the origin toward the new cube, while the points remain in place. This new cube in fact offers an equally good representation of the data, but is more interesting; for, if the 12 points have an organized pattern, e.g., in the form of a cigar, then the new cube fits the points better, because the first component runs in the direction of the lengthwise axis of the cigar and the other components in the direction of the minor axis. The latter is not the case if the three variables are mutually uncorrelated; for, the point concentration then appears as a sphere and any cube is just as good as any other. In Figure 9.2, we show how the cube is rotated for the marital adjustment data, while the points remain in place.

9.1.5 Objectives of the Technique

During this century, factor analysis, and especially principal components analysis, have been used for a variety of objectives, including:

1. Reducing multiplicity to unity: untangling a complex pattern of intervariable associations, thus finding the essence.
2. Latent structure analysis: identification of latent characteristics which conceal a hidden structure in the data.
3. Developing empirical typologies of variables.
4. Dimension-reduction: reducing a space of n variables to a space of p dimensions, $p < n$.
5. Index-construction or scaling: examining whether the n variables can be reduced to one dimension and, if so, constructing a one-dimensional index or scale (special case of dimension-reduction with $p = 1$).
6. Orthogonalization of predictors: transformation of the matrix of independent variables in a multiple regression analysis with substantial multicollinearity.

These uses of factor analysis represent a general line of thought. More particularly, the objectives of PCA are:

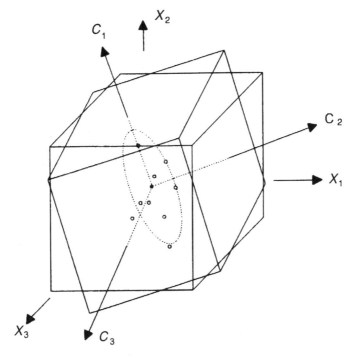

Figure 9.2   PCA as the rotation of a cube

1. Finding as many components as original variables in such a way that the components are mutually orthogonal and sequentially extract maximal variance from the variables. This comes down to examining the eigenstructure of the data matrix **X** or of the correlation matrix **R**. The eigenvalues are the variances of the projections of points on each of the components. The eigenvectors are the direction cosines, which indicate how far the original variable space has to be rotated (see geometric approach).
2. Reducing the number of dimensions by examining which variables have high loadings on each of the components and by looking for a 'simple structure'. This comes down to an examination of matrix **A** of component loadings, as well as the calculation of the measure of redundance of each component.
3. Rotating the resulting component space to a new space, which may offer a still simpler structure and a better interpretation in terms of content.

9.1.6   *Examining the Eigenstructure of* **X** *or* **R***: Introductory Remarks on Singular Value Decomposition*

In PCA one must look for a maximum, because the first component has to extract maximum variance from the set of variables and each next component a maximum from the remaining variance, under the restriction of orthogonality. This is a typical eigenstructure problem.

In order to find the eigenstructure of matrix **X** we can make use of singular value decomposition, abbreviated as SVD. This is an operation according to which any matrix **M** is expressed as the product of three matrices: $\mathbf{M} = \mathbf{P\Delta U'}$.

If we performed such an operation on $\mathbf{X}$, so that $\mathbf{X} = \mathbf{P\Delta U'}$, then $\mathbf{P}$ would be equal to the matrix of eigenvectors of $\mathbf{XX'}$ and $\mathbf{U}$ would be equal to the matrix of eigenvectors of $\mathbf{X'X}$. Matrix Δ contains the square roots of the eigenvalues of $\mathbf{XX'}$ as well as $\mathbf{X'X}$.

As the eigenvalues of $\mathbf{XX'}$ and $\mathbf{X'X}$ are the same, it is of course more sensible in practice to work on the (3×3) matrix $\mathbf{X'X}$, for it is much smaller than the (12×12) matrix $\mathbf{XX'}$, because there are less variables than individuals.

Other simplifications can be made. We know that $\mathbf{X'X}/(n-1)$ is equal to the correlation matrix $\mathbf{R}$ (where $n-1$ is the number of individuals diminished by 1). Hence, we might as well examine the eigenstructure of $\mathbf{R}$, for the eigenvalues of $\mathbf{R}$ are simply the eigenvalues of $\mathbf{X'X}$ divided by $n-1$. Moreover, $\mathbf{R}$ is a square, symmetric matrix. In such a case, the SVD operation is greatly simplified, because in the product $\mathbf{P\Delta U'}$ it holds for symmetric matrices that $\mathbf{P} = \mathbf{U}$.

It follows that:

$$\boxed{\mathbf{R} = \mathbf{UDU'}}$$

in which:

$\mathbf{U}$ = the matrix of eigenvectors of $\mathbf{R}$ and
$\mathbf{D}$ = the matrix of eigenvalues of $\mathbf{R}$
$\quad$ = the matrix of eigenvalues of $\mathbf{X'X}$ divided by $n-1$
$\quad$ = $\Delta^2/(n-1)$ = the matrix of squares of eigenvalues of $\mathbf{X}$ divided by $n-1$.

What becomes clear from this whole story is that finding the eigenstructure of $\mathbf{X}$ amounts to the same as finding the eigenstructure of $\mathbf{R}$. This is the reason why computer programs offer the opportunity to use the correlation matrix $\mathbf{R}$ instead of the original data matrix $\mathbf{X}$ as the input of a principal components analysis.

9.1.7 Eigenvalues and Eigenvectors of the Marital Adjustment Data

The eigenstructure of $\mathbf{R}$ is now calculated for the mini example. The correlation matrix $\mathbf{R}$ follows:

$$\mathbf{R} = \begin{bmatrix} 1 & 0.056 & -0.932 \\ 0.056 & 1 & -0.100 \\ -0.932 & -0.100 & 1 \end{bmatrix}$$

For finding the eigenstructure of $\mathbf{R}$, we apply a strategy which we encountered in the preceding chapter on discriminant analysis. There we examined the eigenstructure of matrix $\mathbf{W^{-1}B}$ and, in doing so, the system of equations $(\mathbf{W^{-1}B} - \lambda\mathbf{I})\mathbf{k} = \mathbf{0}$ had to be solved. The latter was done by forming the characteristic equation: $|\mathbf{W^{-1}B} - \lambda\mathbf{I}| = 0$. From this, the maximal eigenvalue λ was calculated and it was substituted in the system to obtain the eigenvector $\mathbf{k}$.

In factor analysis, the matrix of which the eigenstructure is examined is not $\mathbf{W^{-1}B}$, but $\mathbf{R}$. In two-group discriminant analysis, there was only one eigenvalue and one eigenvector, because only one discriminant function t was calculated. Now there are several eigenvalues and eigenvectors (three in our example, because we are looking for three components). Whence there are also several systems of equations. Such a system of equations has the form $(\mathbf{R} - \lambda\mathbf{I})\,\mathbf{u} = \mathbf{0}$. The characteristic equation is $|\mathbf{R} - \lambda\mathbf{I}| = 0$:

$$\left|\begin{bmatrix} 1 & 0.056 & -0.932 \\ 0.056 & 1 & -0.100 \\ -0.932 & -0.100 & 1 \end{bmatrix} - \lambda \begin{bmatrix} 1 & 0 & 0 \\ 0 & 1 & 0 \\ 0 & 0 & 1 \end{bmatrix}\right| = 0$$

$$\begin{vmatrix} 1-\lambda & 0.056 & -0.932 \\ 0.056 & 1-\lambda & -0.100 \\ -0.932 & -0.100 & 1-\lambda \end{vmatrix} = 0$$

$$(1-\lambda)\begin{bmatrix} 1-\lambda & -0.100 \\ -0.100 & 1-\lambda \end{bmatrix} - 0.056\begin{bmatrix} 0.056 & -0.932 \\ -0.100 & 1-\lambda \end{bmatrix} - 0.932\begin{bmatrix} 0.056 & -0.932 \\ 1-\lambda & -0.100 \end{bmatrix} = 0$$

$$(1-\lambda)[(1-\lambda)^2 - 0.100^2] - 0.056[0.056(1-\lambda) - (0.100)(0.932)]$$
$$- 0.932[(0.056)(-0.100) + 0.932(1-\lambda)] = 0$$

$$(1-\lambda)^3 - (0.100)^2(1-\lambda) - (0.056)^2(1-\lambda) + 2(0.056)(0.100)(0.932)$$
$$- (0.932)^2(1-\lambda) = 0$$

$$(1-\lambda)^3 - 0.882(1-\lambda) + 0.010 = 0$$

The solution of this equation yields $1 - \lambda = -0.945$, $1 - \lambda = 0.012$ and $1 - \lambda = 0.933$, whence $\lambda = 1.945$, $\lambda = 0.988$ and $\lambda = 0.067$. These three lambdas are the eigenvalues of $\mathbf{R}$.

The eigenvectors are found by substituting each of these three lambdas in the matrix equation $(\mathbf{R} - \lambda\mathbf{I})\,\mathbf{u} = \mathbf{0}$. We will now do this for the first eigenvalue $\lambda = 1.945$ or $1 - \lambda = -0.945$:

$$\begin{bmatrix} -0.945 & 0.056 & -0.932 \\ 0.056 & -0.945 & -0.100 \\ -0.932 & -0.100 & -0.945 \end{bmatrix} \begin{bmatrix} u_1 \\ u_2 \\ u_3 \end{bmatrix} = \begin{bmatrix} 0 \\ 0 \\ 0 \end{bmatrix}$$

$$-0.945u_1 + 0.056u_2 - 0.932u_3 = 0$$
$$0.056u_1 - 0.945u_2 - 0.100u_3 = 0$$
$$-0.932u_1 - 0.100u_2 - 0.945u_3 = 0$$

The solution of this system is not unique. The equations are not linearly independent. Therefore, u_1, u_2 and u_3 cannot be determined exactly. It is only possible to indicate what proportion they bear to one another, i.e., $\mathbf{u}' = (-0.886 \quad -0.147 \quad 0.889)$. After normalization, i.e., division by the square root of the sum of squares of u_1, u_2 and u_3, we obtain:

$$\mathbf{u}' = (-0.701 \quad -0.116 \quad 0.704)$$

For the second eigenvalue $\lambda = 0.988$ or $1 - \lambda = 0.012$, we form the matrix equation in an analogous fashion and, after solving the system and normalizing, we obtain the corresponding eigenvector:

$$\mathbf{u}' = (-0.106 \quad 0.993 \quad 0.058)$$

For the third eigenvalue $\lambda = 0.067$ or $1 - \lambda = 0.933$, the eigenvector is:

$$\mathbf{u}' = (0.705 \quad 0.034 \quad 0.708)$$

We bring these three eigenvectors **u** together in one matrix, thus obtaining the promised matrix **U**:

$$U = \begin{bmatrix} -0.701 & -0.106 & 0.705 \\ -0.116 & 0.993 & 0.034 \\ 0.704 & 0.058 & 0.708 \end{bmatrix}$$

Matrix **D** of eigenvalues is written as a diagonal matrix:

$$D = \begin{bmatrix} 1.945 & 0 & 0 \\ 0 & 0.988 & 0 \\ 0 & 0 & 0.067 \end{bmatrix}$$

The reader can now verify that $R = UDU'$:

$$\begin{bmatrix} 1 & 0.056 & -0.932 \\ 0.056 & 1 & -0.100 \\ -0.932 & -0.100 & 1 \end{bmatrix} =$$
$$\begin{bmatrix} -0.701 & -0.106 & 0.705 \\ -0.116 & 0.993 & 0.034 \\ 0.704 & 0.058 & 0.708 \end{bmatrix} \begin{bmatrix} 1.945 & 0 & 0 \\ 0 & 0.988 & 0 \\ 0 & 0 & 0.067 \end{bmatrix} \begin{bmatrix} -0.701 & -0.116 & 0.704 \\ -0.106 & 0.993 & 0.058 \\ 0.705 & 0.034 & 0.708 \end{bmatrix}$$

One can also verify that $UU' = I$, which means that **U** is an orthogonal matrix, i.e., a matrix of which the inverse is equal to the transpose: $U^{-1} = U'$. This matrix **U** rotates the original three X axes to the three component axes, as is shown in Figure 9.2.

9.1.8 *Matrix C of Component Scores*

To obtain the (12×3) matrix **C**, the data matrix **X** (in standardized scores) is multiplied by the transformation matrix **U**: $C = XU$.

$$\begin{bmatrix} 1.436 & 1.713 & -1.713 \\ 0.000 & -0.000 & -0.000 \\ -0.479 & -0.428 & -0.000 \\ 1.436 & 0.856 & -1.285 \\ 0.957 & -1.713 & -0.428 \\ -0.479 & -0.000 & 0.856 \\ 0.000 & -0.000 & -0.000 \\ -1.436 & 0.428 & 1.285 \\ 0.479 & -0.000 & -0.856 \\ -0.957 & -1.285 & 0.428 \\ -1.436 & 1.285 & 1.713 \\ 0.479 & -0.856 & -0.000 \end{bmatrix} \begin{bmatrix} -0.701 & -0.106 & 0.705 \\ -0.116 & 0.993 & 0.034 \\ 0.704 & 0.058 & 0.708 \end{bmatrix} =$$

$$
= \begin{bmatrix}
-2.411 & 1.449 & -0.142 \\
0.000 & 0.000 & 0.000 \\
0.385 & -0.374 & -0.352 \\
-2.011 & 0.623 & 0.132 \\
-0.773 & -1.827 & 0.314 \\
0.938 & 0.100 & 0.268 \\
0.000 & 0.000 & 0.000 \\
1.862 & 0.652 & -0.089 \\
-0.938 & -0.100 & -0.268 \\
1.121 & -1.150 & -0.415 \\
2.064 & 1.528 & 0.243 \\
-0.236 & -0.901 & 0.308
\end{bmatrix} = \mathbf{C}
$$

It is interesting to take a closer look at this matrix $\mathbf{C}$ of component scores. One can verify that the means of C_1, C_2 and C_3 are equal to 0. Indeed, the transformation matrix $\mathbf{U}$ rotates the X_1–X_2–X_3 cube around the origin (see Figure 9.2), so that the axes of the C_1–C_2–C_3 cube still have their mean in the origin.

The intercomponent associations are equal to 0. Indeed, matrix $\mathbf{U}$ rotates in such a way that the components are mutually perpendicular (requirement of orthogonality).

The variances of C_1, C_2 and C_3 are equal to the three eigenvalues within rounding-errors: $\lambda_1 = 1.945$, $\lambda_2 = 0.988$ and $\lambda_3 = 0.067$. Hence, the eigenvalues are the dispersions of the projections of points onto each of the three components. These dispersions have an order: the first component has the highest variance, the second a smaller one, and the third the smallest.

The sum of the three eigenvalues (component variances) is equal to $1.945 + 0.988 + 0.067 = 3$. This is also equal to the sum of variances of the three original variables (which are standardized and thus have a variance of 1, by definition): $1 + 1 + 1 = 3$. This means that the components extract 'all' variance from the variables.

The component scores of matrix $\mathbf{C}$ can also be standardized. As their means are already equal to 0, we only have to divide by each of the standard deviations of C_1, C_2 and C_3, i.e., by the square roots of the eigenvalues. In matrix algebra this comes down to multiplying $\mathbf{C}$ by the square root of the inverse of the diagonal matrix $\mathbf{D}$. Consequently, matrix $\mathbf{C}$ of standardized component scores is equal to:

$$
\boxed{\mathbf{C} = \mathbf{X}\mathbf{U}\mathbf{D}^{-1/2}}
$$

In this formula, $\mathbf{X}$ is the (12×3) matrix of original scores in standardized form. $\mathbf{U}$ is the (3×3) matrix of eigenvectors, which rotates the three original X axes towards the three new C axes (from old to new cube). $\mathbf{D}^{-1/2}$ is the (3×3) diagonal matrix with the three eigenvalues on the main diagonal and zeros everywhere else; this matrix makes all variances of point-projections onto the C axes (in the new cube) equal to 1. It was suggested above to first calculate $\mathbf{X}\mathbf{U}$ and to multiply by $\mathbf{D}^{-1/2}$ afterwards. However, in the computer output that follows, the product $\mathbf{U}\mathbf{D}^{-1/2}$ is calculated first. This matrix is called a 'factor score coefficient matrix' and $\mathbf{X}$ is multiplied by this matrix to obtain $\mathbf{C}$. Hence: in the computer output we see that not $\mathbf{C} = (\mathbf{X}\mathbf{U})\mathbf{D}^{-1/2}$, but rather

$\mathbf{C} = \mathbf{X}(\mathbf{UD}^{-1/2})$ is calculated. The 'factor score coefficient matrix' $\mathbf{UD}^{-1/2}$ is given below:

$$\mathbf{UD}^{-1/2} = \begin{bmatrix} -0.701 & -0.106 & 0.705 \\ -0.116 & 0.993 & 0.034 \\ 0.704 & 0.058 & 0.708 \end{bmatrix} \begin{bmatrix} 1.945 & 0 & 0 \\ 0 & 0.988 & 0 \\ 0 & 0 & 0.067 \end{bmatrix}^{-1/2}$$

$$= \begin{bmatrix} -0.503 & -0.107 & 2.718 \\ -0.083 & 0.999 & 0.131 \\ 0.505 & 0.058 & 2.730 \end{bmatrix}$$

We can now derive the (12×3) matrix of standardized component scores, which is also given in the computer output:

$$\mathbf{C} = \mathbf{X}(\mathbf{UD}^{-1/2}) = \begin{bmatrix} -1.729 & 1.458 & -0.548 \\ 0.000 & 0.000 & 0.000 \\ 0.276 & -0.376 & -1.357 \\ -1.442 & 0.627 & 0.509 \\ -0.554 & -1.838 & 1.213 \\ 0.673 & 0.101 & 1.036 \\ 0.000 & 0.000 & 0.000 \\ 1.335 & 0.656 & -0.343 \\ -0.673 & -0.101 & -1.036 \\ 0.804 & -1.157 & -1.601 \\ 1.480 & 1.537 & 0.937 \\ -0.169 & -0.906 & 1.191 \end{bmatrix}$$

The matrix of component scores is used in research practice for, among other things, the orthogonalization of predictors in a multiple regression analysis. Suppose, for example, that the three indicators of marital adjustment (X_1: give and take, X_2: agreement on finances, X_3: both prefer stay at home) are included in a multiple regression analysis with the dependent variable Y: well-being. Then the correlation $r_{13} = -0.932$ between the independent variables X_1 and X_3 is much too high (multi-collinearity) and, therefore, one can decide to replace matrix $\mathbf{X}$ by matrix $\mathbf{C}$ of components, because the latter are uncorrelated. In our example, two of the three components will suffice, for the third eigenvalue is very small. These two components will then have to be given an appropriate substantial interpretation, like 'companion-ship' and 'agreement'. After that, the new multiple regression analysis can be performed, with Y as the dependent variable and C_1 and C_2 as the independent variables.

9.1.9   Matrix **A** of Component Loadings

The component loadings are the coefficients a_{ij} of matrix $\mathbf{A}$ in the model $\mathbf{X} = \mathbf{CA}'$ (Notice that $\mathbf{A}$ is transposed, because we make a practice of placing the components in the heading and the variables in front of the matrix). Hence, these component loadings are in fact regression coefficients in a model with a variable as the dependent variable and components as the independent variables. Such a matrix of regression coefficients is called a **factor pattern**. However, in PCA, in which the variables are standardized and the components are orthogonal, these beta weights are equal to the correlation coefficients. (Compare with path analysis: path coefficients are equal to correlation coefficients if multicollinearity is absent.)

The matrix of correlations between variables and components is called a factor structure. In PCA, factor pattern and **factor structure** are equivalent. The distinction is only relevant in a context of oblique rotation, i.e., if the factors (components) are no longer orthogonal. The factor structure is now calculated.

To calculate the correlation coefficient between any x and y, the sum of products of standardized scores z_x and z_y is divided by $n - 1$. Applied to correlations between variables (matrix **X**) and components (matrix **C**) the factor structure is as follows:

$$A = \frac{1}{n-1}X'C$$

In this formula, **X** is the original data matrix in standardized form. **C** is the matrix of standardized component scores, which was calculated in the foregoing section and is equal to $XUD^{-1/2}$. Matrix **U** rotates the old cube towards the new one and $D^{-1/2}$ sets the variances of the components scores to 1.

Hence, $A = (1/n - 1)X'(XUD^{-1/2})$. And as $(1/n - 1)X'X = R$, this becomes:

$$A = RUD^{-1/2}$$
$$= UDU'UD^{-1/2}, \text{ for } R = UDU'$$
$$= UDID^{-1/2}, \text{ for U is orthogonal } (U'U = I)$$
$$= UDD^{-1/2}$$

Consequently: $\boxed{A = UD^{1/2}}$

$$A = \begin{bmatrix} -0.701 & -0.106 & 0.705 \\ -0.116 & 0.993 & 0.034 \\ 0.704 & 0.058 & 0.708 \end{bmatrix} \begin{bmatrix} 1.945 & 0 & 0 \\ 0 & 0.988 & 0 \\ 0 & 0 & 0.067 \end{bmatrix}^{1/2}$$

$$A = \begin{bmatrix} -0.977 & -0.105 & 0.183 \\ -0.162 & 0.987 & 0.009 \\ 0.981 & 0.058 & 0.183 \end{bmatrix}$$

The three columns of this matrix stand for C_1, C_2 and C_3 and the three rows represent X_1, X_2 and X_3. We see that X_1 and X_3 have high loadings on the first component with opposite signs (-0.977 and 0.981, respectively). X_2 has a high loading on the second component (0.987). The third component appears to be insignificant.

This result corresponds with the notion we had formed of the original data. Questions X_1 (give and take) and X_3 (prefer stay at home) are both related to 'companionship', on the understanding that X_3 is formulated negatively as the measure of marital 'mal'adjustment. (If we were to read the high scores of X_3 as low, and the low scores as high, then the negative correlation between X_1 and X_3 would become positive.)

Question X_2 (agreement on finances) is one from the group of agreement variables. To agree on all sorts of questions does not mean that a relationship is companionable, and vice versa. Therefore, variable X_2 represents a separate dimension of 'agreement'. The separateness of this dimension also follows from the fact that component C_2 (with a high loading for X_2) is perpendicular to the first component C_1 (with high loadings for X_1 and X_3).

9.1.10   The Measure of Redundancy of a Component

In our example, a third component, C_3, is redundant. Geometrically, this means that we did not really need a cube for a proper representation of the 12 points in a new space, but that a new surface could have sufficed. John van de Geer (1971) gives an expressive image of this idea when he compares it with an umbrella of which the ribs are curved, but with which we would be properly sheltered from the rain if we pulled the ribs into a flat plane.

The measure of redundancy of C_3 can also be calculated. For, as we know, correlation matrix $\mathbf{R}$ can be exactly reproduced as $\mathbf{UDU}'$, making use of eigenvalues ($\mathbf{D}$) and eigenvectors ($\mathbf{U}$). This reproduction can also be performed step by step, because $\mathbf{UDU}'$ can be partitioned as $\mathbf{u}_1\lambda_1\mathbf{u}_1' + \mathbf{u}_2\lambda_2\mathbf{u}_2' + \mathbf{u}_3\lambda_3\mathbf{u}_3'$, where λ_1, λ_2 and λ_3 denote the three eigenvalues and $\mathbf{u}_1$, $\mathbf{u}_2$ and $\mathbf{u}_3$ the three eigenvectors. When using only two components, C_1 and C_2, we see that $\mathbf{R}$ is then reproduced reasonably well:

$$\hat{\mathbf{R}} = \mathbf{u}_1\lambda_1\mathbf{u}_1' + \mathbf{u}_2\lambda_2\mathbf{u}_2'$$

$$\mathbf{u}_1\lambda_1\mathbf{u}_1' = \begin{bmatrix} -0.701 \\ -0.116 \\ 0.704 \end{bmatrix} (1.945) \; (-0.701 \quad -0.116 \quad 0.704)$$

$$= \begin{bmatrix} 0.956 & 0.158 & -0.960 \\ 0.158 & 0.026 & -0.159 \\ -0.960 & -0.159 & 0.964 \end{bmatrix}$$

$$\mathbf{u}_2\lambda_2\mathbf{u}_2' = \begin{bmatrix} -0.106 \\ 0.993 \\ 0.058 \end{bmatrix} (0.988) \; (-0.106 \quad 0.993 \quad 0.058)$$

$$= \begin{bmatrix} 0.011 & -0.104 & -0.006 \\ -0.104 & 0.974 & 0.057 \\ -0.006 & 0.057 & 0.003 \end{bmatrix}$$

$$\hat{\mathbf{R}} = \mathbf{u}_1\lambda_1\mathbf{u}_1' + \mathbf{u}_2\lambda_2\mathbf{u}_2' = \begin{bmatrix} 0.967 & 0.054 & -0.966 \\ 0.054 & 1.000 & -0.102 \\ -0.966 & -0.102 & 0.967 \end{bmatrix}$$

9.1.11   Matrix $\mathbf{A}$ of Component Loadings and the Explained Variance

The conclusion that two components suffice, can be even better explained if we read the proportions of explained variance in matrix $\mathbf{A}$ of component loadings (Table 9.2).

Table 9.2   Matrix A

Variables	Components		
	C_1	C_2	C_3
X_1	−0.977	−0.105	0.183
X_2	−0.162	0.987	0.009
X_3	0.981	0.058	0.183
λ_i	1.945	0.988	0.067
% explained variance	64.8	32.9	2.2
cumulative %	64.8	97.8	100.0

We know that this matrix contains the correlations between components and variables. We also know that the square of a correlation coefficient can be interpreted as a proportion of explained variance. The loading of X_1 on C_1 is −0.977. The square $(−0.977)^2 = 0.955$ means that 96% of the variance of variable X_1 (give and take) is explained by the first component C_1 (companionship). Component C_2 only adds $(−0.105)^2$, i.e., 1%, and component C_3 another $(0.183)^2$, i.e., 3%. The sum is 100%, because 100% of the dispersion of X_1 can be explained in all, and the three components together do this exhaustively. Looking at rows, we can give a similar explanation for X_2 and X_3.

The sum of squared loadings on a *row of the matrix* is called **communality**. The communality of a variable with 'all' components is equal to 1 in PCA. In our example, the communality of variable X_2 with the first two components, C_1 and C_2, is already maximal: $(−0.162)^2 + (0.987)^2 = 1$. The concept of communality will be especially important in techniques of factor analysis, in which, in contrast with PCA, there are less factors than variables.

We can also look at the *columns of matrix* A. The sum of squared loadings of a column, C_1 for example, is the sum of the variance proportions of each of the three variables that are explained by component C_1. This sum is equal to the eigenvalue of the relating component: $(−0.977)^2 + (−0.162)^2 + (0.981)^2 = 1.945$.

A similar explanation can be given for C_1 and C_2.

The eigenvalues appear to have an interesting interpretation. Geometrically, they indicate to what extent the projections of the 12 points onto a component are dispersed, i.e., how well a component is capable of tracing the common variance from the original variables.

In PCA the sum of eigenvalues is equal to the sum of variances of (standardized!) variables: $1.945 + 0.988 + 0.067 = 1 + 1 + 1 = 3$. (Hence, this sum is also equal to the number of variables and also to the sum of elements on the principal diagonal of **R**: see PFA for this.)

Making use of this property, each eigenvalue can be expressed as a proportion of this sum. For the first eigenvalue, this proportion is $\lambda_1 / \sum \lambda_i = 1.945/3 = 0.648$, which means that the first component has extracted 64.8% from the total variance of the three variables together. For the second component, this is 32.9%. C_1 and C_2 together explain $64.8 + 32.9 =$ (rounded off) 97.8% of the variance of original variables. The third component, which adds only 2.2%, is redundant.

9.1.12 How Many Components?

It is clear in this mini example how many components have to be retained. The three-dimensional space (three variables, old cube) was reduced to a two-dimensional space (two components, flat plane). Keep John van de Geer's flattened umbrella in mind. Otherwise, this conclusion could have been derived from the correlation matrix. The high correlation between X_1 and X_3 (-0.932), together with the low correlations with X_2 (0.056 and -0.100), have already pointed to two separate clusters of variables, which represent the dimensions of companionship and agreement. In an analysis of all 20 variables (sometimes hundreds of them in research practice!), the determination of the number of components can be disappointing. Therefore, in addition to the reproduction of the correlation matrix and the analysis of the matrix of component loadings, a great number of criteria have been developed by several authors.

The simplest **criterion** comes from Kaiser (1959). It says: retain only the components of which the eigenvalue is greater than 1. This criterion is the default option in most computer programs. If we had chosen it in our example, the result would have been a one-component solution, for the second eigenvalue 0.988 is smaller than 1. It goes without saying that this criterion is not appropriate here, because the second component really had to be included. We derived this from matrix **A** of component loadings (high loading of X_2 on C_2), as well as from the reproduction of **R** (unsatisfactory reproduction if only $\mathbf{u}_1\lambda_1\mathbf{u}_1'$ is used). However, it should be pointed out that Kaiser's criterion ($\lambda > 1$) can also result in the opposite: more components may be retained than appears necessary according to other criteria.

Another simple criterion is given by plotting the eigenvalues. This is called the **scree test**, developed by Cattell (1966). Suppose we have 14 components, of which the eigenvalues are 2.7, 2.6, 2.5, 2.4, 2.2, 1.7, 0.9, 0.4, etc., descending gradually to 0.1. Then a plot of these eigenvalues would show a kink (elbow), as can be seen in Figure 9.3.

The elbow in the figure indicates that sufficient, i.e., eight, components have been retained. As this criterion is rather subjective, other authors have tried to give it an inferential basis.

By way of illustration, we present an example of the inferential approach introduced by Bartlett (1950). The author asks whether it makes any sense at all to perform PCA as a technique of dimension reduction. According to Bartlett, the quantity $-[n - 1 - (1/6)(2p + 5)] \ln |\mathbf{R}|$ is distributed as chi-square with $0.5(p^2 - p)$ degrees of freedom, where n = the number of units, p = the number of variables and $\ln |\mathbf{R}|$ = the natural logarithm of the determinant of the correlation matrix. This determinant $|\mathbf{R}|$ can also be calculated as the product of all eigenvalues.

The null hypothesis of this χ^2 test is that the correlation matrix of the population of units is the identity matrix, i.e., that the variables are uncorrelated. If this null hypothesis is not rejected, then there is no sense in performing a factor analysis, because the original space cannot be reduced. In our example: $\chi^2 = -[12 - 1 - (1/6)(6 + 5)] \ln[(1.945)(0.988)(0.067)] = 18.79$ with $0.5(9 - 3) = 3$ degrees of freedom.

The null hypothesis is rejected, even for a type I error of $\alpha = 0.001$, which means that it does make sense to perform a reduction of the three-dimensional space.

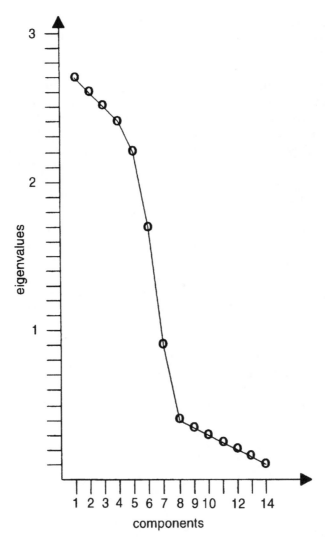

Figure 9.3   Cattell's scree test

9.1.13   *Component Rotation*

After having found a PCA solution, we can rotate the component space to a new
space, which might result in an even simpler structure and a better interpretation in
terms of content. The concept of 'simple structure' ought to be explained first.

Let us look again at matrix **A** of component loadings. In our example, variables X_1
and X_3 had high loadings on component C_1 and variable X_2 had a high loading on
component C_2. Such a pattern, in which only a few high loadings appear for each
component (per column), in which the high loadings on the components refer to
different variables and in which only one high loading appears for each variable (per
row), is called a 'simple structure', after Thurstone (1947).

There is, however, a tendency in PCA according to which the first component is a general factor with high loadings for all variables and the subsequent components are bipolar factors, on which some variables have positive and others negative loadings. This tendency is of course contained in the logic of the technique itself, for, in constructing our new cube according to the principal axis method, the first axis had to fit with the entire set of variables as best it could. Therefore, it is understandable that some variables (geometrically conceived of as vectors) lie to one side and others to the other side of the first component. As the second component is perpendicular to the first, these variables will have positive and negative loadings, respectively.

Consequently, PCA does not always offer the most elucidating solution. For, if the variables can be subdivided in a number of separate, strongly grouped clusters, then the first component will stand midway between these clusters, rather than fitting in with one of the clusters. In such a case, **rotation** of the components is a means of finding a solution in which C_1 fits in with a first cluster, C_2 with a second cluster, etc.

In our example, a rotation will not bring about much improvement, because the PCA solution has already displayed a 'simple structure' *à la Thurstone*. For that reason we draw a second figure (Figure 9.4) of a hypothetical example in which four variables form a first cluster and four other variables a second cluster, and in which the two components C_1 and C_2 are rotated to C_1' and C_2' (coordinates are component loadings).

In Figure 9.4 we read from the marital adjustment example that X_1 and X_3 fit in well with C_1 and that X_2 fits in with C_2. A rotation is unnecessary. On the other hand, in the hypothetical example it is only after rotation that a first cluster of variables fits in with C_1' and a second cluster with C_2', whereas this connection was absent for components C_1 and C_2.

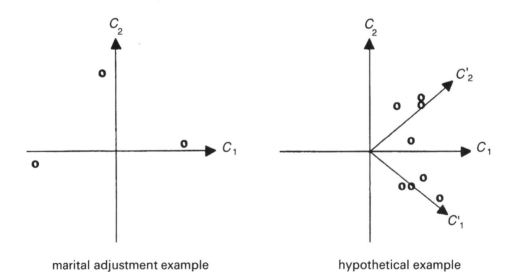

marital adjustment example   hypothetical example

Figure 9.4   Rotation of a two-components solution in PCA

9.1.14   Orthogonal Rotation

In the hypothetical example of Figure 9.4, the two components were rotated in such a way that they remained perpendicular. This is called orthogonal rotation.

Examples of orthogonal rotation are VARIMAX, QUARTIMAX and EQUIMAX. As a series of iterations are involved in these rotation procedures, they cannot be calculated here. The objective of each of these rotations consists of reducing matrix **A** of factor loadings to a 'simple structure'. VARIMAX simplifies the columns of **A**. (The variance of squared loadings of each column is maximized.) QUARTI-MAX aims at a simplification of rows. EQUIMAX is a solution of compromise, in which the calculation involves rows as well as columns.

Notice that the proportions of explained variance (relative eigenvalues) are differently distributed over components after rotation. Before rotation the first component has the highest eigenvalue, by definition. After rotation it can be another component which explains most of the variance. The sum of eigenvalues will, however, be the same, for the same amount of variance is explained.

9.1.15   Oblique Rotation

After having performed an orthogonal rotation, one may still examine whether an oblique rotation results in a better solution. For, it might be possible that the clusters of variables are not situated in perpendicular directions. In oblique rotation, this perpendicularity of factors is no longer a requirement (oblique = askew, slanting, cunning).

If the researcher opts for an oblique rotation, (s)he has to reckon with a number of problems and greater complexity. Firstly, as the factors are no longer perpendicular, they are mutually correlated and, consequently, there is an extra matrix of **factor correlations**.

Secondly, in the matrix of factor loadings **A**, which contains associations between variables and factors, regression coefficients were equal to correlation coefficients in the orthogonal case. The **factor pattern** and the **factor structure** were equal. This is no longer the case for oblique factors. In Figure 9.5, one variable, X_1, is situated in an oblique two-factor solution. The loadings of X_1 in the 'factor pattern' are a_{11} and a_{12}. These are the regression coefficients of a regression analysis of X_1 as a function of the (mutually correlated) factors. The loadings of X_1 in the 'factor structure' are r_{11} and r_{12}. These are the correlations between variable X_1 and each of the factors (components). The latter partly contain the factor correlation and, consequently, cannot be interpreted unambiguously.

There are more difficulties in oblique rotation. A third is that the **communality** of a variable can no longer be calculated as the sum of squared factor loadings of a row of matrix **A**. Fourthly and analogously, the proportion of **explained variance** of a factor can no longer be calculated as the sum of squared loadings of a column of **A**.

We see that there is a reverse to every medal. The advantage of oblique rotation, i.e., a clearer interpretation when clusters of variables belonging together are not perpendicular, appears to be accompanied by a great number of drawbacks.

Therefore, it is recommended that an orthogonal rotation be performed prior to any oblique rotation.

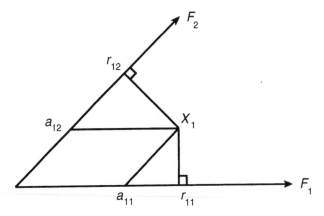

Figure 9.5   Oblique rotation

9.1.16   SPSS for Windows Output of PCA

For the mini example of marital adjustment we now present the SPSS for Windows output. The reader can easily verify whether our results calculated by hand coincide with the output.

Choosing or creating a data file

How to open an SPSS session and how to choose a data file or, if a data file does not yet exist, how to enter data, to choose name, type and label of variables and to save the data file with extension *.sav*, is shown in Chapter 4.

Running the principal components analysis

Click on Statistics. Click on Data Reduction. Click on Factor. This opens the Factor Analysis dialog box. Click on the variables X_1, X_2 and X_3 (either separately or together by means of the click and drag technique) and click on the ▶ push button to select these variables.

Click on Descriptives. Click on Everything. Click on Continue to return to the Factor Analysis dialog box.

Click on Extraction. This opens a Factor Analysis Extraction dialog box. You will see a radio button at Eigenvalues over 1. This means that the program's default choice is Kaiser's criterion (eigenvalue at least 1), whence it comes to a one-component solution. Click on Number of Factors and type 3 to obtain a solution with all three components. Click on Scree Plot. Please notice that the method (PCA) and an unrotated factor solution are already selected. This will suit you. Click on Continue.

Click on Scores. This opens a Factor Analysis Factor Scores dialog box. Click on Save as Variables. The Method Regression is already selected. Click on Display Factor Score Coefficient Matrix. Click on Continue.

You have now returned to the Factor Analysis dialog box. Click on OK. SPSS now runs the statistical procedure and an output window appears with the results of principal components analysis. You may also want to include a data matrix with the component scores in the output. Click on Statistics. Click on Summarize. Click on List Cases. Select the variables Fac1_1, Fac2_1 and Fac3_1 from the source list and click on OK.

Do not forget to save the output: click on File, click on Save as, type *marriage.lst* and click on OK.

As you already know, the computer output of principal components analysis can also be obtained by opening a syntax window and typing SPSS commands. Click on File, click on New, click on SPSS Syntax, type the statements, put the cursor anywhere in the first command line and click on ▶ of the icon bar (or click on Run if you still work with the SPSS for Windows 5.0 version).

You will use the following statements:

```
1 LIST.
2 FACTOR /VARIABLES X1 X2 X3
3   /PRINT ALL
4   /PLOT EIGEN
5   /CRITERIA FACTORS (3)
6   /EXTRACTION PC
7   /ROTATION NOROTATE
8   /SAVE REGRESSION (ALL C).
9 LIST /VARIABLES C1 C2 C3.
```

In statement 1, the data matrix is requested with 'list'.

Statements 2 to 8 request the principal components analysis. Statement 2 indicates which variables are presented. If a subset of this list of variables is analysed, then an extra 'analysis' statement is necessary. All variables are included in the analysis when such an 'analysis' statement is absent, as was the case here. In statement 3, all statistics are requested with 'print = all': numbers, means, standard deviations, communalities, eigenvalues, proportions of explained variance, correlations and their significance, the determinant and the inverse of the correlation matrix, the anti-image covariance and correlation matrices, the reproduced correlations, the factorscore coefficients and others. The anti-image correlation matrix, which was not discussed in our text, contains (the negative of) the partial correlations of every pair of variables controlling for all other variables. If these partial correlations are high, then a dimension reduction is not possible. Thus, the anti-image correlation matrix indicates whether it makes sense to perform a factor analysis. The Kaiser–Meyer–Olkin measure and Bartlett's test serve the same purpose. Bartlett's test, discussed in our text, examines whether the sample correlation matrix comes from a population correlation matrix, which is the identity matrix. The Kaiser–Meyer–Olkin measure looks at the same matter from a different angle.

In statement 4, Cattell's scree test is requested with 'plot = eigen'. The components are situated on the X-axis and the eigenvalues on the Y-axis in descending order. A break between the steep slope of the large factors and the gradual trailing off of the rest of the factors (elbow pattern) indicates the possibility of dimension reduction.

Criteria statement 5 is included to obtain a solution with all three components. For, the program's default choice is Kaiser's criterion (eigenvalue at least 1), whence it comes to a one-component solution.

In statement 6, the expression 'extraction = pc' requests a principal components analysis, abbreviated as pc.

Statement 7 explicitly requests no rotation, because the default option of the computer program would perform a varimax rotation and because the requested component scores would then be the scores *after* rotation.

Statements 8 and 9 belong together. In statement 8, we requested that the component scores be saved in the active file, in the form of all three components with 'rootname' = C (i.e., C_1, C_2 and C_3). In statement 9, a data matrix with these three components is requested with 'list'. Notice that this data matrix contains standardized component scores, which are obtained by multiplying the original data matrix X by the (3×3) matrix $UD^{-1/2}$ of factor score coefficients. The latter matrix is printed as 'Factor Score Coefficient Matrix'.

The output is as follows:

```
X1 X2 X3

    8  9  1
    5  5  5
    4  4  5
    8  7  2
    7  1  4
    4  5  7
    5  5  5
    2  6  8
    6  5  3
    3  2  6
    2  8  9
    6  3  5

Number of cases read =      12    Number of cases listed =      12


Analysis Number  1  Listwise deletion of cases with missing values

                    Mean      Std Dev    Label

X1              5.00000      2.08893    give and take
X2              5.00000      2.33550    agreement on finances
X3              5.00000      2.33550    prefer both stay at home

Number of Cases  =      12


Correlation Matrix:

                  X1          X2          X3

X1            1.00000
X2             .05590    1.00000
X3            -.93169    -.10000    1.00000


Determinant of Correlation Matrix =      .1292361
```

Inverse of Correlation Matrix:

	X1	X2	X3
X1	7.66040		
X2	.28837	1.02096	
X3	7.16599	.37077	7.71359

Kaiser-Meyer-Olkin Measure of Sampling Adequacy = .49551

Bartlett Test of Sphericity = 18.75605, Significance = .00031

There are   2 (33.3%) off-diagonal elements of AIC Matrix > 0.09

Anti-Image Covariance Matrix:

	X1	X2	X3
X1	.13054		
X2	.03687	.97947	
X3	.12127	.04708	.12964

Anti-Image Correlation Matrix:

	X1	X2	X3
X1	.49757		
X2	.10311	.31846	
X3	.93223	.13212	.49761

Measures of sampling adequacy (MSA) are printed on the diagonal.

Correlation 1-tailed Significance Matrix:
' . ' is printed for diagonal elements.

	X1	X2	X3
X1	.		
X2	.43150	.	
X3	.00001	.37858	.

Extraction 1 for Analysis 1, Principal-Components Analysis (PC)

Initial Statistics:

Variable	Communality	*	Factor	Eigenvalue	Pct of Var	Cum Pct
		*				
X1	1.00000	*	1	1.94457	64.8	64.8
X2	1.00000	*	2	.98818	32.9	97.8
X3	1.00000	*	3	.06726	2.2	100.0

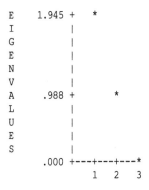

```
E    1.945 +   *
I          |
G          |
E          |
N          |
V          |
A     .988 +        *
L          |
U          |
E          |
S          |
     .000 +---+---+---*
           1   2   3
```

PC Extracted   3 factors.

Factor Matrix:

	FACTOR 1	FACTOR 2	FACTOR 3
X1	.97749	-.10518	.18291
X2	.16174	.98680	.00873
X3	-.98129	.05787	.18364

Final Statistics:

Variable	Communality	*	Factor	Eigenvalue	Pct of Var	Cum Pct
		*				
X1	1.00000	*	1	1.94457	64.8	64.8
X2	1.00000	*	2	.98818	32.9	97.8
X3	1.00000	*	3	.06726	2.2	100.0

Reproduced Correlation Matrix:

	X1	X2	X3
X1	.99999*	.00000	.00000
X2	.05590	.99999*	.00000
X3	-.93169	-.10000	.99999*

The lower left triangle contains the reproduced correlation matrix;   The
diagonal, communalities; and the upper right triangle, residuals between
the observed correlations and the reproduced correlations.

There are   0 (.0%) residuals (above diagonal) that are > 0.05

Skipping Rotation 1, Extraction 1, Analysis 1

```
Factor Score Coefficient Matrix:

                FACTOR  1      FACTOR  2      FACTOR  3

X1                .50268       -.10644         2.71963
X2                .08317        .99860          .12974
X3               -.50463        .05857         2.73048


Covariance Matrix for Estimated Regression Factor Scores:

                FACTOR  1      FACTOR  2      FACTOR  3

FACTOR   1       1.00000
FACTOR   2        .00000       1.00000
FACTOR   3        .00000        .00000         1.00000




  3 PC   EXACT   FACTOR SCORES WILL BE SAVED WITH ROOTNAME: C


FOLLOWING FACTOR SCORES WILL BE ADDED TO THE ACTIVE FILE:

   NAME        LABEL

   C1          REGR FACTOR SCORE    1 FOR ANALYSIS    1
   C2          REGR FACTOR SCORE    2 FOR ANALYSIS    1
   C3          REGR FACTOR SCORE    3 FOR ANALYSIS    1


         C1           C2            C3

     1.72864      1.45714        -.54851
      .00000       .00000         .00000
     -.27625      -.37662       -1.35748
     1.44135       .62706         .50951
      .55489     -1.83729        1.21252
     -.67278       .10111        1.03632
      .00000       .00000         .00000
    -1.33451       .65566        -.34286
      .67278      -.10111       -1.03632
     -.80418     -1.15574       -1.60138
    -1.47935      1.53589         .93737
      .16941      -.90610        1.19082


Number of cases read =     12    Number of cases listed =     12
```

9.2   Principal Factor Analysis

9.2.1   *The Research Problem and the Diagram*

Let us consider the same example we used in principal components analysis (PCA). Three statements about marital adjustment were presented to 12 persons (X_1: give and take, X_2: agreement on finances, X_3: both prefer to stay at home). In PCA we looked for as many components as original variables (i.e., three components C_1, C_2 and C_3), in such a way that the components were perpendicular and sequentially extracted maximal variance from the variables. Each component was supposed to represent subgroups of strongly interrelated variables with high loadings on the relating component. However, in considering as many components as variables (even after rotation) a situation emerged in which a small number of components represented the gross of variables. The result was that nothing more than small subgroups of variables or even 'singletons' were left for the great number of remaining components. Such a component, on which only one or a few variables have high loadings, does not indicate the 'common' parts, but, rather, the 'unique' parts of the research materials. And, as it is the very purpose of factor analyses to reveal the common parts, we looked for a solution with less components than variables in the preceding section under the heading 'How Many Components?' The latter, however, was an *ad hoc* strategy. This is not the case in principal factor analysis, because dimension reduction is built-in in this technique from the beginning.

In principal factor analysis (PFA), we no longer speak of 'components', but of 'factors'. In PFA, too, we want the factors to be orthogonal and to sequentially extract a maximal variance from the variables. But we now want the 'factors' to really be 'factors' which represent the 'common' parts of the original variables. For that reason PFA is sometimes called 'common factor analysis'. The new element in PFA is that not only common factors but also 'unique factors' (E_i), which trace the unique part of each variable, are included in the model. The common factors (F_i) are generally smaller in number than the original variables (except of course when the data structure does not display communality).

In our mini example a two-factor solution is obvious. Therefore, we draw two common factors, F_1 and F_2, in the diagram. To emphasize the inclusion of unique parts (in addition to common parts) we also draw unique factors, one for each of the three variables (i.e., E_1, E_2 and E_3). The choice of letter E stems from the idea that these unique factors are in fact error terms (E for error). For, in principal factor analysis, the original variables X_i are 'explained' by the common factors (F_i) and the 'unexplained' (error) part of these X variables is considered to be the unique part (E_i). The diagram is represented in Figure 9.6.

9.2.2   *The Data Matrix*

The (fictitious) mini data set is the same as in PCA.

9.2.3   *The Model of Principal Factor Analysis*

The PCA model was $\mathbf{X} = \mathbf{CA'}$. Components ($C_i$) now become factors ($F_i$). So, using F instead of C, the PCA model is $\mathbf{X} = \mathbf{FA'}$. This is a system of three equations in

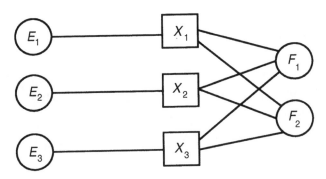

Figure 9.6   Principal factor analysis (PFA) diagram

which each variable is expressed as a linear combination of the (three) factors:

$$X_1 = a_{11}F_1 + a_{12}F_2 + a_{13}F_3$$
$$X_2 = a_{21}F_1 + a_{22}F_2 + a_{23}F_3$$
$$X_3 = a_{31}F_1 + a_{32}F_2 + a_{33}F_3$$

To determine the factor loadings a_{ij}, an SVD operation was first performed on $\mathbf{R}$, in such a way that $\mathbf{R} = \mathbf{UDU'}$, and matrix $\mathbf{A}$ of factor loadings was calculated as $\mathbf{A} = \mathbf{UD}^{1/2}$. In principal factor analysis, the same calculation method will be used, but the model will be different.

The **PFA model** not only contains common factors F_i, but unique factors E_i as well:

$$\boxed{\mathbf{X} = \mathbf{FA'} + \mathbf{E}}$$

We let $\mathbf{F}$ denote the matrix of scores of the common factors and $\mathbf{E}$ the matrix of scores of the unique factors. We have already mentioned that the model is sometimes called the 'common factor model' to indicate that the common factors are really common, i.e., not contaminated with the unique character of each separate variable. A unique factor E_i can be still further split into the separate character of the relating variable (specific factor) and the random noise of that variable (error term).

In a first step, we will include all factors in the model, i.e., as many common factors as variables (three here), but in practice we try to find an economical model, in which a small number of factors together explain a substantial amount of variance of the variables.

With all common factors, the model is represented by the following algebraic system:

$$X_1 = a_{11}F_1 + a_{12}F_2 + a_{13}F_3 + E_1$$
$$X_2 = a_{21}F_1 + a_{22}F_2 + a_{23}F_3 + E_2$$
$$X_3 = a_{31}F_1 + a_{32}F_2 + a_{33}F_3 + E_3$$

The model is constrained by a few assumptions. Firstly, the unique factors E_i are mutually uncorrelated. In matrix terminology this means that $\mathbf{E'E}/(n-1)$ is diagonal.

Secondly, unique and common factors are uncorrelated, in other words matrix $\mathbf{E}'\mathbf{F}$ is equal to $\boldsymbol{\phi}$, the null matrix.

9.2.4   The Reduced Correlation Matrix

Starting from the PFA model and the two assumptions, we can rewrite the correlation matrix $\mathbf{R}$ as follows:

$$\mathbf{R} = \frac{\mathbf{X}'\mathbf{X}}{n-1} = \frac{(\mathbf{FA}'+\mathbf{E})'(\mathbf{FA}'+\mathbf{E})}{n-1}, \quad \text{for} \quad \mathbf{X} = \mathbf{FA}'+\mathbf{E}$$

$$\mathbf{R} = \frac{(\mathbf{AF}'+\mathbf{E}'))(\mathbf{FA}'+\mathbf{E})}{n-1}$$

$$\mathbf{R} = \frac{\mathbf{AF}'\mathbf{FA}'+\mathbf{AF}'\mathbf{E}+\mathbf{E}'\mathbf{FA}'+\mathbf{E}'\mathbf{E}}{n-1}$$

$$\mathbf{R} = \frac{\mathbf{AF}'\mathbf{FA}'+\phi+\phi+\mathbf{E}'\mathbf{E}}{n-1}, \quad \text{for } F_i \text{ and } E_i \text{ are uncorrelated}$$

$$\mathbf{R} = \mathbf{A}\frac{\mathbf{F}'\mathbf{F}}{n-1}\mathbf{A}' + \frac{\mathbf{E}'\mathbf{E}}{n-1}$$

where $\mathbf{F}'\mathbf{F}/(n-1) = \mathbf{I}$ if the factors are uncorrelated. Hence:

$$\boxed{\mathbf{R} = \mathbf{AA}' + \frac{\mathbf{E}'\mathbf{E}}{n-1}}$$

where $\mathbf{E}'\mathbf{E}/(n-1)$ is the diagonal matrix of variances $\sigma^2_{E_i}$ of the unique factors. Thus, if these variances are subtracted from the diagonal elements (1) of the correlation matrix $\mathbf{R}$, the result is $\mathbf{AA}'$:

$$\mathbf{AA}' = \mathbf{R} - \mathbf{E}'\mathbf{E}/(n-1)$$

$$\mathbf{AA}' = \begin{bmatrix} 1 & r_{12} & r_{13} \\ r_{12} & 1 & r_{23} \\ r_{13} & r_{23} & 1 \end{bmatrix} - \begin{bmatrix} \sigma^2_{E_1} & 0 & 0 \\ 0 & \sigma^2_{E_2} & 0 \\ 0 & 0 & \sigma^2_{E_3} \end{bmatrix}$$

$$\mathbf{AA}' = \begin{bmatrix} 1-\sigma^2_{E_1} & r_{12} & r_{13} \\ r_{12} & 1-\sigma^2_{E_2} & r_{23} \\ r_{13} & r_{23} & 1-\sigma^2_{E_3} \end{bmatrix}$$

It follows that $\mathbf{AA}'$ is a matrix of correlations between the original variables, in which the elements (1) of the principal diagonal are diminished by the variances of unique factors. As the variables are standardized, which means that their variance is equal to 1, these new diagonal elements express the total minus the unique, i.e., the common variance of each variable, which is the communality h^2. Therefore, matrix $\mathbf{AA}'$ will be indicated as $\bar{\mathbf{R}}$, which is the matrix of correlations between the original variables, in which the diagonal elements (1) are replaced by communalities:

$$\bar{\mathbf{R}} = \mathbf{AA}' = \begin{bmatrix} h_1^2 & r_{12} & r_{13} \\ r_{12} & h_2^2 & r_{23} \\ r_{13} & r_{23} & h_3^2 \end{bmatrix}$$

Principal factor analysis is simply the performance of the SVD operation on this **reduced correlation matrix $\bar{\mathbf{R}}$**. In other words, not the total variance (1) of the original variables, but, rather, their common variance is analysed in PFA. Just as in PCA, the correlation matrix will be decomposed as the product of three matrices: $\bar{\mathbf{R}} = \mathbf{UDU}'$, where $\mathbf{U}$ contains the eigenvectors and $\mathbf{D}$ the eigenvalues.

However, there are two important **differences with PCA**.

Firstly, in practice **not all factors** are included in the model. Theoretically this may be done, but it is understandable that little is learnt from an analysis in which the number of common factors is equal to the number of original variables. It would mean that the multiplicity of variables had not been brought to unity. It has already become obvious in PCA that a few components together can explain a great amount of variance of the variables. But there the basic model essentially contained as many components as variables. In PFA, on the other hand, the purpose is to take a basic model with less factors than variables as the starting point, which means that principal factor analysis is a technique of dimension reduction.

Secondly, in the PFA model in which the calculations refer to the reduced correlation matrix, the **communalities** (diagonal elements h^2) have to be **estimated**. In a first step it is actually a guess, rather than an estimation, for one is in the dark about the common part of the variables, which is the very thing one is looking for. An often used first guess as to the communality of a variable is the squared multiple correlation coefficient of this variable with all others. If these multiple determination coefficients R_i^2 are substituted in the diagonal of $\bar{\mathbf{R}}$, then the SVD operation $\bar{\mathbf{R}} = \mathbf{UDU}'$ can be performed in a first step and the factor matrix $\mathbf{A}$ can be calculated. In this way $\bar{\mathbf{R}} = \mathbf{AA}'$ can be reproduced. But, as the communalities were merely first guesses, this reproduction in a first step will often be unsatisfactory. For this reason an iterative process is set up. The communalities resulting from the first step (i.e., the diagonal elements $h^2 = \sum a_{ij}^2$ of the reproduced correlation matrix $\bar{\mathbf{R}} = \mathbf{AA}'$) are used again to perform the same operation. This iterative process ends as soon as the communalities converge sufficiently.

9.2.5 *Eigenvalues and Eigenvectors of the Marital Adjustment Data*

We will now calculate the principal factor analysis of our mini example. The correlation matrix was:

$$\mathbf{R} = \begin{bmatrix} 1 & 0.056 & -0.932 \\ 0.056 & 1 & -0.100 \\ -0.932 & -0.100 & 1 \end{bmatrix}$$

The reduced correlation matrix is obtained by replacing the diagonal elements (1) by estimated communalities. For instance, the element at the top left is replaced by the multiple determination coefficient, which is calculated in a regression analysis of X_1 as a function of X_2 and X_3 together. The same is done for the other diagonal elements.

$$\bar{\mathbf{R}} = \begin{bmatrix} h_1^2 & r_{12} & r_{13} \\ r_{12} & h_2^2 & r_{23} \\ r_{13} & r_{23} & h_3^2 \end{bmatrix} = \begin{bmatrix} R_{1.23}^2 & 0.056 & -0.932 \\ 0.056 & R_{2.13}^2 & -0.100 \\ -0.932 & -0.100 & R_{3.12}^2 \end{bmatrix}$$

$$= \begin{bmatrix} 0.869 & 0.056 & -0.932 \\ 0.056 & 0.021 & -0.100 \\ -0.932 & -0.100 & 0.870 \end{bmatrix}$$

The eigenstructure of this reduced correlation matrix is examined in the familiar way: form the characteristic equation $|\bar{\mathbf{R}} - \lambda\mathbf{I}| = 0$, solve for the lambdas λ_i, substitute them in the matrix equation $(\bar{\mathbf{R}} - \lambda\mathbf{I})\mathbf{u} = \mathbf{0}$ and find the eigenvectors $\mathbf{u}_i$. This SVD operation results in the following decomposition, which can be considered a revision exercise for the reader:

$$\bar{\mathbf{R}} = \mathbf{UDU}' = \begin{bmatrix} -0.705 & -0.280 & 0.652 \\ -0.062 & 0.939 & 0.337 \\ 0.707 & -0.197 & 0.679 \end{bmatrix} \begin{bmatrix} 1.808 & 0 & 0 \\ 0 & 0.025 & 0 \\ 0 & 0 & -0.073 \end{bmatrix}$$

$$\begin{bmatrix} -0.705 & -0.062 & 0.707 \\ -0.280 & 0.939 & -0.197 \\ 0.652 & 0.337 & 0.679 \end{bmatrix}$$

9.2.6 The Factor Matrix **A** for all Factors: The Problem of Negative Eigenvalues

Making use of matrix **U** of eigenvectors and diagonal matrix **D** of eigenvalues, we would now have to calculate factor matrix $\mathbf{A} = \mathbf{UD}^{1/2}$. To that end, i.e., to determine $\mathbf{D}^{1/2}$, the square roots of the eigenvalues would have to be calculated. But, the last eigenvalue is negative, whence the third factor will be imaginary. It is important that we touch on this subject.

If a matrix results not only in positive eigenvalues but in negative eigenvalues as well, then we say that it is not positive semi-definite. It can easily be shown that the correlation matrix **R** in PCA, with elements (1) on the principal diagonal, is always positive semi-definite, which means that all eigenvalues are non-negative. If communalities are substituted on the main diagonal, then the reduced correlation matrix will nearly always produce negative eigenvalues. And as an eigenvalue can be interpreted as a proportion of explained variance, which naturally has to be positive, it follows that a negative eigenvalue is absolutely senseless.

In the original correlation matrix the sum of eigenvalues is equal to $1 + 1 + 1 = 3$, i.e., the total variance of the three variables together. In the reduced correlation matrix it is $0.869 + 0.021 + 0.870 = 1.760$, which is equal to the sum of communalities, i.e., the total 'common' variance of the three variables together. The sum of eigenvalues, $\sum \lambda_i = 1.808 + 0.025 + (-0.073)$, yields the same result, for each eigenvalue expresses the proportion of variance that is extracted by the relating factor from the total common variance of variables. Therefore, their sum must be that total common variance. We thus find ourselves in the unlikely situation in which the first two factors together explain $(1.808 + 0.025)/1.760 = 104\%$ of the total common variance, whereas 100% is explained by the three factors together. On the other hand, the negative eigenvalues will generally be extremely small (close to zero). Moreover, a few factors will often suffice to explain the common part of the variables. In our mini example the second eigenvalue is already small ($\lambda_2 = 0.025$), so that a one-factor solution suffices.

9.2.7 Substantial Difference Between PFA and PCA

It is interesting to compare the one factor solution of PFA with the two-components solution of PCA. The first component, which referred to variables X_1 (give and take) and X_3 (both prefer stay at home), represented the dimension of companionship. The second component, on which variable X_2 (agreement on finances) had a high loading, was interpreted as a separate dimension, called 'agreement'.

It appears that the PFA model no longer provides for a second factor. The separate character of variable X_2 is almost entirely attributed to the unique factor E_2 and is not seen as belonging to the common parts. This was impossible in PCA, because the model did not provide for unique factors. We see that the difference between the logic of the PCA model and the PFA model can be translated in terms of content.

9.2.8 Factor Matrix A for the First Factor and Further Iterations

It was impossible to calculate factor matrix A for a three-factor solution because we were pestered by the negative eigenvalue. We will now restrict ourselves to the first factor with an eigenvalue of $\lambda_1 = 1.808$. The reproduction of $\bar{R}$ is then as follows:

$$\bar{R} = u_1 \lambda_1 u_1' = \begin{bmatrix} -0.705 \\ -0.062 \\ 0.707 \end{bmatrix} \quad (1.808) \quad (-0.705 \quad -0.062 \quad 0.707)$$

And the first column of factor matrix A is:

$$a_{i1} = u_1 \lambda_1^{1/2} = \begin{bmatrix} -0.705 \\ -0.062 \\ 0.707 \end{bmatrix} \quad (1.808)^{1/2} = \begin{bmatrix} -0.948 \\ -0.083 \\ 0.950 \end{bmatrix}$$

As was expected, variables X_1 and X_3 have high loadings on this first (and only) factor: -0.948 and 0.950, respectively. The squares of these loadings (0.899 and 0.902) are the communalities of X_1 and X_3 with factor F_1. The sum of the three squared loadings is equal to the eigenvalue of the first factor: $0.899 + 0.007 + 0.902 = 1.808$.

The three calculated communalities are very different from the first guesses: 0.899, 0.007 and 0.902 as against 0.869, 0.021 and 0.870. Therefore, these three new communalities are substituted again in the principal diagonal of the correlation matrix and the whole SVD operation is performed once more. This iterative process is repeated until the communalities converge. After 99 iterations they are 0.935, 0.007 and 0.948.

9.2.9 The Communalities

It goes without saying that the **first estimation** of the communalities will determine the number of iterations: the better the first estimations, the sooner convergence will occur. Thus, we should not be surprised that a great number of propositions have been formulated by several authors. In the foregoing, the squared multiple correlation of a variable with all others was used as a first estimation of its communality. A few other propositions follow below:

(a) Take for each variable the highest out of the correlations with other variables (Thurstone).
(b) Take for each variable the mean of correlations with other variables.
(c) First perform a PCA, retain only the components of which the corresponding eigenvalue is greater than 1 and take for each variable the proportion explained by these components together (a proposition of Kaiser's, called the 'Little Jiffy').

According to some authors the problem of estimating the communalities can be avoided by fixing the number of factors of the PFA model *a priori*. Kaiser's 'Little Jiffy' is in fact an illustration of this strategy.

We would now like to insert a warning and a remark with respect to communalities. Firstly, if the PFA model contains only one common factor (and a unique factor for each variable), then the remarkable situation can occur whereby a communality becomes greater than 1. This would mean that the relating variable and the factor have more than 100% in common, which is of course senseless. This odd situation is called the '**Heywood case**'. It is an alarm signal, which makes us conclude that the rank of the reduced correlation matrix is greater than 1. If more than one common factor is included in the analysis, then no communality will be greater than 1.

Secondly, the reduction of a great number of variables to a small number of common factors is subject to a number of **conditions**. Let us touch briefly on this subject. In PCA all diagonal elements of the correlation matrix were equal to 1. There were as many components as variables. On the other hand, in PFA, the elements on the principal diagonal are replaced by communalities, which means that only the common variance of the variables (separated from unique factors) is analysed. Moreover, the model generally contains less factors than variables. The latter, the dimension reduction, is only possible if certain conditions are fulfilled with regard to the intervariable correlations.

Without pursuing this subject too far, as it merely concerns a theoretical remark, we give an illustration of such conditions. Let us consider a model with four variables and one common factor. And let us conceive of factor analysis as if it were a path analysis, in which factors were latent causal variables. Then the arrow diagram would be as in Figure 9.7.

Form the structural equations and the r equations and it will become clear that $r_{12}r_{34} = r_{14}r_{23}$, as well as $r_{13}r_{24} = r_{14}r_{23}$, must hold. These are the conditions without which the four variables cannot be reduced to one dimension, i.e., without which the rank of **R** cannot be reduced to 1.

9.2.10 Rotations and Factor Scores

The following is not different from what was already explained in PCA. In addition to factor loadings we can also calculate factor scores as $\mathbf{F} = \mathbf{XUD}^{-1/2}$.

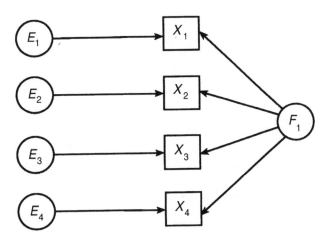

Figure 9.7   Arrow diagram of four variables and one common factor

A rotation can be performed, either orthogonal or oblique, to obtain a factor matrix with 'simple structure'. The concept of 'simple structure' (stemming from Thurstone) has been explained in the foregoing sections. Roughly speaking, it means that each factor is represented by a separate cluster of high loading variables. In this respect we argued that an oblique rotation should always be preceded by an orthogonal rotation. This was naturally not a condemnation of oblique rotation as such. For, in the social sciences it is often the case that factors (like companionship and agreement in our example) cannot be perfectly separated. The warnings against oblique rotation were rather technical in nature. Careful watch must be kept to make certain that the factor correlations are not immoderately high. Besides, in oblique rotation it is recommendable to focus upon the loadings of the factor pattern (regression coefficients), rather than the coefficients of the factor structure (correlations between variables and factors), because the latter are contaminated with factor correlations.

9.2.11   *SPSS for Windows Output of PFA*

Principal factor analysis is called 'principal axis factoring' (PAF) in the SPSS computer program, because of the principal axis method that is used.

The cumbersome output with univariate statistics, the correlation matrix and its inverse, the anti-image correlation matrix, the significances and the scree plot of eigenvalues, as well as the factor scores, is not requested now. A rotation cannot be requested as PAF and the built-in Kaiser criterion (default) extract only one factor, and a one-factor solution cannot be rotated.

Choosing or creating a data file
How to open an SPSS session and how to choose or create and save a data file is shown in Chapter 4.

Running the statistical procedure

Click on Statistics. Click on Data Reduction. Click on Factor. This opens the Factor Analysis dialog box. Click on the variables X_1, X_2 and X_3 (either separately or together by means of the click and drag technique) and click on the ▶ push button to select these variables.

Click on Descriptives. You will see that Initial Solution is already selected. Click on Reproduced Correlation Matrix. Click on Continue to return to the Factor Analysis dialog box.

Click on Extraction. This opens a Factor Analysis Extraction dialog box. You will see that the default selection under Method is principal components analysis. To change this, click on the arrow next to Method and click on Principal Axis Factoring. Click on Maximum Iterations for Convergence. If you want only one iteration for comparison with the results calculated by hand, use the ← backspace key to eliminate the numeral 25 and type 1. Click on Continue.

You have now returned to the Factor Analysis dialog box. Click on OK. SPSS now runs the statistical procedure and an output window appears with the results of principal factor analysis.

Do not forget to save the output: click on File, click on Save as, type the file name with extension *.lst* and click on OK.

As you already know, the computer output can also be obtained by opening a syntax window and typing SPSS commands. Click on File, click on New, click on SPSS Syntax, type the statements, put the cursor anywhere in the first command line and click on ▶ of the icon bar (or click on Run if you still work with the SPSS for Windows 5.0 version).

You will use the following statements:

```
1 FACTOR /VARIABLES X1 X2 X3
2      /PRINT INITIAL EXTRACTION REPR
3      /CRITERIA ITERATE (1)
4      /EXTRACTION PAF.
```

In the last statement, 4, a principal factor analysis (principal axis factoring) is requested with 'extraction'.

Statement 3 is odious in research practice. The default setting for the computer program is 25 iterations. Another number of *n* iterations can be requested with 'criteria iterate (*n*)'. In practice one generally makes use of this possibility if more than 25 iterations (*n* > 25) are needed for the communalities to converge. Here, we have set *n* at 1 for the simple didactical reason that we have only performed one iteration in our calculations by hand, so that the computer results can be compared with ours.

In statement 2, a number of statistics are requested with 'print'. With 'initial' we obtain the initial communalities, eigenvalues and percentages of explained variance. This output is the same as in PCA, except for the communalities. For, the communalities are not equal to 1 now, but in PFA they are initially estimated as the multiple determination coefficients .869, .021 and .870. After one iteration they are .899, .007 and .903, which can be requested with 'extraction' and which can be verified in the output under the heading 'final statistics'. With 'repr' the reproduced correlation matrix is requested.

The output is as follows.

```
Analysis Number   1  Listwise deletion of cases with missing values
Extraction  1  for Analysis  1, Principal Axis Factoring (PAF)
```

Initial Statistics:

Variable	Communality	*	Factor	Eigenvalue	Pct of Var	Cum Pct
		*				
X1	.86946	*	1	1.94457	64.8	64.8
X2	.02053	*	2	.98818	32.9	97.8
X3	.87036	*	3	.06726	2.2	100.0

```
   PAF Attempted to extract   1 factors.
```

```
More than   1 iterations required. Convergence =     .03270
```

Factor Matrix:
```
              FACTOR  1
```

```
X1               .94789
X2               .08279
X3              -.95030
```

Final Statistics:

Variable	Communality	*	Factor	Eigenvalue	Pct of Var	Cum Pct
		*				
X1	.89849	*	1	1.80840	60.3	60.3
X2	.00685	*				
X3	.90306	*				

Reproduced Correlation Matrix:

	X1	X2	X3
X1	.89849*	-.02257	-.03092
X2	.07848	.00685*	-.02133
X3	-.90077	-.07867	.90306*

The lower left triangle contains the reproduced correlation matrix; The diagonal, communalities; and the upper right triangle, residuals between the observed correlations and the reproduced correlations.

There are   0 (.0%) residuals (above diagonal) that are > 0.05

9.3   Variations of Factor Analysis Methods

During this century, a great number of factor analysis methods have been developed. Following the example of Harman *et al.* we also make a distinction between a *model* and a *method*. The PCA *model* $X = CA'$ (with the inclusion of all components) and the PFA model $X = FA' + E$ (with the inclusion of unique factors and generally far fewer common factors than variables) are two examples of linear models. They can be represented by a system of structural equations or by an arrow diagram, as in path analysis. On the other hand, a *method* is a calculation technique, which gives us the opportunity to find a factor solution, i.e., to calculate the loadings, factor scores, factor correlations, etc. In PCA and PFA the same method is used, notably the principal axis method, according to which the first factor extracts a maximum of variance from the variables, the second factor extracts a maximum from the remaining variance and is perpendicular to the first factor, and the third factor extracts a maximum from the remaining variance and is perpendicular to the foregoing two. In PCA this process goes on until all variance is used up. In PFA it goes on until all 'common' variance is used up, because PFA analyses only the non-unique part of the variance, as the diagonal of the correlation matrix does not contain the total variances (1), but the estimated common variances (h^2). Apart from this, there is no difference between the methods used in PCA and PFA. The correlation matrix, not reduced and reduced, respectively, is examined for its eigenstructure by means of an SVD operation. This examination of the eigenstructure really 'is' the principle axis method, for the eigenvalues are the proportions of variance mentioned above that are extracted by the factors from the variables. The eigenvectors simply indicate the directions of these factors.

In addition to the principal axis method (which should not be confused with the principal factor model, which is a model), many other methods have been developed for finding a factor solution. In this section we take a selection from the rich world of factor analysis methods. Some of these methods have been rendered out of date.

9.3.1   The Diagonal Method

The diagonal method (= square root method = triangular method) is one of the oldest in history). It stems from a time without computers and can easily be calculated by hand. No analysis of the eigenstructure of the correlation matrix is made. The decomposition is much simpler: the correlation matrix is decomposed as the product of a lower triangular matrix and its transpose, an upper triangular matrix (whence the name triangular method). What is meant here is in fact the formula $\mathbf{R} = \mathbf{AA}'$, which we have already encountered in PCA, with the difference that $\mathbf{A}$ is now a lower triangular matrix, i.e., a matrix with zeros above the principal diagonal.

How such a factor matrix $\mathbf{A}$ is calculated can be demonstrated quickly. In our marital adjustment example we had the following correlation matrix:

$$\mathbf{R} = \begin{bmatrix} 1 & 0.056 & -0.932 \\ 0.056 & 1 & -0.100 \\ -0.932 & -0.100 & 1 \end{bmatrix}$$

Take the first column of $\mathbf{R}$ as the first column of factor matrix $\mathbf{A}$:

$$\mathbf{a}_1 = \begin{bmatrix} 1 \\ 0.056 \\ -0.932 \end{bmatrix}$$

As the first column of $\mathbf{R}$ stands for the first variable and as the first column of $\mathbf{A}$ stands for the first factor, this means that the first variable is considered to be the first factor. The reproduction of **R** using this first factor would then be a_1a_1':

$$
a_1a_1' = \begin{bmatrix} 1 \\ 0.056 \\ -0.932 \end{bmatrix} (1 \quad 0.056 \quad -0.932) = \begin{bmatrix} 1 & 0.056 & -0.932 \\ 0.056 & 0.003 & -0.052 \\ -0.932 & -0.052 & 0.868 \end{bmatrix}
$$

The residual correlation matrix, which is calculated by subtracting the reproduced from the original correlation matrix, is as follows:

$$
R_1 = R - a_1a_1' = \begin{bmatrix} 0 & 0 & 0 \\ 0 & 0.997 & -0.048 \\ 0 & -0.048 & 0.132 \end{bmatrix}
$$

The first row and column of this first residual correlation matrix contain exclusively zeros. This means that the following factors will only relate to the last two variables.

In other words, the first variable is eliminated in a way that is comparable to partial correlation calculus. The second column of the residual correlation matrix R_1 contains all correlations with the second variable after the first variable (=first factor) is partialled out.

In the next step, the second column of factor matrix **A** is formed by taking the second column of the residual correlation matrix R_1 and by dividing all these elements by the square root of the diagonal element of that column:

$$
a_2 = \begin{bmatrix} 0/(0.997)^{1/2} \\ 0.997/(0.997)^{1/2} \\ -0.048/(0.997)^{1/2} \end{bmatrix} = \begin{bmatrix} 0 \\ 0.998 \\ -0.048 \end{bmatrix}
$$

Hence, the second reproduced correlation matrix becomes:

$$
a_2a_2' = \begin{bmatrix} 0 \\ 0.998 \\ -0.048 \end{bmatrix} (0 \quad 0.998 \quad -0.048) = \begin{bmatrix} 0 & 0 & 0 \\ 0 & 0.997 & -0.048 \\ 0 & -0.048 & 0.002 \end{bmatrix}
$$

And the second residual correlation matrix is:

$$
R_2 = R_1 - a_2a_2' = \begin{bmatrix} 0 & 0 & 0 \\ 0 & 0 & 0 \\ 0 & 0 & 0.130 \end{bmatrix}
$$

The first two rows and columns contain exclusively zeros. It can easily be shown that all remaining correlations of R_2 (only one here) are partial correlations, in which the first two variables are partialled out. This process is repeated until the residual correlations are sufficiently small. The number of important factors is then the number at which the process stops. In our mini example, the third and last step is as follows:

$$\mathbf{a}_3 = \begin{bmatrix} 0/(0.130)^{1/2} \\ 0/(0.130)^{1/2} \\ 0.130/(0.130)^{1/2} \end{bmatrix} = \begin{bmatrix} 0 \\ 0 \\ 0.360 \end{bmatrix}$$

$$\mathbf{a}_3\mathbf{a}_3' = \begin{bmatrix} 0 & 0 & 0 \\ 0 & 0 & 0 \\ 0 & 0 & 0.130 \end{bmatrix}$$

$$\mathbf{R}_3 = \begin{bmatrix} 0 & 0 & 0 \\ 0 & 0 & 0 \\ 0 & 0 & 0 \end{bmatrix}$$

Matrix **A** of factor loadings, the ultimate result of this three factor solution, is composed of the three vectors $\mathbf{a}_1$, $\mathbf{a}_2$ and $\mathbf{a}_3$:

$$\mathbf{A} = \begin{bmatrix} 1 & 0 & 0 \\ 0.056 & 0.998 & 0 \\ -0.932 & -0.048 & 0.360 \end{bmatrix}$$

We notice that $\mathbf{AA}'$ is indeed equal to **R**.

In summary, the diagonal method considers the first variable as the first factor. The second factor is the second variable, after the first has been partialled out. The third factor is the third variable, freed from contamination by the first two, and so on.

It can easily be shown that this procedure is the same as the path analysis with the following triangular system of structural equations without residual terms:

$$X_1 = F_1$$
$$X_2 = a_{21}F_1 + a_{22}F_2$$
$$X_3 = a_{31}F_1 + a_{32}F_2 + a_{33}F_3$$

As no residual terms occur in this diagonal method, it follows that the model is the same as in PCA. Indeed, if we were to first perform PCA followed by a rotation, with the restriction that factor matrix **A** had to be a lower triangular matrix, then we would obtain the same solution.

However, the diagonal method can also be applied to the model with residual terms, as in PFA, i.e., $\mathbf{X} = \mathbf{FA}' + \mathbf{E}$. In that case, it is not the original correlation matrix, but the reduced correlation matrix, with communalities on the main diagonal, which is taken as the starting point of the calculations. And, just as in PFA, the procedure is then burdened by the problem of the first communality estimations (guesses!). Apart from this, the arithmetic is exactly the same.

It goes without saying that the value of the diagonal method is only historical and didactical. One of the weaknesses of the method is that it depends on the order in which the variables are introduced. If the order in the correlation matrix **R** were not

X_1, X_2, X_3 but X_1, X_3, X_2, then factor matrix **A** would have contained different factor loadings:

$$R = \begin{bmatrix} 1 & -0.932 & 0.056 \\ -0.932 & 1 & -0.100 \\ 0.056 & -0.100 & 1 \end{bmatrix} \qquad A = \begin{bmatrix} 1 & 0 & 0 \\ -0.932 & 0.363 & 0 \\ 0.056 & -0.132 & 0.990 \end{bmatrix}$$

9.3.2 The Centroid Method

The same is true of the centroid method. Its value is predominantly historical in nature. It reached its peak in the 1930s and 1940s, but since the rise of the computer has been pushed aside by principal factor analysis (PFA). It is of didactical value because it can easily be calculated by hand.

A first step, just as in the diagonal method, starts from the provisional hypothesis that all intercorrelations can be explained by one factor. In the diagonal method this first factor is the first variable (depending on the order in which the variables are introduced). On the other hand, in the centroid method, all intercorrelations of **R** are involved in the calculation when determining the first factor. As it is not customary to take the line of the PCA model, with elements (1) on the principal diagonal, but, rather, the PFA model, with communalities, we will start from the reduced correlation matrix. (We could have done this in the diagonal method as well.)

Let us estimate the communality of each variable as the highest of correlations with other variables (with a positive sign).

$$\bar{R} = \begin{bmatrix} 0.932 & 0.056 & -0.932 \\ 0.056 & 0.100 & -0.100 \\ -0.932 & -0.100 & 0.932 \end{bmatrix}$$

Then the provisional hypothesis of the first step is: $\bar{R} = a_1 a_1'$.

Before explaining how the factor loadings a_1 are determined (in the diagonal method this is simply the first column of **R** or $\bar{R}$), we will first turn the negative correlations of $\bar{R}$ into positive coefficients. We do this by reversing the contents of variable X_3: not 'both prefer *not* to stay at home', but 'both prefer stay at home'. In doing so, the correlations -0.932 and -0.100 both lose their minus sign. The method can also be applied to negative correlations, but becomes more laborious in that case.

In matrix $\bar{R}$ with positive correlations, we find the sum of each row, i.e., the sum $\sum r_{ij}$ of correlations of each variable i with all others, itself included, and then find the sum of these sums, i.e., the sum T of all intercorrelations of $\bar{R}$:

$$\bar{R} = \begin{bmatrix} 0.932 & 0.056 & 0.932 \\ 0.056 & 0.100 & 0.100 \\ 0.932 & 0.100 & 0.932 \end{bmatrix} \qquad \begin{aligned} \sum_j r_{1j} &= 1.920 \\ \sum_j r_{2j} &= 0.256 \\ \sum_j r_{3j} &= 1.964 \\ \hline T &= 4.140 \end{aligned}$$

Now, the ratios $(\sum_j r_{ij})/T^{1/2}$ are considered to be the factor loadings, i.e., the elements of a_1. Many **justifications** can be given for this formula. We present two of them, one formal and one geometrical.

The **formal** derivation runs as follows. We know that $\bar{\mathbf{R}} = \mathbf{a}_1\mathbf{a}_1'$:

$$\bar{\mathbf{R}} = \begin{bmatrix} r_{11} & r_{12} & r_{13} \\ r_{21} & r_{22} & r_{23} \\ r_{31} & r_{32} & r_{33} \end{bmatrix} = \mathbf{a}_1\mathbf{a}_1' = \begin{bmatrix} a_{11} \\ a_{21} \\ a_{31} \end{bmatrix} (a_{11} \quad a_{21} \quad a_{31})$$

$$= \begin{bmatrix} a_{11}^2 & a_{11}a_{21} & a_{11}a_{31} \\ a_{21}a_{11} & a_{21}^2 & a_{21}a_{31} \\ a_{31}a_{11} & a_{31}a_{21} & a_{31}^2 \end{bmatrix}$$

It follows that the sum of all elements of $\bar{\mathbf{R}}$ is equal to the sum of all elements of $\mathbf{a}_1\mathbf{a}_1'$:

$$r_{11} + r_{22} + r_{33} + 2r_{12} + 2r_{13} + 2r_{23} = a_{11}^2 + a_{21}^2 + a_{31}^2 + 2a_{11}a_{21} + 2a_{11}a_{31} + 2a_{21}a_{31}$$

$$\sum_i \sum_j r_{ij} = (a_{11} + a_{21} + a_{31})^2$$

$$T = \left(\sum_i a_{i1} \right)^2$$

Thus, the sum T of all intercorrelations is equal to the squared sum of factor loadings, whence $\sum_i a_{i1} = T^{1/2}$. This is the denominator of the formula that must be derived.

For variable i the numerator is equal to $\sum_j r_{ij}$, i.e., the sum of correlations with other variables: $r_{i1} + r_{i2} + r_{i3}$. And as $\bar{\mathbf{R}} = \mathbf{a}_1\mathbf{a}_1'$, each correlation will be equal to the product of two loadings ($r_{ij} = a_{i1}a_{j1}$), so that:

$$r_{i1} + r_{i2} + r_{i3} = a_{i1}a_{11} + a_{i1}a_{21} + a_{i1}a_{31}$$

$$\sum_j r_{ij} = a_{i1}(a_{11} + a_{21} + a_{31}) = a_{i1} \sum_i a_{i1}$$

Hence $a_{i1} = \sum_j r_{ij}/\sum_i a_{i1}$. And as $\sum_i a_{i1} = T^{1/2}$ (see above), it follows that $a_{i1} = (\sum_j r_{ij})/T^{1/2}$. This is the formal justification of the calculation of loadings on the first factor.

The **geometrical** justification refers to the name 'centroid method'. We regard the variables as three vectors in the space of perpendicular factors. The maximal number of factors is of course equal to the number of variables (three here).

In a space of two factors, F_1 and F_2, the coordinates of the three variables would be as shown in Figure 9.8.

These coordinates are, by definition, the loadings of variables on factors. For this we refer to the discussion in PCA: loadings are regression coefficients of a regression with variables as dependent variables and factors as independent variables (factor pattern), which, in this case, are equal to coefficients of correlation between variables and factors (factor structure) as the factors are orthogonal. These loadings a_{ij} are the unknowns, which means that the factor axes (provisionally indicated as F_1' and F_2') are not yet fixed. In the diagonal, method F_1 was equated with variable X_1. In the figure this would mean that the F_1 axis would run from the origin to point X_1 ($=$ endpoint of

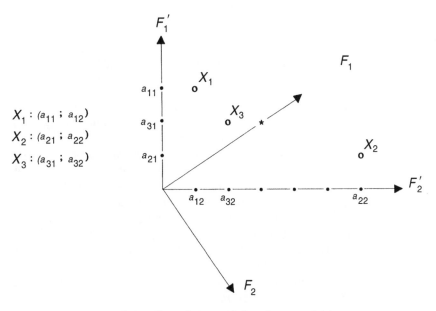

$X_1 : (a_{11} ; a_{12})$

$X_2 : (a_{21} ; a_{22})$

$X_3 : (a_{31} ; a_{32})$

Figure 9.8   Coordinates of the three variables

vector X_1). However, in the centroid method the F_1 axis is chosen in such a way that it runs through the centroid, whence the name. In the figure, the centroid, i.e., the point where the means come together, is indicated by an asterisk *:

$$* = \left(\tfrac{1}{3} \sum a_{i1}; \ \tfrac{1}{3} \sum a_{i2} \right)$$
$$= \left(\frac{a_{11} + a_{21} + a_{31}}{3}; \ \frac{a_{12} + a_{22} + a_{32}}{3} \right)$$

The coordinates of the centroid on other factors (only F_2 here) will be equal to zero. In our example, with axes F_1 and F_2 as the reference system, the quantity $\sum a_{i2} = a_{12} + a_{22} + a_{32}$ is indeed equal to zero. If we substitute this in the basic formula $\bar{\mathbf{R}} = \mathbf{a}_1 \mathbf{a}_1'$ we obtain the same result as above for the loadings on the first factor: $a_{i1} = (\sum_j r_{ij})/T^{1/2}$.

Moving on from the logic of the centroid method, formally and geometrically, we can now proceed to the calculations. The loadings on the first factor are obtained by dividing each sum of a row of the reduced correlation matrix by $T^{1/2}$:

$$\mathbf{a}_1 = \begin{bmatrix} 1.920/(4.140)^{1/2} \\ 0.256/(4.140)^{1/2} \\ 1.964/(4.140)^{1/2} \end{bmatrix} = \begin{bmatrix} 0.944 \\ 0.126 \\ 0.965 \end{bmatrix}$$

From this the first reproduction of $\bar{\mathbf{R}}$ is derived:

$$\mathbf{a}_1 \mathbf{a}_1' = \begin{bmatrix} 0.944 \\ 0.126 \\ 0.965 \end{bmatrix} (0.944 \quad 0.126 \quad 0.965) = \begin{bmatrix} 0.891 & 0.119 & 0.911 \\ 0.119 & 0.016 & 0.122 \\ 0.911 & 0.122 & 0.931 \end{bmatrix}$$

This yields the first residual correlation matrix:

$$\mathbf{R}_1 = \bar{\mathbf{R}} - \mathbf{a}_1\mathbf{a}_1' = \begin{bmatrix} 0.041 & -0.063 & 0.021 \\ -0.063 & -0.084 & -0.022 \\ 0.021 & -0.022 & 0.001 \end{bmatrix}$$

Notice that the sum of each row (or of each column) is equal to zero, because positive and negative correlations are equilibrated. Consequently, we can no longer apply the summation method. Therefore, we will reduce the number of negative correlations to a minimum, using a process called 'reflection'. Above, we made all correlations positive in a first step by reversing variable X_3. In the next steps of the centroid methods we apply the following technical trick. For each variable, determine the sum of positive correlations with other variables (S^+) and the (absolute value of the) sum of negative correlations with other variables (S^-) and reflect that variable for which $S^- - S^+$ has the largest value (ignoring entries in the principal diagonal); repeat this procedure successively until all the $S^- - S^+$ values are negative or until no further reduction of minus signs is possible.

This is very simple in our mini example. We can see at a first glance that reflection of variable X_2 will make all correlations positive. If we had applied the reflection technique, the values $S^- - S^+$ would have been $0.063 - 0.021 = 0.042$, $0.085 - 0 = 0.085$ and $0.022 - 0.021 = 0.001$ for the three variables respectively. The value of X_2 is indeed the highest.

The procedure goes on in a similar fashion:

$$\mathbf{R}_1 = \begin{bmatrix} 0.041 & 0.063 & 0.021 \\ 0.063 & 0.084 & 0.022 \\ 0.021 & 0.022 & 0.001 \end{bmatrix} \qquad \begin{aligned} \sum r_{1j} &= 0.125 \\ \sum r_{2j} &= 0.169 \\ \sum r_{3j} &= 0.044 \\ \hline & 0.338 \end{aligned}$$

$$\mathbf{a}_2 = \begin{bmatrix} 0.125/(0.338)^{1/2} \\ 0.169/(0.338)^{1/2} \\ 0.044/(0.338)^{1/2} \end{bmatrix} = \begin{bmatrix} 0.215 \\ 0.291 \\ 0.076 \end{bmatrix}$$

$$\mathbf{a}_2\mathbf{a}_2' = \begin{bmatrix} 0.215 \\ 0.291 \\ 0.076 \end{bmatrix} (0.215 \quad 0.291 \quad 0.076) = \begin{bmatrix} 0.046 & 0.063 & 0.016 \\ 0.063 & 0.085 & 0.022 \\ 0.016 & 0.022 & 0.006 \end{bmatrix}$$

$$\mathbf{R}_2 = \mathbf{R}_1 - \mathbf{a}_2\mathbf{a}_2' = \begin{bmatrix} -0.005 & 0.000 & 0.005 \\ 0.000 & -0.001 & 0.000 \\ 0.005 & 0.000 & -0.005 \end{bmatrix}$$

The residual correlations are very small, which means that two factors suffice. One should not be alarmed by the fact that negative values appear on the principal diagonal, which is of course theoretically unacceptable and impossible, as it concerns communalities, i.e., squares that are always positive. It simply means that the communalities were incorrectly estimated in the first step. Another procedure which is sometimes used consists of estimating the communalities at each step, high enough so that no negative values are left on the principal diagonal of the residual correlation matrix. All of this, however, remains a form of trial and error. The superiority of principal factor analysis, with its built-in iteration procedure until communalities converge, is obvious here.

Our two-factor approach according to the centroid method results in the following factor matrix, consisting of the two columns a_1 and a_2:

$$\mathbf{A} = \begin{bmatrix} 0.944 & 0.215 \\ 0.126 & 0.291 \\ 0.965 & 0.076 \end{bmatrix}$$

Considering the fact that our starting point was the PFA model, it holds here, too, that a one-factor solution would have sufficed. If we compare the loadings on the first factor with those of principal factor analysis, we see that Thurstone's manual centroid method is a good approximation of modern computer methods.

9.3.3 The Minimum Residuals Method (MINRES)

In both the diagonal method and the centroid method, the concept of 'residual correlation matrix' was used.

Starting from the basic formula $\mathbf{R} = \mathbf{A}\mathbf{A}'$, the factor loadings a_{i1} were determined in a first step and the products $a_{i1}a_{j1}$ (from $\mathbf{A}\mathbf{A}'$) were considered reproduced correlations. The difference of $\mathbf{R} - \mathbf{A}\mathbf{A}'$ produced a matrix $\mathbf{R}_1$ with elements $r_{ij} - a_{i1}a_{j1}$, which was called the first residual correlation matrix. If all the elements of this residual matrix were approximately zero, the process was stopped; if these elements were still substantial, this meant that the factors were still too small in number and, therefore, the first step was repeated to obtain a second residual correlation matrix $\mathbf{R}_2$, and so on.

It is clear that this procedure aims at making the residual correlations as small as possible. Hence, the name 'minimum residuals method' would not have been unbecoming for the foregoing two methods. But, although the same principle is followed in the MINRES method, it still differs from the foregoing methods because the diagonal elements of the correlation matrices (communalities) are not involved in the calculation of the residuals. In other words, a procedure is followed in which the principal diagonal elements of each correlation matrix are left out of consideration and the other elements are minimized.

The model we started with is the PFA model $\mathbf{X} = \mathbf{F}\mathbf{A}' + \mathbf{E}$. In the basic formula $\bar{\mathbf{R}} = \mathbf{A}\mathbf{A}'$, the diagonal elements are omitted in $\bar{\mathbf{R}}$ as well as in $\mathbf{A}\mathbf{A}'$:

$$\mathbf{R} - \mathbf{I} = \begin{bmatrix} 1 & r_{12} & r_{13} \\ r_{21} & 1 & r_{23} \\ r_{31} & r_{32} & 1 \end{bmatrix} - \begin{bmatrix} 1 & 0 & 0 \\ 0 & 1 & 0 \\ 0 & 0 & 1 \end{bmatrix} = \begin{bmatrix} 0 & r_{12} & r_{13} \\ r_{21} & 0 & r_{23} \\ r_{31} & r_{32} & 0 \end{bmatrix}$$

$$\mathbf{A}\mathbf{A}' - \mathrm{diag}(\mathbf{A}\mathbf{A}') = \begin{bmatrix} h_1^2 & \hat{r}_{12} & \hat{r}_{13} \\ \hat{r}_{21} & h_2^2 & \hat{r}_{23} \\ \hat{r}_{31} & \hat{r}_{32} & h_3^2 \end{bmatrix} - \begin{bmatrix} h_1^2 & 0 & 0 \\ 0 & h_2^2 & 0 \\ 0 & 0 & h_3^2 \end{bmatrix} = \begin{bmatrix} 0 & \hat{r}_{12} & \hat{r}_{13} \\ \hat{r}_{21} & 0 & \hat{r}_{23} \\ \hat{r}_{31} & \hat{r}_{32} & 0 \end{bmatrix}$$

Each reproduced correlation $\hat{r}_{ij}$ is equal to a sum of products of factor loadings:

$$\hat{r}_{ij} = a_{i1}a_{j1} + a_{i2}a_{j2} + \ldots + a_{im}a_{jm} = \sum_{p=1}^{m} a_{ip}a_{jp} \qquad \text{(for } m \text{ factors)}$$

The differences between the original correlations r_{ij} and the correlations reproduced via factor loadings $\hat{r}_{ij}$ ($\hat{}$ for estimation) are calculated and the sum of squares of these differences is made as small as possible, i.e., function $f = \sum(r_{ij} - \sum a_{ip}a_{jp})^2$ is minimized. As this function depends on the number of correlations [$n\,(n-1)/2$ when there are n variables], not f itself but, rather, $[2f/n(n-1)]^{1/2}$ is used. The factor loadings are those for which this function reaches a minimum. The diagonal matrix of communalities is derived from these loadings, in the familiar way.

The procedure will not be elaborated here, because many iterative steps are involved. A provisional matrix **A** is taken as the starting point and for any row in **A** increments are added to each factor loading in such a way that function f is minimized. The new loadings give rise to a new reproduced correlation matrix (without diagonal elements). Then function $f = \sum(r_{ij} - \hat{r}_{ij})^2$ is minimized again, and so on. This iterative process is continued until the loadings converge.

For details of the procedure, including the avoidance of Heywood cases (in which communalities become greater than 1), we refer to Harman and Jones (1966). Contrary to the diagonal and centroid methods, which are merely of didactical value, MINRES is a real alternative for the most used principal factor analysis of today.

9.3.4 Canonical Factor Analysis

Another intelligent method for obtaining a factor solution is canonical factor analysis (CFA).

The term 'canonical' clearly stems from Hotelling's canonical correlation analysis. In canonical correlation calculus two (or several) sets of variables are investigated and for each set a linear combination is looked for in such a way that the (canonical) correlation between these linear combinations is maximized.

The special feature of CFA is that a parallel procedure is followed.

Take for instance our mini data set with three variables (fictitious and in fact too small) and suppose that the PFA model with two factors (companionship and agreement) holds. Then, in CFA, the three variables are regarded as a first set, **x** and the two factors as a second set, **f**, and between these two sets a canonical correlation analysis is performed as shown in Figure 9.9.

For the **x** set as well as for the **f** set a linear combination is formed in such a way that the (canonical) correlation between these two linear combinations is the highest possible. Hence, the correlation matrix shown in Table 9.3 is examined.

In this matrix, correlations between variables and factors are factor loadings ($\mathbf{R}_{xf} = \mathbf{A}$). The interfactor-correlations constitute the identity matrix, for the factors are supposed to be uncorrelated ($\mathbf{R}_{ff} = \mathbf{I}$). In canonical correlation calculus the eigenstructure of matrix $\mathbf{R}_{xx}^{-1}\mathbf{R}_{xy}\mathbf{R}_{yy}^{-1}\mathbf{R}_{yx}$ is investigated. If this is applied to canonical factor analysis, in which the y set is now the f set, this matrix becomes $\mathbf{R}_{xx}^{-1}\mathbf{R}_{xf}\mathbf{R}_{ff}^{-1}\mathbf{R}_{fx} = \mathbf{R}_{xx}^{-1}\mathbf{AIA}' = \mathbf{R}_{xx}^{-1}\mathbf{AA}'$. The resulting characteristic equation and matrix equation are: $|\mathbf{R}_{xx}^{-1}\mathbf{AA}' - \lambda\mathbf{I}| = 0$ and $(\mathbf{R}_{xx}^{-1}\mathbf{AA}' - \lambda\mathbf{I})\mathbf{b} = \mathbf{0}$, respectively.

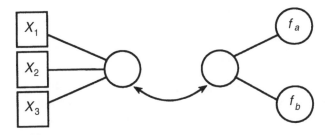

Figure 9.9   Canonical factor analysis (CFA) diagram

Table 9.3   Correlation matrix

	x_1	x_2	x_3	f_a	f_b
x_1	1	r_{12}	r_{13}	r_{1a}	r_{1b}
x_2	r_{21}	1	r_{23}	r_{2a}	r_{2b}
x_3	r_{31}	r_{32}	1	r_{3a}	r_{3b}
f_a	r_{a1}	r_{a2}	r_{a3}	1	0
f_b	r_{b1}	r_{b2}	r_{b3}	0	1

$$= \begin{bmatrix} \mathbf{R}_{xx} & \mathbf{R}_{xf} = \mathbf{A} \\ \mathbf{R}_{fx} = \mathbf{A}' & \mathbf{R}_{ff} = \mathbf{I} \end{bmatrix}$$

In these formulae, λ stands for an eigenvalue, i.e., a squared canonical correlation between the x set and the f set, and $\mathbf{b}$ stands for an eigenvector. In practice, all this is elaborated as follows. Matrix $\mathbf{A}$ is of course unknown as the factor loadings are the very quantities we are looking for. However, $\mathbf{AA}'$ can be estimated as correlation matrix $\bar{\mathbf{R}}_{xx}$ with communalities on the principal diagonal. Instead of communalities h^2, it is also possible to estimate the unique variances $u^2 = 1 - h^2$. In other words, $\bar{\mathbf{R}}_{xx}$ is also equal to $\mathbf{R}_{xx} - \mathbf{U}^2$, in which $\mathbf{U}$ is a diagonal matrix with variances of unique factors. The matrix equation then becomes:

$$[\mathbf{R}_{xx}^{-1}(\mathbf{R}_{xx} - \mathbf{U}^2) - \lambda \mathbf{I}]\mathbf{b} = 0$$

Whence:

$$\mathbf{R}_{xx}^{-1}(\mathbf{R}_{xx} - \mathbf{U}^2)\mathbf{b} = \lambda \mathbf{Ib}$$
$$\mathbf{R}_{xx}\mathbf{R}_{xx}^{-1}(\mathbf{R}_{xx} - \mathbf{U}^2)\mathbf{b} = \mathbf{R}_{xx}\lambda \mathbf{Ib}$$
$$\bar{\mathbf{R}}_{xx}\mathbf{b} = \lambda \mathbf{R}_{xx}\mathbf{b}$$
$$\bar{\mathbf{R}}_{xx}\mathbf{b} = \lambda(\bar{\mathbf{R}}_{xx} + \mathbf{U}^2)\mathbf{b} \text{ because } \mathbf{R}_{xx} = \bar{\mathbf{R}}_{xx} + \mathbf{U}^2$$
$$\bar{\mathbf{R}}_{xx}\mathbf{b} - \lambda \bar{\mathbf{R}}_{xx}\mathbf{b} = \lambda \mathbf{U}^2\mathbf{b}$$
$$(1 - \lambda)\bar{\mathbf{R}}_{xx}\mathbf{b} = \lambda \mathbf{U}^2\mathbf{b}$$
$$\bar{\mathbf{R}}_{xx}\mathbf{b} = \frac{\lambda}{1 - \lambda}\mathbf{U}^2\mathbf{b}$$

Suppose $\lambda/(1 - \lambda) = v$ and $\mathbf{Ub} = \mathbf{q}$ (or $\mathbf{b} = \mathbf{U}^{-1}\mathbf{q}$):

$$\bar{\mathbf{R}}_{xx}\mathbf{U}^{-1}\mathbf{q} = v\mathbf{Uq}$$

Premultiply by $\mathbf{U}^{-1}$:

$$\mathbf{U}^{-1}\bar{\mathbf{R}}_{xx}\mathbf{U}^{-1}\mathbf{q} = v\mathbf{q}$$

$$(\mathbf{U}^{-1}\bar{\mathbf{R}}_{xx}\mathbf{U}^{-1} - v\mathbf{I})\mathbf{q} = \mathbf{0}$$

This is the matrix equation which can be used in practice. $\mathbf{U}$ contains the square roots of the unique variances u^2 and $\bar{\mathbf{R}}_{xx}$ is the correlation matrix in which the elements $1 - u^2$ are now the entries in the principal diagonal.

Analysis of the eigenstructure of $\mathbf{U}^{-1}\bar{\mathbf{R}}_{xx}\mathbf{U}^{-1}$ provides the eigenvalues v and the eigenvectors $\mathbf{q}$, from which the original λ and $\mathbf{b}$ can be calculated back. If the eigenvalues v are collected in a diagonal matrix Λ and the eigenvectors $\mathbf{q}$ in a matrix $\mathbf{Q}$, then equation $\mathbf{U}^{-1}\bar{\mathbf{R}}_{xx}\mathbf{U}^{-1}\mathbf{q} = v\mathbf{q}$ becomes $\mathbf{U}^{-1}\mathbf{R}\bar{\mathbf{R}}_{xx}\mathbf{U}^{-1}\mathbf{Q} = \Lambda\mathbf{Q}$. Premultiplication by $\mathbf{U}$ and postmultiplication by $\mathbf{Q}'$ and $\mathbf{U}$ yields:

$$\bar{\mathbf{R}}_{xx} = \mathbf{U}\mathbf{Q}\Lambda\mathbf{Q}'\mathbf{U} \quad \text{(with } \mathbf{Q}'\mathbf{Q} = \mathbf{I} \text{ if the eigenvectors are normalized)}$$

$$\bar{\mathbf{R}}_{xx} = (\mathbf{U}\mathbf{Q}\Lambda^{1/2})(\Lambda^{1/2}\mathbf{Q}'\mathbf{U})$$

$$\bar{\mathbf{R}}_{xx} = (\mathbf{U}\mathbf{Q}\Lambda^{1/2})(\mathbf{U}\mathbf{Q}\Lambda^{1/2})'$$

And as $\bar{\mathbf{R}}_{xx} = \mathbf{A}\mathbf{A}'$ we can deduce the factor loadings:

$$\boxed{\mathbf{A} = \mathbf{U}\mathbf{Q}\Lambda^{1/2}}$$

It can be shown that these loadings are unaffected by arbitrarily rescaling the observed variables (Van de Geer, 1971, p. 179).

What we have illustrated thus far constitutes a first step. Rao developed an iterative procedure in which $\mathbf{U}^2$ is estimated in a first step on the basis of an assumed number of factors. After calculation of the first factor matrix $\mathbf{A}$, the population correlation matrix is estimated and from this a new estimation of $\mathbf{U}^2$ is derived, and so on until stable $\mathbf{U}^2$ estimations are obtained.

9.3.5 The Maximum Likelihood Method

The maximum likelihood method (ML) is the first which deals with real inferential statistics, for it makes a clear distinction between sample and population. It is true that the foregoing procedures provide for tests of significance of the model or of the number of included factors like Bartlett's test, which was illustrated in PCA but concerns merely *ad hoc* tests which are detached from the procedures for determining the loadings. In the ML method, on the other hand, the distinction between the intercorrelations of the sample and the (hypothetical) intercorrelations of the population is made from the beginning and this distinction remains during the whole process of estimation.

The PFA model $\mathbf{X} = \mathbf{F}\mathbf{A}' + \mathbf{E}$ serves as the starting point, but this model now refers to the population and the elements of $\mathbf{A}$ are now population factor loadings. The population parameters are estimated in such a way that the observed sample data are least surprising (most likely).

The concept of **likelihood** should first be explained. It is the probability of sample results for given population parameters. As an example, let us take one variable, X. Suppose that X is normally distributed in the population with population parameters

μ and σ (the mean and the standard deviation). Then the probability that a randomly chosen individual, i, will obtain score X_i for variable X is the likelihood of score X_i for given μ and σ. If all observations, X_i are considered to be mutually independent, then their joint likelihood is equal to the product of these individual probabilities, i.e., $\prod p(X_i|\mu, \sigma)$. This product is called the likelihood function, L, and it indicates the likelihood of all sample data X_i, taken together and for given population parameters μ and σ. The latter are of course unknown, but one may try different values of μ and σ and calculate the value of the likelihood function L at each trial. The values μ and σ for which L reaches a maximum are called maximum likelihood estimates, whence the name.

In practice, not the maximum of L itself, but that of its logarithm is calculated:

> To gain real insight into the concept of likelihood we have to confront it with the concepts in Bayes' theorem of prior and posterior probability. The likelihood is the probability of the sample data, given the population data. As the latter are hypothetical, it concerns the probability of the data (D), given the hypothesis (H), i.e., $p(D|H)$. However, in Bayes' theorem not $p(D|H)$ but, rather, $p(H|D)$ is calculated. The idea is that a researcher wants to investigate the probability of an hypothesis in the light of the observed data and not vice versa.
>
> The probability $p(H|D)$ is determined as follows.
>
> We know that
>
> $$p(HD) = p(H)p(D|H)$$
>
> and
>
> $$p(HD) = p(D)p(H|D)$$
>
> Consequently
>
> $$p(D)p(H|D) = p(H)p(D|H)$$
>
> As $p(D)$ is in fact a constant, for we have only one sample and therefore the data are fixed, it will be omitted, and the equal sign $=$ will be replaced by the proportionality sign $\propto$ which means: 'is equal to, with the exception of a multiplication factor'.
>
> We then obtain $p(H|D) \propto p(H)p(D|H)$, which is Bayes' theorem.
>
> The term $p(H)$ is the prior probability, i.e., the probability that the hypothesis is true, regardless of the data. The term $p(H|D)$ is the posterior probability, which means the probability that the hypothesis is true, given the data (after cognizance of the data). The term $p(D|H)$ is the likelihood of the data, i.e., the probability of the data, given the hypothesis. It is this likelihood which is used in the ML method.

If this concept of likelihood is applied in multivariate analysis, the situation naturally becomes more complex.

In the foregoing we supposed that X was normally distributed in the population. For more variables we will assume that they constitute a multivariate normal distribution. In that case there will be more than two population parameters: means, variances as well as covariances. All these population parameters can be collected in a matrix, called the population covariance matrix Σ.

When the variables are standardized this will be the population correlation matrix. (The supposition of standardized variables is not necessary, because the ML methods can also be applied on Σ.)

In this complex situation, the likelihood function L indicates the likelihoods of the sample correlation matrices for given population correlation matrices. In the ML method the population parameters are estimated in such a way that L is as high as possible, which means that they are maximum likelihood estimates.

To obtain population factor loadings (elements of **A**), an iterative procedure is required. As a great amount of calculation is involved, this can be better done by the computer. The same basic formula, i.e., $\mathbf{R} = \mathbf{AA'} + \mathbf{U}^2$, is the starting point, but it now refers to population estimates.

The ML method has all the advantages of other intelligent methods (a provision for Heywood cases, a test of the number of factors, and so on).

It is similar to CFA in that the loadings are unaffected by the arbitrary rescaling of the original variables (Lawley, 1940). That is in fact the reason why Σ as well as **R** can be used.

For more details we refer to the original work of Lawley and to the more recent work of Jöreskog (1967).

It is worth mentioning that there is a close relationship between canonical factor analysis (CFA) and the maximum likelihood method (ML).

This relationship can be indicated in an intuitive fashion. CFA aims at finding the highest (canonical) correlation between observed variables and factors. As the reduced correlation matrix $\mathbf{R} - \mathbf{U}^2$ is used, the factors will be free of sample errors if the unique variances ($\mathbf{U}^2$) are known. Therefore, thinking in terms of the ML method in which the idea of sample errors is included in the procedure, canonical factor analysis will provide the maximum likelihood estimates of the factor loadings if the unique variances $\mathbf{U}^2$ are known. But, as $\mathbf{U}^2$ is seldom known, the ML method represents an improved version of CFA, because the question of sample errors is systematically incorporated in the procedure.

The ML method has gained in importance thanks to the work of Jöreskog and the increasing possibilities of the computer. An advantage of the method which should not be underestimated is that, if the number of factors is priorally fixed, the goodness of fit of the ML solution can be tested by means of a χ^2 test. The latter is all too often neglected in research applications.

9.3.6   Alpha Factor Analysis

In alpha factor analysis we are dealing with yet another viewpoint. The roles of variables and units of the data matrix are now interchanged. In the classical viewpoint a sample was always a set of 'units' sampled from a population of 'units' and the number of variables was fixed. We now reverse the argument. We consider the number of individuals as fixed and the set of 'variables' is now conceived of as a sample from a population of 'variables'.

To understand what happens here one can imagine that a group of persons might be submitted to an infinite number of tests, but that they are tested only n times. Then the n tests constitute a sample of tests from an infinite population of tests. Having an

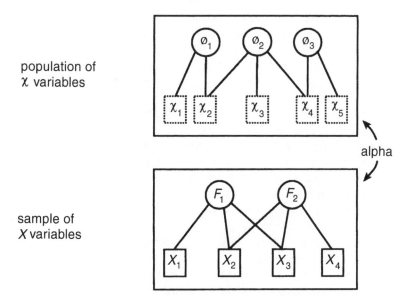

Figure 9.10   The two factor analyses in alpha factor analysis

inquiry in mind, one can imagine that n questions of a questionnaire on the same subject form only a sample of an infinite series of questions.

It follows from this viewpoint that two factor analyses can be considered, one on the sample of X variables and one on the population of χ variables (Greek letters for the population). The common factors of the X variables in the sample are indicated as F and those of the population of χ variables as ϕ. The two factor analyses are visualized in Figure 9.10 (in which the χ variables are represented by squares with dashed lines, because not all of them are measured).

In alpha factor analysis the factors $\mathbf{F}$ are determined in such a way that the squared correlation with the corresponding factors ϕ of the variable population is as high as possible. This (squared) correlation between $\mathbf{F}$ and ϕ is called Cronbach's 'coefficient alpha (α)' (1951), whence the name alpha factor analysis. We can write this coefficient α in the following fashion. Remember that a squared correlation coefficient expresses a proportion of explained variance and is equal to the (squared) covariance, corrected for the variances of each of the variables:

$$r_{xy}^{2} = \frac{[\text{covariance } (x, y)]^{2}}{(\text{variance } x)(\text{variance } y)}$$

For factors $\mathbf{F}$ and the corresponding factors ϕ the covariances are equal to $\mathbf{F}'\phi/m$ and the variances are $\mathbf{F}'\mathbf{F}/m$ and $\phi'\phi/m$ (where m is the number of individuals). This means that coefficient α is:

$$\alpha = \frac{[\mathbf{F}'\phi/m]^{2}}{(\mathbf{F}'\mathbf{F}/m)(\phi'\phi/m)} = \frac{(\mathbf{F}'\phi)^{2}}{(\mathbf{F}'\mathbf{F})(\phi'\phi)}$$

It will be the objective to select the factors **F** for which α reaches a maximum. Coefficient α expresses which proportion of the variance of the ϕ factors (of the variable population) is explained by the **F** factors (of the variable sample). Therefore, it is a measure of the generalizability of the variables, sometimes called reliability. Maximizing α thus means calculating the maximal reliability that can be extracted from the original variables.

The factors **F** are linear combinations of the X variables, hence: $\mathbf{F} = \mathbf{Xw}$, where **w** is the vector of weights (regression coefficients). Analogously, we have $\phi = \chi\omega$ (Greek letters for the population). But, even if we substitute this in the above formula for α, we have not got any further, for only **X** is known. It follows that we will have to make assumptions. It will be assumed that the covariances between the sample and population variables (elements of $\mathbf{F'\phi}$) are, on the average, equal to the harmonic mean of the sample covariances (off-diagonal elements of $\mathbf{F'F}$) and the population covariances (off-diagonal elements of $\phi'\phi$).

In other words, $\overline{(\mathbf{F'\phi})}^2 = \overline{(\mathbf{F'F})}\overline{(\phi'\phi)}$, where — stands for the mean and - - - - for the mean of the off-diagonal elements.

As $\mathbf{F} = \mathbf{Xw}$ refers to the nX variables and $\phi = \chi\omega$ to an infinite number of χ variables, the above forumla for α can be simplified as follows:

$$\alpha = \frac{(\mathbf{F'\phi})^2}{(\mathbf{F'F})(\phi'\phi)} = \frac{1}{\mathbf{F'F}}\frac{(\mathbf{F'\phi})^2}{\phi'\phi} = \frac{1}{\mathbf{F'F}}\frac{(n\,\infty)^2}{\infty^2}\frac{\overline{(\mathbf{F'\phi})^2}}{\overline{(\phi'\phi)}}$$

$$= \frac{1}{\mathbf{F'F}}n^2\overline{\mathbf{F'}}\overline{\mathbf{F}} = n^2\frac{\overline{\mathbf{F'F}}}{\mathbf{F'F}} = n^2\frac{\overline{\mathbf{w'X'X}}\mathbf{w}}{\mathbf{w'X'Xw}}$$

In the denominator, $\mathbf{X'X}$ is the correlation matrix (multiplied by m), provided that the variables are standardized. Yet, it is also possible to take the reduced correlation matrix, with communalities on the principal diagonal. The same holds for the numerator, but here a mean - - - - is used which refers only to the off-diagonal elements, i.e. $\bar{\mathbf{R}} - \mathbf{H}^2$ (where $\mathbf{H}^2$ is the diagonal matrix of communalities). And as $n(n-1)$ covariances are involved in the calculation of such a mean - - - -, the formula becomes:

$$\alpha = n^2\frac{\mathbf{w'}(\bar{\mathbf{R}} - \mathbf{H}^2)\mathbf{w}/n(n-1)}{\mathbf{w'\bar{R}w}}$$

$$\alpha = \frac{n}{n-1}\left(1 - \frac{\mathbf{w'H}^2\mathbf{w}}{\mathbf{w'\bar{R}w}}\right)$$

The search for a maximum of α comes down to finding a minimum of the term $\mathbf{w'H}^2\mathbf{w}/\mathbf{w'\bar{R}w}$ or a maximum of the inverse ratio $\mathbf{w'\bar{R}w}/\mathbf{w'H}^2\mathbf{w}$. If the latter is equated to λ the formula becomes:

$$\alpha = \frac{n}{n-1}\left(1 - \frac{1}{\lambda}\right)$$

so that α can always be calculated back. The maximization of $\lambda = \mathbf{w'\bar{R}w}/\mathbf{w'H}^2\mathbf{w}$ proceeds according to the familiar mathematical process, i.e., by forming the matrix equation and the corresponding characteristic equation. The matrix equation (exercise for the reader) is the following: $[\mathbf{H}^{-1}\bar{\mathbf{R}}\mathbf{H}^{-1} - \lambda\mathbf{I}]\mathbf{q} = \mathbf{0}$, where, as in CFA, $\mathbf{q} = \mathbf{H}\omega$ (in CFA we had $\mathbf{q} = \mathbf{Ub}$). We can see that a formal analogy of canonical factor analysis has emerged. The only difference is that matrix $\mathbf{U}^{-1}\bar{\mathbf{R}}\mathbf{U}^{-1}$, of which the eigenstructure had to be examined, is now $\mathbf{H}^{-1}\bar{\mathbf{R}}\mathbf{H}^{-1}$. Unique variances ($\mathbf{U}$) are replaced by communalities ($\mathbf{H}$).

All this is understandable if we keep in mind that alpha factor analysis is related to a sample of n variables from an infinite population of variables. Consequently, we focus on the common, and not the unique, part of the variables. An analysis in terms of unique variances refers to the error component of each variable and therefore depends on the number of individuals (m). On the other hand, an analysis in terms of communalities refers to the common components and strongly depends on the number of variables (n).

This analogy can also be seen in the calculation of the factor loadings. In CFA we had $\mathbf{A} = \mathbf{U}\mathbf{Q}\mathbf{\Lambda}^{1/2}$. In alpha factor analysis the $\mathbf{U}$ is replaced by $\mathbf{H}$: $\mathbf{A} = \mathbf{H}\mathbf{Q}\mathbf{\Lambda}^{1/2}$.

It also holds for alpha factor analysis that the loadings are unaffected by arbitrary rescaling of the variables, just as in CFA and ML.

Here, too, as in all other methods of factor analysis, the communalities have to be estimated (euphemism for guessed) in a first step. Kaiser and Caffrey (1965) developed an iterative procedure which is continued until covergence is reached.

9.3.7 Image Analysis

The viewpoint of alpha factor analysis, in which the variables are conceived of as a sample from a population of variables, also holds for Guttman's image analysis (1953).

The 'image' of a variable X_i is the part that this variable has in common with the other variables. The anti-image is the unique part, which is not associated with other variables. The image and anti-image are calculated by means of a multiple regression of variable X_i as a function of all others, i.e., $X_i \sum_{j=1}^{n-1} b_{ij}X_j + e_i$, in which the predicted part $\hat{X}_i = \sum_{j=1}^{n-1} b_{ij}X_j$, is equal to the image, and the error term e_i to the anti-image. Hence, the image is the total of projections on the regression plane and the anti-image is perpendicular to this plane. A number of assumptions follow from this: $\text{cov}(e_i, X_j) = 0$ and $\text{cov}(e_i, \hat{X}_i) = 0$.

Thus far the concepts of 'image' and 'anti-image' were used in their general meaning. But Guttman goes a step further. He makes the distinction between the sample of n variables and the infinite population of variables, a distinction that was explained in alpha factor analysis. In the sample of variables he speaks of partial image and partial anti-image, respectively. In the population of variables he makes an analogous distinction between total image and total anti-image. We can visualize these distinctions as follows:

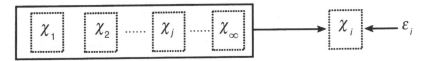

The population contains ∞ variables. The total image of χ_i is $\sum_{j=1}^{\infty} \beta_{ij}\chi_j$. The total anti-image of χ_i is ε_i.

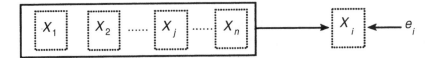

The sample contains n variables. The partial image of X_i is $\sum_{j=1}^{n-1} b_{ij}X_j$. The partial anti-image of X_i is e_i.

Guttman showed that if the whole population of variables is considered, the communality of each variable X_i is equal to the squared multiple correlation with other variables. Therefore, the best estimate of the part that X_i shares with other variables is equal to the image $\hat{X}_i = \sum b_{ij}X_j$, i.e., the predicted part of regression analysis (where the variables are standardized, so that the weights b_{ij} are standardized regression coefficients). The best estimate of the unique part of X_i is equal to the anti-image: $e_i = X_i - \hat{X}_i$.

In image analysis the covariance matrix $\mathbf{G}$ of image scores and the covariance matrix $\mathbf{\Gamma}$ of anti-image scores are used. Guttman showed that the correlation matrix of the original n variables is equal to: $\mathbf{R} = \mathbf{G} - \mathbf{\Gamma} + 2\mathbf{S}^2$, in which $\mathbf{S}^2 =$ the diagonal matrix of anti-image variances.

He also showed that the image analysis in the population of ∞ variables becomes identical to factor analysis. For, if $n \to \infty$, and, consequently, if the ratio of the number of factors and the number of variables $m/n \to 0$, then $\mathbf{S}^2$ tends to the diagonal matrix $\mathbf{U}^2$ of unique variances, which has been dealt with in other sections. The reduced correlation matrix $\mathbf{R} - \mathbf{U}^2$ is then approximated by $\mathbf{R} - \mathbf{S}^2$. The procedure, which will not be elaborated further here, comes down to examining the eigenstructure of the matrix $\mathbf{R} - \mathbf{S}^2$. Guttman showed that the diagonal elements of this reduced correlation matrix, i.e., the squared multiple correlations, are theoretically the smallest possible communalities. The unique variances in $\mathbf{S}^2$ are then the highest possible. In the examination of the eigenstructure, one runs up against a problem which we have already encountered in PFA, i.e., the production of negative eigenvalues as a result of incorrect communality estimates. In that case the reduced correlation matrix is not positive semi-definite. (We can also say that the matrix is not fair or that it is not a Gram matrix, named after Mr Gram.) What is original about Guttman's image analysis is the rescaling of the reduced correlation matrix in such a way that it remains fair. For details we refer to Kaiser (1963) and Muliak (1972).

In summary: the extraction of factors is performed by examining the eigenstructure of the image covariance matrix with squared multiple correlations on the principal diagonal and with adjusted correlation coefficients in the off-diagonal entries, in which the adjustment is a procedure which guarantees a (fair) Gram matrix.

It goes without saying that the elements of the anti-image covariance matrix will all be approximately zero if the factor analytic assumptions of the variable structure are correct.

The rest of the procedure, i.e., finding the factor loadings, determining the number of factors, iterating, etc., is comparable to the other methods that have been discussed.

It is also worth mentioning that Jöreskog (1969) proposed an improved version of Guttman's method, which was given the name 'image factor analysis'.

9.3.8 The Multiple Group Method

It will have become clear by now that factor analysis can be approached from many different viewpoints: the selection of factors one by one which extract a maximum of variance from the variables (PCA and PFA), the selection of factors one by one according to a system of partial relation calculus (diagonal method), the selection of factors one by one which run through the centroid (centroid method), the selection of factors one by one in such a way that the residual correlations between 'different' variables are minimized (MINRES), the application of canonical correlation analysis on a set of variables and a set of factors (CFA), the generalization to a population of individuals (ML), the generalization to a population of variables (alpha and image analysis).

The multiple group method is another example of a new viewpoint, according to which the variables are subdivided in groups or clusters with strong within-associations. It is in fact a form of cluster analysis, just like the B coefficient method and linkage analysis, which are not elaborated here. And as the clusters of variables are not necessarily situated in perpendicular directions, it is obvious that an oblique solution will be chosen.

All the foregoing methods resulted in orthogonal factors and an oblique solution was obtained only afterwards, by means of an oblique rotation. On the other hand, in the multiple group method an oblique factor matrix is obtained directly and all factors are extracted simultaneously. It follows that factor correlations will be part of the model and the aforementioned distinction between factor structure (correlations between factors and variables) and factor pattern (regression coefficients) will be included in the procedure.

The essence of the multiple group method consists of choosing the factors in such a way that their axes run through the centroids of the clusters of variables. To start the procedure one must begin with a grouping of the n variables into m clusters, which can be done on the basis of theoretical considerations or by using the results of another method (e.g., the method of B coefficients).

If the variables are standardized, then each factor can be calculated as the sum of variables in the related cluster, for such a sum variable runs through the centroid.

For example, for cluster k with p variables: $F_k = \sum_{j=1}^{p} x_j$ (where $k = 1, 2, \ldots, m$ if there are m clusters).

In preparing a factor solution we first calculate two sums of correlations in the reduced correlation matrix (which contains communality estimates on the principal diagonal). The first is the sum of correlations of each variable with all variables (itself included) in each cluster. For variable x_i of cluster k this sum is $s_{ik} = \sum_{j=1}^{p} r_{ij}$, where correlation r_{ii} of x_i with itself is equal to the communality h_i^2. The second is the sum of correlations between the variables of cluster l and cluster k (including the case $l = k$). The sum S_{lk} is easily calculated by adding together the foregoing sums s_{ik} for each of q variables of cluster l: $S_{lk} = \sum_{i=1}^{q} \sum_{j=1}^{p} r_{ij} = \sum_{i=1}^{q} s_{ik}$. A special case is the sum S_{kk}.

We can now calculate the factor correlation which will be collected in matrix ϕ. To determine the correlation between factor F_k and factor F_l we simply use the well-known formula of a correlation coefficient:

$$r_{xy} = \frac{\text{covariance}\,(x, y)}{s_x s_y}$$

$$r_{F_k F_l} = \frac{\sum F_k F_l}{N s_{F_k} s_{F_l}}$$

In this formula, N is the number of individuals. Notice that the denominator contains the standard deviations of factors, for it is not because the variables x_j are standardized that this is also the case for their sums F_k.

A simplification is straightforward. The variance $(s_{F_k})^2$ of a factor F_k is equal to the sum S_{kk}, which can be derived by writing F_k as a sum of standardized variables x_j and by elaborating on the variance of that sum, taking into account that $r_{jj} = (h_j)^2$.

An analaogous simplification holds for the covariance: $(\sum F_k F_l)/N = S_{kl}$.

Consequently, the correlation between factors F_k and F_l can be written in terms of sums of correlations:

$$r_{F_k F_l} = \frac{S_{kl}}{(S_{kk} \quad S_{ll})^{1/2}}$$

In addition to these factor correlations (collected in matrix ϕ), the correlations between variables and factors can also be expressed in terms of the foregoing sums:

$$r_{x_j F_k} = \frac{\sum x_j F_k}{N s_{x_j} s_{F_k}} = \frac{S_{jk}}{(S_{kk})^{1/2}}$$

These correlations are collected in a factor matrix $\mathbf{S}$ which represents the factor structure. The loadings of $\mathbf{S}$ are contaminated with the factor correlations. Making use of $\mathbf{S}$ and ϕ, the factor pattern $\mathbf{A}$ can be calculated as follows:

$$\mathbf{A} = \mathbf{S}\phi^{-1}.$$

The loadings of $\mathbf{A}$ are the coordinates of the variables in an oblique reference system of factor axes. They are not correlations (as in $\mathbf{S}$), but regression coefficients in a system of linear equations of the form $\mathbf{X} = \mathbf{F}\mathbf{A}'$, in which the variables are the dependent variables and the factors are the independent variables. The loadings of the factor pattern are freed from contamination by the factor correlations (as they are 'partial' regression coefficients).

Once the factor loadings are known, the same procedure that was used in other methods can be applied, i.e., the calculation of the reproduced and residual correlation matrix in several iterative steps. However, there is an important difference from all of the foregoing methods: the factors are not orthogonal but oblique. In an orthogonal solution the reproduced correlation matrix was equal to the product $\mathbf{A}\mathbf{A}'$. This was derived in the section on PFA. There, the following formula was used:

$$\mathbf{R} = \mathbf{A}\frac{\mathbf{F}'\mathbf{F}}{n-1}\mathbf{A}' + \frac{\mathbf{E}'\mathbf{E}}{n-1}$$

where $\mathbf{F'F}/(n-1) = \mathbf{I}$ if the factors are uncorrelated. But in the multiple group method, in which factor correlations are included in the procedure, matrix $\boldsymbol{\phi} = \mathbf{F'F}/(n-1)$ will generally not be equal to the identity matrix and, consequently, the reproduced correlation matrix will no longer be equal to $\mathbf{AA'}$, but, rather to $\mathbf{A}\boldsymbol{\phi}\mathbf{A'}$. As $\mathbf{A} = \mathbf{S}\boldsymbol{\phi}^{-1}$, we can also write:

$$\mathbf{A}\boldsymbol{\phi}\mathbf{A'} = \mathbf{S}\boldsymbol{\phi}^{-1}\boldsymbol{\phi}\boldsymbol{\phi}^{-1}\mathbf{S'} = \mathbf{S}\boldsymbol{\phi}^{-1}\mathbf{S'}$$

where $\boldsymbol{\phi}^{-1}$ takes care of undoing the contamination with factor correlations (which is contained in the factor structure $\mathbf{S}$). The residual correlation matrix is naturally equal to the original minus the reproduced correlation matrix, i.e., $\mathbf{R} - \mathbf{A}\boldsymbol{\phi}\mathbf{A'}$. If this approximates the null matrix, then we are finished. One can only hope that the factor pattern contains a 'simple structure *á la* Thurstone', so that the clusters can be clearly distinguished. If, on the other hand, the residual correlations are too high, then an iterative procedure is set up, which continues until the magnitudes of the residual correlations are negligible.

In this section we have taken the line that the multiple group method produces an oblique solution by definition. However, in practice, preference is given to an orthogonal solution which is obtained by orthogonalizing the oblique solution. This is done by means of a Gram–Schmidt-orthogonalization, a procedure according to which non-orthogonal factors are made orthogonal and for which we refer to any textbook in linear algebra. In the foregoing methods an orthogonal solution was produced and only afterwards, via rotation, was it examined as to whether an oblique solution corresponded better with reality. Here, the reverse takes place: an oblique solution forms the starting point and afterwards it is made orthogonal. The advantage of an orthogonal solution is, as we know, that the common variance explained by the factors can be determined unambiguously. It is therefore up to the researcher to decide whether (s)he wants to take this orthogonal step. For details we refer to Harman (1967) and Bennett and Bowers (1976).

9.4 Other Methods in the World of Factor Analysis

The methods dealt with so far constitute only a selection of the rich world of factor analysis procedures. In this selection we have predominantly focussed upon the line of thought.

The PCA model without unique factors is different from the PFA model.

Minimizing the residuals (MINRES) is different from maximizing the variance (PCA and PFA).

Generalizing to a population of individuals (ML) is different from generalizing to a population of variables (alpha and image analysis).

Finding an orthogonal solution, after which an oblique rotation may follow (in almost all methods), is different from finding an oblique solution, after which orthogonalization follows (multiple group method).

The selection of factors one by one (centroid and diagonal method) is different from the simultaneous extraction of factors (multiple group method).

Considering a factor analysis as a form of canonical correlation analysis between a set of latent and a set of observed variables (CFA) is different from considering factor analysis as a form of cluster analysis, in which the observed variables are subdivided into distinct groups (multiple group method).

The interreliability of a series of items (alpha factor analysis) is different from the claim on validity of a factor model (factor analysis as a path analysis with latent variables).

And so on. Many other distinctions exist. We will mention three more.

9.4.1   *R and Q Factor Analysis*

All methods discussed in this chapter are *R* factor analyses. The *n* variables of the data matrix form the starting point and an $n \times n$ correlation matrix **R** is calculated, on which an operation of dimension reduction is performed.

On the other hand, in *Q* factor analysis the *m* persons form the starting point and the correlation matrix is then an $m \times m$ matrix. Having the data matrix in mind, it is not the variable side, but, rather, the individual side which is investigated (see Figure 9.11).

Thinking in terms of content, it is not difficult to imagine that in certain research problems the individual side receives more attention than the variable side. For example, political science research on nations often aims at grouping the countries, making use of the scores on a series of variables. In such cases the subdivision in groups of countries is a form of cluster analysis of the units rather than the variables.

The technical side of *Q* analysis is fairly simple, as the SVD operation for examining the eigenstructure, which was explained in PCA, can also be performed on the transposed data matrix. It naturally goes without saying that a sufficient number of variables have to be on hand in a *Q* analysis. For, statistics is still the theory of great numbers and, as the role of individuals is now taken over by variables, an analysis on a small number of variables will produce unstable interperson correlations. As a result, the application possibilities of *Q* factor analysis are rather

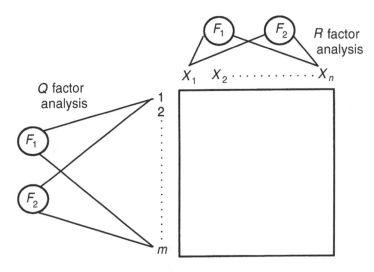

Figure 9.11   *Q* factor analysis

limited. Moreover, other techniques of the cluster analysis of units exists which are designed for this specific purpose of grouping.

9.4.2   *Non-linear and Non-metric Factor Analysis*

In all of the foregoing methods, the measurement level of the variables remained undiscussed. As means and variances were involved in the calculations, it was taken for granted that the variables were measured at the interval or ratio level. It was also assumed that the relationships between variables and factors represented in a system of equations were all linear, for the loadings of a factor pattern were the regression coefficients of a linear regression analysis.

These two requirements can, however, be relaxed. The computer program PRIN-CALS (see Gifi, 1980) performs a principal components analysis, which is non-metric as well as non-linear.

A treatment of this technique falls beyond the reach of this text, but it should be pointed out that non-metric and non-linear PCA is a promising new development which deserves our attention. The interested reader is referred to Gifi (1980)

9.4.3   *Higher-order Factor Analysis*

According to some authors, our theoretical buildings have open ceilings. Therefore, a factor analysis might be performed in several different steps. The oblique factors of a first analysis could be conceived of as variables, on which a new factor analysis is performed. The latter would then provide second-order factors. This process could be continued to obtain third-order factors and so on.

It is understandable that higher-order factor analysis is not often used in practice. To begin with, the first-order factors must be oblique in order to proceed with the second step. They must also be sufficiently numerous to be conceived of as variables.

Canonical Correlation Analysis: The Study of Economic Inequality and Political Instability

10.1 The Research Problem and the Causal Diagram

In a study by the political scientist Russett, an analysis was made of the associations between the economic and political characteristics of 47 countries. Five indicators were used for the measure of economic inequality: the division of farmland, the GINI index, the percentage of tenant farmers, the GNP per capita and the percentage of farmers. Russett used the following four indicators for the measure of political instability: the instability of leadership, the level of internal group violence, the occurrence of internal war and the stability of democracy. The research hypothesis was that Alexis de Tocqueville was right: there is not one nation that is capable of maintaining a democratic form of government for an extensive period of time if the most important sources of income are unevenly distributed among its citizens. In other words, there is a significant association between the economic *in*equality and the political *in*stability of nations.

The two theoretical concepts in this research problem are 'economic inequality' (X^*) and 'political instability' (Y^*). They are called canonical variables and the expectation is that they are strongly correlated. The correlation between the two is known as 'canonical correlation'. The first canonical variable, X^*, is measured by $p = 5$ indicators, X_1 to X_5, and we will consider X^* as a linear combination (a weighted sum) of these X variables. In an analogous fashion, Y^*, the second canonical variable, is a linear combination of the $q = 4$ indicators Y_1 to Y_4. In the most general case, in which the X set contains p variables and the Y set contains q variables, the diagram can be represented as shown in Figure 10.1.

In Russett's research problem, the canonical correlation between the canonical variables X^* and Y^* is in fact a causal relationship, because he asserts that nations with great economic (in)equality display great political (in)stability. The arrow in the other direction, according to which the political characteristics would influence the economic characteristics, is not implied in de Tocqueville's or Russett's view. However, considering the fact that a canonical correlation is a 'correlation', the statistical analysis is not asymmetrical. For this reason we do not draw a causal arrow from X^* to Y^* in the figure, but, rather, a double-sided, curved arrow, indicating that the question of causality remains an open one.

For the sake of simplicity, let us limit ourselves in our mini data set to two indicators of economic inequality, the GINI index and the percentage of farmers, and

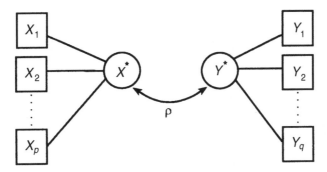

Figure 10.1   Causal diagram: general

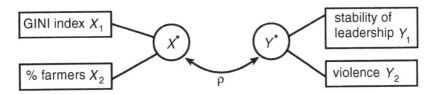

Figure 10.2   Causal diagram: specific

two indicators of political instability, the instability of leadership and the level of internal group violence. The diagram would then be as shown in Figure 10.2.

10.2   The Data Matrix

The units of analysis are countries. Since Russett included the data for the 47 countries in his publication, we have not had to construct the data ourselves. We have taken a random sample of $n = 12$ countries from the original data matrix. As mentioned, we will limit ourselves to two variables from the X set and two variables from the Y set. We will call these X_1, X_2, Y_1 and Y_2, respectively. All of the variables have been measured at the interval level.

The GINI index (X_1) tells us to what degree the actual distribution of income in a country deviates from an ideal distribution in a condition of complete equality. It is a number between 1 and 100. The higher the number, the more inequality there is.

The percentage of the labour force employed in the agricultural sector (X_2) is also a number between 1 and 100. It is not a measure of inequality, but an extra economic variable which tells us something about the absence of industrialization.

The instability of leadership (Y_1) is an index $[17 - a/b]$. Here, the numerator, a, is the number of years a country has been independent in the period between 1945–1961; the denominator, b, is the number of political leaders in that same period; 17 is the number of years observed. The index varies from 0 to 17. The higher the index, the more unstable the leadership.

The level of internal group violence (Y_2) is the number of deaths per million, as the

Table 10.1   Data matrix

	GINI index	% farmers	Leadership	Violence
Yugoslavia	43.7	67	0	0
Poland	45.0	57	8.5	5
Japan	47.0	40	15.7	0.1
India	52.2	71	3.0	14.0
Philippines	56.4	59	14.0	292.0
Sweden	57.7	13	8.5	0
New Zealand	77.3	16	12.8	0
Spain	78.0	50	0	0.2
Italy	80.3	29	15.5	0.2
Iraq	88.1	81	16.2	344.0
Venezuela	90.9	42	14.9	111.0
Bolivia	93.8	72	15.3	663.0

result of rioting, revolutions and civil wars in the period between 1950 and 1962. A high number here, needless to say, indicates greater instability.

Our random sample of $n = 12$ countries resulted in the data matrix shown in Table 10.1.

10.3 The Model of Canonical Correlation Analysis

In canonical correlation analysis, we want to see if there is a significant association between a set of X variables and a set of Y variables. For this reason we look for a linear combination, X^*, of the X set and a linear combination, Y^*, of the Y set, in such a way that X^* and Y^* are maximally correlated. The two linear combinations, X^* and Y^*, are not observed and, for the moment, are unknown. They are called canonical variables. In our example they have been given a name *a priori*: economic inequality and political instability. Sometimes such an *a priori* theory is absent at the start of research and a name must be devised afterwards. The correlation ρ between X^* and Y^* is called a canonical correlation.

The simplest way to explain the logic of canonical correlation analysis is by means of multiple regression analysis. In multiple regression, there is one dependent variable, Y, and a set of independent variables, X_i. We then attempt to find a linear combination in the form of $X^* = a_1 X_1 + a_2 X_2 + \ldots$, in such a way that X^* and Y are maximally correlated. (Please note: in Chapter 5, $\hat{y}$ was used as a symbol instead of X^*.)

In canonical correlation analysis there isn't only one, but an entire set of Y variables. These, too, will be represented by a linear combination in the form of $Y^* = b_1 Y_1 + b_2 Y_2 + \ldots$. The two linear combinations (canonical variables), X^* and Y^*, are of course unknown. To find these, the a and b weights must be calculated. Canonical correlation analysis aims at determining these weights in such a way that the canonical correlation ρ is as high as possible. The square of this canonical correlation is the proportion of variance in one set (e.g., political characteristics) that is explained by the variance in the other set (e.g., economic characteristics).

Just as in principal components analysis, where not one but several uncorrelated components could be determined, here, various pairs of canonical variables can be found. Each pair is uncorrelated with the preceding pair and is calculated each time so that the canonical correlation is maximal. The number of pairs of canonical variables or, which comes down to the same thing, the number of canonical correlations, is equal to the number of variables in the smallest set, i.e., min $[p, q]$.

In our example, $p = q = 2$. Two pairs of canonical variables can therefore be calculated as well as two corresponding canonical correlations. The canonical variables are $X^* = a_1 X_1 + a_2 X_2$ and $Y^* = b_1 Y_1 + b_2 Y_2$. In vector notation this would be: $\mathbf{x}^* = \mathbf{xa}$ and $\mathbf{y}^* = \mathbf{yb}$.

As with the techniques in the preceding chapters, the calculation of each of the canonical correlations and of the a and b weights will be done by examining the eigenstructure of a typical matrix. In discriminant analysis and principal components analysis, this typical matrix was $\mathbf{W}^{-1}\mathbf{B}$ and $\mathbf{R}$, respectively. In canonical correlation analysis this matrix is $\mathbf{R}_{yy}^{-1}\mathbf{R}_{xy}'\mathbf{R}_{xx}^{-1}\mathbf{R}_{xy}$. Why this involves this particularly complex matrix will become clear later when we treat the canonical correlation between X^* and Y^* as a multiple correlation between the canonical variable Y^* and the set of X variables. Before explaining this, let us first distinguish between different types of within- and between-correlation matrices, and also discuss the geometric approach and the objectives of the technique.

10.4 Three Types of Correlations

A legitimate method for examining the correlations between the economic and political characteristics is an analysis of the separate correlations between the GINI index and the (in)stability of leadership (X_1, Y_1), between the GINI index and the level of violence (X_1, Y_2), between the percentage of farmers and the (in)stability of leadership (X_2, Y_1), and between the percentage of farmers and level of violence (X_2, Y_2). These are the correlations between X and Y variables and are therefore called **between-correlations**.

Canonical correlation analysis, however, goes a step further than this examination of separate correlations.

First of all, in canonical correlation analysis one aims to examine to what degree two batteries, X variables on the one hand and Y variables on the other, show association 'as a whole'. To this end, each battery is replaced by a linear combination. The correlation between these two linear combinations forms the subject of the research.

Secondly, in canonical correlation analysis one controls for the associations within each of the sets, as it is possible that the variables within the X set of economic characteristics are also correlated in pairs. These types of correlations are called **within-correlations**. They form a problem that is comparable to multicollinearity in multiple regression analysis. There, the regression coefficients that were calculated were partial coefficients, i.e., we controlled each variable for association with the other variables in the X set. Something similar is done in canonical correlation analysis, only here we don't just control on the side of the X set, but on the side of the Y set of political characteristics as well, because we now have various Y variables that could also be correlated in pairs.

Table 10.2   Correlation matrix

$$
\begin{array}{c}
\begin{array}{cccc}
x_1 & x_2 & y_1 & y_2
\end{array} \\
\begin{array}{c}
x_1 \\ x_2 \\ \\ y_1 \\ y_2
\end{array}
\begin{bmatrix}
1 & r_{x_1 x_2} & r_{x_1 y_1} & r_{x_1 y_2} \\
r_{x_2 x_1} & 1 & r_{x_2 y_1} & r_{x_2 y_2} \\
\\
r_{y_1 x_1} & r_{y_1 x_2} & 1 & r_{y_2 y_2} \\
r_{y_2 x_1} & r_{y_2 x_2} & r_{y_2 y_1} & 1
\end{bmatrix}
=
\begin{bmatrix}
\mathbf{R}_{xx} & \mathbf{R}_{xy} \\
\\
\mathbf{R}_{yx} & \mathbf{R}_{yy}
\end{bmatrix}
\end{array}
$$

We can, therefore, discern three types of correlations:

1. Correlations between X variables; the correlation matrix is $\mathbf{R}_{xx}$.
2. Correlations between Y variables; the correlation matrix is $\mathbf{R}_{yy}$.
3. Correlations between X and Y variables; the correlation matrix is $\mathbf{R}_{xy} = \mathbf{R}'_{yx}$.

In other words, if we put the correlations between all the variables, X_1, X_2, Y_1 and Y_2, in one big correlation matrix, it would be broken down as shown in Table 10.2.

The fact that canonical correlation analysis aims to examine the between-correlations and not the within-correlations, can be illustrated more clearly by comparing this technique to double principal component analysis (PCA twice). PCA looks for the correlations within one set of variables, i.e., within-correlations. If we were to perform two PCAs, one on the X set and one on the Y set, we would obtain a first principal component in each PCA. The correlation between these two principal components is not the same as the (first) canonical correlation. For, the correlation between the two components measures to what degree the within-associations between the economic characteristics are comparable to the within-associations between the political characteristics. Canonical correlation, on the other hand, measures to what degree the economic and political characteristics are correlated, controlling for (i.e., assuming the absence of) within-associations within the economic set on the one hand and within the political set on the other.

10.5   Geometric Approach

In order to explain canonical correlation from a geometric viewpoint, we create two coordinate systems: one with the two x variables as axes, x_1 and x_2; and one with the two y variables as axes, y_1 and y_2 (see Figure 10.3). The variables have been standardized.

The linear combinations x_1^* and x_2^* are situated in the (x_1, x_2) space and the linear combinations y_1^* and y_2^* have been situated in the (y_1, y_2) space. Note that a canonical variable, x_1^*, for example, is not the same as the regression function of x_2 on the function of x_1, as the latter pertains to the correlation and regression within the x set, while the canonical variable x_1^* is constructed so that it is maximally correlated with y_1^* from the 'other' set. This distinction has been shown in the figure by indicating the canonical variable x_1^* with a solid line, and the regression function of x_2 on x_1 with a dashed line through the points of the scatterplot. The same has been done for the other three canonical variables.

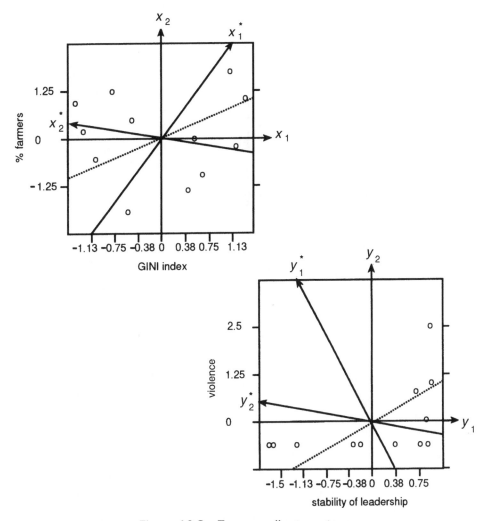

Figure 10.3   Two coordinate systems

Canonical correlation analysis aims at finding a first pair of canonical variables, one x^* in (x_1, x_2) space and one y^* in (y_1, y_2) space, in such a way that the correlation between x^* and y^* is maximal. Afterwards one looks for a second pair of canonical variables, uncorrelated with the first pair, in such a way that the (canonical) correlation between this second pair is as high as possible.

One can see that the canonical correlations between the first pair, x_1^* and y_1^*, as well as the second pair, x_2^* and y_2^* (uncorrelated with the first), are indeed extremely high by looking at the representation given in Figure 10.4 of the coordinate systems where the canonical variables are axes.

The fact that x_1^* and x_2^* (as well as y_1^* and y_2^*) are uncorrelated does not necessarily mean that they are orthogonal in (x_1, x_2) space. It does mean that the regression line in (x_1^*, x_2^*) space has a zero slope. This is shown in Figure 10.5.

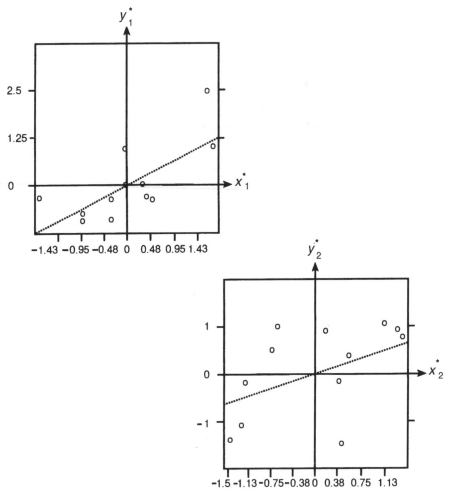

Figure 10.4   Coordinate systems where canonical variables are axes

10.6   Objectives of the Technique

Three goals are pursued in canonical correlation analysis. With Russett's study of countries in mind, these goals can be described as the following:

1. We look for a first pair of linear combinations, one from the set of economic variables and one from the set of political variables, in such a way that the correlation between both of the linear combinations is maximal. Next we look for a second pair of linear combinations, also maximally correlated and uncorrelated with the first pair. We do this as many times as there are variables in the smallest set. We call the linear combinations 'canonical variables'. The weights are known as 'canonical weights'. The maximized correlations are called 'canonical correlations'. On the basis of the canonical weights, we attempt to interpret the

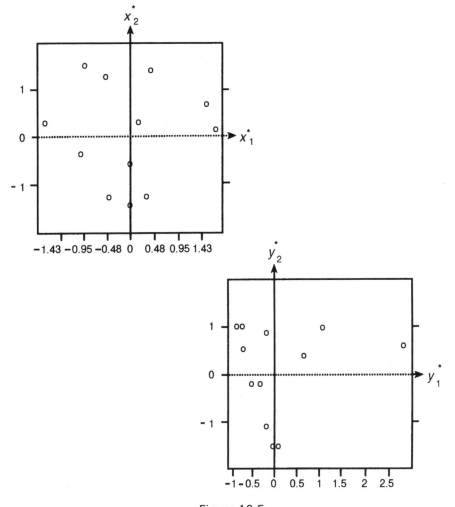

Figure 10.5

associations 'between' the sets. One can also attempt to give a name to each canonical variable per pair.

2. Making use of the canonical weights, the scores of the canonical variables are calculated. The correlations between the original variables and the canonical variables often offer better possibilities for interpretation. These are called 'structure correlations'.

3. We check to see whether the associations between the two sets can be generalized to the population of the countries. This is done by testing the canonical correlations for significance. We can perform this test for all of the canonical correlations together or for each of the separate canonical correlations or their subgroups. Since the first canonical correlation is the largest and the following correlations become smaller and smaller, it seems obvious to test these separately, and only to interpret the ones which give us the most significant result.

10.7 Examination of the Eigenstructure of the $R_{yy}^{-1}R_{xy}'R_{xx}^{-1}R_{xy}$ Matrix

It was stated above that a multiple regression approach can be helpful in explaining the logic of canonical correlation analysis. Let us now look at this approach. Let us take the Y set as the set of dependent variables. (We could just as easily have done this exercise with the X set.) We will use vector and matrix notation. For the sake of simplicity let us consider the X and Y variables as standardized and, instead of the time-consuming notation in z scores, z_x and z_y, let us write the lower case letters x and y.

We consider the linear combination $\mathbf{y}^* = \mathbf{yb}$; this on the assumption that vector $\mathbf{b}$ is known and that the entire set of y variables could be replaced by one y^*, so that multiple regression analysis with one dependent (canonical) variable, y^*, and various independent x variables could be applied.

The first step is the calculation of the correlations of dependent variable y^* with the x variables, as follows:

$$\text{correlation } r_{xy^*} = \frac{\text{covariance } (x, y^*)}{(\text{standard deviation } x)(\text{standard deviation } y^*)}$$

What we need is the covariance between each x_i and y^*, and the standard deviations of x_i and y^*. In vector and matrix notation the covariances between the independent variables x_i and the dependent variable y^* are equal to $\mathbf{x}'\mathbf{y}^*/(n-1) = \mathbf{x}'\mathbf{yb}/(n-1) = \mathbf{R}_{xy}\mathbf{b}$, where $n =$ the number of units (countries here).

The variances of x variables are equal to $\mathbf{x}'\mathbf{x}/(n-1)$ and their standard deviations are $[\mathbf{x}'\mathbf{x}/(n-1)]^{1/2}$. These are all equal to 1 if the x variables are standardized. This is also the case for the y variables, but not for the linear combination y^*.
The variance of y^*

$$= \frac{1}{n-1}\mathbf{y}^{*\prime}\mathbf{y}^* = \frac{1}{n-1}(\mathbf{yb})'(\mathbf{yb})$$
$$= \frac{1}{n-1}\mathbf{b}'\mathbf{y}'\mathbf{yb} = \mathbf{b}'\mathbf{R}_{yy}\mathbf{b}$$

The standard deviation of y^*

$$= (\mathbf{b}'\mathbf{R}_{yy}\mathbf{b})^{1/2}$$

Now the matrix of zero-order correlations between the canonical variable y^* and each of the x variables can be set up (note: if only one canonical variable y^* is being observed, then this is not a matrix but a vector; in the case of several canonical variables, which are collected in a $\mathbf{y}^*$ vector, these are put together in a matrix):

$$\mathbf{R}_{y^*x} = (\mathbf{R}_{xy}\mathbf{b})/(\mathbf{b}'\mathbf{R}_{yy}\mathbf{b})^{1/2}$$

The next step is the calculation of multiple correlation coefficient R of y^* on the function of the set of x variables. This will be the canonical correlation. In multiple regression analysis it holds that the multiple determination coefficient, R^2 (the square of the multiple correlation coefficient), is equal to: $R^2 = \mathbf{r}'(y)\mathbf{R}_{xx}^{-1}\mathbf{r}(y)$, where $\mathbf{r}(y) =$ the vector of correlations of y with x variables and $\mathbf{R}_{xx}^{-1} =$ the inverse of the matrix of correlations between the x variables mutually. In the more complex situation of canonical correlation analysis, $\mathbf{r}(y)$ is replaced by $\mathbf{R}_{y^*x'}$, so that a canonical correlation (squared) can be calculated as follows:

$$\rho^2 = R^2_{y^* \cdot x_1 x_2 \dots x_p} = \mathbf{R}'_{y^*x}\mathbf{R}_{xx}^{-1}\mathbf{R}_{y^*x} = [(\mathbf{R}_{xy}\mathbf{b})/(\mathbf{b}'\mathbf{R}_{yy}\mathbf{b})^{1/2}]'\mathbf{R}_{xx}^{-1}[(\mathbf{R}_{xy}\mathbf{b})/(\mathbf{b}'\mathbf{R}_{yy}\mathbf{b})^{1/2}]$$

$$\rho^2 = \frac{\mathbf{b}'\mathbf{R}'_{xy}\mathbf{R}_{xx}^{-1}\mathbf{R}_{xy}\mathbf{b}}{\mathbf{b}'\mathbf{R}_{yy}\mathbf{b}}$$

The **b** coefficients are those for which the above ratio, the squared canonical correlation, is maximal. For the maximization of this ratio, the partial derivatives must be taken and set to zero. The derivative of any ratio u/v is equal to $(uv' - u'v)/v^2$. This derivative is zero if its numerator is zero, i.e., if $uv' = u'v$. Applied to the ratio ρ^2, this results in:

$$(\mathbf{b}'\mathbf{R}'_{xy}\mathbf{R}_{xx}^{-1}\mathbf{R}_{xy}\mathbf{b})(2\mathbf{R}_{yy}\mathbf{b}) = (2\mathbf{R}'_{xy}\mathbf{R}_{xx}^{-1}\mathbf{R}_{xy}\mathbf{b})(\mathbf{b}'\mathbf{R}_{yy}\mathbf{b})$$

$$\mathbf{R}'_{xy}\mathbf{R}_{xx}^{-1}\mathbf{R}_{xy}\mathbf{b} = \frac{\mathbf{b}'\mathbf{R}'_{xy}\mathbf{R}_{xx}^{-1}\mathbf{R}_{xy}\mathbf{b}}{\mathbf{b}'\mathbf{R}_{yy}\mathbf{b}}\mathbf{R}_{yy}\mathbf{b}$$

$$\mathbf{R}'_{xy}\mathbf{R}_{xx}^{-1}\mathbf{R}_{xy}\mathbf{b} = \rho^2\mathbf{R}_{yy}\mathbf{b}$$

$$\mathbf{R}_{yy}^{-1}\mathbf{R}'_{xy}\mathbf{R}_{xx}^{-1}\mathbf{R}_{xy}\mathbf{b} = \rho^2\mathbf{b}$$

$$(\mathbf{R}_{yy}^{-1}\mathbf{R}'_{xy}\mathbf{R}_{xx}^{-1}\mathbf{R}_{xy} - \rho^2\mathbf{I})\mathbf{b} = 0$$

We encountered the structure of this last equation earlier. It is a typical eigenstructure problem, where **b** are the eigenvectors and ρ^2 the eigenvalues of the $\mathbf{R}_{yy}^{-1}\mathbf{R}'_{xy}\mathbf{R}_{xx}^{-1}\mathbf{R}_{xy}$ matrix.

In most textbooks this matrix is simply presented. The intention of the preceding technical digression was to show that this matrix logically follows from the design of canonical correlation calculation, i.e., the maximization of the between-correlation ρ between the linear combinations x^* and y^* of two sets of variables, controlling for the within-correlations in each of the sets. This control of the within-correlations can be seen by the inverse of $\mathbf{R}_{xx}$ and $\mathbf{R}_{yy}$ in the formula of the complex matrix, the eigenstructure of which will be examined.

We have explained the foregoing from the logic of multiple regression analysis.[1] In doing so, we replaced y with the linear combination y^*. We could, of course, have calculated from the other direction, using x^* as a point of departure and building on the regression analysis of x^* on the function of y variables. We would then have found the $\mathbf{R}_{xx}^{-1}\mathbf{R}'_{yx}\mathbf{R}_{yy}^{-1}\mathbf{R}_{yx}$ matrix, in which x and y have changed places. The canonical correlations would have been the same (ρ^2 = the eigenvalues) and the weights would not have been **b** but **a** (eigenvectors).

---

[1] In many textbooks another method is followed. A function is defined:

$$F = \mathbf{a}'\mathbf{R}_{xy}\mathbf{b} - \tfrac{1}{2}\rho_1(\mathbf{a}'\mathbf{R}_{xx}\mathbf{a} - 1) - \tfrac{1}{2}\rho_2(\mathbf{b}'\mathbf{R}_{yy}\mathbf{b} - 1)$$

This function is maximized by equating the partial derivatives with zero. This procedure, known as the Lagrange multiplier method with several shadow conditions ($\mathbf{a}'\mathbf{R}_{xx}\mathbf{a} = 1$ and $\mathbf{b}'\mathbf{R}_{yy}\mathbf{b} = 1$ here), produces the same results but is, in terms of the logic of the technique, less clear.

Apart from the canonical correlations (ρ^2), finding the eigenstructure of the complex matrix $\mathbf{R}_{yy}^{-1}\mathbf{R}_{xy}'\mathbf{R}_{xx}^{-1}\mathbf{R}_{xy}$ only gives us the $\mathbf{b}$ vector of weights of the canonical variable y^*. In order to calculate $\mathbf{a}$, however, one doesn't have to perform the operation all over again in the other direction. For, by expressing the canonical correlation as a simple correlation between $\mathbf{x}^* = \mathbf{xa}$ and $\mathbf{y}^* = \mathbf{yb}$ and by entering this in the formula found for ρ, and provided that $\mathbf{a}'\mathbf{R}_{xx}\mathbf{a} = 1$ and $\mathbf{b}'\mathbf{R}_{yy}\mathbf{b} = 1$ (which means that x^* and y^* must be standardized), it can easily be calculated that:

$$\mathbf{a} = \mathbf{R}_{xx}^{-1}\mathbf{R}_{xy}\mathbf{b}\frac{1}{\rho}$$

We derive this formula from the comparison of two formulas for ρ^2, one from the multiple regression of y^* on the x set and one from the zero-order correlation of x^* and y^*.

Firstly:

$$\rho^2 = \frac{\mathbf{b}'\mathbf{R}_{xy}'\mathbf{R}_{xx}^{-1}\mathbf{R}_{xy}\mathbf{b}}{\mathbf{b}'\mathbf{R}_{yy}\mathbf{b}}$$

$$= \frac{\mathbf{b}'}{(\mathbf{b}'\mathbf{R}_{yy}\mathbf{b})^{1/2}}\mathbf{R}_{xy}'\mathbf{R}_{xx}^{-1}\mathbf{R}_{xy}\frac{\mathbf{b}}{(\mathbf{b}'\mathbf{R}_{yy}\mathbf{b})^{1/2}}$$

$$= \mathbf{b}'\mathbf{R}_{xy}'\mathbf{R}_{xx}^{-1}\mathbf{R}_{xy}\mathbf{b} \text{ with } \mathbf{b} \text{ normalized}$$

Secondly:

$$\rho = \frac{[(\mathbf{xa})'(\mathbf{yb})]/(n-1)}{(\mathbf{a}'\mathbf{R}_{xx}\mathbf{a})^{1/2}(\mathbf{b}'\mathbf{R}_{yy}\mathbf{b})^{1/2}}$$

$$= \frac{\mathbf{a}'}{(\mathbf{a}'\mathbf{R}_{xx}\mathbf{a})^{1/2}}\mathbf{R}_{xy}\frac{\mathbf{b}}{(\mathbf{b}'\mathbf{R}_{yy}\mathbf{b})^{1/2}}$$

$$= \mathbf{a}'\mathbf{R}_{xy}\mathbf{b} \text{ with } \mathbf{a} \text{ and } \mathbf{b} \text{ normalized}$$

Consequently:

$$\mathbf{b}'\mathbf{R}_{xy}'\mathbf{R}_{xx}^{-1}\mathbf{R}_{xy}\mathbf{b} = \rho\mathbf{a}'\mathbf{R}_{xy}\mathbf{b}$$

$$\mathbf{a}' = \frac{1}{\rho}\mathbf{b}'\mathbf{R}_{xy}'\mathbf{R}_{xx}^{-1}$$

$$\mathbf{a} = \mathbf{R}_{xx}^{-1}\mathbf{R}_{xy}\mathbf{b}\frac{1}{\rho}$$

With more than one (two here) canonical correlations, the $\mathbf{a}_i$ vectors are brought together in matrix $\mathbf{A}$:

$$\boxed{\mathbf{A} = \mathbf{R}_{xx}^{-1}\mathbf{R}_{xy}\mathbf{B}\Delta^{-1/2}}$$

It can be verified that $\mathbf{A}'\mathbf{R}_{xx}\mathbf{A} = \mathbf{I}$, which means that each canonical variable x^* is standardized.

10.8   Examination of the Eigenstructure of Russett's Data

Let us now apply the foregoing to our mini data set. Our task is to find the eigenstructure of the matrix $\mathbf{M} = \mathbf{R}_{yy}^{-1}\mathbf{R}_{xy}'\mathbf{R}_{xx}^{-1}\mathbf{R}_{xy}$.

We stated earlier that by means of singular value decomposition (SVD) every matrix, $\mathbf{M}$, can be expressed as the product of three matrices, $\mathbf{M} = \mathbf{P}\Delta\mathbf{U}'$, where Δ is the diagonal matrix of the eigenvalues of $\mathbf{M}$. From the study of the eigenstructure of the correlation matrix $\mathbf{R}$ (in PCA), we know that it holds for (square) symmetrical matrices that $\mathbf{P} = \mathbf{U} = $ the matrix of eigenvectors. The matrix above, $\mathbf{M}$, is square but not symmetrical. In such a case it holds that not $\mathbf{M} = \mathbf{U}\Delta\mathbf{U}'$, but that $\mathbf{M} = \mathbf{U}\Delta\mathbf{U}^{-1}$. In other words, $\mathbf{U}$ is not necessarily orthogonal (because in the case of orthogonality, we have $\mathbf{U}^{-1} = \mathbf{U}'$).

It follows that we can simply examine the eigenstructure of $\mathbf{M}$ in the classical manner, with Lagrange multipliers. Only the SVD result is slightly different than it would be in the case of symmetrical matrices.

The matrix equation is the one that was derived above. Eigenvalues ρ^2 are now represented as λ and eigenvectors as $\mathbf{u}$:

$$(\mathbf{R}_{yy}^{-1}\mathbf{R}_{xy}'\mathbf{R}_{xx}^{-1}\mathbf{R}_{xy} - \lambda\mathbf{I})\mathbf{u} = 0 \quad \text{or} \quad (\mathbf{M} - \lambda\mathbf{I})\mathbf{u} = 0$$

The lambdas are found by the characteristic equation:

$$|\mathbf{R}_{yy}^{-1}\mathbf{R}_{xy}'\mathbf{R}_{xx}^{-1}\mathbf{R}_{xy} - \lambda\mathbf{I}| = 0 \quad \text{or} \quad |\mathbf{M} - \lambda\mathbf{I}| = 0$$

What we need first is the correlation matrix $\mathbf{R}$, which is divided into the submatrices $\mathbf{R}_{xx}$, $\mathbf{R}_{xy}$, and $\mathbf{R}_{yy}$. For the mini data set of $n = 12$ countries, this is the following:

$$\mathbf{R} = \left[\begin{array}{cc|cc} 1.0000 & 0.0027 & 0.4643 & 0.5348 \\ 0.0027 & 1.0000 & -0.1526 & 0.5388 \\ \hline 0.4643 & -0.1526 & 1.0000 & 0.4663 \\ 0.5348 & 0.5388 & 0.4663 & 1.0000 \end{array}\right] = \left[\begin{array}{cc} \mathbf{R}_{xx} & \mathbf{R}_{xy} \\ \mathbf{R}_{xy} & \mathbf{R}_{yy} \end{array}\right]$$

We first calculate $\mathbf{R}_{yy}^{-1}$ and $\mathbf{R}_{xx}^{-1}$:

$$\mathbf{R}_{yy}^{-1} = \begin{bmatrix} 1.000 & 0.466 \\ 0.466 & 1.000 \end{bmatrix}^{-1} = \frac{1}{0.783}\begin{bmatrix} 1.000 & -0.466 \\ -0.466 & 1.000 \end{bmatrix}'$$

$$= \begin{bmatrix} 1.278 & -0.596 \\ -0.596 & 1.278 \end{bmatrix}$$

$$\mathbf{R}_{xx}^{-1} = \begin{bmatrix} 1.000 & 0.003 \\ 0.003 & 1.000 \end{bmatrix}^{-1} = \frac{1}{0.999}\begin{bmatrix} 1.000 & -0.003 \\ -0.003 & 1.000 \end{bmatrix}'$$

$$= \begin{bmatrix} 1.000 & -0.003 \\ -0.003 & 1.000 \end{bmatrix}$$

We now calculate the complex matrix $\mathbf{M} = \mathbf{R}_{yy}^{-1}\mathbf{R}'_{xy}\mathbf{R}_{xx}^{-1}\mathbf{R}_{xy}$:

$$\mathbf{M} = \begin{bmatrix} 1.278 & -0.596 \\ -0.596 & 1.278 \end{bmatrix}\begin{bmatrix} 0.464 & -0.153 \\ 0.535 & 0.539 \end{bmatrix}\begin{bmatrix} 1.000 & -0.003 \\ -0.003 & 1.000 \end{bmatrix}\begin{bmatrix} 0.464 & 0.535 \\ -0.153 & 0.539 \end{bmatrix}$$

$$= \begin{bmatrix} 0.207 & -0.131 \\ 0.069 & 0.636 \end{bmatrix}$$

The characteristic equation is then:

$$|\mathbf{M} - \lambda\mathbf{I}| = \begin{vmatrix} 0.207 - \lambda & -0.131 \\ 0.069 & 0.636 - \lambda \end{vmatrix} = 0$$

$$(0.207 - \lambda)(0.636 - \lambda) - (0.069)(-0.131) = 0$$

$$\lambda^2 - 0.843\lambda + 0.141 = 0$$

$$\lambda_i = \frac{0.843 \pm (0.710 - 0.563)^{1/2}}{2}$$

The two eigenvalues are $\lambda_1 = 0.614$ and $\lambda_2 = 0.229$.

The eigenvectors of $\mathbf{M}$ are found by the matrix equation of: $(\mathbf{M} - \lambda\mathbf{I})\mathbf{u} = \mathbf{0}$.
First we enter $\lambda = 0.614$:

$$\begin{bmatrix} 0.207 - 0.614 & -0.131 \\ 0.069 & 0.636 - 0.614 \end{bmatrix}\begin{bmatrix} u_1 \\ u_2 \end{bmatrix} = \begin{bmatrix} 0 \\ 0 \end{bmatrix}$$

$$(0.207 - 0.614)u_1 - 0.131u_2 = 0$$
$$0.069u_1 + (0.636 - 0.614)u_2 = 0$$

$$-0.407u_1 - 0.131u_2 = 0$$
$$0.069u_1 + 0.022u_2 = 0$$

$$\begin{bmatrix} u_1 \\ u_2 \end{bmatrix} = \begin{bmatrix} -0.131 \\ 0.407 \end{bmatrix} \quad \text{normalized:} \quad \begin{bmatrix} u_1 \\ u_2 \end{bmatrix} = \begin{bmatrix} -0.306 \\ 0.952 \end{bmatrix}$$

We then enter $\lambda = 0.229$ in the matrix equation:

$$\begin{bmatrix} 0.207 - 0.229 & -0.131 \\ 0.069 & 0.636 - 0.229 \end{bmatrix}\begin{bmatrix} u_1 \\ u_2 \end{bmatrix} = \begin{bmatrix} 0 \\ 0 \end{bmatrix}$$

$$(0.207 - 0.229)u_1 - 0.131u_2 = 0$$
$$0.069u_1 + (0.636 - 0.229)u_2 = 0$$

$$-0.022u_1 - 0.131u_2 = 0$$
$$0.069u_1 + 0.407u_2 = 0$$

$$\begin{bmatrix} u_1 \\ u_2 \end{bmatrix} = \begin{bmatrix} 0.131 \\ -0.022 \end{bmatrix} \quad \text{normalized:} \quad \begin{bmatrix} u_1 \\ u_2 \end{bmatrix} = \begin{bmatrix} 0.986 \\ -0.168 \end{bmatrix}$$

We collect the two eigenvectors of $\mathbf{M}$ in a matrix, $\mathbf{U}$:

$$\mathbf{U} = \begin{bmatrix} -0.306 & 0.986 \\ 0.952 & -0.168 \end{bmatrix}$$

The two eigenvalues are brought together in the diagonal matrix Δ:

$$\Delta = \begin{bmatrix} 0.614 & 0 \\ 0 & 0.229 \end{bmatrix}$$

The reader can verify that $\mathbf{U}\Delta\mathbf{U}^{-1} = \mathbf{M}$.

10.9 The A and B Matrices of Canonical Weights

The eigenvalues of $\mathbf{M}$ are the squared canonical correlations. The eigenvectors, however, are not yet the vectors, $\mathbf{b}$, of b coefficients, because the shadow condition that $\mathbf{b}'\mathbf{R}_{yy}\mathbf{b} = 1$ has not been met, i.e., that each canonical variable, y^*, must be standardized. To include this condition, each eigenvector, $\mathbf{u}$ of $\mathbf{M}$ is divided by the corresponding standard deviation, $(\mathbf{u}'\mathbf{R}_{yy}\mathbf{u})^{1/2}$. For the first eigenvector, $\mathbf{u}'\mathbf{R}_{yy}\mathbf{u}$ is equal to:

$$\mathbf{u}_1'\mathbf{R}_{yy}\mathbf{u}_1 = \begin{bmatrix} -0.306 & 0.952 \end{bmatrix}\begin{bmatrix} 1 & 0.466 \\ 0.466 & 1 \end{bmatrix}\begin{bmatrix} -0.306 \\ 0.952 \end{bmatrix} = 0.728$$

so that

$$\mathbf{b}_1 = \frac{1}{(0.728)^{1/2}}\begin{bmatrix} -0.306 \\ 0.952 \end{bmatrix} = \begin{bmatrix} -0.359 \\ 1.116 \end{bmatrix}$$

For the second eigenvector, $\mathbf{u}'\mathbf{R}_{yy}\mathbf{u}$ is equal to:

$$\mathbf{u}_2'\mathbf{R}_{yy}\mathbf{u}_2 = \begin{bmatrix} 0.986 & -0.168 \end{bmatrix}\begin{bmatrix} 1 & 0.466 \\ 0.466 & 1 \end{bmatrix}\begin{bmatrix} 0.986 \\ -0.168 \end{bmatrix} = 0.846$$

Hence

$$\mathbf{b}_2 = \frac{1}{(0.846)^{1/2}}\begin{bmatrix} 0.986 \\ -0.168 \end{bmatrix} = \begin{bmatrix} 1.072 \\ -0.182 \end{bmatrix}$$

We bring the two vectors, $\mathbf{b}_i$, together in a matrix, $\mathbf{B}$, of b coefficients:

$$\mathbf{B} = \begin{bmatrix} -0.359 & 1.072 \\ 1.116 & -0.182 \end{bmatrix}$$

We verify that $\mathbf{B}'\mathbf{R}_{yy}\mathbf{B} = \mathbf{I}$, so that each y^* is standardized.

In order to calculate the $\mathbf{A}$ matrix of a coefficients, we could follow the same time-consuming route we took for $\mathbf{B}$. However, a formula for $\mathbf{A}$ was derived above, making use of the knowledge of $\mathbf{B}$:

$$\mathbf{A} = \mathbf{R}_{xx}^{-1}\mathbf{R}_{xy}\mathbf{B}\Delta^{-1/2}$$

$$\mathbf{A} = \begin{bmatrix} 1 & -0.003 \\ -0.003 & 1 \end{bmatrix}\begin{bmatrix} 0.464 & 0.535 \\ -0.153 & 0.539 \end{bmatrix}\begin{bmatrix} -0.359 & 1.072 \\ 1.116 & -0.182 \end{bmatrix}$$

$$\times \begin{bmatrix} 1/(0.614)^{1/2} & 0 \\ 0 & 1/(0.229)^{1/2} \end{bmatrix}$$

$$= \begin{bmatrix} 0.547 & 0.837 \\ 0.836 & -0.549 \end{bmatrix}$$

We verify that $\mathbf{A'R}_{xx}\mathbf{A} = \mathbf{I}$, which means that each canonical variable x^* is standardized.

10.10   The Canonical Variables x^* and y^*

Now that we have calculated matrices $\mathbf{A}$ and $\mathbf{B}$, the scores of canonical variables x^* and y^* can be determined. We take these from the equations $\mathbf{X}^* = \mathbf{XA}$ and $\mathbf{Y}^* = \mathbf{YB}$. (Note: for one single pair of canonical variables this is a vector notation: $\mathbf{x}^* = \mathbf{xa}$ and $\mathbf{y}^* = \mathbf{yb}$.)

Algebraically, these are the following equations:

$$x_1^* = 0.547x_1 + 0.836x_2$$
$$x_2^* = 0.837x_1 - 0.549x_2$$
$$y_1^* = -0.359y_1 + 1.116y_2$$
$$y_2^* = 1.072y_1 - 0.182y_2$$

Here, x_1^* and y_1^* are the first pair of canonical variables which display the highest canonical correlation ($\sqrt{0.614}$). From the equations we see that the most weight appears to be attributed to variables x_2 and y_2, 0.836 and 1.116, respectively. The first pair of canonical variables, therefore, refers predominantly to the relationship between the percentage of farmers and the level of violence.

The second pair, x_2^* and y_2^*, attributes a large weight to x_1 and y_1. The between-correlation between the GINI index and stability of leadership is represented in particular by this second pair.

From the above equations, the scores of the canonical variables can now be calculated. In order to do this, the values of x_1, x_2, y_1 and y_2 must first be standardized. For example, take the first unit from the data matrix: Yugoslavia. The scores on X_1 and X_2 are 43.7 and 67, in z scores -1.253 and 0.776. By substituting these values in the x_1^* equation, we get the score for Yugoslavia for the first canonical variable from the first set: $0.547(-1.253) + 0.836(0.776) = -0.037$. All of the canonical variable scores for the 12 individual countries can be calculated in the same way. To illustrate this procedure, we first give the data matrix in the form of z scores (Table 10.3). From this, the matrix of scores of canonical variables can be derived (Table 10.4).

In the next step, the correlations between the canonical variables and the original variables can be examined. These are sometimes called **structure correlations**. They can offer the possibility for a better interpretation of the canonical variables. In Table 10.5 we see the matrix for all the correlations between the four variables and the two pairs of canonical variables. The quadrant above and to the left is the original correlation matrix. The quadrant below and to the right contains the correlations between the canonical variables. There we find the canonical correlations ($\sqrt{0.614} = 0.783$ and $\sqrt{0.229} = 0.479$). We can also see that the second pair is indeed uncorrelated with the first pair. The quadrant below and to the left (or above and to the right) contains the structure correlations. We can see that the first pair of canonical variables displays the highest correlation with x_2 (% of farmers) and y_2 (level of violence), while the second pair is predominantly linked to x_1 (GINI index)

Table 10.3   *z* scores

z_{x1}	z_{x2}	z_{y1}	z_{y2}
−1.253	0.776	−1.660	−0.567
−1.185	0.326	−0.299	−0.543
−1.079	−0.439	0.854	−0.567
−0.806	0.956	−1.180	−0.500
−0.585	0.416	0.582	0.823
−0.517	−1.653	−0.299	−0.567
0.513	−1.518	0.390	−0.567
0.550	0.011	−1.660	−0.566
0.671	−0.934	0.822	−0.566
1.081	1.406	0.934	1.070
1.228	−0.349	0.726	−0.039
1.381	1.001	0.790	2.589

Table 10.4   Canonical variables

x_1^*	x_2^*	y_1^*	y_2^*
−0.04	−1.47	−0.04	−1.68
−0.38	−1.17	−0.50	−0.22
−0.96	−0.66	−0.94	1.02
0.36	−1.20	−0.14	−1.17
0.03	−0.72	0.71	0.47
−1.67	0.48	−0.53	−0.22
−0.99	1.26	−0.77	0.52
0.31	0.45	−0.04	−1.68
−0.41	1.07	−0.93	0.98
1.77	0.13	0.86	0.81
0.38	1.22	−0.30	0.79
1.59	0.61	2.61	0.38

Table 10.5   All correlations

	x_1	x_2	y_1	y_2	x_1^*	x_2^*	y_1^*	y_2^*
x_1	1.000	0.003	0.464	0.535	0.549	0.836	0.430	0.400
x_2	0.003	1.000	−0.153	0.539	0.837	−0.547	0.656	−0.262
y_1	0.464	−0.153	1.000	0.466	0.126	0.473	0.161	0.987
y_2	0.535	0.539	0.466	1.000	0.743	0.152	0.948	0.318
x_1^*	0.549	0.837	0.126	0.743	1.000	0.000	0.783	0.000
x_2^*	0.836	−0.547	0.473	0.152	0.000	1.000	0.000	0.479
y_1^*	0.430	0.656	0.161	0.948	0.783	0.000	1.000	0.000
y_2^*	0.400	−0.262	0.987	0.318	0.000	0.479	0.000	1.000

and y_1 (stability of leadership). We had already derived this from the matrices of standardized canonical weights (**A** and **B**).

10.11   A Causal Approach to Canonical Correlation Analysis

In 1968, Stewart and Love developed an asymmetrical version of canonical correlation analysis. The canonical correlations calculated above are, after all, symmetrical coefficients. For example, the eigenvalue $\lambda_1 = 0.614$, which represents the squared correlation between the first pair of canonical variables, can be interpreted as the proportion of variance in the y set (political characteristics) that is explained by the x set (economic characteristics). One could, however, just as easily reason the other way round: λ_1 is also the proportion of variance in economic inequality that is explained by political instability. In other words, no distinction is made between independent and dependent variables, between cause and effect. For this reason Stewart and Love proposed an '**index of redundancy**'. This index measures to what degree the y set can be reconstructed on the basis of the knowledge of the x set. It appears that this index is equal to the arithmetic mean of all multiple determination coefficients that are obtained by multiple regression analyses with one y variable repeatedly on the function of the entire x set.

10.12 The Significance Tests

In order to test whether the canonical correlations are significant, we make use of Wilks's lambda (Λ), a measure, just like Student's t, Hotelling's T and Fisher's F, that confronts the ratio of the between-dispersion and the within-dispersion from the sample in this ratio under the null hypothesis. Wilks's Λ is the multivariate analogous of this ratio in its most general form, so that t, T and F are special cases of Λ. This measure is therefore used for more complex multivariate analysis techniques, like multiple discriminant analysis, multivariate analysis of variance and covariance (see below) and canonical correlation analysis.

In canonical correlation analysis, Wilks's Λ can be calculated as the product of error variances, where the error variances are determined by the eigenvalues (i.e., the squared canonical correlations, therefore the proportions of explained variance) subtracted from 1. In our example:

$$\Lambda = \prod_{i=1}^{2}(1 - \lambda_i) = (1 - 0.614)(1 - 0.229) = 0.298$$

Bartlett constructed a V measure that is distributed as chi square with pq degrees of freedom, where p and q represent the number of variables of the x set and the y set:

$$V = -[n - 1 - (p + q + 1)/2]\ln \Lambda$$
$$= -[12 - 1 - (2 + 2 + 1)/2]\ln 0.298$$
$$= 10.29$$

For $pq = 4$ degrees of freedom, this value is slightly greater than the critical χ^2-value $= 9.488$ that is found under the null hypothesis for a significance level of $\alpha = 0.05$. Therefore, there is a significant association between the economic inequality and the political instability of countries. De Tocqueville and Russett's hypothesis is empirically supported.

The V measure can also be split additively, so that a separate test can be performed as to whether the significant correlation between the economic and political characteristics also holds for the second canonical correlation (that was predominantly linked to the GINI index and stability of leadership). For this purpose the first canonical correlation is left out in Wilks's lambda, so that in this mini example only $(1 - \lambda_2)$ remains:

$$V_2 = -[12 - 1 - (2 + 2 + 1)/2] \ln(1 - 0.229) = 2.21$$

For $(p - 1)(q - 1) = 1$ degree of freedom, this value is not significant. In our mini example, where we are punished by the small numbers, the second canonical correlation does not appear to be significant.

This can also be seen by reviewing the separate multiple regression analyses where one y variable is repeatedly analysed on the function of the entire x set. From this it appears that only y_2 (level of violence) is significantly associated with the economic characteristics, while this is not the case for y_1 (stability of leadership). It is therefore the predominantly political variable y_1 that disrupts an ideal canonical structure, as it is not significantly associated with each of the economic variables (between-association is too weak) and is rather strongly associated with the other political variable (within-association is too strong).

10.13 SPSS for Windows Output of Canonical Correlation Analysis

When trying to get the computer output for canonical correlation analysis in SPSS, a problem arises. SPSS used to have separate software for canonical correlation analysis, under the name of 'CANCORR'. With the switch to SPSSX in 1986 'CANCORR' was simply removed and today's user is told that (s)he can perform canonical correlation analysis with the subprogram 'MANOVA' (multivariate analysis of variance and covariance). MANOVA is equipped for several dependent variables of interval measurement level as well as factors of lower measurement level and covariates of interval measurement level. By not requesting factors, but only dependent variables and covariates, one finds oneself in the 'CANCORR' design. All this will become clearer to the reader after the treatment of MANOVA in the following chapter. We apologize for any confusion caused by the regretful decision of the SPSS designers to eliminate a good 'CANCORR' program in the old SPSS, with elegant and compact output. In the interest of maintaining unity with the other chapters, we have, none the less, decided to work with SPSS and not with other programs such as SAS or BMDP.

Choosing or creating a data file
How to open an SPSS session and how to choose or create and save a data file is shown in Chapter 4.

Running the statistical procedure
Click on Statistics. Click on ANOVA Models. Click on Multivariate. This opens the dialog box of multivariate analysis of variance. To perform a canonical correlation analysis, you will select no factors, but only dependent variables and covariates. Click on Y_1 and Y_2 in the Source Variable list and click on the ▶ push button of Dependent Variables. Click on X_1 and X_2 in the Source Variable list and click on the ▶ push button of Covariates.

Click on Model. Select Discriminant Analysis: this will result in a canonical correlation analysis. Select Eigenvalues. Don't worry about interactions: they are not calculated when no factors are selected (unless, of course, you define products of covariates with the compute facility). Click on Continue to return to the main dialog box. Click on OK. SPSS now runs the statistical procedure and an output window appears with the results of canonical correlation analysis.

Do not forget to save the output: click on File, click on Save as, type the file name with extension *.lst* and click on OK.

As you already know, the computer output can also be obtained by opening a syntax window and typing SPSS commands. Click on File, click on New, click on SPSS Syntax, type the statements, put the cursor anywhere in the first command line and click on ▶ of the icon bar (or click on Run if you still work with the SPSS for Windows 5.0 version).

The statements are as follows:

```
1     MANOVA Y1 Y2 WITH X1 X2
2     /DISCRIM STANDARD CORRELATIONS ALPHA (1)
3     /PRINT SIGNIF (EIGEN)
4     /DESIGN.
```

The expression 'MANOVA' in statement 1 requests a multivariate analysis of variance. The dependent variables are y_1 and y_2. The absence of the word 'BY' indicates that there are no factors with lower measurement level present. The word 'WITH' indicates that the covariates with an interval measurement level will follow; these are x_1 and x_2.

In statement 2, a canonical correlation analysis is requested with 'DISCRIM'. 'STANDARD' means that we would like to have the standardized canonical weights. With 'CORRELATIONS' we request the correlations between the original variables and the canonical variables; these are the structure correlations. With 'ALPHA' we establish the significance level of the canonical variables. The default for this is 0.15. By setting the maximum at 1 ('ALPHA (1)'), we can be certain that all of the canonical variables, even the insignificant ones, will be included in the analysis.

'PRINT = SIGNIF (EIGEN)' in statement 3 requests the eigenvalues (squared canonical correlations). This statement isn't really necessary since the default setting includes the printing of eigenvalues.

The problem with MANOVA is that the default setting results in a gigantic amount of output, superfluous for our purposes here as there is no need in a canonical correlation analysis for information within and between cells, because there are no cells (cfr. absence of factors). We have omitted this output below. And we must ask the reader to please ignore anything pertaining to 'cells' or 'analysis of variance designs'. The output is as follows:

```
* * ANALYSIS  OF  VARIANCE -- DESIGN   1 * *

EFFECT .. WITHIN CELLS Regression
Multivariate Tests of Significance (S = 2, M = -1/2, N = 3 )
```

```
Test Name        Value  Approx. F Hypoth. DF  Error DF Sig. of F

Pillais          .84278   3.27723     4.00      18.00    .035
Hotellings      1.88474   3.29829     4.00      14.00    .042
Wilks            .29789   3.32878     4.00      16.00    .036
Roys             .61349
```

Eigenvalues and Canonical Correlations

```
Root No.   Eigenvalue      Pct.   Cum. Pct.  Canon Cor.   Sq. Cor

    1        1.587       84.215     84.215       .783       .613
    2         .298       15.785    100.000       .479       .229
```

* * ANALYSIS OF VARIANCE -- DESIGN   1 * *

EFFECT .. WITHIN CELLS Regression (CONT.)
Univariate F-tests with (2,9) D. F.

```
Variable   Sq. Mul. R    Mul. R Adj. R-sq.  Hypoth. MS     Error MS

Y1           .23929      .48917   .07024     51.32790    36.26121
Y2           .57477      .75814   .48027 139502.6540 22935.17716
```

```
Variable        F  Sig. of F

Y1         1.41550     .292
Y2         6.08248     .021
```

* * ANALYSIS OF VARIANCE -- DESIGN   1 * *

Standardized canonical coefficients for DEPENDENT variables
        Function No.

```
Variable         1        2

Y1            -.359    1.072
Y2            1.116    -.182
```

Correlations between DEPENDENT and canonical variables
        Function No.

```
Variable         1        2

Y1             .161     .987
Y2             .948     .317
```

```
* * ANALYSIS  OF  VARIANCE -- DESIGN   1 * *

Variance explained by canonical variables of DEPENDENT variables

CAN. VAR.  Pct Var DE Cum Pct DE Pct Var CO Cum Pct CO

       1       46.262      46.262      28.381      28.381
       2       53.738     100.000      12.321      40.703


Standardized canonical coefficients for COVARIATES
                    CAN. VAR.

COVARIATE            1          2

X1                 .547       .837
X2                 .836      -.549


* * ANALYSIS  OF  VARIANCE -- DESIGN   1 * *

Correlations between COVARIATES and canonical variables
                    CAN. VAR.

Covariate            1          2

X1                 .549       .836
X2                 .837      -.547


Variance explained by canonical variables of the COVARIATES

CAN. VAR.  Pct Var DE Cum Pct DE Pct Var CO Cum Pct CO

       1       30.749      30.749      50.122      50.122
       2       11.436      42.186      49.878     100.000

* * ANALYSIS  OF  VARIANCE -- DESIGN   1 * *

Regression analysis for WITHIN CELLS error term  (CONT.)
Dependent variable .. Y1              stability of leadership

COVARIATE          B        Beta    Std. Err.    t-Value   Sig. of t

X1               .15259    .46476      .095       1.599       .144
X2              -.04322   -.15384      .082       -.529       .610

COVARIATE   Lower -95%  CL- Upper

X1               -.063      .369
X2               -.228      .142
```

```
* * ANALYSIS  OF  VARIANCE -- DESIGN   1 * *

Regression analysis for WITHIN CELLS error term  (CONT.)
Dependent variable .. Y2                 violence

COVARIATE            B        Beta    Std. Err.    t-Value    Sig. of t

X1              5.89064     .53339     2.401       2.454        .037
X2              5.07855     .53734     2.054       2.472        .035


COVARIATE    Lower -95%  CL- Upper

X1                 .460     11.321
X2                 .431      9.726
```

11

Techniques with Multiple Dependent Variables

In this last chapter, two techniques of analysis with multiple dependent variables are treated. Multivariate analysis of variance (MANOVA) is an extension of the ANOVA design, as not only one, but multiple dependent variables measured at the interval level are involved. Analysis of covariance (ANCOVA) is changed in the same way to multivariate analysis of covariance (MANCOVA).

Our research example is the problem from Raoul Naroll's *The Moral Order* (1982), in which he asks: where is the best place on earth to live?

A second analysis technique, multiple discriminant analysis (MDA), is an extension of two-group discriminant analysis, because, instead of two, multiple groups are analysed. With dummy coding, this comes down to the entry of more than one dummy dependent variable.

Our research example is the study by Kenneth L. Wilson (1980), in which a triple labour market model is recommended after an analysis of immigrant enclaves of Cubans in Miami.

To end, we illustrate again how classical techniques of multivariate analysis form one family. The dummy dependent variables of multiple discriminant analysis are considered as a set of dependent variables. The independent (discriminating) variables are also considered as a set and a canonical correlation analysis will be performed between the two sets. The results appear to be identical to those from the multiple discriminant analysis. We could have bridged multivariate variance analysis with canonical correlation analysis in the same way. And this is precisely why canonical correlation analysis has been omitted from the SPSS/PC computer program and placed under MANOVA.

11.1 Multivariate Analysis of Variance: Where is the Best Place on Earth to Live?

11.1.1 The Research Problem and the Causal Diagram

In his book *The Moral Order* (1982), Raoul Naroll collects statistical data about mental illness, alcoholism, divorce, suicide, child abuse, homicide and other problems for a large number of countries in the world. He comes to the conclusion that these problems can be decreased by strict 'moralnets'. By 'moralnet' he means a primary group which functions as a normative reference group. One of the typical 'moralnets' is the extended family. According to Naroll, the moralnet theory dates back to Moses and Confucius, but neither Moses nor Confucius could have realized that so much evidence was available to support the theory.

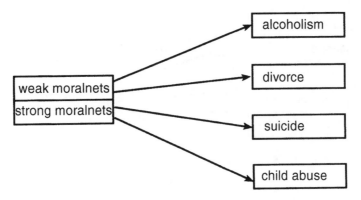

Figure 11.1   Multivariate analysis of variance diagram

The research problem presented here has the following structure. The units of analysis are countries. There are many dependent variables measured at the interval level (alcohol use, divorce rate, etc.) and there is one dichotomous independent variable (strong versus weak moralnets). The diagram is shown in Figure 11.1.

If we took just one dependent variable, suicide, for example, we would then have a simple one-way ANOVA design. And, since the independent variable is a dichotomy, the *F* test is reduced to a simple *t* test of the difference between two means (see Chapter 4) as shown in Figure 11.2.

Because more dependent variables are included in Naroll's moralnet theory than merely suicide, we speak of a *MANOVA* instead of an ANOVA. The *M* stands for *M*ultiple dependent variables measured at the interval level.

From the moment another nominal or ordinal independent variable is introduced (in addition to the independent variable already present), we have, just as with an ANOVA, the transition from a one-way to a two-way design. An example of such a variable is homogeneity. According to Naroll, countries are homogeneous if there are no great differences in religion, race and language, and heterogeneous if the opposite is the case. Belgium and the Netherlands are heterogeneous nations, the former because of linguistic diversity, the latter because of religious diversity. Denmark, Norway and Sweden are examples of homogeneous nations.

Assuming that not only weak moralnets, but heterogeneity, too, offers an explanation for the social problems presented, we have a two-way design with two independent variables. In addition to the effects of moralnets and homogeneity, such a design can also show possible effects of interaction. We therefore have a two-way 2 × 2 MANOVA design: 'two-way' because there are two independent variables and '2 × 2' because they are dichotomies. Restricting ourselves to two of the many

Figure 11.2   Structure of a one-way ANOVA design

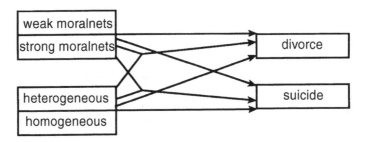

Figure 11.3   Structure of a two-way MANOVA design

dependent variables, the divorce rate and the suicide rate, the structure of this two-way MANOVA design is as represented in Figure 11.3.

It will be clear that the model can become more complex in many ways. Firstly, the independent variables do not have to be dichotomies. The strength of the moralnets could, for example, be measured as the strength of the ties within the extended family (which functions as the normative reference group), i.e., as family strength. More than two categories could be provided for this, for example weak, medium and strong, so that a trichotomy is brought about. In the case of such polytomies, multiple dummies are needed (one dummy less than the number of categories), making the analysis much more complex. Secondly, when there are multiple dependent variables, which are mutually correlated, the analysis does not only contain the variations and variances of these variables, but the two-by-two covariations and covariances as well. Thirdly, with more than two independent variables, one will have to consider higher-order interactions as well as second-order interactions. These do not only demand more complex calculation, but are generally difficult to interpret theoretically. Simply trying to express them causes problems. Fourthly, if some independent variables are measured at the interval level, we then have a multivariate analogue of ANCOVA, i.e., multivariate analysis of covariance (MANCOVA), a design that is more complicated than MANOVA.

11.1.2   The Data Matrix

The principles of MANOVA will now be illustrated by means of a model with two dependent variables of interval measurement level, the divorce rate (Y_1) and the suicide rate (Y_2), and two independent variables, family strength (A) with three categories 1, 2 and 3 (3 = strong) and homogeneity (B) with two categories 1 and 2 (2 = homogenous). The cross-table, in which the values for the dependent variables are contained in the cells (no frequencies!), is shown in Table 11.1. The corresponding data matrix is shown in Table 11.2.

11.1.3   Objectives of the Technique

In order to explain which questions the researcher asks in MANOVA, we go back to analysis of variance with one dependent variable, which, in our example, is the divorce rate. In a two-way ANOVA design we would ask:

Table 11.1   Values for dependent variables

B	1			2		
A → ↓		Y_1	Y_2		Y_1	Y_2
1	Czechoslovakia	21	239	Sweden	31	215
	Finland	18	219	Austria	13	219
2	Great Britain	20	098	Norway	12	081
	Switzerland	12	173	Poland	12	112
3	Netherlands	13	063	Italy	03	055
	Belgium	11	155	Ireland	03	025

Table 11.2   Data matrix

A	B	Y_1	Y_2
1	1	21	239
1	1	18	219
1	2	31	215
1	2	13	219
2	1	20	098
2	1	12	173
2	2	12	081
2	2	12	112
3	1	13	063
3	1	11	155
3	2	03	055
3	2	03	025

1. Is there a significant difference between the **mean** divorce rates of countries with weak, medium and strong family strength? (effect of *A*)
2. Is there a significant difference between the **mean** divorce rates of homogenous and heterogeneous countries? (effect of *B*)
3. Is there a significant effect of interaction, i.e., is the effect of family strength on the divorce rate different in homogenous and heterogeneous countries? Or, which comes down to the same thing, is the effect of homogeneity different in nations with weak, medium and strong family strength? (effect of *A* × *B*)

In MANOVA we alter these three questions in the following way. The dependent variable divorce is now replaced by two (or more) dependent variables, divorce and suicide. Therefore the adjective '**mean**' is replaced by '**centroid**'; this is the vector of multiple means.

11.1.4   *Student's t, Fisher's F, Hotelling's T and Wilks's* Λ

In order to answer these MANOVA questions, the *F* test from ANOVA is replaced by Wilks's lambda test. To explain what Wilks's lambda (Λ) entails, let us think back to Student's *t*, Fisher's *F* and Hotelling's T^2 (or Mahalanobis' D^2).

variables

		one	multiple
groups	two	Student's t	Hotelling's T^2
	multiple	Fisher's F	Wilks's lambda

Figure 11.4   Tests in multivariate analysis

For one variable and two groups we used t. The example in Chapter 4 (Experimental Design) was the financial concession in the humour group and the no-humour group.

For one variable and multiple groups we used F. The example in Chapter 7 (Analysis of Variance) was the intrinsic motivation in the three groups of task interest.

For multiple variables and two groups we used T^2 (or D^2). The example in Chapter 8 (Two-Group Discriminant Analysis) was the financial situation and the level of services in the group of poor and rich neighbourhoods.

For multiple variables and multiple groups we use Λ. Consequently, t, T and F are special cases of Λ. (We encountered Wilks's lambda earlier, in the discussion of canonical correlation analysis. The reader will note that there are other uses for this test.) The above is summarized in Figure 11.4 (see also Figure 8.4).

11.1.5 Preparatory Calculations: the Matrices W, B and T

In MANOVA Λ is used to check whether the centroids (vectors of means of dependent variables) of the various groups (formed by the categories of independent variables) differ significantly. Here, too, we are looking for the greatest possible (between-)dispersion between the groups. We shall therefore, just as with other techniques of analysis, have to calculate the matrices **W**, **B** and **T**, i.e., the within-groups, between-groups and total matrices of variations and covariations. These are sometimes called SSCP matrices (Sum of Squares and Cross Products matrices). Let us, true to tradition, begin with matrix **W**.

Our example of the moralnet theory with variables A (family strength), B (homogeneity), Y_1 (divorce) and Y_2 (suicide), is a 3×2 design with six cells, A_1B_1, A_1B_2, A_2B_1, A_2B_2, A_3B_1 and A_3B_2. Each cell contains values for two dependent variables, Y_1 and Y_2. The number of observations in this mini example is of course much too small (only two countries in each cell), so the reader must imagine that we are dealing with larger numbers.

In order to obtain **W** we calculate the mean and the dispersion (variation) in each cell and for each dependent variable.

For example, in cell A_1B_1: $\bar{Y}_1 = (21 + 18)/2 = 19.5$ and

$$\sum (Y_1 - \bar{Y}_1)^2 = (21 - 19.5)^2 + (18 - 19.5)^2 = 4.5$$

In the same cell, the mean and the dispersion of Y_2 is 229 and 200, respectively. But there is more. Because there is more than one dependent variable, the possibility exists that these are mutually associated. As stated above, this makes MANOVA more complex than ANOVA and it is extremely important that this association be taken into account. This means that the covariation between Y_1 and Y_2 must also be calculated in each cell. For cell A_1B_1 this is:

$$\sum(Y_1 - \bar{Y}_1)(Y_2 - \bar{Y}_2) = (21 - 19.5)(239 - 229) + (18 - 19.5)(219 - 229) = 30$$

In summary: we can calculate two means for each cell, one for Y_1 and one for Y_2, which together form a centroid or vector of means; and for each cell we can also calculate two variations and one covariation, collected in a cell-SSCP matrix with the variations on the principal diagonal. For the first cell, A_1B_1, the results calculated above are shown in Table 11.3. If we perform these operations for each cell,

Table 11.3

cell A_1B_1	$(19.5 \quad 229)$	centroid
	$\begin{bmatrix} 4.5 & 30 \\ 30 & 200 \end{bmatrix}$	SSCP matrix

Table 11.4

	B_1	B_2
A_1	$(19.5 \quad 229)$ $\begin{bmatrix} 4.5 & 30 \\ 30 & 200 \end{bmatrix}$	$(22 \quad 217)$ $\begin{bmatrix} 162 & -36 \\ -36 & 8 \end{bmatrix}$
A_2	$(16 \quad 135.5)$ $\begin{bmatrix} 32 & -300 \\ -300 & 2812.5 \end{bmatrix}$	$(12 \quad 96.5)$ $\begin{bmatrix} 0 & 0 \\ 0 & 480.5 \end{bmatrix}$
A_3	$(12 \quad 109)$ $\begin{bmatrix} 2 & -92 \\ -92 & 4232 \end{bmatrix}$	$(03 \quad 40)$ $\begin{bmatrix} 0 & 0 \\ 0 & 450 \end{bmatrix}$

Table 11.4 results, which sets us up for the calculation of **W**. Matrix **W** of within-variations and covariations is simply calculated as the sum of all six cell matrices from Table 11.4:

$$\mathbf{W} = \begin{bmatrix} 200.5 & -398 \\ -398 & 8183 \end{bmatrix}$$

Let us go now to the calculation of matrix **B**. This one is different for each of the three questions that must be answered in MANOVA (effect of A, effect of B and the interaction effect). Let us illustrate question 1, the effect of factor A. According to the null hypothesis, there is no centroid difference between countries with weak, medium and strong family ties. Taking the cross-table with the original data as a starting point, we can calculate the means and collect these per row in a row centroid as shown in Table 11.5.

Table 11.5

		Y scores				$\bar{Y}$	row centroid
A_1	Y_1	21	18	31	13	20.75	(20.75 223)
	Y_2	239	219	215	219	223.00	
A_2	Y_1	20	12	12	12	14.00	(14 116)
	Y_2	098	173	081	112	116.00	
A_3	Y_1	13	11	03	03	7.50	(7.50 74.50)
	Y_2	063	155	055	025	74.50	

In order to calculate the between-variations and covariations, these three row centroids are situated around the total-sample centroid. This is (14.08   137.83) and is obtained by calculating the grand mean of Y_1 and Y_2 for all 12 countries.

The calculations are simple because there are only three row centroids. We will have to multiply by a factor of 4, because, as we know from sample theory, the dispersion of means of groups of four values is four times too small (variances $\sigma^2/4$ against σ^2!).

The between-variation of Y_1 is:

$$4[(20.75 - 14.08)^2 + (14 - 14.08)^2 + (7.50 - 14.08)^2] = 351.17$$

The between-variation of Y_2 is:

$$4[(223 - 137.83)^2 + (116 - 137.83)^2 + (74.50 - 137.83)^2] = 46\,964.67$$

The between-covariation of Y_1 and Y_2 is:

$$4[(20.75 - 14.08)(223 - 137.83) + (14 - 14.08)(116 - 137.83)$$
$$+ (7.50 - 14.08)(74.50 - 137.83)] = 3946.17$$

These results are collected in matrix **B** of between-variations and -covariations:

$$\mathbf{B} = \begin{bmatrix} 351.17 & 3946.17 \\ 3946.17 & 46\,964.67 \end{bmatrix}$$

The reader can verify that $\mathbf{T} = \mathbf{W} + \mathbf{B}$.

11.1.6   Wilks's Lambda Test

Wilks's Λ is calculated as the ratio of two determinants:

$$\Lambda = |\mathbf{W}|/|\mathbf{T}|$$

Considering the fact that $\mathbf{T} = \mathbf{W} + \mathbf{B}$ this ratio can also be rewritten as follows:

$$\Lambda = |\mathbf{W}|/|\mathbf{W} + \mathbf{B}|$$

Rewriting **T** as **W** + **B** is important, because matrix **B** will be different for each of the three questions answered (effect of A, B and $A \times B$). Matrix **W**, however, will remain the same. The preparatory calculations for question 1, the effect of family strength, were performed above, therefore:

$$\Lambda = \frac{|\mathbf{W}|}{|\mathbf{W} + \mathbf{B}|} = \frac{\begin{bmatrix} 200.5 & -398 \\ -398 & 8183 \end{bmatrix}}{\begin{bmatrix} 551.67 & 3548.17 \\ 3548.17 & 55\,147.67 \end{bmatrix}} = 0.083$$

Note that in this ratio (in contrast to the F ratio), the 'withins' are in the numerator and the 'betweens' in the denominator, and therefore a smaller Λ will indicate a greater centroid difference. A ratio of $\Lambda = 1$ means of course that the null hypothesis is not rejected because, in that case, $\mathbf{B}$ in the denominator adds nothing to $\mathbf{W}$.

To test the significance of Λ, we follow Bartlett. He showed that the following statistic, denoted by V, is χ^2 distributed with pd_B degrees of freedom:

$$V = -[d_W + d_B - (p + d_B + 1)/2]\ln \Lambda$$

Here p = the number of dependent variables and d_B = one less than the number of centroids compared, i.e., the number of between-degrees of freedom. The value d_W indicates the number of within-degrees of freedom. In each cell we have calculated with two observations. So there are $(2 - 1)$ degrees of freedom per cell. There are six cells. Consequently $d_W = 6(2 - 1) = 6$.

Bartlett's V can now be derived:

$$V = -[6 + 2 - (2 + 2 + 1)/2]\ln(0.083) = 13.68$$

For $pd_B = (2)(2) = 4$ degrees of freedom, this value is greater than the critical χ^2 value (9.49) that was found under the null hypothesis for $\alpha = 0.05$. There is, therefore, a significant difference between the mean divorce and suicide rates (considered together and in mutual association) in countries with various degrees of family strength. The null hypothesis that the centroids are equal or that they differ solely by chance is refuted.

We can answer questions (2) and (3) analogously. Matrix $\mathbf{W}$ remains the same. For matrix $\mathbf{B}$, column centroids (situated around the total-sample centroid) are used for question (2), and for question (3) we use the differences between cell centroids and the corresponding row centroid (situated around the differences between the corresponding column centroids and the total-sample centroid). The results are shown in Table 11.6.

The positive answer to question (1) gives support to Naroll's moralnet theory in terms of family strength. The other two effects (of B and $A \times B$) are, however, not significant. The difference between the centroids of homogenous and heterogeneous countries is not more than one of chance. There is also no significant interaction effect: the centroid difference between countries with divergent family ties is not

Table 11.6

	Λ	V	$\chi^2_{critical}$	$df\ (pd_B)$
Question 1 (effect of A)	0.08	13.68	9.49	4
Question 2 (effect of B)	0.48	3.66	5.99	2
Question 3 (effect of $A \times B$)	0.57	3.09	9.49	4

significantly different in homogenous and heterogeneous countries. In other words, the combination of homogeneity and family strength offers no additional explanation for divorce and suicide.

11.1.7   *Alternatives for Wilks's lambda Test: Multivariate Analysis of Variance as the Reverse of Discriminant Analysis*

In addition to the tests described above on the basis of Wilks's Λ and Bartlett's V, other test criteria have been developed by various authors. All of these criteria are operations on the eigenvalues from an eigenstructure analysis of the matrix $\mathbf{W}^{-1}\mathbf{B}$. Let us first discuss this approach seperately, i.e., the calculation of MANOVA according to the principles of discriminant analysis.

If we remember from Chapter 8, in the 1930s Fisher saw discriminant analysis as the reverse of analysis of variance, since in discriminant analysis the independent variables are measured at the interval level and the dependent variable is measured at a lower level. In analysis of variance this is reversed. If we take our example from the moralnet theory and limit ourselves, as above, to the effect of family strength (A), then the one-way MANOVA design would look as shown in Figure 11.5.

Reversing the arrows would result in a discriminant analysis, with Y_1 and Y_2 as discriminating variables and with the three categories of A as groups. Such a discriminant analysis would be performed by examining the eigenstructure of matrix $\mathbf{W}^{-1}\mathbf{B}$, with the objective of maximizing the ratio of the dispersion between the groups and the dispersion within the groups (see Chapter 8 and the second part of this chapter). This is exactly the same objective as in analysis of variance. In terms of the calculations, it makes no difference whether the arrows of the model go in one direction or the other.

Matrices $\mathbf{W}$ and $\mathbf{B}$ were worked out above for the effect of family strength (A). The product $\mathbf{W}^{-1}\mathbf{B}$ is the following:

$$\mathbf{W}^{-1}\mathbf{B} = \begin{bmatrix} 200.5 & -398 \\ -398 & 8183 \end{bmatrix}^{-1} \begin{bmatrix} 351.17 & 3946.17 \\ 3946.17 & 46\,964.67 \end{bmatrix} = \begin{bmatrix} 2.998 & 34.395 \\ 0.628 & 7.414 \end{bmatrix}$$

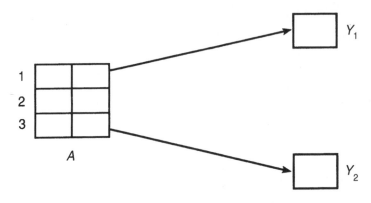

Figure 11.5   One-way MANOVA design

The eigenvalues are the roots of the characteristic equation:

$$|\mathbf{W}^{-1}\mathbf{B} - \lambda\mathbf{I}| = 0$$

$$\begin{vmatrix} 2.998 - \lambda & 34.395 \\ 0.628 & 7.414 - \lambda \end{vmatrix} = 0$$

$$(2.998 - \lambda)(7.414 - \lambda) - (0.628)(34.395) = 0$$

$$\lambda^2 - 10.412\lambda - 0.621 = 0$$

With $g = 3$ groups and $p = 2$ variables, a number of $\min(g - 1, p) = 2$ discriminant functions can be calculated. Consequently two eigenvalues can be found, which are obtained by solving the above quadratic equation: $\lambda_1 = 10.35$ and $\lambda_2 = 0.06$.

On the basis of these eigenvalues, various authors have formulated propositions for testing the null hypothesis that the centroids of countries with different family ties are either equal or differ solely by chance.

The first author, Wilks, was discussed above. His Λ measure was calculated as the ratio $|\mathbf{W}|/|\mathbf{W} + \mathbf{B}|$ and the measure derived from this, Bartlett's V, was distributed as χ^2. Wilks's Λ, however, is also a function of the eigenvalues of $\mathbf{W}^{-1}\mathbf{B}$, i.e., the product of $1/(1 + \lambda_i)$. In our example with two eigenvalues: $\Lambda = [1/(1 + 10.35)][1/(1 + 0.06)] = 0.083$, the same result as above! It is also worth mentioning that, in addition to Bartlett, Rao developed a measure based on Λ which also follows an F distribution. This has been entered in the SPSS computer output. Hotelling takes the sum of the eigenvalues of λ_i as a criterion, which is equal to the sum of values on the principal diagonal of $\mathbf{W}^{-1}\mathbf{B}$. Pillai considers the sum of $\lambda_i/(1 + \lambda_i)$. From the ratio $\lambda_i/(1 + \lambda_i)$, Roy selects that for which λ_i is the greatest.

All these criteria, by Wilks, Hotelling, Pillai and Roy, can be transformed into a measure which follows the F-distribution. The results can be found in the standard MANOVA output of the SPSS computer program.

11.1.8   Multivariate Analysis of Variance, an Entire World

What was explained above is merely the core of MANOVA. One could safely say that the possibilities for further analysis form an entire world of their own. In addition to testing the separate effects, estimations can be made of each of the effects, with the associated confidence intervals. Special contrasts can be treated. Analyses of residuals can be performed by means of plots. (Compare multiple regression analysis.) Every possible design can be tried out by specifying the effects subject to an analysis. Stepdown analyses are possible by entering the dependent variables one by one.

There are also possibilities for special designs, with repeated measurements, with incomplete measurements, with grouped measurements (block design), with hierarchical ordering (nested design) and others.

Non-orthogonal designs can also be dealt with. In our example the number of observations was the same in each cell. In that case, independent variables A and B are uncorrelated, as one obtains a cross-table with equal frequencies in the cells. Our design, in other words, was orthogonal. In the case of unequal numbers of observations in the cells, one speaks of non-orthogonal designs. These can be treated by entering properly determined contrasts in what is called a design matrix.

11.1.9 Assumptions

We conclude with two recommendations: the use of plots for the analysis of residuals and Box's M test for the control of the homogeneity assumption.

Firstly, just as in regression analysis, in MANOVA one starts from the assumption that the residuals are randomly distributed. In the absence of a significant interaction effect, the interaction term can be added to the residual term. A plot of the standardized residual values against the values expected from the model gives a good idea of the accuracy of this normality assumption. One should be suspicious of any systematic pattern.

Secondly, just as in ANOVA, here, too, the assumption of homoscedasticity (an equal dispersion in each cell), must be examined. In MANOVA there is the added factor that one is dealing with multiple dependent variables that are mutually associated. These 'co'variations shouldn't differ too much per cell either. Box's M test examines this homogeneity of within-variations and covariations. An F value with corresponding empirical significance level (significance $= \ldots$) is printed by the computer. The value of p must not be smaller than a postulated $\alpha = 0.05$, as the variations and covariations should 'not' differ significantly if one wants to apply the MANOVA model responsibly. The logic of a significance test is therefore reversed here!

The numbers in our mini example are, however, too small (only two observations per cell) to perform this test.

11.1.10 SPSS for Windows Output of Multivariate Analysis of Variance

The use of MANOVA was already discussed in canonical correlation analysis. To perform a multivariate analysis of variance, you will now select no covariates, but factors and dependent variables.

Choosing or creating a data file
How to open an SPSS session and how to choose or create and save a data file is shown in Chapter 4.

Running the statistical procedure
Click on Statistics. Click on ANOVA Models. Click on Multivariate. This opens the dialog box of multivariate analysis of variance. Click on Y_1 and Y_2 in the Source Variable list and click on the ▶ push button of Dependent Variables. Click on A and click on the ▶ push button of Factors. Click on Define Range. Type the minimum value 1. Click on Maximum and type 3. Click on Continue. Click on B and click on the ▶ push button of Factors. Click on Define Range. Type the minimum value 1. Click on Maximum and type 2. Click on Continue.

Click on Model. You will see that Multivariate Tests and Univariate Tests are already selected. So is the Full Factorial Model. Click on Eigenvalues. Click on Continue to return to the main dialog box. Click on OK. SPSS now runs the statistical procedure and an output window appears with the results of multivariate analysis of variance.

Do not forget to save the output: click on File, click on Save as, type the file name with extension .lst and click on OK.

As you already know, the computer output can also be obtained by opening a syntax window and typing SPSS commands. Click on File, click on New, click on SPSS Syntax, type the statements, put the cursor anywhere in the first command line and click on ▶ of the icon bar (or click on Run if you still work with the SPSS for Windows 5.0 version).

The following statements are entered:

```
1 MANOVA Y1 Y2 BY A (1,3) B (1,2)
2    /PRINT SIGNIF (EIGEN)
3    /METHOD NOCONSTANT
4    /DESIGN.
```

The command MANOVA in statement 1 indicates that a multivariate analysis of variance is being performed. The dependent variables are Y_1 and Y_2. The absence of the word 'WITH' indicates that there are no covariates. The word 'BY' indicates that the factors measured at the lower level will follow afterwards. Factor A has three categories, 1, 2 and 3. The lowest and highest category are entered between parentheses. Factor B has two categories, 1 and 2.

- 'PRINT = SIGNIF (EIGEN)' in statement 2 requests the eigenvalues.
- 'METHOD = NOCONSTANT' in statement 3 specifies a model without a constant term, so that a good deal of output is suppressed.

The (intentionally limited) output is as follows:

```
* * ANALYSIS  OF  VARIANCE -- DESIGN   1 * *
EFFECT .. A BY B
Multivariate Tests of Significance (S = 2, M = -1/2, N = 1 1/2)
Test Name        Value  Approx. F Hypoth. DF   Error DF  Sig. of F
Pillais          .43339    .82993      4.00      12.00      .531
Hotellings       .76266    .76266      4.00       8.00      .578
Wilks            .56707    .81989      4.00      10.00      .541
Roys             .43233


Eigenvalues and Canonical Correlations

Root No.    Eigenvalue      Pct.   Cum. Pct.  Canon Cor.
   1           .762      99.861     99.861       .658
   2           .001        .139    100.000       .033
* * ANALYSIS  OF  VARIANCE -- DESIGN   1 * *
EFFECT .. A BY B (CONT.)
Univariate F-tests with (2,6) D. F.

Variable   Hypoth. SS  Error SS Hypoth. MS   Error MS        F  Sig. of F

Y1           66.50000  200.50000   33.25000   33.41667    .99501     .423
Y2         1626.00000 8183.00000  813.00000 1363.83333    .59611     .581
```

```
* * ANALYSIS  OF  VARIANCE -- DESIGN   1 * *
EFFECT .. B
Multivariate Tests of Significance (S = 1, M = 0, N = 1 1/2)
Test Name        Value  Approx. F Hypoth. DF   Error DF  Sig. of F
Pillais          .51870   2.69422      2.00        5.00      .161
Hotellings      1.07769   2.69422      2.00        5.00      .161
Wilks            .48130   2.69422      2.00        5.00      .161
Roys             .51870


Eigenvalues and Canonical Correlations


Root No.    Eigenvalue       Pct.    Cum. Pct.  Canon Cor.
     1          1.078    100.000      100.000        .720
* * ANALYSIS  OF  VARIANCE -- DESIGN   1 * *
EFFECT .. B (CONT.)
Univariate F-tests with (1,6) D. F.
Variable   Hypoth. SS   Error SS Hypoth. MS   Error MS         F  Sig. of F
Y1           36.75000  200.50000   36.75000   33.41667   1.09975      .335
Y2         4800.00000 8183.00000 4800.00000 1363.83333   3.51949      .110


* * ANALYSIS  OF  VARIANCE -- DESIGN   1 * *
EFFECT .. A
Multivariate Tests of Significance (S = 2, M = -1/2, N = 1 1/2)
Test Name        Value  Approx. F Hypoth. DF   Error DF  Sig. of F
Pillais          .96848   2.81667      4.00       12.00      .074
Hotellings     10.41037  10.41037      4.00        8.00      .003
Wilks            .08312   6.17149      4.00       10.00      .009
Roys             .91190


Eigenvalues and Canonical Correlations


Root No.    Eigenvalue       Pct.    Cum. Pct.  Canon Cor.
     1         10.350     99.424       99.424        .955
     2           .060       .576      100.000        .238
* * ANALYSIS  OF  VARIANCE -- DESIGN   1 * *
EFFECT .. A (CONT.)
Univariate F-tests with (2,6) D. F.
Variable   Hypoth. SS   Error SS Hypoth. MS   Error MS         F  Sig. of F
Y1          351.16667  200.50000  175.58333   33.41667   5.25436      .048
Y2        46964.6667 8183.00000 23482.3333 1363.83333  17.21789      .003
```

11.2 Multiple Discriminant Analysis: Enclaves of Cubans in Miami: The Triple Labour Market Model

In its technical aspects, multiple discriminant analysis is a special case of MANOVA (first part of this chapter) and an extension of two-group discriminant analysis (Chapter 8). We will assume a knowledge of both chapters. We will also examine its links with canonical correlation analysis.

11.2.1   The Research Problem and the Causal Diagram

Multiple discriminant analysis (MDA) can be well illustrated by means of the following research example. Kenneth L. Wilson (1980) reacts against the dual labour market model, according to which two separate labour markets exist, a primary market with positive characteristics like stability, promotional opportunities, high wages and interesting working conditions, and a secondary market with negative characteristics like high turnover, absence of promotion schemes, low wages and unfavourable working conditions.

This dual theory was also intended to apply to immigrants in developed nations. According to the theory, legal immigrant cohorts contain a high percentage of professionals and technically educated workers who find their way to the primary labour market and for whom upward occupational mobility (promotion) and absence of discrimination are the rule. Illegal and non-registered immigration, on the other hand, is made up primarily of unskilled workers who find themselves in the secondary labour market, with low wages and poor working conditions.

According to Wilson, the dual labour market theoreticians have concerned themselves almost exclusively (and erroneously) with this latter category of immigrants in the secondary circuit. His assertion is that immigrants cannot be limited to two circuits. There is, according to him, a third labour market made up of those living in immigrant enclaves that can be empirically distinguished from the primary and secondary labour markets.

Workers from enclaves and workers from the primary sector have in common a significant economic return from past human capital investments. Such returns are absent in the 'open' secondary labour market. The reader need only refer to the Chinese restaurants in the Netherlands and the Jewish diamond industry in Antwerp in order to form an idea of this third labour market. Wilson's example are the enclaves of Cubans in Miami, Florida. Businesses in the Cuban enclaves in Miami are usually small in size, but extremely profitable. They are concentrated on textile, leather, furniture, cigar production, the construction industry and banking. In the service sector they comprise flourishing restaurants, supermarkets, private clinics, funeral parlours and private schools.

In order to test his concepts, Wilson made use of a three-group discriminant analysis. Cuban immigrants were classified into the first or second labour market on the basis of data on the mean salary, the size of the business and the promotion schemes in the company. Cuban immigrants from enclaves were placed in the third labour market. In order to assess whether there was an empirical difference between these three labour markets, a dozen discriminating variables were selected: occupational prestige; home ownership as a measure of economic stability; number of relatives in the United States; knowledge of the United States; satisfaction with income; desire to change occupation; desire to return to country of origin; plans to go to another country; preparedness to go to the United States if one had the opportunity to relive one's life; experience and perception of discrimination; the opportunities for relating with Anglo-Americans.

The causal diagram which corresponds to such a three-group discriminant analysis is shown in Figure 11.6. The independent variables are the 12 discriminating characteristics. The dependent variable is the classification into three labour markets. If the arrows were reversed, we would be dealing with a one-way MANOVA, which, as stated above, can be seen as the reverse of discriminant analysis. In our calculations we will follow the same procedure, i.e., an eigenstructure analysis of matrix $\mathbf{W}^{-1}\mathbf{B}$.

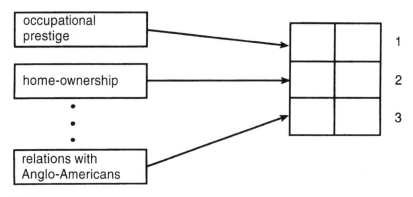

Figure 11.6   Causal diagram

The logic is the same as in a two-group discriminant analysis. The only difference is that there are now three groups instead of two and that the F test of centroid differences is now replaced by Wilks's lambda, just as in MANOVA.

11.2.2   The Data Matrix

As an example, we take Wilson's triple labour market model, but for the sake of simplicity let us limit ourselves to two discriminating variables: $X_1 =$ the number of relatives in the United States and $X_2 =$ income satisfaction. For both variables the values vary from 1 to 10. The dependent variable is a trichotomy, consisting of the three categories of Cuban immigrants from the first, second and third labour markets (codes 1, 2 and 3).

The data matrix is shown in Table 11.7.

11.2.3   Wilks's Lambda Test

In order to perform Wilks's lambda test, we must calculate the ratio of the determinant of **W**, the matrix of within-group variations and covariations, and the

Table 11.7   Data matrix

	Y	X_1	X_2
primary labour market	1	2	6
	1	4	9
	1	1	8
	1	2	9
secondary labour market	2	4	3
	2	2	4
	2	3	5
	2	2	1
enclaves	3	9	7
	3	6	8
	3	8	9
	3	8	7

Table 11.8

group 1	(2.25 8)	centroid
	$\begin{bmatrix} 4.75 & 2 \\ 2 & 6 \end{bmatrix}$	SSCP matrix
group 2	(2.75 3.25)	centroid
	$\begin{bmatrix} 2.75 & 1.25 \\ 1.25 & 8.75 \end{bmatrix}$	SSCP matrix
group 3	(7.75 7.25)	centroid
	$\begin{bmatrix} 4.75 & -1.25 \\ -1.25 & 2.75 \end{bmatrix}$	SSCP matrix
total	(4.25 6.33)	overall centroid
	$\begin{bmatrix} 86.25 & 27 \\ 27 & 74.67 \end{bmatrix}$	SSCP matrix

determinant of **T**, the matrix of total variations and covariations. In order to obtain **W** we calculate, just as in MANOVA, the means of X_1 and X_2 values for each group, which together form a within-group centroid, as well as the SSCP matrix of variations and covariations. The result is shown in Table 11.8.

Matrix **W** is the sum of the preceding three within-SSCP matrices:

$$\mathbf{W} = \begin{bmatrix} 12.25 & 2 \\ 2 & 17.50 \end{bmatrix}$$

Matrix **T** is the matrix of total-sample variations and covariations indicated at the bottom of the table, leaving the groups outside consideration:

$$\mathbf{T} = \begin{bmatrix} 86.25 & 27 \\ 27 & 74.67 \end{bmatrix}$$

Matrix **B** of between-groups variations and covariations can be obtained by a calculation of the group centroids in relation to the total centroid, but considering the fact that $\mathbf{T} = \mathbf{W} + \mathbf{B}$, **B** could just as well be calculated as the difference between **T** and **W**:

$$\mathbf{B} = \mathbf{T} - \mathbf{W} = \begin{bmatrix} 74 & 25 \\ 25 & 57.17 \end{bmatrix}$$

Wilks's lambda can now be calculated in three ways. The most simple formula is $\Lambda = |\mathbf{W}|/|\mathbf{T}|$. A second approach is the eigenstructure examination of $\mathbf{W}^{-1}\mathbf{B}$, where Λ is equal to the product of $1/(1 + \lambda_i)$. All of this is analogous to the calculation procedures in MANOVA. A third approach, based on the principles of canonical correlation calculation, will be explained later.

Let us now follow the three approaches. Using Wilks's lambda we aim to test whether the three labour markets among Cuban immigrants in Miami, Florida can be empirically distinguished from one another. In our mini example this means determining whether there is a significant difference between the centroids of the three groups, where each centroid is made up of the mean number of relatives and the mean income satisfaction, seen together, and keeping their dispersion and mutual association in mind.

11.2.4 Wilks's Lambda as the Ratio $|W|/|T|$

According to the first formula, Wilks's lambda is equal to:

$$\Lambda = \frac{|W|}{|T|} = \frac{\begin{vmatrix} 12.25 & 2 \\ 2 & 17.50 \end{vmatrix}}{\begin{vmatrix} 86.26 & 27 \\ 27 & 74.67 \end{vmatrix}} = \frac{210.38}{5711.29} = 0.037$$

We know from the section on MANOVA that the smaller the lambda is, the greater the centroid difference.

With Bartlett's V we can test whether the centroid difference is significant:

$$V = -[d_W + d_B - (p + d_B + 1)/2] \ln \Lambda$$

where

p = the number of discriminating variables = 2
d_B = one less than the number of centroids being compared = $3 - 1 = 2$
d_W = one less than the number of observations per group, to be multiplied by the number of groups = $3(4 - 1) = 9$.

$$V = -[9 + 2 - (2 + 2 + 1)/2] \ln 0.037 = 28.06$$

This value is distributed as χ^2 with $pd_B = (2)(2) = 4$ degrees of freedom. It is greater than the critical χ^2 value (9.49) found under the null hypothesis for $\alpha = 0.05$. Therefore there is a significant difference between the three labour markets for Cuban immigrants in Miami. The dual labour market theory was refuted by Wilson. The means of the discriminating variables (number of relatives and income satisfaction, considered together and in mutual association) do indeed display more than random differences between the three groups.

11.2.5 Wilks's Lambda Test from the Eigenstructure of $W^{-1}B$

The preceding calculation of Wilks's Λ is rather general. The test for centroid differences results in the conclusion that there is a difference between the three labour markets, but what we don't yet know is whether the enclaves are distinguished chiefly from the primary or secondary labour markets. The second method of calculation, via the examination of the eigenstructure of $W^{-1}B$ (completely analogous with two-group discriminant analysis and with MANOVA in the inverse direction), will give us the opportunity to carry out a more refined analysis.

$$W^{-1}B = \begin{bmatrix} 12.25 & 2 \\ 2 & 17.50 \end{bmatrix}^{-1} \begin{bmatrix} 74 & 25 \\ 25 & 57.17 \end{bmatrix} = \begin{bmatrix} 5.92 & 1.54 \\ 0.75 & 3.09 \end{bmatrix}$$

The eigenvalues are the roots of the characteristic equation:

$$|\mathbf{W}^{-1}\mathbf{B} - \lambda\mathbf{I}| = 0$$

$$\begin{vmatrix} 5.92 - \lambda & 1.54 \\ 0.75 & 3.09 - \lambda \end{vmatrix} = 0$$

$$(5.92 - \lambda)(3.09 - \lambda) - (0.75)(1.54) = 0$$

$$\lambda^2 - 9.01\lambda + 17.14 = 0$$

The roots are

$$\lambda_1 = 6.28 \quad \text{and} \quad \lambda_2 = 2.73$$

What was calculated above as the value for Wilks's lambda, $|\mathbf{W}|/|\mathbf{T}|$ is also equal to the product of $1/(1 + \lambda_i)$:

$$\Lambda = [1/(1 + 6.28)][1/(1 + 2.73)] = 0.037$$

So far, nothing new. However, the advantage of this eigenstructure examination, when compared to the preceding general approach, is that we can now apply a decomposition. This is done as follows:

$$\Lambda = [1/(1 + \lambda_1)][1/(1 + \lambda_2)]$$

Therefore $1/\Lambda = (1 + \lambda_1)(1 + \lambda_2)$. Taking the logarithms of both sides gives us:

$$\ln 1/\Lambda = \ln[(1 + \lambda_1)(1 + \lambda_2)] = \ln(1 + \lambda_1) + \ln(1 + \lambda_2)$$

$$-\ln \Lambda = \sum \ln(1 + \lambda_i)$$

The formula of Bartlett's V can now be modified:

$$V = -[d_W + d_B - (p + d_B + 1)/2] \ln \Lambda$$

$$= [d_W + d_B - (p + d_B + 1)/2] \sum \ln(1 + \lambda_i)$$

Now we find the decomposition. First we perform the general test by entering both of the eigenvalues, λ_1 and λ_2, in the formula for V:

$$V = [9 + 2 - (2 + 2 + 1)/2][\ln(1 + 6.28) + \ln(1 + 2.73)] = 28.06$$

This value is the same as above. It is distributed as χ^2 with $pd_B = 4$ degrees of freedom and the conclusion is that there is a significant difference between the three labour markets. The decomposition is now applied as follows:

There are two discriminant functions. Remember, the number of discriminant functions is equal to $\min(g - 1, p)$ with $g = 3$ groups and $p = 2$ variables. The second function stands for the part that the second eigenvalue represents. This part can be tested seperately because of the characteristics of additive partition of χ^2. Therefore, in the formula for V (that is distributed as χ^2), we can enter λ_2 separately and this way test whether the second discriminant function also represents a significant centroid difference:

$$V = [9 + 2 - (2 + 2 + 1)/2] \ln(1 + 2.73) = 11.19$$

With $(p-1)(g-2) = (2-1)(3-2) = 1$ degree of freedom, this value is significant, because the critical value of χ^2 for $\alpha = 0.05$ and $df = 1$ is equal to 3.84 and therefore smaller than 11.19.

Now we have gained more insight. Not only does there appear to be a significant difference between the three groups, there are also two specific differences, expressed by the two discriminant functions. It is therefore interesting to examine the two functions themselves, in addition to the two eigenvalues. For that purpose we will calculate the eigenvectors. We enter the values $\lambda_1 = 6.28$ and $\lambda_2 = 2.73$ one by one in the matrix equation $(\mathbf{W}^{-1}\mathbf{B} - \lambda\mathbf{I})\mathbf{k} = \mathbf{0}$ and we solve the equations in order to determine the weights, $\mathbf{k}$. These weights are normalized and give us the two discriminant functions (exercise for the reader):

$$t_1 = 0.973x_1 + 0.230x_2$$
$$t_2 = -0.391x_1 + 0.920x_2$$

The reason the coefficients in the computer output differ slightly from these is that a standardization procedure is applied (important in the case of strongly correlated predictors).

We can see that the first function attributes a great deal of weight to variable x_1 (the number of relatives) and the second function to x_2 (income satisfaction).

If we look at the group centroids as well, we get more insight into our data. The means of variable x_1 are 2.25, 2.75 and 7.75, respectively. For this variable, which receives a high weight for the first discriminant function, the Cuban enclaves are sharply distinguished from the first two labour markets. The immigrants of the primary and the secondary labour markets are not easily distinguished from one another in this first discriminant function, but are empirically different from the immigrants of the enclaves.

The second discriminant function arranges the groups differently. The means of variable x_2, which receives a high weight for the second discriminant function, are 8, 3.25 and 7.75, respectively. In this second dimension, predominantly determined by the income satisfaction, the second labour market is sharply distinguished from the other two. Immigrants from the enclaves show a great resemblance to those from the first circuit.

11.2.6 Classification

One can see from the computer output that the classification of each of the 12 persons in the three groups is perfect. There is no overlap. For the treatment of this classification problem, see two-group discriminant analysis (Chapter 8).

11.2.7 Homoscedasticity

Let us not forget to check Box's M test. The within-covariance matrices of the three groups mustn't differ significantly from each other. The fact that this is indeed the case (empirical significance level $p = 0.9645 \gg 0.05$) means that we are allowed to apply the technique.

11.3 Multiple Discriminant Analysis as Canonical Correlation Analysis

As promised above, we will now discuss another approach from the principles of canonical correlation calculation. Multiple discriminant analysis can also be calculated by means of canonical correlation analysis, for the following reason. Let us take our mini example of Cuban immigrants once again. The structure of the research problem was as shown in Figure 11.7. The three groups of labour markets together form a trichotomous variable with the categories 1, 2 and 3. This trichotomy can be replaced by two dummies, D_1 and D_2, as is indicated in the figure. Seen in this light, we have the structure of canonical correlation analysis technique, as shown in Figure 11.8.

It follows that we will have to give the computer another data matrix than the one given above. There are now four, instead of three, variables (Table 11.9).

We now return to canonical correlation analysis (Chapter 10). The calculations are an exercise for the reader. We will present the results in telegram style.

Our point of departure is the correlation matrix:

$$\mathbf{R} = \left[\begin{array}{cc|cc} 1 & -0.50 & 0.92 & 0.40 \\ -0.50 & 1 & -0.40 & -0.87 \\ \hline 0.92 & -0.40 & 1 & 0.34 \\ 0.40 & -0.87 & 0.34 & 1 \end{array} \right] = \left[\begin{array}{c|c} \mathbf{R}_{xx} & \mathbf{R}_{xy} \\ \hline \mathbf{R}_{yx} & \mathbf{R}_{yy} \end{array} \right]$$

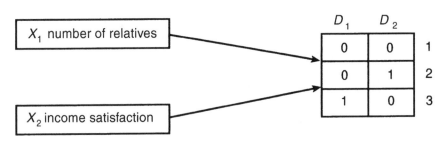

Figure 11.7   Structure of the research problem

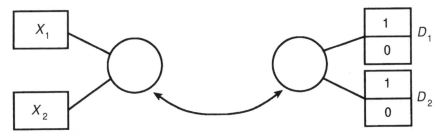

Figure 11.8   Canonical correlation analysis diagram

Table 11.9   Data matrix with four variables

	D_1	D_2	X_1	X_2
primary labour market	0	0	2	6
	0	0	4	9
	0	0	1	8
	0	0	2	9
secondary labour market	0	1	4	3
	0	1	2	4
	0	1	3	5
	0	1	2	1
enclaves	1	0	9	7
	1	0	6	8
	1	0	8	9
	1	0	8	7

The matrix for which the eigenstructure is being examined is $\mathbf{M} = \mathbf{R}_{yy}^{-1}\mathbf{R}_{xy}'\mathbf{R}_{xx}^{-1}\mathbf{R}_{xy}$:

$$\mathbf{M} = \begin{bmatrix} 1 & 0.34 \\ 0.34 & 1 \end{bmatrix}^{-1} \begin{bmatrix} 0.92 & -0.40 \\ 0.40 & -0.87 \end{bmatrix} \begin{bmatrix} 1 & -0.50 \\ -0.50 & 1 \end{bmatrix}^{-1} \begin{bmatrix} 0.92 & 0.40 \\ -0.40 & -0.87 \end{bmatrix}$$

$$= \begin{bmatrix} 0.849 & 0.061 \\ 0.026 & 0.745 \end{bmatrix}$$

The characteristic equation $|\mathbf{M} - \lambda\mathbf{I}| = 0$ gives us the following eigenvalues: $\lambda_1 = 0.863$ and $\lambda_2 = 0.732$. These two eigenvalues are the squared canonical correlations between the first and second pair of canonical variables, respectively. Both canonical correlations are high. Here, too, we see that the discrimination between the three labour markets is not determined from one single dimension, but from two. (Compare this with the two discriminant functions.)

The eigenvalues for M are not equal to the eigenvalues calculated earlier for $\mathbf{W}^{-1}\mathbf{B}$ (6.28 and 2.73). It can, however, be shown that a fixed relationship exists between both. If we indicate the eigenvalues of the canonical correlation analysis by λ_{cc}, then: $\lambda_{cc} = \lambda/(\lambda + 1)$ or $\lambda = \lambda_{cc}/(1 - \lambda_{cc})$. Indeed: $0.863 = 6.28/(6.28 + 1)$ and $0.732 = 2.73/(2.73 + 1)$.

Wilks's lambda was calculated above as the product of $1/(1 + \lambda_i)$. From the above fixed relationship it follows that $1/(1 + \lambda) = 1 - \lambda_{cc}$. Consequently Wilks's Λ is also the product of the values $1 - \lambda_{cc}$: $\Lambda = \Pi(1 - \lambda_{cc}) = (1 - 0.863)(1 - 0.732) = 0.037$.

It is worth noting that $1 - \lambda_{cc}$ has an interesting interpretation. Considering the fact that λ_{cc} is the squared canonical correlation, i.e., the proportion of the variance in one set which is explained by the other set, $1 - \lambda_{cc}$ is the unexplained part, i.e., the residual variance. Wilks's lambda is therefore the product of these residual variances.

The further progression of the analysis is identical to the preceding. Making use of Bartlett's V, Wilks's Λ indicates that there is a significant difference between the three groups. The two canonical correlations can be tested separately and both appear to be significant.

The matrix of eigenvectors can be calculated and, with the help of this, the coefficients of the canonical variables (as linear combinations of the variables from a set) can be determined. Please refer to the computer output for these coefficients. Here, too, it appears that the first dimension (the first pair of canonical variables) is predominantly determined by the number of relatives (X_1) and causes a division between the enclaves and the other labour markets (dummy D_1). The second pair displays high coefficients for the income satisfaction (X_2) and causes a division between the second labour market and the others (dummy D_2).

The same conclusions have thus been reached by another method of calculation.

11.3.1   SPSS for Windows Output of Multiple Discriminant Analysis

The computer output is the same as in two-group discriminant analysis, the only difference being that there are now three instead of two groups.

Choosing or creating a data file

How to open an SPSS session and how to choose a data file or, if a data file does not yet exist, how to enter data, to choose name, type and label of variables and to save the data file with extension *.sav*, is shown in Chapter 4.

Running the discriminant analysis

Click on Statistics. Click on Classify. Click on Discriminant. Click on variable *Y* in the Source Variable list on the left and click on the ▶ push button of the Grouping Variable. Click on Define Range. Type the minimum value 1. Click on the value of Maximum and type 3. Click on Continue. You now return to the Discriminant Analysis dialog box. Click on the variables X_1 and X_2 in the Source Variable list (either separately or together by means of the click and drag technique) and click on the ▶ push button of the Independents.

Click on Statistics. A Discriminant Analysis Statistics dialog box appears. Click on Box's M. Click on Continue.

You don't have to click on Method, because we are not going to select a stepwise analysis. Click on Classify. A Discriminant Analysis Classification dialog box appears. You will see under Prior Probabilities that All Groups Equal is chosen. You may click on Compute from Group Sizes here and a radio button will show that you have chosen this option, but this will not change the output now, because the groups are equal in size. You may also choose some plots and display options. Click on Continue.

If you now click on OK in the main Discriminant Analysis dialog box, SPSS will run the statistical procedure and an output window will appear with the results of discriminant analysis.

Do not forget to save the output: click on File, click on Save as, type the file name with extension *.lst* and click on OK.

Running the statistical procedures with SPSS commands

As you already know, you can run the foregoing statistical procedures by opening a syntax window and typing SPSS commands. Click on File, click on New, click on SPSS Syntax, type the statements, put the cursor anywhere in the first command line and click on ▶ (or on Run for the 5.0 version).

The limited statements are as follows:

```
1 DISCRIMINANT /GROUPS Y (1,3)
2    /VARIABLES X1 X2
3    /STATISTICS MEAN BOXM TABLE.
```

'DISCRIMINANT' in statement 1 requests a discriminant analysis, and 'GROUPS = Y (1,3)' indicates that the dependent variable Y represents the groups (minimum score 1 = first group, maximum score 3 = last group).

In statement 2 the discriminating variables X_1 and X_2 are specified. These are measured at the interval level.

'STATISTICS = MEAN BOXM TABLE' in statement 3 requests three things: the group means, Box's M test for homogeneity of the covariance matrices (test of homoscedasticity) and the table with the % of correct classifications.

The output is as follows.

```
- - - - - - - -   D I S C R I M I N A N T   A N A L Y S I S   - - - - - - - -

On groups defined by Y        labour market
            12 (unweighted) cases were processed.
             0 of these were excluded from the analysis.
            12 (unweighted) cases will be used in the analysis.

Number of Cases by Group
                Number of Cases
   Y         Unweighted     Weighted  Label
        1         4           4.0
        2         4           4.0
        3         4           4.0
     Total       12          12.0

Group Means
   Y            X1                X2
   1         2.25000          8.00000
   2         2.75000          3.25000
   3         7.75000          7.75000
  Total      4.25000          6.33333

On groups defined by Y          labour market

Analysis number       1
Direct method:  All variables passing the tolerance test are entered.
       Minimum Tolerance Level.................  .00100

Canonical Discriminant Functions
       Maximum number of functions.............     2
       Minimum cumulative percent of variance...  100.00
       Maximum significance of Wilks' Lambda....  1.0000
Prior probability for each group is  .33333
                   Canonical Discriminant Functions
```

```
             Pct of   Cum Canonical After  Wilks'
  Fcn Eigenvalue Variance Pct    Corr   Fcn  Lambda Chisquare  DF  Sig
                                     :    0  .0368   28.061     4  .0000
   1*   6.2803   69.71  69.71    .9288 :    1  .2682   11.187     1  .0008
   2*   2.7288   30.29 100.00    .8555 :
   * marks the   2 canonical discriminant functions remaining in the analysis.
```

```
Standardized Canonical Discriminant Function Coefficients
             FUNC  1     FUNC  2
X1            .92988    -.39285
X2            .26215     .97483
```

```
Structure Matrix:
Pooled-within-groups correlations between discriminating variables
and canonical discriminant functions
(Variables ordered by size of correlation within function)
             FUNC  1     FUNC  2
X1            .96569*   -.25969
X2            .38917     .92117*
```

```
Canonical Discriminant Functions evaluated at Group Means (Group Centroids)
  Group      FUNC  1    FUNC  2
    1       -1.28076    1.83860
    2       -1.77522   -1.65043
    3        3.05598    -.18817
```

```
Test of equality of group covariance matrices using Box's M
The ranks and natural logarithms of determinants printed are those
of the group covariance matrices.
     Group Label              Rank   Log Determinant
          1                    2         1.001449
          2                    2          .916291
          3                    2          .245122
        Pooled Within-Groups
        Covariance Matrix      2          .954442
    Box's M      Approximate F Degrees of freedom Significance
    2.1014          .23677       6,        2018.8      .9645
```

```
Classification Results -
                     No. of   Predicted Group Membership
     Actual Group    Cases       1         2         3
     --------------- ------    --------  --------  --------
  Group    1           4          4         0         0
                                100.0%      .0%       .0%

  Group    2           4          0         4         0
                                  .0%     100.0%      .0%

  Group    3           4          0         0         4
                                  .0%       .0%     100.0%

Percent of 'grouped' cases correctly classified: 100.00%
```

11.3.2   SPSS for Windows Output of Multiple Discriminant Analysis as Canonical Correlation Analysis

We now offer the computer another data matrix. The two discriminating variables, X_1 = the number of relatives in the United States and X_2 = the income satisfaction, remain the same. The trichotomous dependent variable is replaced by the two dummies D_1 and D_2. For the requesting of a canonical correlation analysis the reader is referred to chapter 10. The statements to be typed in the syntax window are as follows.

```
1 MANOVA D1 D2 WITH X1 X2
2  /DISCRIM
3  /PRINT SIGNIF (EIGEN)
4  /DESIGN.
```

In statements 1 and 2 a canonical correlation analysis is requested and in statement 3 the eigenvalues are requested.

The output, parts of it omitted, is as follows.

```
* * ANALYSIS  OF  VARIANCE -- DESIGN   1 * *

EFFECT .. WITHIN CELLS Regression
Multivariate Tests of Significance (S = 2, M = -1/2, N = 3 )

Test Name        Value  Approx. F Hypoth. DF   Error DF  Sig. of F
Pillais        1.59446   17.69261      4.00      18.00      .000
Hotellings     9.00911   15.76594      4.00      14.00      .000
Wilks           .03684   16.84102      4.00      16.00      .000
Roys            .86264


Eigenvalues and Canonical Correlations
Root No.    Eigenvalue       Pct.    Cum. Pct.  Canon Cor.    Sq. Cor
       1         6.280      69.711      69.711        .929       .863
       2         2.729      30.289     100.000        .855       .732


* * ANALYSIS  OF  VARIANCE -- DESIGN   1 * *
EFFECT .. WITHIN CELLS Regression (CONT.)
Univariate F-tests with (2,9) D. F.
Variable    Sq. Mul. R     Mul. R  Adj. R-sq.  Hypoth. MS    Error MS
D1             .86151      .92818      .83074     1.14868      .04103
D2             .77558      .88067      .72571     1.03411      .06649


Variable            F   Sig. of F
D1           27.99374      .000
D2           15.55179      .001


* * ANALYSIS  OF  VARIANCE -- DESIGN   1 * *

Raw canonical coefficients for DEPENDENT variables
           Function No.
Variable            1           2
D1              1.913       1.356
D2              -.218       2.335
```

```
Standardized canonical coefficients for DEPENDENT variables
          Function No.
Variable           1          2
D1               .942       .668
D2              -.107      1.150
```

* * ANALYSIS OF VARIANCE -- DESIGN 1 * *

```
Correlations between DEPENDENT and canonical variables
          Function No.
Variable           1          2
D1               .996       .093
D2              -.578       .816
```

```
Variance explained by canonical variables of DEPENDENT variables
CAN. VAR.  Pct Var DE Cum Pct DE Pct Var CO Cum Pct CO
      1       66.294     66.294     57.188     57.188
      2       33.706    100.000     24.667     81.855
```

* * ANALYSIS OF VARIANCE -- DESIGN 1 * *

```
Raw canonical coefficients for COVARIATES
          Function No.
COVARIATE          1          2
X1               .327       .193
X2               .077      -.400
```

```
Standardized canonical coefficients for COVARIATES
          CAN. VAR.
COVARIATE          1          2
X1               .914       .540
X2               .201     -1.043
```

* * ANALYSIS OF VARIANCE -- DESIGN 1 * *
```
Correlations between COVARIATES and canonical variables
          CAN. VAR.
Covariate          1          2
X1               .982       .189
X2               .508      -.861
```

```
Variance explained by canonical variables of the COVARIATES
 CAN. VAR.  Pct Var DE Cum Pct DE Pct Var CO Cum Pct CO
      1       52.738     52.738     61.135     61.135
      2       28.442     81.180     38.865    100.000
Regression analysis for WITHIN CELLS error term
```

```
* * ANALYSIS  OF  VARIANCE -- DESIGN   1 * *
Regression analysis for WITHIN CELLS error term  (CONT.)
Dependent variable .. D1                dummy 1
COVARIATE              B        Beta   Std. Err.    t-Value   Sig. of t
X1              .15625      .88861        .023      6.746        .000
X2              .01939      .10261        .025       .779        .456


COVARIATE    Lower -95%  CL- Upper
X1                 .104        .209
X2                -.037        .076



* * ANALYSIS  OF  VARIANCE -- DESIGN   1 * *
Regression analysis for WITHIN CELLS error term  (CONT.)
Dependent variable .. D2                dummy2
COVARIATE              B        Beta   Std. Err.    t-Value   Sig. of t
X1             -.02014     -.11452        .029      -.683        .512
X2             -.15790     -.83551        .032     -4.983        .001


COVARIATE    Lower -95%  CL- Upper
X1                -.087        .047
X2                -.230       -.086
```

Appendix

Required Mathematical and Statistical Knowledge

A.1 Elementary Algebra

A knowledge of **number theory** is required: natural numbers, integers, rational and real numbers, calculations (addition, subtraction, multiplication, division, involution), properties (associative, commutative, distributive), the concept of absolute value ($|-9| = 9$); **set theory** (set, subset, union, intersection, complement, disjunction); **logarithms** (base 10, base e, rules); the **solving of equations** (quadratic equations and polynomials of the n-th degree) and of systems of equations; **permutations**, **combinations** and **variations**, Newton's binomial theorem; the **theory of functions** (linear function, quadratic function, polygon, exponential function, logarithmic function); number series: arithmetic and geometric progressions; the **summation** or **sigma sign** (calculation and rules); **differentiating** and **integrating** (the determining of an optimum, maximum or minimum).

A.2 Elementary Statistics

Since in this volume only the classical techniques are treated, whereby the variables are either measured at the interval level or can be considered as the interval by means of dummy-operations, we limit ourselves here to those elements of statistics that are relevant to our purposes: the mean, the weighted mean, variation, variance, standard deviation, covariation, covariance, correlation and, in addition, the corresponding concepts of sampling theory and test theory: the partition of the variance in a within and between component, as well as that of the covariance; standardization; sampling theory including the distinction between the distribution of the population, the distribution of the sample and the sampling distribution; the type I and type II error; the estimating and testing of a hypothesis; the t test and the treatment of degrees of freedom; the probability distributions z, t, χ^2, F.

Let us begin with the measures of central tendency.

A.2.1 Measures of Central Tendency ($\bar{X}$ and $\bar{X}_g$)

In all studies it is advisable to carry out a separate study for each variable independently. The frequency distribution of a variable must display sufficient dispersion. It can be unimodal, bimodal or multimodal. Unimodality is in many cases a requirement and can sometimes be reached by making the class intervals slightly wider. A unimodal distribution can be either skewed or symmetrical. Symmetrical distributions can be a good approximation of the normal distribution, but can also deviate from it; if they are more peaked than the normal curve, then they are referred to as leptokurtic, and if they are flatter than normal, as platykurtic. The approximation of a normal distribution is in some cases a requirement and the test of normality, designed especially for this, is unfortunately too often disregarded.

One of the first measures that is calculated in such a separate study of an individual variable is the measure of central tendency: the arithmetic mean, the mode, the median and others. The mode is only useful in the case of a unimodal distribution. It is the value that occurs most frequently. The median is the value of the middle unit, that is, half of the units will have a lower value than it and half will have a higher value.

In this book, where the variables are usually measured at the interval level, we will be calculating mostly by arithmetic means. The arithmetic mean ($\bar{X}$ for the random sample, μ for the population) is the sum of all values divided by the number of values: $\sum X/n$.

When a frequency distribution is subdivided into classes, each class midpoint (X_{mi}) is considered as a representative of the class concerned and is multiplied by the number of elements (f_i) of that class: $(\sum f_i X_{mi})/\sum f_i = (\sum f_i X_{mi})/n$.

Such an operation strongly resembles the calculation of the weighted mean, a procedure that we will encounter frequently. If n elements are distributed in different groups and if varying weights are attributed to the groups (g_i for the i-th group), the weighted mean is then $\bar{X}_g = (\sum g_i X_i)/\sum g_i$. In the frequency distribution with grouped data, the class frequencies f_i are the weights and their sum $\sum f_i$ is the total number of elements n.

A.2.2 Measures of Dispersion

A frequency distribution must display sufficient dispersion. A variable must vary. When all persons in a country adhere to the same religion, then religious affiliation within that country is not open to statistical study. Outside that country, however, it is, because a comparison with other countries, where other religions are acknowledged, provides for variation. The measures of dispersion, just as the measures of central tendency, are greatly dependent on the measurement level of the variables. In combination with the median, the interquartile distance or the 10–90-percentile distance is sometimes used, because the median is equal to the second quartile and the 50th percentile. The measures that are especially important for our aims are those used in combination with the arithmetic mean: variation, variance and standard deviation.

Variation, also known as the sum of squares (SS), is the summation of the squared deviations of the mean: $SS = \sum(X - \bar{X})^2$. The squaring is intended to make the dispersion positive, because a square is always positive. Instead of the square, one could also take the absolute value in order to obtain the absolute deviation of the mean: $AA = \sum |X - \bar{X}|$, but the squared deviation SS provides the opportunity for more interesting interpretation, because of the possibility of the additive partition into a between- and within-component, something that is of vital importance for multivariate analysis, as is apparent in the treatment of many techniques.

Variance s^2 is simply equal to the variation divided by the number of degrees of freedom; this is the number of cases minus 1, thus $s^2 = SS/(n - 1)$. The reason why we do not divide by the number of items in a sample (n), but by ($n-1$), is that the sample mean is fixed and therefore removes a degree of freedom.

Standard deviation s is equal to the square root of the variance: $s = [\sum(X - \bar{X})^2/(n-1)]^{1/2}$. The three concepts — variation, variance and standard deviation — play a crucial role in the treatment of each of the techniques in multivariate analysis. This can even be seen in a bivariate analysis, where the concepts of covariation, covariance and correlation form an analogy with the three concepts of variation, variance and standard deviation. These concepts form the basis for each of the following expansions and refinements. A thorough study of all the ins and outs of these concepts is therefore advisable. While more attention paid to the basis may seem like a loss of time, the result in the end will be an enormous gaining of time.

A.2.3 Measures of Association

At the point where we start dealing with more than one variable, the problem of association becomes relevant, between income and consumption, for example. It must be understood that a study of the association between two variables implies the study of each individual variable, with its mean and dispersion. An enormous number of association measures have been constructed, depending on the measurement level of the variables. An overview of the most important measures can be found in Tacq (1977, 1980). For our intentions, we limit ourselves to the measures that are related to the measures of central tendency ($\bar{X}$) and of dispersion (SS, s^2, s) for variables measured at the interval level, as indicated above. In connection with variation (SS), variance (s^2) and standard deviation (s), we will treat covariation (SS_{xy}), covariance (s_{xy}) and correlation (r_{xy}), respectively.

Covariation SS_{xy} is the sum of the products of deviations of X values from their mean on one hand, and that of Y values from their mean on the other: $SS_{xy} = \sum(X - \bar{X})(Y - \bar{Y})$. When X and Y are equal, covariation is transformed into variation.

Covariance s_{xy} is equal to the covariation divided by the number of degrees of freedom, i.e., the number of cases minus 1, thus: $s_{xy} = [\sum(X - \bar{X})(Y - \bar{Y})]/(n-1)$.

Correlation r_{xy} is equal to the covariance of X and Y in standardized form. The standardization of a variable calls for some explanation. A variable X is standardized by subtracting each value of X by the mean (so that the mean of values becomes 0) and by dividing the result by the standard deviation (so that the standard deviation becomes 1). The standardized value z_x then becomes $z_x = (X - \mu)/\sigma$. This is analogous for z_y. The correlation between the two variables is therefore $r_{xy} = (\sum z_x z_y)/(n-1)$. This is Pearson's well-known product–moment–correlation coefficient, which can also be written as the covariation divided by the square root of the product of variations:

$$r_{xy} = \frac{\sum(X - \bar{X})(Y - \bar{Y})}{[\sum(X - \bar{X})^2 \sum(Y - \bar{Y})^2]^{1/2}}$$

The formula which shows that the correlation is equal to the covariance of the standardized variables $r_{xy} = (\sum z_x z_y)/(n-1)$ forms the basis for many calculations in multivariate analyses. The reader is advised to memorize this formula. Here is an example to assist the memory.

Someone who goes out a lot (X) can afford little sleep (Y). Consider each variable as quantitative: $X =$ the number of evenings out per week and $Y =$ the number of hours of sleep per night. Let's say that the mean number of evenings out for n persons is 3 and the standard deviation is 1.5. The mean number of hours of sleep is 8 and standard deviation is 2. We make z scores for all the values, i.e., we subtract each value by the mean and we divide by the standard deviation. Someone with 8 hours of sleep would then receive a score of 0; 6 hours of sleep becomes $(6 - 8)/2 = -1$; 12 hours of sleep is 2, and so on. Such a z score is the number of standard deviations that the value is removed from the mean: someone with 12 hours of sleep is 2 standard deviations above the mean of 8 hours. For each person the product of the z score for going out and the z score for sleep is calculated. All these products are added up and the sum is divided by the number of persons minus 1. This results in a number between -1 and 1, usually known in another form as the correlation coefficient.

It is worth mentioning that while the correlation coefficient can only be calculated for variables of interval measurement level, dichotomous variables form an exception. By applying dummy-coding, for example gender: male $= 0$, female $= 1$, the formula of the correlation coefficient can still be employed. The measure of association is then called the 'fourfold point correlation coefficient'.

A.2.4 Partition of Variance

An important principle which will be applied to almost every multivariate analysis is the partition of the variance into a between- and a within-component. We will illustrate this principle here as the partition of the variation (sum of squares SS). For the respective variances, one simply has to divide by the degrees of freedom in a modified manner.

Consider the following series of scores for a variable X:

$$2 \quad 2 \quad 3 \quad 4 \quad 4 \quad 5 \quad 6 \quad 7 \quad 8 \quad 9$$

The mean is 5 and the **total variation** is 54. Let us now divide the ten scores into two groups of five.

The first group is:

$$2 \quad 2 \quad 3 \quad 4 \quad 4$$

The mean is 3 and the variation is 4.

The second group is:

$$5 \quad 6 \quad 7 \quad 8 \quad 9$$

The mean is 7 and the variation is 10.

The sum of the variation within the first group and the variation within the second group is called **within-group variation** and is $4 + 10 = 14$.

The mean 3 from the first group and the mean 7 from the second group together form a series of two numbers which make it possible for us to calculate the variation 'between' the two group means. The series is:

$$3 \quad 7$$

The mean of this is 5 and the variation is 8. This variation, however, has been calculated on the basis of means and not individual values. A leap in level, as it were, has been made from individuals to groups with five individuals each. The probability of dispersion of these groups is five times smaller than the probability of dispersion of their individual members. The variation 8 is therefore deceitfully small. In order to realize comparability on the same level, we multiply this number by the size of the group 5 and we have $8 \times 5 = 40$. This is the **between-group variation**. It is the variation between the two group means, corrected for its artificially low probability of dispersion compared to individuals.

We note:

the total variation   SST = 54
the within-group variation   SSW = 14
the between-group variation   SSB = 40

And we see that $54 = 14 + 40$ or SST = SSW + SSB.

The total variation can thus be additively partitioned into the within- and between-group variation.

Algebraically, this principle can be represented as follows. We represent each individual score as X, the total mean as $\bar{X}$ and the group means as $\bar{X}_i$ for the i-th group. Thus:

$$X - \bar{X} = X - \bar{X}$$
$$X - \bar{X} = X - \bar{X}_i + \bar{X}_i - \bar{X}$$
$$(X - \bar{X})^2 = (X - \bar{X}_i)^2 + (\bar{X}_i - \bar{X})^2 + 2(X - \bar{X}_i)(\bar{X}_i - \bar{X})$$
$$\sum(X - \bar{X})^2 = \sum(X - \bar{X}_i)^2 + \sum(\bar{X}_i - \bar{X})^2 + 2\sum(X - \bar{X}_i)(\bar{X}_i - \bar{X})$$

The last term becomes zero because for each group i it holds that $\bar{X}_i - \bar{X}$ is a constant and $\sum(X - \bar{X}_i) = 0$. Therefore:

$$\sum(X - \bar{X})^2 = \sum(X - \bar{X}_i)^2 + \sum(\bar{X}_i - \bar{X})^2$$

The last term must be multiplied by the group size as $\sum$ is a summation of scores of individuals j and not of groups i:

$$\sum(X - \bar{X})^2 = \sum(X - \bar{X}_i)^2 + n_i \sum(\bar{X}_i - \bar{X})^2$$
$$\text{SST} = \text{SSW} + \text{SSB}$$

A.2.5 Sampling Theory

From sampling theory one should have a ready knowledge of the most important concepts: population, random sample, sampling distribution, estimation theory, the testing of a hypothesis, most especially the t test of difference of means, the type I error, the type II error, degrees of freedom and some knowledge of a few probability distributions. What follows is an ultra-concise treatment of the themes that are most relevant for this book.

When a random sample of $n = 2000$ items is taken from a population of N items (if N is high, knowledge of the exact number is superfluous), then there are three distributions involved: population distribution, sample distribution, and sampling distribution. If we consider a quantitative variable, age X for example, and assume that the ages are 'normally' distributed in the population, then the three distributions would be as shown in Figure A.1.

The distribution of age in the sample strongly resembles the distribution of the population. On the X axis we see age values, on the Y axis the corresponding numbers of persons (frequencies f). The mean and the standard deviation of the population are indicated by Greek letters (μ and σ), while this is not the case with the sample ($\bar{X}$ and s). The sample mean ($\bar{X}$) is an unbiased estimator of the population mean (μ). This is somewhat more subtle for the variance. The variance σ^2 of the population is calculated as $\sum(X - \mu)^2/N$. One could then intuitively expect that $S^2 = \sum(X - \bar{X})^2/n$ from the sample is a good approximation of the population variance. This estimation is, however, on the low side. Considering that in random sampling there is a tendency to choose values nearer to the mean than to the extremes, the sample variance turns out to be a bit smaller. This is corrected by choosing $n - 1$, and not n, in the denominator. The value $s^2 = S^2[n/(n-1)]$ is therefore an unbiased estimator of the population variance σ^2. Why the denominator must be precisely $n - 1$ is proven exactly in mathematical statistics.

The sampling distribution differs greatly from the last two distributions. Now the items are not persons, with an age X, but many samples with the size n which could have been sampled from the same population. On the X axis, therefore, are mean ages that could have been found in each of the samples, and on the Y axis are the proportions of samples (p), that correspond with each mean. These proportions of samples are viewed as probabilities (p), so that the sampling distribution is in fact a probability distribution, in this case a normal distribution. Its mean is the mean of the means of all the samples, which is indicated by the two bars above the X. The expected value of this is μ. The standard deviation of the sampling distribution, also known as the standard error, is not equal to the standard deviation of the population σ, but is $\sqrt{n}$ smaller. Mathematically it can be shown that $\sigma_{\bar{x}}^2 = \sigma^2/n$. This is why the dispersion of the sampling distribution, as can be seen in the diagram, is smaller than

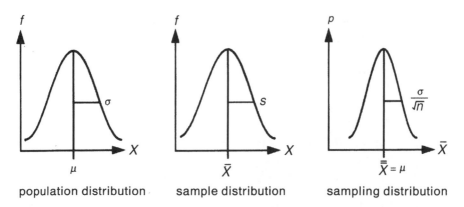

population distribution   sample distribution   sampling distribution

Figure A.1   Normal distribution curves

the dispersion of the other two distributions. Intuitively this means that group means have a much smaller chance of dispersion than do individual values (X). We encountered something similar in the partition of variance: the probability of dispersion is n times smaller with a group size n.

The three distributions indicated, the population, the sample and the sampling distribution, form the basis for all inferential statistics. Each time one draws conclusions about the population from sample data, these three distributions must be kept in mind, for each variable individually.

With this basis in mind let us begin our overview of sampling theory. This can be divided into two parts: **estimation theory** and **test theory**.

An example of **statistical estimation** is the following. One week before the French presidential elections, a random sample survey establishes that the preference for the two candidates, Giscard d'Estaing and Mitterand, is very close: 48% and 52%. If the estimation of 52% for Mitterand, which is based on a survey of 2000 eligible voters, produces a confidence interval of 50–54, then, with a postulated probability of, for example 99%, we are able to predict that Mitterand will win. With a greater interval of 48–56, or a lower postulated probability of 90%, our prediction is less certain. There will always be uncertainty. If we take a lower postulated probability, for example 90%, then while the confidence interval will be smaller, for example 51–53, it can only support our prediction that Mitterand will most likely win with a probability of 90%. We might as well ask the reader if (s)he would be prepared to put his/her hand into a bag containing 90 eels and 10 poisonous rattlesnakes. For, that is the probability we are dealing with. If we maintain our strict requirement of 99%, then we must, in order to boost the interval of 48–56 to a media-friendlier interval of 50–54, raise our sample of 2000 to 5000, something that implies more than twice the cost.

The problem with statistical estimation is thus the attempt to generalize a sample statistic (a sample mean or sample proportion) to the whole population. A combination of uncertainties is involved here. The size of the confidence interval i, the postulated probability p $(= 1 - \alpha =$ see further) and the sample size n are the three most important spoilsports.

A confidence interval was considered above as a margin of uncertainty around a proportion of votes for Mitterand (52%), but it can be calculated for every conceivable sample quantity: a mean (for one variable measured at the interval level), a correlation coefficient (for two variables measured at the interval level), an eta-coefficient (for two variables, one interval and one nominal), etc.

The statistical estimation theory is also closely related to the statistical test theory. A statistical test of a hypothesis can usually be considered as a statistical estimation and it can even be proved that the latter in fact provides more information than the former. We first give a concise review of statistical testing.

Statistical testing has to do with the testing of a hypothesis. Such a hypothesis can involve one single variable, for example the hypothesis that Mitterand will receive more than half the votes in France $(H : \pi > 0.50$, variable voting behaviour). But usually such a hypothesis involves more than one variable, for example the hypothesis that persons with a lower income are more likely to vote for Mitterand than persons with a higher income (variables voting behaviour and income). In this book hypotheses involving more than two variables are treated, but bivariate hypotheses consistently form the point of departure and in order to explain a number of important concepts, the type I and the type II error, we must even resort to univariate hypotheses. Let us do this first.

Let us once again take the unambiguous univariate hypothesis that Mitterand will receive more than half the votes in France ($H : \pi > 0.50$). Testing of such an hypothesis is a bit of a *reductio ad absurdum*. We start from the assumption that we are wrong, in other words, that Mitterand can only count on the support of 50% of the eligible voting population. We call this the null hypothesis ($H_0 : \pi = 0.50$). Starting from this supposition, we reason further and, in doing so, make use of our knowledge of random sampling and probability distributions.

If we, with H_0 as a point of departure, take an enormous amount of samples of $n = 2000$ from the French population and determine the proportion of Mitterand voters for each sample, we would then obtain a sampling distribution of proportions which would have the form of a binomial probability distribution. In view of the fact that n is large and that $\pi = 0.50$ we know that such a binomial probability distribution will tend toward the normal distribution with a mean of $\mu = \pi$ and standard error of $\sigma_p = [\pi(1 - \pi)/n]^{1/2}$, thus $\mu = 0.50$ and $\sigma_p = 0.0112$. For percentages instead of proportions the order of size is 100 times greater: $\mu = 50\%$ and $\sigma_p = 1.12\%$.

From the characteristics of the normal distribution we can deduce that 95% of the area under the curve, i.e., 95% of the samples, are situated between $1.96\sigma_p$ to the right and $1.96\sigma_p$ to the left of the mean μ. Consequently, 95% of the samples should yield a proportion between 47.8 and 52.2.

In order to realize an actual *reductio ad absurdum* we would have to observe 100% of the samples, but let us be satisfied with a 5% probability of error. This error is called a **type I error**. Our reasoning is as follows.

Assuming that the null hypothesis is correct and that our sample would yield a percentage of Mitterand voters of, say, 60%, then such a result, together with even more extreme results, would have so little chance under the null hypothesis that we, with the postulated 5% probability of making a mistake, would have to reject the null hypothesis. If, however, we were to find 51% in the sample, then this result, together with more extreme results, would have a fairly good chance under the null hypothesis, so that we couldn't reject it.

In our example we found 52%, so that, with an *a priori* fixed probability of a type I error of 5%, we are just short of being able to reject the null hypothesis, because 95% of the samples yield a proportion between 47.8 and 52.2 and 52 just falls within that range (see Figure A.2). The chance of finding a result of 52 or a more extreme result

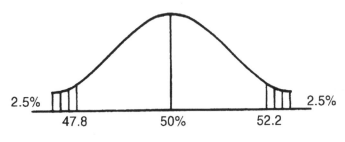

2.5%   2.5%
    47.8   50%   52.2

Figure A.2

under the null hypothesis is therefore slightly higher than 5%, and thus just high enough so that we cannot reject the null hypothesis.

If, however, we are absolutely certain that Mitterand will win no less than half of the votes and therefore only want to test to the right of 50%, then we perform a one-tailed test. In that case the 5% probability of a type I error would not be distributed over the two extremes of the sampling distribution, but could be completely demarcated to the right side of the distribution, at $1.65\sigma_p$ to the right of the mean μ, therefore to the right of the value $50 + (1.65)(1.12) = 51.8$. In the case that we — for whatever reason — are absolutely certain that Mitterand cannot lose significantly and we are only uncertain as to whether his success will be significant or one of chance, we *could* then reject the null hypothesis of merely random deviations of 50%. For our sample result of 52%, together with higher results, would then have slightly less than a 5% chance under the null hypothesis (Figure A.3).

Let us now move on from this short review of the testing of a 'specific' hypothesis, in which the concept of the 'postulated type I error' was explained, i.e., the probability that the null hypothesis is erroneously rejected.

In order to explain the 'type II error' our problem will have to be made still more specific, something that may make a rather scholastic impression.

The univariate hypothesis that Mitterand will win more than half of the votes ($H : \pi > 50\%$), where the null hypothesis is $H_0 : \pi = 50\%$, leaves room for many alternatives, especially all values greater than 50% and up to 100%. From this we take one alternative as an example: $H_a : \pi = 53\%$. This extremely specific alternative hypothesis H_a must now compete with the null hypothesis H_0, which is just as specific. On the assumption that H_0 was correct, we observed an enormous amount of samples of size $n = 2000$, that together formed a 'normal' sampling distribution with $\mu_0 = 50\%$ and $\sigma_p = [(50)(50)/2000]^{1/2} = 1.12$. We can now do the same for H_a with $\mu_a = 53\%$ and $\sigma_p = [(53)(47)/2000]^{1/2} = 1.12$.

Above, in the discussion of the type I error, the sample result of 52% was situated under the H_0 distribution. A one-tailed test with an *a priori* type I error of 5% revealed that a value of 52% significantly differed from 50%, as the probability of finding that value or even higher values was smaller than the assumed 5%. This probability is calculated by using tables for the area under the curve of the normal distribution. At 52%, the corresponding z score is $(52 - 50)/1.12 = 1.79$ and the area is 3.67%. We will now do the same for the alternative hypothesis. The sample result of 52% is now situated under the H_a distribution. The probability of finding 52% or

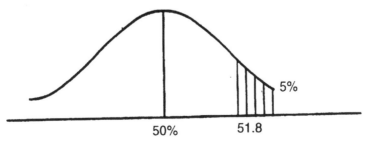

50%   51.8   5%

Figure A.3

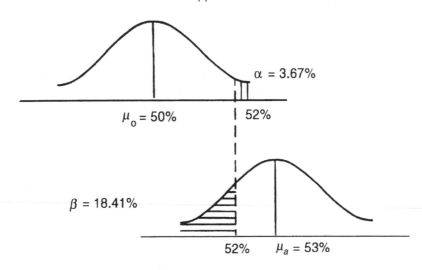

Figure A.4

smaller values is now calculated. At 52%, the corresponding z score is $(52 - 53)/1.12 = 0.90$ and the area is 18.41%. The latter is the probability of a **type II error**. This is the probability that the null hypothesis is accepted in the erroneous assumption that the alternative hypothesis is correct, in other words, the probability of an error of acceptance. This is visualized in Figure A.4.

The probability of a type I error is indicated here by the symbol α, and the probability of a type II error by the symbol β. The two distributions, under H_0 and H_a are situated under each other, as experience shows us that students are not always able to tell them apart. Note that in this case α is not the normative *a priori* type I error of 5%, but the factually realized area of 3.67% to the right of the sample result under H_0. This could also be called the likelihood of exceeding.

With intertwined H_0 and H_a distributions, the curves are as shown in Figure A.5.

The probability β of a type II error can of course be calculated for each of the many alternative hypotheses, so for $H_a : \pi = 54\%$, for $H_a : \pi = 55\%$ and so on up to $H_a : \pi = 100\%$. All these probabilities for a type II error can be brought together in a β distribution. It is, however, customary to construct not a β, but a $(1 - \beta)$ distribution. The probability $1 - \beta$ is the probability of the correct rejection of the null hypothesis (i.e., not making the mistake of accepting it). It is the probability of distinguishing, also known as power, because it indicates the power with which the

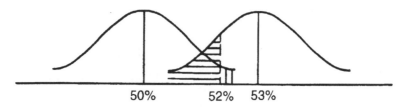

Figure A.5

actual situation

	H_0 is correct	H_0 is incorrect
accept H_0	$1 - \alpha$	β
reject H_0	α	$1 - \beta$

decision

Figure A.6   The four probabilities

alternative hypothesis can compete with the null hypothesis. This power is greater the further away the alternative hypothesis is from the null hypothesis. The power is also greater when the sample is larger. If one wants to ensure a small probability of a type II error, then the sample in the study must be sufficiently large. The power is also greater in a one-tailed test than in a two-tailed test, provided that one tests in the correct direction. Moreover, the power is greater the larger the α is. In other words, there is a play of give and take between the type I and the type II error. If α becomes greater then β becomes smaller, and vice versa. This situation is comparable to that of a legal trial. There are four probabilities: finding the suspect guilty when (s)he is innocent is α, finding him/her innocent when (s)he is guilty is β, finding him/her innocent when (s)he is innocent is $1 - \alpha$, and finding him/her guilty when (s)he is guilty is $1 - \beta$. This is summarized in Figure A.6.

A.2.6   Expansion of Sampling Theory

We limited ourselves above to the statistical testing of a univariate hypothesis with regard to a proportion (the proportion of Mitterand voters). Such a proportion is obtained from a dichotomous variable (votes for or against). The sampling distribution of proportions is a binomial probability distribution, which tends toward the normal distribution if the sample size n is large and/or if π is in the neighbourhood of 50%. In our example both conditions were met.

With a variable measured at the interval level, like age, it is not the proportion that is calculated but the mean. An example of a test for a mean will be given later, when we discuss the normal distribution. The sampling distribution is now a distribution of means. This sampling distribution is normal if the population is normally distributed and/or if the sample size n is large. With small numbers, a normality test is advisable, something that is unfortunately all too often neglected in practice.

In this book we limit ourselves to variables measured at the interval level and to dichotomies. The latter are viewed as dummy variables with 0–1 coding. Polytomous variables can be converted into a series of such dummies (one less than the number of categories). Little attention is paid to ordinal variables in classical random sample theory. A separate treatment of this would take us too far from our objectives at this time, but it is sufficient for our purposes to also view these ordinal variables as polytomous and to convert them into a series of dummies.

Another expansion of the theory of random sampling is the step from univariate to bivariate and multivariate hypotheses. If we were to literally carry out this expansion, we would become tangled in a net of formulae, as even a bivariate hypothesis

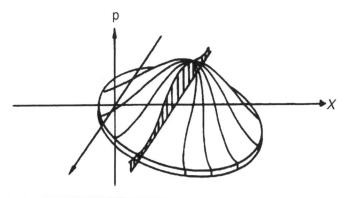

Figure A.7

pertaining to the statistical association between two variables X and Y would imply three sampling distributions, one for X, one for Y and one for the combination of X and Y. The latter, provided that the sample size is sufficient, is the so-called bivariate normal distribution and must be situated in three dimensional space, as shown in Figure A.7. It is normally distributed in all directions. The multivariate normal distribution can of course no longer be represented visually as it implies multi-dimensional space.

The confidence interval in the statistical estimation is now an entire confidence ellipsis at the foot of a mountain of normal distributions. One of the many confidence intervals (for variable Y) is drawn in the figure for a fixed value of X.

For statistical estimation and testing, however, we seldom have to make use of this entire bivariate normal distribution in all its ins and outs, because a separate sampling distribution is constructed — albeit under the assumption of bivariate normal distribution — for most association measures which indicate the strength of the relationship between X and Y. We would then speak, for example, of a sampling distribution of correlation coefficients, in which the sample correlation coefficient r is situated for the purpose of testing the null hypothesis $H_0 : \rho = 0$. The details of such a test can be found in any statistics textbook; for the testing of association measures see Tacq (1977).

A.2.7 The t Test of Difference of Means

An example of a bivariate test that forms the basis for most classical multivariate analyses is the t test of difference of means. Fisher's F test from the analysis of variance, Hotelling's T test from two-group discriminant analysis and Wilks's Λ test from multivariate analysis of variance and multiple discriminant analysis are three examples of such extensions of the t test. It is therefore extremely important that the reader have a thorough command of the t test. For this reason the test is explicitly treated in Chapter 4.

A.2.8 Sample Distributions as Probability Distributions

It was explained above that the sampling distribution is a probability distribution that, in turn, is either a normal, a binomial or a t distribution. The study of the existing probability distributions is therefore essential for the application of statistical tests. It is therefore recommended that the reader brush up on his/her knowledge especially of the binomial, normal, t, χ^2 and F distributions. Without going into too much detail on this subject, let us intuitively sketch a few relevant basic characteristics of the most important probability distributions.

The **binomial distribution**, as the word suggests, pertains to a nominal characteristic with two categories, i.e., a dichotomy, like gender with the categories male and female. In the case of such a dichotomy one can calculate a proportion, e.g. the proportion of women. From an entire population of millions of persons one can draw a sample of $n = 2000$ and within that arises a certain proportion of women, let's say 45%. Of course, one has only taken one sample, which contains 45% women. Another sample of $n = 2000$ could have contained a proportion of 53%. And another, a proportion of 49%. Taking this to the extreme, one could take a sample containing only women, which would mean a proportion of 100%, but the probability of such a sample is, of course, extremely small. If one imagines that a gigantic number of samples is taken and that for each sample the proportion of women is noted, then one has conjured up a sampling distribution of proportions. A sampling distribution like this is hypothetical. It cannot be compiled even in this present age of computers. But it can be theoretically grasped, on the condition that an assumption is made about the proportion of women (π) in the population of millions of persons. Such an assumption pertaining to a city like New York, where we know that there is a surplus of women, would be $\pi = 55\%$. Now, with an *a priori* hypothesis about π and a postulated sample size n, the sampling distribution of proportions takes on the form of a binomial distribution, where the numbers of proportions of women are on the X axis and the probabilities on the Y axis, i.e., the proportions of samples in which each of the proportions of women occur. Such a binomial distribution is a probability distribution in which the probabilities are calculated as $\binom{n}{r}\pi^r(1-\pi)^{n-r}$, where r is the number of women in the sample. It is very skewed if π is extremely small or large and/or if the sample size n is small. It almost corresponds to the normal distribution if π is close to 50% and/or the sample size n is large.

The latter, the tendency of the binomial toward the normal distribution, is nicely illustrated by Galton's board (see Figure A.8). At the top is a funnel in which balls are dropped. In the middle we see metal bars at an equal distance from each other. At the bottom are receptacles. Each time a ball hits a bar it has just as much probability of falling to the right as to the left ($\pi = 50\%$). In order for a ball to fall into the receptacle at the extreme left, it must fall to the left each time it hits a bar. The probability that this will occur is, of course, small. The same holds for the extreme right. The probability of landing in a centrally located receptacle is very great, because a ball may fall first to the right then to the left, and so on. The result with a large number of balls is the Gauss-curve of normal distribution, shown in Figure A.8.

Replace the ball with a sample, the number or proportion of balls with a number or proportion of samples, the probability of half falling to the left with the postulated probability of $\pi = 50\%$ being a woman and you have the sampling distribution of the proportions of women, which is a binomial distribution and in this case corresponds with the normal distribution because $\pi = 50\%$ and because n is large.

The **normal distribution** is a nicely formed unimodal and symmetric distribution. Its peak is in the middle, so that the mode, the median and the arithmetic mean coincide.

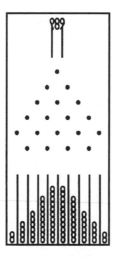

Figure A.8   Galton's board

According to some, examples of normal distributions are rare, and to others innumerable. The distribution of intelligence quotients would be such an example, where pure coincidence or nature's game of chance brings about a normal distribution. Many people have an IQ of 100. An IQ of 80 and 120 is far less frequent. And extreme IQs of 60 and 140 are rare. If, for example, the standard deviation is equal to 10, then in a normal distribution 68% of the population would be situated between an IQ of 90 and 110, in other words, between one standard deviation to left and to the right of the mean. And 95.5% of the population would be situated between 80 and 120, i.e., between two standard deviations to the left and to the right of the mean. A careful study of the normal distribution requires insight into its formula (where exp[*y*] is equal to e^y):

$$f(X) = \frac{1}{\sigma\sqrt{2\pi}}\exp\left[-\frac{(X-\mu)^2}{2\sigma^2}\right]$$

For our purposes we need only note that this formula contains three elements: the numbers 2, π and e are constants, the Greek letters μ and σ are parameters and X is a variable. A constant is fixed, e.g., $\pi = 3.14$, and a variable varies freely, e.g., the intelligence quotient X is different for each person within the population. A parameter, on the other hand, can be both: for a defined distribution it is fixed, but it varies across distributions. This demands some explanation. Let us take our IQ distribution of probability with mean $\mu = 100$ and standard deviation $\sigma = 10$. Suppose that the physical height for the same population also forms a normal distribution with $\mu = 170\,\mathrm{cm}$ and $\sigma = 12\,\mathrm{cm}$. The parameters μ and σ are then fixed for a defined distribution, but vary across distributions. It is for this last reason that scores are usually standardized. For each person the IQ score X_1 is transformed to $(X_1 - 100)/10$ and the physical height X_2 to $(X_2 - 170)/12$. The two normal distributions will then coincide, because they are both reduced to the so-called 'standard' normal distribution with mean $\mu = 0$ and standard deviation $\sigma = 1$. The areas under the curve of the standard normal distribution are included in the appendix of all statistics textbooks, so that for every normal distribution, after transforming the X values into z scores, valuable use can be made of these appendices.

The use of the normal distribution is especially important in the estimating and testing of hypotheses for variables of at least the interval measurement level. This can be extremely profitable particularly when the sampling distribution is normal. This is the case if the population distribution is normal, but also with unevenly distributed populations, on the condition that the sample size n is large. An extreme example of this is the testing of an hypothesis as to the mean income by means of a random sample (e.g., $H_0 : \mu = 2000$ as opposed to $H_a : \mu > 2000$). We know that the incomes in the population are extremely unevenly distributed, as many have very little and but a few have a lot. But with a sufficiently large sample of $n = 530$ the sampling distribution of mean incomes will still be normally distributed. In such a sampling distribution the mean incomes are on the X axis and the probabilities are on the Y axis, i.e., the proportions of samples in which each of the mean incomes occur. The mean of this sampling distribution of means, also called the expected value $E(X)$, is equal to the mean of the population that is postulated in the null hypothesis. The standard deviation of this sampling distribution, also known as the standard error, is equal to $\sigma/\sqrt{n}$ and is estimated as $S/\sqrt{(n-1)}$ or, which comes down to the same, as $s/\sqrt{n}$, because $s^2 = S^2[n/(n-1)]$. If in our sample we find a mean income of 2200, with a standard deviation S of 920, then we enter this mean in the sampling distribution of means in the form of a z score: $z = (2200 - 2000)/(920/\sqrt{529}) = 5$. The probability under the null hypothesis $\mu = 2000$ of finding such an extreme or a more extreme sample result $[p(z \geq 5H_0)]$ can be read in the table of areas under the curve of the standard normal distribution. This probability is only $0.000\,000\,3$ and, therefore so small that H_0 can be rejected in favour of H_a. As one can see, grateful use is made here of the fact that the sampling distribution for large samples approximates the normal distribution. For small samples, the sampling distribution of means does not follow the normal distribution, but the t distribution.

Student's t distribution was developed at the start of this century by William Gosset, an employee of the Guiness brewery in Dublin who published statistical articles under the pseudonym Student. During a study of the relationship between the quality of the ingredients of beer, like barley and hops, the production conditions and the final product, Gosset recognized the need for a small sample theory. His t distribution is in many ways comparable to the standard normal distribution. It is as nicely formed, unimodal and symmetrical. Its mean is also equal to 0. An important difference, however, is that its dispersion, the standard error, is not equal to 1, as in the standard normal distribution, and is not even fixed. With small samples, this standard error varies along with the sample size. If we call df the number of degrees of freedom (in most applications $df = n - 1$), then the variance of the t distribution appears to be equal to $df/(df - 2)$ for $df > 2$. This variance is greater the smaller df is. The t distribution is then flatter in the middle and denser at the extremes in comparison with the normal distribution. For large samples, i.e., for large df, the variance $df/(df - 2)$ approximates to 1, the variance of the standard normal distribution. The consequence of all of this is that not only one standard t distribution exists, as is the case in the family of normal distributions, but many t distributions depending on the number of degrees of freedom. The general formula, up to a constant, is:

$$f(t) = (1 + t^2/df)\exp[-(df + 1)/2] \quad \text{with } -\infty < t < \infty \text{ and } df > 0$$

Another important point is that the sampling distribution of means only follows a t distribution if the population distribution is normal. The moral of the story is the following. If you are asked to carry out the foregoing test of the null hypothesis $H_0 : \mu = 2000$ with regard to the mean income of a population with a sample of $n = 26$, then you would have to refuse, because σ is unknown, n is small and the population is extremely skewed. But imagine that the population of incomes, for whatever reason, *could* be regarded as normal, because, for example, the sample withstood the normality test, even in this case you would be punished statistically. For, in the case of numbers so small the power, i.e., the probability of confirming H_a if it is correct, is naturally extremely small. Our sample with mean 2200 and standard deviation 920, would then have a t score of $(2200 - 2000)/(920/\sqrt{25}) = 1.09$. The probability under H_0 that we would find this result or a greater value is, even with a one-tailed test, much greater than 10%, for, with a postulated type I error of 10%, according to the t table, a minimum critical t value of 1.32 is required. With such a small sample of $n = 26$ we are therefore not able to reject the null hypothesis.

Two other distributions that we will use frequently are the χ^2 and the F distribution. As with the t distribution, it is also the case for these distributions that the tables in the appendices of statistics textbooks only show critical values for different degrees of freedom and for a number of often used type I errors. For an exact treatment of these distributions, the reader is referred to advanced textbooks in distribution theory. Here we will discuss succinctly in which applications χ^2 and F are used.

The χ^2 **distribution** will be relevant each time an idealized series of values is compared to a factually realized series. A simple example is the testing of the null hypothesis that the marks earned by a series of students form a normal distribution against the alternative hypothesis that the distribution significantly deviates from the normal. If the factual numbers of students who earn a 5, 6, 7, 8, 9 are 26, 35, 18, 15, 6 (O_i), respectively, then the expected numbers under the null hypothesis of a normal distribution are 6, 25, 38, 25, 6 (E_i), respectively. The statistical quantity $G = \sum[(O_i - E_i)^2/E_i]$ is equal to 15.67. The sampling distribution of this quantity is χ^2-distributed for $5 - 1 = 4$ degrees of freedom (one degree of freedom less than the number of frequencies in the equation). The χ^2 table gives a critical value of 9.49 for $\alpha = 0.05$ and $df = 4$. The value found is greater, so that the null hypothesis with a postulated probability of 0.95 can be rejected.

An example of the application of the χ^2 test in multivariate analysis is the testing of the null hypothesis that the covariance matrices of the different groups in discriminant analysis are equal to each other, against the alternative hypothesis that these differ significantly.

The *F* **distribution** becomes relevant each time the ratio of variances or variance-like quantities is considered. A simple example is the testing of whether the variance between groups is significantly larger than the variance within groups. The general notion here is that the differences between individuals within groups are only random differences (error variance), but that the differences between group means stand out above chance. An example of calculating this can be found in section A.2.4, where the partition of variance is dealt with. A series of scores 2 2 3 4 4 5 6 7 8 9 with mean 5 and variation 54 is partitioned into two groups. The first group 2 2 3 4 4 has a mean of 3 and a variation of 4. The second group 5 6 7 8 9 has a mean of 7 and a variation of 10. The within-group variation is $4 + 10 = 14$. The between-group variation is defined by examining the group means 3 and 7. Their mean is 5 and their variation 8. The between-group variation entirely determined by the group is obtained by multiplying the variation between groups by the number of individuals per group: $8 \times 5 = 40$. It appears that $54 = 40 + 14$ or $SST = SSB + SSW$. An analogous division of the total into a between- and a within-component can be carried out for the degrees of freedom. One degree of freedom is lost to the mean of a series. There are, therefore, nine degrees of freedom for the total of 10 scores. For the between component we calculate for two groups, so that there is one degree of freedom. For the within component, we calculate for 2×5 individuals, each time losing a degree of freedom to the group mean, so that $2(5 - 1) = 8$ remain. We see here, too, that total $=$ between $+$ within, because $9 = 1 + 8$. Should one now want to work with variances instead of variations (Mean squares MS instead of Sum of Squares SS), then one must divide each of the variations concerned by the corresponding degrees of freedom: $MSB = 40/1$ and $MSW = 14/8$. The ratio of the between-variance MSB and the within-variance MSW is a statistical quantity $F = (40/1)/(14/8) = 22.86$, for which the sampling distribution for the degrees of freedom, one for the numerator and eight for the denominator, is distributed as F (F for Sir Ronald Fisher). The critical value of F for one degree of freedom for the numerator and eight degrees of freedom for the denominator is equal to 5.32 for a postulated α of 0.05. The value we found is greater, and we can therefore, even with these small numbers (!), reject the null hypothesis with a probability of 95%. The null hypothesis states that the ratio MSB/MSW is equal to 1, in other words, that the differences between groups (MSB) are not greater than the randomly assumed differences between individuals within groups ($MSW = $ error variance).

In multivariate analysis the F distribution will frequently be used in more complicated situations than the example above. The test of difference of groups in analysis of variance, the test for the significance of the regression model in multiple regression analysis and the test for centroid differences in discriminant analysis are just a few of the many examples of application. Rao especially seems extremely charmed by the F distribution and has developed an F variant for most of the applications in multivariate analysis.

We add a final remark for reasons of mathematical esthetics. The attentive reader will already have seen that instead of the F test for this example, we could just as easily have used the t test of difference of means from A.2.7 (see Chapter 4). We could have situated the difference obtained (-4) between the mean of the first group (3) and the mean of the second group (7) in a sampling distribution of differences of means with the estimated standard error $= (s_w^2/n_1 + s_w^2/n_2)^{1/2}$ and where s_w^2 is equal to $(4 + 10)/((5 - 1) + (5 - 1)) = 1.75$ and $n_1 = n_2 = 5$. The t value for the difference of means found in our pair of samples would be equal to $t = (4 - 0)/[1.75/5 + 1.75/5]^{1/2} = 4.78$. From the t table a significant difference would then appear between the means of the two groups. Mathematical esthetics is involved here because the F value of 22.86 which was obtained is equal to the square of the t value found of 4.78.

One can also see in the F and t table that the critical values of F for a numerator of one degree of freedom (only two groups!) are equal to the squares of the corresponding values of t.

A.3 Matrix Algebra

At the end of Chapter 5 on regression analysis and in all of the following chapters use is made of matrix notation. We limit ourselves here to a concise overview of the most important definitions and operations that the reader must grasp in order to read the chapters. For a more extensive treatment see Green (1976) or any textbook on linear algebra.

A.3.1 Vectors

A **column vector** of order $m \times 1$ is an ordered m-tuple of real numbers (called scalars), that are collected in a column:

$$\mathbf{a} = \begin{bmatrix} a_1 \\ a_2 \\ a_3 \\ \vdots \\ a_m \end{bmatrix}$$

The a_i's are called elements or components of $\mathbf{a}$. Two column vectors are equal to each other if they are equal element by element. A vector is indicated by a bold-face lower-case letter $\mathbf{a}, \mathbf{b}, \mathbf{c}, \ldots$. For matrices, bold-faced capitals $\mathbf{A}, \mathbf{B}, \mathbf{C}, \ldots$ are used. The column vector $\mathbf{a}$ has m rows and 1 column. For this reason it is of order $m \times 1$.

A **row vector** of order $1 \times m$ is the transpose of the $m \times 1$ column vector. Transposition is indicated with a prime and means laying flat, so that a column becomes a row: $\mathbf{a}' = (a_1, a_2, a_3, \ldots, a_m)$. Here, too, two row vectors are equal if they are equal element by element.

The row vector $\mathbf{a}'$ has 1 row and m columns. This is why it is of order $1 \times m$. If one transposes the row vector again one obtains the column vector $\mathbf{a} : (\mathbf{a}')' = \mathbf{a}$.

A **zero vector** is filled with zeros and is indicated by a bold-faced zero, therefore $\mathbf{0}$ as a column vector and $\mathbf{0}'$ as a row vector.

A **unit vector** is filled with ones and is indicated by a bold-faced one, therefore $\mathbf{1}$ as a column vector and $\mathbf{1}'$ as a row vector.

For the **adding** or **subtracting** of two or more vectors the corresponding elements are added (or subtracted). For example:

$$\mathbf{a} = \begin{bmatrix} 2 \\ 4 \\ 3 \end{bmatrix} \qquad \mathbf{b} = \begin{bmatrix} 1 \\ 3 \\ 2 \end{bmatrix} \qquad \mathbf{a} + \mathbf{b} = \begin{bmatrix} 3 \\ 7 \\ 5 \end{bmatrix}$$

$$\mathbf{a}' = (2, 4, 3) \qquad \mathbf{b}' = (1, 3, 2) \qquad \mathbf{a}' - \mathbf{b}' = (1, 1, 1) = \mathbf{1}'$$

Naturally, vectors must be of the same order if they are to be added or subtracted. For example, the adding of $\mathbf{c}' = (5, 2, 1)$ and $\mathbf{d}' = (3, 4)$ is impossible. Subtracting row vector $\mathbf{b}'$ from column vector $\mathbf{a}$ is also out of the question.

The **addition** (or substraction) of vectors has a number of **properties**.

It is commutative: $\mathbf{a} + \mathbf{b} = \mathbf{b} + \mathbf{a}$.

It is associative: $\mathbf{a} + (\mathbf{b} + \mathbf{c}) = (\mathbf{a} + \mathbf{b}) + \mathbf{c}$.

A property of the zero vector is that $\mathbf{a} + \mathbf{0} = \mathbf{0} + \mathbf{a} = \mathbf{a}$.

The sum of a vector $\mathbf{a}$ and its opposite $-\mathbf{a}$ (in which all the elements are negative numbers) is equal to the zero vector: $\mathbf{a} + (-\mathbf{a}) = (-\mathbf{a}) + \mathbf{a} = \mathbf{0}$.

The **multiplication of a vector with a scalar k** is the multiplication of each element of the vector with that real number:

$$k\mathbf{a} = k \begin{bmatrix} a_1 \\ a_2 \\ a_3 \\ \vdots \\ a_m \end{bmatrix} = \begin{bmatrix} ka_1 \\ ka_2 \\ ka_3 \\ \vdots \\ ka_m \end{bmatrix}$$

For example, the product of the row vector $\mathbf{a}' = (2, 4, 3)$ and the real number $k = 2$ is $k\mathbf{a}' = (4, 8, 6)$.

The multiplication by a scalar has a number of **properties**:

It is associative: $k_1(k_2\mathbf{a}) = (k_1 k_2)\mathbf{a}$.

It is, in combination with addition, distributive: $k(\mathbf{a} + \mathbf{b}) = k\mathbf{a} + k\mathbf{b}$ and also $(k_1 + k_2)\mathbf{a} = k_1\mathbf{a} + k_2\mathbf{a}$.

Multiplication with the number 1 produces the vector itself: $1\mathbf{a} = \mathbf{a}$.

Multiplication with the number 0 produces the zero vector: $0\mathbf{a} = \mathbf{0}$.

Multiplication with the number -1 produces the opposite vector: $-1\mathbf{a} = -\mathbf{a}$.

Addition and multiplication with a scalar are brought together in the concept **linear combination**, a concept that we repeatedly encounter in multivariate analysis.

If $\mathbf{a}_1, \mathbf{a}_2, \mathbf{a}_3, \ldots, \mathbf{a}_m$ are m vectors and $k_1, k_2, k_3, \ldots, k_m$ are m real numbers, then the vector $\mathbf{y} = k_1\mathbf{a}_1 + k_2\mathbf{a}_2 + k_3\mathbf{a}_3 + \ldots + k_m\mathbf{a}_m$ is a linear combination of the m vectors. This is therefore a weighted sum of the vectors, in which the scalars are the weights. The discriminant functions from discriminant analysis, the canonical variables from canonical correlation analysis and the principal components from principal components analysis are three examples.

The **scalar product** of the two **vectors a** and **b** (sometimes called the inner product) is the product of the transposed vector $\mathbf{a}'$ and the vector $\mathbf{b}$, as follows:

$$\mathbf{a} = \begin{bmatrix} a_1 \\ a_2 \\ \vdots \\ a_m \end{bmatrix} \qquad \mathbf{b} = \begin{bmatrix} b_1 \\ b_2 \\ \vdots \\ b_m \end{bmatrix} \qquad \mathbf{a}'\mathbf{b} = a_1 b_1 + a_2 b_2 + \ldots + a_m b_m$$

For example:

$$\mathbf{a} = \begin{bmatrix} 2 \\ 4 \\ 3 \end{bmatrix} \qquad \mathbf{b} = \begin{bmatrix} 1 \\ 3 \\ 2 \end{bmatrix} \qquad \mathbf{a'b} = 20$$

The multiplication of two column vectors $\mathbf{a}$ and $\mathbf{b}$ is not possible, because their orders are $(m \times 1)$ and $(m \times 1)$, respectively, and these do not display any correspondence. After the transposing of $\mathbf{a}$, this correspondence *is* present, as follows: $(1 \times m)(m \times 1)$. This will be discussed more extensively when we treat the multiplication of matrices. We can see that the scalar product of two vectors produces a real number.

A special case is the scalar product of a vector with itself. One then obtains the sum of the squares of the elements:

$$\mathbf{a} = \begin{bmatrix} 2 \\ 4 \\ 3 \end{bmatrix} \qquad \mathbf{a'a} = 29$$

Another special case is the scalar product of the unit vector $\mathbf{1}$ and the vector $\mathbf{a}$. One then obtains the sum of the elements:

$$\mathbf{1} = \begin{bmatrix} 1 \\ 1 \\ 1 \end{bmatrix} \qquad \mathbf{a} = \begin{bmatrix} 2 \\ 4 \\ 3 \end{bmatrix} \qquad \mathbf{1'a} = 9$$

A.3.2 Matrices

A **matrix A** of order $m \times n$ is a rectangular array of real numbers in m rows and n columns:

$$\mathbf{A} = \begin{bmatrix} a_{11} & a_{12} & \cdots & a_{1n} \\ a_{21} & a_{22} & \cdots & a_{2n} \\ \vdots & \vdots & & \vdots \\ a_{m1} & a_{m2} & & a_{mn} \end{bmatrix}$$

While bold-faced lower-case letters are used for vectors $\mathbf{a}, \mathbf{b}, \mathbf{c}, \ldots$, matrices are indicated by bold-faced capitals $\mathbf{A}, \mathbf{B}, \mathbf{C}, \ldots$. A vector is a special case of a matrix. For, if $m = 1$, the $m \times n$ matrix is transformed into a $1 \times m$ row vector and if $n = 1$ it is transformed into an $m \times 1$ column vector.

Even a scalar, taken to the extreme, is a special case of a matrix with $m = n = 1$. In other words, a real number is a 1×1 matrix.

A matrix is **rectangular** if the number of rows (m) differs from the number of columns (n). On the other hand, if $m = n$ we speak of a **square** matrix.

Take, for example, the matrices below. The 3×3 matrix $\mathbf{A}$ is square and the 2×3 matrix $\mathbf{B}$ is rectangular.

$$\mathbf{A} = \begin{bmatrix} 2 & 1 & 5 \\ 4 & 3 & 2 \\ 3 & 2 & 1 \end{bmatrix} \qquad \mathbf{B} = \begin{bmatrix} 7 & 9 & 3 \\ 3 & -1 & 1 \end{bmatrix}$$

The **principal diagonal** of a square matrix is the set of elements from the top left to the bottom right. For **A** this is {2, 3, 1}. The sum of the elements on the principal diagonal of a square matrix **A** is called the **trace**: $\text{tr}(\mathbf{A}) = \sum_i a_i$.

A **diagonal matrix** is a square matrix which contains zeros everywhere off the principal diagonal. Elements on the principal diagonal themselves can either be zero or not. For example:

$$\mathbf{C} = \begin{bmatrix} 2 & 0 & 0 \\ 0 & 3 & 0 \\ 0 & 0 & 1 \end{bmatrix} \qquad \mathbf{D} = \begin{bmatrix} -3 & 0 \\ 0 & 0 \end{bmatrix}$$

The **transpose** of a matrix **A** is the matrix **A′** that is obtained by exchanging rows and columns. For example:

$$\mathbf{A} = \begin{bmatrix} 2 & 1 & 5 \\ 4 & 3 & 2 \\ 3 & 2 & 1 \end{bmatrix} \qquad \mathbf{A'} = \begin{bmatrix} 2 & 4 & 3 \\ 1 & 3 & 2 \\ 5 & 2 & 1 \end{bmatrix}$$

$$\mathbf{B} = \begin{bmatrix} 7 & 9 & 3 \\ 3 & -1 & 1 \end{bmatrix} \qquad \mathbf{B'} = \begin{bmatrix} 7 & 3 \\ 9 & -1 \\ 3 & 1 \end{bmatrix}$$

If we once again transpose the transposed matrix, we would, of course, obtain the original matrix, so that $(\mathbf{A'})' = \mathbf{A}$.

A square matrix is **symmetric** if it is equal to its transpose, i.e., if $\mathbf{A} = \mathbf{A'}$. This means that the mirror images of the triangles to the top right and bottom left of the principal diagonal contain the same numbers; in other words, $a_{ij} = a_{ji}$. The matrix **E** below, for example, is a symmetric matrix and the matrix **A** above is a non-symmetric matrix.

$$\mathbf{E} = \begin{bmatrix} 3 & 1 & 2 \\ 1 & 7 & 4 \\ 2 & 4 & 5 \end{bmatrix}$$

Symmetric matrices are extremely common in multivariate analysis. A typical example is the correlation matrix **R**, which contains the zero-order correlation coefficients off the principal diagonal, so that $r_{ij} = r_{ji}$.

A rectangular matrix, of course, cannot be symmetric; the condition for symmetry is that a matrix be square. A diagonal matrix is always symmetric.

The **zero matrix** is filled with zeros and is indicated by a bold-faced phi: ϕ. If it is square, the zero matrix is both symmetric and diagonal.

Two other special cases of diagonal matrices are the scalar matrix and the identity matrix.

A **scalar matrix** is a diagonal matrix with equal elements on the principal diagonal. For example:

$$\mathbf{F} = \begin{bmatrix} 3 & 0 & 0 \\ 0 & 3 & 0 \\ 0 & 0 & 3 \end{bmatrix} \qquad \mathbf{G} = \begin{bmatrix} -2 & 0 \\ 0 & -2 \end{bmatrix}$$

The **identity matrix**, always indicated by **I**, is a square matrix with 1s on the principal diagonal and 0s everywhere else. It is therefore a special case of a scalar matrix. For example:

$$\mathbf{I} = \begin{bmatrix} 1 & 0 & 0 \\ 0 & 1 & 0 \\ 0 & 0 & 1 \end{bmatrix} \qquad \mathbf{I} = \begin{bmatrix} 1 & 0 \\ 0 & 1 \end{bmatrix}$$

In summary, a matrix is either rectangular or square. A square matrix can be symmetric or not. A symmetric matrix can be diagonal or not. A diagonal matrix can be scalar or not. A scalar matrix can be the identity matrix **I** or not.

A.3.3 Operations with Matrices

For the **addition** (or subtraction) of two or more matrices, the corresponding elements are added (or subtracted).

In order to perform these operations the matrices must naturally be of the same order. For example:

$$\mathbf{A} = \begin{bmatrix} 2 & 1 & 5 \\ 4 & 3 & 2 \\ 3 & 2 & 1 \end{bmatrix} \quad \mathbf{E} = \begin{bmatrix} 3 & 1 & 2 \\ 1 & 7 & 4 \\ 2 & 4 & 5 \end{bmatrix} \quad \mathbf{A} + \mathbf{E} = \begin{bmatrix} 5 & 2 & 7 \\ 5 & 10 & 6 \\ 5 & 6 & 6 \end{bmatrix}$$

The **addition** of matrices has the same **properties** as the addition of vectors:

It is commutative: $\mathbf{A} + \mathbf{B} = \mathbf{B} + \mathbf{A}$.
It is associative: $\mathbf{A} + (\mathbf{B} + \mathbf{C}) = (\mathbf{A} + \mathbf{B}) + \mathbf{C}$.
A property of the zero matrix is that $\mathbf{A} + \phi = \phi + \mathbf{A} = \mathbf{A}$.
The sum of the matrix **A** and its opposite $-\mathbf{A}$ (in which all elements are negative numbers) is equal to the zero matrix: $\mathbf{A} + (-\mathbf{A}) = (-\mathbf{A}) + \mathbf{A} = \phi$.

The **multiplication of a matrix with a scalar** k is also the same as with vectors. Each element is multiplied by the real number k. For example:

$$\mathbf{B} = \begin{bmatrix} 7 & 9 & 3 \\ 3 & -1 & 1 \end{bmatrix} \qquad k = 2 \qquad k\mathbf{B} = \begin{bmatrix} 14 & 18 & 6 \\ 6 & -2 & 2 \end{bmatrix}$$

The multiplication by a scalar has the same properties as for vectors.

It is associative: $k_1(k_2\mathbf{A}) = (k_1 k_2)\mathbf{A}$.
It is, in combination with addition, distributive: $k(\mathbf{A} + \mathbf{B}) = k\mathbf{A} + k\mathbf{B}$ and also $(k_1 + k_2)\mathbf{A} = k_1\mathbf{A} + k_2\mathbf{A}$.
Multiplication by the number 1 produces the matrix itself: $1\mathbf{A} = \mathbf{A}$.
Multiplication by the number 0 produces the zero matrix: $0\mathbf{A} = \phi$.
Multiplication by the number -1 produces the opposite matrix: $-1\mathbf{A} = -\mathbf{A}$.
Multiplication by a scalar gives us the opportunity to define a subtraction, for example $\mathbf{A} - \mathbf{E}$, as an addition: $\mathbf{A} + (-\mathbf{E})$. Here **E** is first multiplied by the scalar -1 and then $-\mathbf{E}$ is added to **A**.

$$\mathbf{A} = \begin{bmatrix} 2 & 1 & 5 \\ 4 & 3 & 2 \\ 3 & 2 & 1 \end{bmatrix} \quad \mathbf{E} = \begin{bmatrix} 3 & 1 & 2 \\ 1 & 7 & 4 \\ 2 & 4 & 5 \end{bmatrix} \quad \mathbf{A} - \mathbf{E} = \begin{bmatrix} -1 & 0 & 3 \\ 3 & -4 & -2 \\ 1 & -2 & -4 \end{bmatrix}$$

Multiplication by a scalar also brings some clarity to the concepts of scalar matrix and identity matrix.

A scalar matrix, for example $\mathbf{F}$, is equal to the product of the identity matrix and the scalar on the principal diagonal:

$$\mathbf{F} = \begin{bmatrix} 3 & 0 & 0 \\ 0 & 3 & 0 \\ 0 & 0 & 3 \end{bmatrix} = 3 \begin{bmatrix} 1 & 0 & 0 \\ 0 & 1 & 0 \\ 0 & 0 & 1 \end{bmatrix} = 3\mathbf{I}$$

Up till now addition and multiplication by a scalar was discussed using vectors and matrices. The similarity with number theory was considerable. This similarity is no longer as evident in the **multiplication of matrices**.

In order to multiply two matrices $\mathbf{A}$ and $\mathbf{B}$ there must be a correspondence. For example, if $\mathbf{A}$ is an $m \times n$ matrix and $\mathbf{B}$ an $n \times p$ matrix, then we have this correspondence because $\mathbf{A}$ has n columns and $\mathbf{B}$ n rows: $(m \times n)(n \times p)$. The product $\mathbf{C} = \mathbf{AB}$ is therefore an $m \times p$ matrix with as many rows as $\mathbf{A}$ and as many columns as $\mathbf{B}$: $(m \times n)(n \times p)$. An element c_{ij} of the product $\mathbf{C}$ is calculated as $c_{ij} = \sum_k a_{ik} b_{kj}$, i.e., multiplying the elements of the i-th row of $\mathbf{A}$ by the corresponding elements of the j-th column of $\mathbf{B}$ and then taking the sum of these products. An example is the product of the 2×3 matrix $\mathbf{B}$ and the 3×2 matrix $\mathbf{H}$:

$$\mathbf{B} = \begin{bmatrix} 7 & 9 & 3 \\ 3 & -1 & 1 \end{bmatrix} \quad \mathbf{H} = \begin{bmatrix} 1 & 5 \\ 3 & 2 \\ 2 & 1 \end{bmatrix} \quad \mathbf{BH} = \begin{bmatrix} 40 & 56 \\ 2 & 14 \end{bmatrix}$$

By way of illustration, the **first** row of $\mathbf{B}$ and the **second** column of $\mathbf{H}$ have been enframed. This produces the number 56 on the **first** row, **second** column of $\mathbf{BH}$ as follows: $(7)(5) + (9)(2) + (3)(1) = 35 + 18 + 3 = 56$. Analogously so for the other three elements.

Note that the product $\mathbf{HB}$ is not equal to $\mathbf{BH}$. This is because $\mathbf{BH}$ is a 2×2 matrix, while $\mathbf{HB}$ is a 3×3 matrix: $(3 \times 2)(2 \times 3)$.

$$\mathbf{H} = \begin{bmatrix} 1 & 5 \\ 3 & 2 \\ 2 & 1 \end{bmatrix} \quad \mathbf{B} = \begin{bmatrix} 7 & 9 & 3 \\ 3 & -1 & 1 \end{bmatrix} \quad \mathbf{HB} = \begin{bmatrix} 22 & 4 & 8 \\ 27 & 25 & 11 \\ 17 & 17 & 7 \end{bmatrix}$$

By way of illustration: the **second** row of $\mathbf{H}$ and the **third** column of $\mathbf{B}$ produces the number 11 on the **second** row, **third** column of $\mathbf{HB}$ as follows: $(3)(3) + (2)(1) = 11$. Analogously so for the other eight elements.

We understand now why a column vector cannot be multiplied by a column vector. There is, after all, no correspondence: $(m \times 1)(m \times 1)$. We *do* find this correspondence in the product of a $1 \times m$ row vector $\mathbf{a}'$ with an $m \times 1$ column vector $\mathbf{b}$ and this produces a 1×1 matrix, a scalar therefore. The product of an $m \times 1$ column vector $\mathbf{b}$ with a $1 \times m$ row vector $\mathbf{a}'$ is, however, something very different; the result of this is an $m \times m$ matrix! For example:

$$\mathbf{a} = \begin{bmatrix} 2 \\ 4 \\ 3 \end{bmatrix} \quad \mathbf{a}' = (2, 4, 3) \quad \mathbf{b} = \begin{bmatrix} 1 \\ 3 \\ 2 \end{bmatrix} \quad \mathbf{a}'\mathbf{b} = 20 \quad \mathbf{ba}' = \begin{bmatrix} 2 & 4 & 3 \\ 6 & 12 & 9 \\ 4 & 8 & 6 \end{bmatrix}$$

We can see that matrix multiplication is generally **not commutative**: $\mathbf{AB} \neq \mathbf{BA}$. The properties of associativity do, however, hold: $(\mathbf{AB})\mathbf{C} = \mathbf{A}(\mathbf{BC})$, as do those of distributivity: $\mathbf{A}(\mathbf{B} + \mathbf{C}) = \mathbf{AB} + \mathbf{AC}$. One must also be careful in transposing with the extension and transferring of properties. Because while it holds for addition that the transpose of the sum is equal to the sum of the transposes: $(\mathbf{A} + \mathbf{B})' = \mathbf{A}' + \mathbf{B}'$, this is not the case for multiplication.

After all, the transpose of the product is equal to the product of the transposes in the reverse order: $(\mathbf{AB})' = \mathbf{B}'\mathbf{A}'$. For example:

$$\mathbf{B} = \begin{bmatrix} 7 & 9 & 3 \\ 3 & -1 & 1 \end{bmatrix} \quad \mathbf{H} = \begin{bmatrix} 1 & 5 \\ 3 & 2 \\ 2 & 1 \end{bmatrix} \quad \mathbf{BH} = \begin{bmatrix} 40 & 56 \\ 2 & 14 \end{bmatrix} \quad (\mathbf{BH})' = \begin{bmatrix} 40 & 2 \\ 56 & 14 \end{bmatrix}$$

$$\mathbf{B}' = \begin{bmatrix} 7 & 3 \\ 9 & -1 \\ 3 & 1 \end{bmatrix} \quad \mathbf{H}' = \begin{bmatrix} 1 & 3 & 2 \\ 5 & 2 & 1 \end{bmatrix} \quad \mathbf{H}'\mathbf{B}' = \begin{bmatrix} 40 & 2 \\ 56 & 14 \end{bmatrix}$$

A.3.4   The Determinant of a Square Matrix

The determinant of a matrix plays an important role in multivariate analysis, for example in the calculation of the inverse. Only square matrices have a determinant.

The **determinant** of an $m \times m$ matrix $\mathbf{A}$, indicated by $\det(\mathbf{A})$ or $|\mathbf{A}|$, is a number that is calculated from the elements of the matrix, as follows.

Construct all of the possible products of m elements so that one and only one element is taken from each row and one and only one element is taken from each column. There are $m!$ of these products. For a 3×3 matrix with elements a_{ij}, for example, there are $3! = (1)(2)(3) = 6$ products. We give these a plus sign or a minus sign: $a_{11}a_{22}a_{33}, a_{12}a_{23}a_{31}, a_{13}a_{21}a_{32}, -a_{13}a_{22}a_{31}, -a_{11}a_{23}a_{32}, -a_{12}a_{21}a_{33}$. The plus sign or minus sign is determined by the number of inversions: $+$ for an even number and $-$ for an odd number of inversions. We speak of an inversion when two column subscripts are not in their natural order, provided that the row subscripts are all placed in their natural order $(i = 1, 2, 3)$. For example, in the fourth product $-a_{13}a_{22}a_{31}$ the row subscripts i are in the natural order 1, 2, 3 and the column subscripts in the order 3, 2, 1. The inversions are $3 > 2, 3 > 1, 2 > 1$. Their number (three) is odd and the product, therefore, is given a minus sign. The numbers of inversions for the six products are 0, 2, 2, 3, 1, 1, respectively. The signs are therefore $+++---$, respectively. The sum of all $m!$ products with their sign is the determinant. For example:

$$\mathbf{A} = \begin{bmatrix} 2 & 1 & 5 \\ 4 & 3 & 2 \\ 3 & 2 & 1 \end{bmatrix} \quad \begin{aligned} |\mathbf{A}| &= (2)(3)(1) + (1)(2)(3) + (5)(4)(2) - (5)(3)(3) - (2)(2)(2) \\ &\quad - (1)(4)(1) = -5 \end{aligned}$$

$$\mathbf{G} = \begin{bmatrix} -2 & 0 \\ 0 & -2 \end{bmatrix} \quad |\mathbf{G}| = g_{11}g_{22} - g_{12}g_{21} = (-2)(-2) - (0)(0) = 4$$

This procedure is too complex for larger matrices, but other methods are available. We will now discuss the calculation of the **determinant with the help of minors and cofactors**.

In an $m \times m$ matrix $\mathbf{A}$ each element a_{ij} has a **minor**, this is the determinant of the submatrix that is obtained by eliminating the i-th row and the j-th column of the matrix $\mathbf{A}$. For example:

$$\mathbf{A} = \begin{bmatrix} a_{11} & a_{12} & a_{13} \\ a_{21} & a_{22} & a_{23} \\ a_{31} & a_{32} & a_{33} \end{bmatrix} \qquad \text{minor}(a_{21}) = \begin{vmatrix} a_{12} & a_{13} \\ a_{32} & a_{33} \end{vmatrix} = a_{12}a_{33} - a_{13}a_{32}$$

Analogously so for the other eight elements of $\mathbf{A}$.

A **cofactor** is a minor with a plus or minus sign. These are attributed as follows. Consider the matrix as a sort of chess or draughts board, give the top left square a plus sign, and change the sign each time you move over one square. In this way, an array of signs emerges according to an alternating pattern:

$$\begin{bmatrix} + & - & + & - & \cdots \\ - & + & - & + & \cdots \\ + & - & + & - & \cdots \\ - & + & - & + & \cdots \\ \vdots & \vdots & \vdots & \vdots & \cdots \end{bmatrix}$$

In the foregoing, the minor of the element a_{21} from the matrix $\mathbf{A}$ was calculated. The cofactor of a_{21} is this minor, given a minus sign: cofactor $(a_{21}) = -(a_{12}a_{33} - a_{13}a_{32})$.

We can now calculate the **determinant**. Take an arbitrary row or column from matrix $\mathbf{A}$, multiply each element of that row (or column) by its cofactor and sum these products. This is the determinant.

If, for example, we choose the second row from the following matrix $\mathbf{A}$, this becomes:

$$\mathbf{A} = \begin{bmatrix} 2 & 1 & 5 \\ 4 & 3 & 2 \\ 3 & 2 & 1 \end{bmatrix} \qquad |\mathbf{A}| = -4 \begin{vmatrix} 1 & 5 \\ 2 & 1 \end{vmatrix} + 3 \begin{vmatrix} 2 & 5 \\ 3 & 1 \end{vmatrix} - 2 \begin{vmatrix} 2 & 1 \\ 3 & 2 \end{vmatrix}$$

$$= -4(1 - 10) + 3(2 - 15) - 2(4 - 3) = -5$$

For those interested in a visual image of what the determinant of a matrix means, see Green (1976, pp. 118 ff.), where the determinant is interpreted in terms of areas, volumes and hypervolumes of geometric figures.

We will discuss two more concepts that play an important role in multivariate analysis: the non-singular matrix and the rank of a matrix. A matrix is **singular** when its determinant is equal to 0. For example:

$$\mathbf{J} = \begin{bmatrix} 1 & 2 & 3 \\ 2 & 4 & 6 \\ 3 & 6 & 9 \end{bmatrix} \qquad |\mathbf{J}| = 1 \begin{vmatrix} 4 & 6 \\ 6 & 9 \end{vmatrix} - 2 \begin{vmatrix} 2 & 6 \\ 3 & 9 \end{vmatrix} + 3 \begin{vmatrix} 2 & 4 \\ 3 & 6 \end{vmatrix}$$

$$= 1(36 - 36) - 2(18 - 18) + 3(12 - 12) = 0$$

We see that the elements in the second row of $\mathbf{J}$ are double those in the first row, and that the elements in the third row are triple those in the first row. With systems of linear equations, often used in multivariate analysis, we speak of linear dependence in such a case. The matrix of coefficients is then singular and this is a problem. One hopes for a non-singular matrix, i.e., a matrix $\mathbf{A}$ where $|\mathbf{A}| \neq 0$.

Linear dependence can be described as follows. The first and third rows of $\mathbf{J}$ are linearly dependent. These rows can be seen as row vectors $\mathbf{j}'_1$ and $\mathbf{j}'_3$. Now, these two row vectors are linearly independent if no set of scalars, k_1 and k_3, can be found that are not each zero, so that the linear combination (weighted sum) of these vectors is the zero vector. In our example, we have $\mathbf{j}'_1 = (1, 2, 3)$ and $\mathbf{j}'_3 = (3, 6, 9)$ and one certainly can find a set of scalars $k_1 = -3$ and $k_3 = 1$ so that $k_1\mathbf{j}'_1 + k_3\mathbf{j}'_3 = -3(1, 2, 3) + 1(3, 6, 9) = (0, 0, 0)$. Thus the two row vectors are linearly dependent.

Now the **rank** of a matrix can be discussed. A matrix, rectangular or square, is rank r if the maximal number of linearly independent rows (or columns) is equal to r. Another, but equivalent, formulation is this: the rank of $\mathbf{A}$ is r if each minor of order $r + 1$ is equal to 0 and at least one minor of order r is not 0.

For example, the rank of the 3×3 matrix $\mathbf{A}$ above is equal to its order 3. The rank of $\mathbf{J}$, on the other hand, is 1, while its order is 3. An intermediate example is the following 3×3 matrix $\mathbf{K}$, with order 3 and rank 2:

$$\mathbf{K} = \begin{bmatrix} 1 & 2 & 3 \\ 2 & 4 & 6 \\ 3 & 6 & 7 \end{bmatrix} \quad |\mathbf{K}| = 1(28 - 36) - 2(14 - 18) + 3(12 - 12) = 0$$

$$\text{and minor} \begin{vmatrix} 4 & 6 \\ 6 & 7 \end{vmatrix} = 28 - 36 = -8 \neq 0$$

We see that a square matrix is singular if its rank is smaller than its order, and vice versa.

A.3.5 The Inverse of a Matrix

We know that for a real number k we can find the inverse number $k^{-1} = 1/k$ so that $k \cdot k^1 = 1$. Similarly, for a square matrix $\mathbf{A}$ we can determine the **inverse matrix**. This is the matrix indicated by $\mathbf{A}^{-1}$, and the rule here is that the product of it and the original matrix $\mathbf{A}$ is equal to the identity matrix $\mathbf{I}$: $\mathbf{A}\mathbf{A}^{-1} = \mathbf{A}^{-1}\mathbf{A} = \mathbf{I}$.

Not all matrices have an inverse. One requirement is that $|\mathbf{A}| \neq 0$, in other words that the matrix $\mathbf{A}$ is non-singular or, which comes down to the same thing, that its rank is equal to its order. This is sometimes referred to as being of 'full rank' or being 'positive definite'.

Many procedures have been developed for calculating the inverse of a matrix, because this becomes too complex for large matrices. Here, we will follow the calculation procedure that makes use of minors, cofactors and the determinant.

The inverse of a matrix $\mathbf{A}$ is the adjoint matrix adj $\mathbf{A}$ divided by its determinant $|\mathbf{A}|$:

$$\mathbf{A}^{-1} = \frac{\text{adj } \mathbf{A}}{|\mathbf{A}|}$$

The determinant is already known. The adjoint matrix (the adjoint of $\mathbf{A}$) is constructed as follows. Replace each element a_{ij} in the matrix $\mathbf{A}$ with its cofactor (minor with a sign). From this matrix of cofactors take the transpose. This is adj $\mathbf{A}$.

For example:

$$A = \begin{bmatrix} 2 & 1 & 5 \\ 4 & 3 & 2 \\ 3 & 2 & 1 \end{bmatrix}$$

$$|A| = 2\begin{vmatrix} 3 & 2 \\ 2 & 1 \end{vmatrix} - 1\begin{vmatrix} 4 & 2 \\ 3 & 1 \end{vmatrix} + 5\begin{vmatrix} 4 & 3 \\ 3 & 2 \end{vmatrix}$$

$$= 2(3-4) - 1(4-6) + 5(8-9) = -5$$

$$\text{adj } A = \begin{bmatrix} \begin{vmatrix} 3 & 2 \\ 2 & 1 \end{vmatrix} & -\begin{vmatrix} 4 & 2 \\ 3 & 1 \end{vmatrix} & \begin{vmatrix} 4 & 3 \\ 3 & 2 \end{vmatrix} \\ -\begin{vmatrix} 1 & 5 \\ 2 & 1 \end{vmatrix} & \begin{vmatrix} 2 & 5 \\ 3 & 1 \end{vmatrix} & -\begin{vmatrix} 2 & 1 \\ 3 & 2 \end{vmatrix} \\ \begin{vmatrix} 1 & 5 \\ 3 & 2 \end{vmatrix} & -\begin{vmatrix} 2 & 5 \\ 4 & 2 \end{vmatrix} & \begin{vmatrix} 2 & 1 \\ 4 & 3 \end{vmatrix} \end{bmatrix} = \begin{bmatrix} -1 & 2 & -1 \\ 9 & -13 & -1 \\ -13 & 16 & 2 \end{bmatrix}$$

$$= \begin{bmatrix} -1 & 9 & -13 \\ 2 & -13 & 16 \\ -1 & -1 & 2 \end{bmatrix}$$

$$A^{-1} = \frac{\text{adj } A}{|A|} \begin{bmatrix} +1/5 & -9/5 & +13/5 \\ -2/5 & +13/5 & -16/5 \\ +1/5 & +1/5 & -2/5 \end{bmatrix}$$

The reader can verify that $AA^{-1} = A^{-1}A = I$.

A.3.6 The Eigenstructure of a Matrix: Eigenvalues and Eigenvectors

In the treatment of advanced multivariate analyses, the understanding of the concepts of eigenvalue and eigenvector will be assumed. The eigenvalue usually indicates an optimum, for example a maximal variance in factor analysis, a maximal squared correlation in canonical correlation analysis and the ratio of the between- and within-variance in discriminant analysis.

In order to understand this optimum, think of the speaker of a stereo system which must be constructed according to specific measurements in order to reach the resonance effect, or of a water tap which squeaks at a certain flow, but spouts water soundlessly when opened or closed further, or of a car which starts to vibrate at 120 km/h, but loses this vibration at 110 km/h and 130 km/h. If we are able to convert such an optimum moment, at which the eigen-frequency of the material is reached, into the form of a determined number, then we have conjured up an eigenvalue. The direction cosines that indicate which direction the tap must be turned are something like eigenvectors.

The eigenstructure problem is as follows. Consider an $m \times 1$ vector **x**. Premultiply **x** by an $m \times m$ matrix **M**. Through this operation (known as linear transformation) the vector **x** is transformed into an $m \times m$ vector **y**:

$$\underset{(m \times m)}{\mathbf{M}} \quad \underset{(m \times 1)}{\mathbf{x}} \quad = \quad \underset{(m \times 1)}{\mathbf{y}}$$

If this premultiplication by **M** results in a vector $\mathbf{y} = \lambda\mathbf{x}$ that is equal to a multiple of **x**, we then obtain:

$$\boxed{\mathbf{Mx} = \lambda\mathbf{x}}$$

Premultiplication by the matrix **M** comes down to the same thing as multiplication by a real number λ. This number λ is called the **eigenvalue** of **M** (also: latent root or characteristic root). A vector **x** for which it holds that $\mathbf{Mx} = \lambda\mathbf{x}$ is called the **eigenvector** (also: latent vector or characteristic vector). It is said of such an eigenvector that it is invariant under transformation.

For example:

$$\mathbf{M} = \begin{bmatrix} -2 & 4 \\ 3 & -1 \end{bmatrix} \quad \mathbf{x}_1 = \begin{bmatrix} 1 \\ 1 \end{bmatrix} \quad \mathbf{x}_2 = \begin{bmatrix} 4 \\ -3 \end{bmatrix} \quad \mathbf{x}_3 = \begin{bmatrix} 2 \\ 4 \end{bmatrix}$$

$$\mathbf{Mx}_1 = \begin{bmatrix} -2 & 4 \\ 3 & -1 \end{bmatrix}\begin{bmatrix} 1 \\ 1 \end{bmatrix} = \begin{bmatrix} 2 \\ 2 \end{bmatrix} = 2\begin{bmatrix} 1 \\ 1 \end{bmatrix} = 2\mathbf{x}_1 \quad (\lambda = 2)$$

$$\mathbf{Mx}_2 = \begin{bmatrix} -2 & 4 \\ 3 & -1 \end{bmatrix}\begin{bmatrix} 4 \\ -3 \end{bmatrix} = \begin{bmatrix} -20 \\ 15 \end{bmatrix} = -5\begin{bmatrix} 4 \\ -3 \end{bmatrix} = -5\mathbf{x}_2 \quad (\lambda = -5)$$

$$\mathbf{Mx}_3 = \begin{bmatrix} -2 & 4 \\ 3 & -1 \end{bmatrix}\begin{bmatrix} 2 \\ 4 \end{bmatrix} = \begin{bmatrix} 12 \\ 2 \end{bmatrix} \neq \lambda\begin{bmatrix} 2 \\ 4 \end{bmatrix}$$

From this example, it appears that $\mathbf{x}_1$ is an eigenvector with eigenvalue $\lambda = 2$ and also that $\mathbf{x}_2$ is an eigenvector with eigenvalue $\lambda = -5$.

The vector $\mathbf{x}_3$, on the other hand, is not an eigenvector, because it is not transformed into a multiple of itself after premultiplication by **M**; in other words it is not invariant under transformation.

The calculation of eigenvalues and eigenvectors is done as follows. We'll use the above matrix equation:

$$\mathbf{Mx} = \lambda\mathbf{x}$$
$$\mathbf{Mx} - \lambda\mathbf{x} = \mathbf{0}$$
$$(\mathbf{M} - \lambda\mathbf{I})\mathbf{x} = \mathbf{0}$$

This is the matrix equation from which the eigenvectors will be determined. If the trivial solution $\mathbf{x} = \mathbf{0}$ is not chosen, then it can be easily proven that $(\mathbf{M} - \lambda\mathbf{I})\mathbf{x}$ is equal to the zero vector if $|\mathbf{M} - \lambda\mathbf{I}| = 0$. This latter equation is called a characteristic equation and from it the eigenvalues λ_i are calculated. Afterwards the eigenvalues are entered into the matrix equation in order to calculate the eigenvectors.

Let us do this for the matrix **M** above.

$$\mathbf{M} = \begin{bmatrix} -2 & 4 \\ 3 & 1 \end{bmatrix}$$

The characteristic equation is $|\mathbf{M} - \lambda\mathbf{I}| = 0$.

$$\left| \begin{bmatrix} -2 & 4 \\ 3 & -1 \end{bmatrix} - \lambda \begin{bmatrix} 1 & 0 \\ 0 & 1 \end{bmatrix} \right| = 0$$

$$\left| \begin{bmatrix} -2 & 4 \\ 3 & -1 \end{bmatrix} - \begin{bmatrix} \lambda & 0 \\ 0 & \lambda \end{bmatrix} \right| = 0$$

$$\begin{vmatrix} -2-\lambda & 4 \\ 3 & -1-\lambda \end{vmatrix} = 0$$

$$(-2-\lambda)\ (-1-\lambda) - (3)(4) = 0$$

$$\lambda^2 + 3\lambda - 10 = 0$$

$$\lambda_2 + 5\lambda - 2\lambda - 10 = 0$$

$$\lambda(\lambda + 5) - 2(\lambda + 5) = 0$$

$$(\lambda - 2)(\lambda + 5) = 0. \qquad \text{Solution:} \quad \lambda_1 = 2, \quad \lambda_2 = -5.$$

We enter the first eigenvalue $\lambda_1 = 2$ into the matrix equation:

$$(\mathbf{M} - \lambda_1\mathbf{I})\mathbf{x} = \mathbf{0}$$

$$\left\{ \begin{bmatrix} -2 & 4 \\ 3 & -1 \end{bmatrix} - 2 \begin{bmatrix} 1 & 0 \\ 0 & 1 \end{bmatrix} \right\} \begin{bmatrix} x_1 \\ x_2 \end{bmatrix} = \begin{bmatrix} 0 \\ 0 \end{bmatrix}$$

$$\begin{bmatrix} -2-2 & 4 \\ 3 & -1-2 \end{bmatrix} \begin{bmatrix} x_1 \\ x_2 \end{bmatrix} = \begin{bmatrix} 0 \\ 0 \end{bmatrix}$$

$$-4x_1 + 4x_2 = 0$$

$$3x_1 - 3x_2 = 0$$

There are an infinite number of solutions for this system, for which $x_1 = x_2$.
Examples of eigenvectors are $\begin{bmatrix} 1 \\ 1 \end{bmatrix}, \begin{bmatrix} 2 \\ 2 \end{bmatrix}, \begin{bmatrix} 3 \\ 3 \end{bmatrix}$ and so forth.

We then enter the second eigenvalue $\lambda_2 = -5$:

$$(\mathbf{M} - \lambda_2\mathbf{I})\mathbf{x} = \mathbf{0}$$

$$\left\{ \begin{bmatrix} -2 & 4 \\ 3 & -1 \end{bmatrix} - (-5) \begin{bmatrix} 1 & 0 \\ 0 & 1 \end{bmatrix} \right\} \begin{bmatrix} x_1 \\ x_2 \end{bmatrix} = \begin{bmatrix} 0 \\ 0 \end{bmatrix}$$

$$\begin{bmatrix} -2+5 & 4 \\ 3 & -1+5 \end{bmatrix} \begin{bmatrix} x_1 \\ x_2 \end{bmatrix} = \begin{bmatrix} 0 \\ 0 \end{bmatrix}$$

$$3x_1 + 4x_2 = 0$$

$$3x_2 + 4x_2 = 0$$

There are an infinite number of solutions for this system, for which x_1 and x_2 have a ratio of 4 to -3.

Examples of eigenvectors are:

$$\begin{bmatrix} 4 \\ -3 \end{bmatrix} \begin{bmatrix} 8 \\ -6 \end{bmatrix} \begin{bmatrix} 12 \\ -9 \end{bmatrix}$$

and so forth.

The problem of indeterminism that arises here because of the infinite number of possible solutions is solved by normalizing the eigenvectors. This is discussed in Chapter 8 on two-group discriminant analysis.

Normalizing means that the vector is divided by its length $||\mathbf{k}||$ to obtain a vector with unit length. The length is calculated as the square root of the sum of squared elements. If we call the first eigenvector $\mathbf{u}_1$, then its length is equal to $[u_1^2 + u_2^2]^{1/2}$. For eigenvector $\begin{bmatrix} 1 \\ 1 \end{bmatrix}$ this is $[1 + 1]^{1/2} = \sqrt{2}$. For the second eigenvector $\mathbf{u}_2 = \begin{bmatrix} 4 \\ -3 \end{bmatrix}$ the length is $[4^2 + (-3)^2]^{1/2} = 5$. Consequently, the two normalized eigenvectors are:

$$\mathbf{u}_1 = \begin{bmatrix} 1/\sqrt{2} \\ 1/\sqrt{2} \end{bmatrix} \qquad \mathbf{u}_2 = \begin{bmatrix} 4/5 \\ -3/5 \end{bmatrix}$$

We can collect them in a matrix $\mathbf{U}$:

$$\mathbf{U} = \begin{bmatrix} 1/\sqrt{2} & 4/5 \\ 1/\sqrt{2} & -3/5 \end{bmatrix}$$

The eigenvalues are collected on the principal diagonal of a diagonal matrix $\mathbf{D}$:

$$\mathbf{D} = \begin{bmatrix} 2 & 0 \\ 0 & -5 \end{bmatrix}$$

We calculate the inverse of $\mathbf{U}$:

$$\mathbf{U}^{-1} = \begin{bmatrix} -3/5 & -1/\sqrt{2} \\ -4/5 & 1/\sqrt{2} \end{bmatrix}' \Big/ \left(-\frac{7}{5\sqrt{2}} \right) = \begin{bmatrix} 3\sqrt{2}/7 & 4\sqrt{2}/7 \\ 5/7 & -5/7 \end{bmatrix}$$

It can now be verified that $\mathbf{UDU}^{-1}$ equals the original matrix $\mathbf{M}$ (exercise for the reader). This decomposition, according to which $\mathbf{M}$ is written as the product of three matrices, is called singular value decomposition (SVD). The SVD operation which was calculated here ($\mathbf{M} = \mathbf{UDU}^{-1}$) holds for matrices that are square and non-symmetric. For other kinds of matrices, see Green (1976).

Statistical Tables

Statistical probabilities for Tables 1–4 have been calculated using PCalc 2.1.

Table 1   Cumulative standard normal distribution

Z	0.00	0.01	0.02	0.03	0.04	0.05	0.06	0.07	0.08	0.09
0.0	0.5000	0.5040	0.5080	0.5120	0.5160	0.5199	0.5239	0.5279	0.5319	0.5359
0.1	0.5398	0.5438	0.5478	0.5517	0.5557	0.5596	0.5636	0.5675	0.5714	0.5753
0.2	0.5793	0.5832	0.5871	0.5910	0.5948	0.5987	0.6026	0.6064	0.6103	0.6141
0.3	0.6179	0.6217	0.6255	0.6293	0.6331	0.6368	0.6406	0.6443	0.6480	0.6517
0.4	0.6554	0.6591	0.6628	0.6664	0.6700	0.6736	0.6772	0.6808	0.6844	0.6879
0.5	0.6915	0.6950	0.6985	0.7019	0.7054	0.7088	0.7123	0.7157	0.7190	0.7224
0.6	0.7257	0.7291	0.7324	0.7357	0.7389	0.7422	0.7454	0.7486	0.7517	0.7549
0.7	0.7580	0.7611	0.7642	0.7673	0.7704	0.7734	0.7764	0.7794	0.7823	0.7852
0.8	0.7881	0.7910	0.7939	0.7967	0.7995	0.8023	0.8051	0.8078	0.8106	0.8133
0.9	0.8159	0.8186	0.8212	0.8238	0.8264	0.8289	0.8315	0.8340	0.8365	0.8389
1.0	0.8413	0.8438	0.8461	0.8485	0.8508	0.8531	0.8554	0.8577	0.8599	0.8621
1.1	0.8643	0.8665	0.8686	0.8708	0.8729	0.8749	0.8770	0.8790	0.8810	0.8830
1.2	0.8849	0.8869	0.8888	0.8907	0.8925	0.8944	0.8962	0.8980	0.8997	0.9015
1.3	0.9032	0.9049	0.9066	0.9082	0.9099	0.9115	0.9131	0.9147	0.9162	0.9177
1.4	0.9192	0.9207	0.9222	0.9236	0.9251	0.9265	0.9279	0.9292	0.9306	0.9319
1.5	0.9332	0.9345	0.9357	0.9370	0.9382	0.9394	0.9406	0.9418	0.9429	0.9441
1.6	0.9452	0.9463	0.9474	0.9484	0.9495	0.9505	0.9515	0.9525	0.9535	0.9545
1.7	0.9554	0.9564	0.9573	0.9582	0.9591	0.9599	0.9608	0.9616	0.9625	0.9633
1.8	0.9641	0.9649	0.9656	0.9664	0.9671	0.9678	0.9686	0.9693	0.9699	0.9706
1.9	0.9713	0.9719	0.9726	0.9732	0.9738	0.9744	0.9750	0.9756	0.9761	0.9767
2.0	0.9772	0.9778	0.9783	0.9788	0.9793	0.9798	0.9803	0.9808	0.9812	0.9817
2.1	0.9821	0.9826	0.9830	0.9834	0.9838	0.9842	0.9846	0.9850	0.9854	0.9857
2.2	0.9861	0.9864	0.9868	0.9871	0.9875	0.9878	0.9881	0.9884	0.9887	0.9890
2.3	0.9893	0.9896	0.9898	0.9901	0.9904	0.9906	0.9909	0.9911	0.9913	0.9916
2.4	0.9918	0.9920	0.9922	0.9925	0.9927	0.9929	0.9931	0.9932	0.9934	0.9936
2.5	0.9938	0.9940	0.9941	0.9943	0.9945	0.9946	0.9948	0.9949	0.9951	0.9952
2.6	0.9953	0.9955	0.9956	0.9957	0.9959	0.9960	0.9961	0.9962	0.9963	0.9964
2.7	0.9965	0.9966	0.9967	0.9968	0.9969	0.9970	0.9971	0.9972	0.9973	0.9974
2.8	0.9974	0.9975	0.9976	0.9977	0.9977	0.9978	0.9979	0.9979	0.9980	0.9981
2.9	0.9981	0.9982	0.9982	0.9983	0.9984	0.9984	0.9985	0.9985	0.9986	0.9986
3.0	0.9987	0.9987	0.9987	0.9988	0.9988	0.9989	0.9989	0.9989	0.9990	0.9990
3.1	0.9990	0.9991	0.9991	0.9991	0.9992	0.9992	0.9992	0.9992	0.9993	0.9993
3.2	0.9993	0.9993	0.9994	0.9994	0.9994	0.9994	0.9994	0.9995	0.9995	0.9995
3.3	0.9995	0.9995	0.9995	0.9996	0.9996	0.9996	0.9996	0.9996	0.9996	0.9997
3.4	0.9997	0.9997	0.9997	0.9997	0.9997	0.9997	0.9997	0.9997	0.9997	0.9998

Table 2   Values of χ^2 corresponding to p

df	$\chi^2_{0.005}$	$\chi^2_{0.01}$	$\chi^2_{0.025}$	$\chi^2_{0.055}$	$\chi^2_{0.10}$	$\chi^2_{0.90}$	$\chi^2_{0.95}$	$\chi^2_{0.975}$	$\chi^2_{0.99}$	$\chi^2_{0.995}$
1	0.000039	0.00016	0.00098	0.0039	0.0158	2.71	3.84	5.02	6.63	7.88
2	0.0100	0.0201	0.0506	0.1026	0.2107	4.61	5.99	7.38	9.21	10.60
3	0.0717	0.115	0.216	0.352	0.584	6.25	7.81	9.35	11.34	12.84
4	0.207	0.297	0.484	0.711	1.064	7.78	9.49	11.14	13.28	14.86
5	0.412	0.554	0.831	1.15	1.61	9.24	11.07	12.83	15.09	16.75
6	0.676	0.872	1.24	1.64	2.20	10.64	12.59	14.45	16.81	18.55
7	0.989	1.24	1.69	2.17	2.83	12.02	14.07	16.01	18.48	20.28
8	1.34	1.65	2.18	2.73	3.49	13.36	15.51	17.53	20.09	21.96
9	1.73	2.09	2.70	3.33	4.17	14.68	16.92	19.02	21.67	23.59
10	2.16	2.56	3.25	3.94	4.87	15.99	18.31	20.48	23.21	25.19
11	2.60	3.05	3.82	4.57	5.58	17.28	19.68	21.92	24.73	26.76
12	3.07	3.57	4.40	5.23	6.30	18.55	21.03	23.34	26.22	28.30
13	3.57	4.11	5.01	5.89	7.04	19.81	22.36	24.74	27.69	29.82
14	4.07	4.66	5.63	6.57	7.79	21.06	23.68	26.12	29.14	31.32
15	4.60	5.23	6.26	7.26	8.55	22.31	25.00	27.49	30.58	32.80
16	5.14	5.81	6.91	7.96	9.31	23.54	26.30	28.85	32.00	34.27
18	6.26	7.01	8.23	9.39	10.86	25.99	28.87	31.53	34.81	37.16
20	7.43	8.26	9.59	10.85	12.44	28.41	31.41	34.17	37.57	40.00
24	9.89	10.86	12.40	13.85	15.66	33.20	36.42	39.36	42.98	45.56
30	13.79	14.95	16.79	18.49	20.60	40.26	43.77	46.98	50.89	53.67
40	20.71	22.16	24.43	26.51	29.05	51.81	55.76	59.34	63.69	66.77
60	35.53	37.48	40.48	43.19	46.46	74.40	79.08	83.30	88.38	91.95
120	83.85	86.92	91.58	95.70	100.62	140.23	146.57	152.21	158.95	163.64

Table 3 Values of *t* for *v* degrees of freedom and *p* = 1 − α

$1 - \alpha$ v	0.75	0.90	0.95	0.975	0.99	0.995	0.9995
1	1.000	3.078	6.314	12.706	31.821	63.657	636.619
2	0.816	1.886	2.920	4.303	6.965	9.925	31.598
3	0.765	1.638	2.353	3.182	4.541	5.841	12.941
4	0.741	1.533	2.132	2.776	3.747	4.604	8.610
5	0.727	1.476	2.015	2.571	3.365	4.032	6.859
6	0.718	1.440	1.943	2.447	3.143	3.707	5.959
7	0.711	1.415	1.895	2.365	2.998	3.499	5.405
8	0.706	1.397	1.860	2.306	2.896	3.355	5.041
9	0.703	1.383	1.833	2.262	2.821	3.250	4.781
10	0.700	1.372	1.812	2.228	2.764	3.169	4.587
11	0.697	1.363	1.796	2.201	2.718	3.106	4.437
12	0.695	1.356	1.782	2.179	2.681	3.055	4.318
13	0.694	1.350	1.771	2.160	2.650	3.012	4.221
14	0.692	1.345	1.761	2.145	2.624	2.977	4.140
15	0.691	1.341	1.753	2.131	2.602	2.947	4.073
16	0.690	1.337	1.746	2.120	2.583	2.921	4.015
17	0.689	1.333	1.740	2.110	2.567	2.898	3.965
18	0.688	1.330	1.734	2.101	2.552	2.878	3.922
19	0.688	1.328	1.729	2.093	2.339	2.861	3.883
20	0.687	1.325	1.725	2.086	2.528	2.845	3.850
21	0.686	1.323	1.721	2.080	2.518	2.831	3.819
22	0.686	1.321	1.717	2.074	2.508	2.819	3.792
23	0.685	1.319	1.714	2.069	2.500	2.807	3.767
24	0.685	1.318	1.711	2.064	2.492	2.797	3.745
25	0.684	1.316	1.708	2.060	2.485	2.787	3.725
26	0.684	1.315	1.706	2.056	2.479	2.779	3.707
27	0.684	1.314	1.703	2.052	2.473	2.771	3.690
28	0.683	1.313	1.701	2.048	2.467	2.763	3.674
29	0.683	1.311	1.699	2.045	2.462	2.756	3.659
30	0.683	1.310	1.697	2.042	2.457	2.750	3.646
40	0.681	1.303	1.684	2.021	2.423	2.704	3.551
60	0.679	1.296	1.671	2.000	2.390	2.660	3.460
120	0.677	1.289	1.658	1.980	2.358	2.617	3.373
∞	0.674	1.282	1.645	1.960	2.326	2.576	3.291

Table 4　Values of F for $\alpha = 0.05$ and v_1 and v_2 degrees of freedom for numerator and denominator

v_2 \ v_1	1	2	3	4	5	6	7	8	9	10	12	15	20	24	30	40	60	120	∞
1	161.4	199.5	215.7	224.6	230.2	234.0	236.8	238.9	240.5	241.9	243.9	245.9	248.0	249.1	250.1	251.1	252.2	253.3	254.3
2	18.51	19.00	19.16	19.25	19.30	19.33	19.35	19.37	19.38	19.40	19.41	19.43	19.45	19.45	19.46	19.47	19.48	19.49	19.50
3	10.13	9.55	9.28	9.12	9.01	8.94	8.89	8.85	8.81	8.79	8.74	8.70	8.66	8.64	8.62	8.59	8.57	8.55	8.53
4	7.71	6.94	6.59	6.39	6.26	6.16	6.09	6.04	6.00	5.96	5.91	5.86	5.80	5.77	5.75	5.72	5.69	5.66	5.63
5	6.61	5.79	5.41	5.19	5.05	4.95	4.88	4.82	4.77	4.74	4.68	4.62	4.56	4.53	4.50	4.46	4.43	4.40	4.36
6	5.99	5.14	4.76	4.53	4.39	4.28	4.21	4.15	4.10	4.06	4.00	3.94	3.87	3.84	3.81	3.77	3.74	3.70	3.67
7	5.59	4.74	4.35	4.12	3.97	3.87	3.79	3.73	3.68	3.64	3.57	3.51	3.44	3.41	3.38	3.34	3.30	3.27	3.23
8	5.32	4.46	4.07	3.84	3.69	3.58	3.50	3.44	3.39	3.35	3.28	3.22	3.15	3.12	3.08	3.04	3.01	2.97	2.93
9	5.12	4.26	3.86	3.63	3.48	3.37	3.29	3.23	3.18	3.14	3.07	3.01	2.94	2.90	2.86	2.83	2.79	2.75	2.71
10	4.96	4.10	3.71	3.48	3.33	3.22	3.14	3.07	3.02	2.98	2.91	2.85	2.77	2.74	2.70	2.66	2.62	2.58	2.54
11	4.84	3.98	3.59	3.36	3.20	3.09	3.01	2.95	2.90	2.85	2.79	2.72	2.65	2.61	2.57	2.53	2.49	2.45	2.40
12	4.75	3.89	3.49	3.26	3.11	3.00	2.91	2.85	2.80	2.75	2.69	2.62	2.54	2.51	2.47	2.43	2.38	2.34	2.30
13	4.67	3.81	3.41	3.18	3.03	2.92	2.83	2.77	2.71	2.67	2.60	2.53	2.46	2.42	2.38	2.34	2.30	2.25	2.21
14	4.60	3.74	3.34	3.11	2.96	2.85	2.76	2.70	2.65	2.60	2.53	2.46	2.39	2.35	2.31	2.27	2.22	2.18	2.13
15	4.54	3.68	3.29	3.06	2.90	2.79	2.71	2.64	2.59	2.54	2.48	2.40	2.33	2.29	2.25	2.20	2.16	2.11	2.07
16	4.49	3.63	3.24	3.01	2.85	2.74	2.66	2.59	2.54	2.49	2.42	2.35	2.28	2.24	2.19	2.15	2.11	2.06	2.01
17	4.45	3.59	3.20	2.96	2.81	2.70	2.61	2.55	2.49	2.45	2.38	2.31	2.23	2.19	2.15	2.10	2.06	2.01	1.96
18	4.41	3.55	3.16	2.93	2.77	2.66	2.58	2.51	2.46	2.41	2.34	2.27	2.19	2.15	2.11	2.06	2.02	1.97	1.92
19	4.38	3.52	3.13	2.90	2.74	2.63	2.54	2.48	2.42	2.38	2.31	2.23	2.16	2.11	2.07	2.03	1.98	1.93	1.88
20	4.35	3.49	3.10	2.87	2.71	2.60	2.51	2.45	2.39	2.35	2.28	2.20	2.12	2.08	2.04	1.99	1.95	1.90	1.84
21	4.32	3.47	3.07	2.84	2.68	2.57	2.49	2.42	2.37	2.32	2.25	2.18	2.10	2.05	2.01	1.96	1.92	1.87	1.81
22	4.30	3.44	3.05	2.82	2.66	2.55	2.46	2.40	2.34	2.30	2.23	2.15	2.07	2.03	1.98	1.94	1.89	1.84	1.78
23	4.28	3.42	3.03	2.80	2.64	2.53	2.44	2.37	2.32	2.27	2.20	2.13	2.05	2.01	1.96	1.91	1.86	1.81	1.76
24	4.26	3.40	3.01	2.78	2.62	2.51	2.42	2.36	2.30	2.25	2.18	2.11	2.03	1.98	1.94	1.89	1.84	1.79	1.73
25	4.24	3.39	2.99	2.76	2.60	2.49	2.40	2.34	2.28	2.24	2.16	2.09	2.01	1.96	1.92	1.87	1.82	1.77	1.71
26	4.23	3.37	2.98	2.74	2.59	2.47	2.39	2.32	2.27	2.22	2.15	2.07	1.99	1.95	1.90	1.85	1.80	1.75	1.69
27	4.21	3.35	2.96	2.73	2.57	2.46	2.37	2.31	2.25	2.20	2.13	2.06	1.97	1.93	1.88	1.84	1.79	1.73	1.67
28	4.20	3.34	2.95	2.71	2.56	2.45	2.36	2.29	2.24	2.19	2.12	2.04	1.96	1.91	1.87	1.82	1.77	1.71	1.65
29	4.18	3.33	2.93	2.70	2.55	2.43	2.35	2.28	2.22	2.18	2.10	2.03	1.94	1.90	1.85	1.81	1.75	1.70	1.64
30	4.17	3.32	2.92	2.69	2.53	2.42	2.33	2.27	2.21	2.16	2.09	2.01	1.93	1.89	1.84	1.79	1.74	1.68	1.62
40	4.08	3.23	2.84	2.61	2.45	2.34	2.25	2.18	2.12	2.08	2.00	1.92	1.84	1.79	1.74	1.69	1.64	1.58	1.51
60	4.00	3.15	2.76	2.53	2.37	2.25	2.17	2.10	2.04	1.99	1.92	1.84	1.75	1.70	1.65	1.59	1.53	1.47	1.39
120	3.92	3.07	2.68	2.45	2.29	2.17	2.09	2.02	1.96	1.91	1.83	1.75	1.66	1.61	1.55	1.50	1.43	1.35	1.25
∞	3.84	3.00	2.60	2.37	2.21	2.10	2.01	1.94	1.88	1.83	1.75	1.67	1.57	1.52	1.46	1.39	1.32	1.22	1.00

Bibliography

Alschuler, L., 1976, Satellization and Stagnation in Latin America, *International Studies Quarterly*, vol. 20, no. 1, 39–82.

Ammerman, C., P. Gluchowski and P. Schmidt, 1975, Rekursive oder nicht-rekursive Modelle? Zum Problem der Testbarkeit von Feedback-Prozessen, *Zeitschrift für Soziologie*, vol. 4, no. 3, 203–220.

Bartlett, M., 1950, Tests of Significance of Factor Analysis, *British Journal of Psychology*, vol. 3, 77–85.

Bennett, S. and D. Bowers, 1976, *An Introduction to Multivariate Techniques for Social and Behavioural Sciences*, London: Macmillan.

Blalock, H., 1961, *Causal Inferences in Nonexperimental Research*, Chapel Hill: The University of North Carolina Press.

Blalock, H., 1960, *Social Statistics*, London: McGraw-Hill.

Blau, P. and O. Duncan, 1967, *The American Occupational Structure*, London: Wiley.

Bodenheimer, S., 1973, Dependency and Imperialism: The Roots of Latin American Under-development, *Politics and Society*, vol. 1, no. 3, 327–357.

Boudon, R., 1965, Méthodes d'analyse causale, *Revue française de sociologie*, vol. VI, 24–43.

Boudon, R., 1967, *L'analyse mathématique des faits sociaux*, Paris: Plon.

Brownlee, K., 1965, *Statistical Theory and Methodology in Science and Engineering*, New York: John Wiley and Sons.

Cattell, R., 1966, *Handbook of Multivariate Experimental Psychology*, Chicago: Rand McNally.

Chase-Dunn, C., 1975, The effects of international economic dependence on development and inequality: a cross-national study, *American Sociological Review*, vol. 40, 720–738.

Chatterjee, S. and B. Price, 1977, *Regression Analysis by Example*, New York: John Wiley and Sons.

Coleman, J., 1964, *Introduction to Mathematical Sociology*, New York: The Free Press of Glencoe.

Colson, F., 1977, *Sociale indikatoren van enkele aspecten van bevolkingsgroei*, Leuven: dissertatie K.U.L., Departement Sociologie.

Cook, T. and T. Campbell, 1979, *Quasi-Experimentation: Design and Analysis Issues for Field Settings*, Chicago: Rand McNally.

Cooley, W. and P. Lohnes, 1971, *Multivariate Data Analysis*, New York: Wiley.

Cronbach, L., 1951, Coefficient Alpha and the Internal Structure of Tests, *Psychometrika*, vol. 16, 297–334.

Daniel, T. and J. Esser, 1980, Intrinsic Motivation as Influenced by Rewards, Task Interests and Task Structure, *Journal of Applied Psychology*, vol. 65, no. 5, 566–573.

De Finetti, B., 1964, Foresight, its Logical laws, its Subjective Sources (1937), in : H. Kyburg and H. Smokler, *Studies in Subjective Probability*, New York: Wiley.

De Jong, G. and R. Sell, 1975, Changes in Childlessness in the United States: A Demographic Path Analysis, *Population Studies*, vol. 31, no. 1, 129–141.

De Jong, M.J., 1982, *Wat hebben ze bereikt?* [What have they achieved?], Rotterdam: Rotterdamse Universitaire Pers.

Duncan, O., 1975, *Introduction to Structural Equation Models*, New York: Academic Press.

Gifi, A., 1980, *Niet-lineaire Multivariate Analyse*, Leiden.

Goldberger, A., 1970, On Boudon's Method of Linear Causal Analysis, *American Sociological Review*, vol. 35, 97–101.

Gordon, R., 1968, Issues in Multiple Regression, *American Journal of Sociology*, vol. 73, 592–616.

Green, P., 1978, *Analyzing Multivariate Data*, Illinois: Dryden.

Green, P., 1976, *Mathematical Tools for Applied Multivariate Analysis*, New York: Academic Press.

Guttman, L., 1953, Image Theory for the Structure of Quantitative Variates, *Psychometrika*, vol. 18, 227–296.

Harman, H., 1967, *Modern Factor Analysis*, Chicago: University of Chicago Press.

Harman, H. and W. Jones, 1966, Factor Analysis by minimizing residuals (Minres), *Psychometrika*, vol. 31, 351–368.

Hays, W., 1972, *Statistics for the Social Sciences*, Holt International Edition.

Hettne, B., 1982, *Development Theory and the Third World*, Stockholm: Swedish Agency for Research Co-operation with Developing Countries.

Hoge, D. and J. Carroll, 1975, Christian Beliefs, Nonreligious Factors and Anti-Semitism, *Social Forces*, vol. 53, no. 4, 581–594.

Hout, W., 1984, *Frank en Vrij in het Zuiden?* [Free as the Wind in the South?], Rotterdam, doctoraalscriptie EUR SSCW.

Houtman, D. and A. Steijn, 1990, *Verkeren niet-werkenden in een sociaal isolement? De maatschappelijke participatie van werkenden, RWW-ers en ABW-ers vergeleken*, Ongepubliceerd werkstuk, Rotterdam.

Jöreskog, K., 1967, Some Contributions to Maximum Likelihood Factor Analysis, *Psychometrika*, vol. 32, 443–482.

Jöreskog, K., 1969, A General Approach to Confirmatory Maximum Likelihood Factor Analysis, *Psychometrika*, vol. 34, no. 2, 183–201.

Jöreskog, K., 1973, A General Method for Estimating a Linear Structural Equation System, in: A. Goldberger and O. Duncan, *Structural Equation Models in the Social Sciences*, London: Seminar Press, pp. 85–112.

Kaiser, H., 1958, The Varimax Criterion for Analytic Rotation in Factor Analysis, *Psychometrika*, vol. 23, 187–200.

Kaiser, H., 1959, The Application of Electronic Computers to Factor Analysis, Symposium on the application of computers to psychological problems, *American Psychological Association*.

Kaiser, H., 1963, Image Analysis, in: C. Harris, *Problems in Measuring Change*, Madison: University of Wisconsin Press.

Kaiser, H. and J. Caffrey, 1965, Alpha Factor Analysis, *Psychometrika*, vol. 30, 1–14.

Kalleberg, A., 1977, Work Values and Job Rewards: a Theory of Job Satisfaction, *American Sociological Review*, vol. 42, 124–143.

Kendall, M. and A. Stuart, 1969, *The Advanced Theory of Statistics. Volume 2: Inference and Relationship; Volume 3: Design and Analysis, and Time Series*, London: Griffin.

Klingemann, H., 1979, Organisationsmobilität in der Großforschung. Eine Analyse inner- und außerorganisatorischer Determinanten der individuellen Bereitschaft zur Organisationsmobilität am Beispiel der Kernforschungsanlage Jülich, *Zeitschrift für Soziologie*, vol. 8, no. 3, 230–253.

Kruijt, D. and M. Vellinga, 1978, Bases sociologiques du militantisme chez les ouvriers et les dirigeants syndicaux: une analyse méthodologique de cas, *Revue française de sociologie*, pp. 125–152.

Kruskal, J. and F. Carmone, 1968, Use and Theory of MONANOVA, a Program to Analyze Factorial Experiments by Estimating Monotone Transformations of the Data, unpublished paper, Bell Laboratories.

Kruskal, J. and M. Wish, 1978, *Multidimensional Scaling*, London: Sage.

Kruskal, W. and W. Wallis, 1952, Use of ranks in one-criterion variance analysis, *Journal of the American Statistical Association*, vol. 47, 583–621.

LaFree, G., 1983, Male Power and Female Victimization: Toward a Theory of Interracial Rape, *American Journal of Sociology*, vol. 88, no. 2, 311–328.

Lange, E., 1978, Determinanten der Entscheidung für das Studium der Soziologie, eine Anwendung der Pfadanalyse, *Zeitschrift für Soziologie*, vol. 8, no. 1, 72–86.

Lazarsfeld, P., 1955, Interpretation of Statistical Relationships as a Research Operation, in: P. Lazarsfeld and M. Rosenberg, *The Language of Social Research*, New York: Macmillan.

Lazarsfeld, P., 1961, The Algebra of Dichotomous Systems, in: H. Solomon, *Studies in Item Analysis and Prediction*, Stanford: Stanford University Press.

Lazarsfeld, P., 1968, The Analysis of Attribute Data, *International Encyclopedia of the Social Sciences*, vol. 15, 419–429.

Lawley, D., 1940, The Estimation of Factor Loading by the Method of Maximum Likelihood, *Proceedings of the Royal Society of Edinburgh 60*, 64–82.

Locke, H. and R. Williamson, 1958, Marital Adjustment: a Factor Analysis Study, *American Sociological Review*, vol. 23, no. 5, 562–569.

McLaughlin, S., 1978, Occupational Sex Identification and the Assessment of Male and Female Earnings Inequality, *American Sociological Review*, vol. 43, 909–921.

Muliak, S., 1972, *The Foundations of Factor Analysis*, New York: McGraw-Hill.

Myles, J., 1978, Institutionalization and Sick Role Identification among the Elderly, *American Sociological Review*, vol. 43, 508–521.

Naroll, R., 1982, *The Moral Order*, London: Sage.

Nie, N. *et al.*, 1975, *Statistical Package for the Social Sciences*, New York: McGraw-Hill.

Norušis, M., 1978, *SPSS Statistical Algorithms*, Release 8.0.

Opp, K-D. and P. Schmidt, 1976, *Einführung in die Mehrvariablenanalyse. Grundlagen der Formulierung und Prüfung komplexer sozialwissenschaftlicher Aussagen*, Reinbek bei Hamburg: Rowohlt Taschenbuch Verlag.

O'Quin, K. and J. Aronoff, 1981, Humor as a Technique of Social Influence, in: *Social Psychology Quarterly*, vol. 44, no. 4, 349–357.

Pappi, F. and I. Pappi, 1978, Sozialer Status und Konsumstil, eine Fallstudie zur Wohnzimmereinrichtung, *Kölner Zeitschrift für Soziologie und Sozialpsychologie*, vol. 30, 60–86.

Philipsen, H., 1969, *Afwezigheid wegens ziekte*. Groningen: Wolters-Noordhoff.

Provoost, F., 1979, *Kansarme Buurten, een onderzoek naar territoriale concentraties van kansarme bevolkingsgroepen in het Nederlandstalig landsgedeelte en Brussel-hoofdstad*, Leuven: Federatie Buurtwerk.

Russett, B., 1969, Inequality and Instability: the Relation of Land Tenure to Politics, in: D. Rowney and J. Graham, *Quantitative History, Selected Readings in the Quantitative Analysis of Historical Data*, Illinois: The Dorsey Press, pp. 356–367.

Schuessler, K. and H. Driver, 1956, A Factor Analysis of Sixteen Primitive Societies, *American Sociological Review*, vol. 21, no. 4, 493–499.

Shingles, R., 1977, Faculty Ratings: Procedures for Interpreting Student Evaluations, *American Educational Research Journal*, vol. 14, no. 4, 459–470.

Siegrist, J. and K. Dittmann, 1981, Lebensveränderungen und Krankheitsausbruch: Methodik und Ergebnisse einer medizinsoziologischen Studie, *Kölner Zeitschrift für Soziologie und Sozialpsychologie*, vol. 33, 132–147.

Simon, H., 1954, Spurious Correlation: a Causal Interpretation, *Journal of the American Statistical Association*, vol. 49, 467–479.

Somers, R., 1968, An Approach to the Multivariate Analysis of Ordinal Data, *American Sociological Review*, vol. 33, 971–977.

Stewart, D. and W. Love, 1968, A General Canonical Correlation Index, *Psychological Bulletin*, vol. 70, 160–163.

Tacq, J., 1977, *Associatiematen voor kruistabellen. Een handleiding bij het interpreteren van SPSS-output*, Leuven: Sociologisch Onderzoeksinstituut.

Tacq, J., 1984, *Causaliteit in sociologisch onderzoek. Een beoordeling van causale analysetechnieken in het licht van wijsgerige opvattingen over causaliteit*, Deventer: Van Loghum Slaterus.

Thurstone, L., 1947, *Multiple Factor Analysis*, Chicago: University of Chicago Press.

Valeriani, R., 1979, *Travels with Henry*, Boston: Houghton Mifflin.

Van de Geer, J., 1971, *Introduction to Multivariate Analysis for the Social Sciences*, San Francisco: Freeman.

Vandenberghe, R., Denoo, H. and De Roo, F. 1978, Onderzoek naar factoren die door leerkrachten basisonderwijs als beïnvloedend en remmend ervaren worden, *Pedagogisch Tijdschrift / Forum van Opvoedkunde*, vol. I: 3, no. 7, 369–385; vol. II: 3, no. 8, 429–443.

Van Raaij, W., 1968, *Geprogrammeerde instructie wiskunde ter voorbereiding voor het vak statistiek*, Voorschoten: Vam.

Wilson, K., 1980, Immigrant Enclaves: An Analysis of the Labor Market Experiences of Cubans in Miami, *American Journal of Sociology*, vol. 86, no. 2, 295–319.

Woelfel, J. and A. Haller, 1971, Significant Others, the Self-reflexive Act and the Attitude Formation Process, *American Sociological Review*, vol. 36, 74–86.

Wold, H., 1954, Causality and Econometrics, *Econometrica*, vol. 22, 162–177.

Wold, H., 1956, Causal Inference from Observational Data, *Journal of the Royal Statistical Society*, Series A, Bd 119, Part I, 28–60.

Wold, H., 1960, A Generalization of Causal Chain Models, *Econometrica*, vol. 28, 443–463.

Wright, S., 1918, On the Nature of Size Factors, *Genetics*, vol. 3, 367–374.

Wright, S., 1921, Correlation and Causation, *Journal of Agricultural Research*, vol. 20, 557–585.

Wright, S., 1934, The Method of Path Coefficients, *Annals of Mathematical Statistics*, vol. 5, 161–215.

INDEX

additivity 40, 126–127, 161, 184, 185
analysis of covariance 36, 38, 39, 40, 41, 43, 48, 49,
    58, 61, 74, 81, 87, 185, 206–209
analysis of variance 35, 36, 38, 39, 40, 41, 42, 43,
    48, 49, 75, 87
  the model 186–188
  geometry 188–192
  objectives 192–193
  calculations in one-way ANOVA 193–196
  Student's t test as F test 196–197
  calculations in two-way ANOVA 197–201
  dummy regression approach 201–206
  factorial design 210–214
  assumptions 214–215
  SPSS for Windows output 215–230

betas, standardization 111–112, 122–124, 161–
    162
bivariate causal structure 8–10, 86

canals 51, 52, 68
canonical correlation analysis 35, 36, 38, 47, 48,
    50, 51, 52, 68, 82–83, 88
  the model 324–325
  geometry 326–328
  objectives 328–329
  calculation of canonical correlations and
      weights 330–335
  scores of canonical variables 336–337
  structure correlations 336
  causal canonical correlation analysis 337–338
  significance tests 338–339
  SPSS for Windows output 339–343
canonical structure 25, 36, 88
capitalization on chance, multiple
    comparisons 176–177
causal relationship/causal analysis 34, 78–79, 80,
    174–176
characteristics 3
  measurement level 5, 160
  nominal dependent 39, 231
  nominal independent 40
  mixed measurement levels 40
  measurement level for non-dependent
      techniques 51–52
cluster analysis 37, 38, 41, 52
convergent causal structure 11–12, 36, 37, 86

correlation coefficient and coefficient of
    determination
  PRE interpretation of r^2 as explained
      variance 106–107
  interpretation of r^2 as explained variance 107–
      108
  three interpretations of r 108–110, 373
covariance, *see* analysis of covariance; multivariate
    analysis of covariance

dependency 34, 35
discriminant analysis 36, 38, 39, 40, 41, 43, 48, 49,
    59, 87
  the model 233–234
  geometry 235–238
  objectives 238–239
  calculation of the discriminant function 239–
      246
  classification and prediction 246–247
  significance tests 248–251
  dummy regression approach 252–254
  Box's M test 254–255
  SPSS for Windows output 255–265
discrimination structure 18, 36, 37, 87
dispersion 3, 6, 372
distinctions 3
dummy variable 32–33
dynamic models 161

effect of interaction 34, 126–128
experiment/experimental design 8, 9, 10, 35, 71,
    90–98

factor analysis 35, 37, 38, 41, 46, 48, 49, 51, 52, 87
  higher-order 50, 321
  confirmatory 51, 52, 62
  explorative 51, 62, 67
  R and Q 53, 69, 320–321
  oblique rotation 62, 283–284
  diagonal method 300–303
  centroid method 303–307
  minimum residuals method 307–308
  canonical 308–310
  maximum likelihood method 310–312
  alpha 312–315
  image analysis 315–317
  multiple group method 317–319
  see also principal components analysis; principal
      factor analysis

homals 51, 52, 53
homoscedasticity and heteroscedasticity 214–215
Hotelling's T^2 test 238, 248, 249–251, 347–348

identification 160
indirect causality 14, 36, 43, 87, 141
interaction, effect of 34, 126–128
interactive structure 16, 36, 37, 40, 87, 184

latent structure 21, 22, 37, 87
   of similarities 28, 29, 37, 88
latent variable 32, 46–50, 160
linearity
   techniques 54, 161
   test 54, 127–128, 214
LISREL 46, 50, 65
loglinear analysis 51, 52

Mahalanobis' distance D^2 251–252
manifest variable 32
matrix algebra 388–400
   vectors 388–390
   matrices 390–392
   operations with matrices 392–394
   determinant 394–396
   linear dependency, singular matrix 396
   inverse of a matrix 396–397
   eigenstructure (eigenvalues and
      eigenvectors) 397–400
measurement models 79–80
multicollinearity 42, 128–130, 162
multidimensional scale analysis 37, 38, 41, 48, 50,
   51, 52, 54, 88
multiple discriminant analysis 37, 38, 64, 80
   situation 356–358
   Wilks's lambda test 358–362
   as canonical correlation analysis 363–365
   SPSS for Windows output 365–370
multiple regression analysis 36, 38, 39, 40, 41, 43,
   46, 48, 49, 51, 72, 86
   preparatory bivariate regression analysis 99–
      115, 118
   the model 115–116
   geometry 116–118
   objectives 118–119
   calculation regression function 119–121
   multiple correlation coefficient and coefficient of
      determination 121–122
   betas 122–124
   significance tests 124–126
   adjusted R^2 125
   tests of additivity and linearity 126–128
   multicollinearity 128–130
   analysis of residuals 131–132
   matrix approach 132–134
   SPSS for Windows output 135–139

multivariate analysis of covariance 37, 38, 41,
   82
multivariate analysis of variance 37, 38, 41, 77
   situation 344–346
   objectives 346–347
   Wilks's lambda test 347–348, 350–353
   MANOVA as the reverse of discriminant
      analysis 352–353
   assumptions 354
   SPSS for Windows output 354–356
multivariate multiple regression analysis 37

non-linear multivariate analysis 52, 321
normality 214

orthogonality
   of independent variables 41–43, 214
   of latent variables 50–51, 66, 281–283

partial correlation analysis 36, 38, 39, 40, 41, 43,
   46, 48, 49, 74, 87
   the model 142–145
   geometry 145–149
   objectives 149
   calculation of partial correlation 149–154
   part correlation 154–157
   SPSS for Windows output 177–182
path analysis 45, 49, 65, 72
   calculation in 13 steps 159–177
   SPSS for Windows output 177–182
princals 51, 52, 321
principal components analysis 51, 80
   the model 268–269
   geometry 269–270
   objectives 270–271
   eigenvalues and eigenvectors 271–274
   component scores 274–276
   component loadings 276–278, 279
   how many components? 278, 280–281
   rotation, orthogonal and oblique 281–284
   SPSS for Windows output 284–289
principal factor analysis
   the model 290–292
   reduced correlation matrix 292–293
   eigenvalues and eigenvectors 293–294
   negative eigenvalues 294–295
   factor loading 295
   communalities 295–296
   factor scores 296–297
   rotations 296–297
   SPSS for Windows output 297–299
problem-relation 43

recursivity 160

sample theory 375–382, 382–388
similarities of data 54–55
Simon–Blalock procedure 43, 46, 157–159
simultaneous equation models 46, 159
split-half procedure 176
spurious causality 12–14, 36, 43, 87, 140–141
statistical relationship 34
Student's *t* test 71, 93–95, 184, 196–197, 249, 345, 347–348

units 3
  level 4
  analysis of 53

variance, *see* analysis of variance; multivariate analysis of variance

Wilks's lambda test 338, 347–348, 350–353, 358–362